JESSICA JONES

THE PULSE

JESSICA JONES: THE PULSE — THE COMPLETE COLLECTION. Contains material originally published in magazine form as PULSE #1-9 and #11-14, and NEW AVENGERS ANNUAL #1. First printing 2014. ISBN# 978-0-7851-9086-8. Published by MARVEL WORLDWIDE, INC., a subsidiary of MARVEL ENTERTAINMENT, LLC. OFFICE OF PUBLICATION: 135 West 50th Street, New York, NY 10020. Copyright © 2004, 2005, 2006 and 2014 Marvel Characters, Inc. All rights reserved. All characters featured in this issue and the distinctive names and likenesses thereof, and all related indicia are trademarks of Marvel Characters, Inc. No similarity between any of the names, characters, persons, and/or institutions in this magazine with those of any living or dead person or institution is intended, and any such similarity which may exist is purely coincidental. **Printed** ... & CMO Marvel Characters B.V.; DAN BUCKLEY, Publisher & President - Print, Animation & Digital Divisions; JOE QUESA... ...perations & Procurement, Publishing; C.B. CEBULSKI, SVP of Creator & Content Development; DAVID GABRIEL, SVP Pri... ...Director of Publishing Technology; SUSAN CRESPI, Editorial Operations Manager; ALEX MORALES, Publishing Operatio... ...arvel Comics or on Marvel.com, please contact Niza Disla, Director of Marvel Partnerships, at ndisla@marvel.com. F... ...7/4/2014 and 8/11/2014 by QUAD/GRAPHICS, VERSAILLES, KY, USA.

10987654321

El Dorado County Library
345 Fair Lane
Placerville, CA 95667

WITHDRAWN

P9-BJW-794
3 1738 00966 4622

Writer
Brian Michael Bendis

Issues #1-5
Penciler: **Mark Bagley**
Inker: **Scott Hanna**
Colorists: **Frank D'Armata** with
Brian Reber (#1-2) & **Pete Pantazis** (#3-5)

Issues #6-7
Artist: **Brent Anderson**
Colorist: **Pete Pantazis**

Issues #8-9
Penciler: **Michael Lark**
Inkers: **Michael Lark** (#8)
& **Stefano Gaudiano** (#9)
Colorist: **Pete Pantazis**

Issues #11-14
Artist: **Michael Gaydos**
Colorist: **Matt Hollingsworth**

New Avengers Annual #1
Penciler: Olivier Coipel
Inkers: **Drew Geraci, Drew Hennessy, Livesay, Rick Magyar, Danny Miki,
Mark Morales, Mike Perkins & Tim Townsend**
Colorists: **June Chung, Richard Isanove & Jose Villarrubia**

Letterers: **Virtual Calligraphy's Cory Petit** (#1-14) &
Comicraft's Albert Deschesne (New Avengers Annual #1)
Cover Art: **Mike Mayhew & Avalon's Andy Troy** (#1 & #2-14);
Gabriele Dell'Otto (#2); and **Olivier Coipel,
Mark Morales & Jose Villarrubia** (New Avengers Annual #1)
Assistant Editors: **Marc Sumerak, Nicole Wiley, Molly Lazer,
Stephanie Moore & Aubrey Sitterson**
Editor: **Andy Schmidt**

The Pulse created by Brian Michael Bendis

Collection Editor: Jennifer Grünwald • Assistant Editor: Sarah Brunstad • Associate Managing Editor: Alex Starbuck
Editor, Special Projects: Mark D. Beazley • Senior Editor, Special Projects: Jeff Youngquist
SVP Print, Sales & Marketing: David Gabriel

Editor in Chief: Axel Alonso • Chief Creative Officer: Joe Quesada • Publisher: Dan Buckley • Executive Producer: Alan Fine

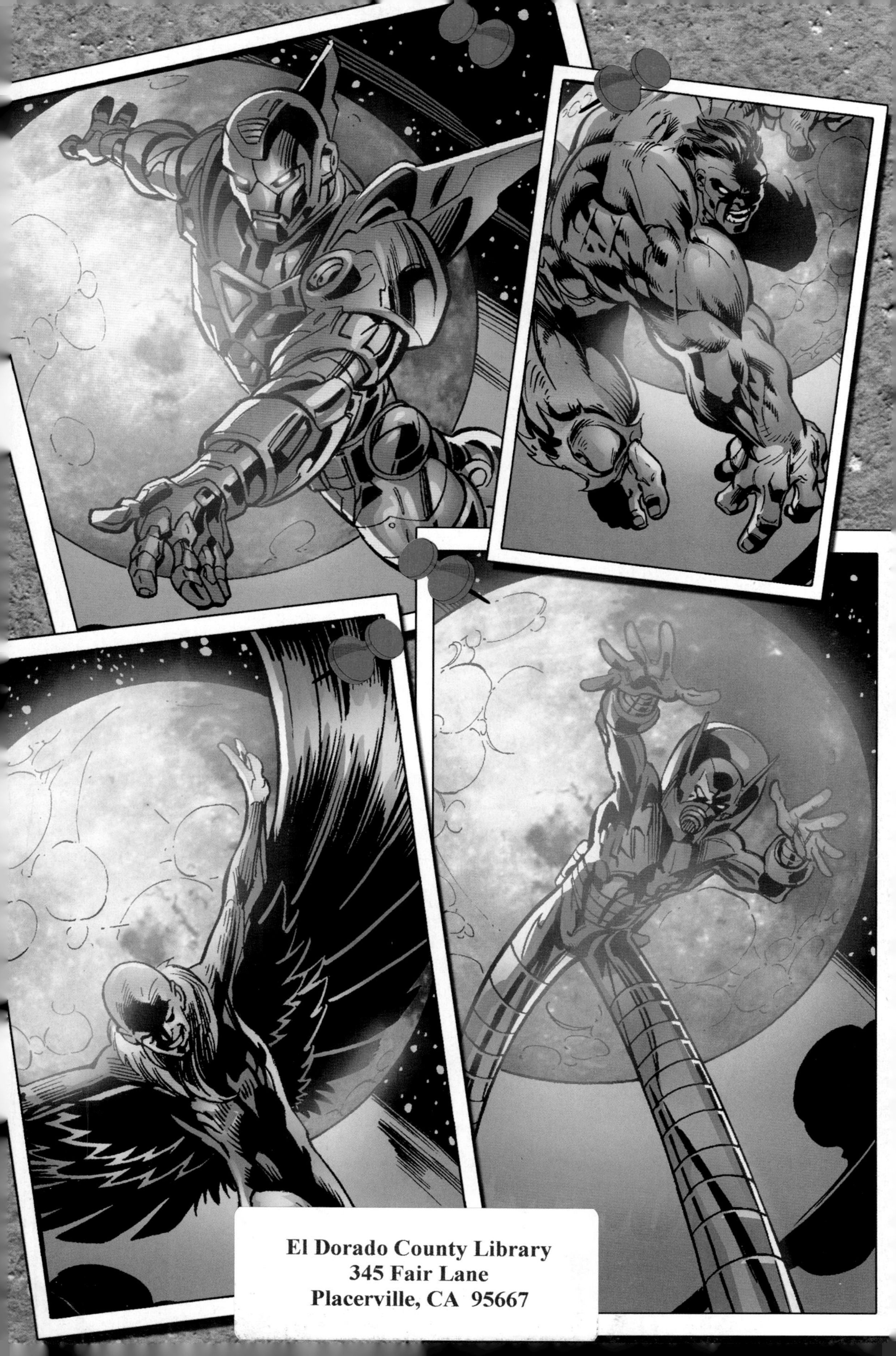

rime in the city plummets 6.5%

Police Commissioner credits cops on the street Page 16

DAILY BUGLE

SPECIAL EDITION

ST 25 CENTS

25¢

www.dailybugle.com

...AY, SEPTEMBER 26, 2003 / Partly Cloudy, 68 / Weather Page 36 ★★ Mike Mayhew

SPIDER-MAN: HERO OR MENACE?

Masked man swings into action amidst urban jungle

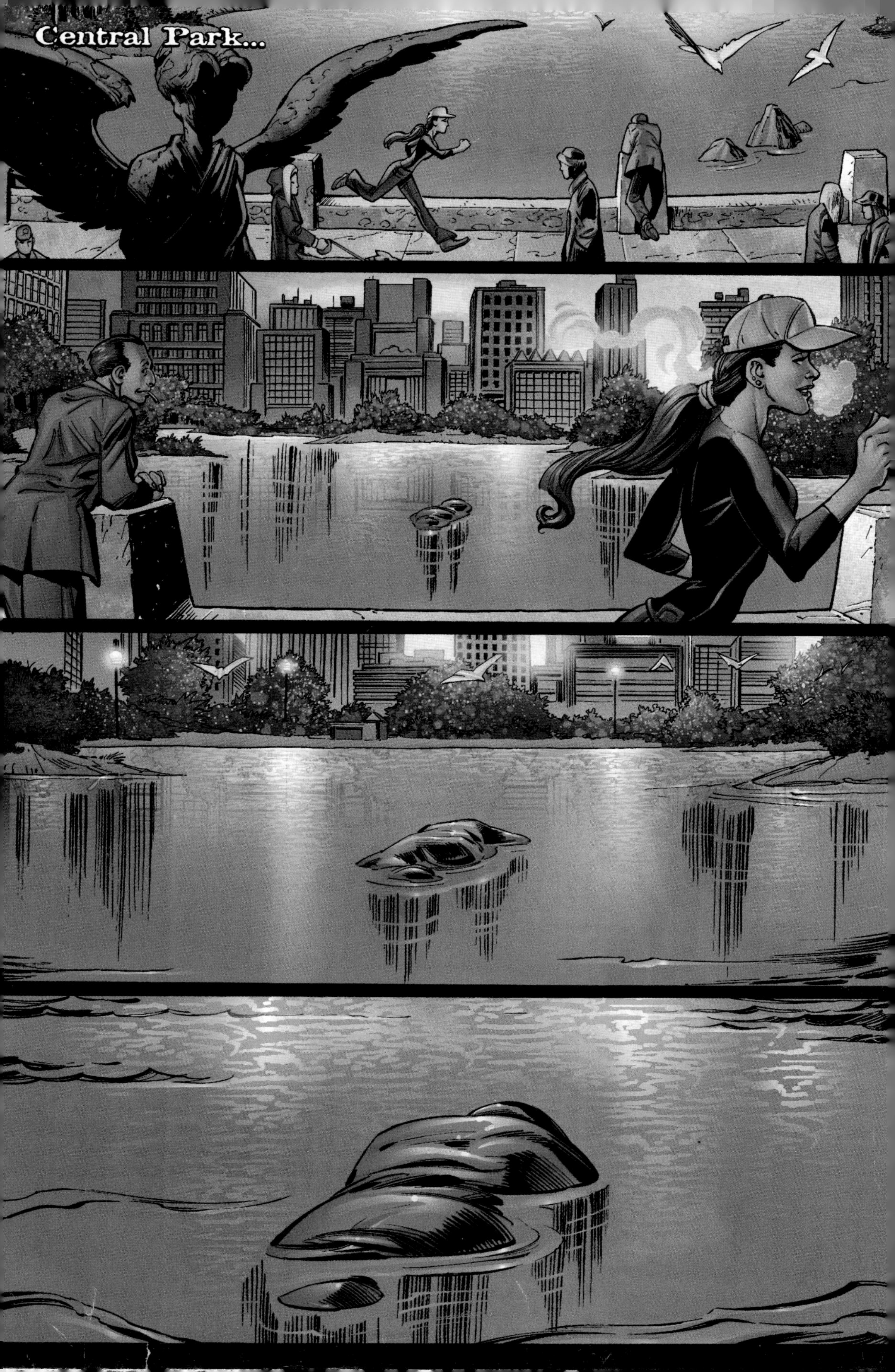
Central Park...

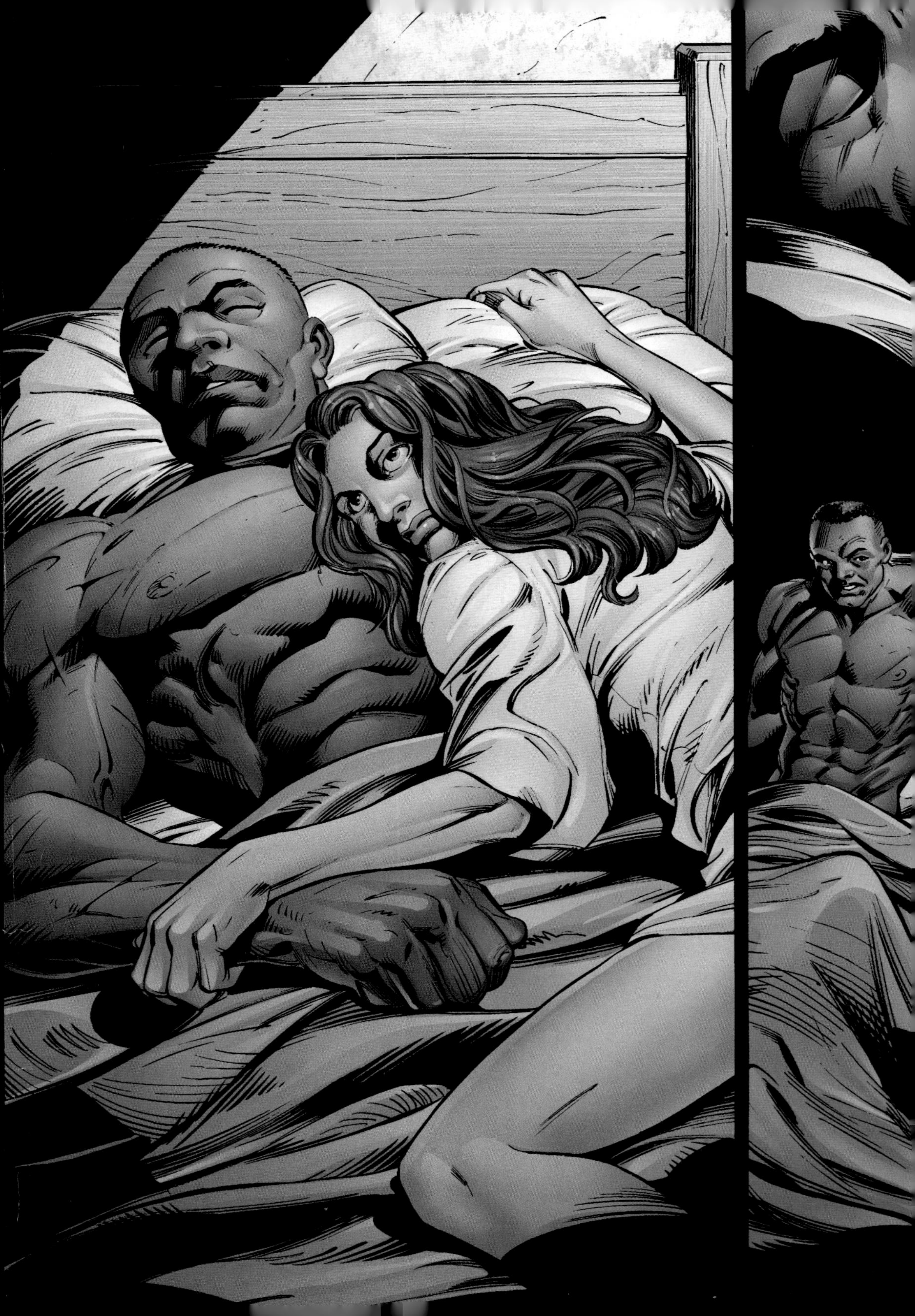

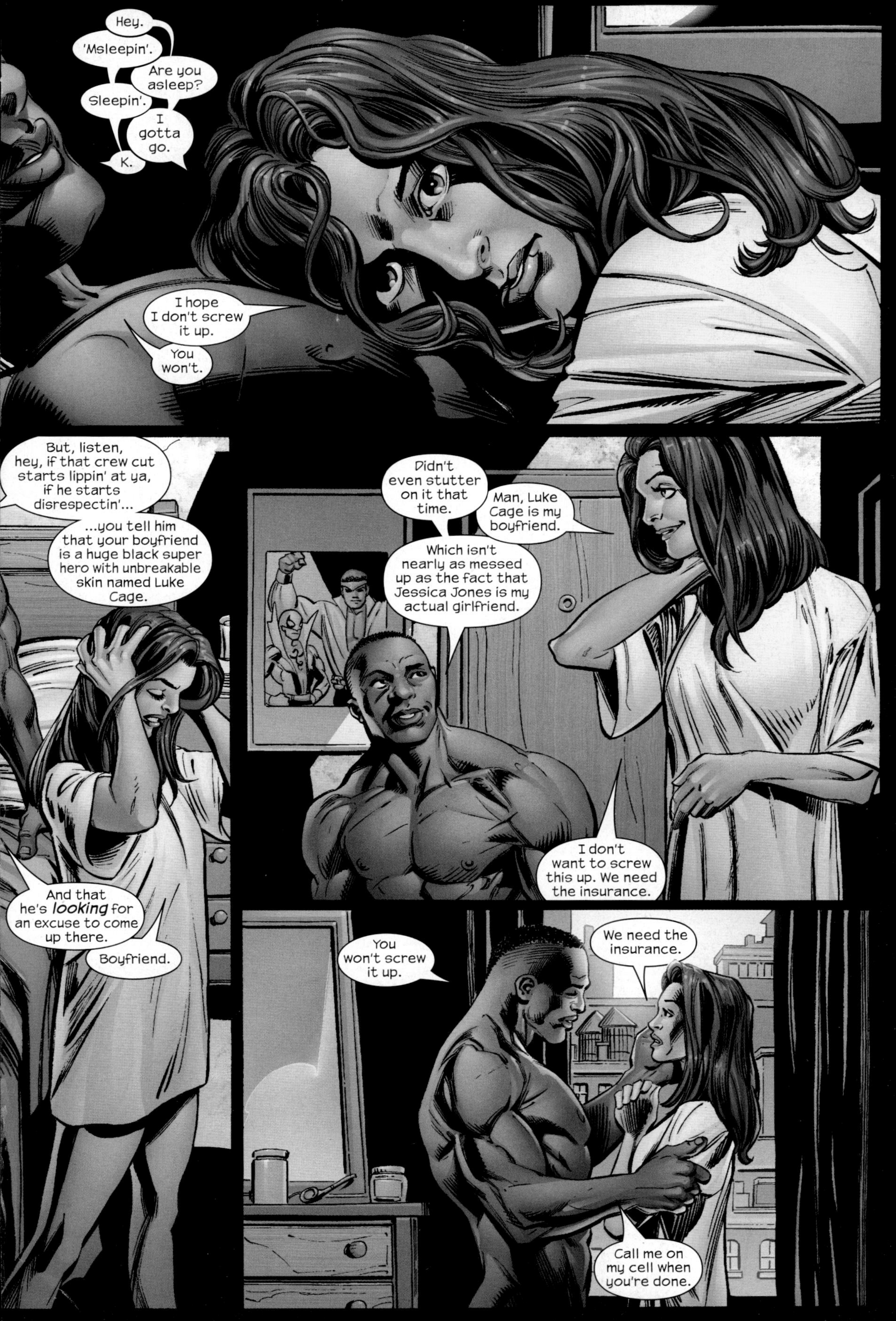
Hey.
'Msleepin'.
Are you asleep?
Sleepin'.
I gotta go.
K.
I hope I don't screw it up.
You won't.
But, listen, hey, if that crew cut starts lippin' at ya, if he starts disrespectin'...
...you tell him that your boyfriend is a huge black super hero with unbreakable skin named Luke Cage.
And that he's *looking* for an excuse to come up there.
Boyfriend.
Didn't even stutter on it that time.
Man, Luke Cage is my boyfriend.
Which isn't nearly as messed up as the fact that Jessica Jones is my actual girlfriend.
I don't want to screw this up. We need the insurance.
You won't screw it up.
We need the insurance.
Call me on my cell when you're done.

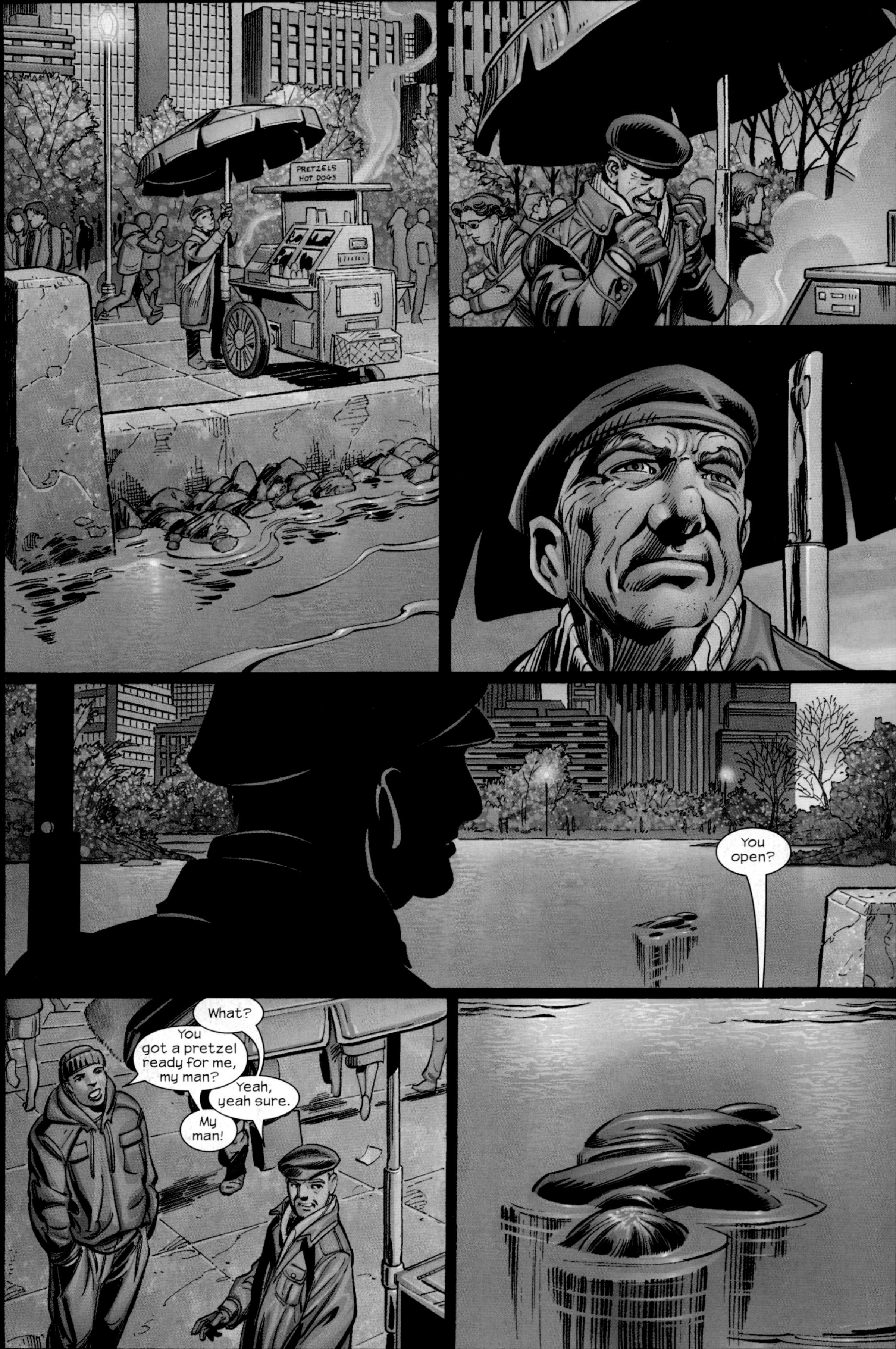
PRETZELS
HOT DOGS
You open?
What?
You got a pretzel ready for me, my man?
Yeah, yeah sure.
My man!

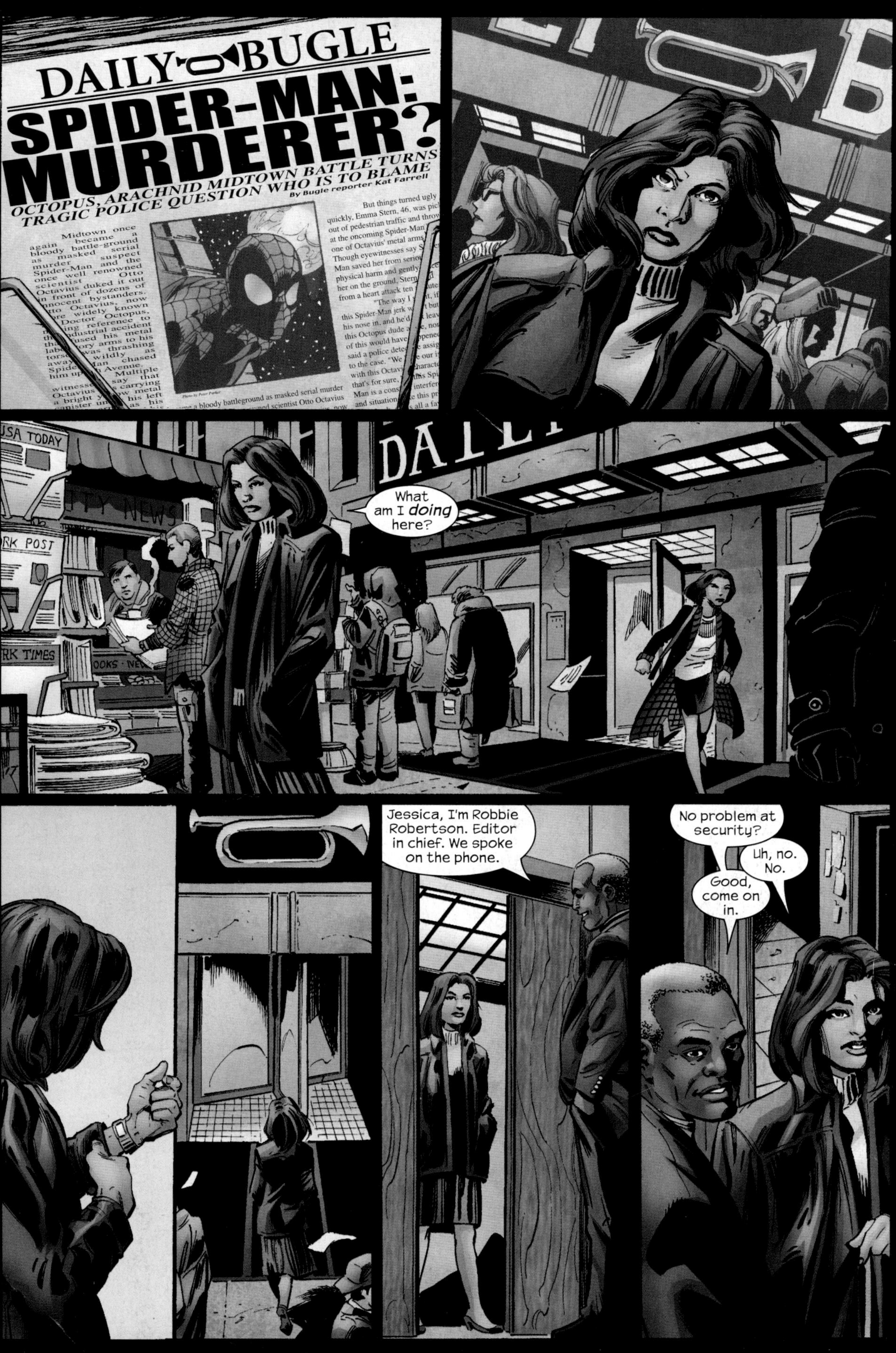
DAILY BUGLE
SPIDER-MAN: MURDERER?
OCTOPUS, ARACHNID MIDTOWN BATTLE TURNS TRAGIC POLICE QUESTION WHO IS TO BLAME
By Bugle reporter Kat Farrell
Photo by Peter Parker
USA TODAY
What am I *doing* here?
Jessica, I'm Robbie Robertson. Editor in chief. We spoke on the phone.
No problem at security?
Uh, no. No.
Good, come on in.

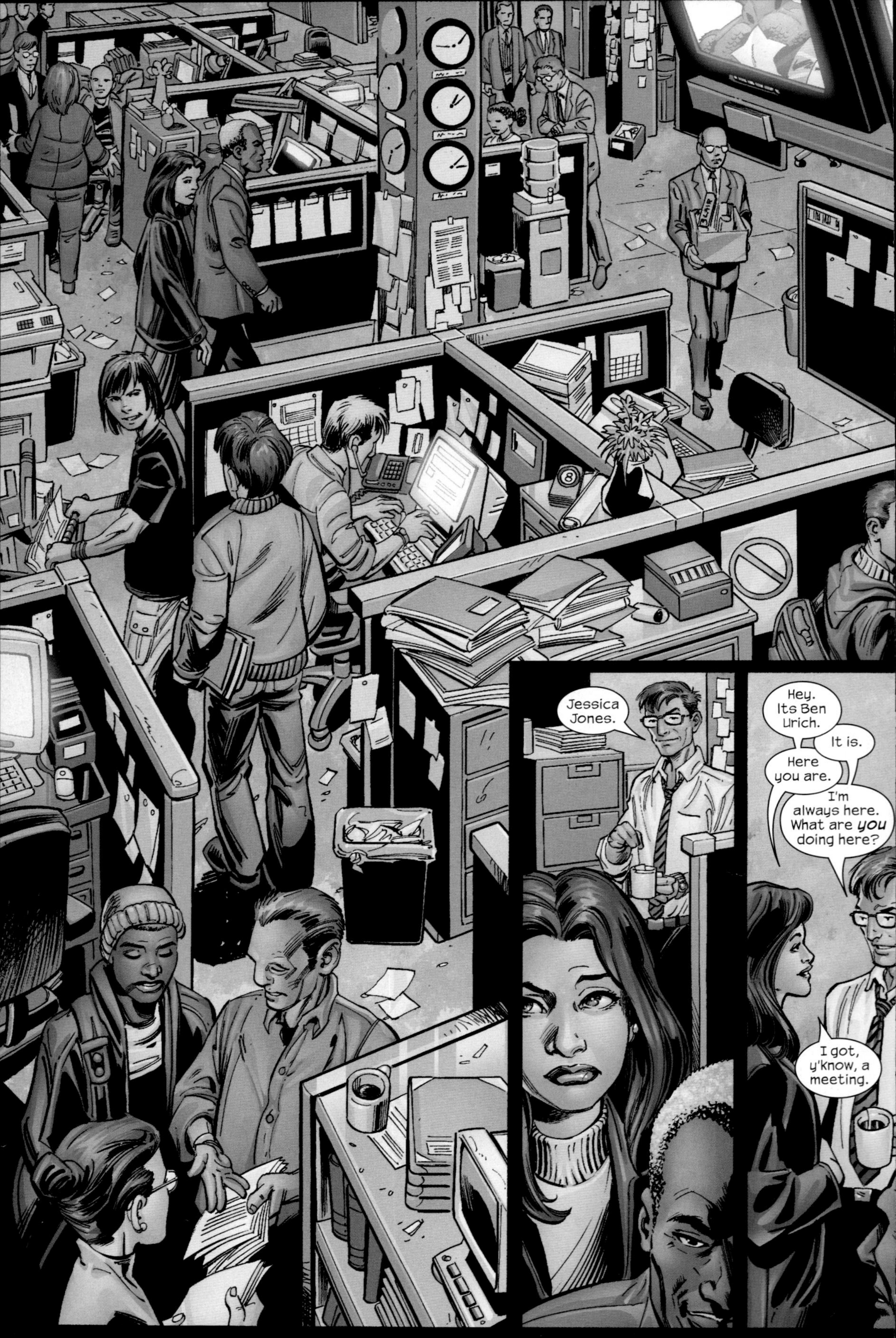

Jessica Jones.
Hey. Its Ben Urich.
It is.
Here you are.
I'm always here. What are *you* doing here?
I got, y'know, a meeting.

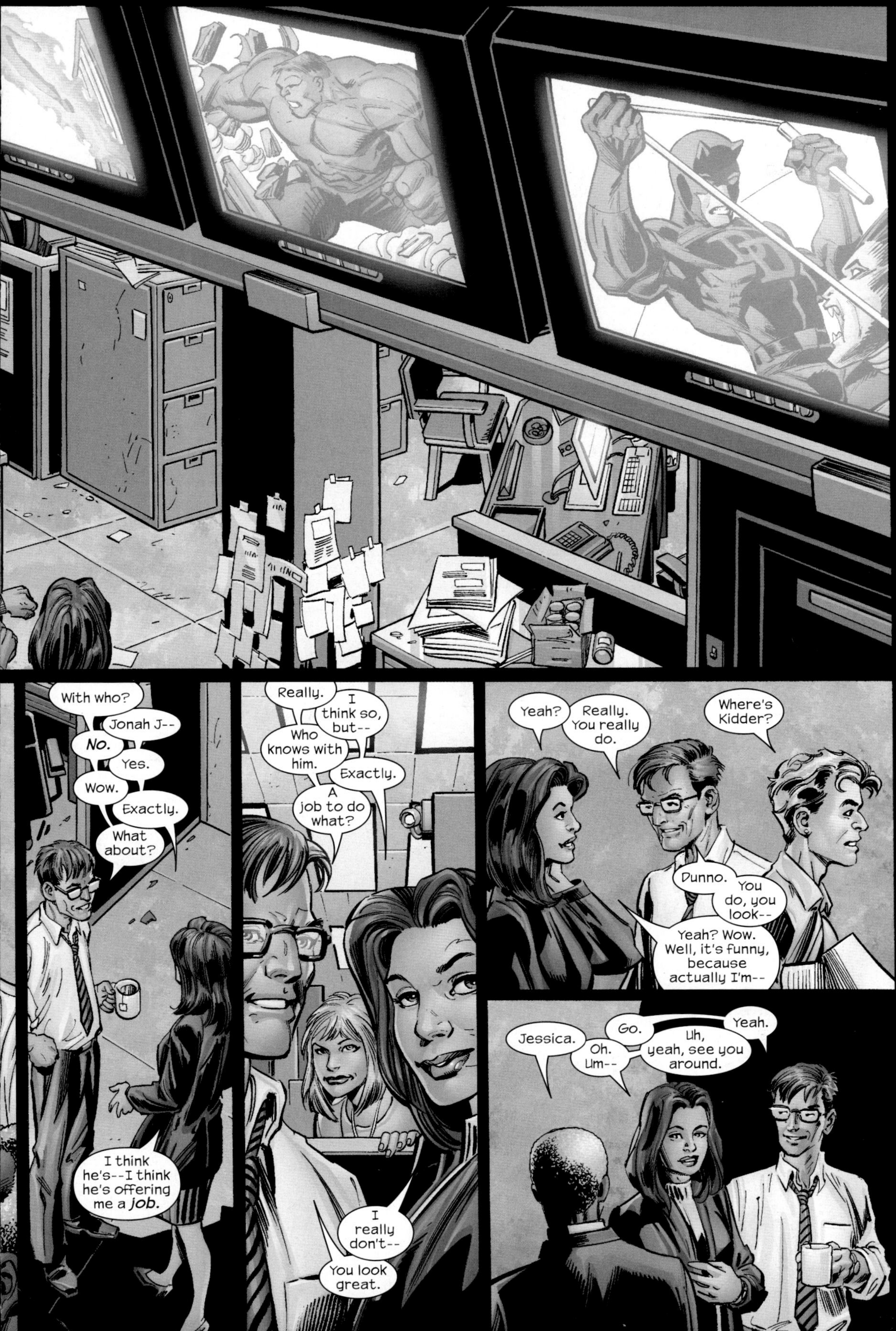
With who?
Jonah J--
No.
Yes.
Wow.
Exactly.
What about?
I think he's--I think he's offering me a job.
Really.
I think so, but--
Who knows with him.
Exactly.
A job to do what?
I really don't--
You look great.
Yeah?
Really. You really do.
Where's Kidder?
Dunno.
You do, you look--
Yeah? Wow. Well, it's funny, because actually I'm--
Jessica.
Oh. Um--
Go.
Uh, yeah, see you around.
Yeah.

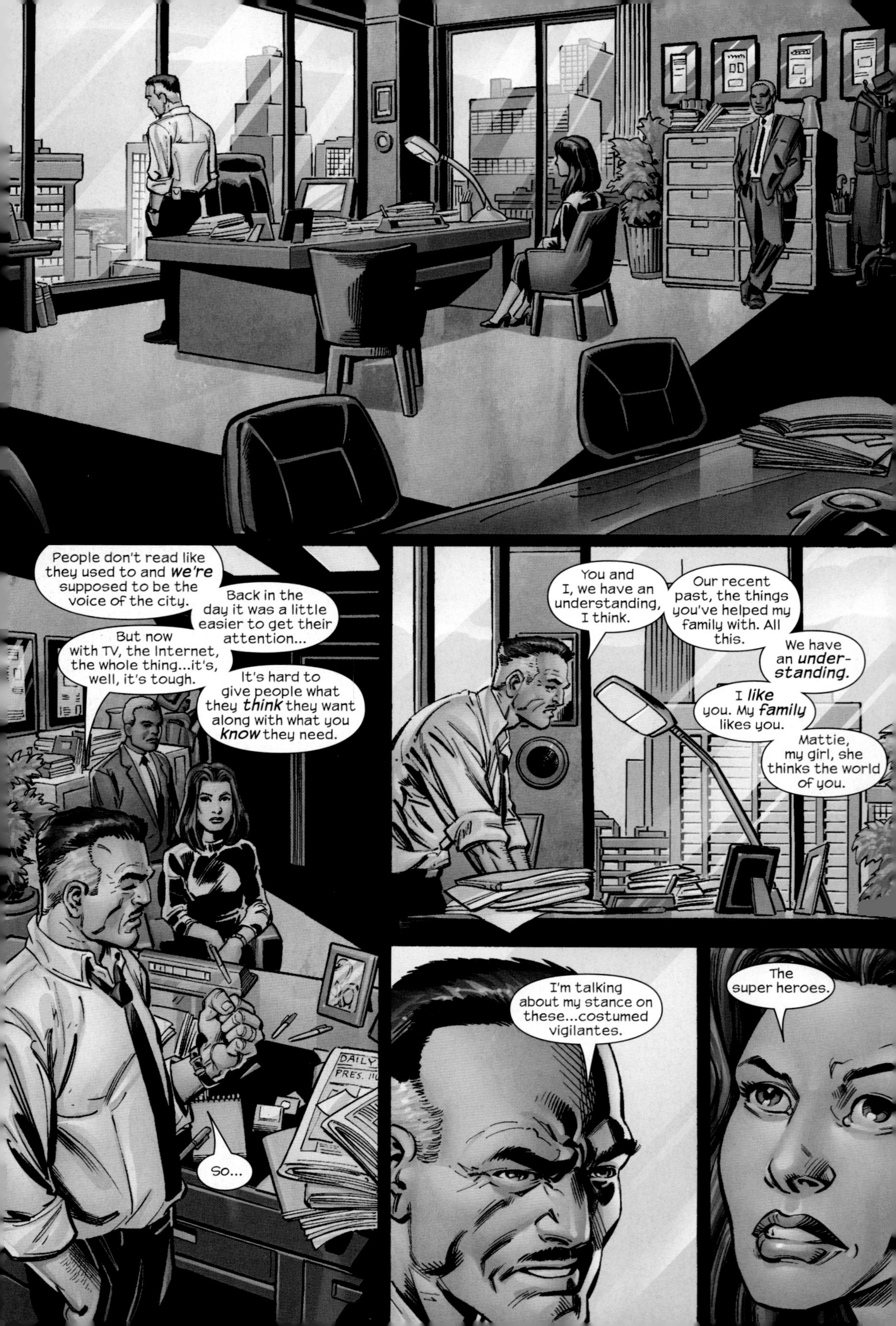
People don't read like they used to and *we're* supposed to be the voice of the city.
Back in the day it was a little easier to get their attention...
But now with TV, the Internet, the whole thing...it's, well, it's tough.
It's hard to give people what they *think* they want along with what you *know* they need.
So...
You and I, we have an understanding, I think.
Our recent past, the things you've helped my family with. All this.
We have an *under-standing.*
I *like* you. My *family* likes you.
Mattie, my girl, she thinks the world of you.
I'm talking about my stance on these...costumed vigilantes.
The super heroes.

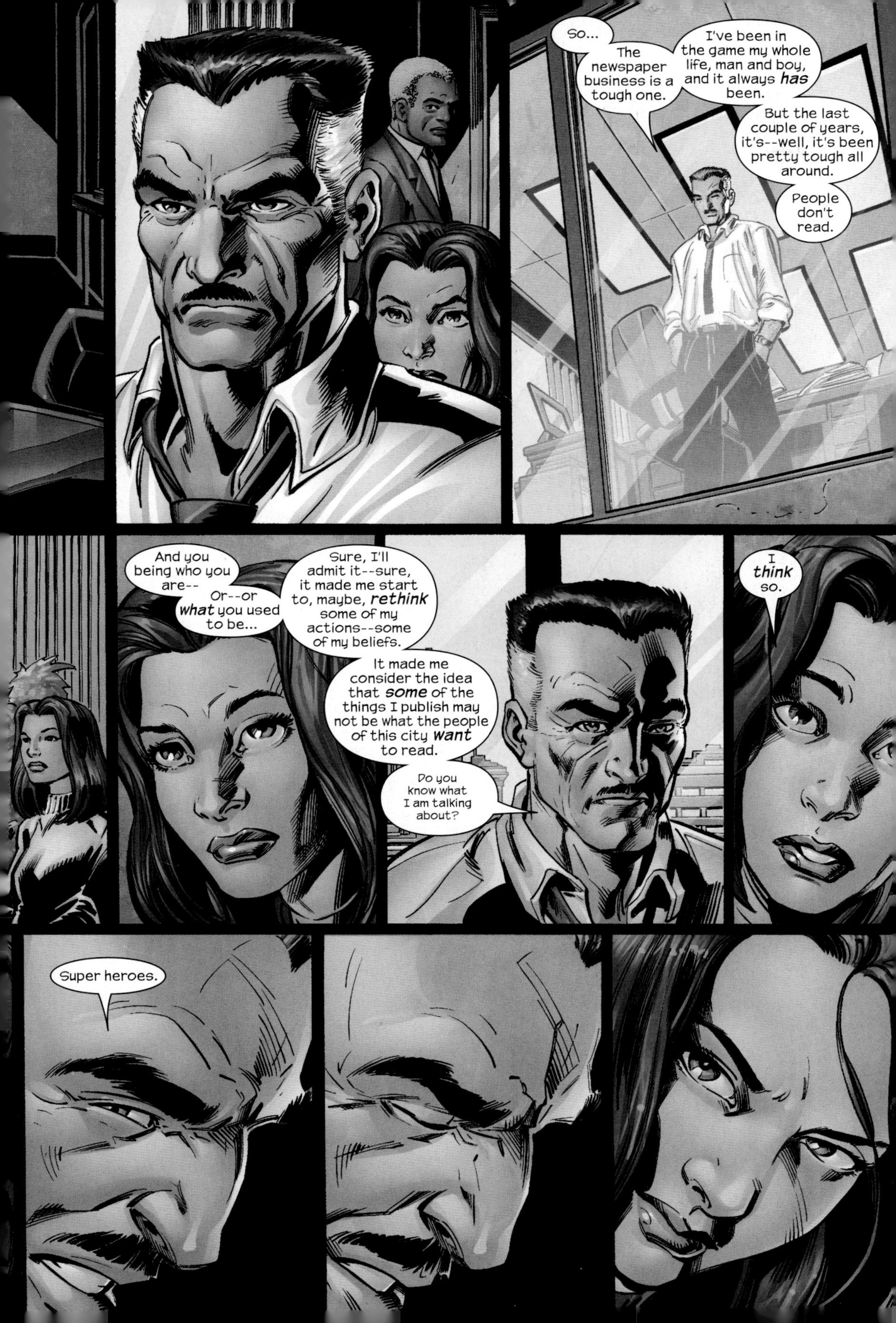
So...
The newspaper business is a tough one.
I've been in the game my whole life, man and boy, and it always *has* been.
But the last couple of years, it's--well, it's been pretty tough all around.
People don't read.
And you being who you are--
Or--or *what* you used to be...
Sure, I'll admit it--sure, it made me start to, maybe, *rethink* some of my actions--some of my beliefs.
It made me consider the idea that *some* of the things I publish may not be what the people of this city *want* to read.
Do you know what I am talking about?
I *think* so.
Super heroes.

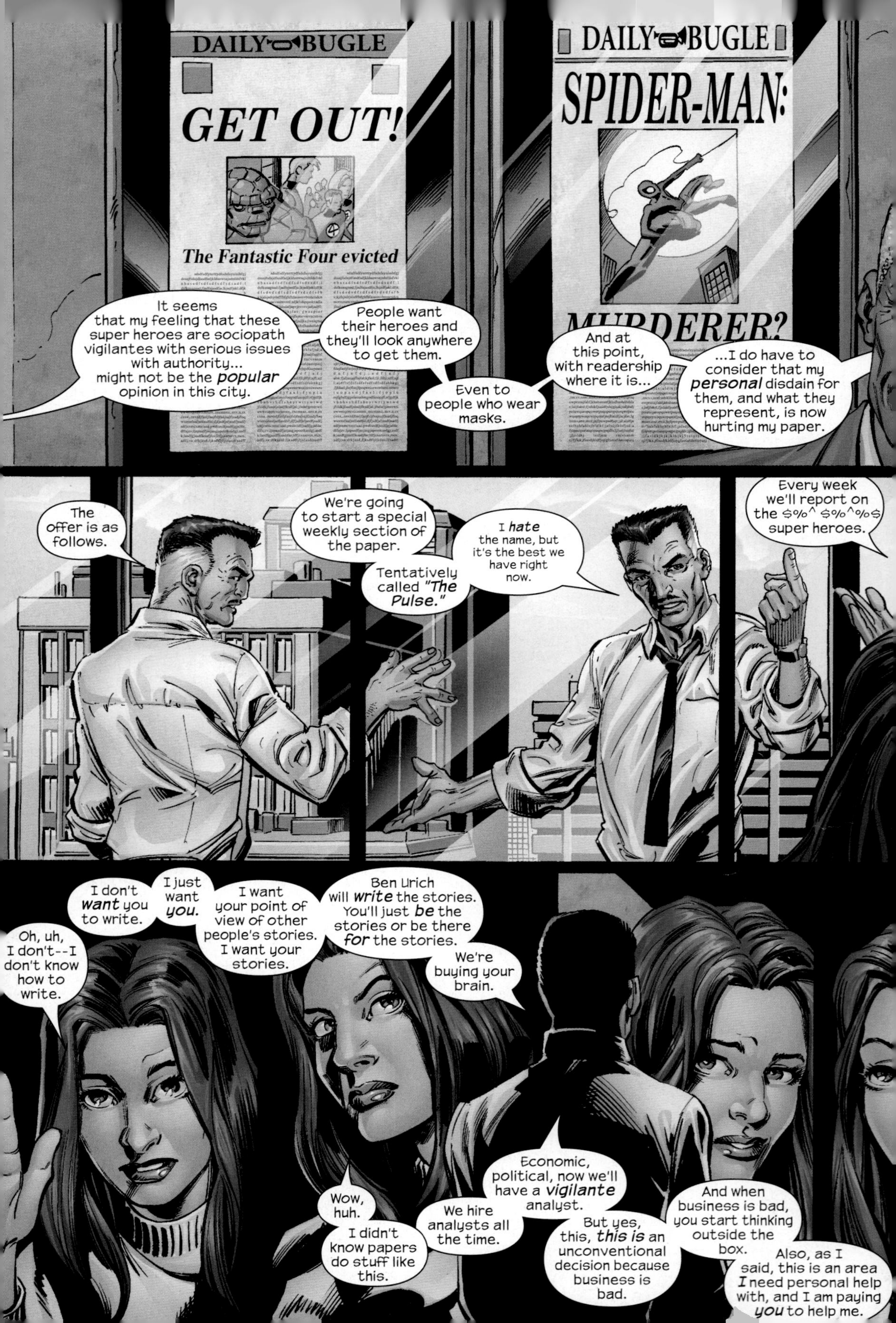

DAILY BUGLE
GET OUT!
The Fantastic Four evicted
DAILY BUGLE
SPIDER-MAN:
MURDERER?
It seems that my feeling that these super heroes are sociopath vigilantes with serious issues with authority... might not be the *popular* opinion in this city.
People want their heroes and they'll look anywhere to get them.
Even to people who wear masks.
And at this point, with readership where it is...
...I do have to consider that my *personal* disdain for them, and what they represent, is now hurting my paper.
The offer is as follows.
We're going to start a special weekly section of the paper.
Tentatively called *"The Pulse."*
I *hate* the name, but it's the best we have right now.
Every week we'll report on the $%^ $%^%$ super heroes.
Oh, uh, I don't--I don't know how to write.
I don't *want* you to write.
I just want *you.*
I want your point of view of other people's stories. I want your stories.
Ben Urich will *write* the stories. You'll just *be* the stories or be there *for* the stories.
We're buying your brain.
Wow, huh.
I didn't know papers do stuff like this.
We hire analysts all the time.
Economic, political, now we'll have a *vigilante* analyst.
But yes, this, *this is* an unconventional decision because business is bad.
And when business is bad, you start thinking outside the box.
Also, as I said, this is an area *I* need personal help with, and I am paying *you* to help me.

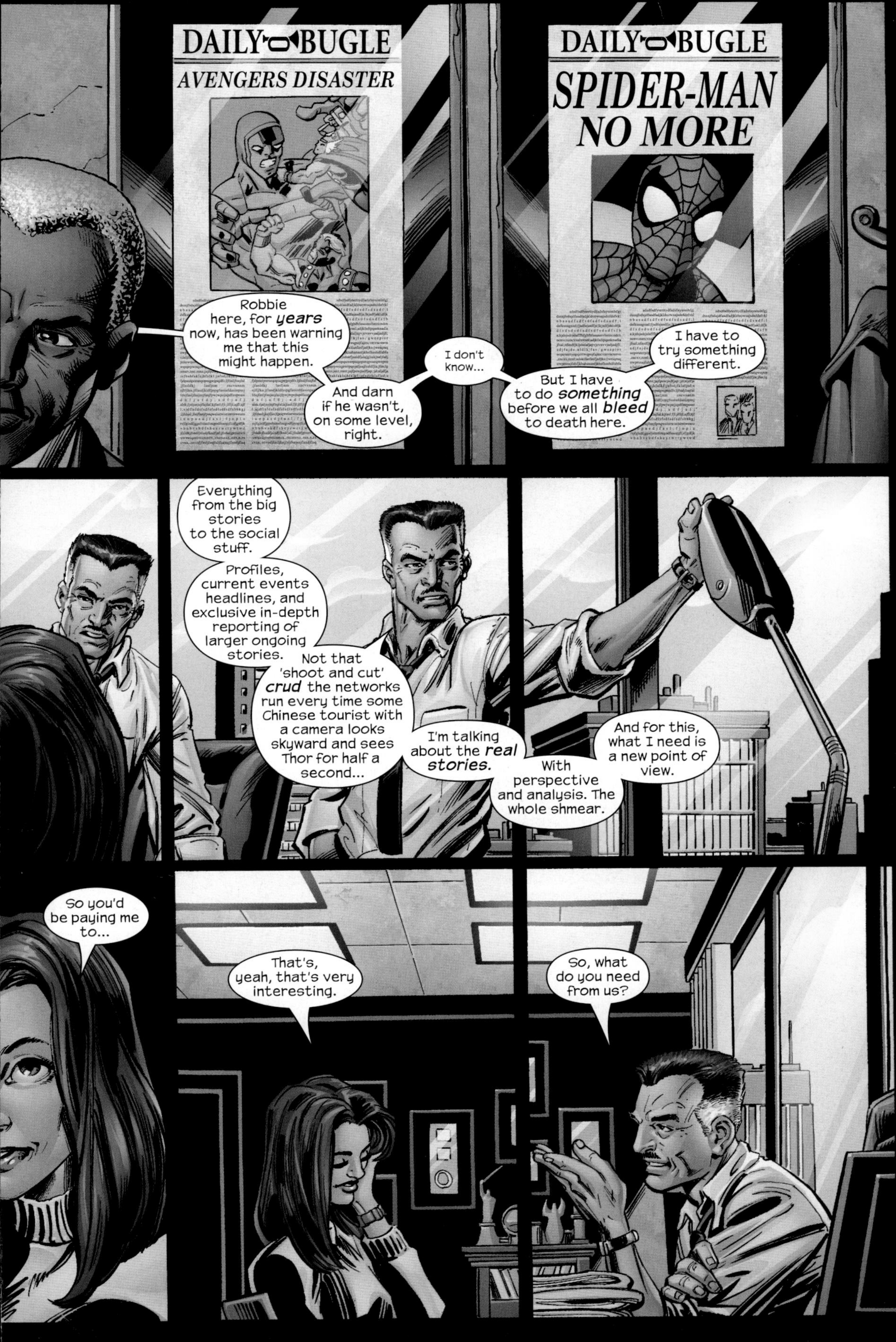
DAILY BUGLE
AVENGERS DISASTER
DAILY BUGLE
SPIDER-MAN NO MORE
Robbie here, for *years* now, has been warning me that this might happen.
And darn if he wasn't, on some level, right.
I don't know...
But I have to do *something* before we all *bleed* to death here.
I have to try something different.
Everything from the big stories to the social stuff.
Profiles, current events headlines, and exclusive in-depth reporting of larger ongoing stories.
Not that 'shoot and cut' *crud* the networks run every time some Chinese tourist with a camera looks skyward and sees Thor for half a second...
I'm talking about the *real stories.*
With perspective and analysis. The whole shmear.
And for this, what I need is a new point of view.
So you'd be paying me to...
That's, yeah, that's very interesting.
So, what do you need from us?

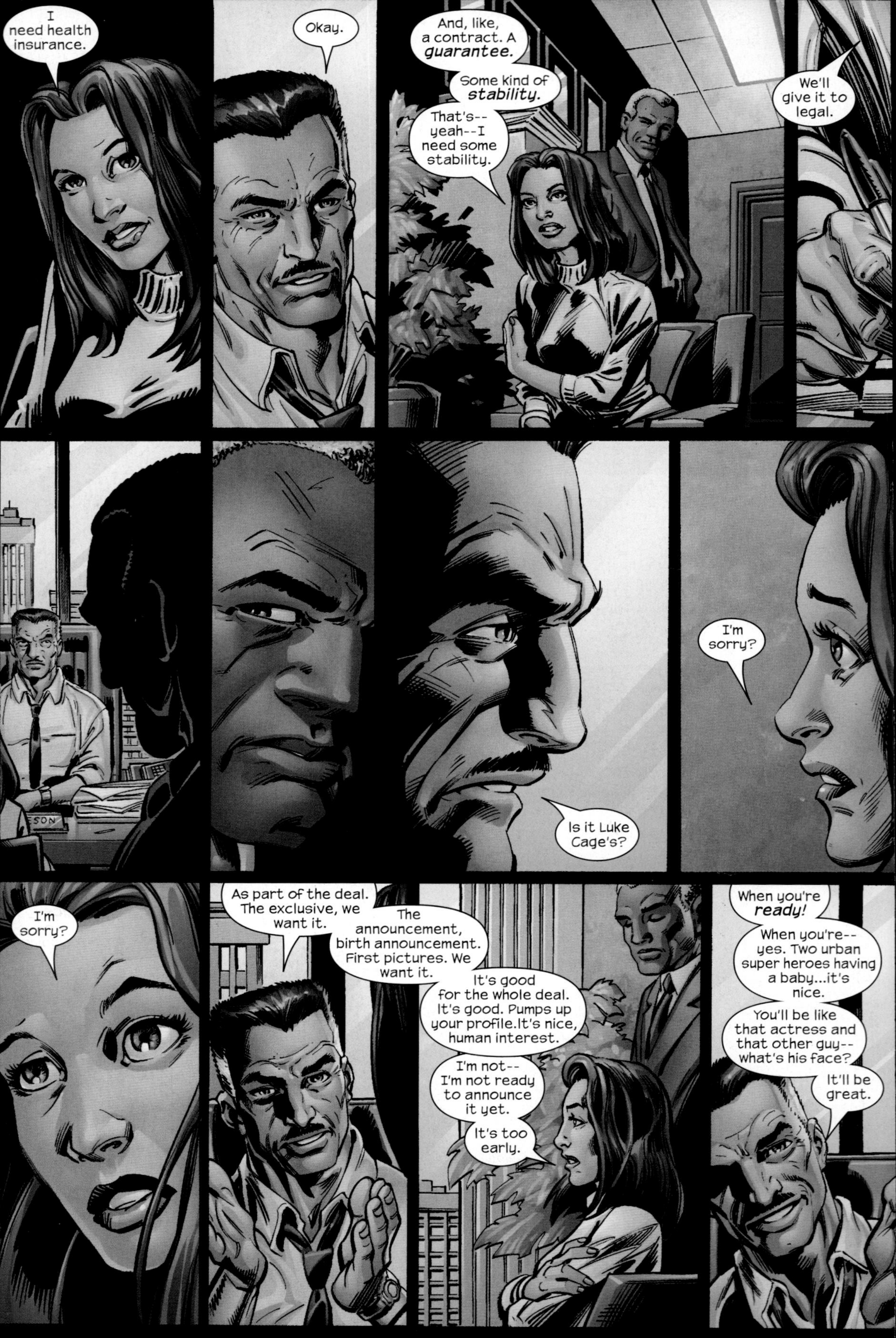
I need health insurance.
Okay.
And, like, a contract. A *guarantee.*
Some kind of *stability.*
That's-- yeah--I need some stability.
We'll give it to legal.
SON
I'm sorry?
Is it Luke Cage's?
I'm sorry?
As part of the deal. The exclusive, we want it.
The announcement, birth announcement. First pictures. We want it.
It's good for the whole deal. It's good. Pumps up your profile. It's nice, human interest.
I'm not-- I'm not ready to announce it yet.
It's too early.
When you're *ready!*
When you're-- yes. Two urban super heroes having a baby...it's nice.
You'll be like that actress and that other guy-- what's his face?
It'll be great.

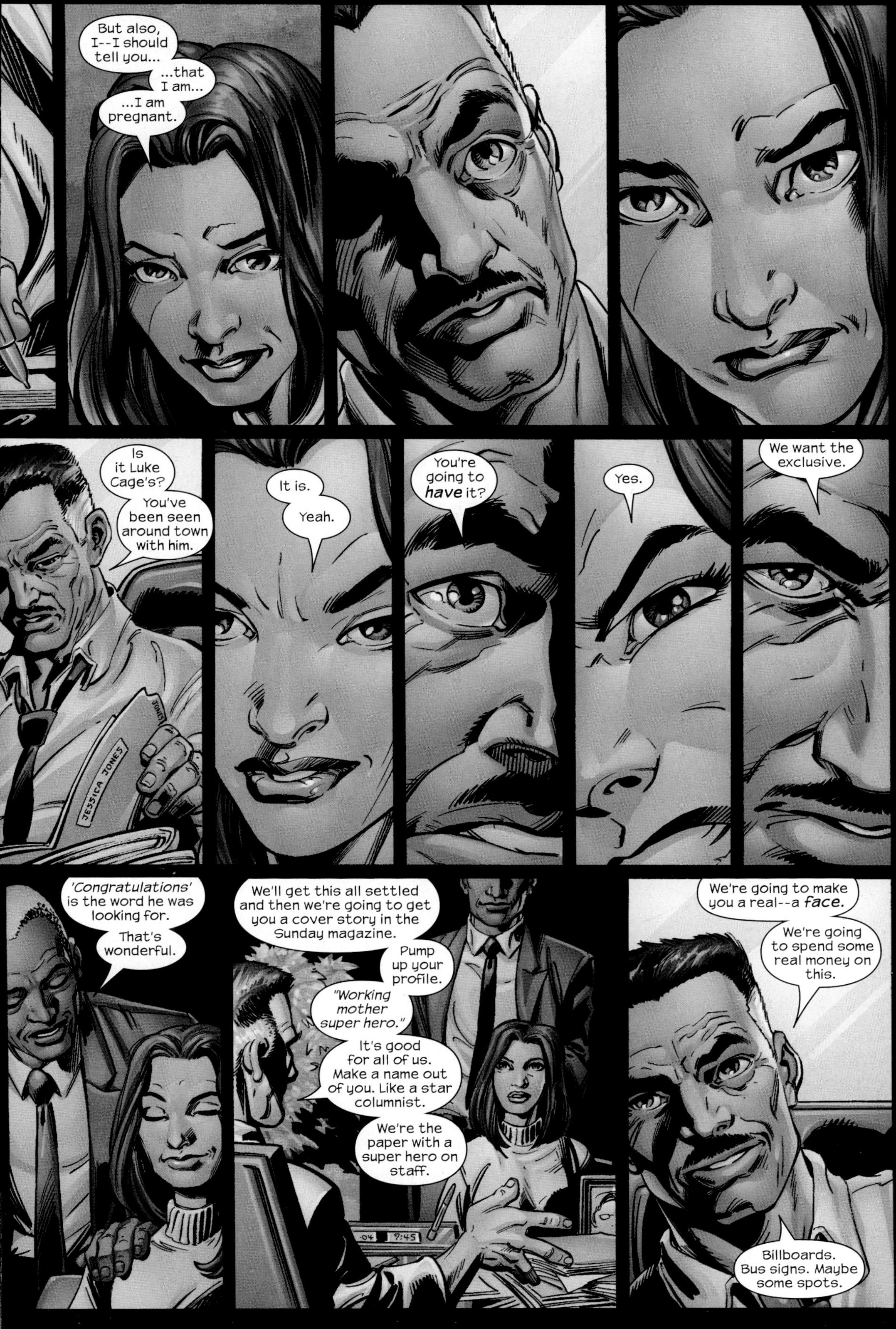

But also, I--I should tell you...
...that I am...
...I am pregnant.
Is it Luke Cage's?
You've been seen around town with him.
JESSICA JONES
It is.
Yeah.
You're going to *have* it?
Yes.
We want the exclusive.
'Congratulations' is the word he was looking for.
That's wonderful.
We'll get this all settled and then we're going to get you a cover story in the Sunday magazine.
Pump up your profile.
"Working mother super hero."
It's good for all of us. Make a name out of you. Like a star columnist.
We're the paper with a super hero on staff.
We're going to make you a real--a *face.*
We're going to spend some real money on this.
Billboards. Bus signs. Maybe some spots.

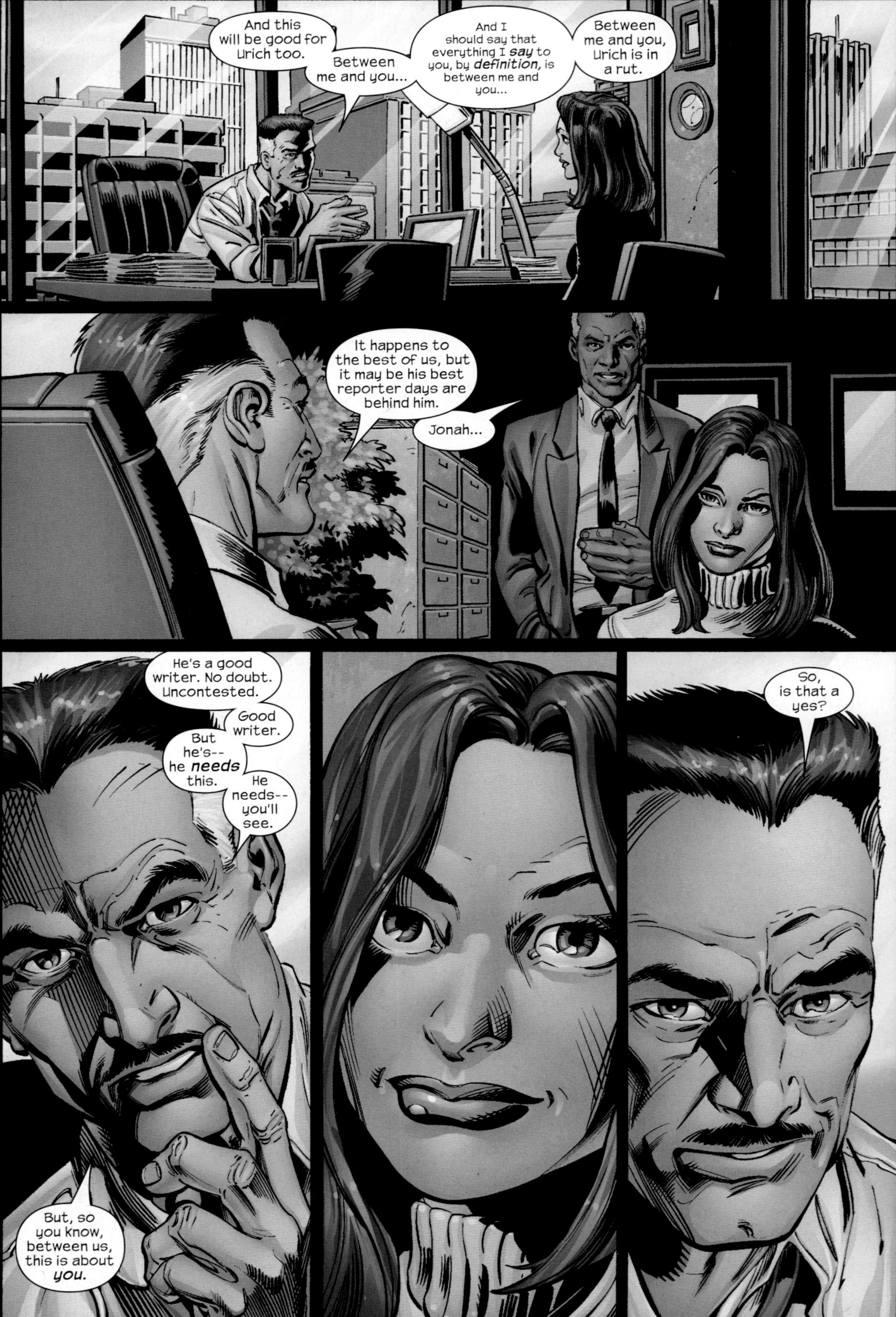
And this will be good for Urich too.
Between me and you...
And I should say that everything I *say* to you, by *definition,* is between me and you...
Between me and you, Urich is in a rut.
It happens to the best of us, but it may be his best reporter days are behind him.
Jonah...
He's a good writer. No doubt. Uncontested.
Good writer.
But he's-- he *needs* this.
He needs-- you'll see.
But, so you know, between us, this is about *you.*
So, is that a yes?

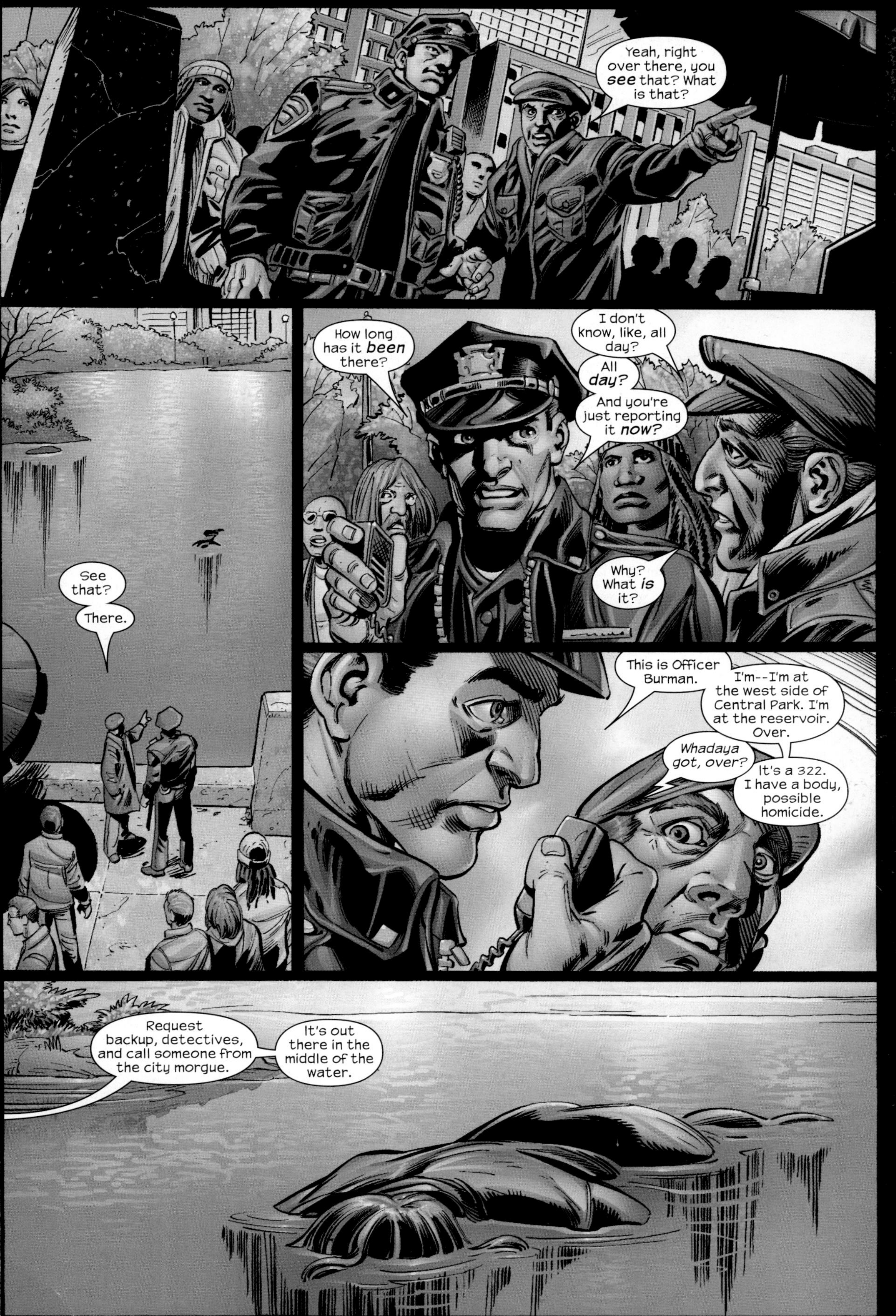
Yeah, right over there, you see that? What is that?
See that?
There.
How long has it been there?
I don't know, like, all day?
All day?
And you're just reporting it now?
Why? What is it?
This is Officer Burman.
I'm--I'm at the west side of Central Park. I'm at the reservoir. Over.
Whadaya got, over?
It's a 322. I have a body, possible homicide.
Request backup, detectives, and call someone from the city morgue.
It's out there in the middle of the water.

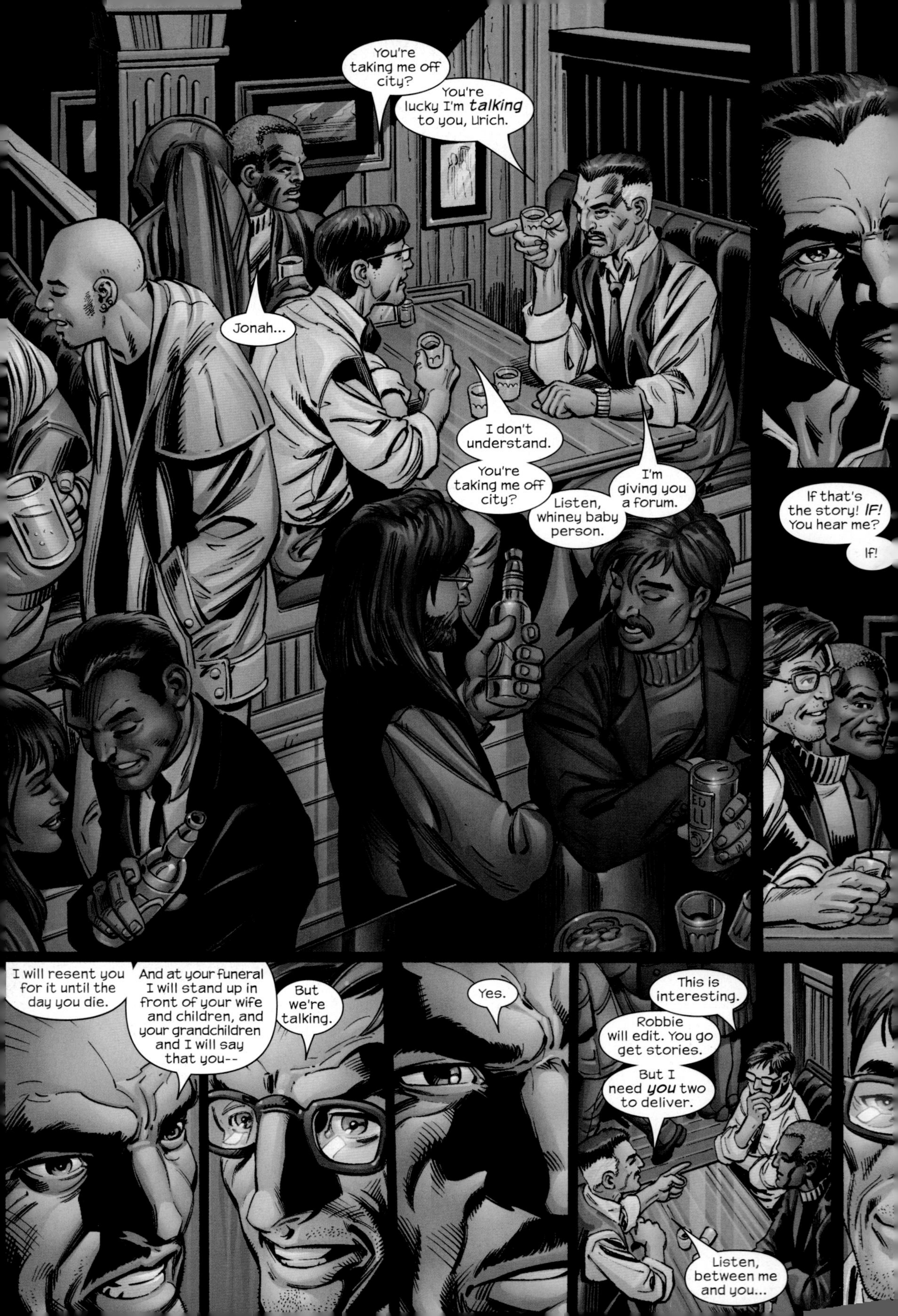
You're taking me off city?
You're lucky I'm *talking* to you, Urich.
Jonah...
I don't understand.
You're taking me off city?
Listen, whiney baby person.
I'm giving you a forum.
If that's the story! *IF!* You hear me?
IF!
I will resent you for it until the day you die.
And at your funeral I will stand up in front of your wife and children, and your grandchildren and I will say that you--
But we're talking.
Yes.
This is interesting.
Robbie will edit. You go get stories.
But I need *you* two to deliver.
Listen, between me and you...

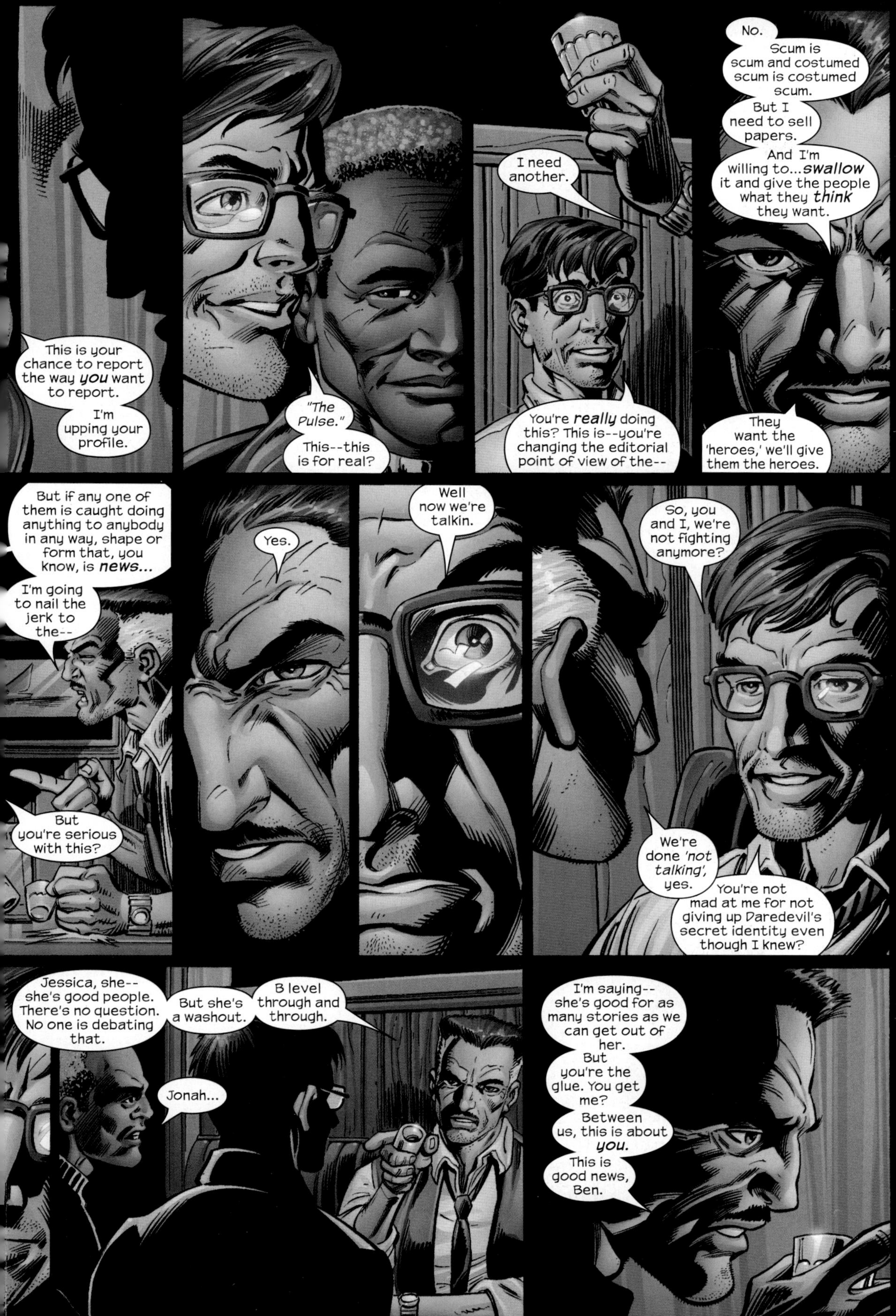
This is your chance to report the way *you* want to report.
I'm upping your profile.
"The Pulse."
This--this is for real?
I need another.
You're *really* doing this? This is--you're changing the editorial point of view of the--
No.
Scum is scum and costumed scum is costumed scum.
But I need to sell papers.
And I'm willing to...*swallow* it and give the people what they *think* they want.
They want the 'heroes,' we'll give them the heroes.
But if any one of them is caught doing anything to anybody in any way, shape or form that, you know, is *news...*
I'm going to nail the jerk to the--
But you're serious with this?
Yes.
Well now we're talkin.
So, you and I, we're not fighting anymore?
We're done *'not talking'*, yes.
You're not mad at me for not giving up Daredevil's secret identity even though I knew?
Jessica, she--she's good people. There's no question. No one is debating that.
But she's a washout.
B level through and through.
Jonah...
I'm saying--she's good for as many stories as we can get out of her.
But you're the glue. You get me?
Between us, this is about *you.*
This is good news, Ben.

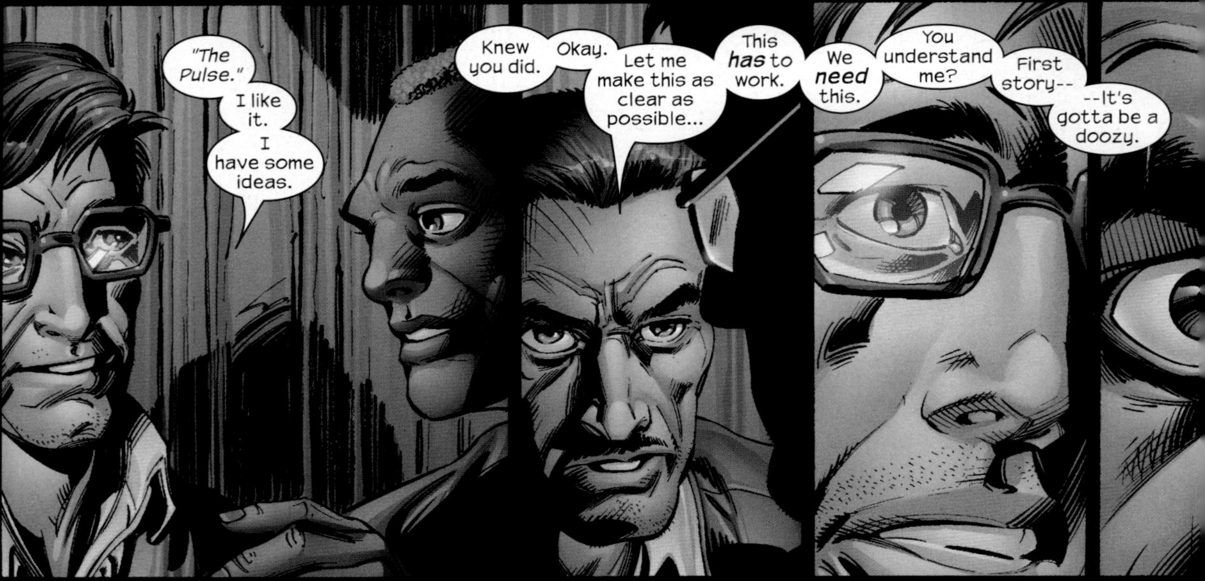
"The Pulse."
I like it.
I have some ideas.
Knew you did.
Okay.
Let me make this as clear as possible...
This **has** to work.
We **need** this.
You understand me?
First story--
--It's gotta be a doozy.

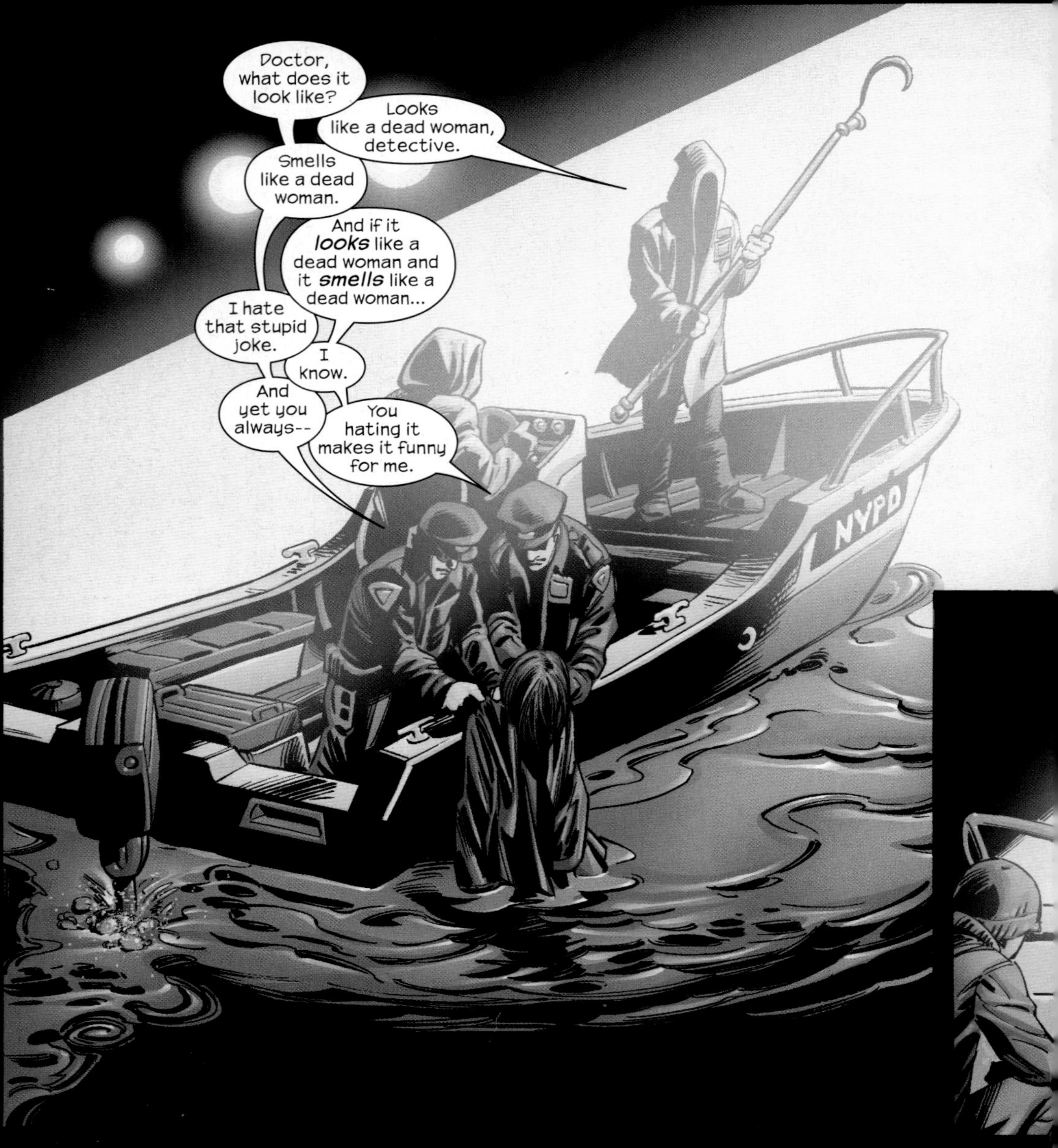
Doctor, what does it look like?
Looks like a dead woman, detective.
Smells like a dead woman.
And if it **looks** like a dead woman and it **smells** like a dead woman...
I hate that stupid joke.
I know.
And yet you always--
You hating it makes it funny for me.
NYPD

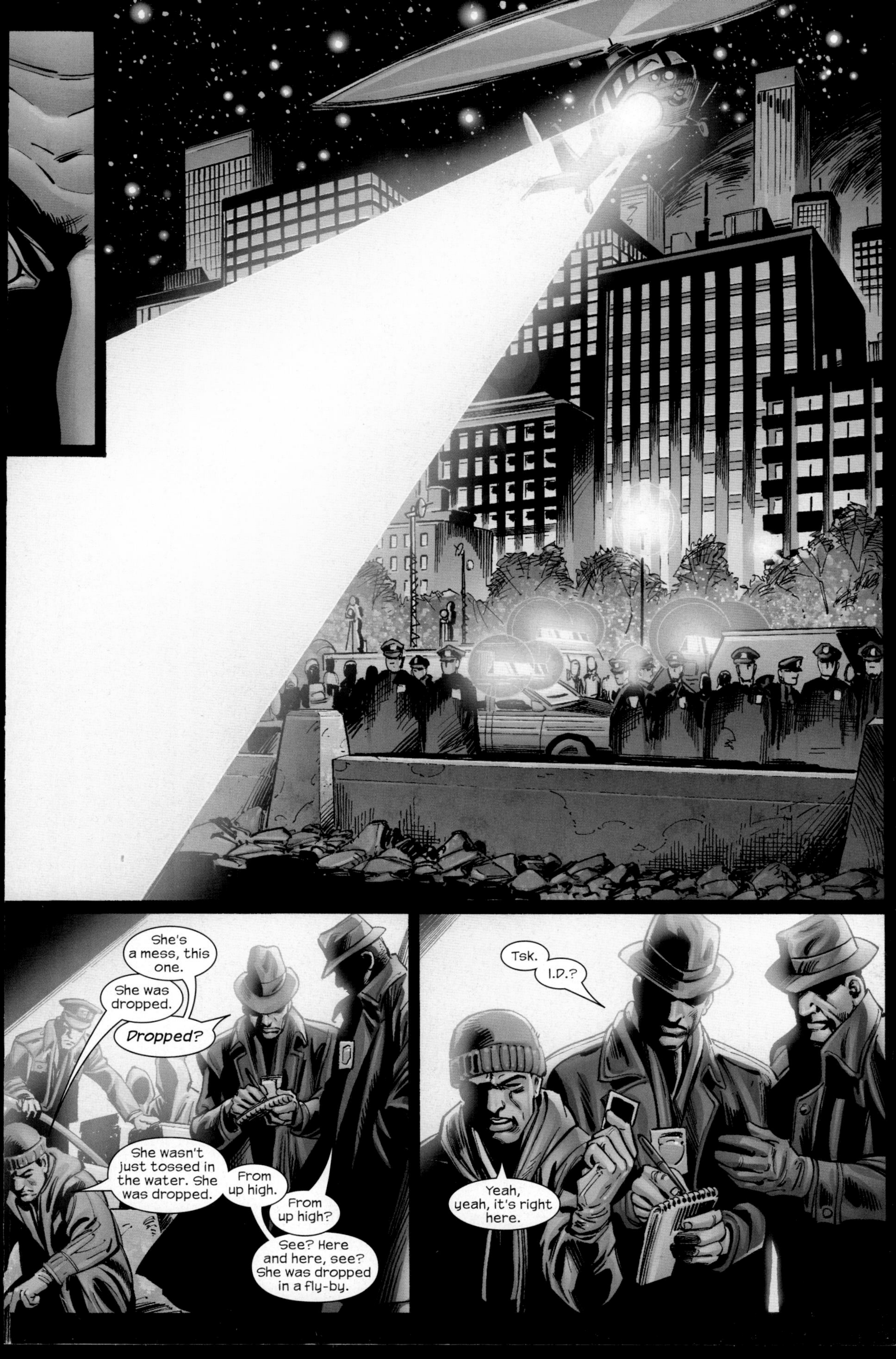
She's a mess, this one.
She was dropped.
Dropped?
She wasn't just tossed in the water. She was dropped.
From up high.
From up high?
See? Here and here, see? She was dropped in a fly-by.
Tsk.
I.D.?
Yeah, yeah, it's right here.

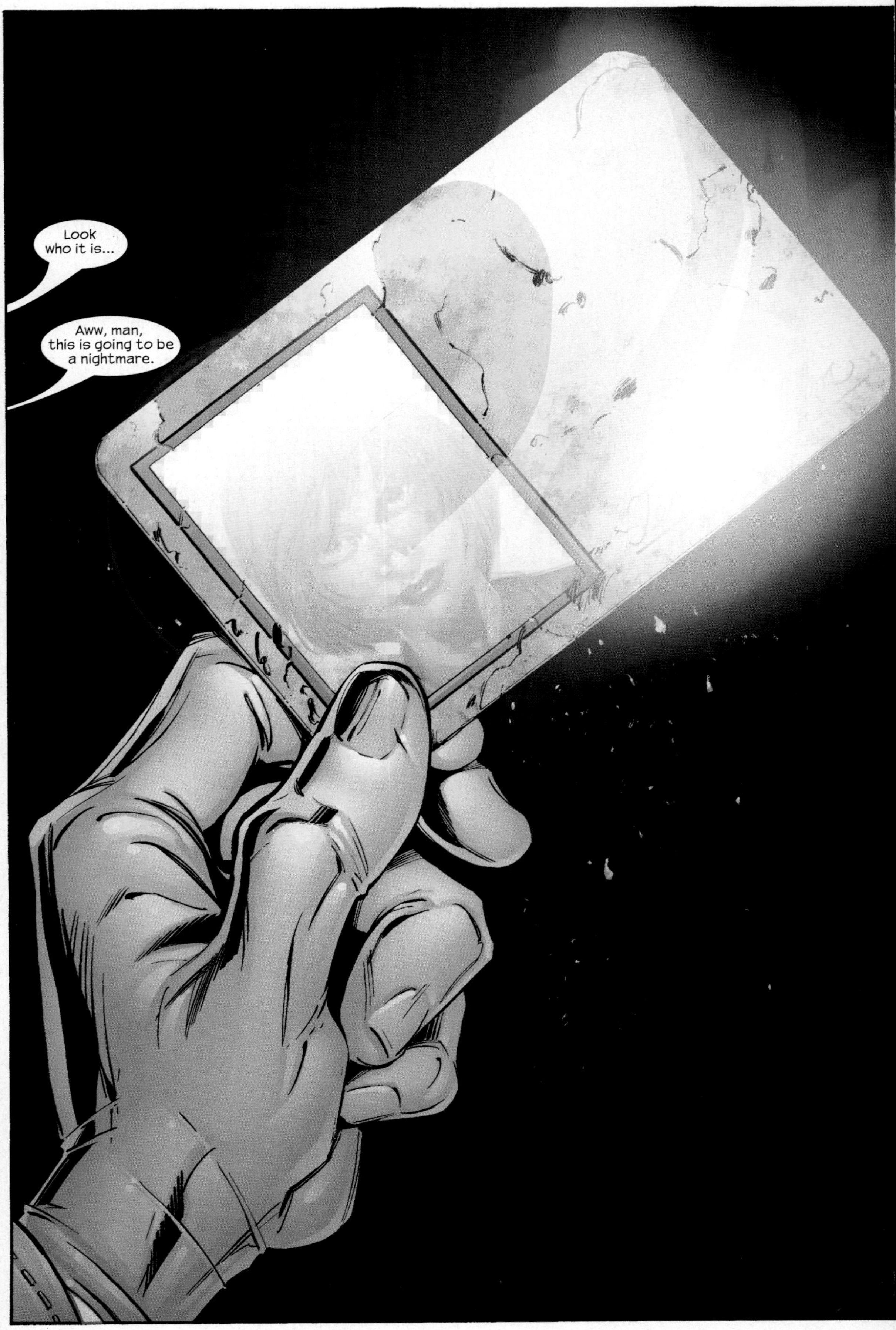
Look who it is...
Aww, man, this is going to be a nightmare.

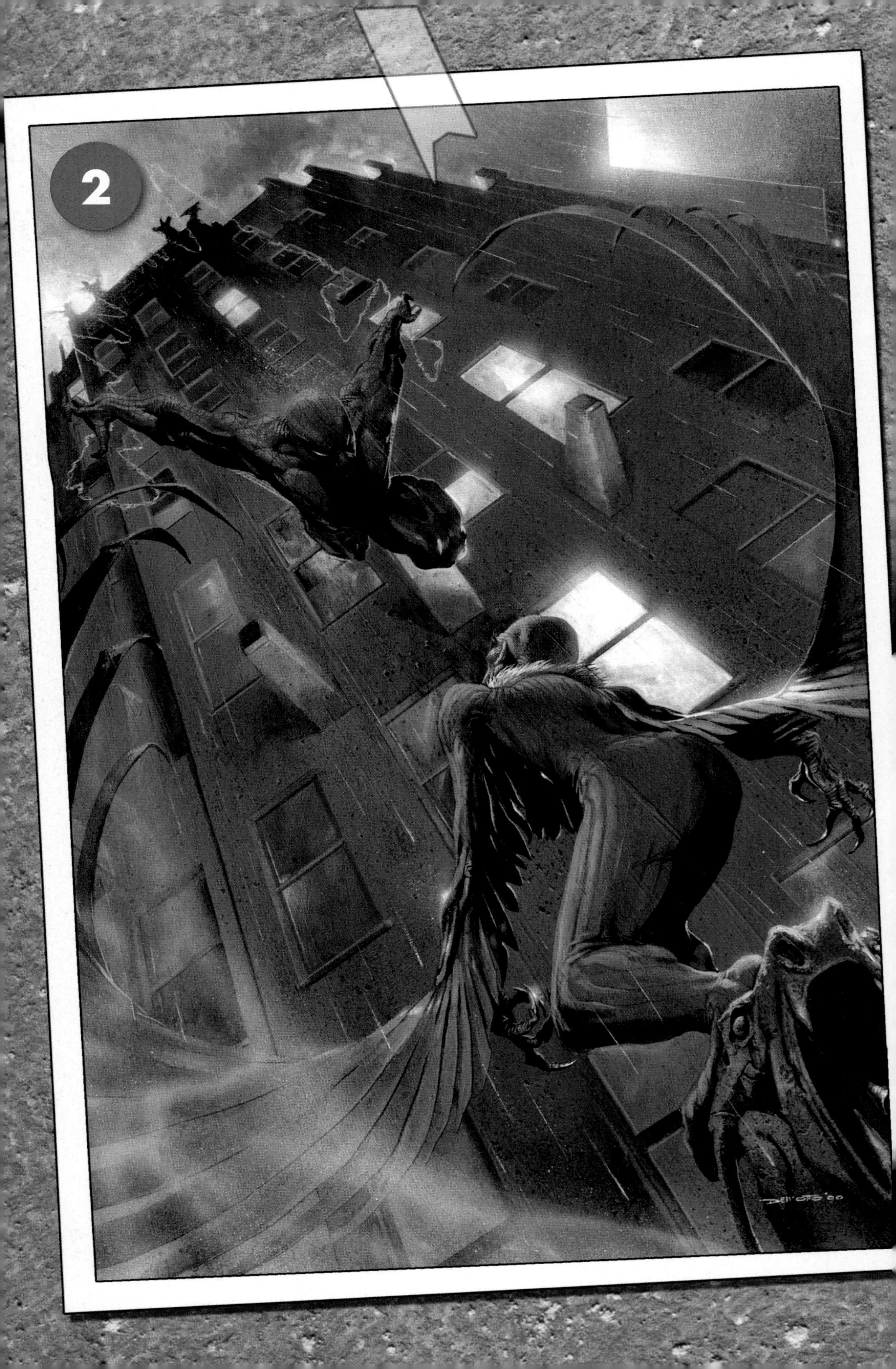
2

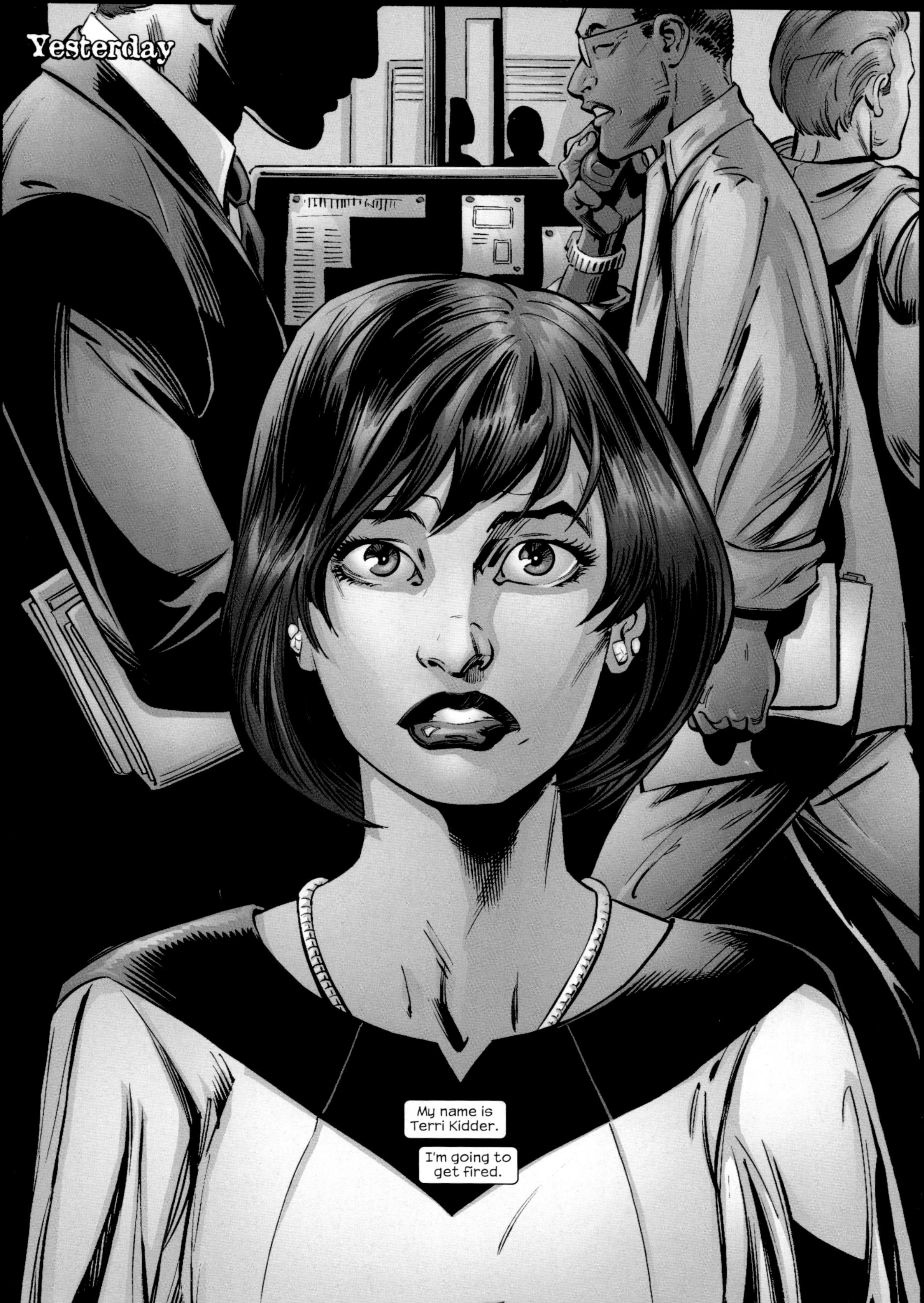
Yesterday
My name is Terri Kidder.
I'm going to get fired.

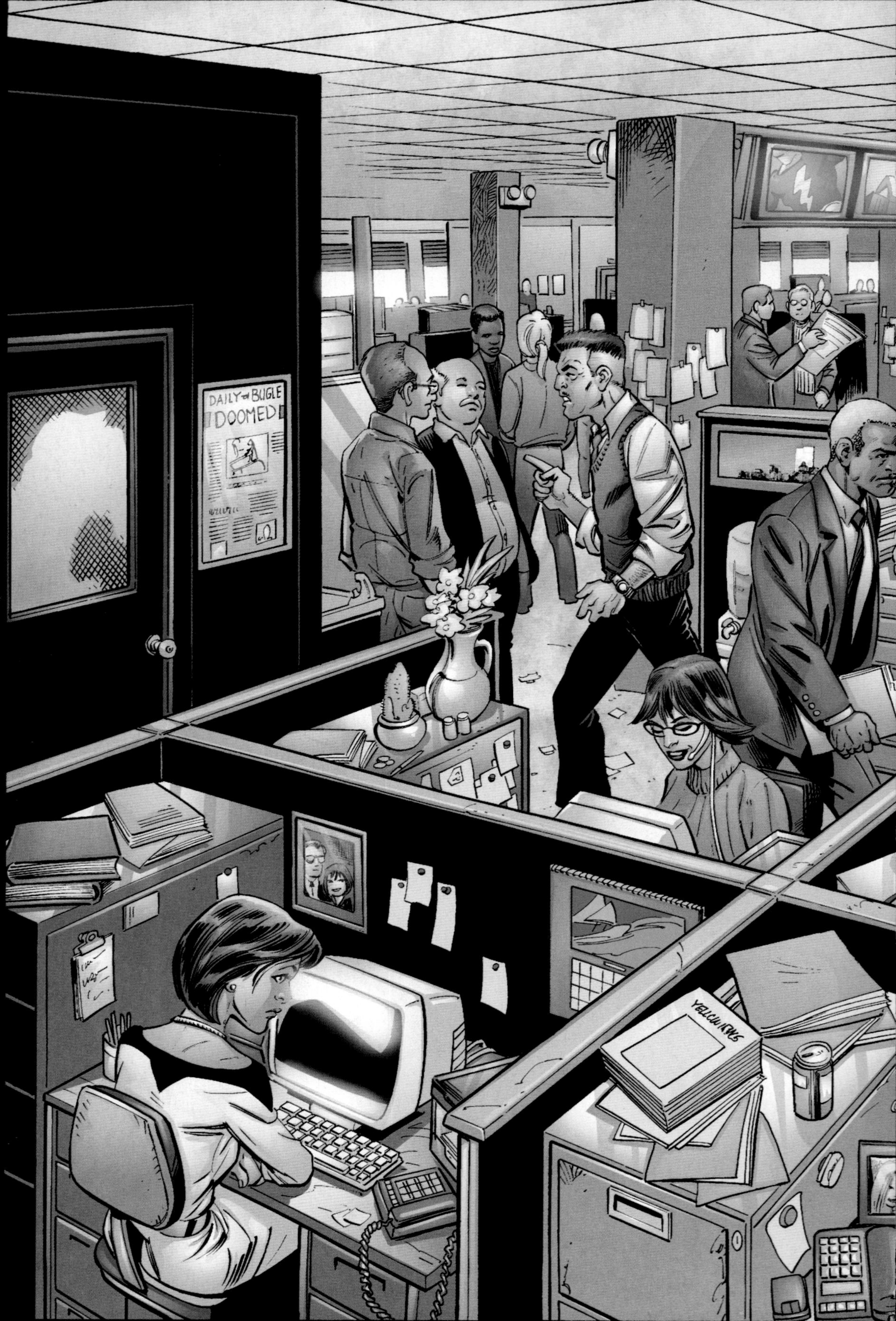
DAILY BUGLE
DOOMED

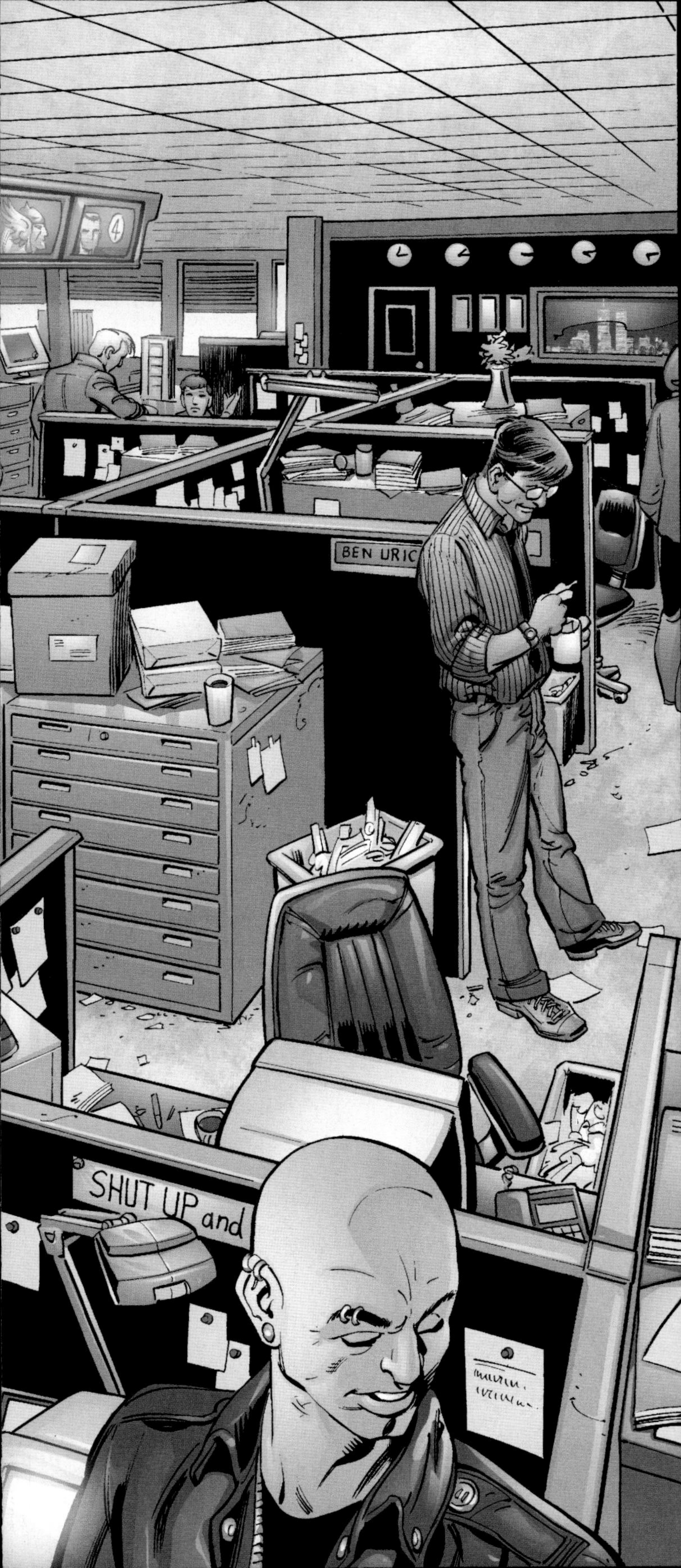
BEN URIC
SHUT UP and

I am.

I can feel it.

It's three o' clock and I have no story.

I need a story. That's what this stupid job is. It's ***all*** it is.

Finding a story. Getting a story. Feeding a story. Making a story.

Four kabillion people in this city.

Every one of them cheating, robbing, killing, stabbing, someone out of something somewhere...and I have *no story!*

Half the people in this ***room*** are probably closet ***mutants*** and I have no story.

I've been here two weeks and I haven't found one story worth publishing.

But I have to find ***something*** or I am out on my toosh by Friday.

No joke. I am so gone it's not even funny.

But I've never worked for a paper like ***this.*** My last job was at one of those big, old-fashioned, great metropolitan newspapers...

...and if you're, basically, ***everyone*** I know...you're asking: "Why on earth would you leave a job at a big, respected newspaper to come work at a tabloid like the frakakta Daily Bugle?"

And by tabloid I'm not talking about 'Princess Di's head is kidnapped by Aliens' or--or 'Reed Richards is sleeping with Madonna,' no.

'Tabloid' gets a crap reputation because people don't know what the ***word*** means.

Tabloid is the format. The folded newspaper format. And it's the only thing we have in common with those pieces of rag trip.

No. This is a real tabloid newspaper.

And I ***wanted*** to work here...in New York City. For exactly ***this*** kind of paper.

My other job felt shallow and--and uninspired. Look at this place! Look how alive it is.

We are the voice of the ***people.*** We're the voice of the common man. The commuter. The coffee guy.

We speak for ***everyone*** in a language they want and understand.

Me personally? No. I'm not speaking for ***anyone*** because I have ***no story!***

I'm just not used to the ***politics*** of this place yet.

I mean, ***every*** place has them, the politics. I just don't understand how this place works.

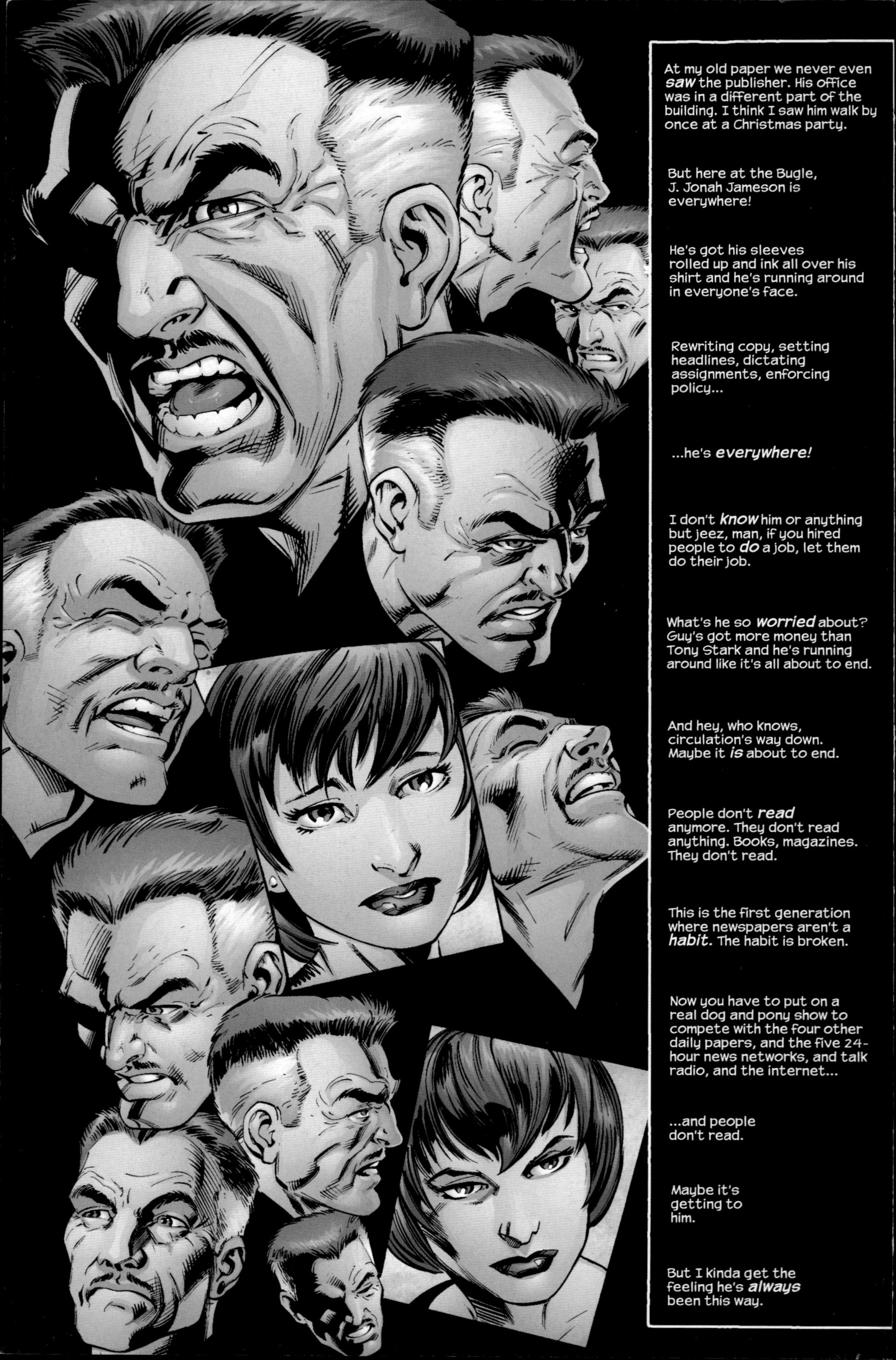
At my old paper we never even saw the publisher. His office was in a different part of the building. I think I saw him walk by once at a Christmas party.
But here at the Bugle, J. Jonah Jameson is everywhere!
He's got his sleeves rolled up and ink all over his shirt and he's running around in everyone's face.
Rewriting copy, setting headlines, dictating assignments, enforcing policy...
...he's everywhere!
I don't know him or anything but jeez, man, if you hired people to do a job, let them do their job.
What's he so worried about? Guy's got more money than Tony Stark and he's running around like it's all about to end.
And hey, who knows, circulation's way down. Maybe it is about to end.
People don't read anymore. They don't read anything. Books, magazines. They don't read.
This is the first generation where newspapers aren't a habit. The habit is broken.
Now you have to put on a real dog and pony show to compete with the four other daily papers, and the five 24-hour news networks, and talk radio, and the internet...
...and people don't read.
Maybe it's getting to him.
But I kinda get the feeling he's always been this way.

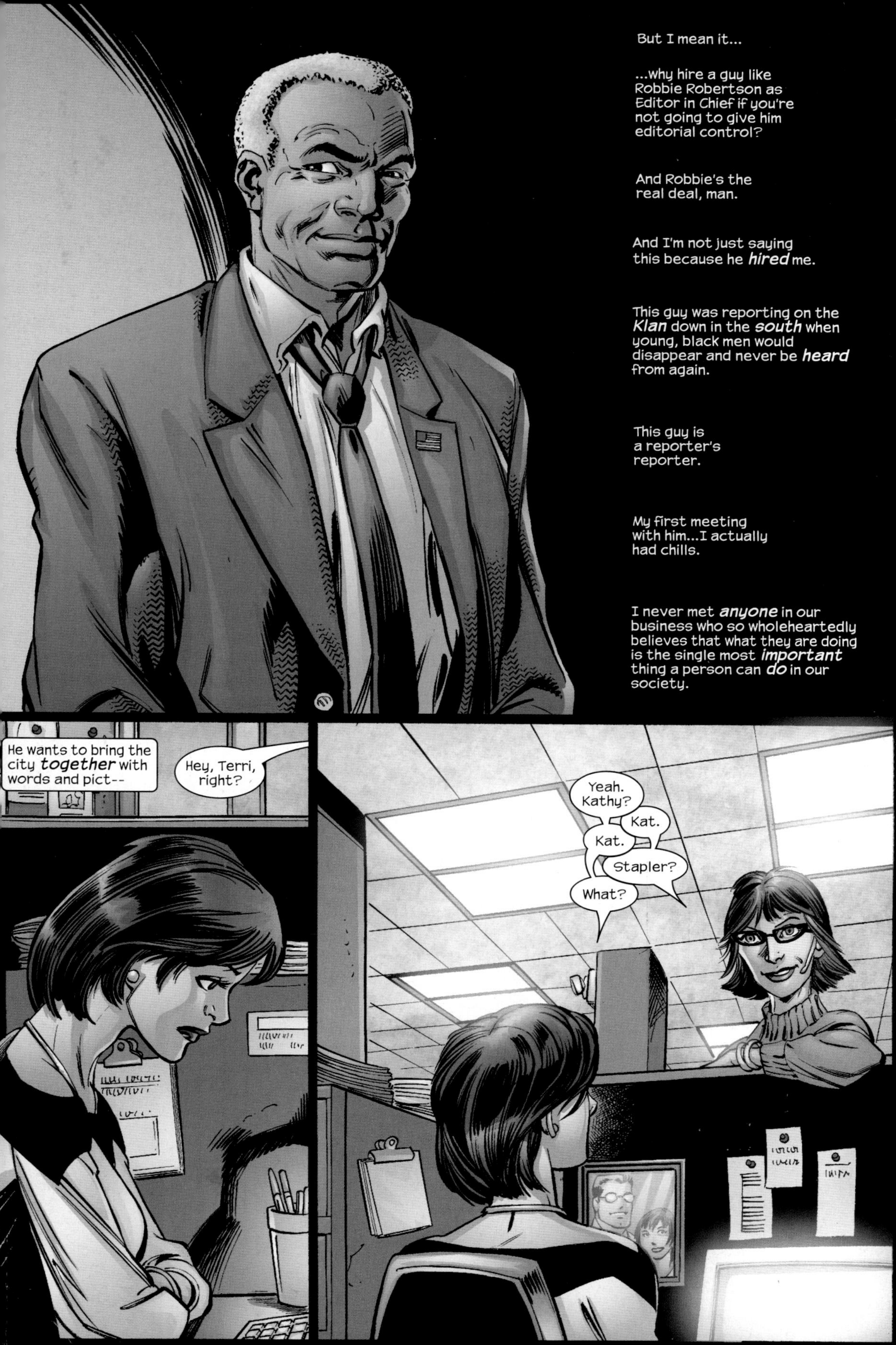
But I mean it...
...why hire a guy like Robbie Robertson as Editor in Chief if you're not going to give him editorial control?
And Robbie's the real deal, man.
And I'm not just saying this because he *hired* me.
This guy was reporting on the *Klan* down in the *south* when young, black men would disappear and never be *heard* from again.
This guy is a reporter's reporter.
My first meeting with him...I actually had chills.
I never met *anyone* in our business who so wholeheartedly believes that what they are doing is the single most *important* thing a person can *do* in our society.
He wants to bring the city *together* with words and pict--
Hey, Terri, right?
Yeah. Kathy?
Kat.
Kat.
Stapler?
What?

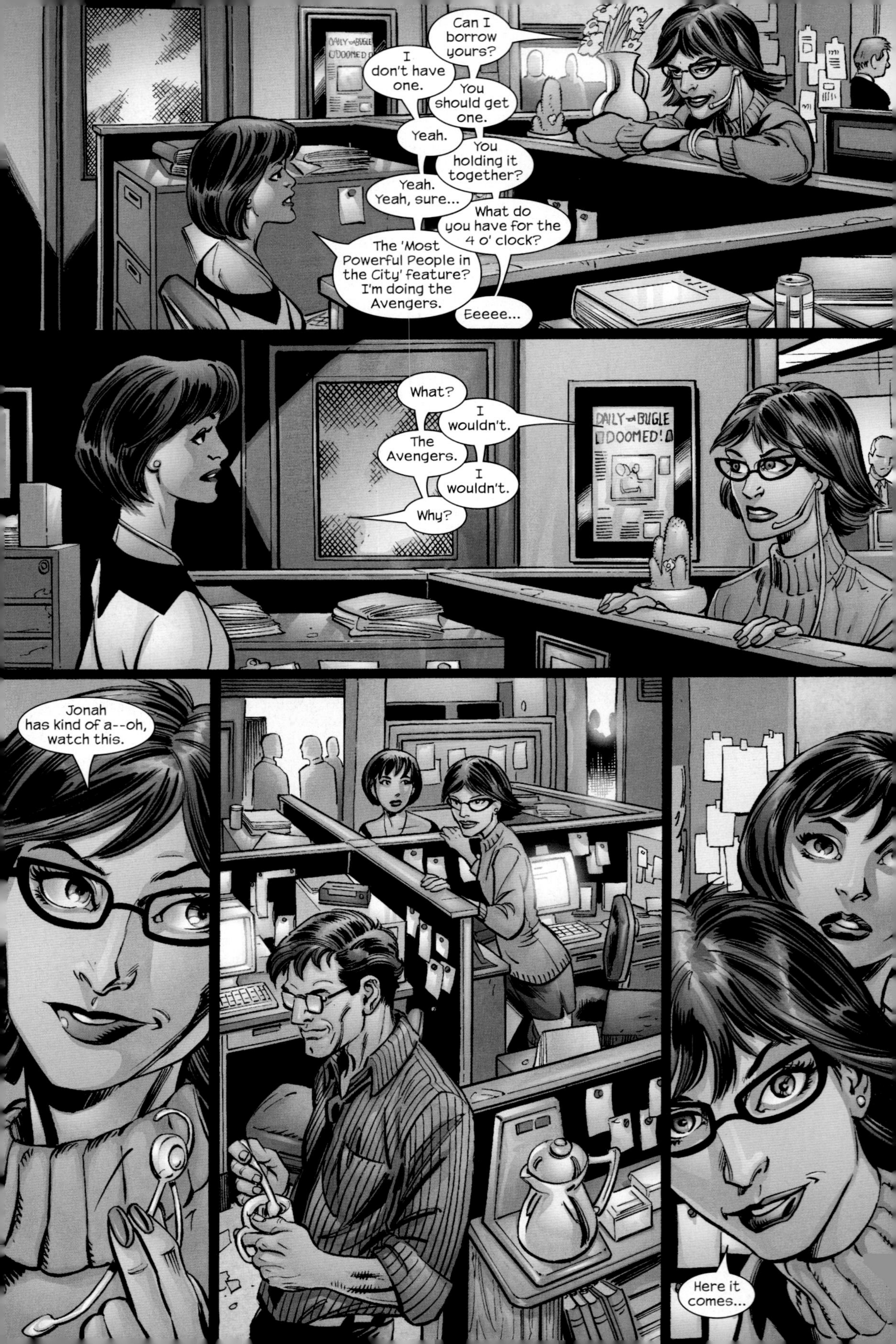
Can I borrow yours?
I don't have one.
You should get one.
Yeah.
You holding it together?
Yeah. Yeah, sure...
What do you have for the 4 o' clock?
The 'Most Powerful People in the City' feature? I'm doing the Avengers.
Eeeee...
What?
I wouldn't.
The Avengers.
I wouldn't.
Why?
Jonah has kind of a--oh, watch this.
Here it comes...

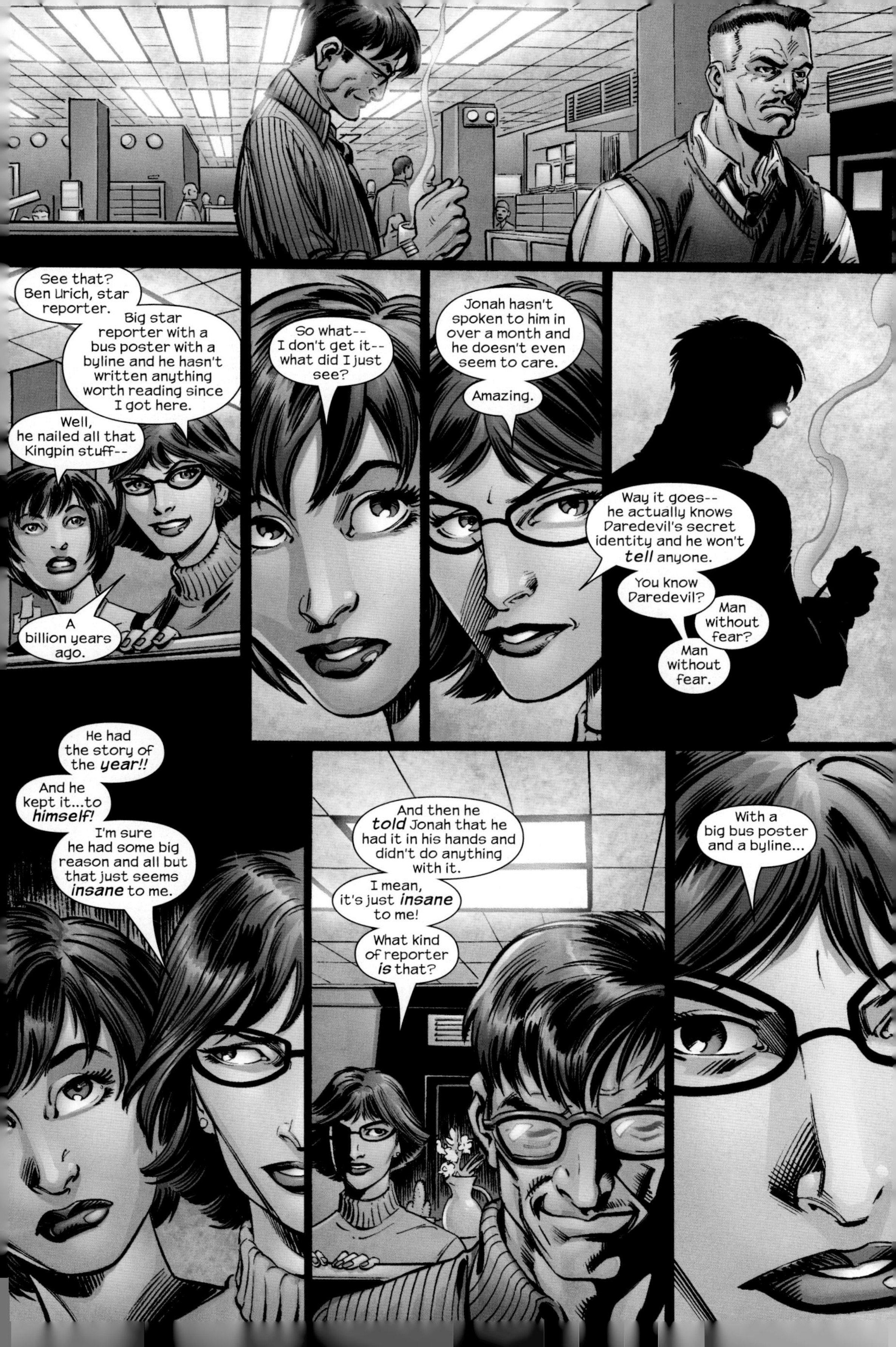
See that? Ben Urich, star reporter.
Big star reporter with a bus poster with a byline and he hasn't written anything worth reading since I got here.
Well, he nailed all that Kingpin stuff--
A billion years ago.
So what-- I don't get it-- what did I just see?
Jonah hasn't spoken to him in over a month and he doesn't even seem to care.
Amazing.
Way it goes-- he actually knows Daredevil's secret identity and he won't *tell* anyone.
You know Daredevil?
Man without fear?
Man without fear.
He had the story of the *year!!*
And he kept it...to *himself!*
I'm sure he had some big reason and all but that just seems *insane* to me.
And then he *told* Jonah that he had it in his hands and didn't do anything with it.
I mean, it's just *insane* to me!
What kind of reporter *is* that?
With a big bus poster and a byline...

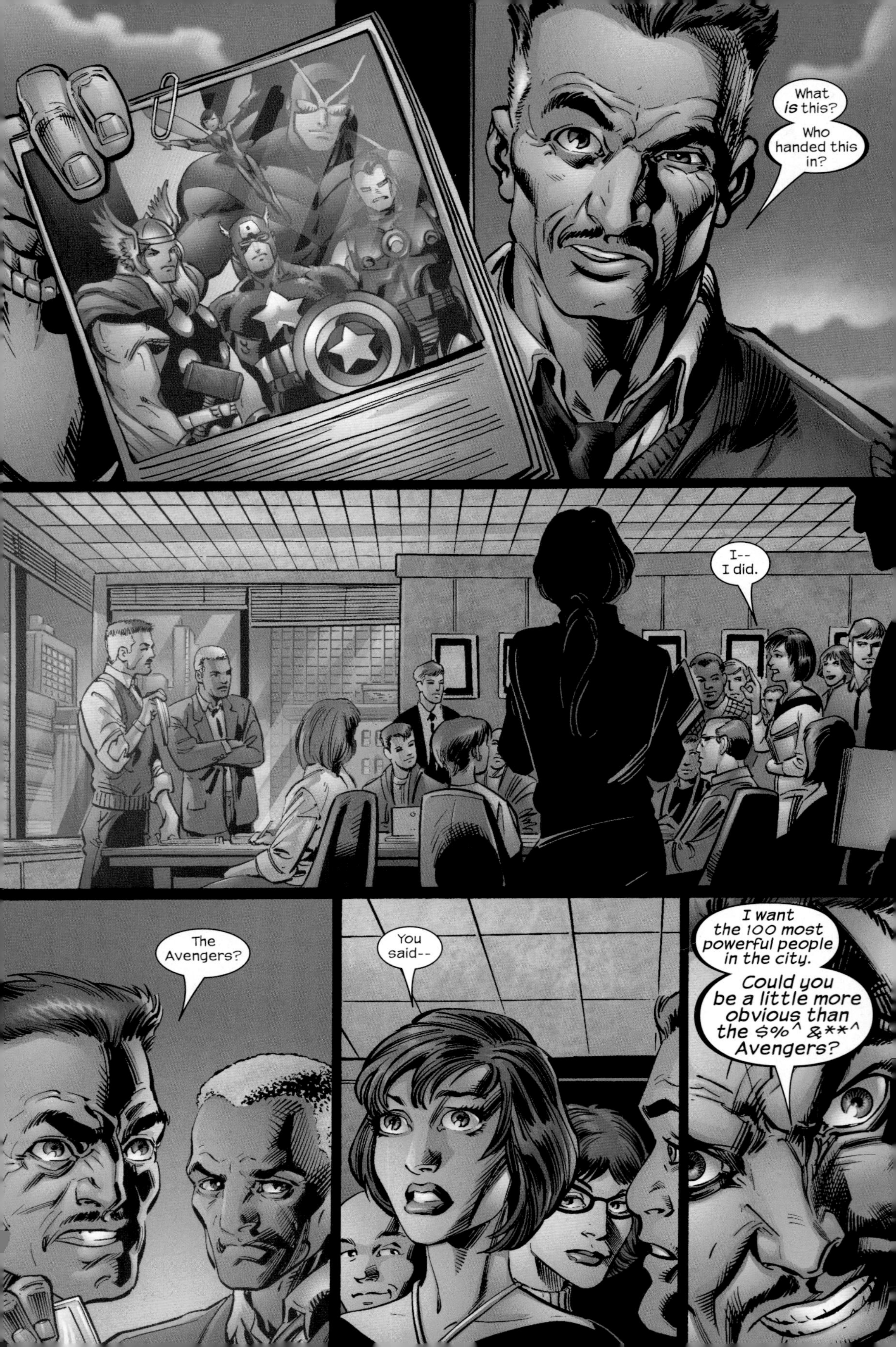

What is this?
Who handed this in?
I-- I did.
The Avengers?
You said--
I want the 100 most powerful people in the city.
Could you be a little more obvious than the $%^ &**^ Avengers?

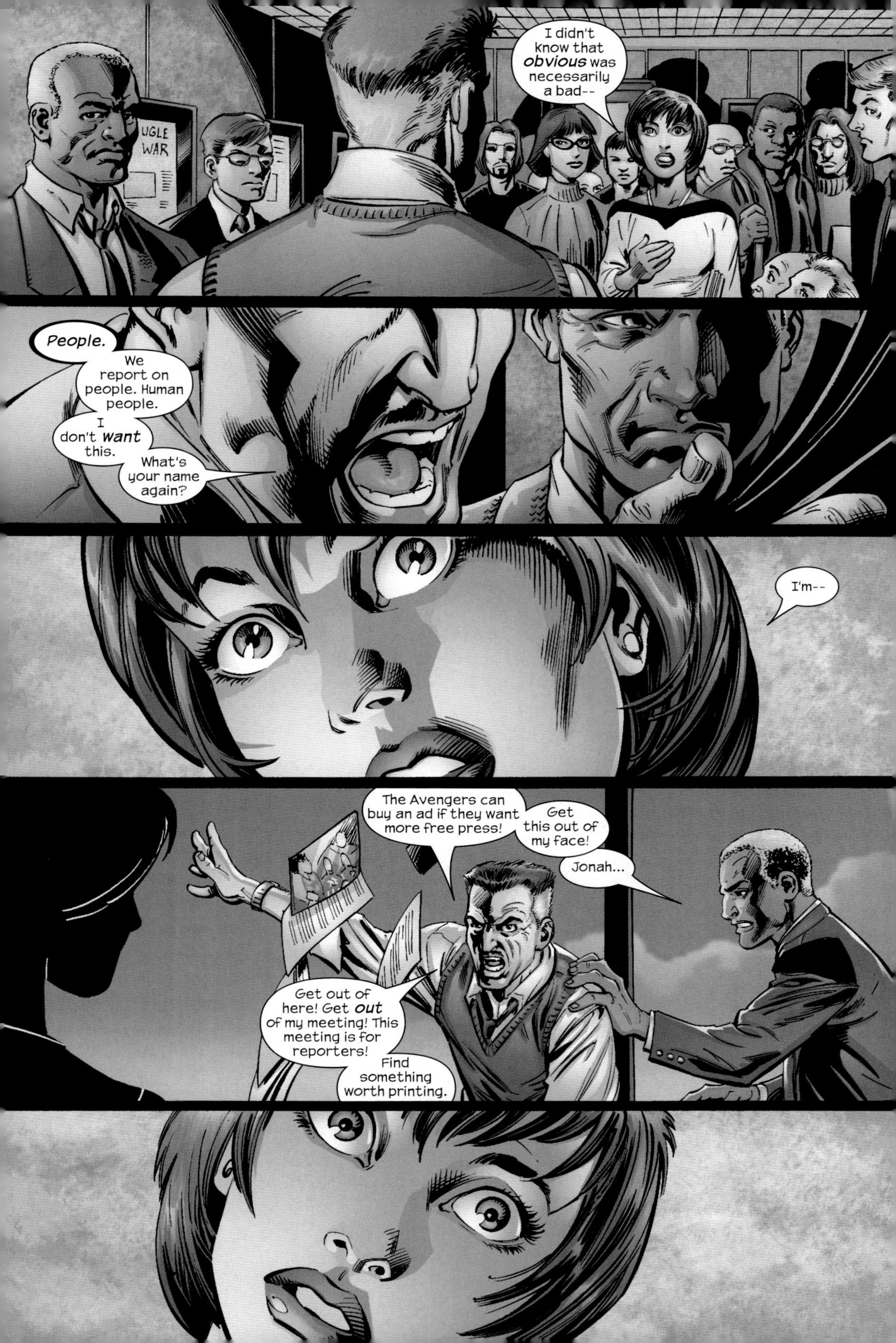
I didn't know that *obvious* was necessarily a bad--
People.
We report on people. Human people.
I don't *want* this.
What's your name again?
I'm--
The Avengers can buy an ad if they want more free press!
Get this out of my face!
Jonah...
Get out of here! Get *out* of my meeting! This meeting is for reporters!
Find something worth printing.

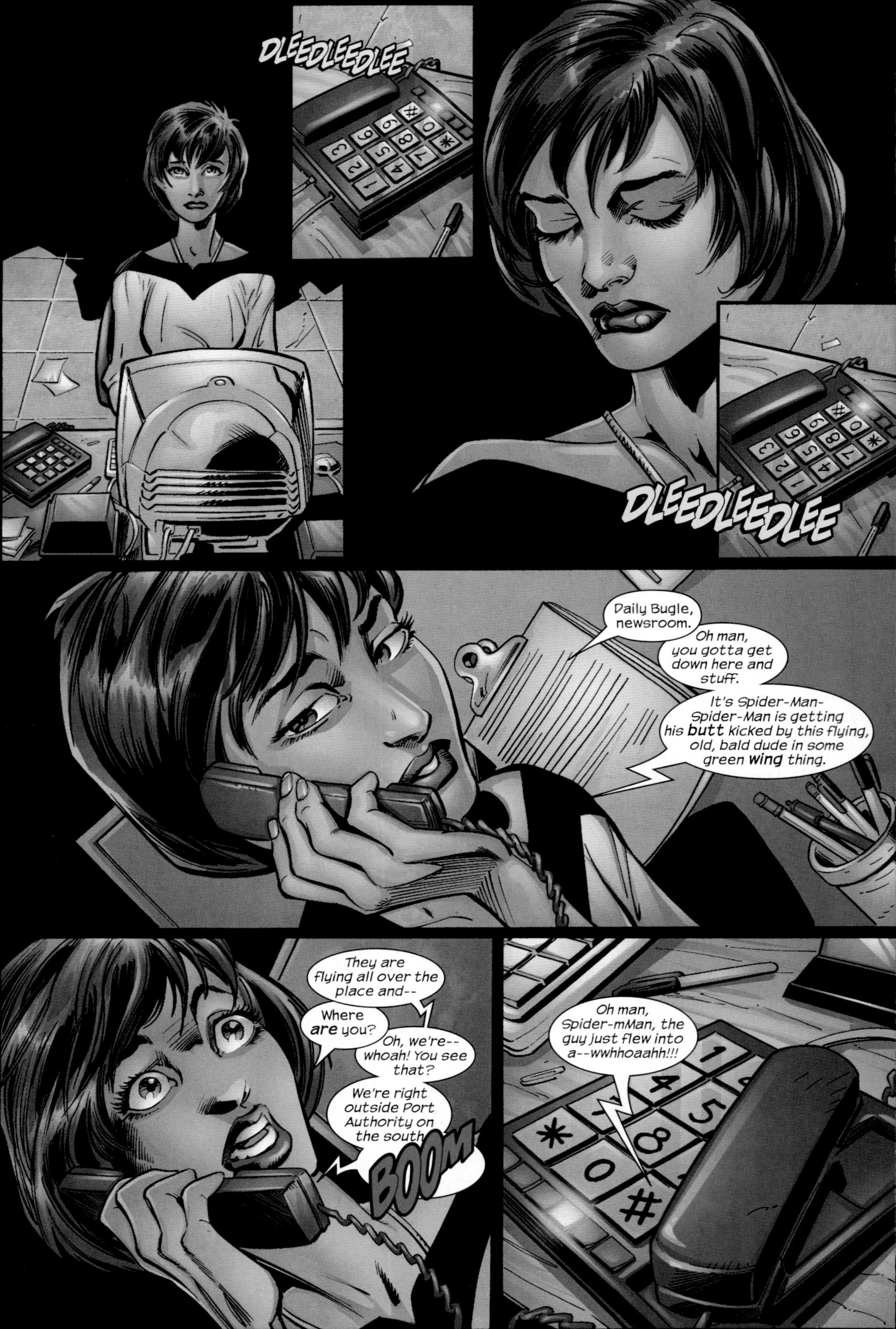
DLEEDLEEDLEE
DLEEDLEEDLEE
Daily Bugle, newsroom.
Oh man, you gotta get down here and stuff.
It's Spider-Man-Spider-Man is getting his **butt** kicked by this flying, old, bald dude in some green **wing** thing.
They are flying all over the place and--
Where **are** you?
Oh, we're-- whoah! You see that?
We're right outside Port Authority on the south
BOOM
Oh man, Spider-mMan, the guy just flew into a--wwhhoaahh!!!

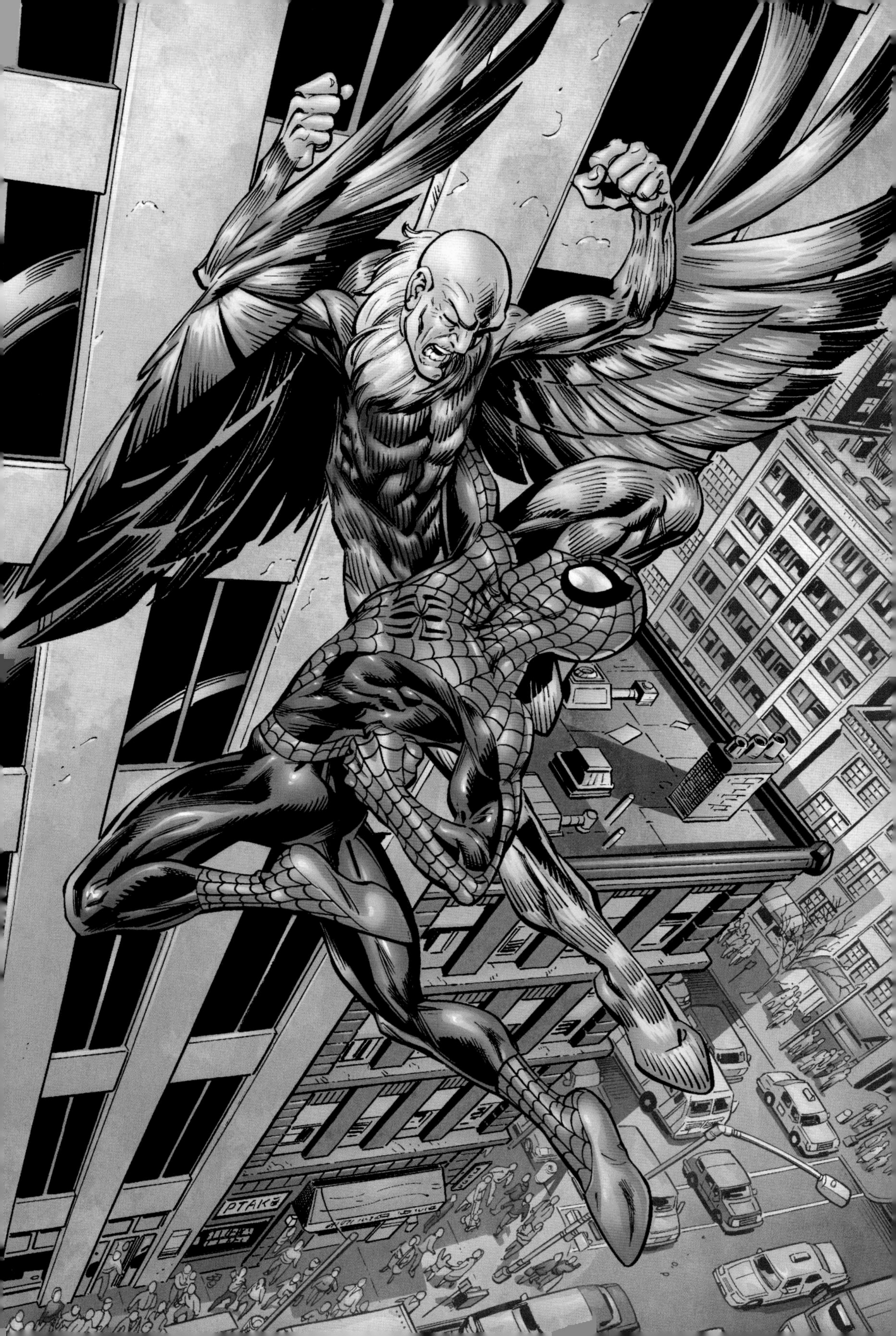

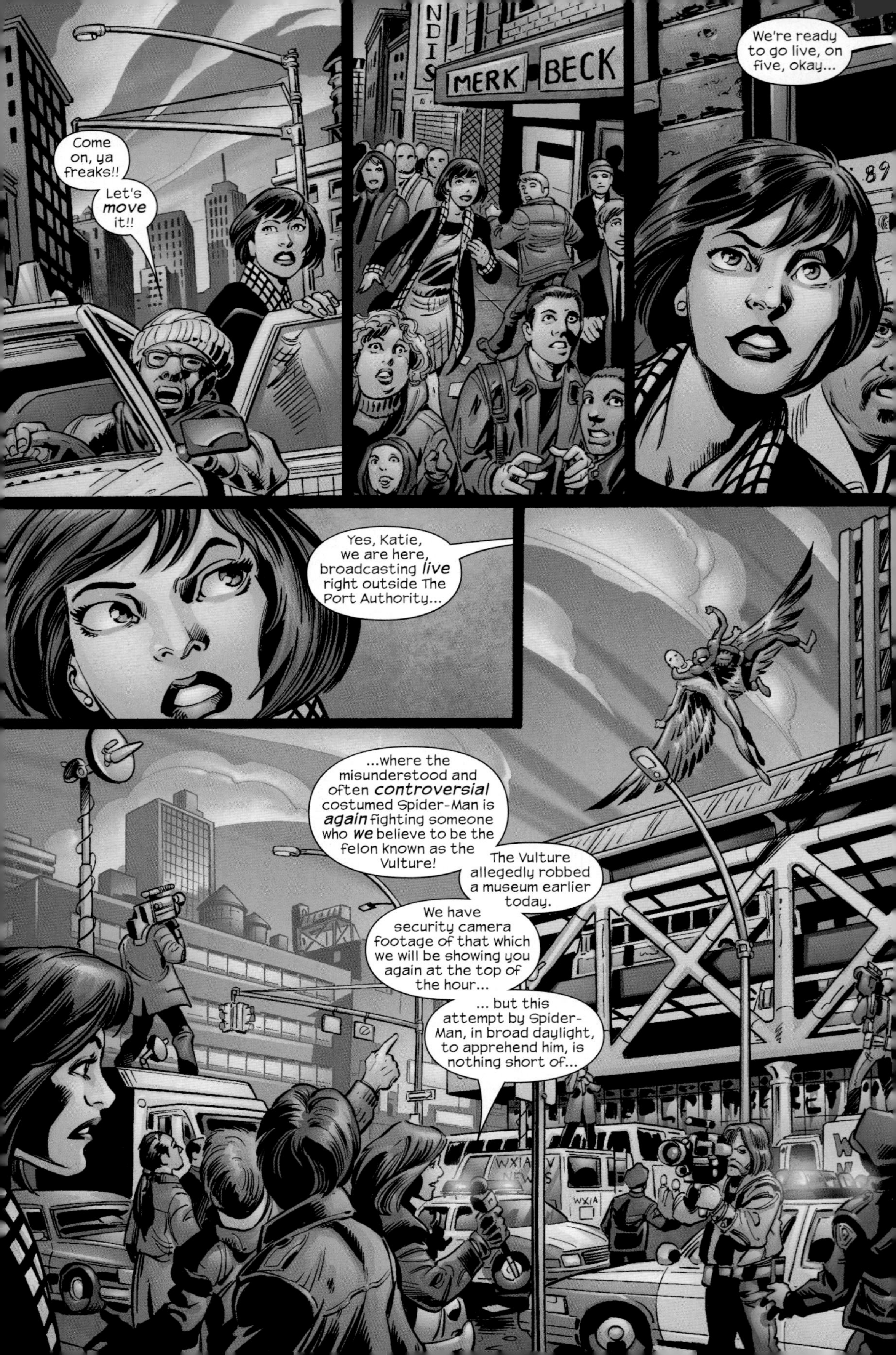

Come on, ya freaks!!
Let's *move* it!!
NDIS
MERK
BECK
We're ready to go live, on five, okay...
Yes, Katie, we are here, broadcasting *live* right outside The Port Authority...
...where the misunderstood and often *controversial* costumed Spider-Man is *again* fighting someone who *we* believe to be the felon known as the Vulture!
The Vulture allegedly robbed a museum earlier today.
We have security camera footage of that which we will be showing you again at the top of the hour...
... but this attempt by Spider-Man, in broad daylight, to apprehend him, is nothing short of...
WXIA

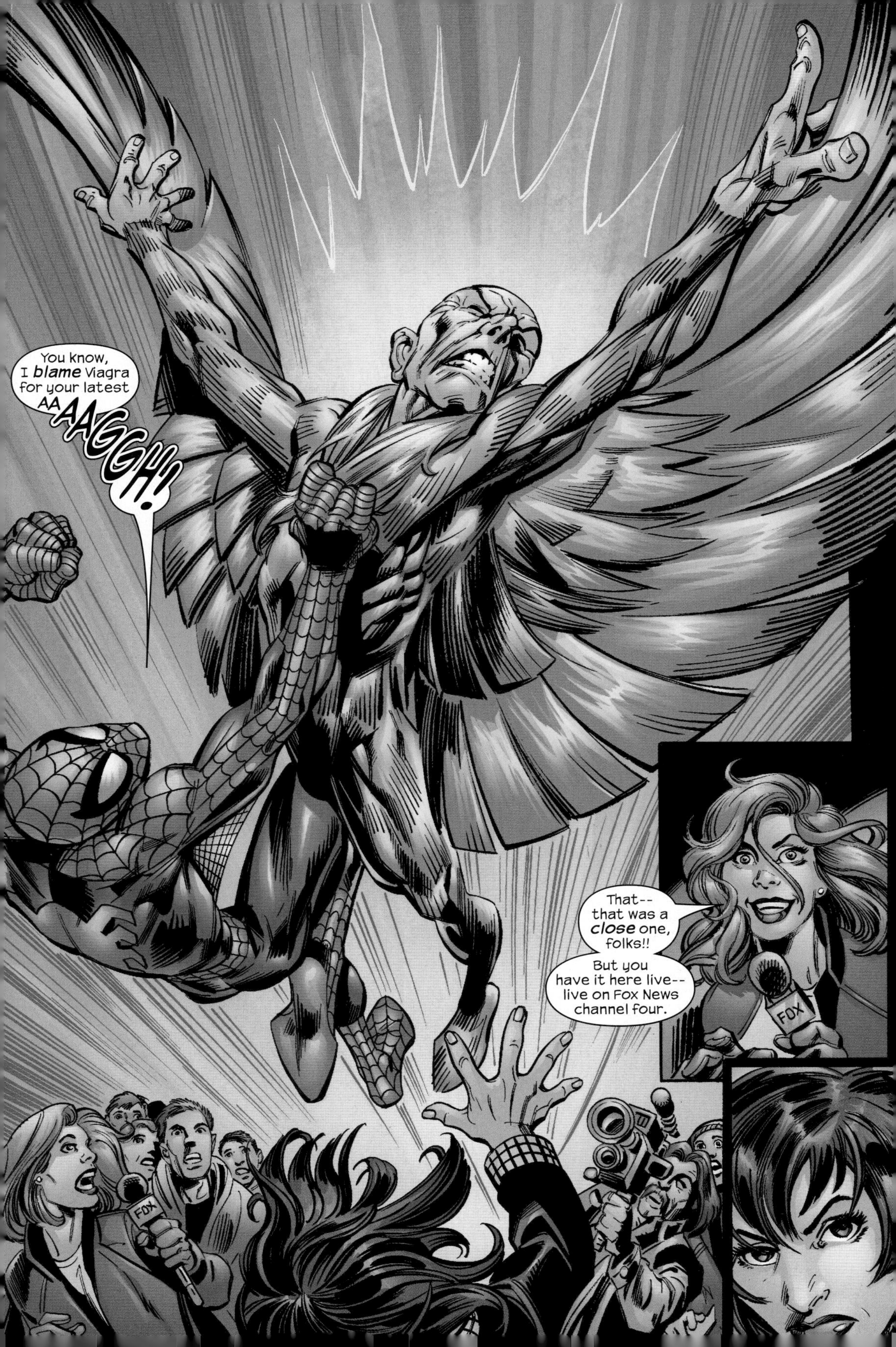
You know, I *blame* Viagra for your latest AA
AAGGH!!
That-- that was a *close* one, folks!!
But you have it here live-- live on Fox News channel four.
FOX
FOX

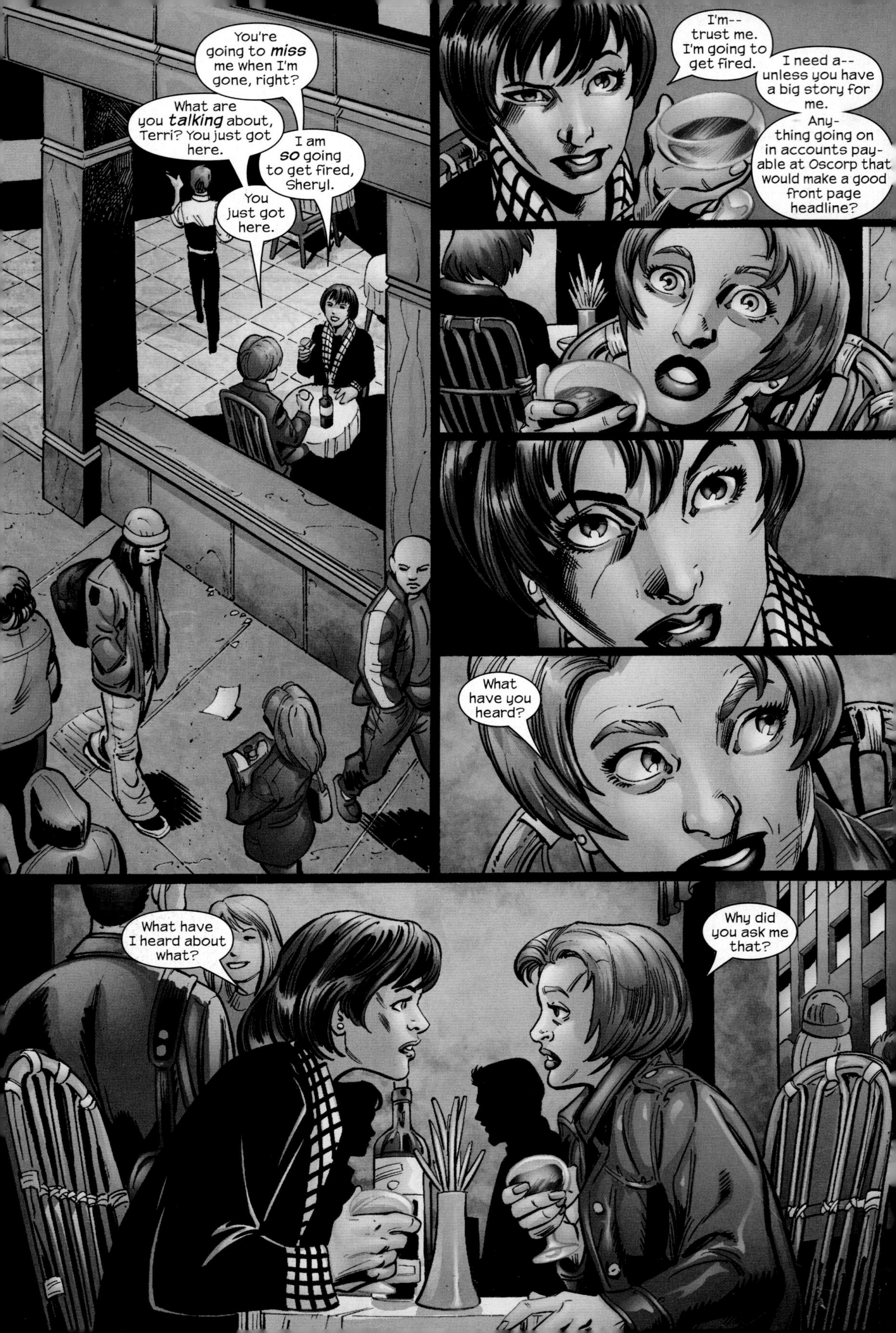

You're going to *miss* me when I'm gone, right?
What are you *talking* about, Terri? You just got here.
I am *so* going to get fired, Sheryl.
You just got here.
I'm-- trust me. I'm going to get fired.
I need a-- unless you have a big story for me.
Any-thing going on in accounts pay-able at Oscorp that would make a good front page headline?
What have you heard?
What have I heard about what?
Why did you ask me that?

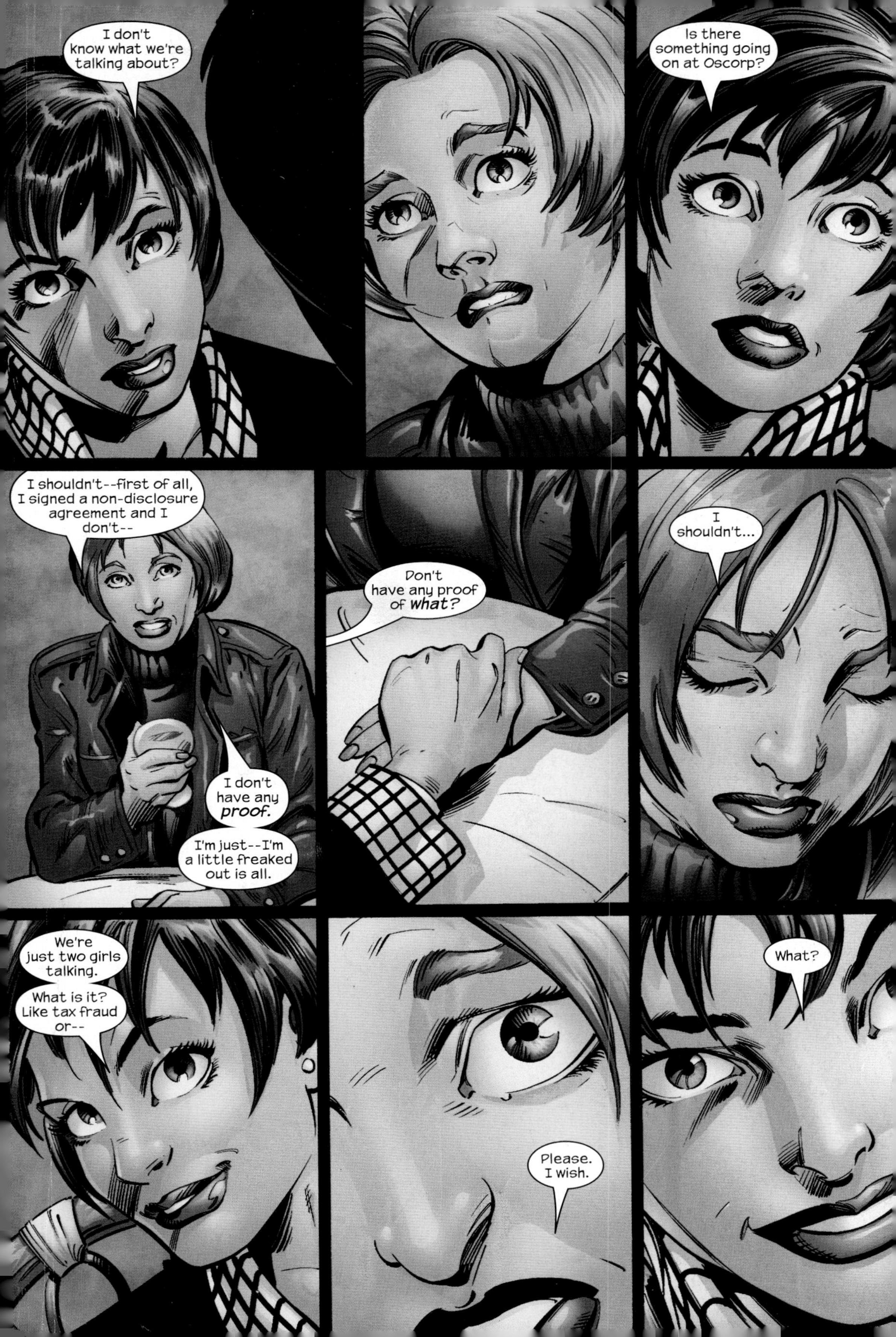

I don't know what we're talking about?
Is there something going on at Oscorp?
I shouldn't--first of all, I signed a non-disclosure agreement and I don't--
I don't have any *proof.*
I'm just--I'm a little freaked out is all.
Don't have any proof of *what?*
I shouldn't...
We're just two girls talking.
What is it? Like tax fraud or--
Please. I wish.
What?

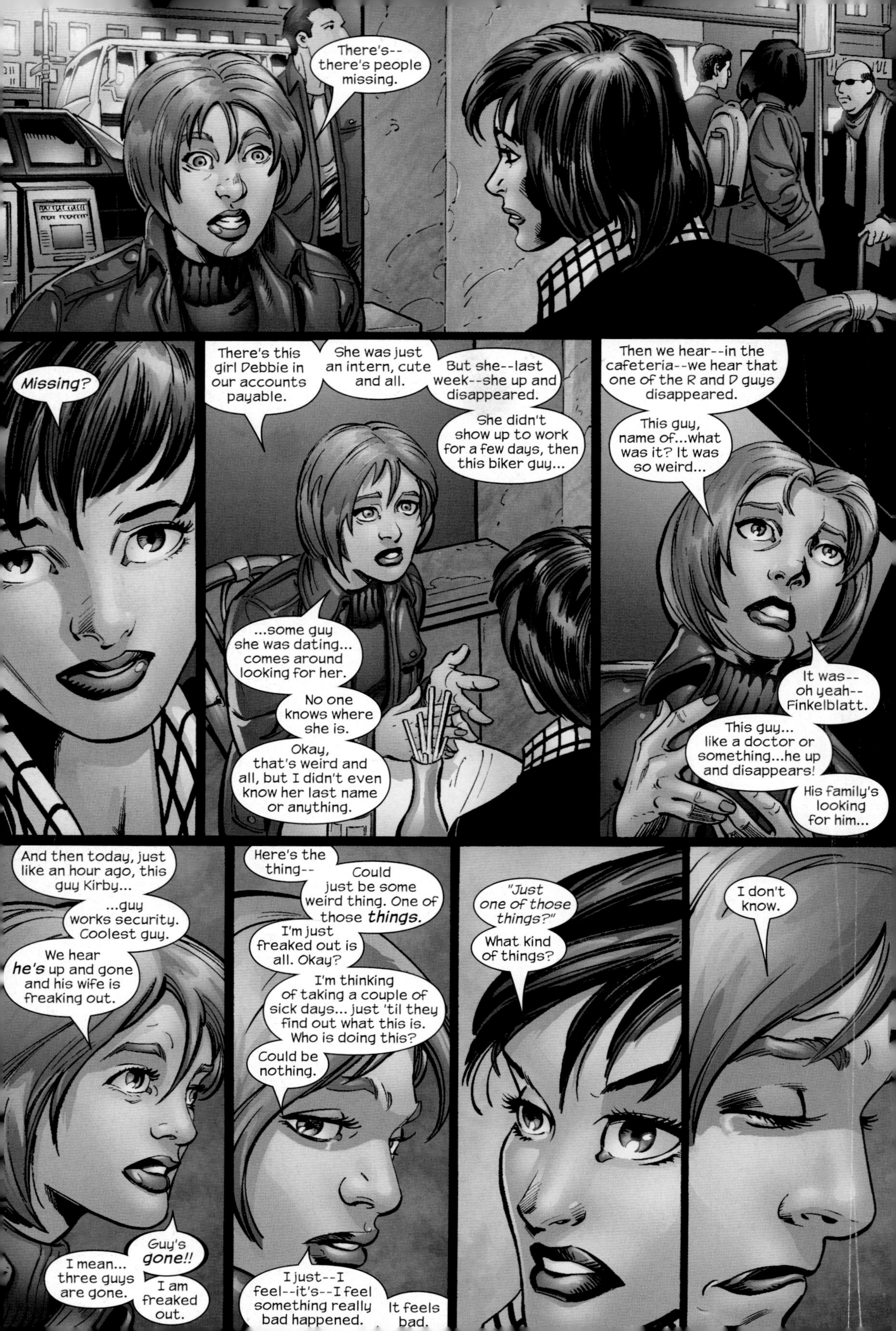
There's--
there's people
missing.
Missing?
There's this
girl Debbie in
our accounts
payable.
She was just
an intern, cute
and all.
But she--last
week--she up and
disappeared.
She didn't
show up to work
for a few days, then
this biker guy...
...some guy
she was dating...
comes around
looking for her.
No one
knows where
she is.
Okay,
that's weird and
all, but I didn't even
know her last name
or anything.
Then we hear--in the
cafeteria--we hear that
one of the R and D guys
disappeared.
This guy,
name of...what
was it? It was
so weird...
It was--
oh yeah--
Finkelblatt.
This guy...
like a doctor or
something...he up
and disappears!
His family's
looking
for him...
And then today, just
like an hour ago, this
guy Kirby...
...guy
works security.
Coolest guy.
We hear
he's up and gone
and his wife is
freaking out.
Guy's
gone!!
I mean...
three guys
are gone.
I am
freaked
out.
Here's the
thing--
Could
just be some
weird thing. One of
those *things.*
I'm just
freaked out is
all. Okay?
I'm thinking
of taking a couple of
sick days... just 'til they
find out what this is.
Who is doing this?
Could be
nothing.
I just--I
feel--it's--I feel
something really
bad happened.
It feels
bad.
*"Just
one of those
things?"*
What kind
of things?
I don't
know.

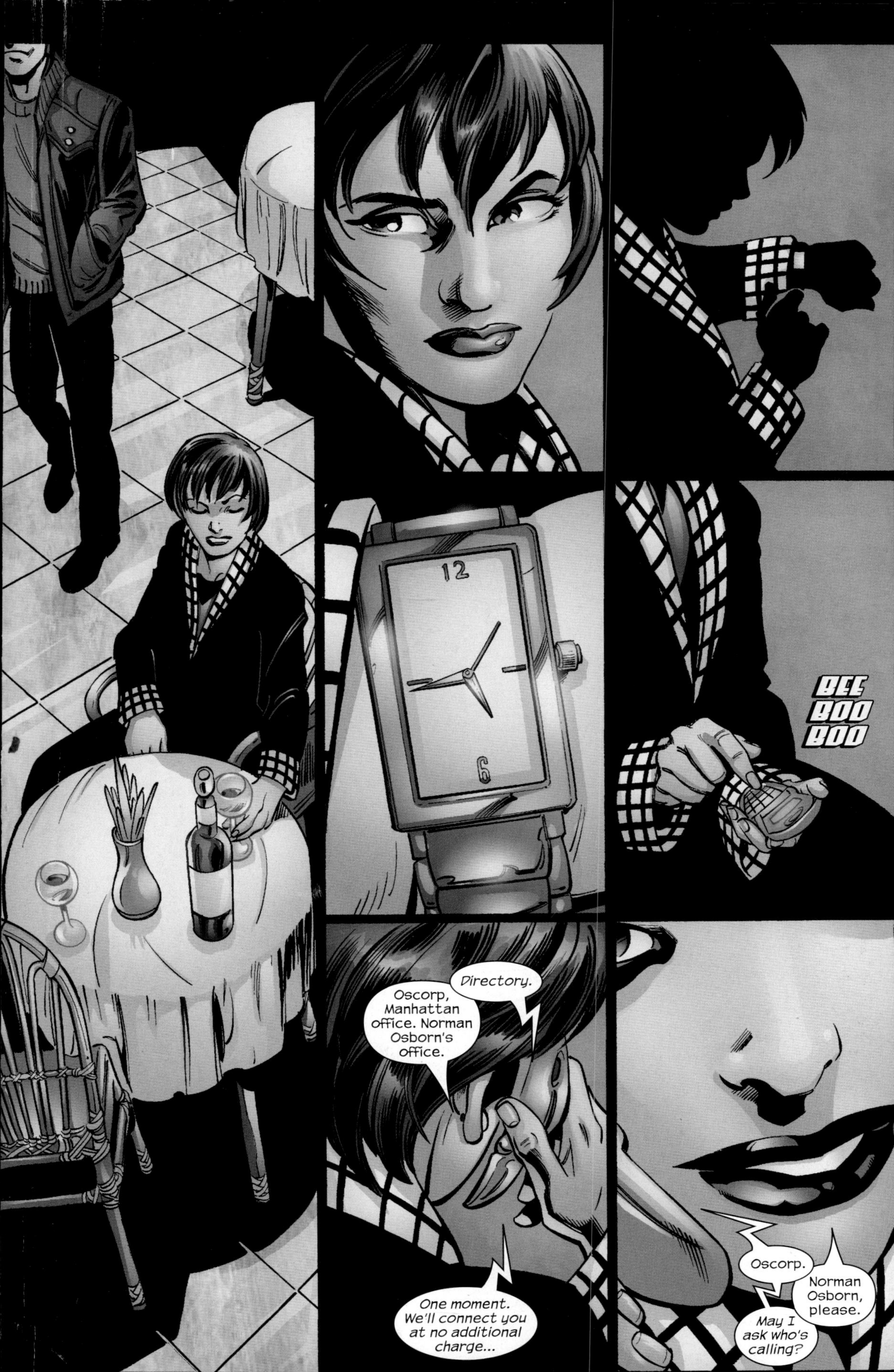
BEE
BOO
BOO
Directory.
Oscorp, Manhattan office. Norman Osborn's office.
One moment. We'll connect you at no additional charge...
Oscorp.
Norman Osborn, please.
May I ask who's calling?

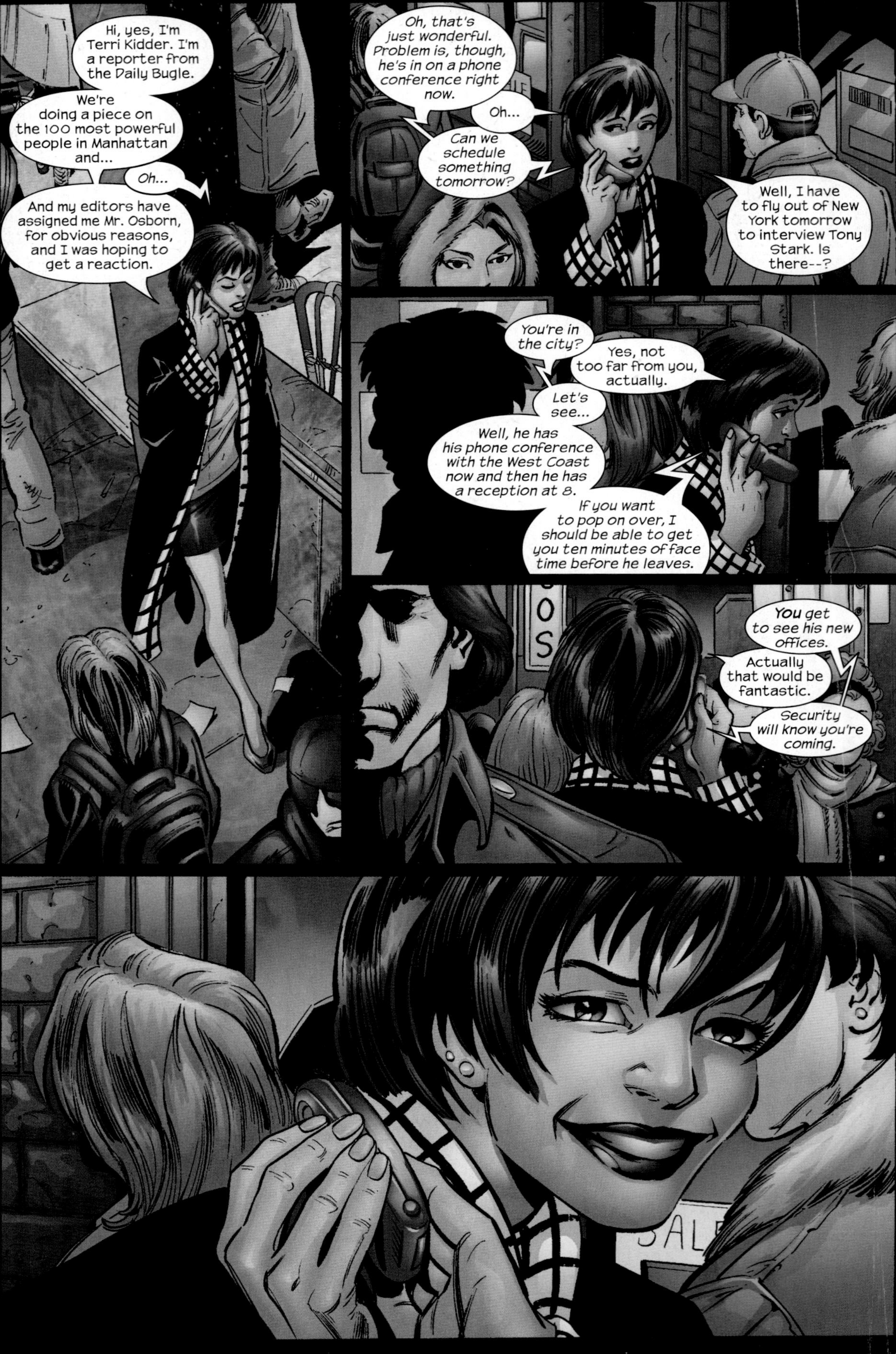
Hi, yes, I'm Terri Kidder. I'm a reporter from the Daily Bugle.
We're doing a piece on the 100 most powerful people in Manhattan and...
Oh...
And my editors have assigned me Mr. Osborn, for obvious reasons, and I was hoping to get a reaction.
Oh, that's just wonderful. Problem is, though, he's in on a phone conference right now.
Oh...
Can we schedule something tomorrow?
Well, I have to fly out of New York tomorrow to interview Tony Stark. Is there--?
You're in the city?
Yes, not too far from you, actually.
Let's see...
Well, he has his phone conference with the West Coast now and then he has a reception at 8.
If you want to pop on over, I should be able to get you ten minutes of face time before he leaves.
You get to see his new offices.
Actually that would be fantastic.
Security will know you're coming.

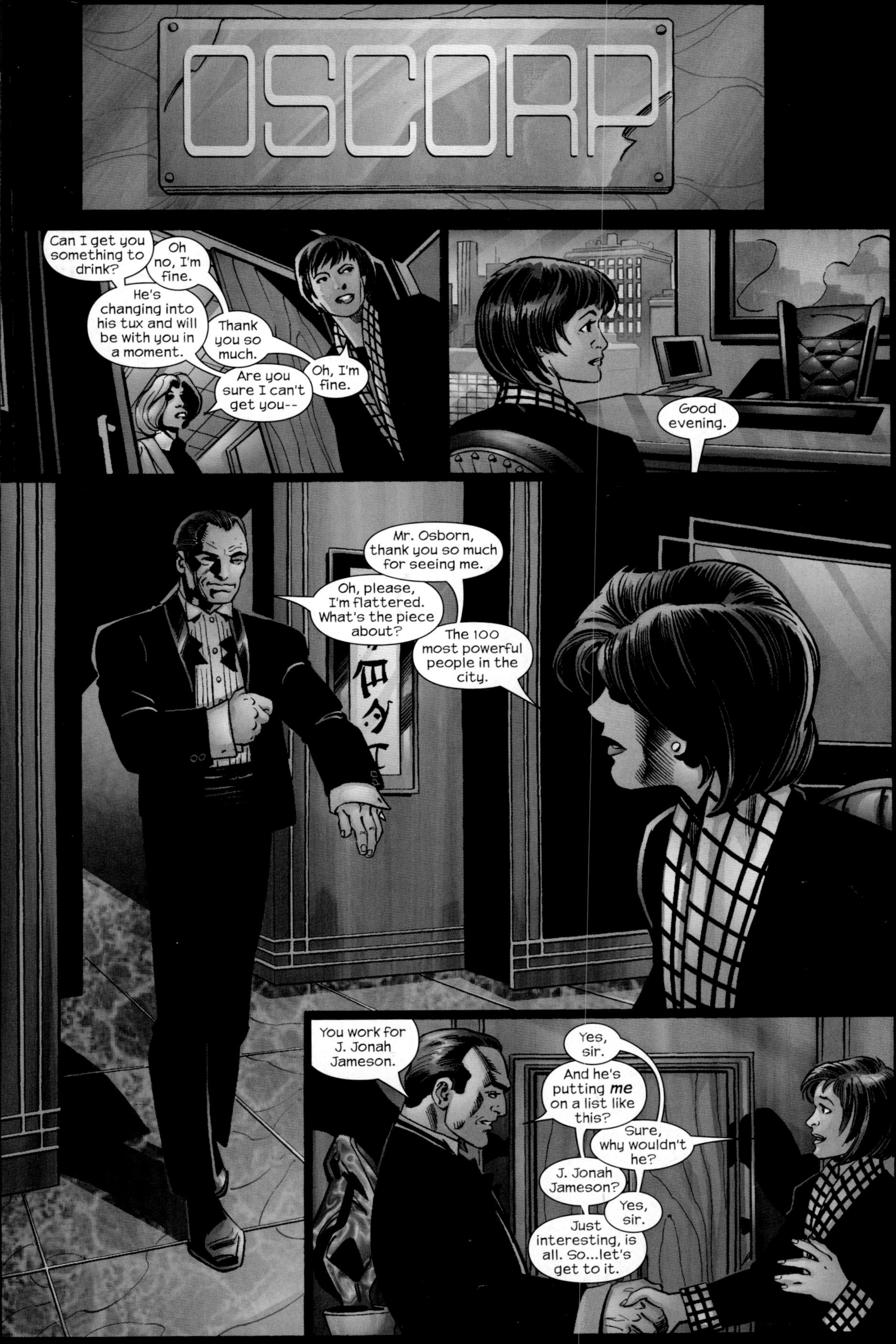
OSCORP
Can I get you something to drink?
Oh no, I'm fine.
He's changing into his tux and will be with you in a moment.
Thank you so much.
Are you sure I can't get you--
Oh, I'm fine.
Good evening.
Mr. Osborn, thank you so much for seeing me.
Oh, please, I'm flattered. What's the piece about?
The 100 most powerful people in the city.
You work for J. Jonah Jameson.
Yes, sir.
And he's putting *me* on a list like this?
Sure, why wouldn't he?
J. Jonah Jameson?
Yes, sir.
Just interesting, is all. So...let's get to it.

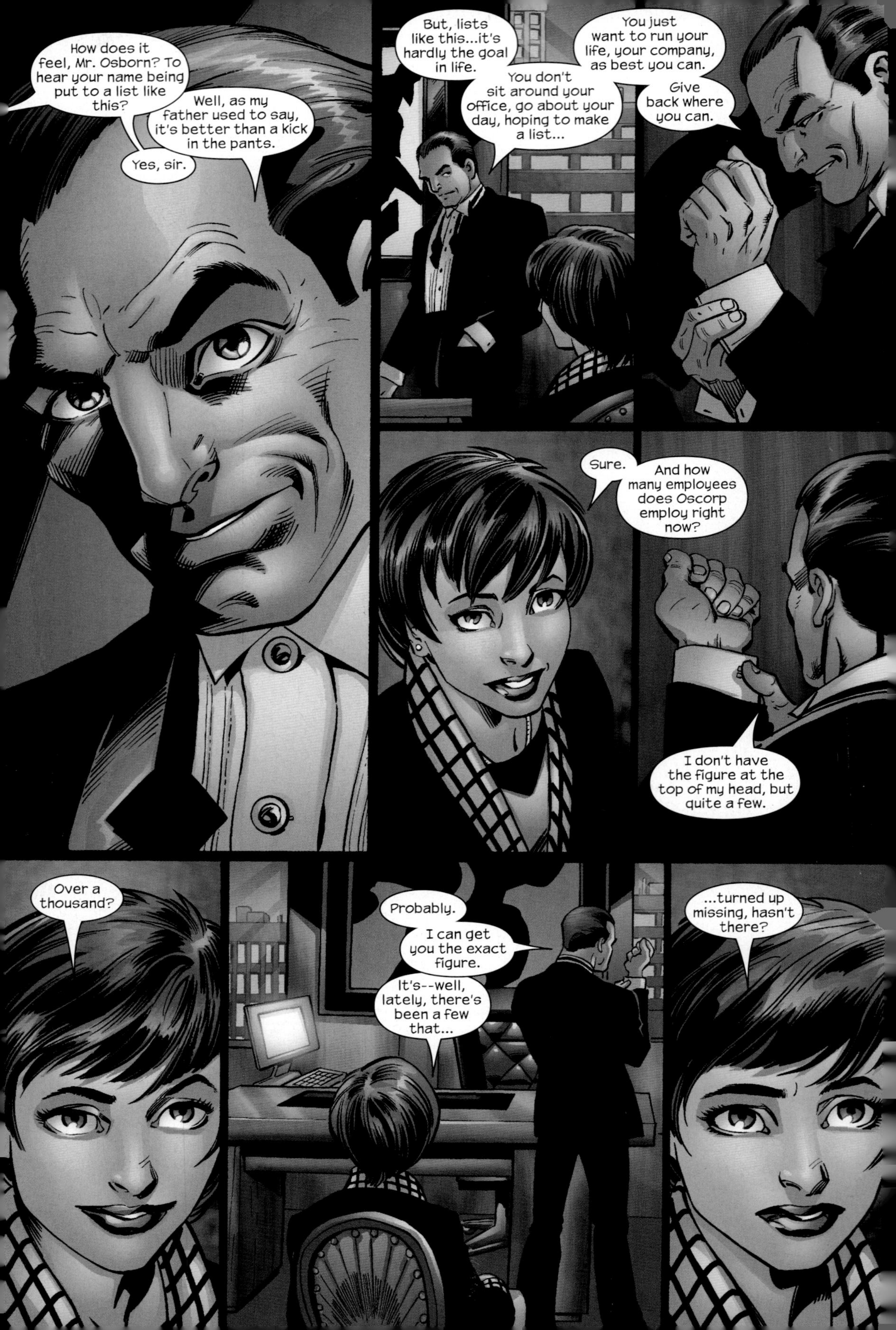
How does it feel, Mr. Osborn? To hear your name being put to a list like this?
Well, as my father used to say, it's better than a kick in the pants.
Yes, sir.
But, lists like this...it's hardly the goal in life.
You don't sit around your office, go about your day, hoping to make a list...
You just want to run your life, your company, as best you can.
Give back where you can.
Sure.
And how many employees does Oscorp employ right now?
I don't have the figure at the top of my head, but quite a few.
Over a thousand?
Probably.
I can get you the exact figure.
It's--well, lately, there's been a few that...
...turned up missing, hasn't there?

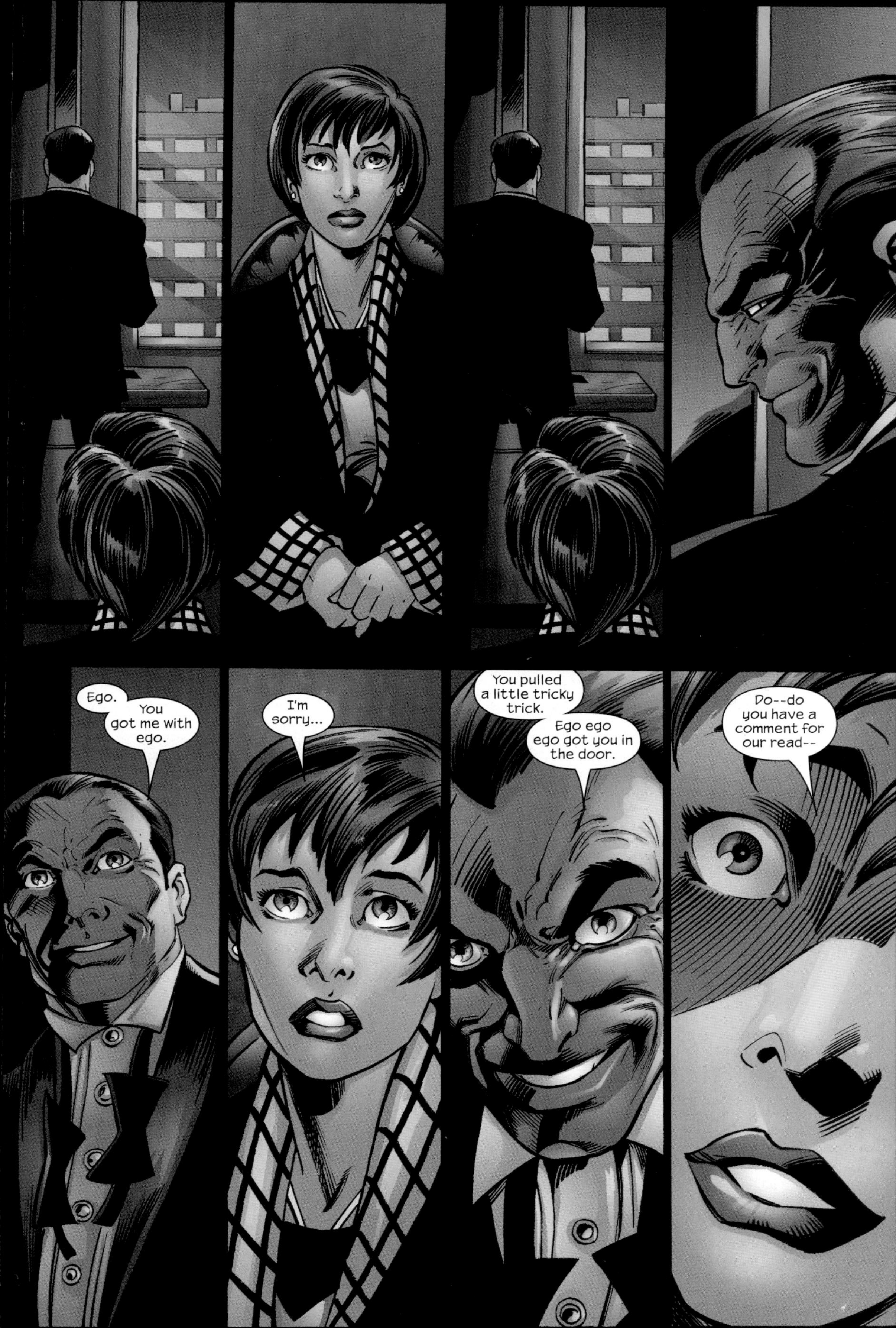

Ego.
You got me with ego.
I'm sorry...
You pulled a little tricky trick.
Ego ego ego got you in the door.
Do--do you have a comment for our read--

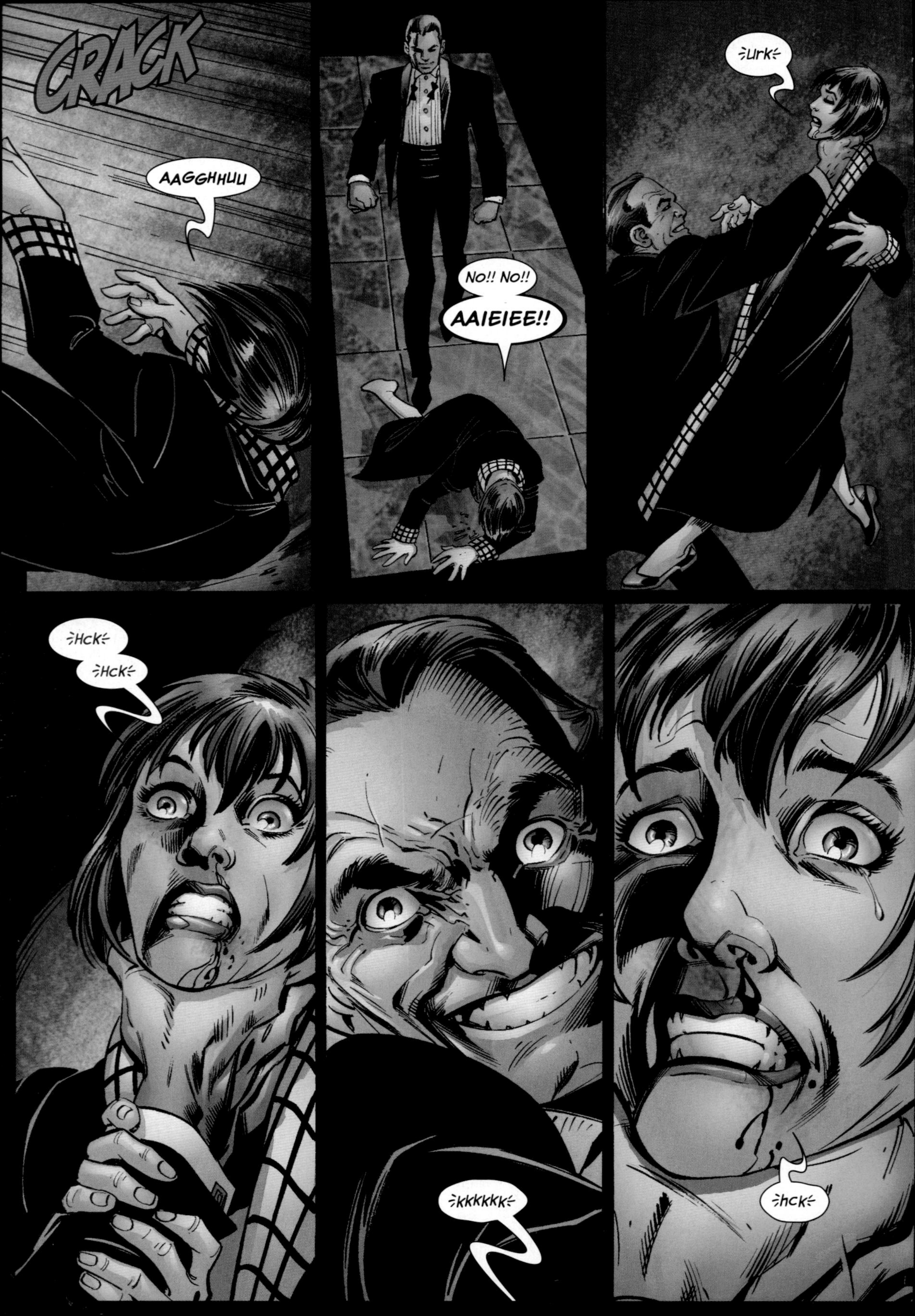
CRACK
AAGGHHUU
No!! No!!
AAIEIEE!!
urk
Hck
Hck
kkkkkk
hck

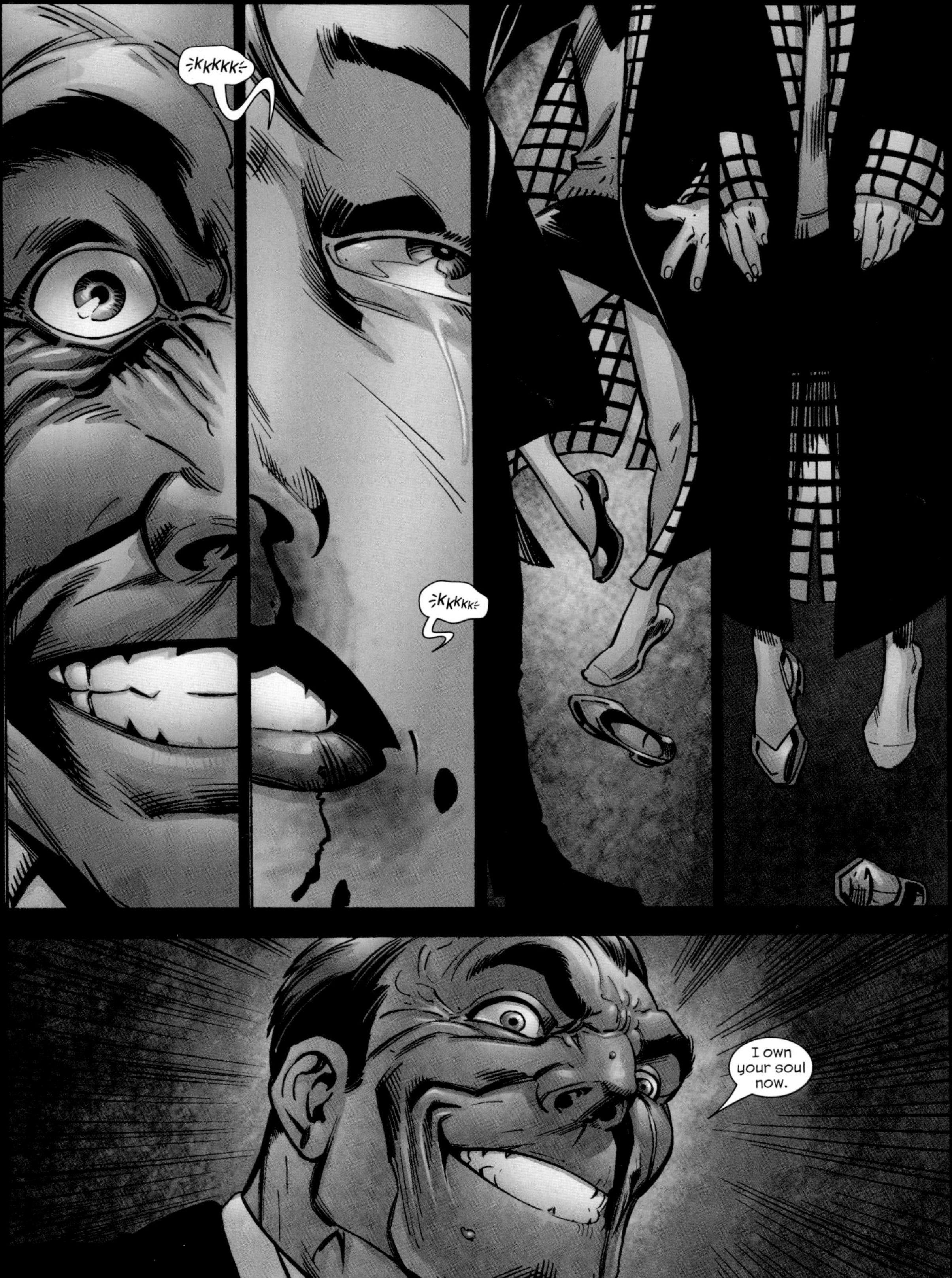
KKKKK
KKKKK
I own your soul now.

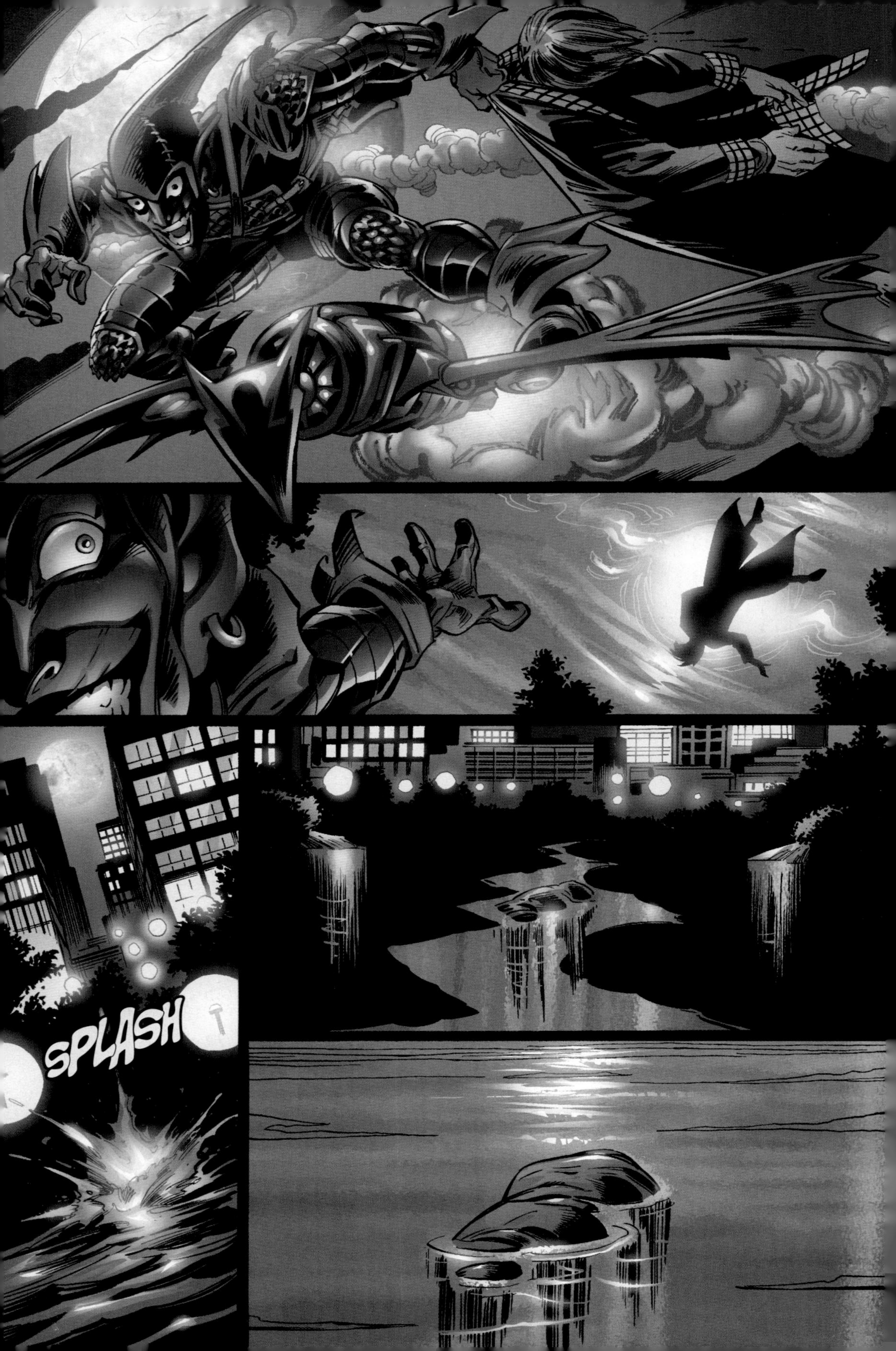
SPLASH

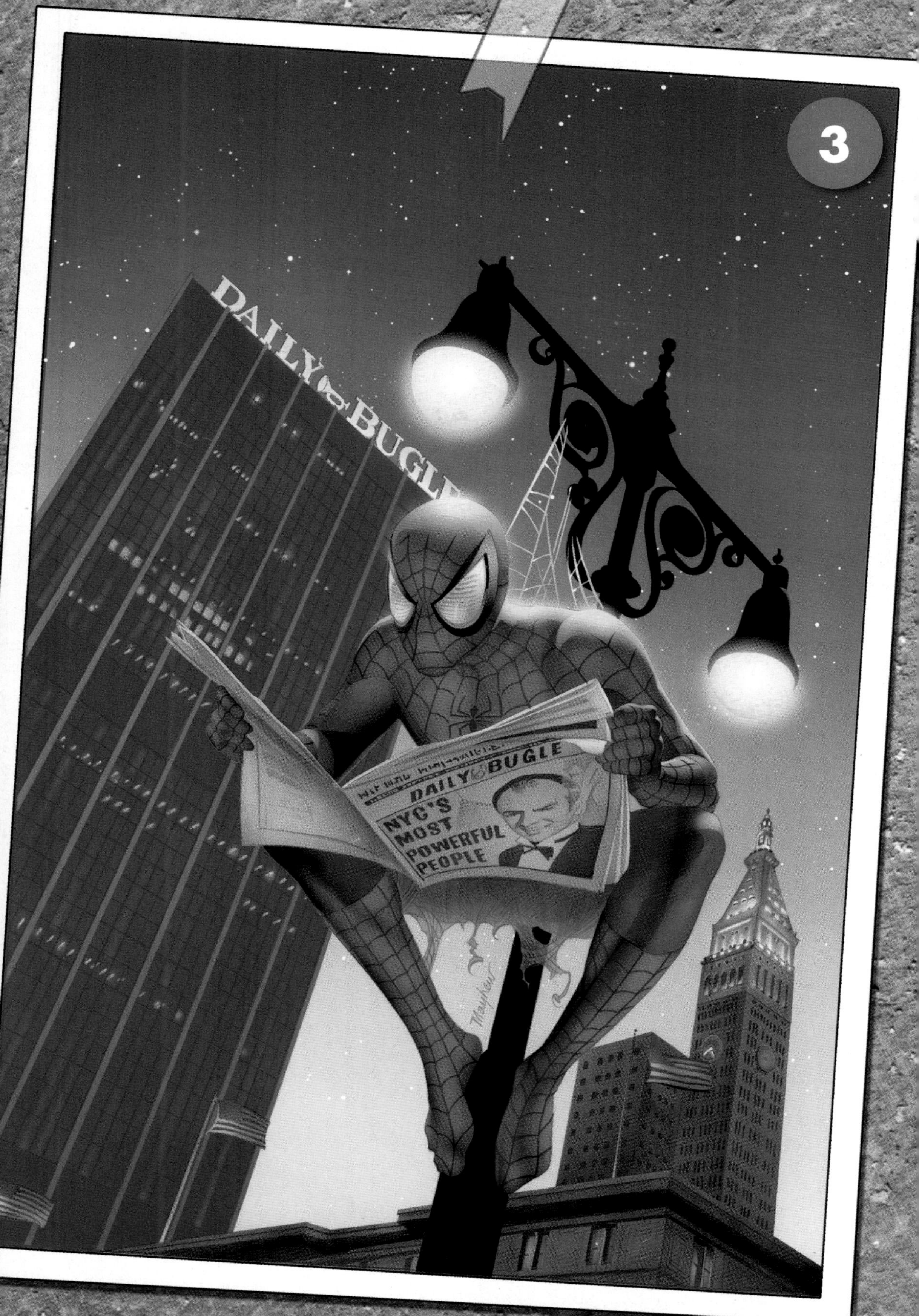
3
DAILY BUGLE
DAILY BUGLE
NYC'S MOST POWERFUL PEOPLE

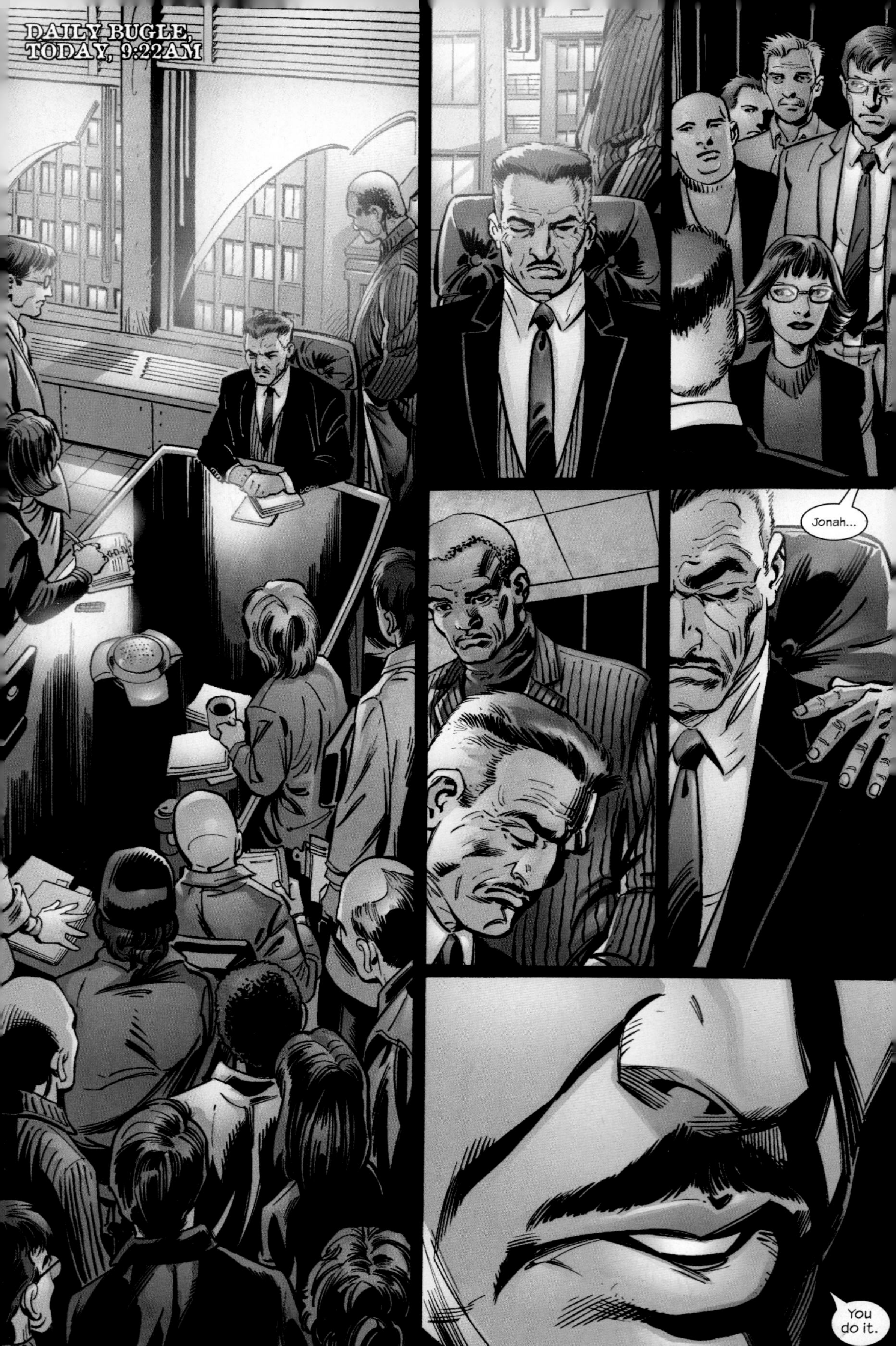
DAILY BUGLE, TODAY, 9:22AM
Jonah...
You do it.

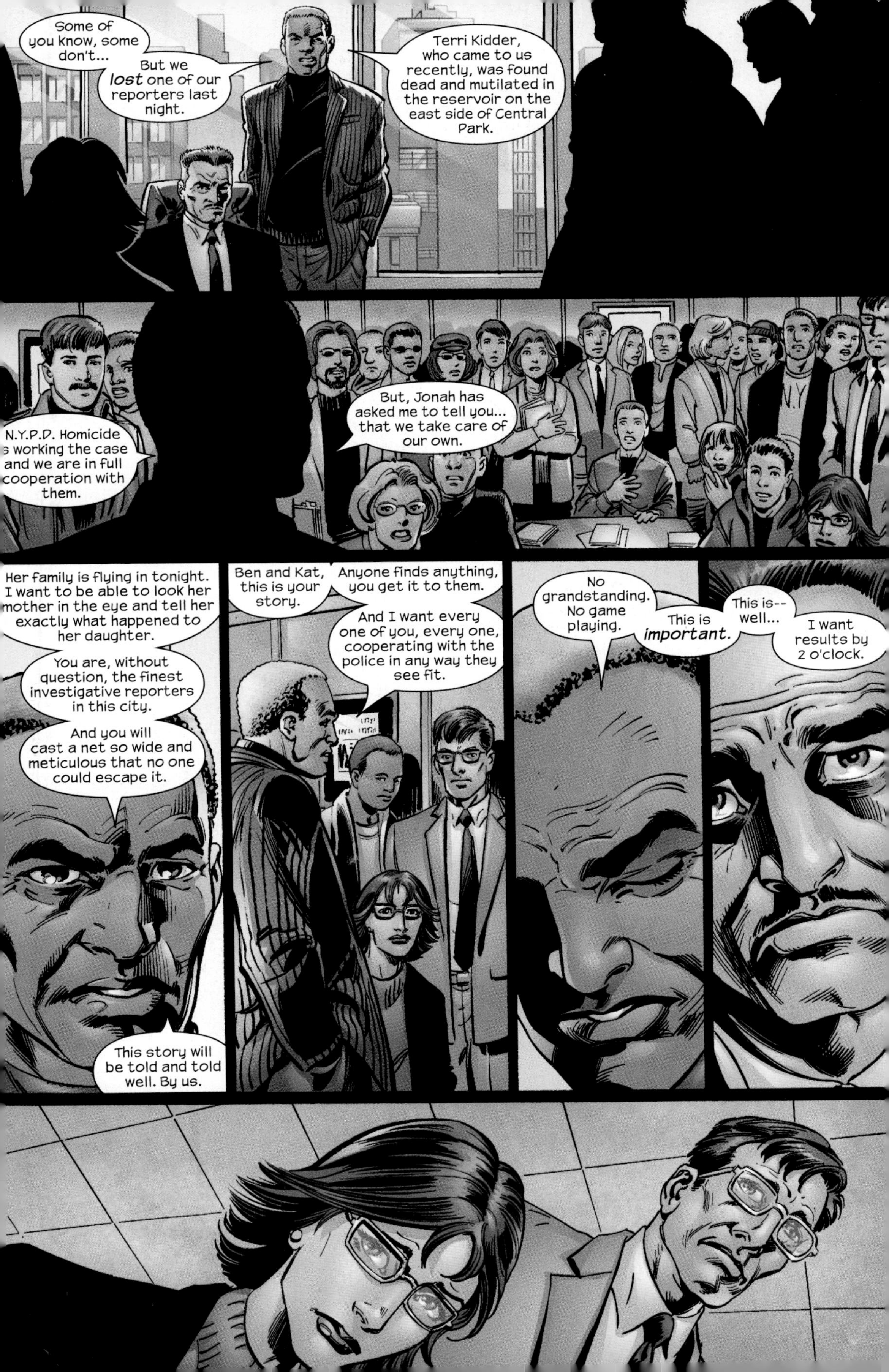

Some of you know, some don't...
But we *lost* one of our reporters last night.
Terri Kidder, who came to us recently, was found dead and mutilated in the reservoir on the east side of Central Park.
N.Y.P.D. Homicide is working the case and we are in full cooperation with them.
But, Jonah has asked me to tell you... that we take care of our own.
Her family is flying in tonight. I want to be able to look her mother in the eye and tell her exactly what happened to her daughter.
You are, without question, the finest investigative reporters in this city.
And you will cast a net so wide and meticulous that no one could escape it.
This story will be told and told well. By us.
Ben and Kat, this is your story.
Anyone finds anything, you get it to them.
And I want every one of you, every one, cooperating with the police in any way they see fit.
No grandstanding. No game playing.
This is *important.*
This is-- well...
I want results by 2 o'clock.

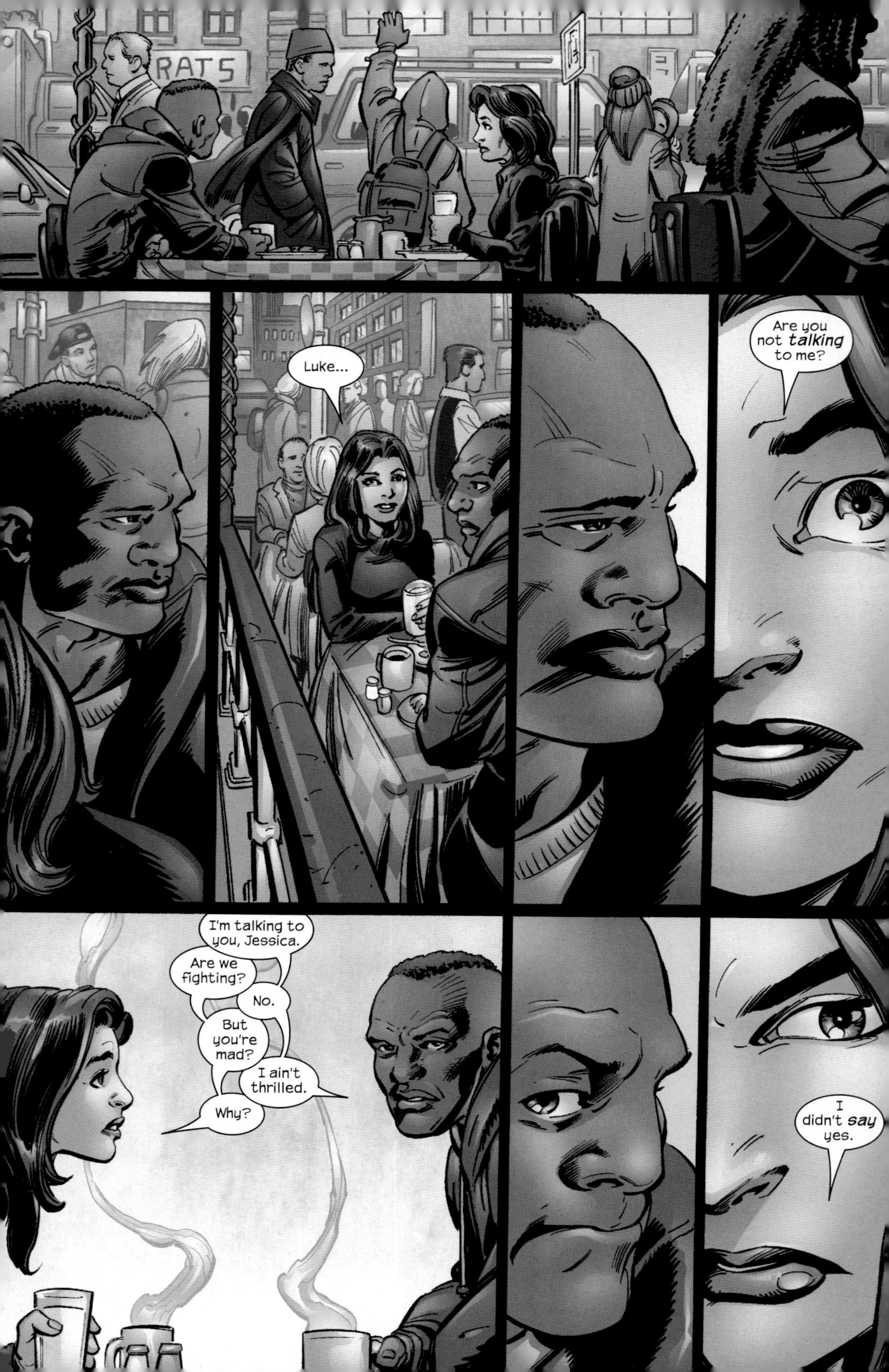
RATS
Luke...
Are you not *talking* to me?
I'm talking to you, Jessica.
Are we fighting?
No.
But you're mad?
I ain't thrilled.
Why?
I didn't *say* yes.

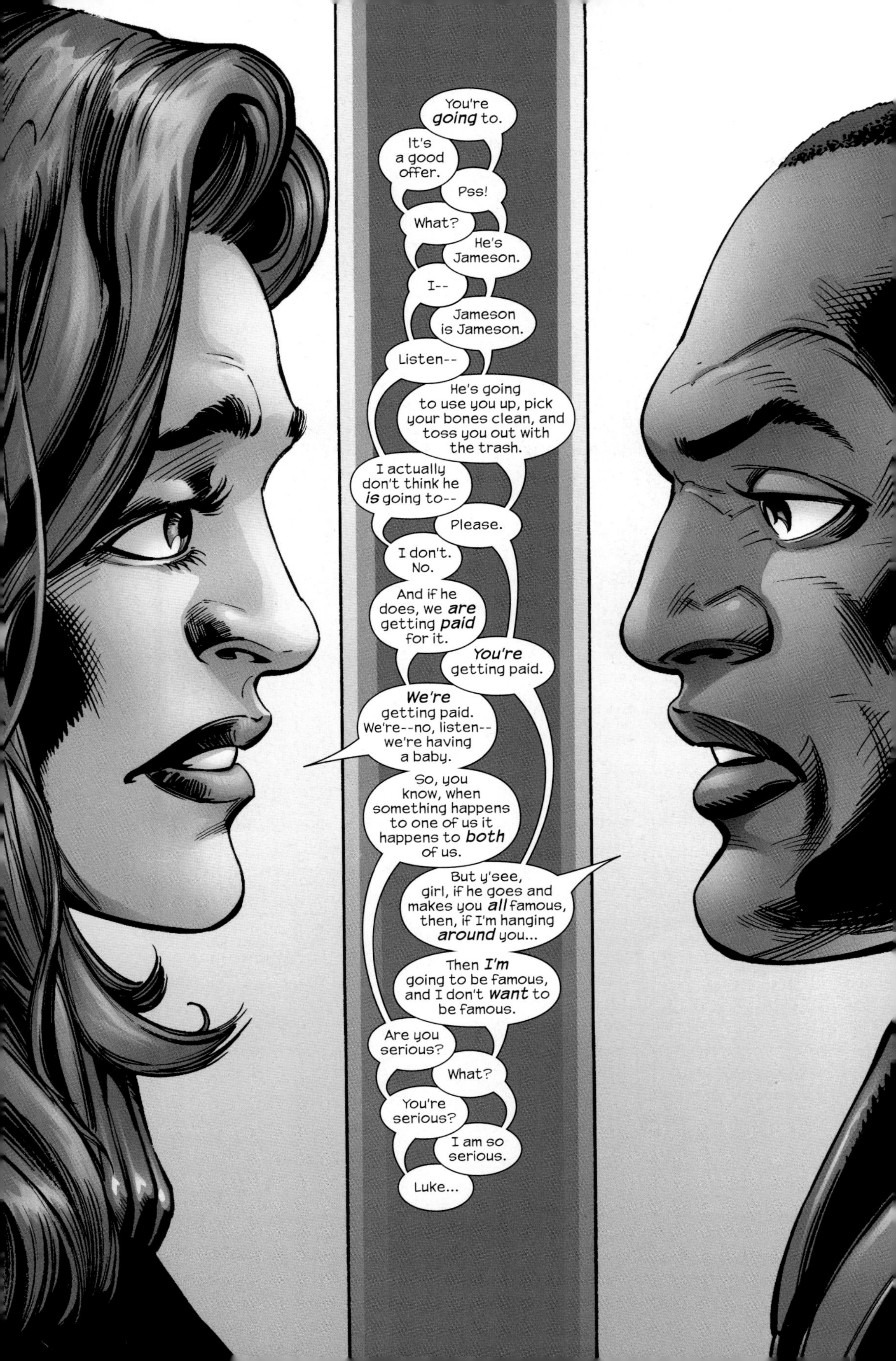
You're *going* to.
It's a good offer.
Pss!
What?
He's Jameson.
I--
Jameson is Jameson.
Listen--
He's going to use you up, pick your bones clean, and toss you out with the trash.
I actually don't think he *is* going to--
Please.
I don't. No.
And if he does, we *are* getting *paid* for it.
You're getting paid.
We're getting paid. We're--no, listen--we're having a baby.
So, you know, when something happens to one of us it happens to *both* of us.
But y'see, girl, if he goes and makes you *all* famous, then, if I'm hanging *around* you...
Then *I'm* going to be famous, and I don't *want* to be famous.
Are you serious?
What?
You're serious?
I am so serious.
Luke...

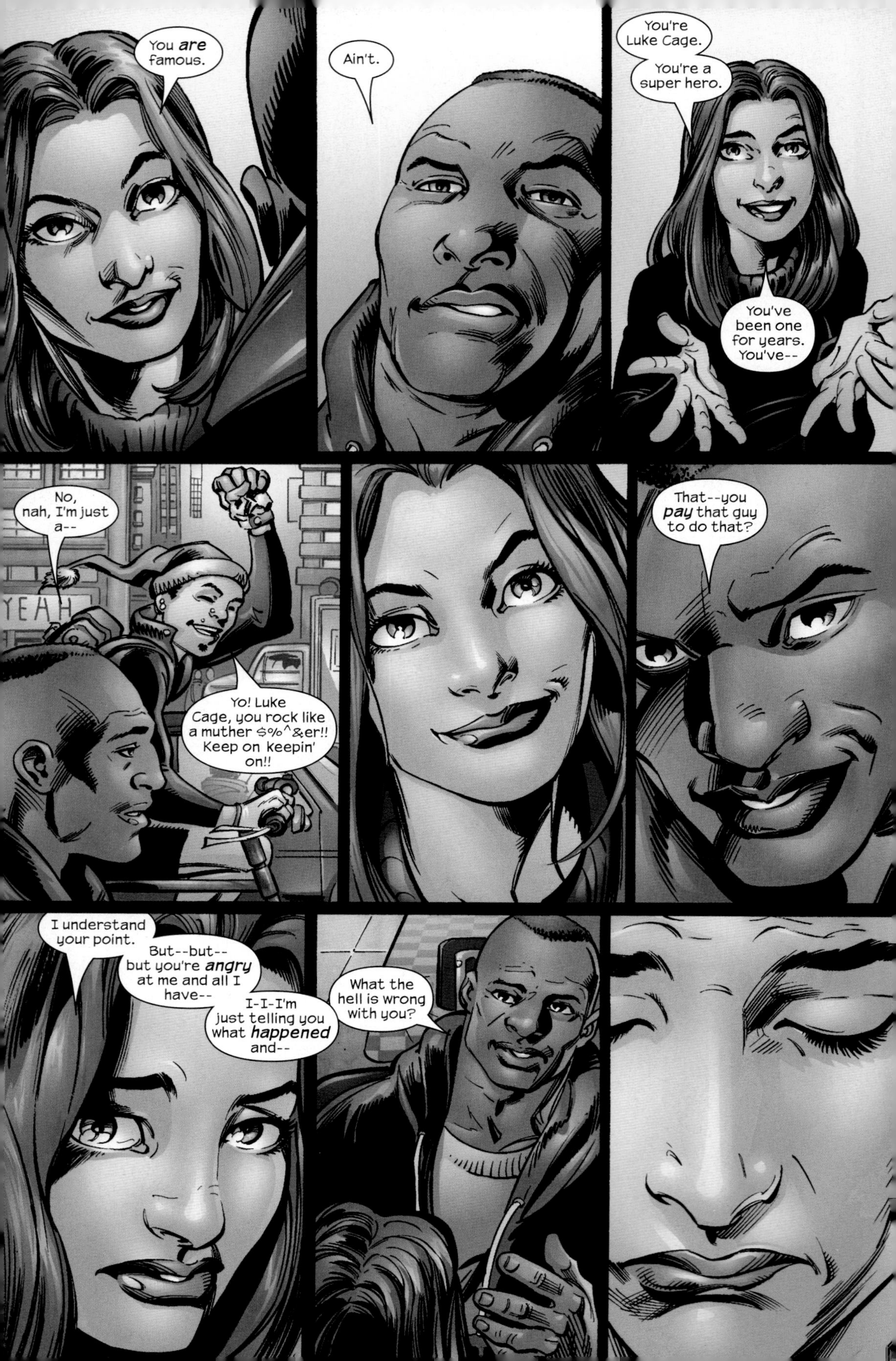
You are famous.
Ain't.
You're Luke Cage.
You're a super hero.
You've been one for years. You've--
No, nah, I'm just a--
YEAH
Yo! Luke Cage, you rock like a muther $%^&er!! Keep on keepin' on!!
That--you pay that guy to do that?
I understand your point.
But--but--but you're angry at me and all I have--
I-I-I'm just telling you what happened and--
What the hell is wrong with you?

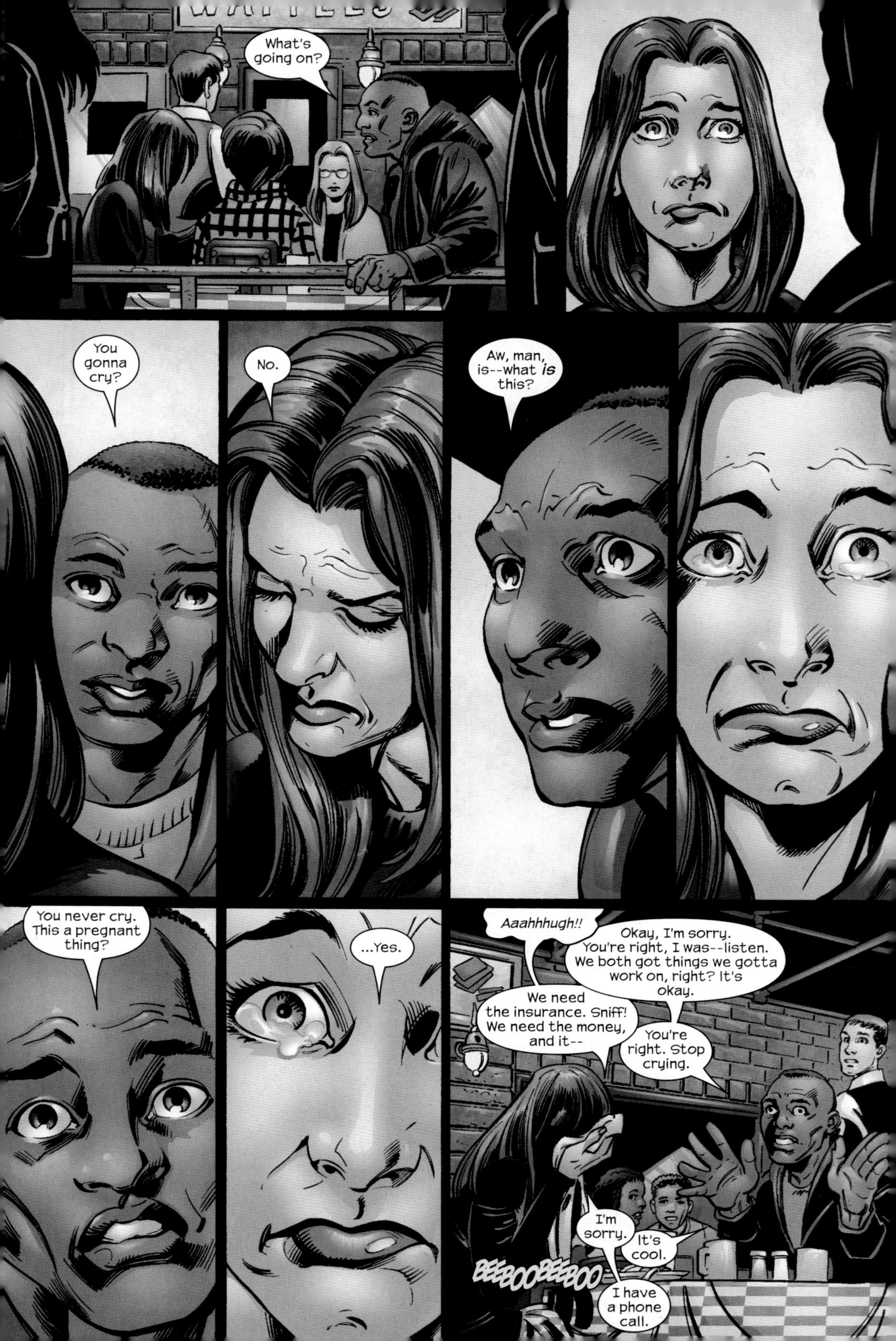
What's going on?
You gonna cry?
No.
Aw, man, is--what *is* this?
You never cry. This a pregnant thing?
...Yes.
Aaahhhugh!!
Okay, I'm sorry. You're right, I was--listen. We both got things we gotta work on, right? It's okay.
We need the insurance. Sniff! We need the money, and it--
You're right. Stop crying.
I'm sorry.
It's cool.
BEEBOOBEEBOO
I have a phone call.

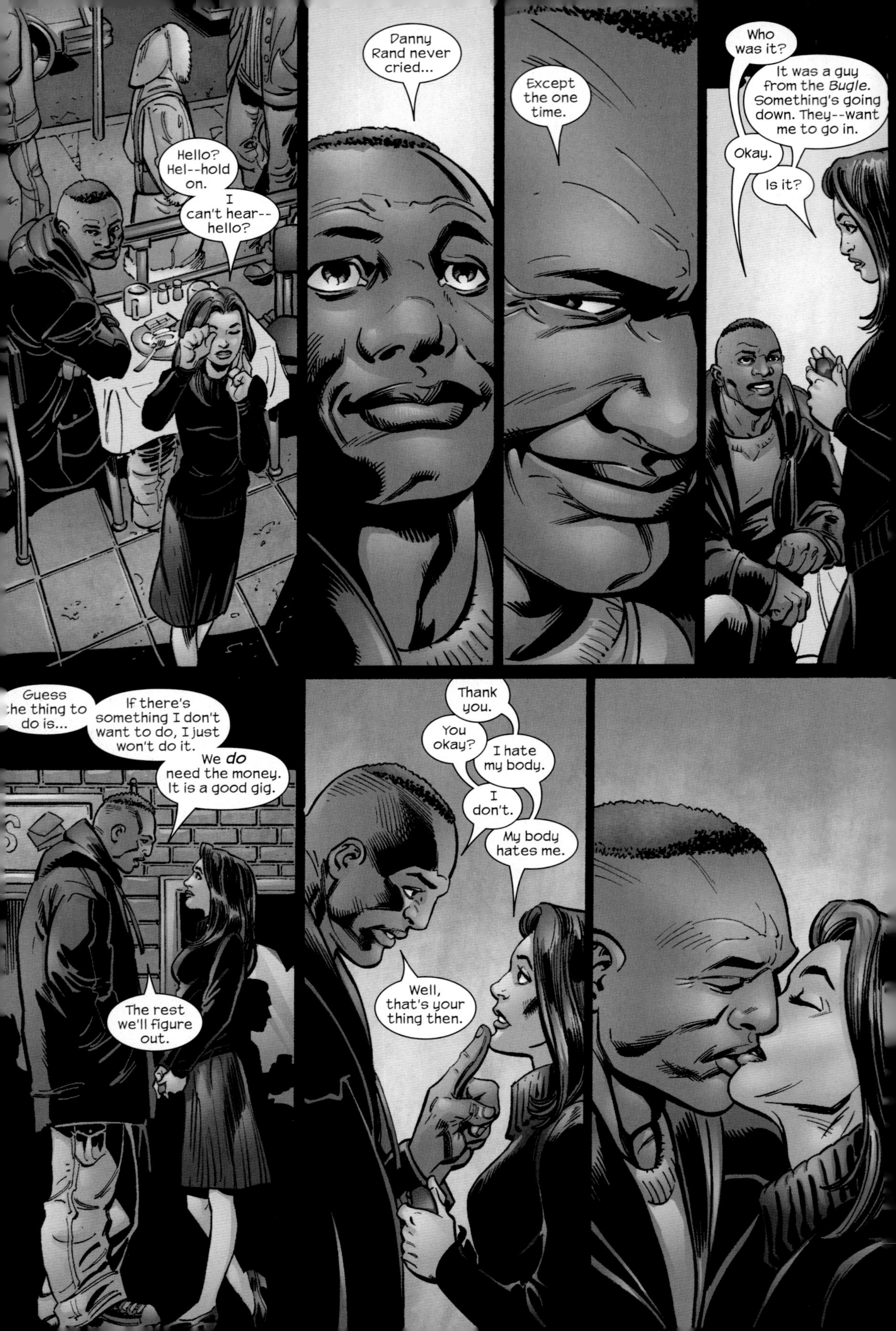
Hello? Hel--hold on.
I can't hear-- hello?
Danny Rand never cried...
Except the one time.
Who was it?
It was a guy from the *Bugle.* Something's going down. They--want me to go in.
Okay.
Is it?
Guess the thing to do is...
If there's something I don't want to do, I just won't do it.
We *do* need the money. It is a good gig.
The rest we'll figure out.
Thank you.
You okay?
I hate my body.
I don't.
My body hates me.
Well, that's your thing then.

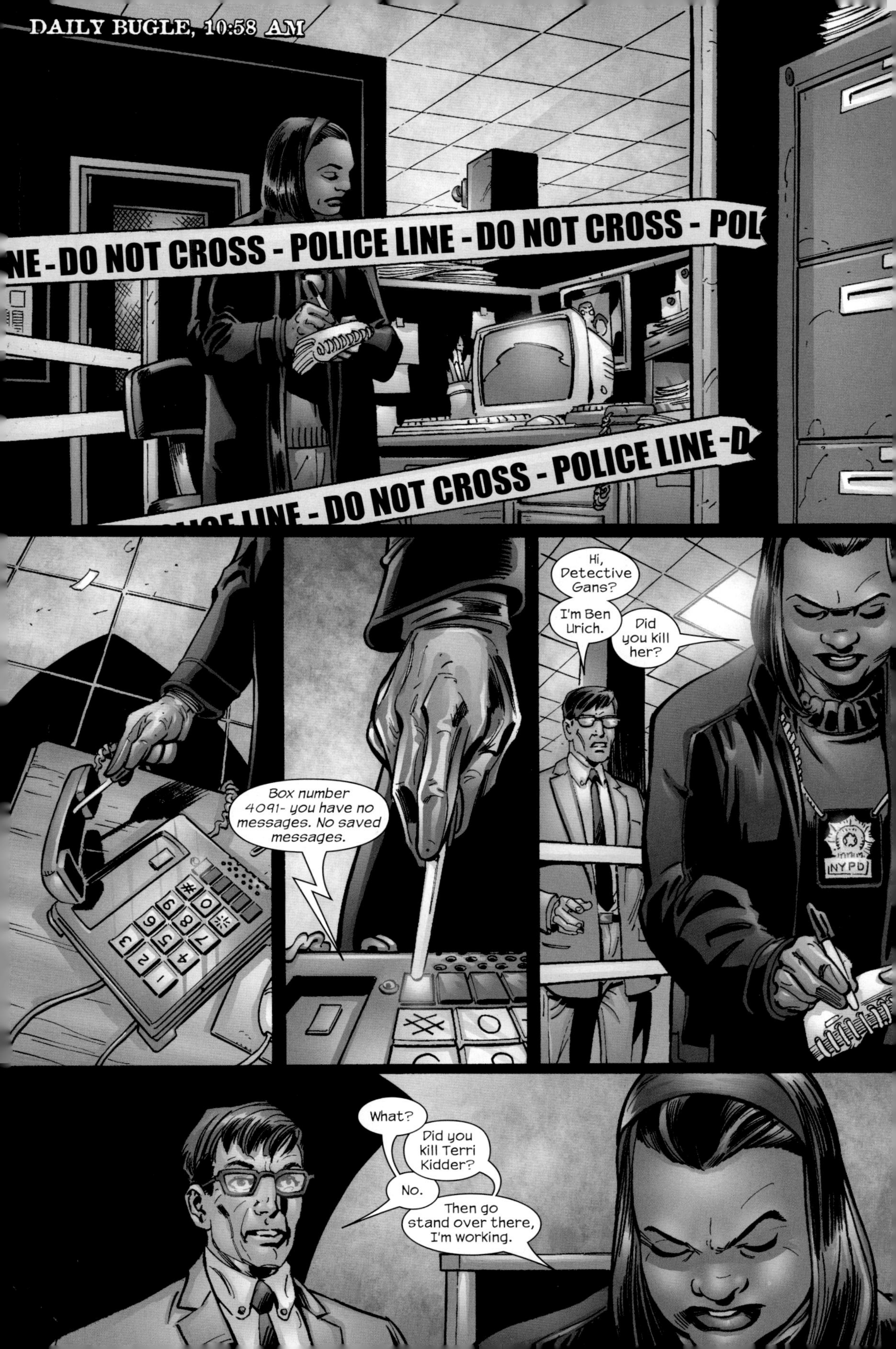
DAILY BUGLE, 10:58 AM
NE - DO NOT CROSS - POLICE LINE - DO NOT CROSS - POL
DO NOT CROSS - POLICE LINE -
Box number 4091- you have no messages. No saved messages.
Hi, Detective Gans?
I'm Ben Urich.
Did you kill her?
NYPD
What?
Did you kill Terri Kidder?
No.
Then go stand over there, I'm working.

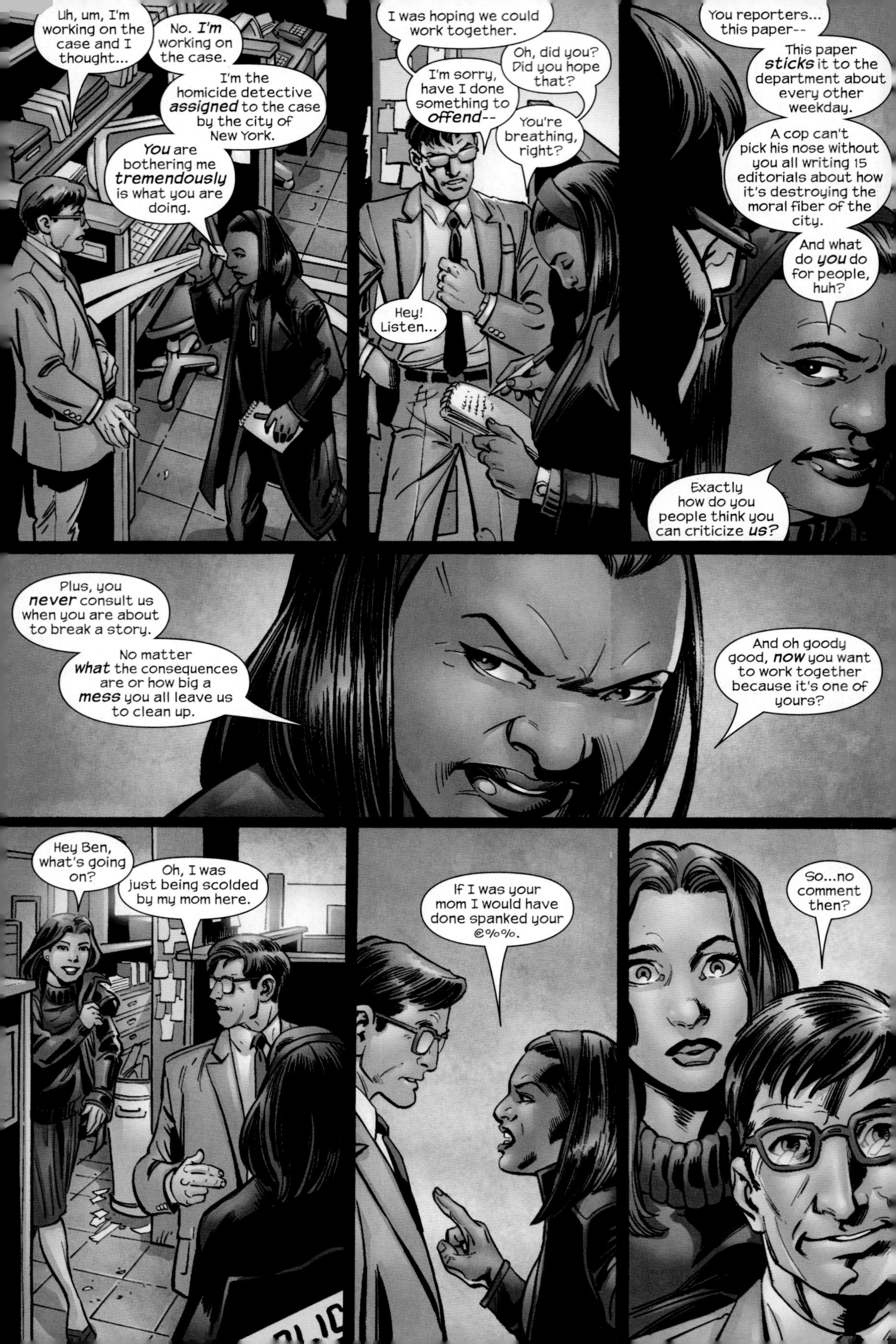
Uh, um, I'm working on the case and I thought...
No. I'm working on the case.
I'm the homicide detective assigned to the case by the city of New York.
You are bothering me tremendously is what you are doing.
I was hoping we could work together.
Oh, did you? Did you hope that?
I'm sorry, have I done something to offend--
You're breathing, right?
Hey! Listen...
You reporters... this paper--
This paper sticks it to the department about every other weekday.
A cop can't pick his nose without you all writing 15 editorials about how it's destroying the moral fiber of the city.
And what do you do for people, huh?
Exactly how do you people think you can criticize us?
Plus, you never consult us when you are about to break a story.
No matter what the consequences are or how big a mess you all leave us to clean up.
And oh goody good, now you want to work together because it's one of yours?
Hey Ben, what's going on?
Oh, I was just being scolded by my mom here.
If I was your mom I would have done spanked your @%%.
So...no comment then?

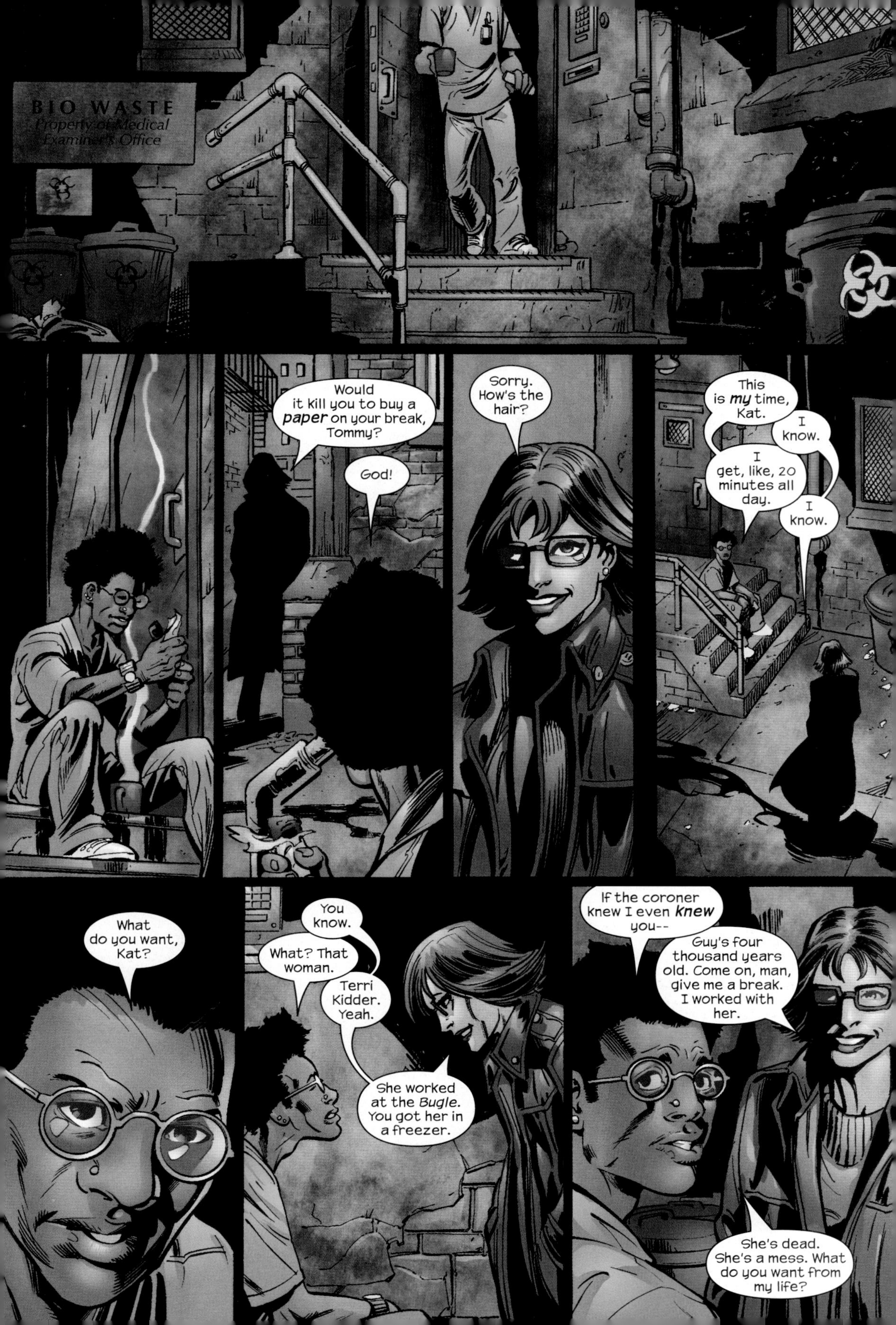
BIO WASTE
Property of Medical Examiner's Office
Would it kill you to buy a *paper* on your break, Tommy?
God!
Sorry. How's the hair?
This is *my* time, Kat.
I know.
I get, like, 20 minutes all day.
I know.
What do you want, Kat?
You know.
What? That woman.
Terri Kidder. Yeah.
She worked at the *Bugle*. You got her in a freezer.
If the coroner knew I even *knew* you--
Guy's four thousand years old. Come on, man, give me a break. I worked with her.
She's dead. She's a mess. What do you want from my life?

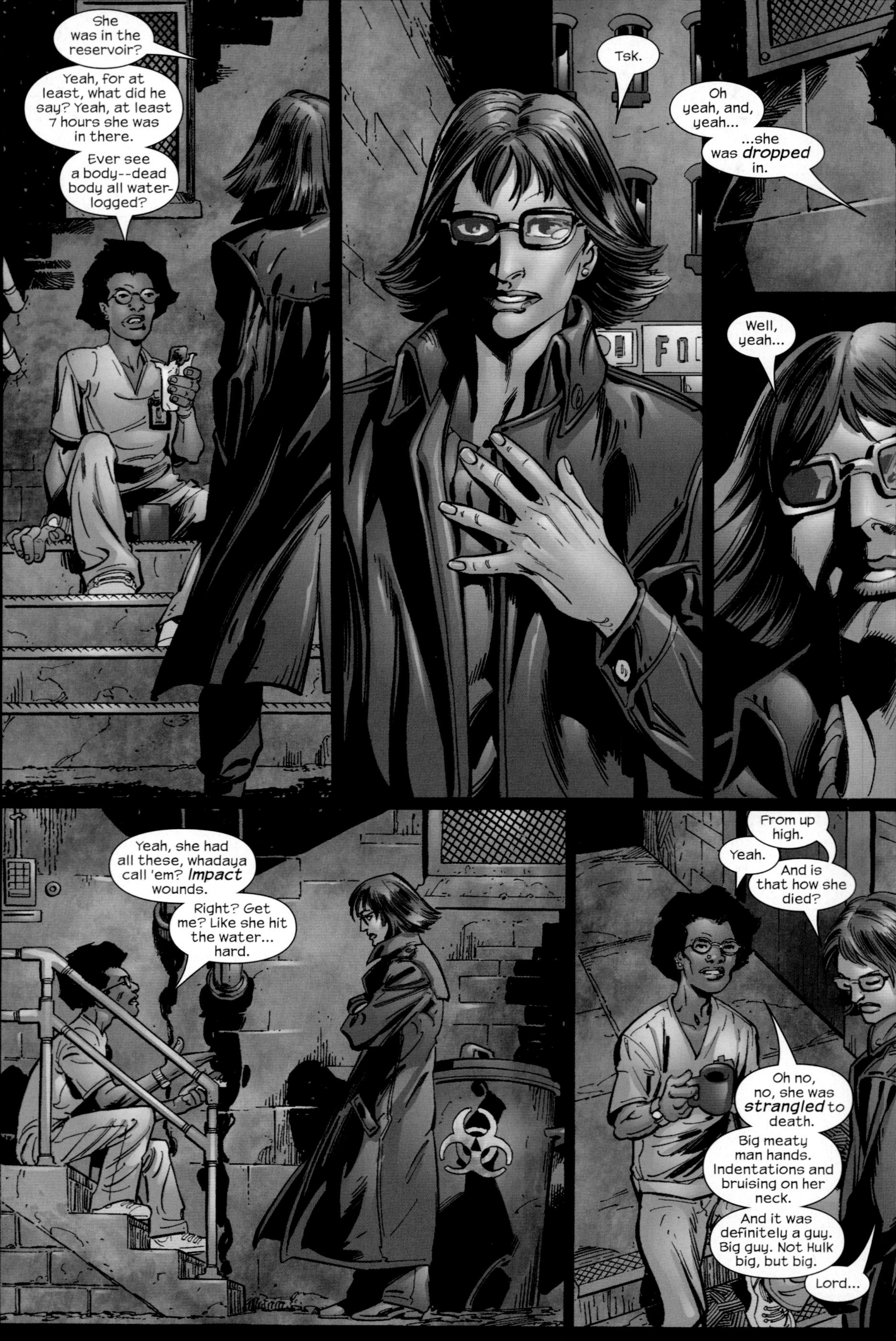
She was in the reservoir?
Yeah, for at least, what did he say? Yeah, at least 7 hours she was in there.
Ever see a body--dead body all water-logged?
Tsk.
Oh yeah, and, yeah...
...she was *dropped* in.
Well, yeah...
Yeah, she had all these, whadaya call 'em? *Impact* wounds.
Right? Get me? Like she hit the water... hard.
From up high.
Yeah.
And is that how she died?
Oh no, no, she was *strangled* to death.
Big meaty man hands. Indentations and bruising on her neck.
And it was definitely a guy. Big guy. Not Hulk big, but big.
Lord...

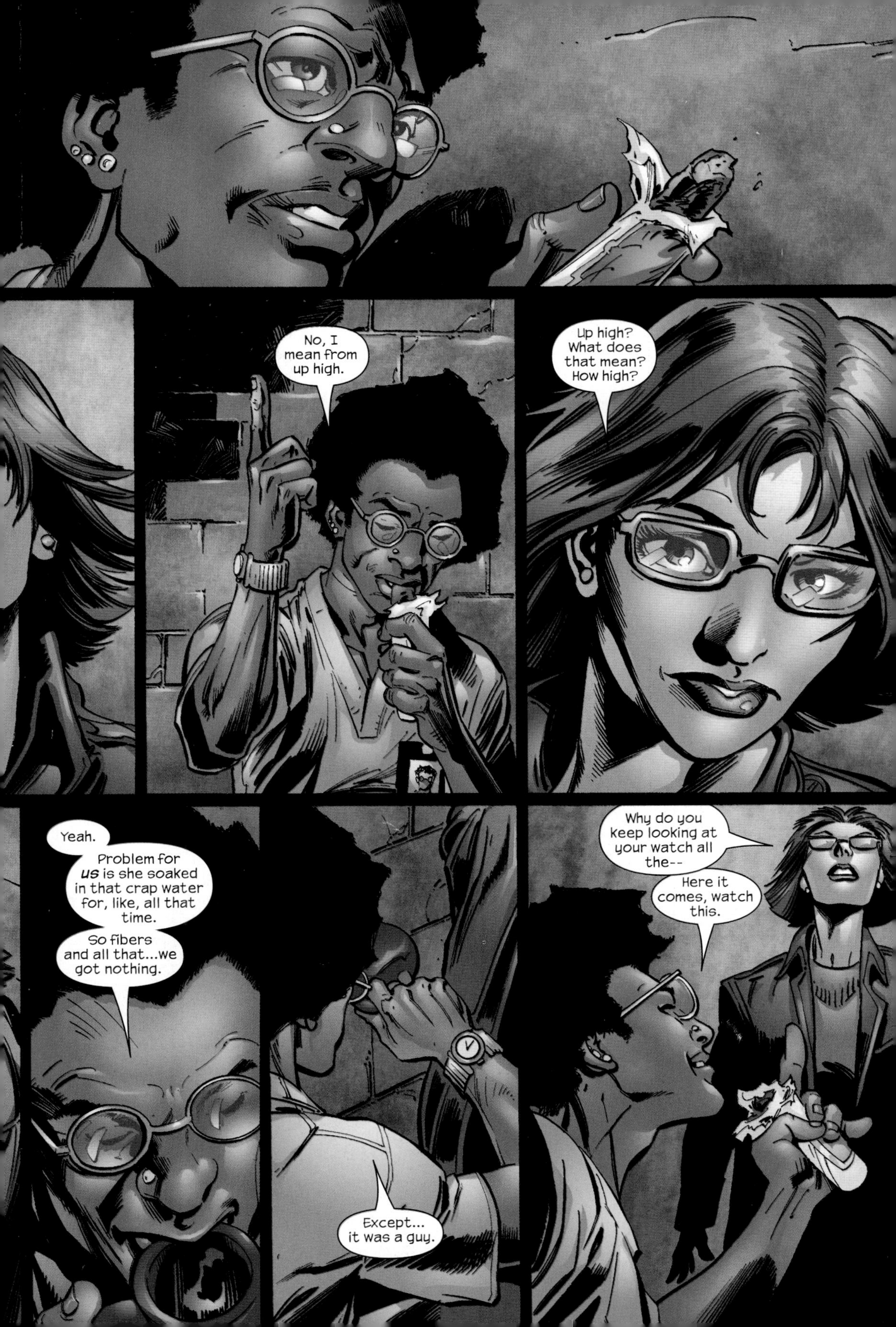
No, I mean from up high.
Up high? What does that mean? How high?
Yeah.
Problem for *us* is she soaked in that crap water for, like, all that time.
So fibers and all that...we got nothing.
Except... it was a guy.
Why do you keep looking at your watch all the--
Here it comes, watch this.

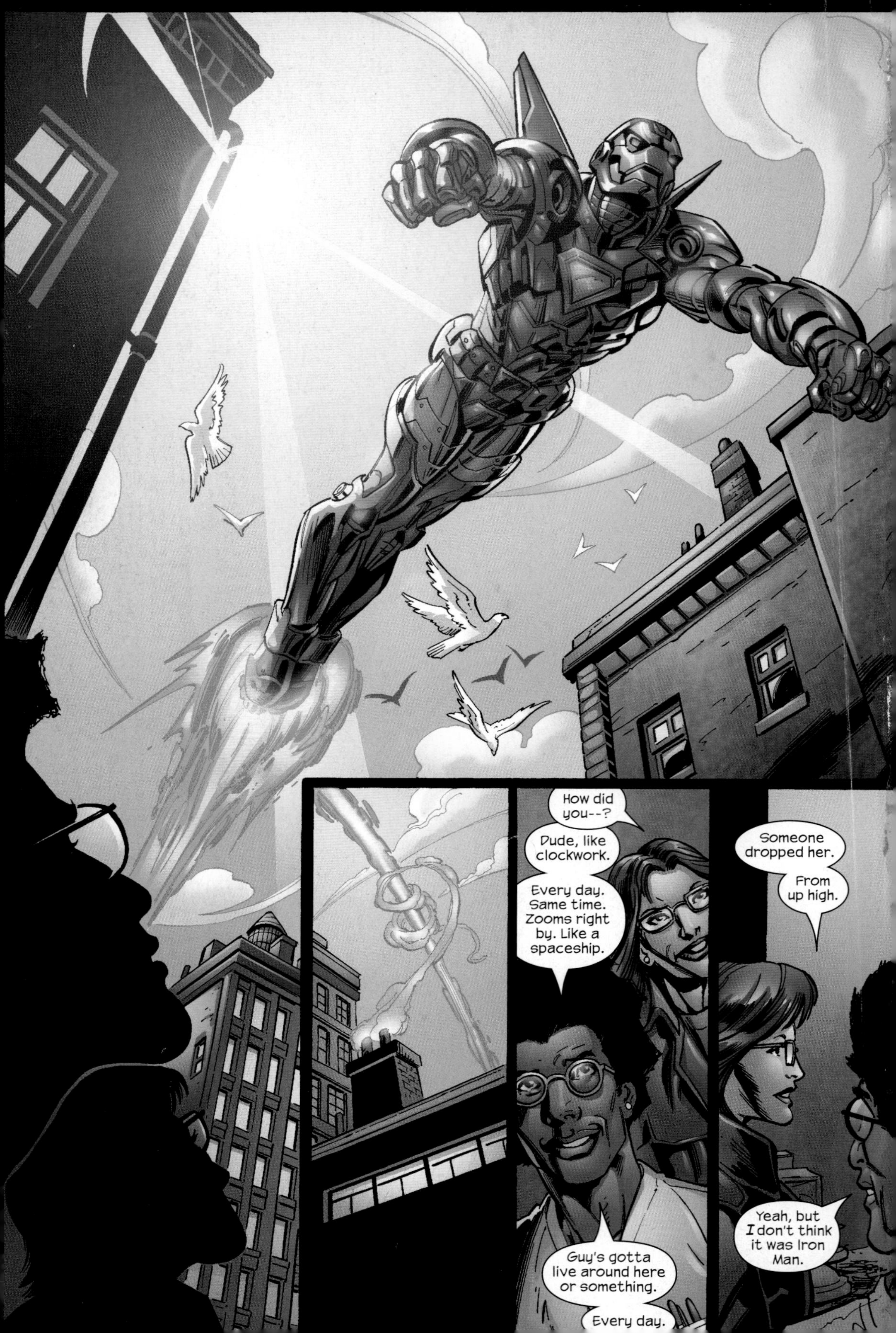
How did you--?
Dude, like clockwork.
Every day. Same time. Zooms right by. Like a spaceship.
Guy's gotta live around here or something.
Every day.
Someone dropped her.
From up high.
Yeah, but I don't think it was Iron Man.

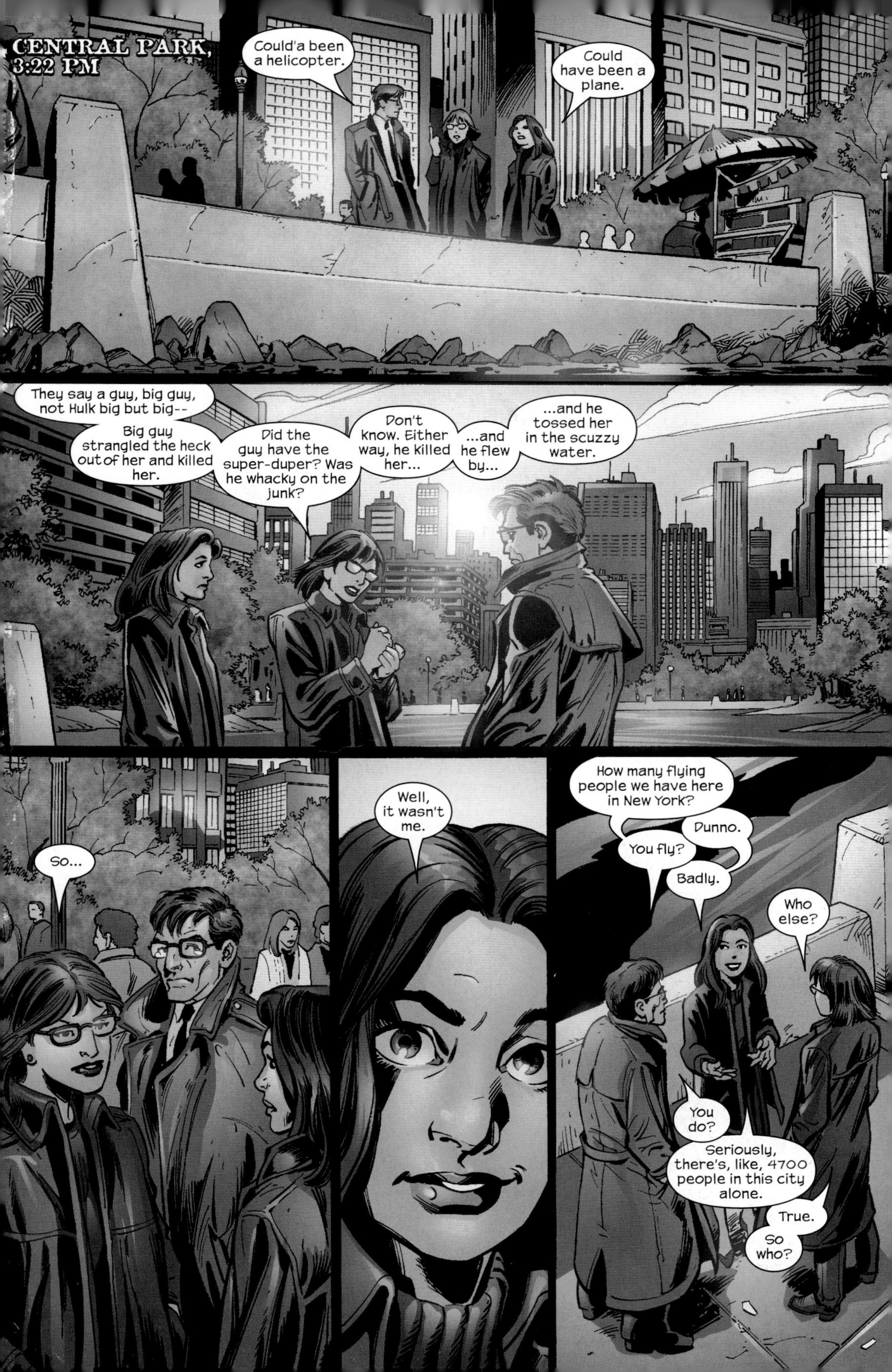
CENTRAL PARK, 3:22 PM
Could'a been a helicopter.
Could have been a plane.
They say a guy, big guy, not Hulk big but big--
Big guy strangled the heck out of her and killed her.
Did the guy have the super-duper? Was he whacky on the junk?
Don't know. Either way, he killed her...
...and he flew by...
...and he tossed her in the scuzzy water.
So...
Well, it wasn't me.
How many flying people we have here in New York?
Dunno.
You fly?
Badly.
Who else?
You do?
Seriously, there's, like, 4700 people in this city alone.
True.
So who?

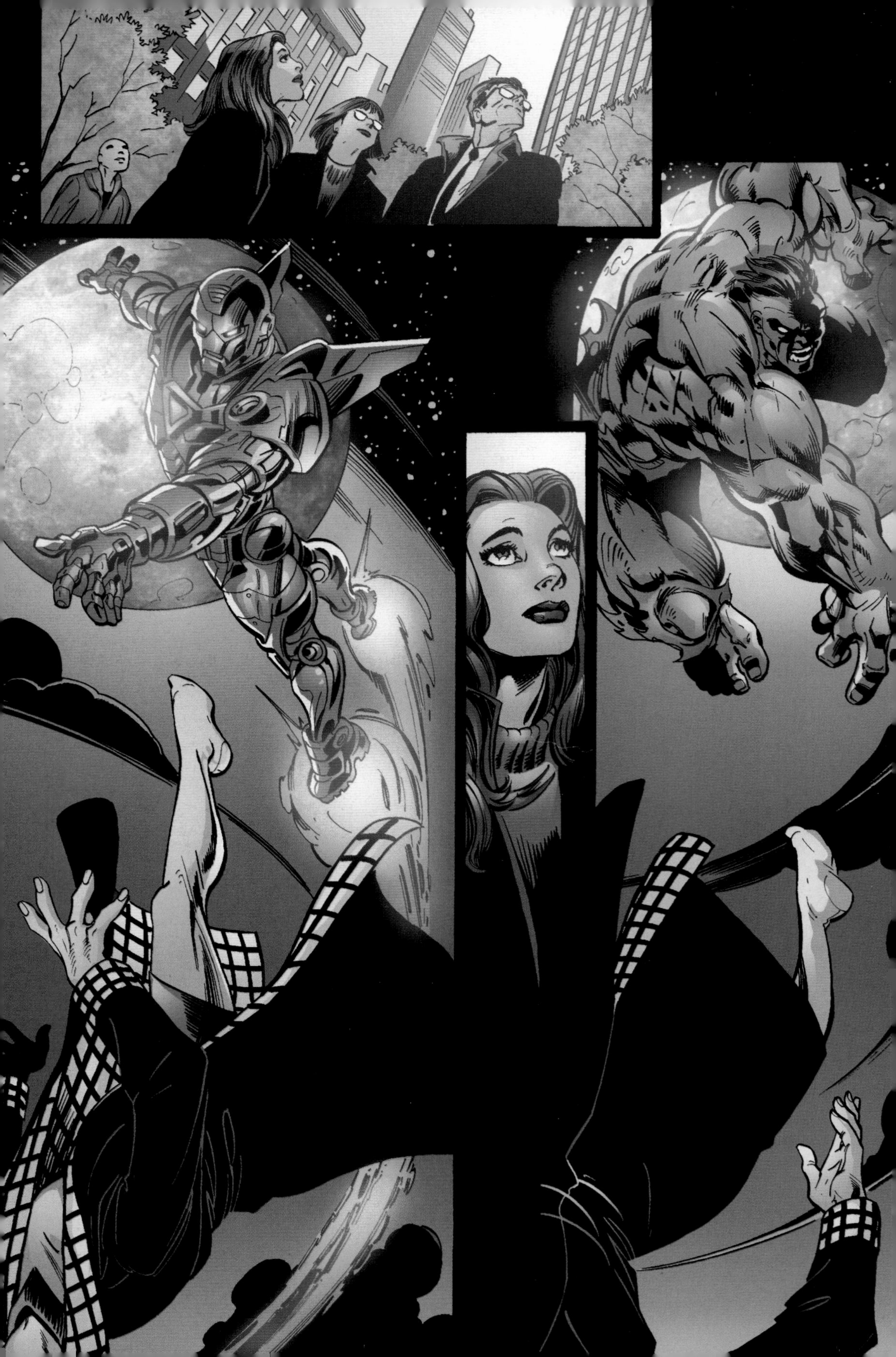

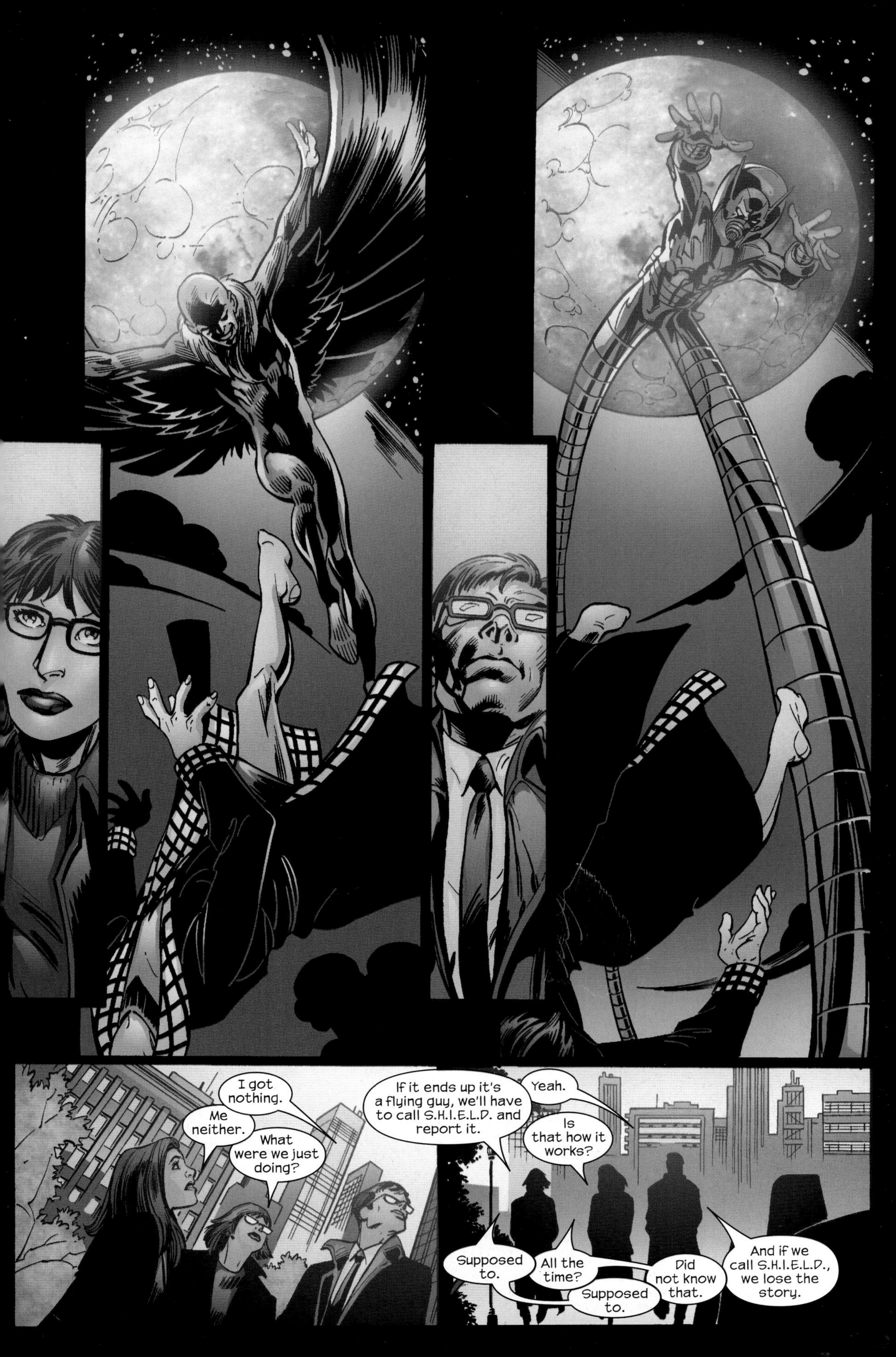

I got nothing.
Me neither.
What were we just doing?
If it ends up it's a flying guy, we'll have to call S.H.I.E.L.D. and report it.
Yeah.
Is that how it works?
Supposed to.
All the time?
Supposed to.
Did not know that.
And if we call S.H.I.E.L.D., we lose the story.

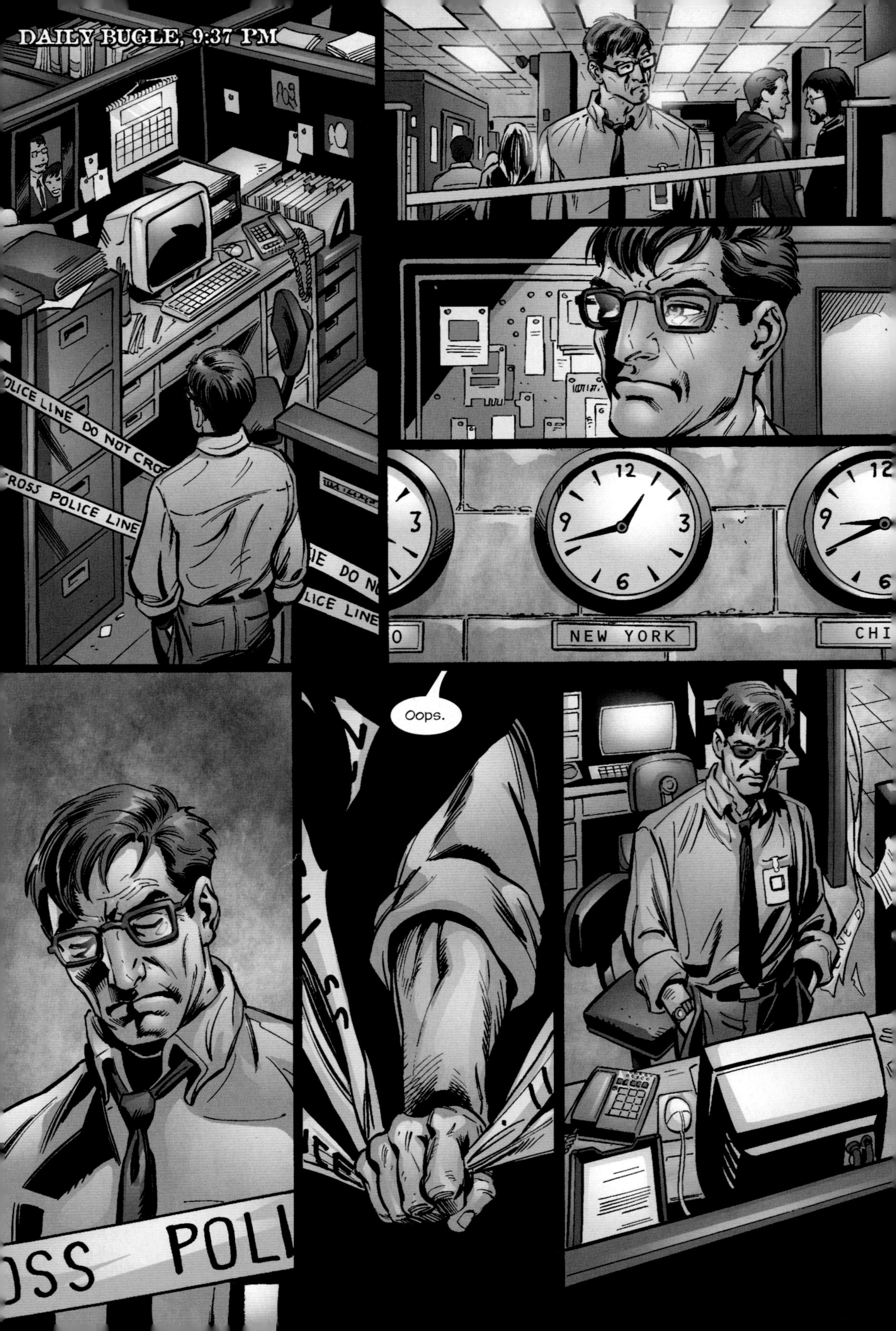
DAILY BUGLE, 9:37 PM
POLICE LINE DO NOT CROSS
CROSS POLICE LINE
NEW YORK
Oops.

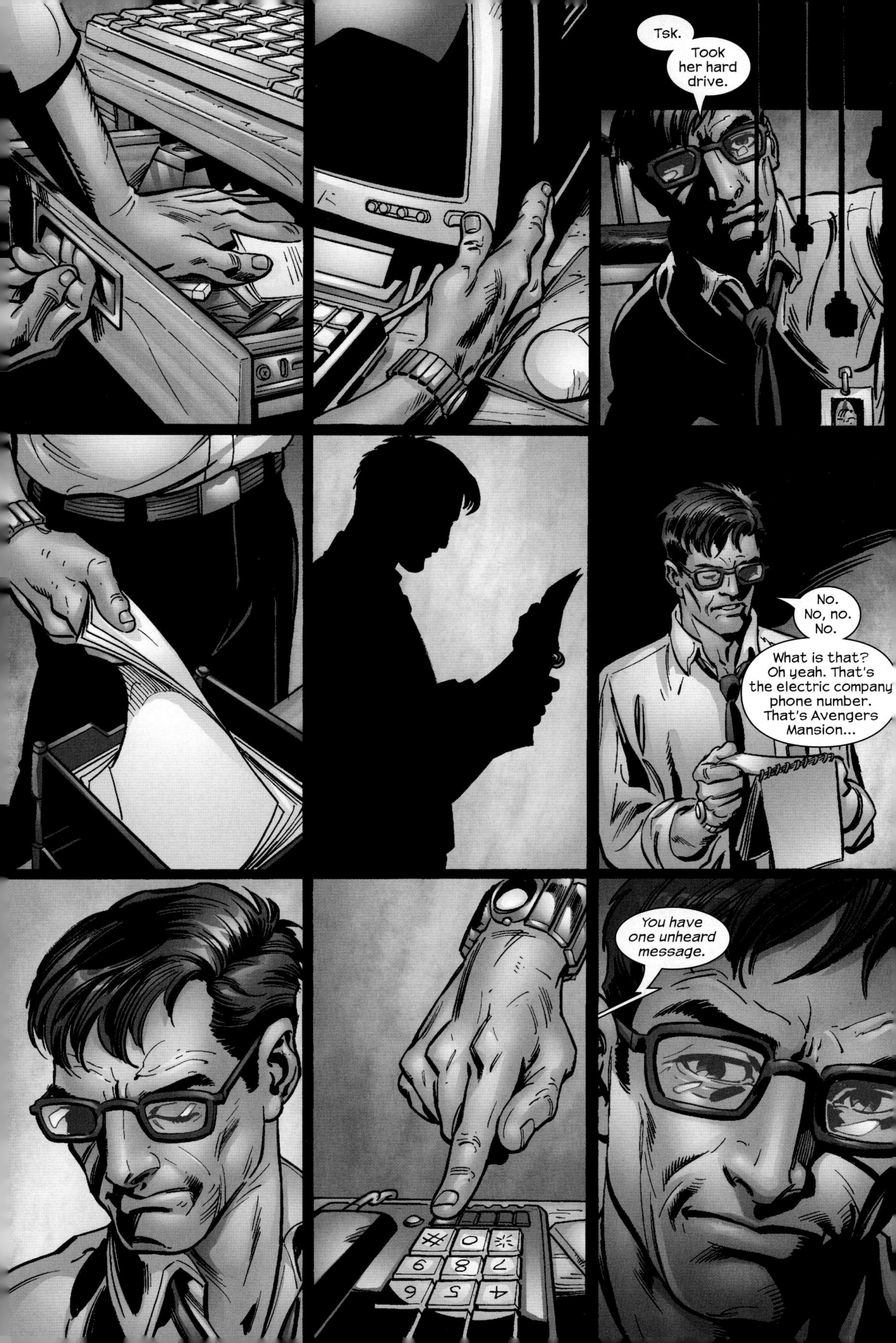
Tsk.
Took her hard drive.
No. No, no. No.
What is that? Oh yeah. That's the electric company phone number. That's Avengers Mansion...
You have one unheard message.

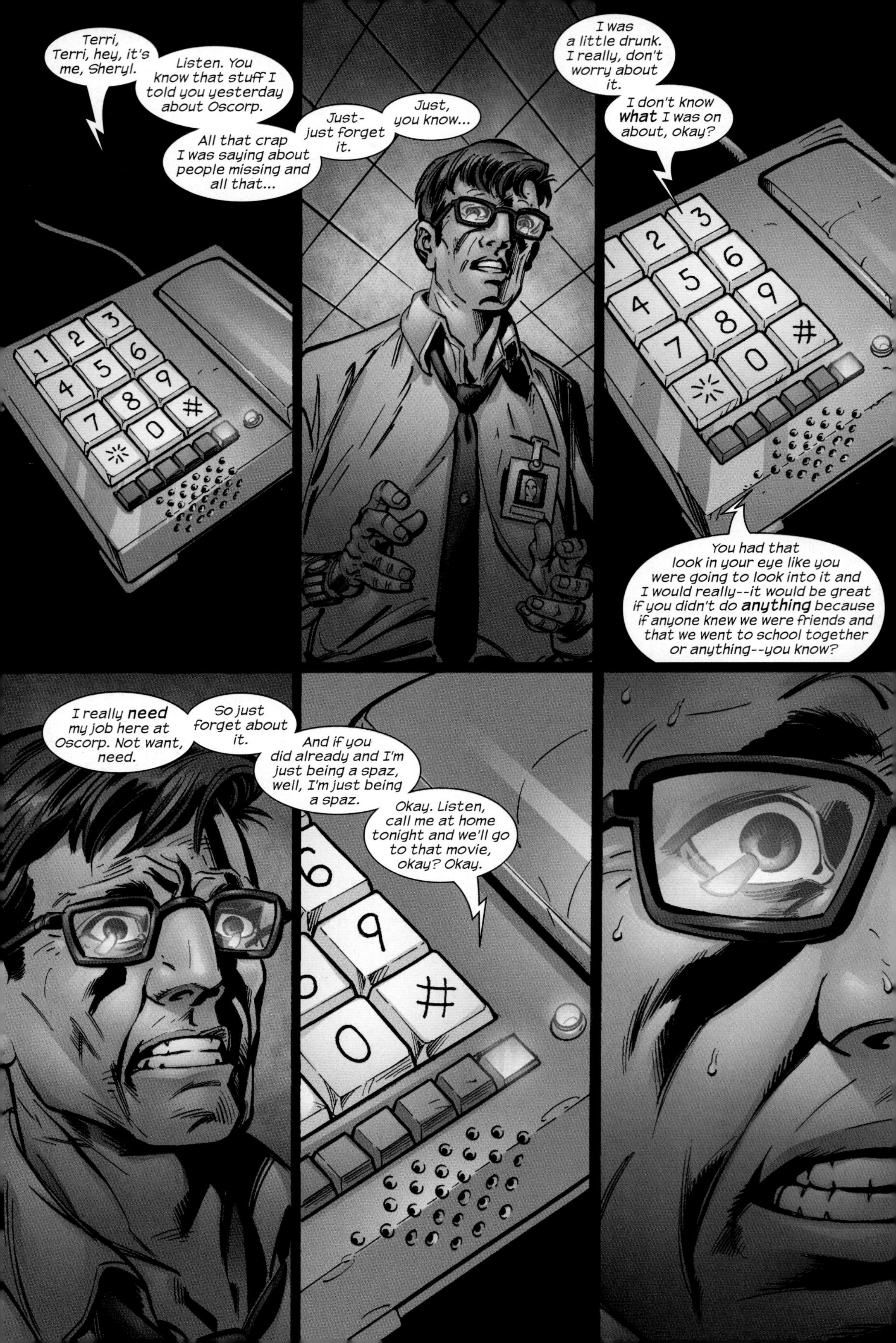

Terri, Terri, hey, it's me, Sheryl.
Listen. You know that stuff I told you yesterday about Oscorp.
All that crap I was saying about people missing and all that...
Just- just forget it.
Just, you know...
I was a little drunk. I really, don't worry about it.
I don't know **what** I was on about, okay?
You had that look in your eye like you were going to look into it and I would really--it would be great if you didn't do **anything** because if anyone knew we were friends and that we went to school together or anything--you know?
I really **need** my job here at Oscorp. Not want, need.
So just forget about it.
And if you did already and I'm just being a spaz, well, I'm just being a spaz.
Okay. Listen, call me at home tonight and we'll go to that movie, okay? Okay.

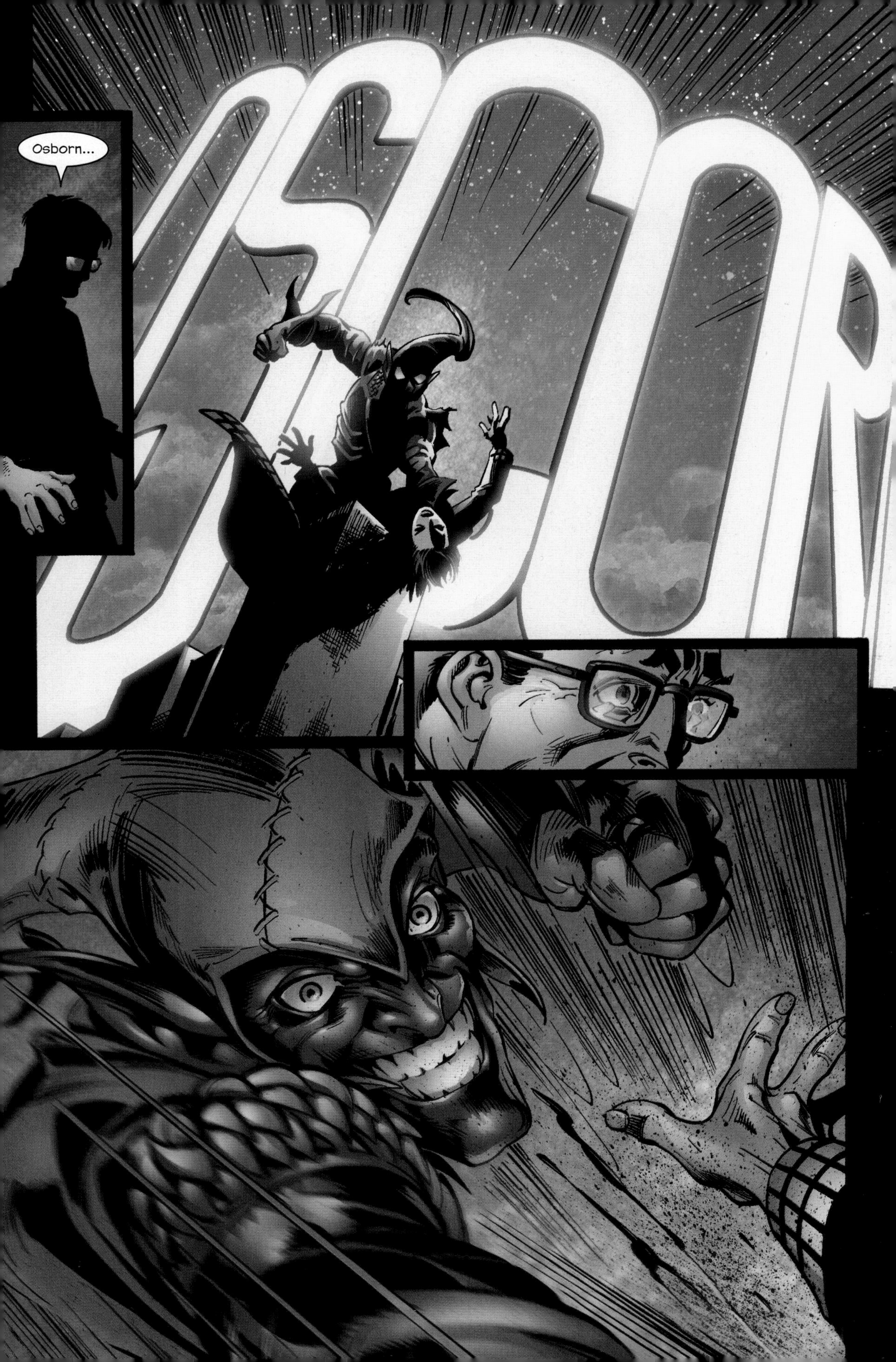
Osborn...

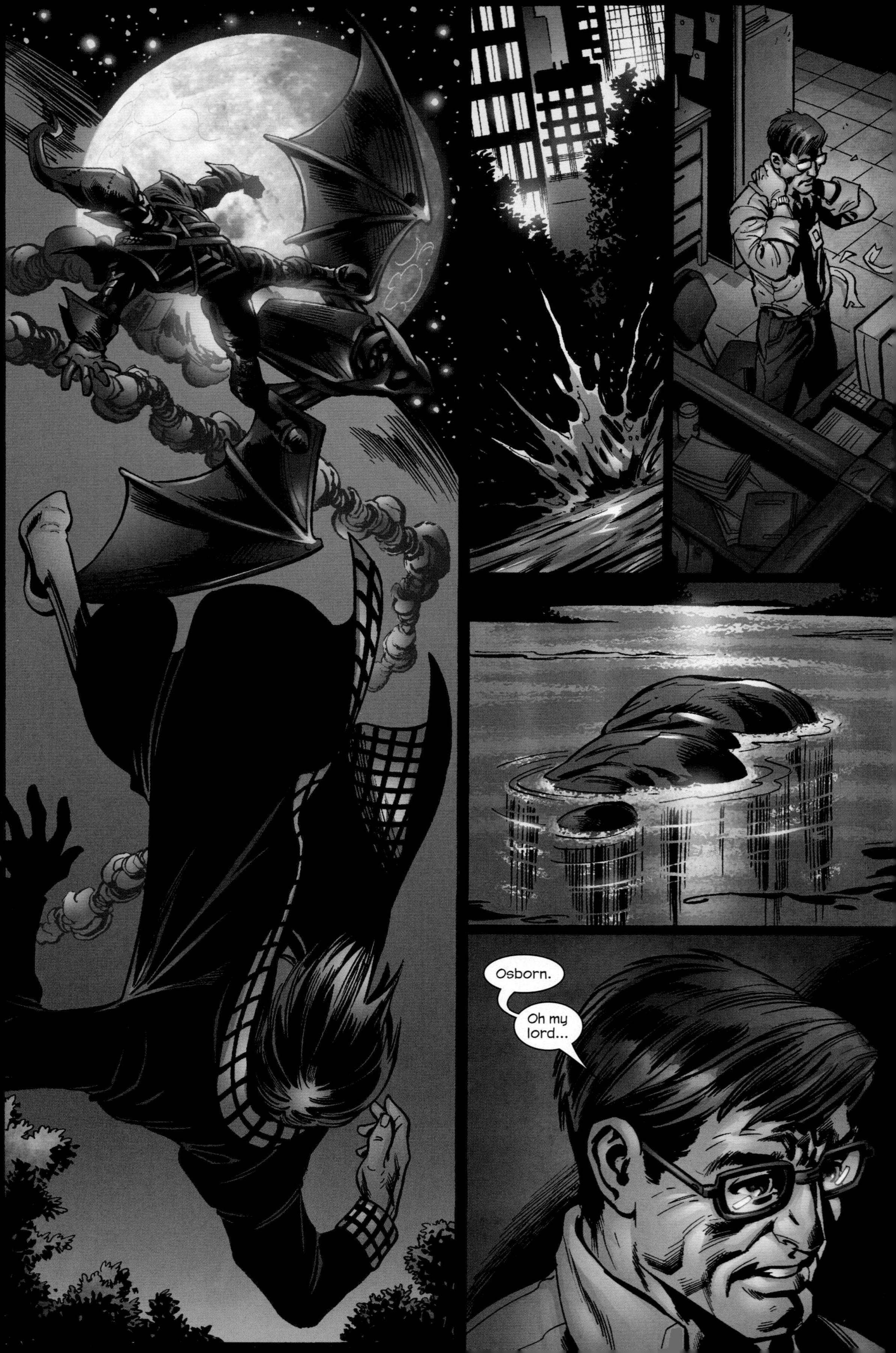
Osborn.
Oh my lord...

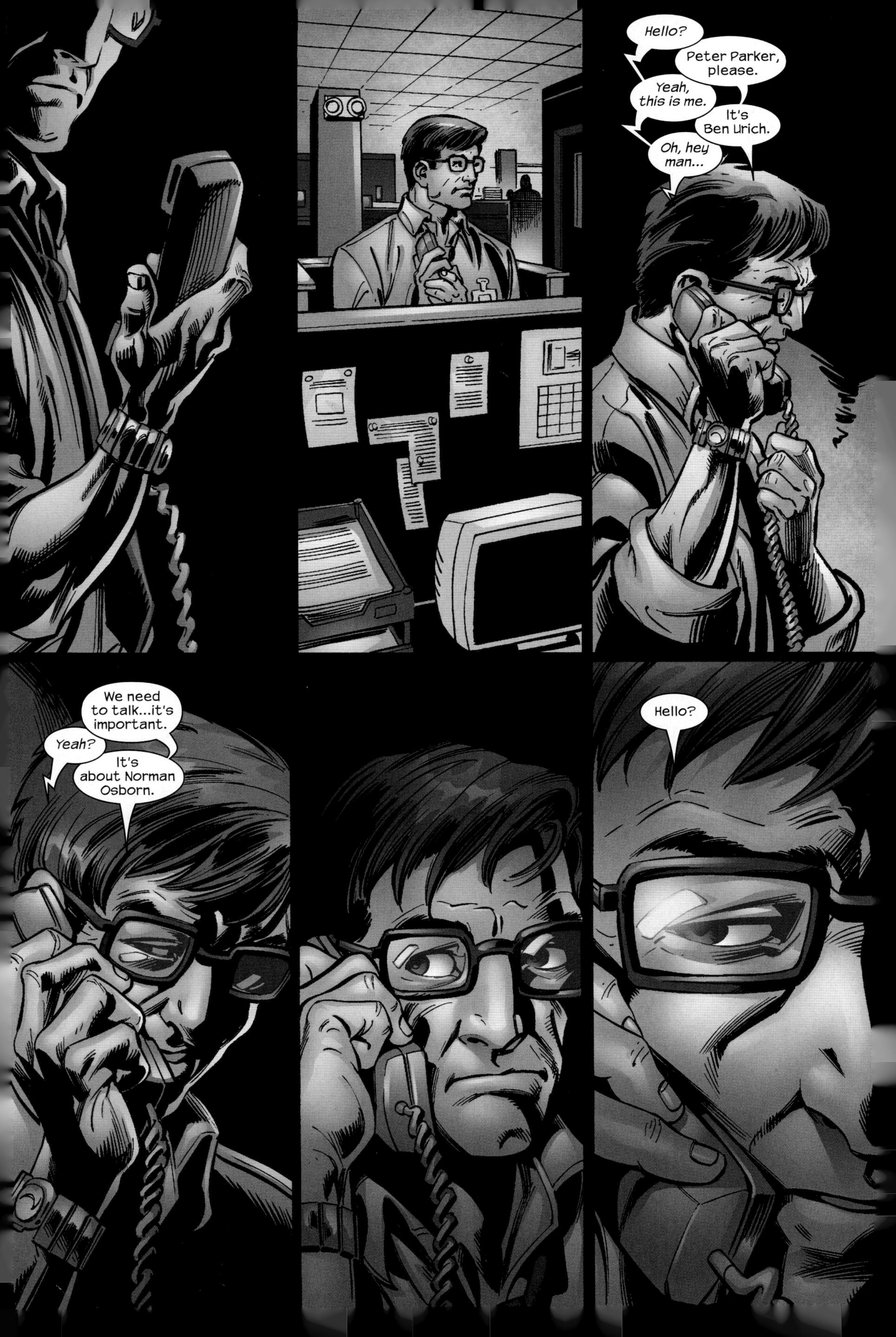
Hello?
Peter Parker, please.
Yeah, this is me.
It's Ben Urich.
Oh, hey man...
We need to talk...it's important.
Yeah?
It's about Norman Osborn.
Hello?

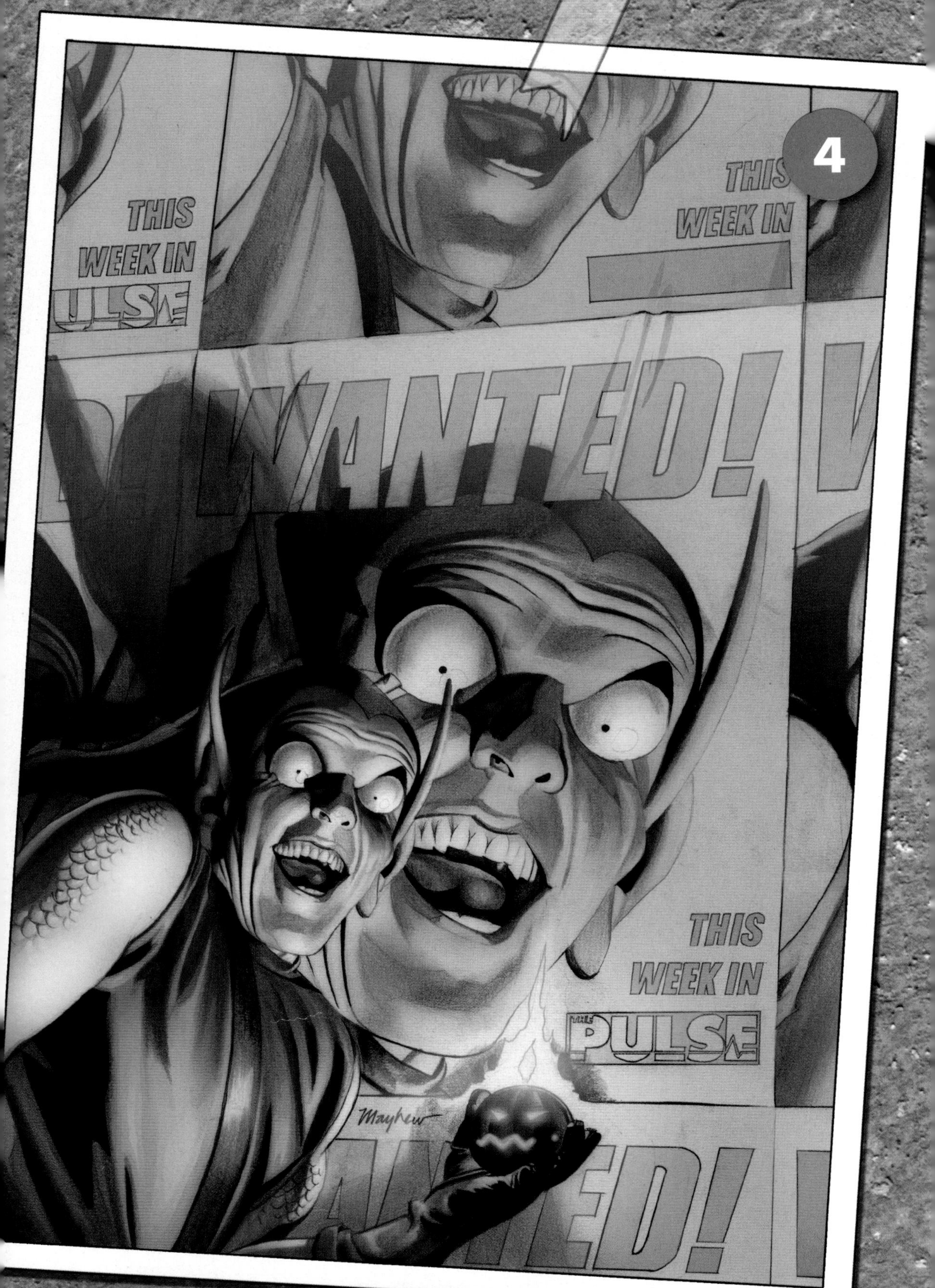
4
THIS
WEEK IN
THIS
WEEK IN
WANTED!
THIS
WEEK IN
THE PULSE
Mayhew

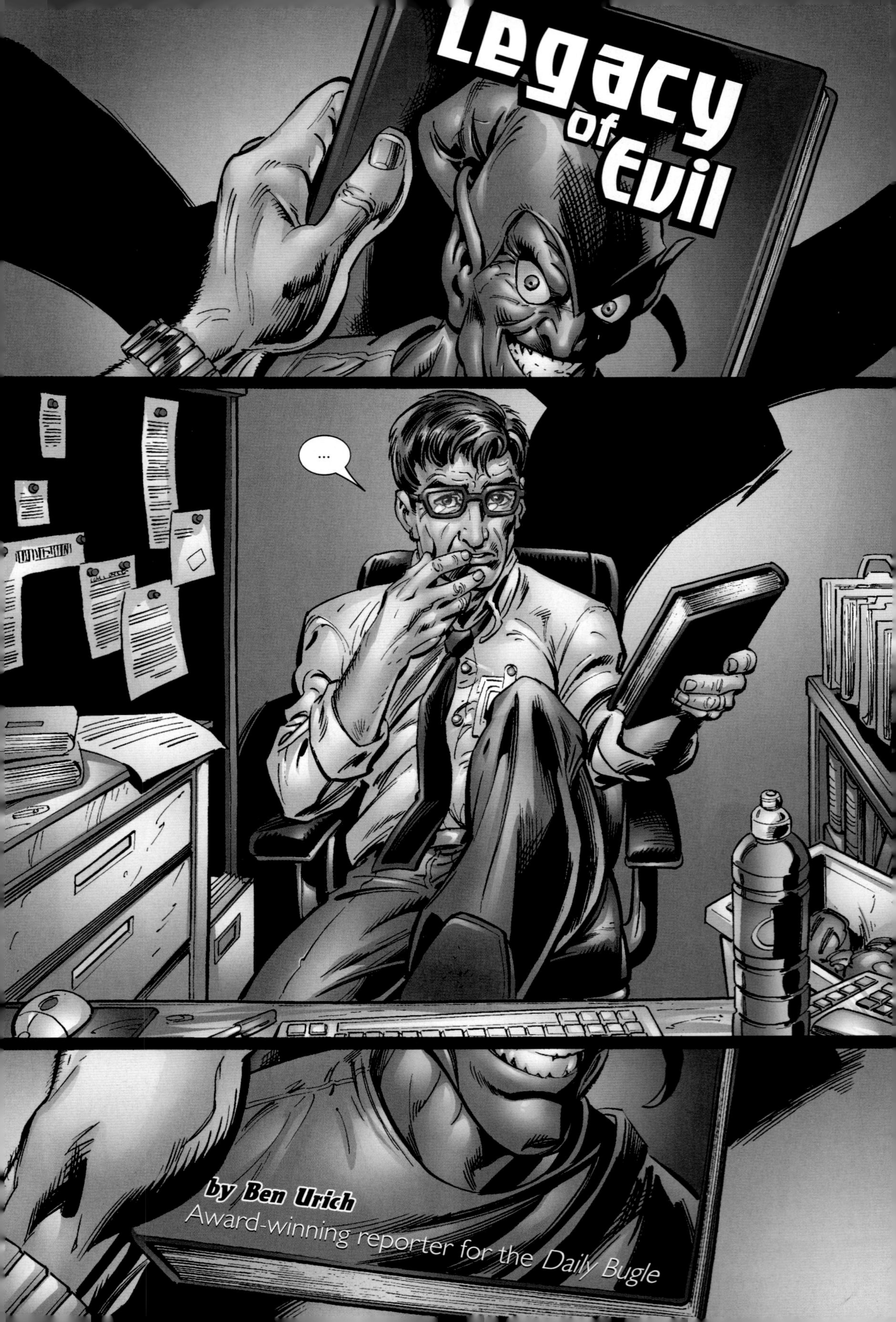

Legacy of Evil
...
by Ben Urich
Award-winning reporter for the Daily Bugle

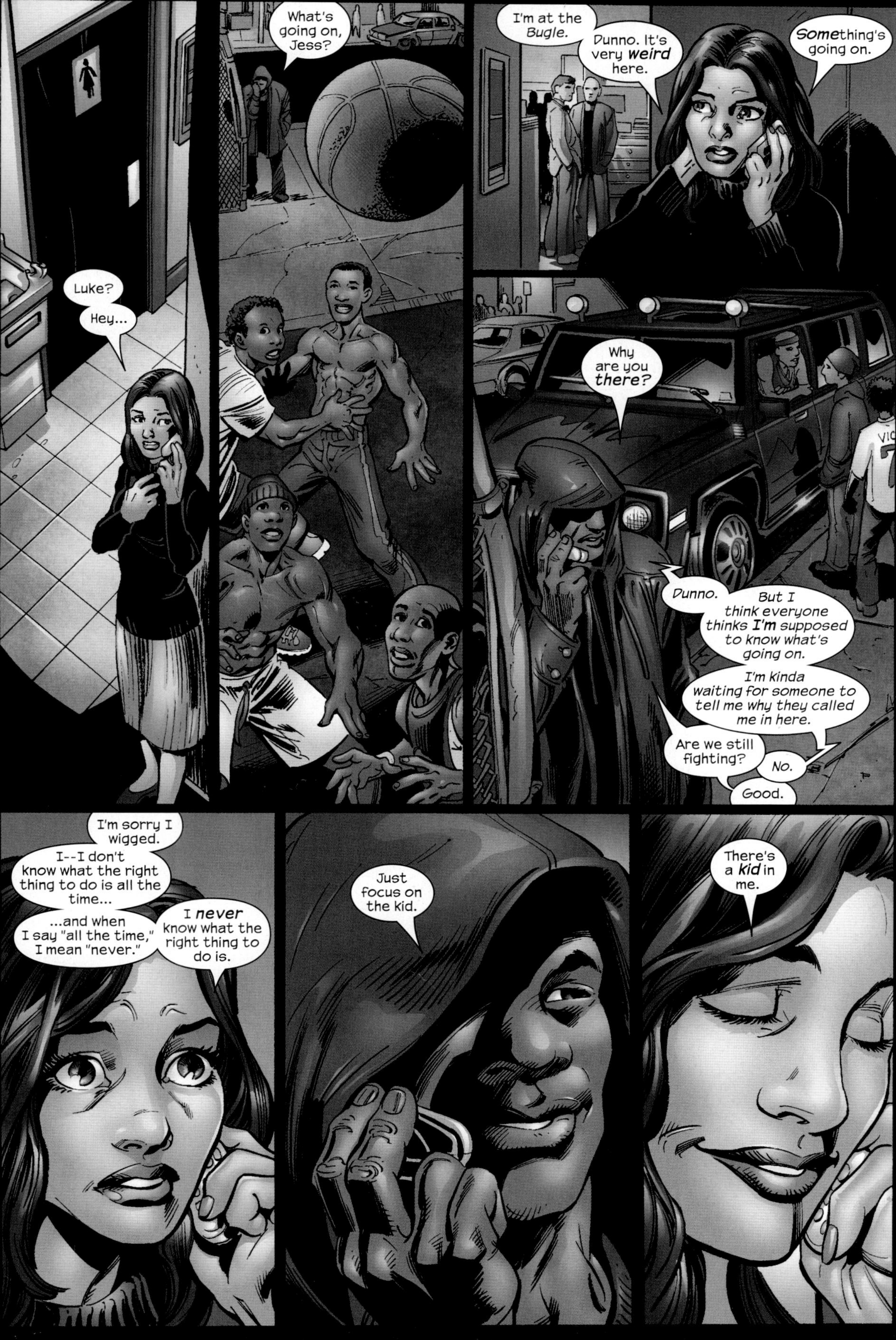
Luke?
Hey...
What's going on, Jess?
I'm at the *Bugle*.
Dunno. It's very **weird** here.
Something's going on.
Why are you **there**?
Dunno.
But I think everyone thinks **I'm** supposed to know what's going on.
I'm kinda waiting for someone to tell me why they called me in here.
Are we still fighting?
No.
Good.
I'm sorry I wigged.
I--I don't know what the right thing to do is all the time...
...and when I say "all the time," I mean "never."
I **never** know what the right thing to do is.
Just focus on the kid.
There's a **kid** in me.

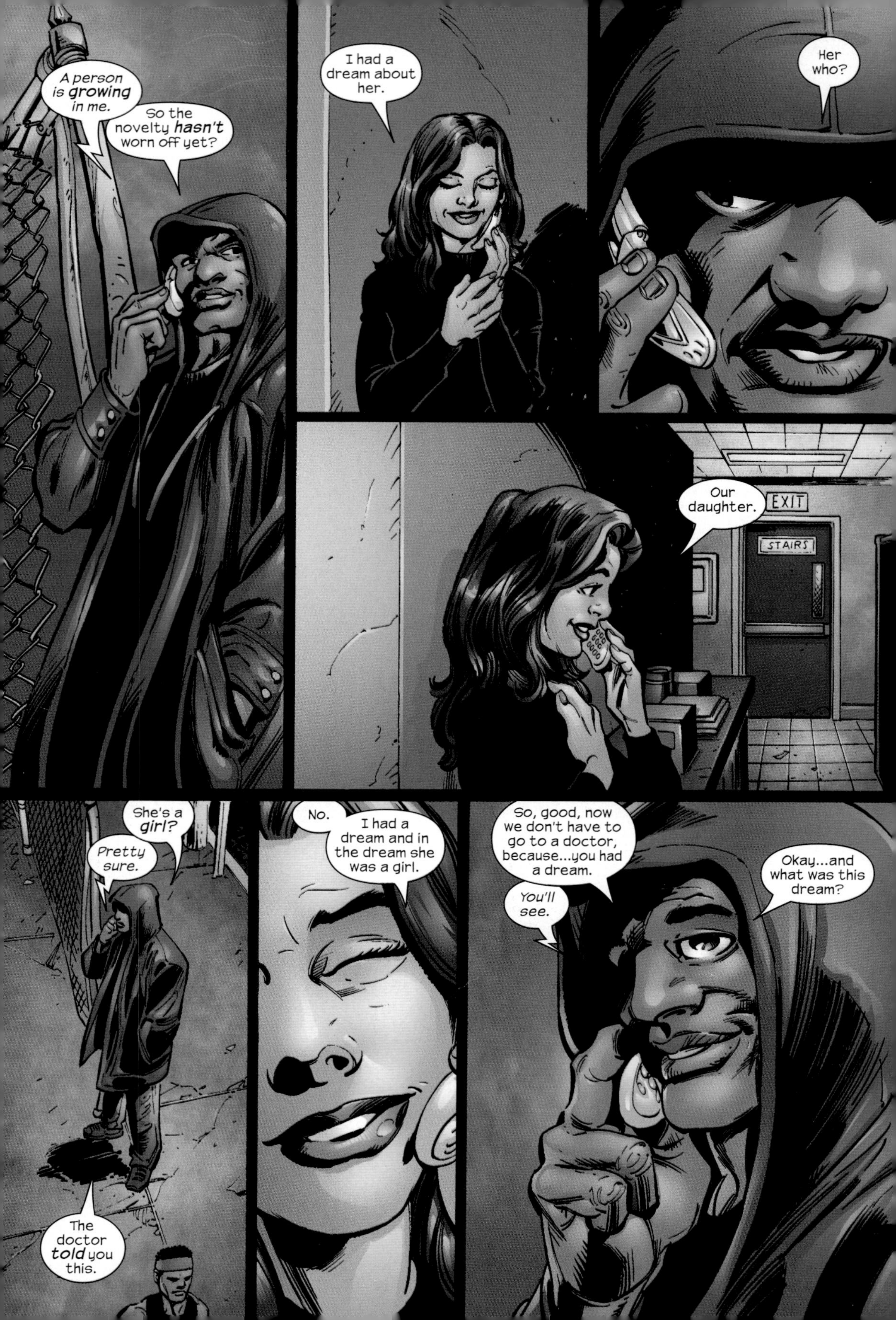
A person is *growing* in me.
So the novelty *hasn't* worn off yet?
I had a dream about her.
Her who?
Our daughter.
EXIT
STAIRS
She's a *girl*?
Pretty sure.
The doctor *told* you this.
No.
I had a dream and in the dream she was a girl.
So, good, now we don't have to go to a doctor, because...you had a dream.
You'll see.
Okay...and what was this dream?

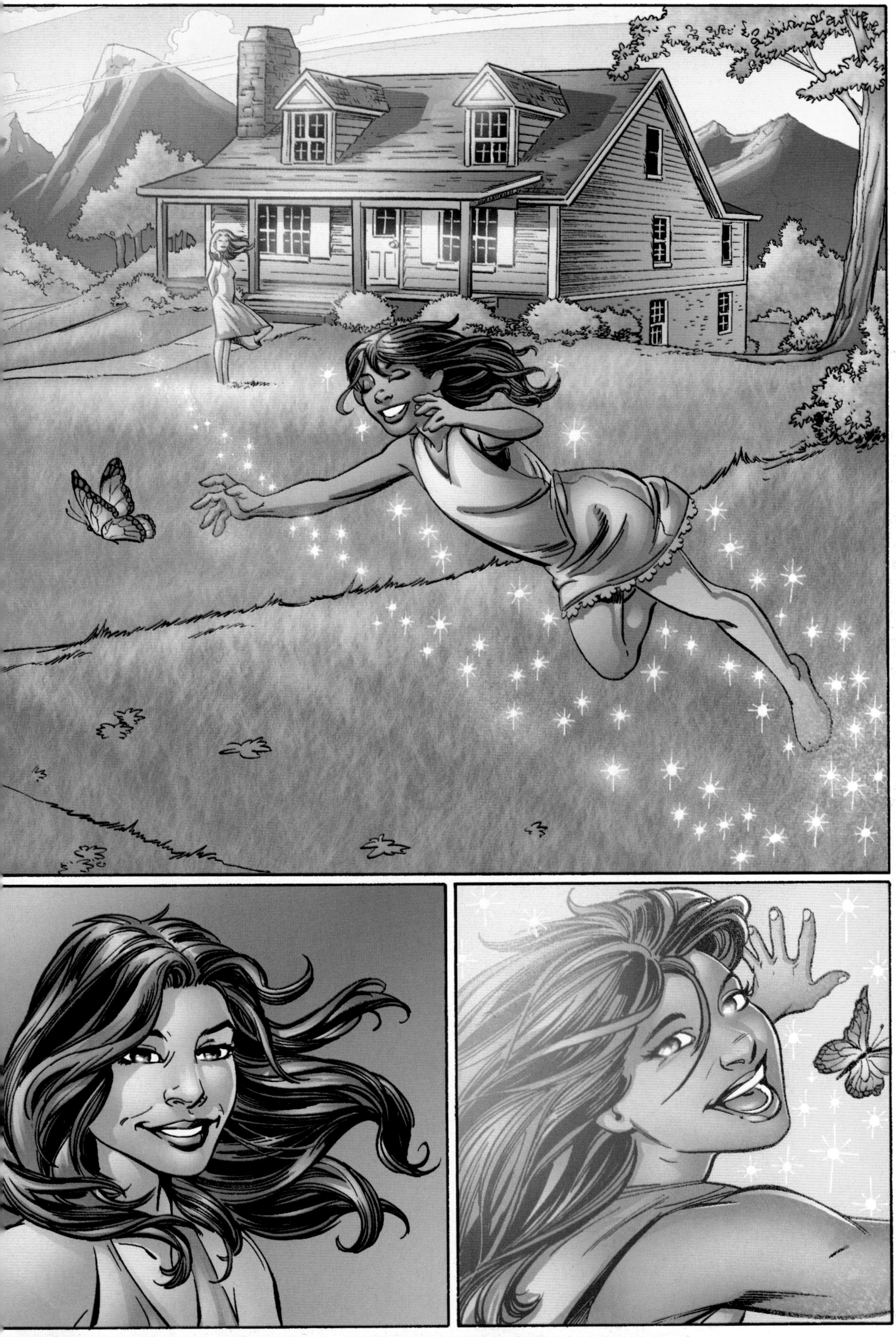

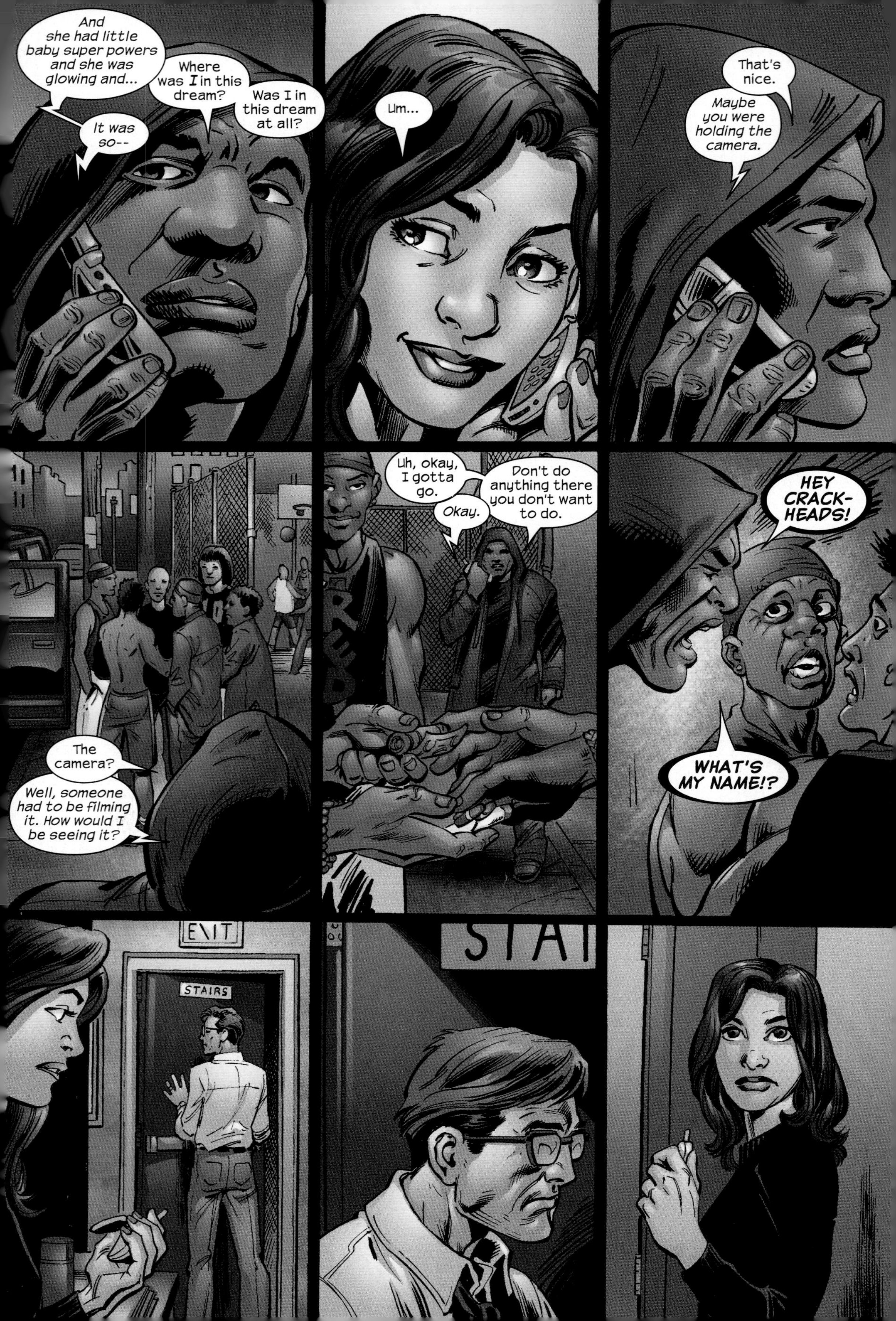
And she had little baby super powers and she was glowing and...
It was so--
Where was I in this dream?
Was I in this dream at all?
Um...
That's nice.
Maybe you were holding the camera.
The camera?
Well, someone had to be filming it. How would I be seeing it?
Uh, okay, I gotta go.
Okay.
Don't do anything there you don't want to do.
HEY CRACK-HEADS!
WHAT'S MY NAME!?
EXIT
STAIRS

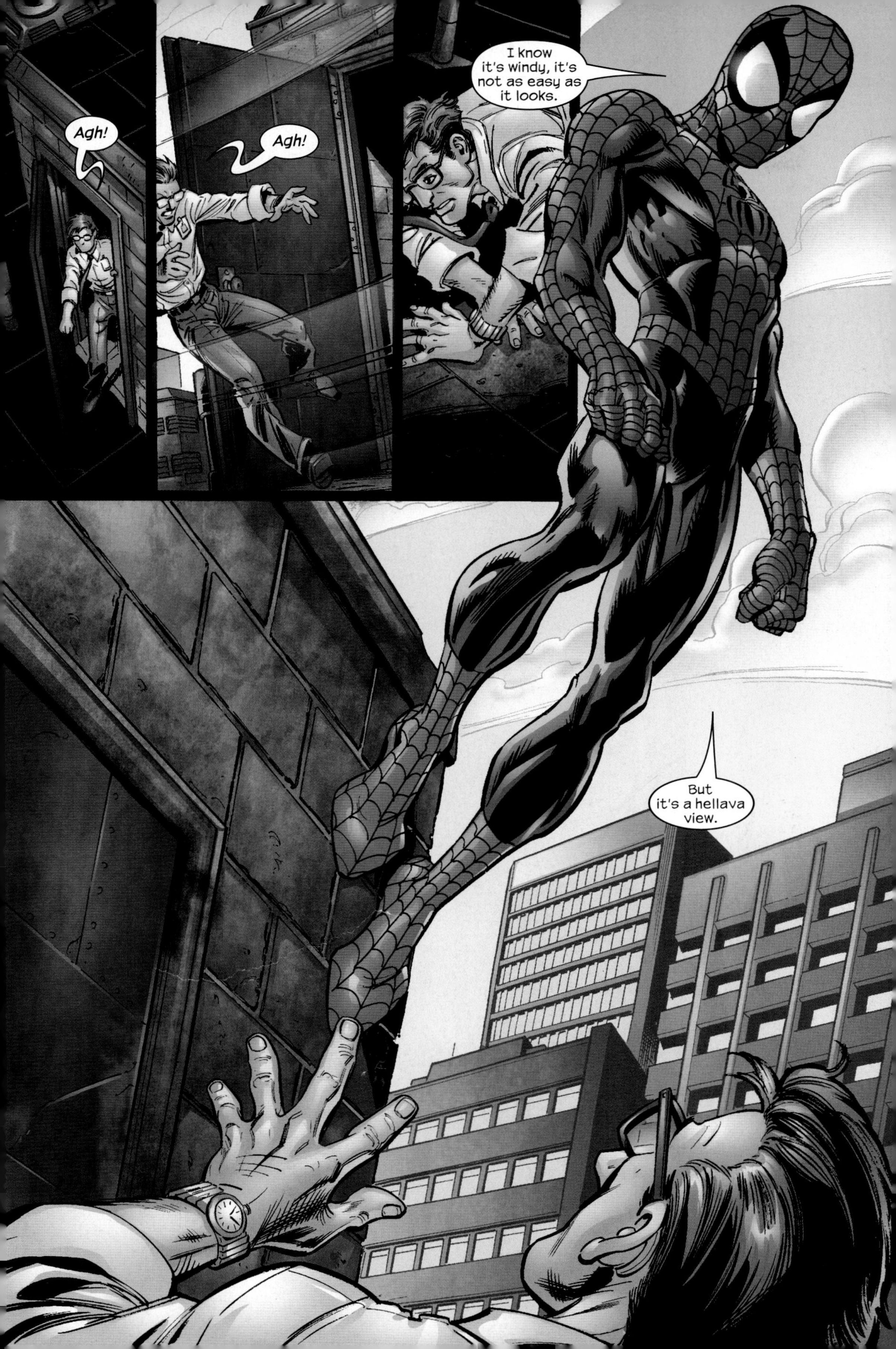
Agh!
Agh!
I know it's windy, it's not as easy as it looks.
But it's a hellava view.

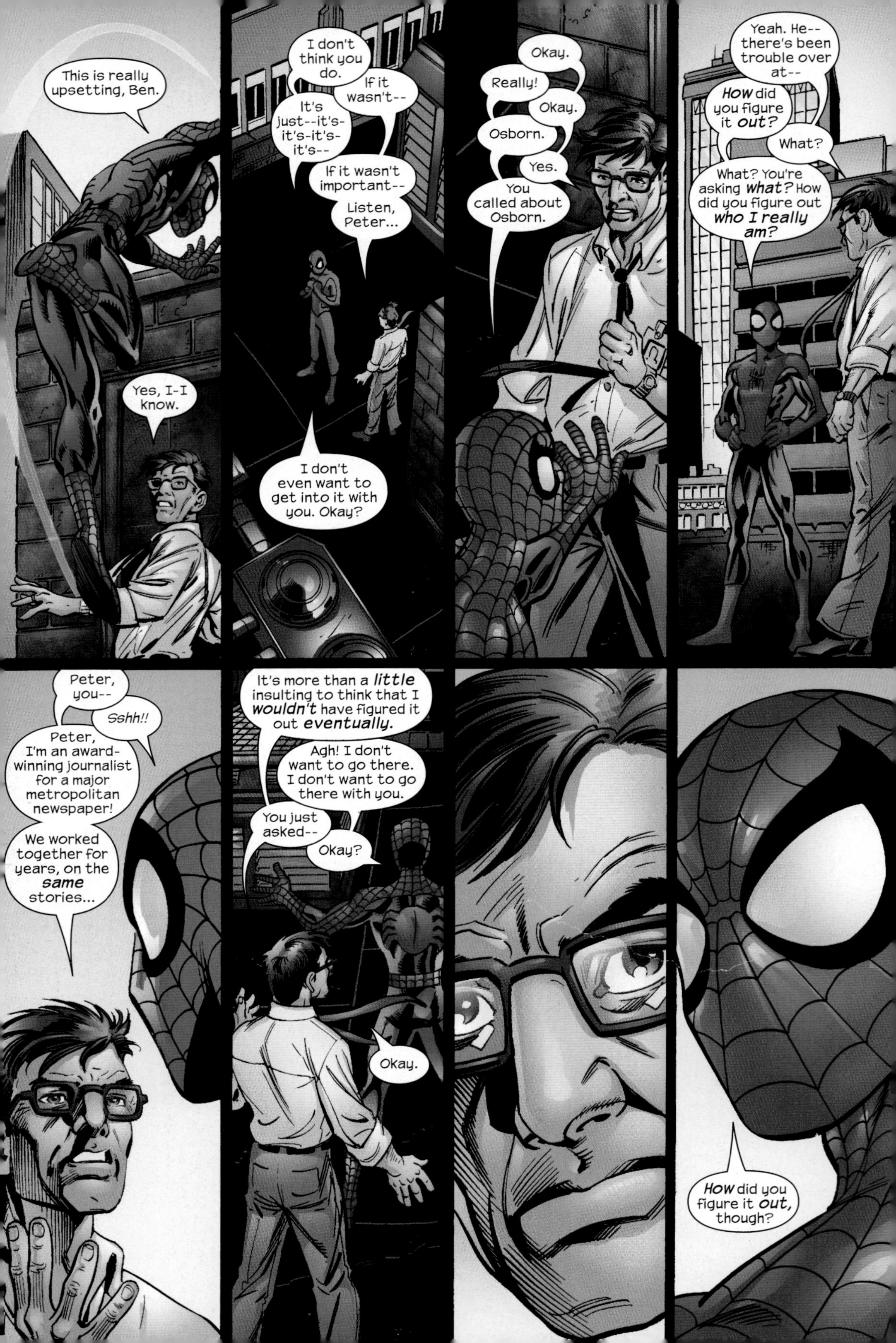
This is really upsetting, Ben.
Yes, I-I know.
I don't think you do.
If it wasn't--
It's just--it's-it's-it's-it's--
If it wasn't important--
Listen, Peter...
I don't even want to get into it with you. Okay?
Okay.
Really!
Okay.
Osborn.
Yes.
You called about Osborn.
Yeah. He--there's been trouble over at--
How did you figure it *out?*
What?
What? You're asking *what?* How did you figure out *who I really am?*
Peter, you--
Sshh!!
Peter, I'm an award-winning journalist for a major metropolitan newspaper!
We worked together for years, on the *same* stories...
It's more than a *little* insulting to think that I *wouldn't* have figured it out *eventually*.
Agh! I don't want to go there. I don't want to go there with you.
You just asked--
Okay?
Okay.
How did you figure it *out*, though?

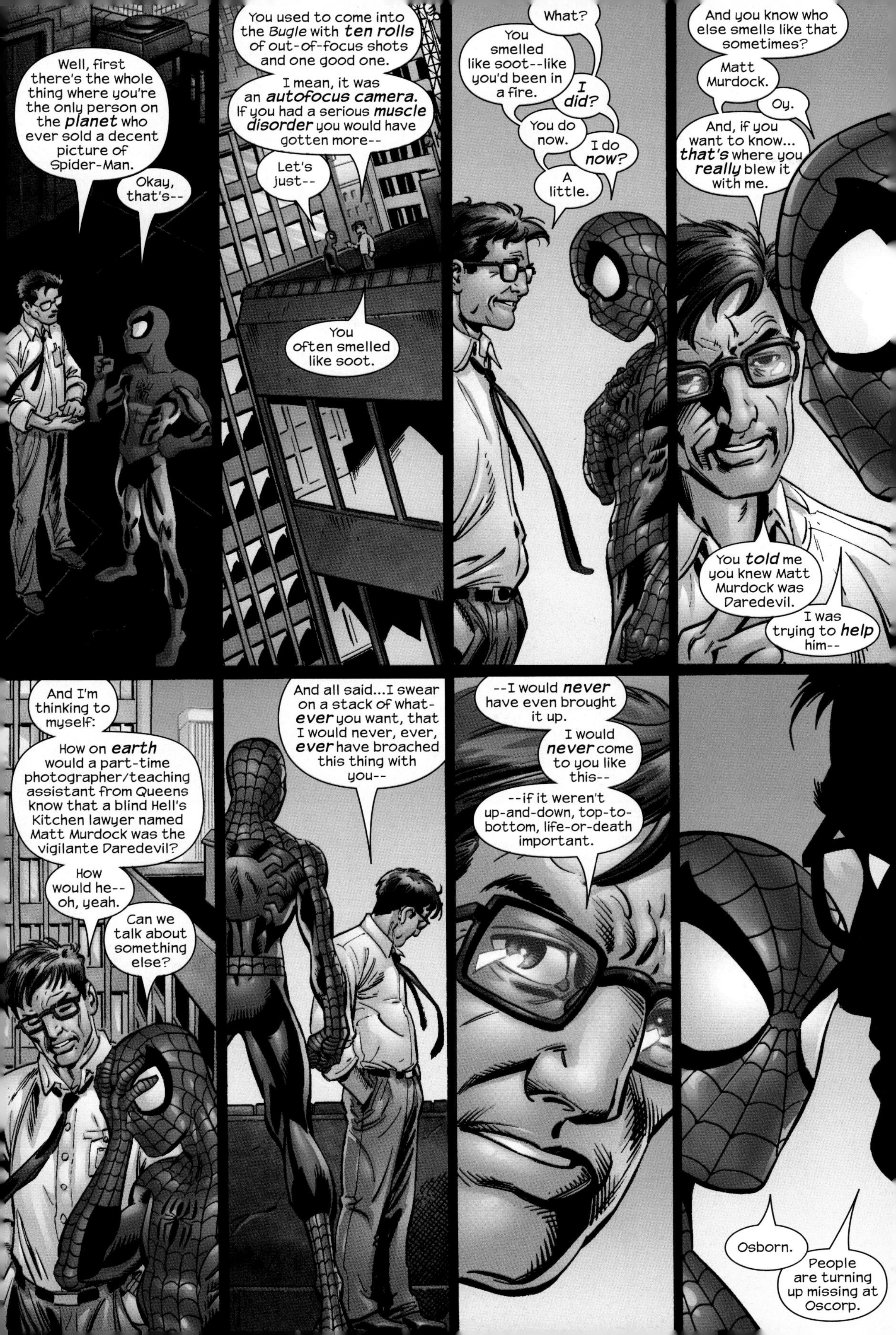
Well, first there's the whole thing where you're the only person on the planet who ever sold a decent picture of Spider-Man.
Okay, that's--
You used to come into the Bugle with ten rolls of out-of-focus shots and one good one.
I mean, it was an autofocus camera. If you had a serious muscle disorder you would have gotten more--
Let's just--
You often smelled like soot.
What?
You smelled like soot--like you'd been in a fire.
I did?
You do now.
I do now?
A little.
And you know who else smells like that sometimes?
Matt Murdock.
Oy.
And, if you want to know... that's where you really blew it with me.
You told me you knew Matt Murdock was Daredevil.
I was trying to help him--
And I'm thinking to myself:
How on earth would a part-time photographer/teaching assistant from Queens know that a blind Hell's Kitchen lawyer named Matt Murdock was the vigilante Daredevil?
How would he--oh, yeah.
Can we talk about something else?
And all said...I swear on a stack of whatever you want, that I would never, ever, ever have broached this thing with you--
--I would never have even brought it up.
I would never come to you like this--
--if it weren't up-and-down, top-to-bottom, life-or-death important.
Osborn.
People are turning up missing at Oscorp.

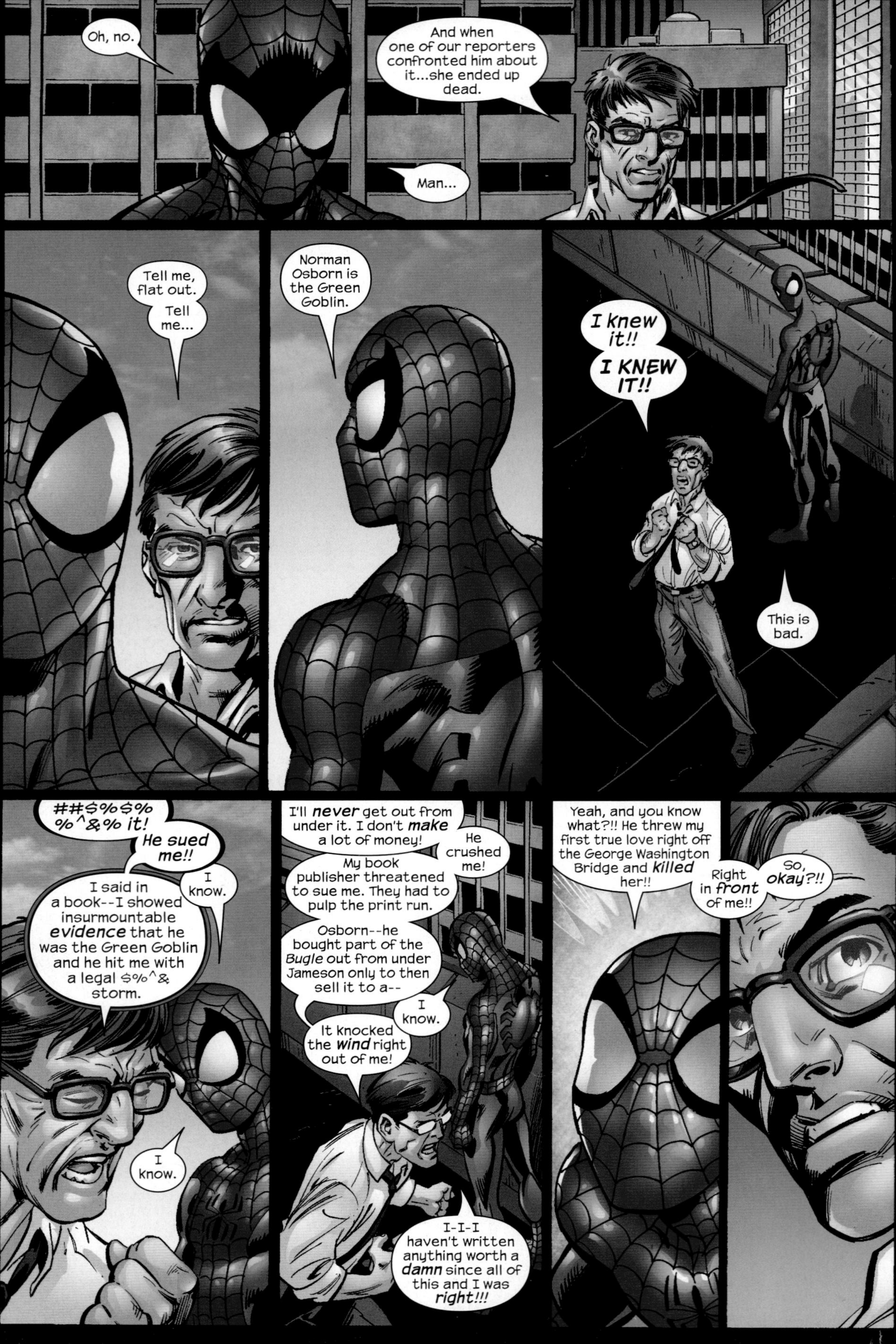

Oh, no.
And when one of our reporters confronted him about it...she ended up dead.
Man...
Tell me, flat out.
Tell me...
Norman Osborn is the Green Goblin.
I knew it!!
I KNEW IT!!
This is bad.
##$%$% %^&% it!
He sued me!!
I know.
I said in a book--I showed insurmountable evidence that he was the Green Goblin and he hit me with a legal $%^& storm.
I know.
I'll never get out from under it. I don't make a lot of money!
He crushed me!
My book publisher threatened to sue me. They had to pulp the print run.
Osborn--he bought part of the Bugle out from under Jameson only to then sell it to a--
I know.
It knocked the wind right out of me!
I-I-I haven't written anything worth a damn since all of this and I was right!!!
Yeah, and you know what?!! He threw my first true love right off the George Washington Bridge and killed her!!
Right in front of me!!
So, okay?!!

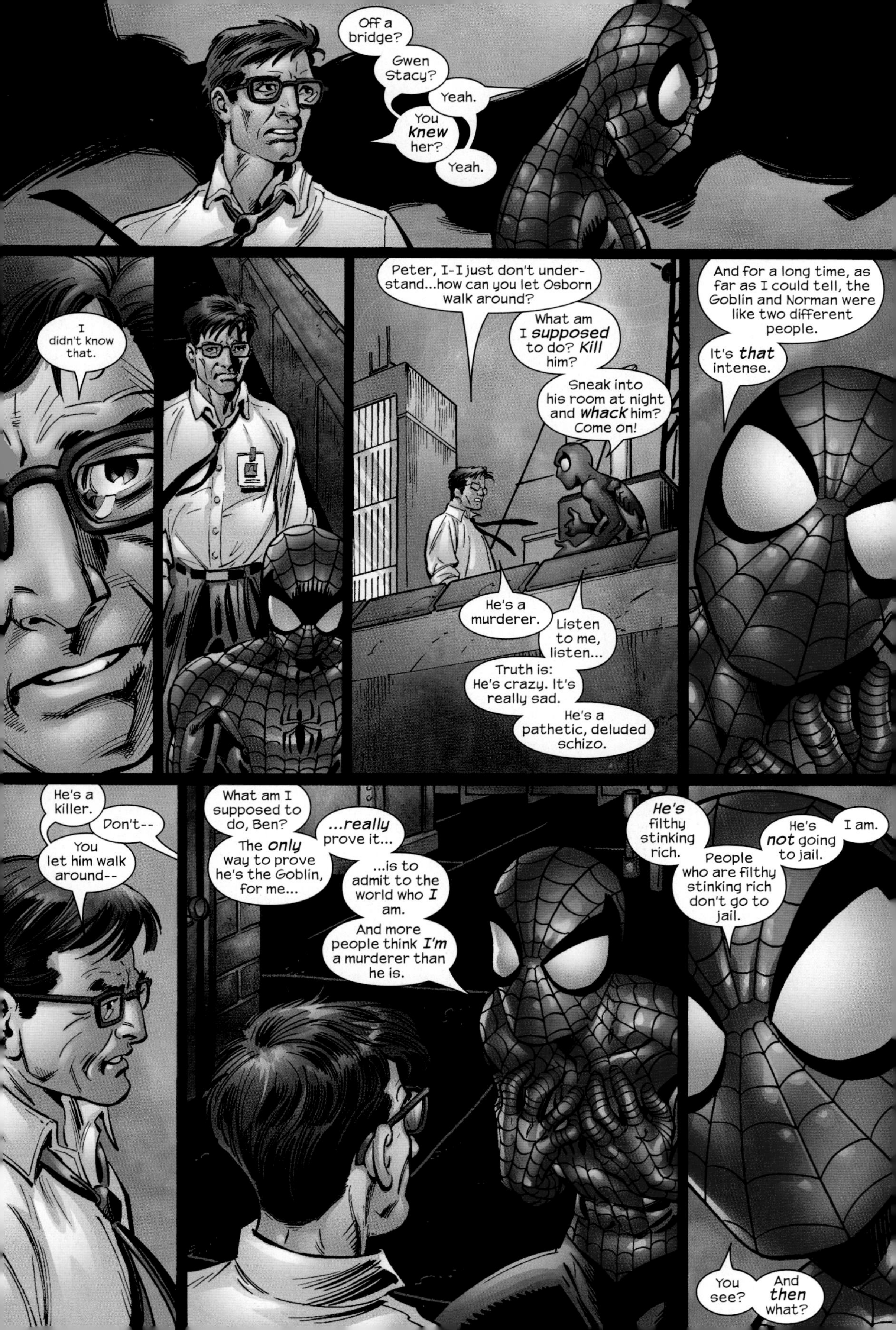
Off a bridge?
Gwen Stacy?
Yeah.
You knew her?
Yeah.
I didn't know that.
Peter, I-I just don't under-stand...how can you let Osborn walk around?
What am I supposed to do? Kill him?
Sneak into his room at night and whack him? Come on!
He's a murderer.
Listen to me, listen...
Truth is: He's crazy. It's really sad.
He's a pathetic, deluded schizo.
And for a long time, as far as I could tell, the Goblin and Norman were like two different people.
It's that intense.
He's a killer.
Don't--
You let him walk around--
What am I supposed to do, Ben?
The only way to prove he's the Goblin, for me...
...really prove it...
...is to admit to the world who I am.
And more people think I'm a murderer than he is.
He's filthy stinking rich.
He's not going to jail.
I am.
People who are filthy stinking rich don't go to jail.
You see?
And then what?

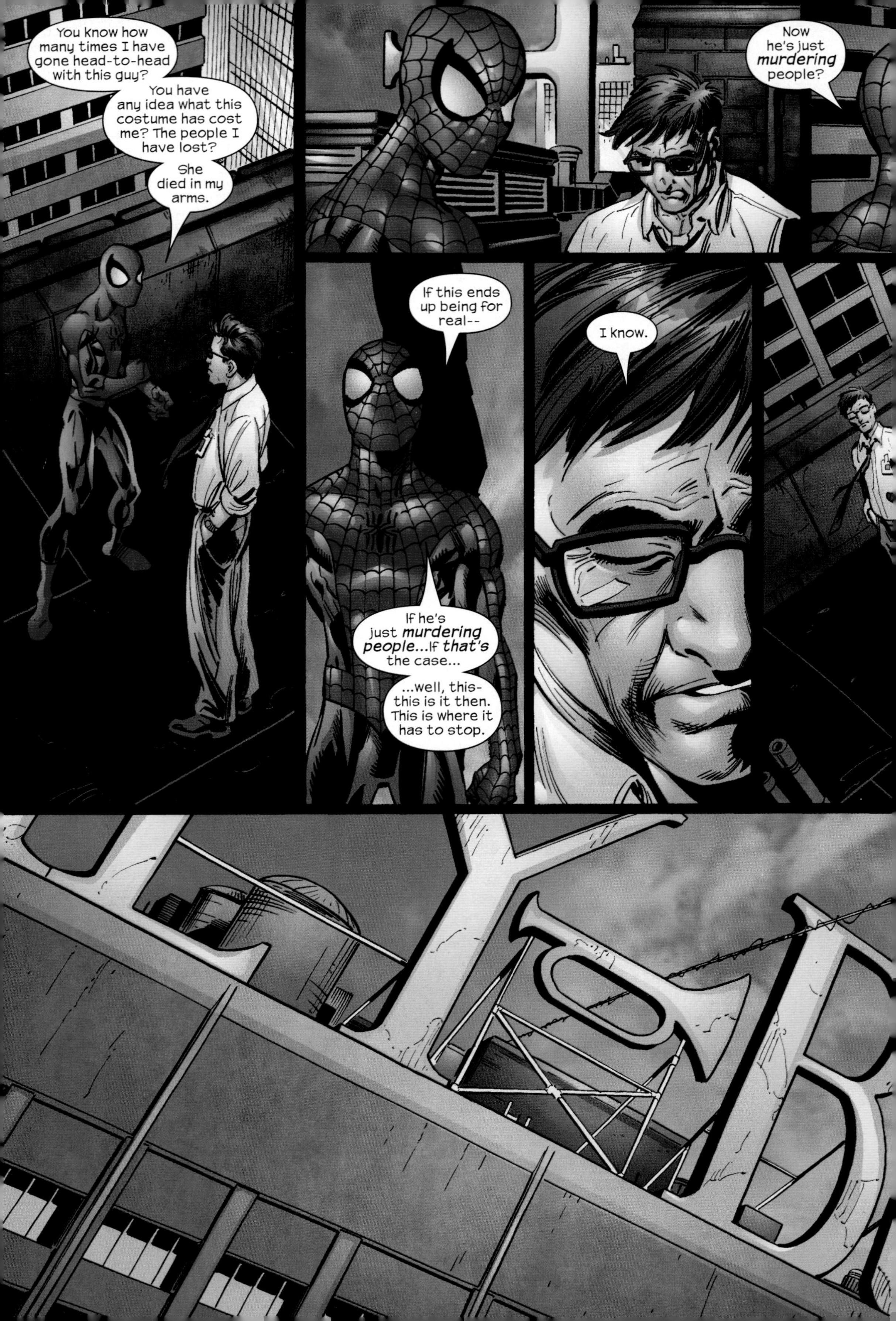
You know how many times I have gone head-to-head with this guy?
You have any idea what this costume has cost me? The people I have lost?
She died in my arms.
Now he's just *murdering* people?
If this ends up being for real--
If he's just *murdering people*...If *that's* the case...
...well, this-this is it then. This is where it has to stop.
I know.

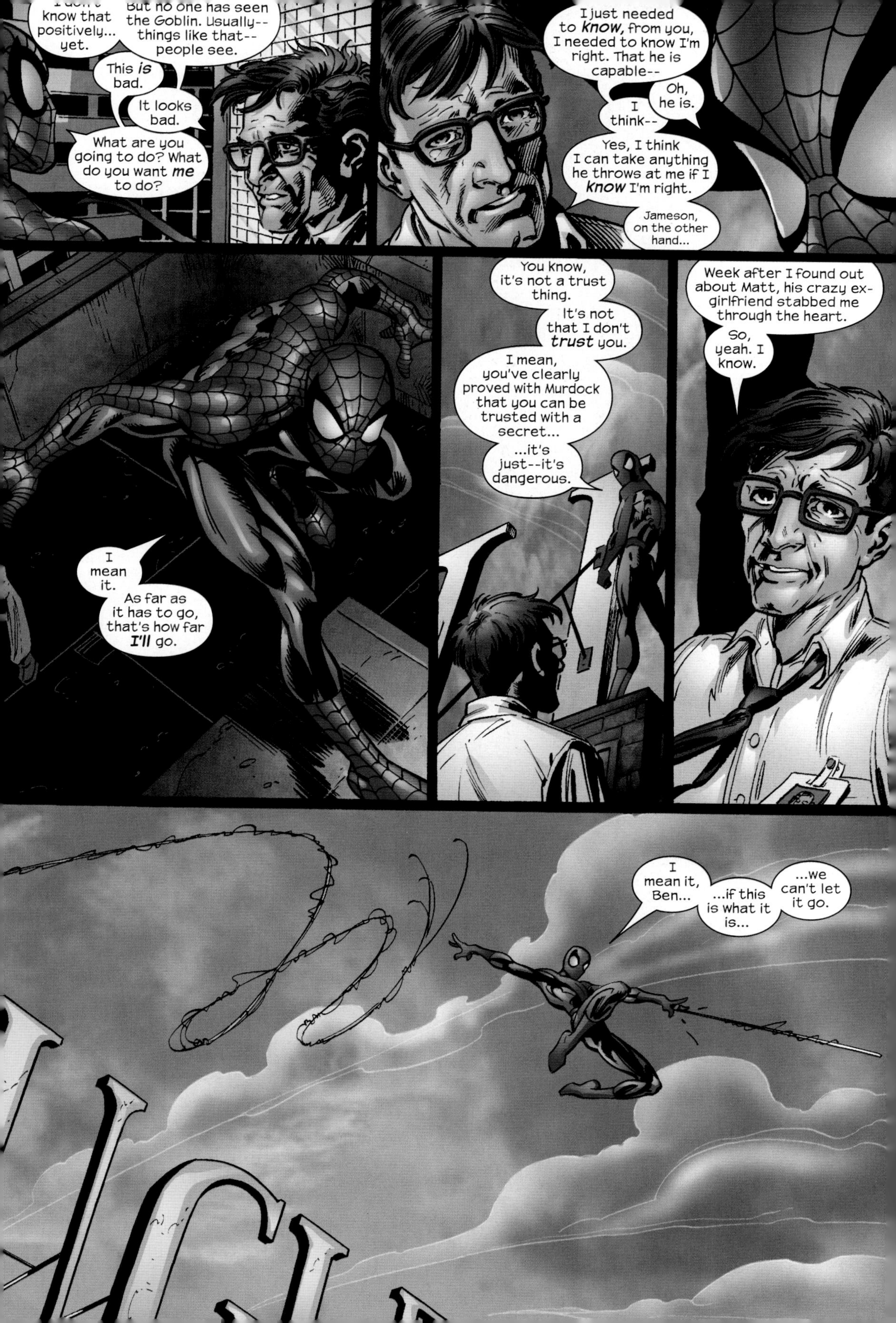

positively... yet.
But no one has seen the Goblin. Usually-- things like that-- people see.
This *is* bad.
It looks bad.
What are you going to do? What do you want *me* to do?
I just needed to *know*, from you, I needed to know I'm right. That he is capable--
Oh, he is.
I think--
Yes, I think I can take anything he throws at me if I *know* I'm right.
Jameson, on the other hand...
I mean it.
As far as it has to go, that's how far *I'll* go.
You know, it's not a trust thing.
It's not that I don't *trust* you.
I mean, you've clearly proved with Murdock that you can be trusted with a secret...
...it's just--it's dangerous.
Week after I found out about Matt, his crazy ex-girlfriend stabbed me through the heart.
So, yeah. I know.
I mean it, Ben...
...if this is what it is...
...we can't let it go.

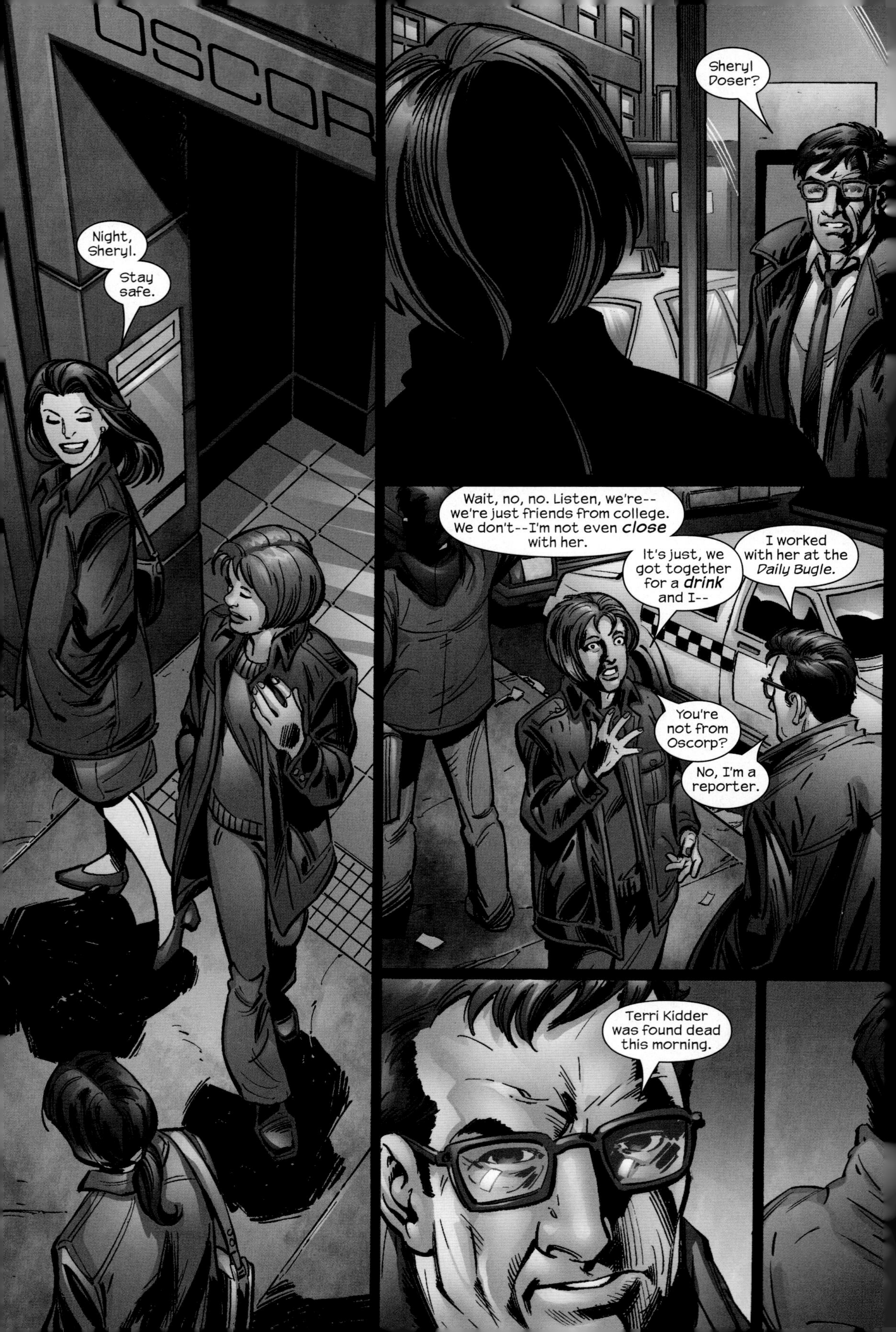
OSCOR
Night, Sheryl.
Stay safe.
Sheryl Doser?
Wait, no, no. Listen, we're--we're just friends from college. We don't--I'm not even *close* with her.
It's just, we got together for a *drink* and I--
I worked with her at the *Daily Bugle.*
You're not from Oscorp?
No, I'm a reporter.
Terri Kidder was found dead this morning.

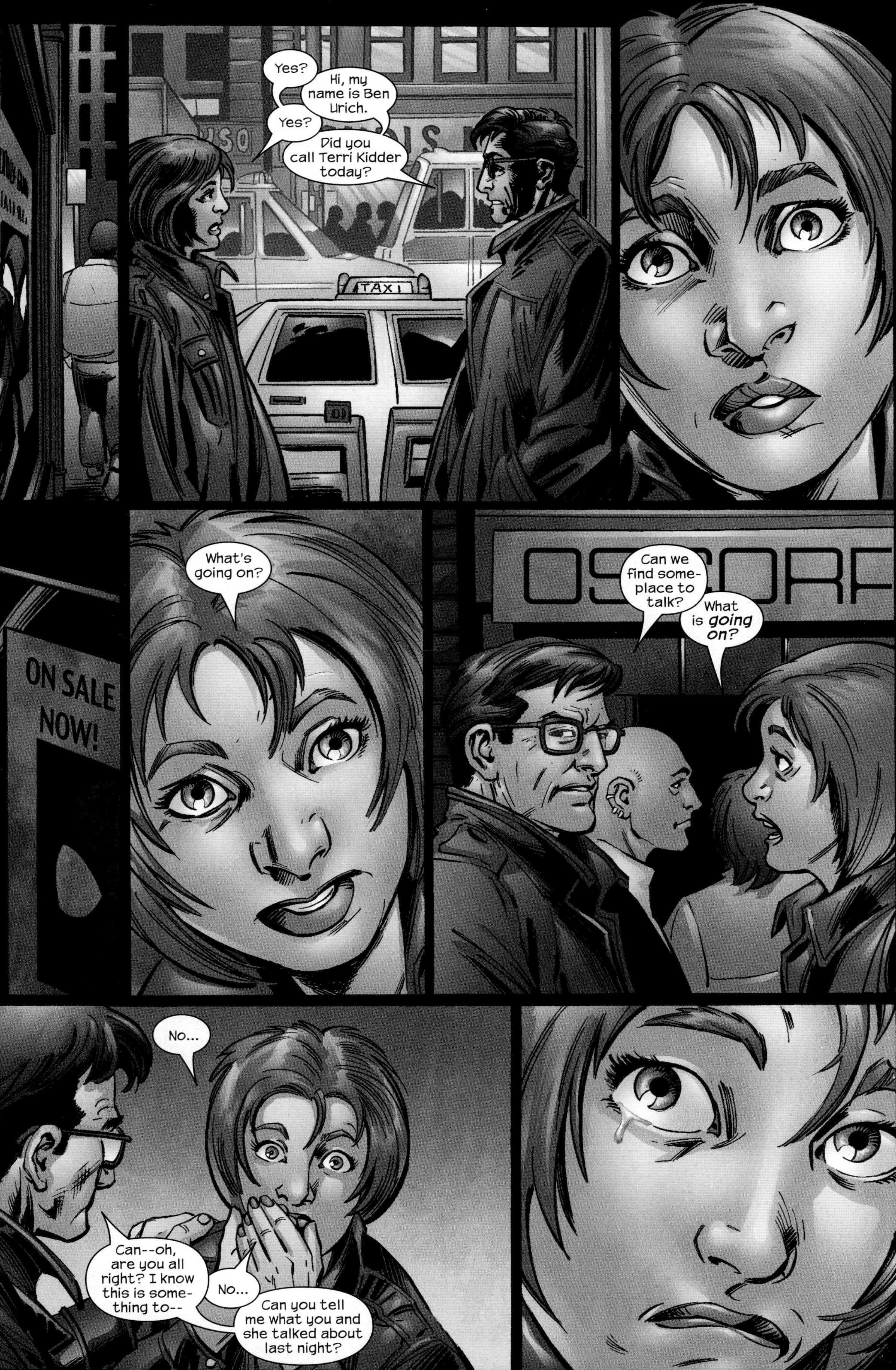

Yes?
Hi, my name is Ben Urich.
Yes?
Did you call Terri Kidder today?
TAXI
What's going on?
ON SALE NOW!
OSCORP
Can we find some-place to talk?
What is *going on?*
No...
Can--oh, are you all right? I know this is some-thing to--
No...
Can you tell me what you and she talked about last night?

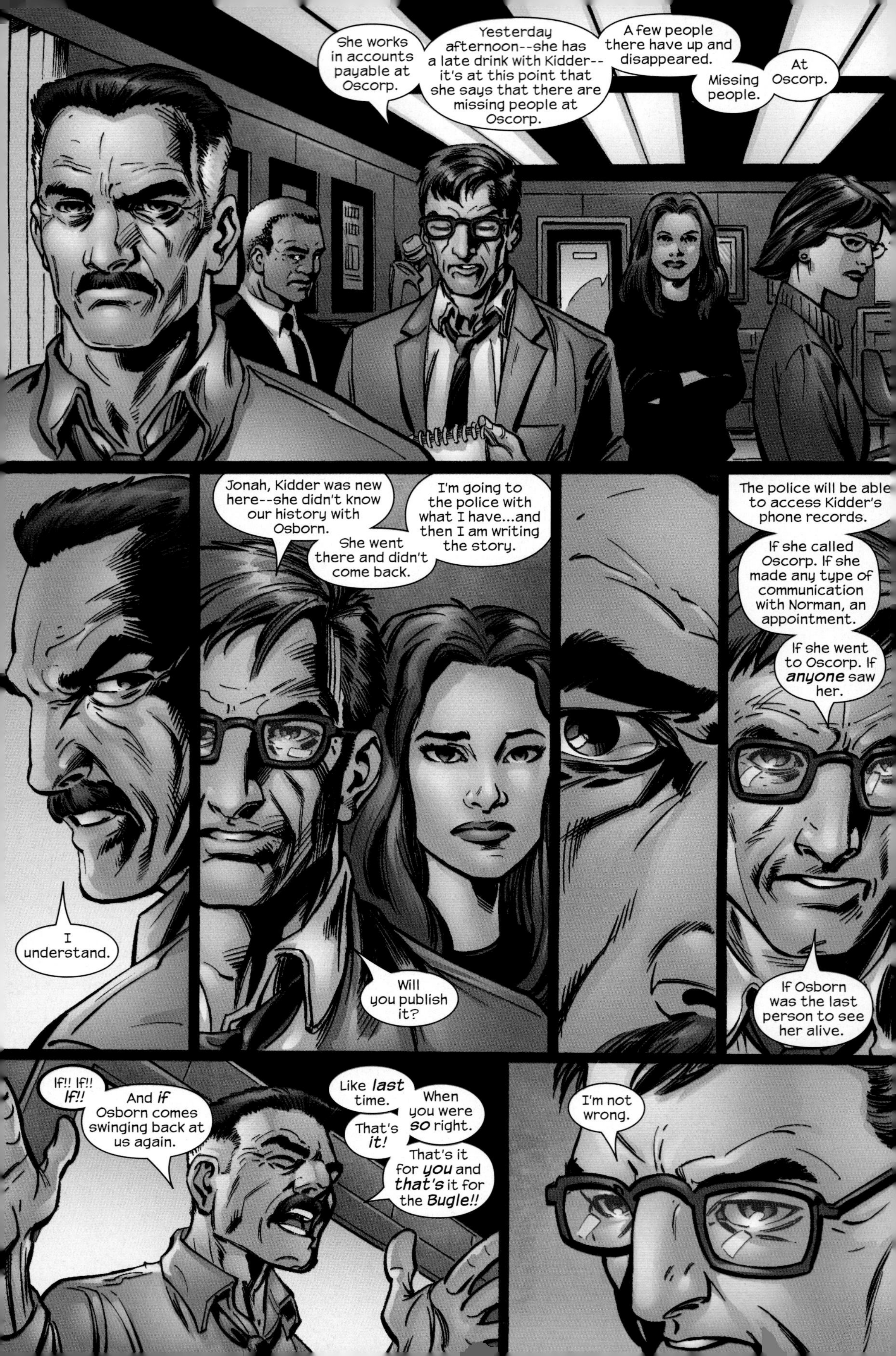
She works in accounts payable at Oscorp.
Yesterday afternoon--she has a late drink with Kidder--it's at this point that she says that there are missing people at Oscorp.
A few people there have up and disappeared.
Missing people.
At Oscorp.
I understand.
Jonah, Kidder was new here--she didn't know our history with Osborn.
She went there and didn't come back.
I'm going to the police with what I have...and then I am writing the story.
Will you publish it?
The police will be able to access Kidder's phone records.
If she called Oscorp. If she made any type of communication with Norman, an appointment.
If she went to Oscorp. If *anyone* saw her.
If Osborn was the last person to see her alive.
If!! If!! *If!!*
And *if* Osborn comes swinging back at us again.
Like *last* time.
When you were *so* right.
That's *it!*
That's it for *you* and *that's* it for the *Bugle!!*
I'm not wrong.

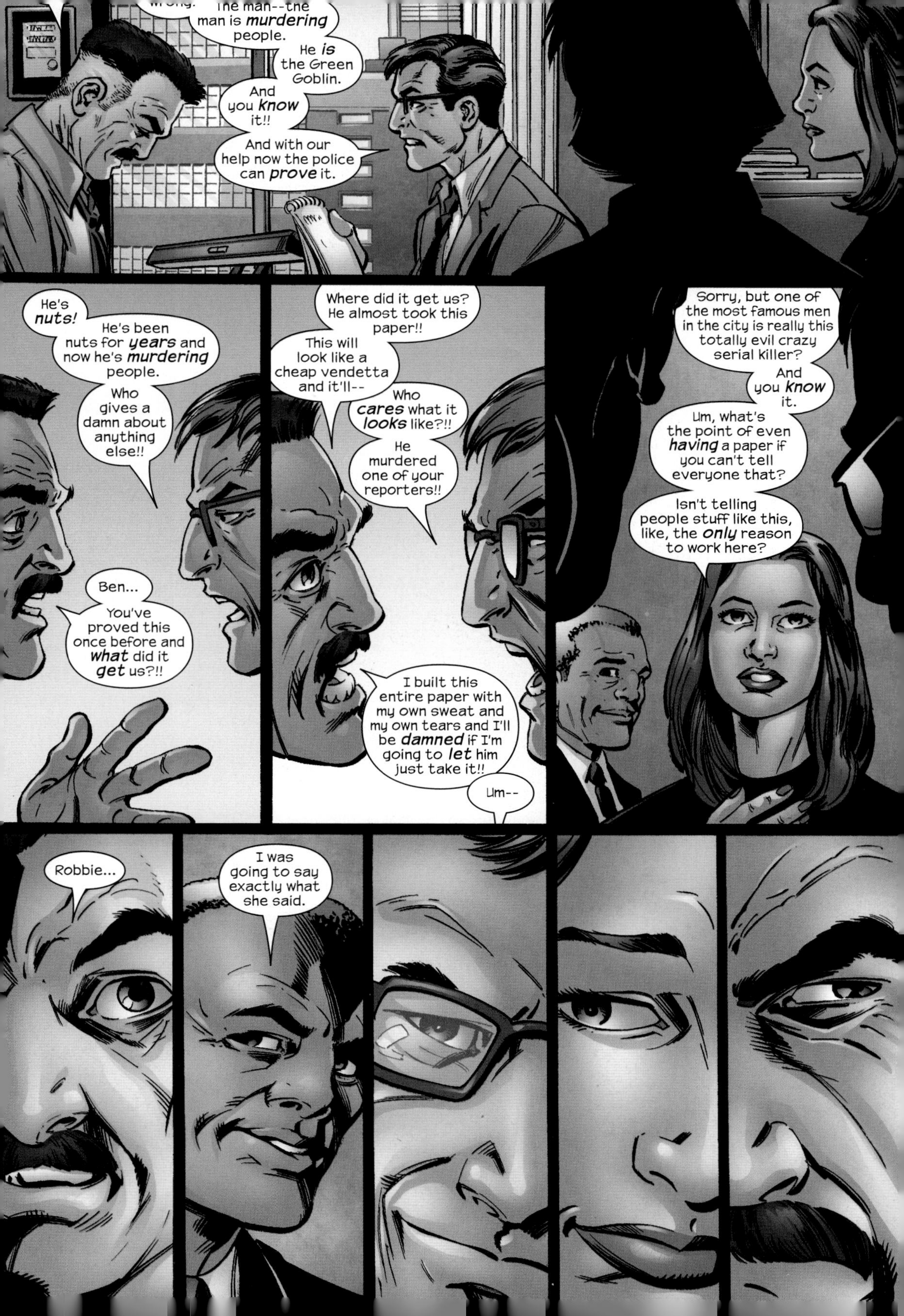

wrong.
The man--the man is *murdering* people.
He *is* the Green Goblin.
And you *know* it!!
And with our help now the police can *prove* it.
He's *nuts!*
He's been nuts for *years* and now he's *murdering* people.
Who gives a damn about anything else!!
Ben...
You've proved this once before and *what* did it *get* us?!!
Where did it get us? He almost took this paper!!
This will look like a cheap vendetta and it'll--
Who *cares* what it *looks* like?!!
He murdered one of your reporters!!
I built this entire paper with my own sweat and my own tears and I'll be *damned* if I'm going to *let* him just take it!!
Um--
Sorry, but one of the most famous men in the city is really this totally evil crazy serial killer?
And you *know* it.
Um, what's the point of even *having* a paper if you can't tell everyone that?
Isn't telling people stuff like this, like, the *only* reason to work here?
Robbie...
I was going to say exactly what she said.

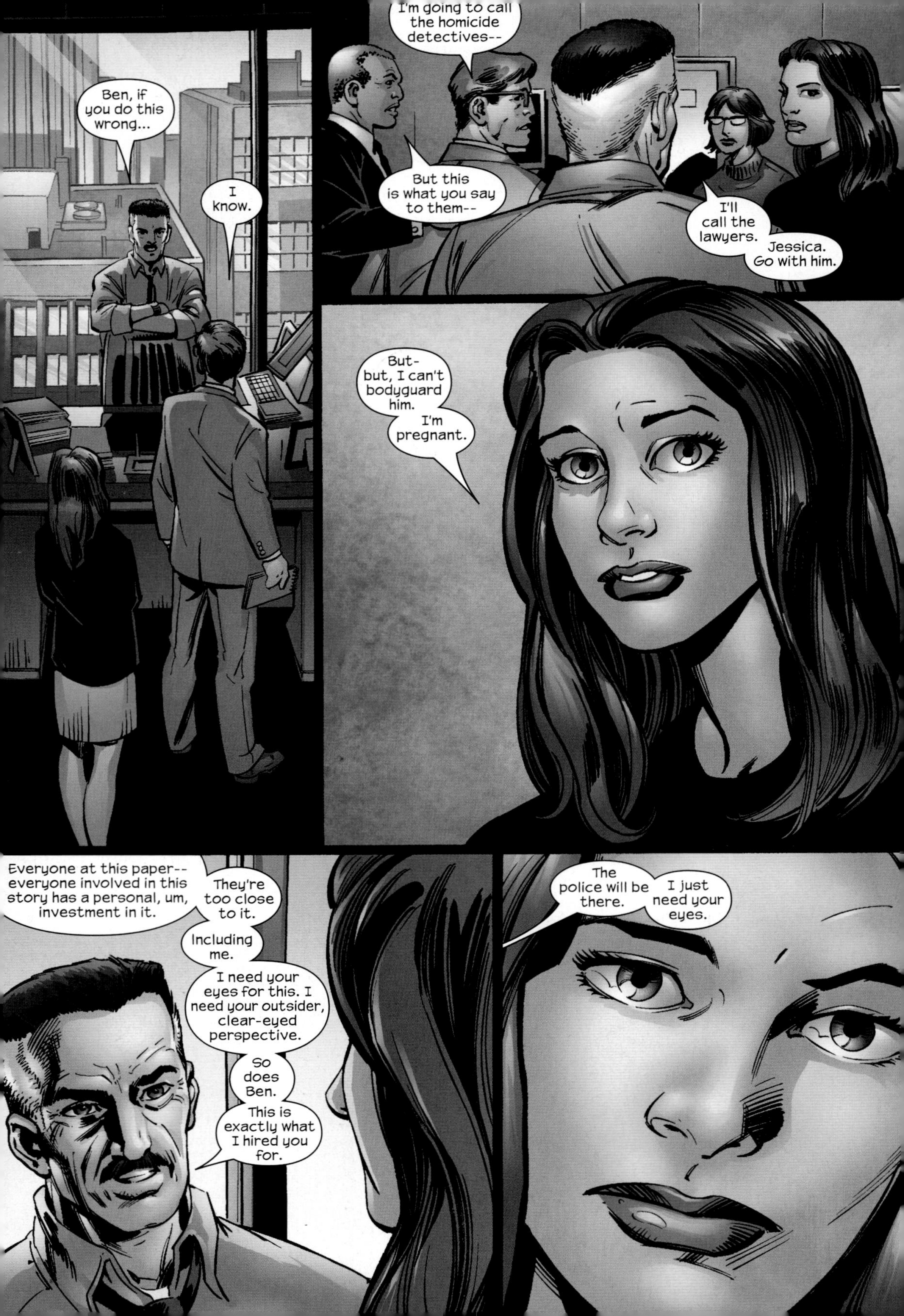
Ben, if you do this wrong...
I know.
I'm going to call the homicide detectives--
But this is what you say to them--
I'll call the lawyers.
Jessica. Go with him.
But-but, I can't bodyguard him.
I'm pregnant.
Everyone at this paper--everyone involved in this story has a personal, um, investment in it.
They're too close to it.
Including me.
I need your eyes for this. I need your outsider, clear-eyed perspective.
So does Ben.
This is exactly what I hired you for.
The police will be there.
I just need your eyes.

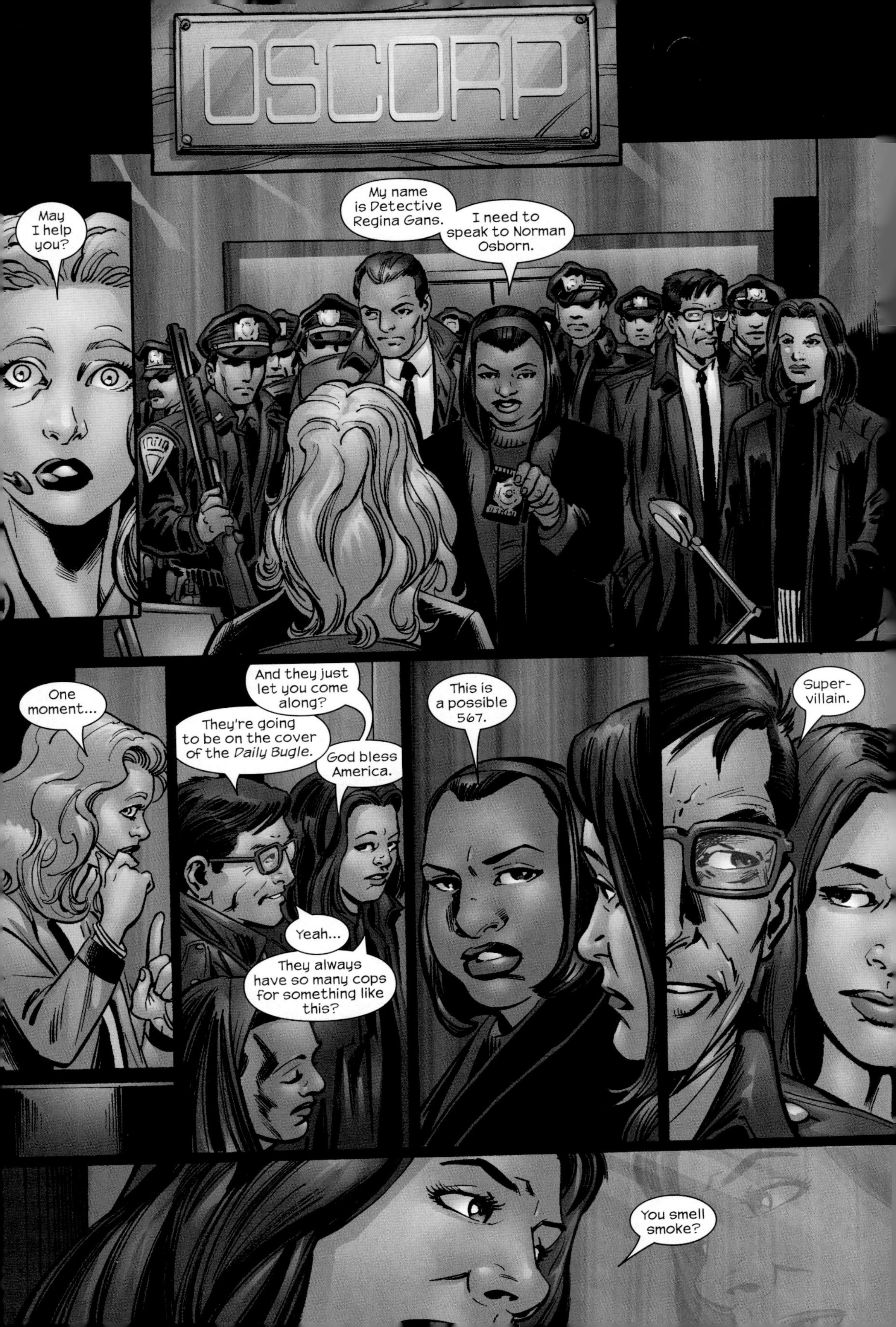
OSCORP
May I help you?
My name is Detective Regina Gans.
I need to speak to Norman Osborn.
One moment...
And they just let you come along?
They're going to be on the cover of the *Daily Bugle*.
God bless America.
Yeah...
They always have so many cops for something like this?
This is a possible 567.
Super-villain.
You smell smoke?

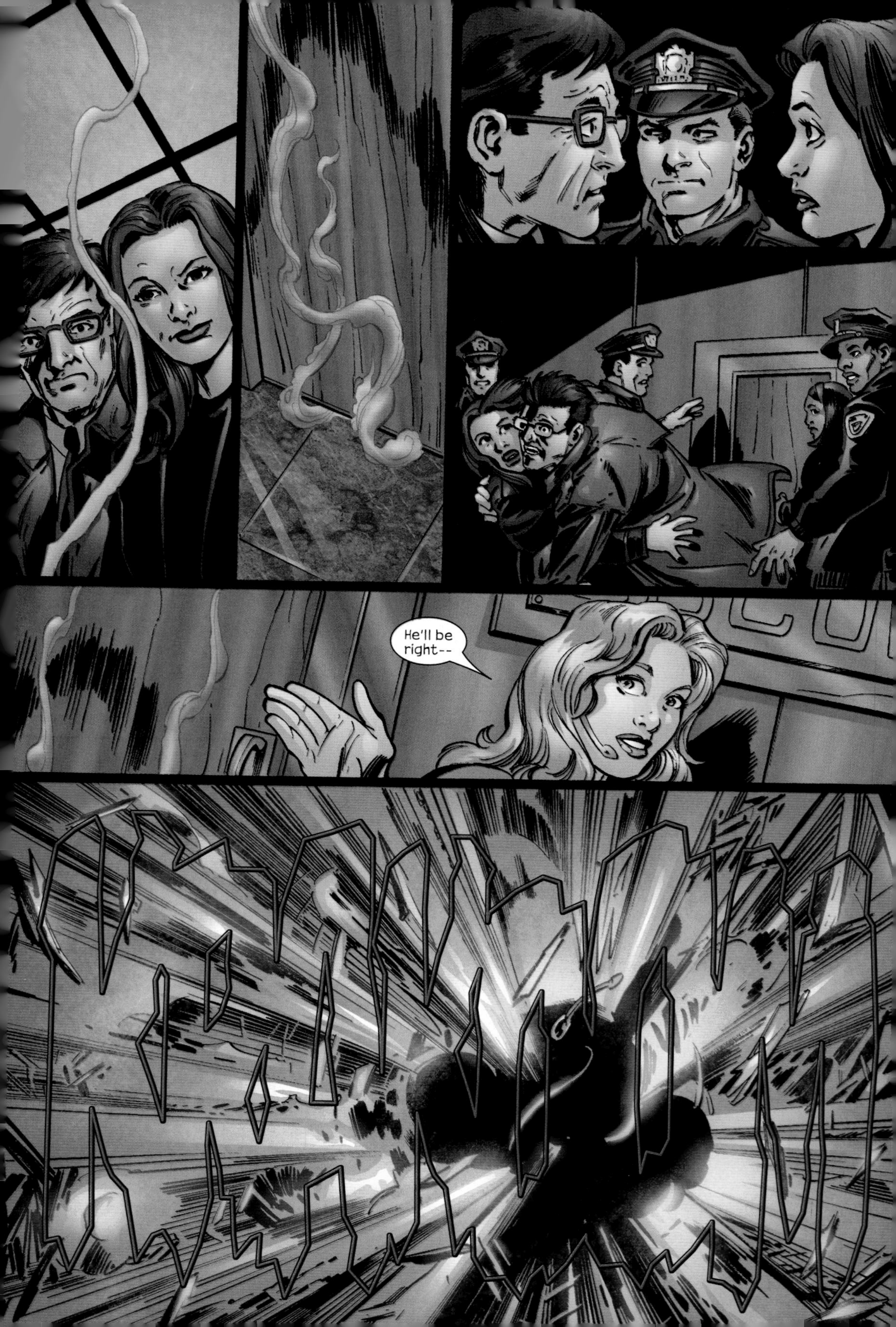
He'll be right--

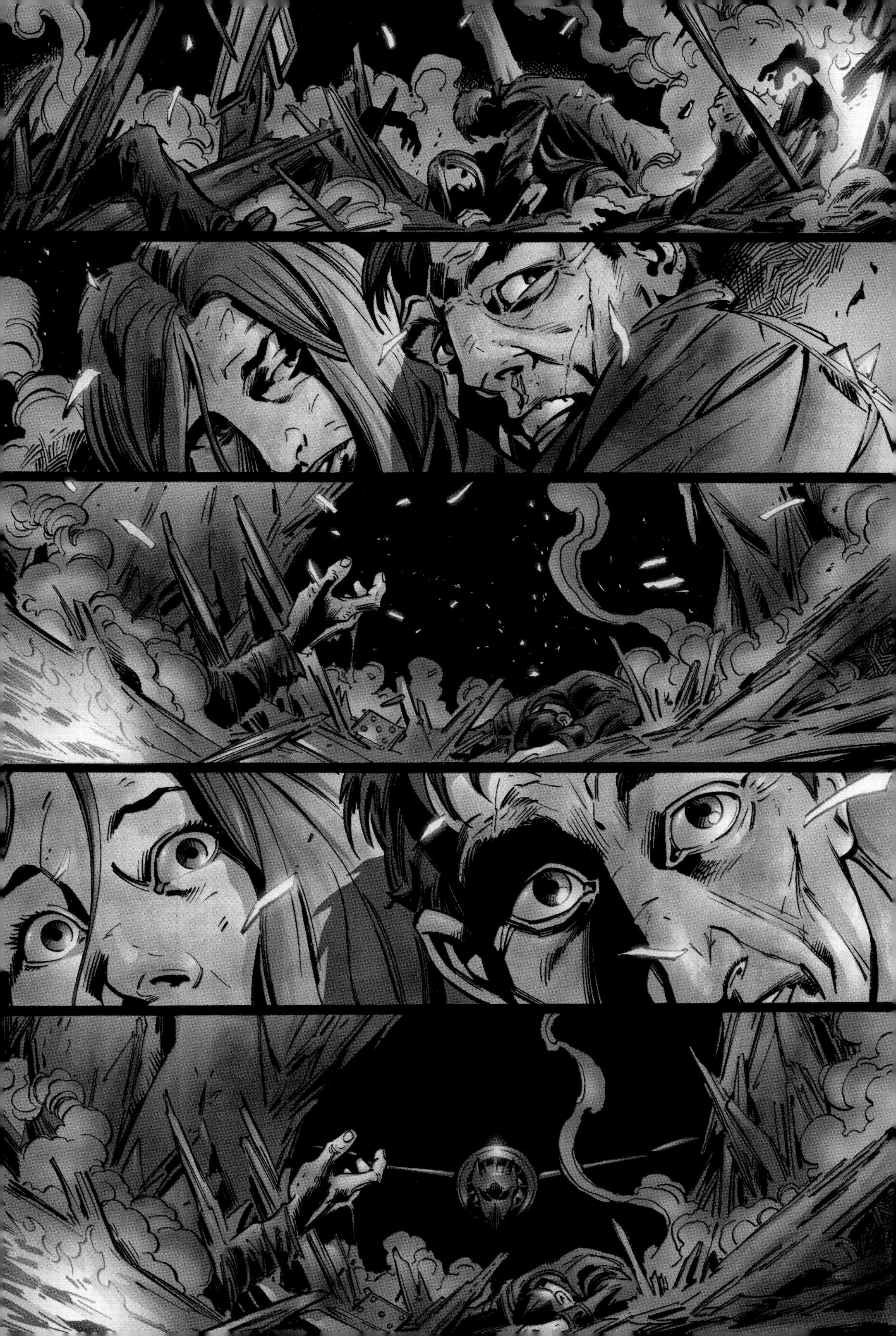

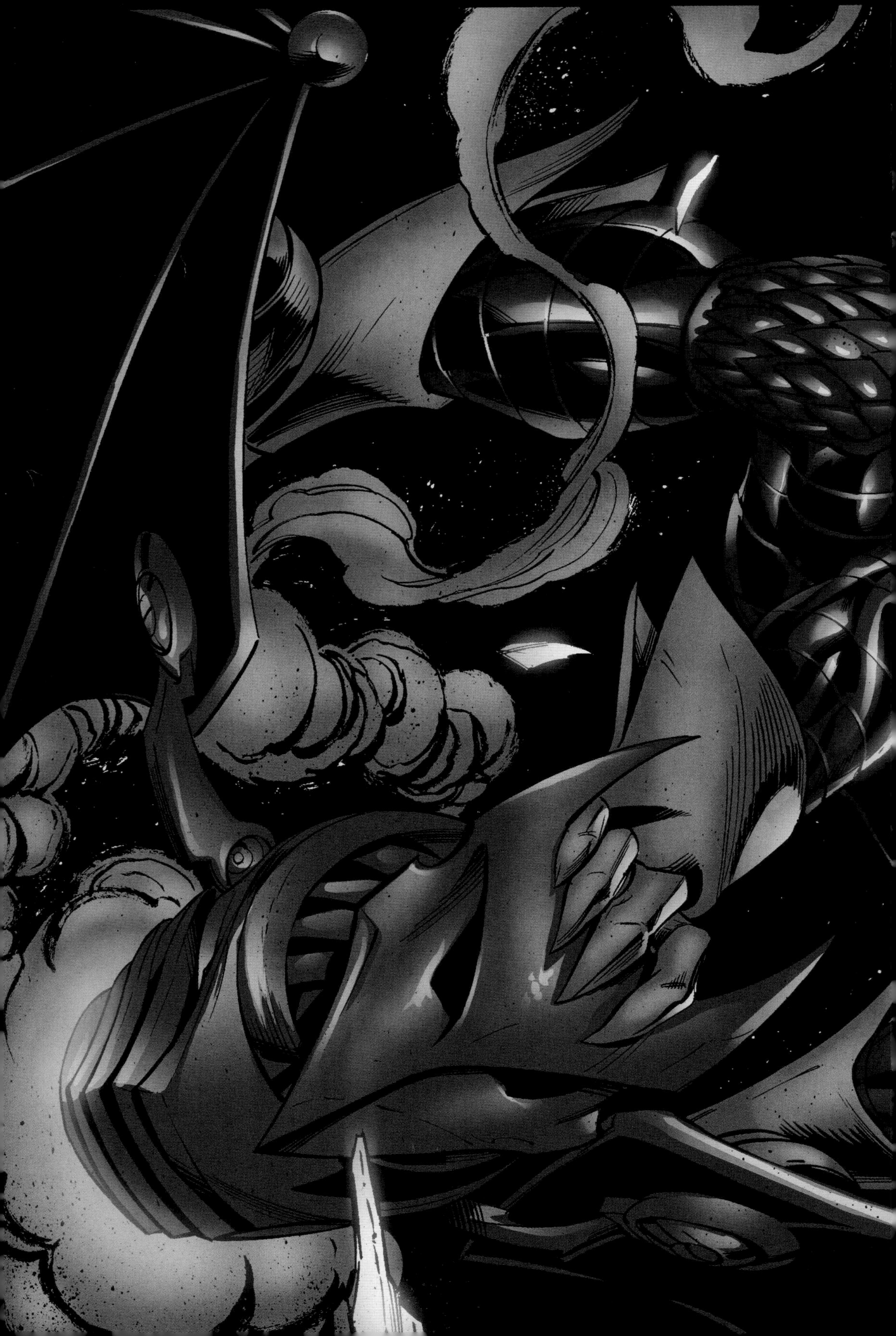

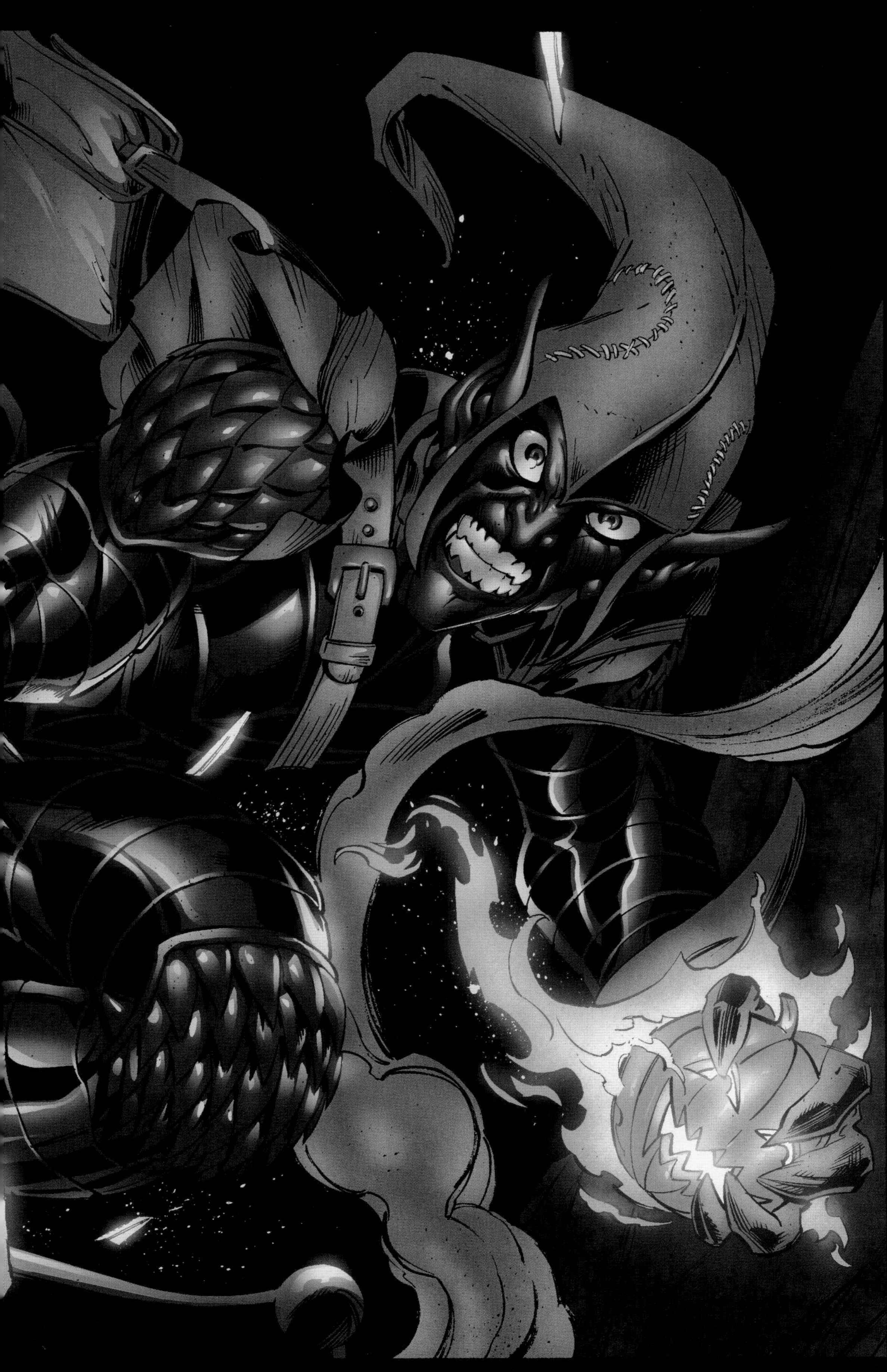

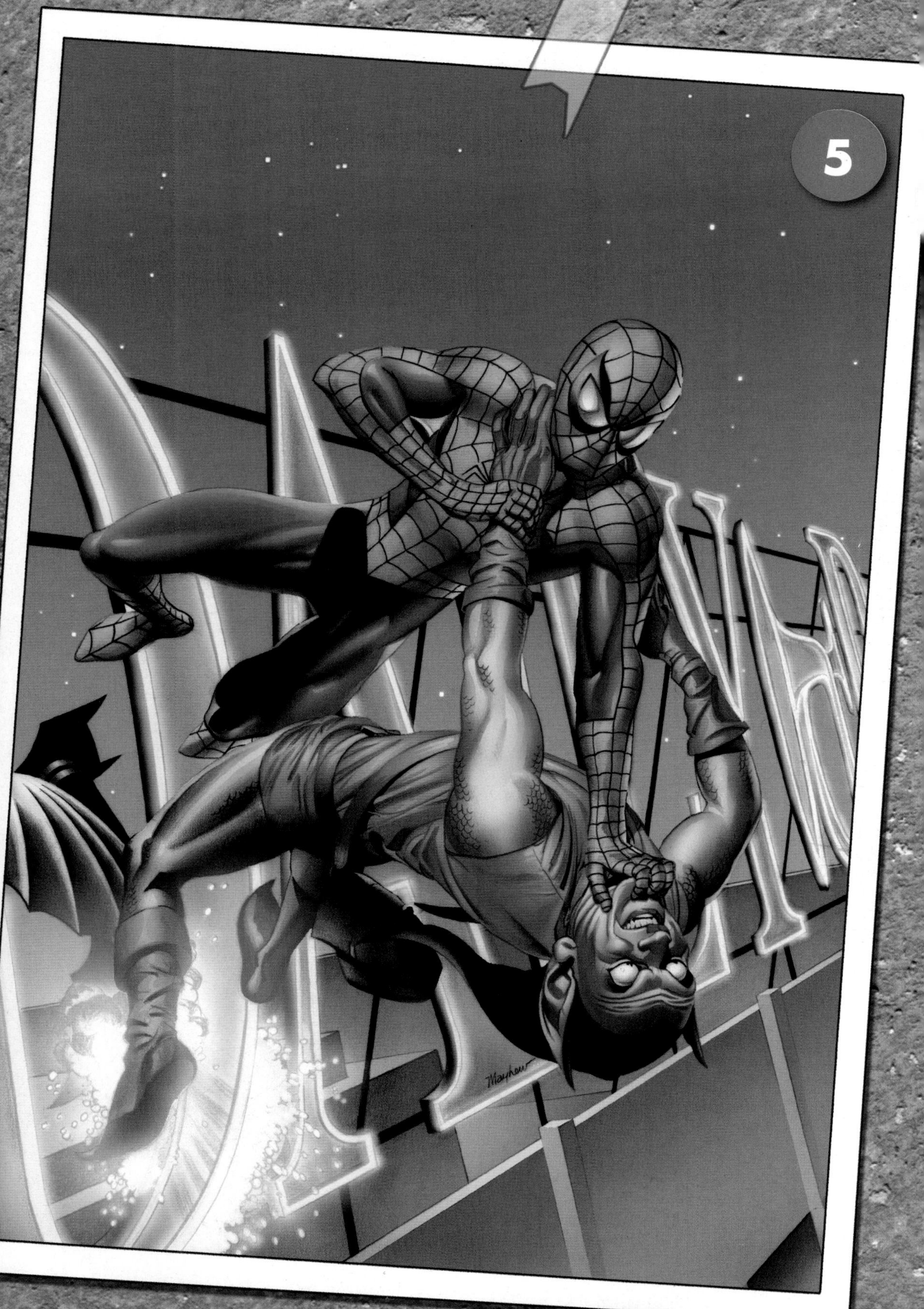
5

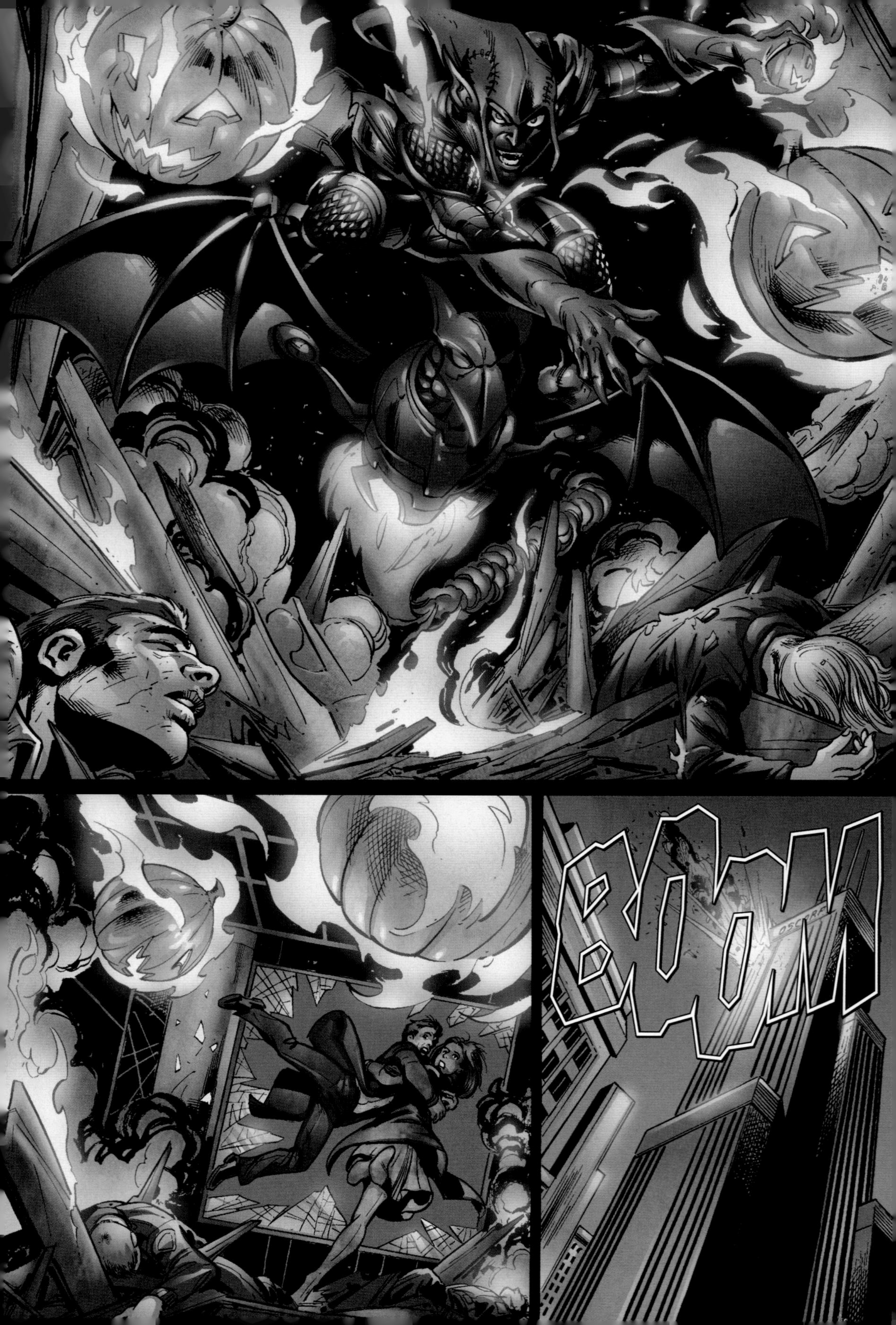
BOOM

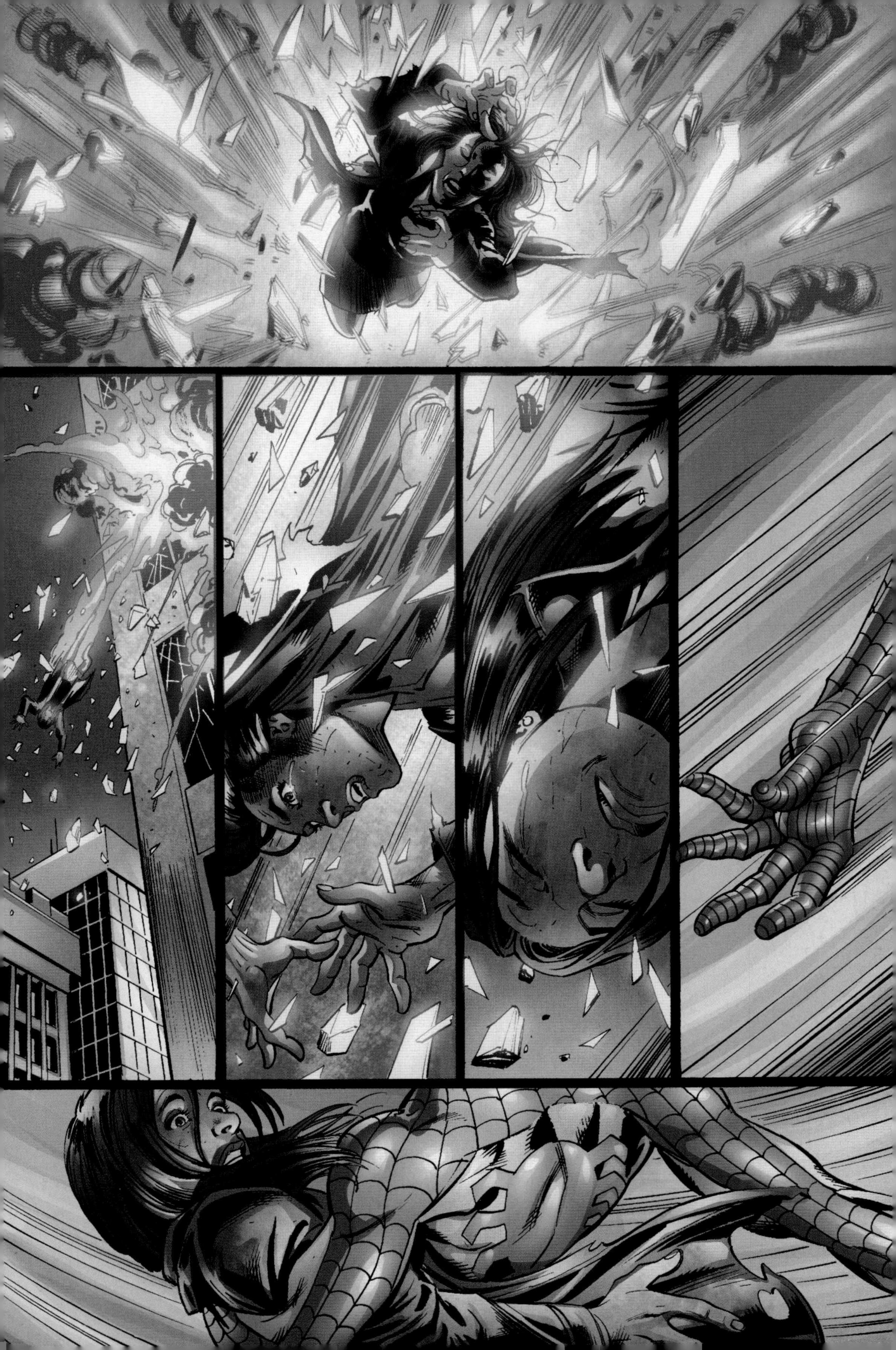

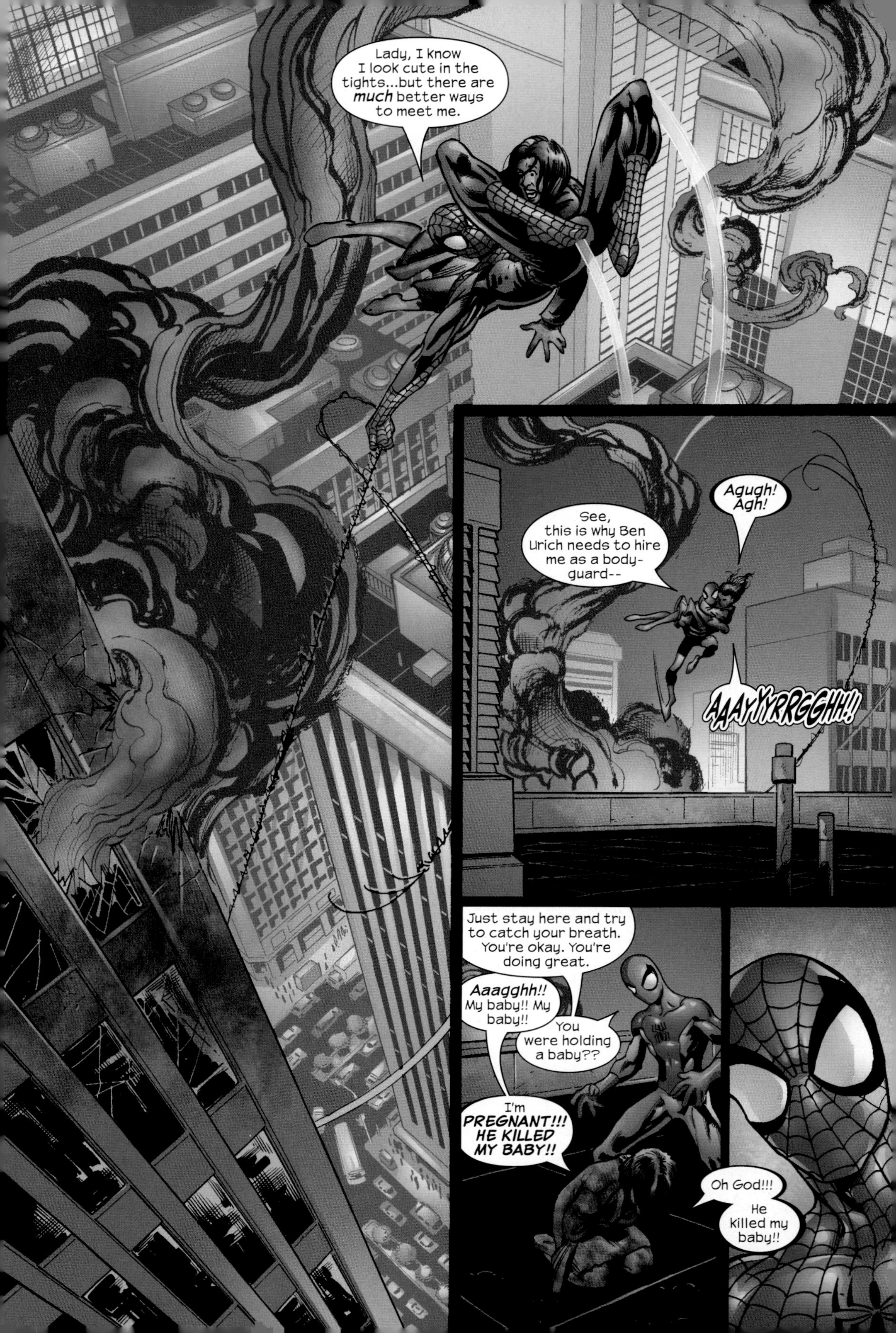
Lady, I know I look cute in the tights...but there are *much* better ways to meet me.
See, this is why Ben Urich needs to hire me as a body-guard--
Agugh! Agh!
AAAYYRRGGHH!!
Just stay here and try to catch your breath. You're okay. You're doing great.
Aaagghh!! My baby!! My baby!!
You were holding a baby??
I'm PREGNANT!!! HE KILLED MY BABY!!
Oh God!!!
He killed my baby!!

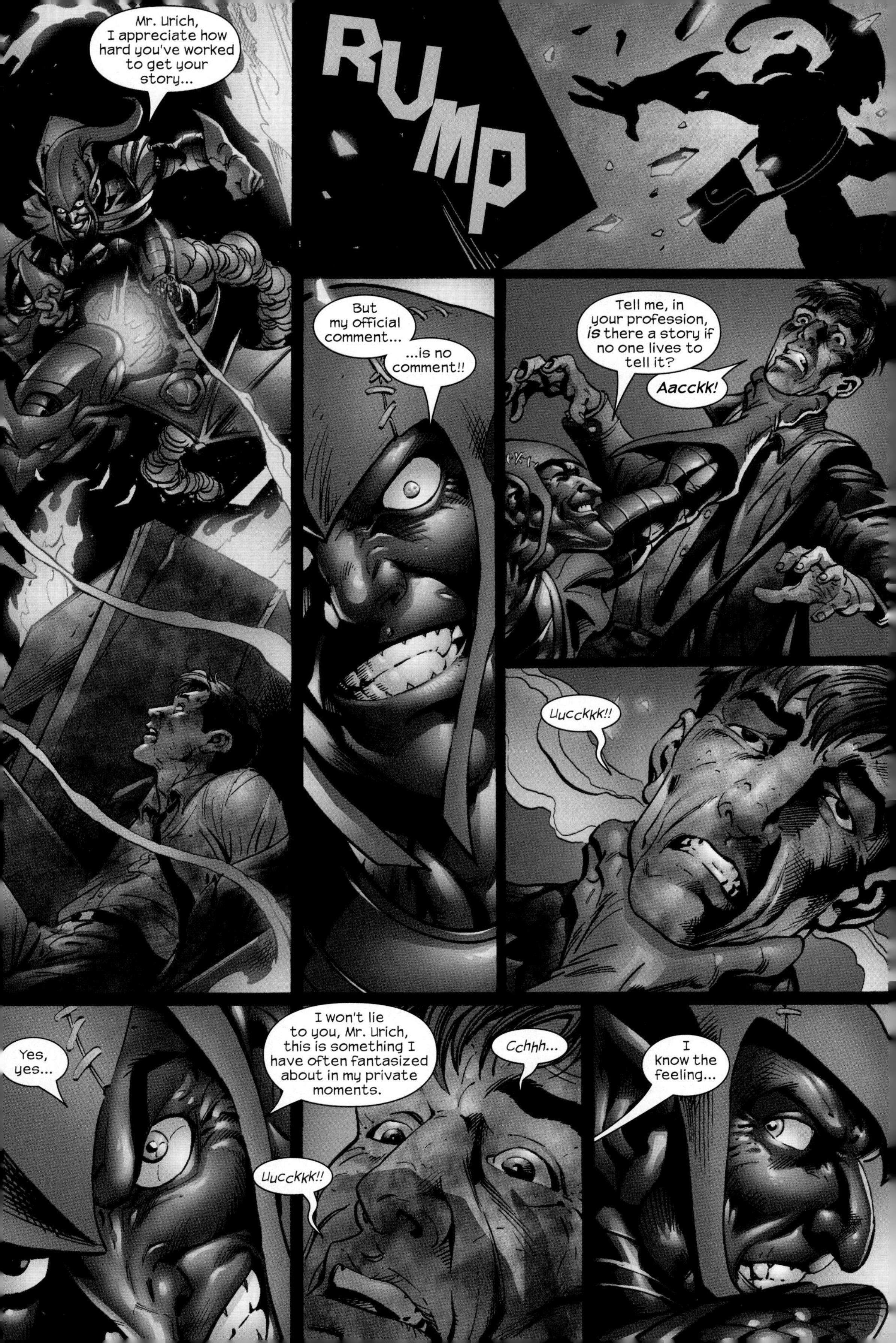
Mr. Urich, I appreciate how hard you've worked to get your story...
RUMP
But my official comment...
...is no comment!!
Tell me, in your profession, *is* there a story if no one lives to tell it?
Aacckk!
Uucckkk!!
Yes, yes...
I won't lie to you, Mr. Urich, this is something I have often fantasized about in my private moments.
Uucckkk!!
Cchhh...
I know the feeling...

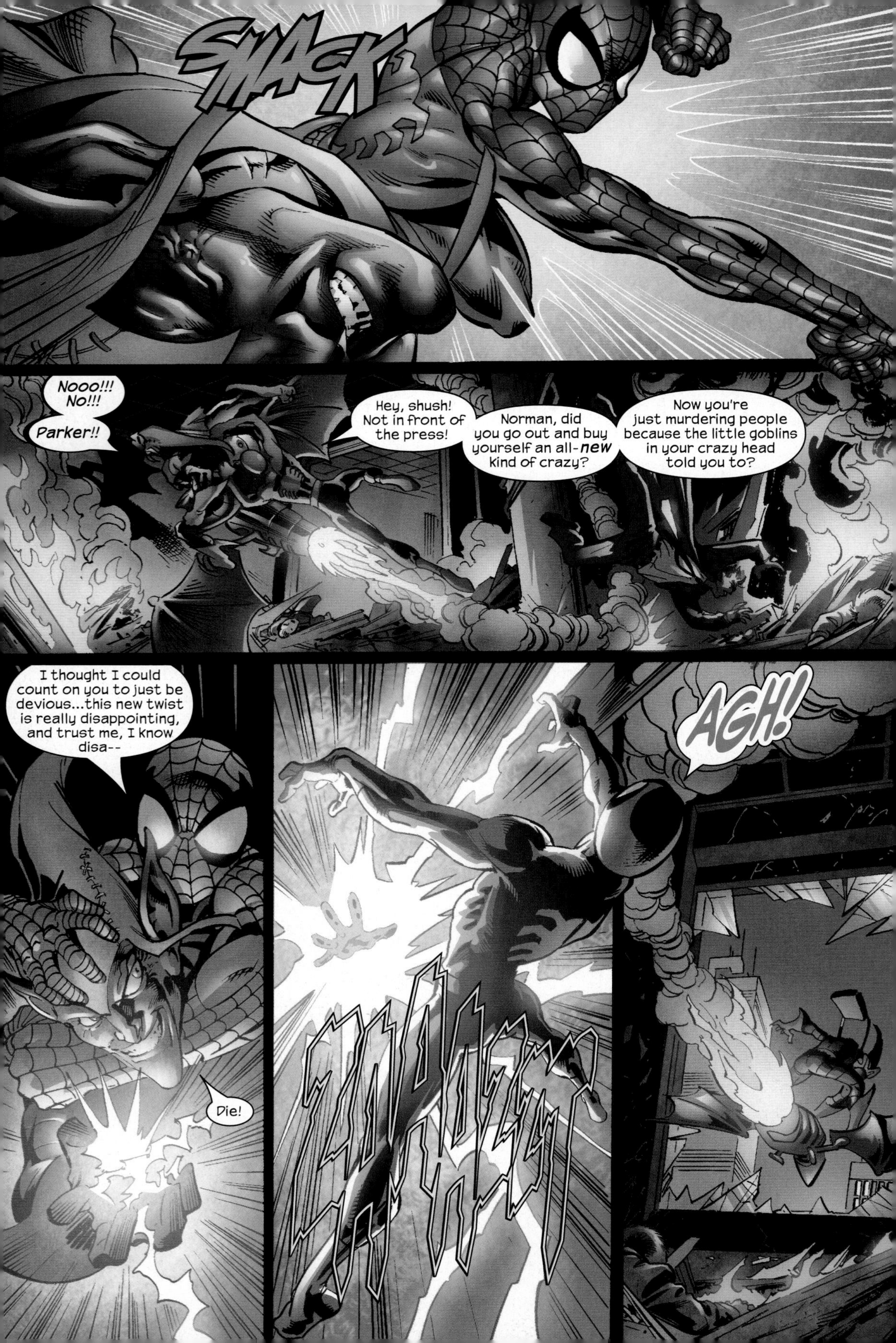

SMACK
Nooo!!! No!!!
Parker!!
Hey, shush! Not in front of the press!
Norman, did you go out and buy yourself an all-*new* kind of crazy?
Now you're just murdering people because the little goblins in your crazy head told you to?
I thought I could count on you to just be devious...this new twist is really disappointing, and trust me, I know disa--
Die!
AGH!

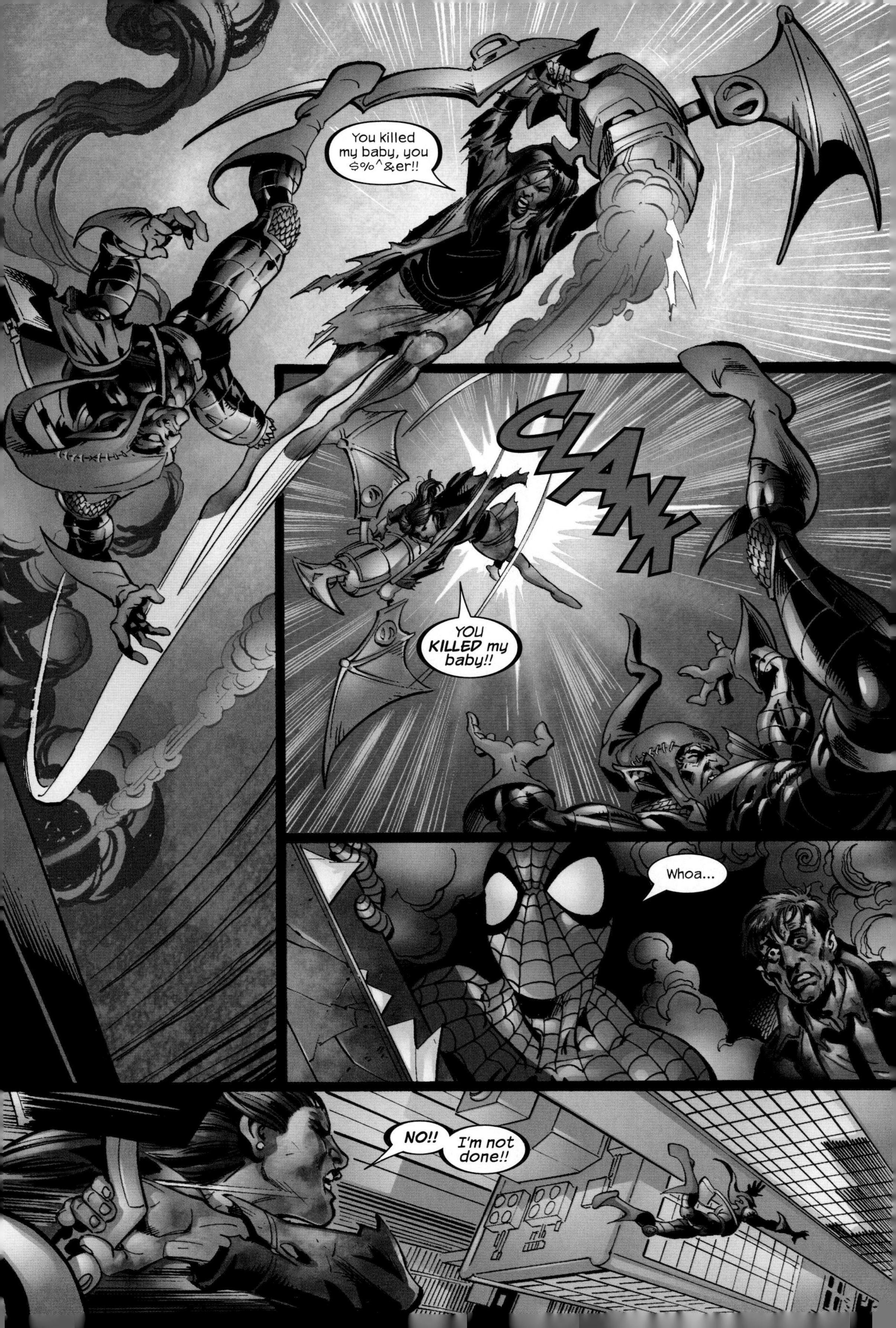
You killed my baby, you $%^&er!!
CLANK
YOU KILLED my baby!!
Whoa...
NO!!
I'm not done!!

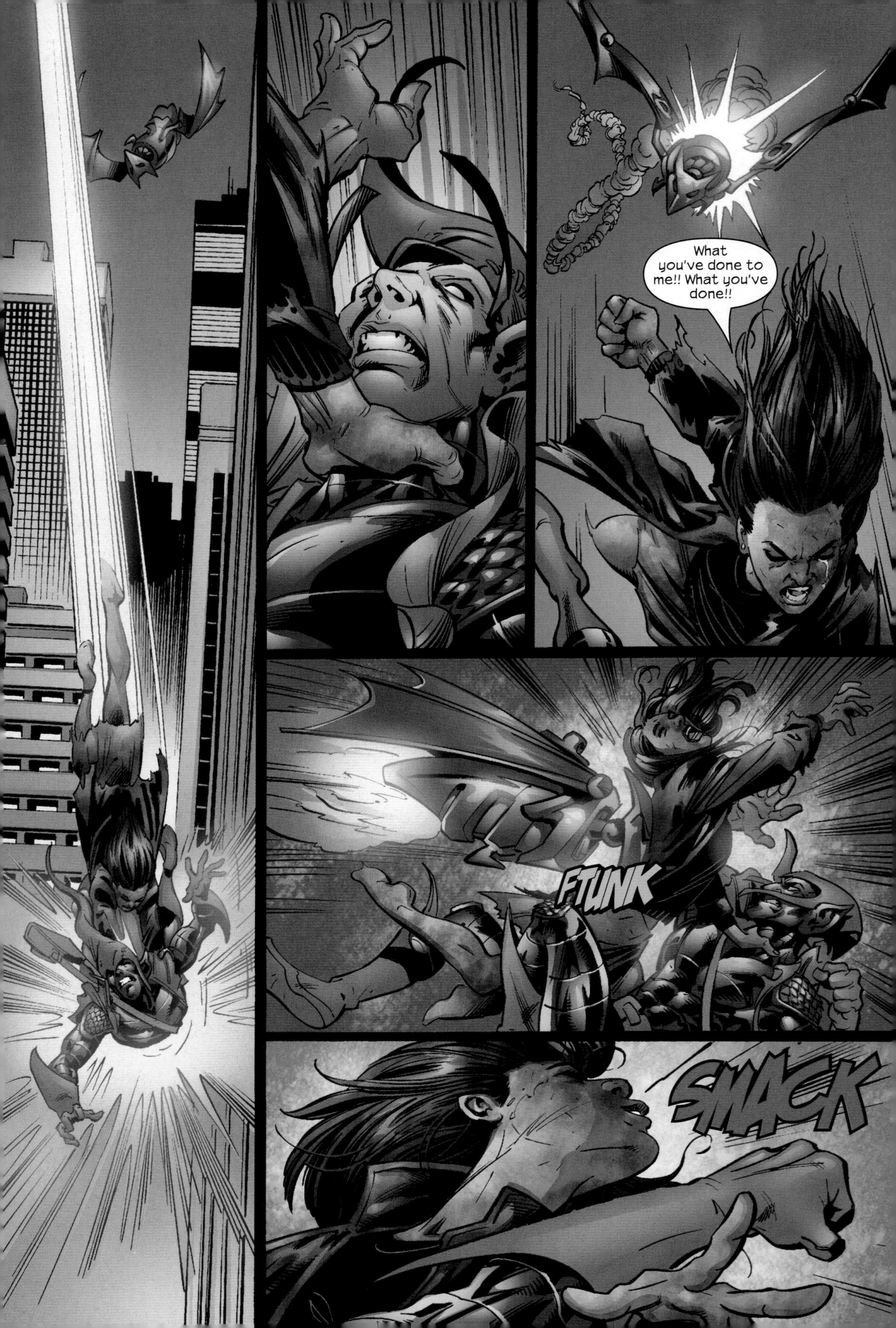

What you've done to me!! What you've done!!
FTUNK
SMACK

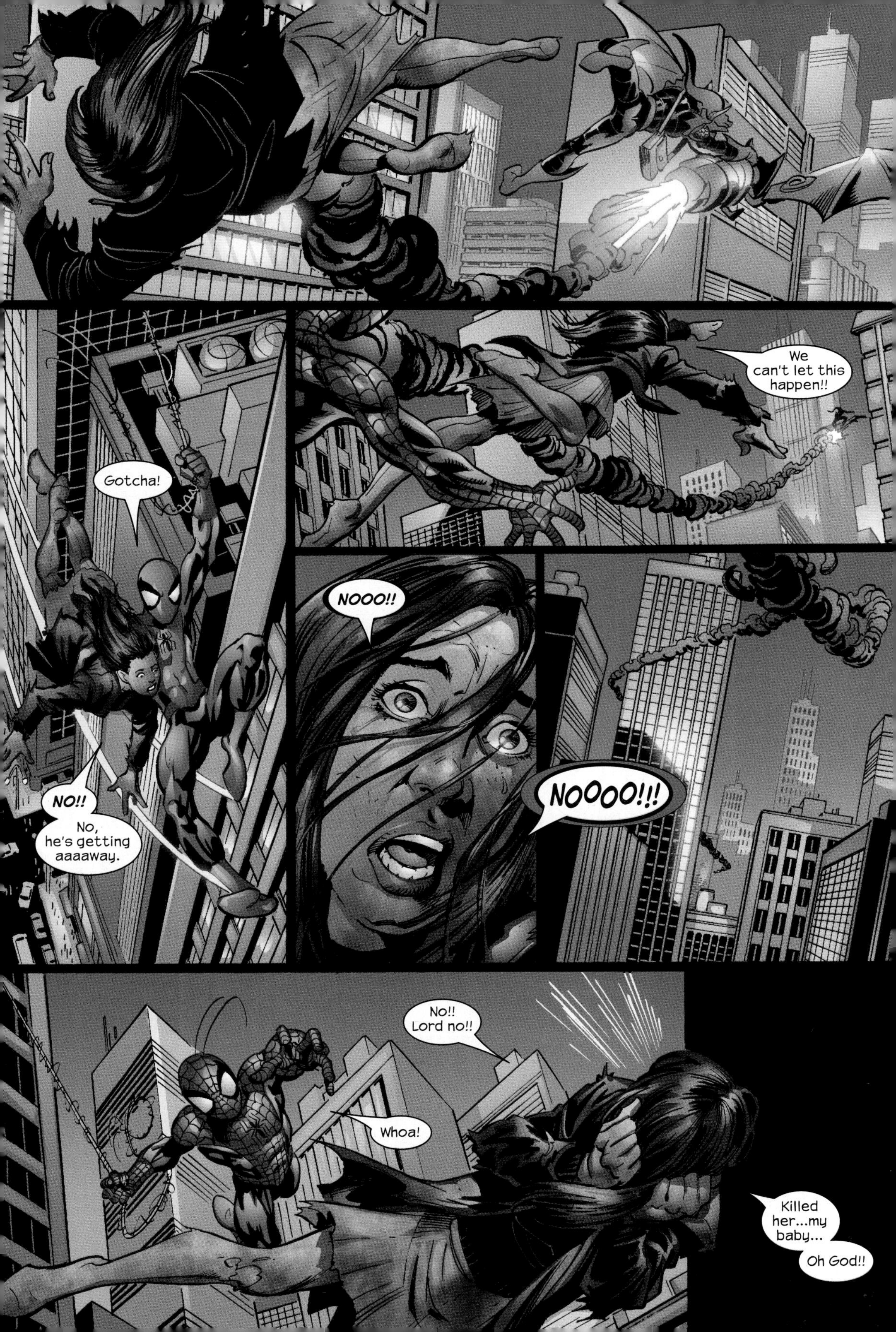
Gotcha!
We can't let this happen!!
NO!!
No, he's getting aaaaway.
NOOO!!
NOOOO!!!
No!! Lord no!!
Whoa!
Killed her...my baby...
Oh God!!

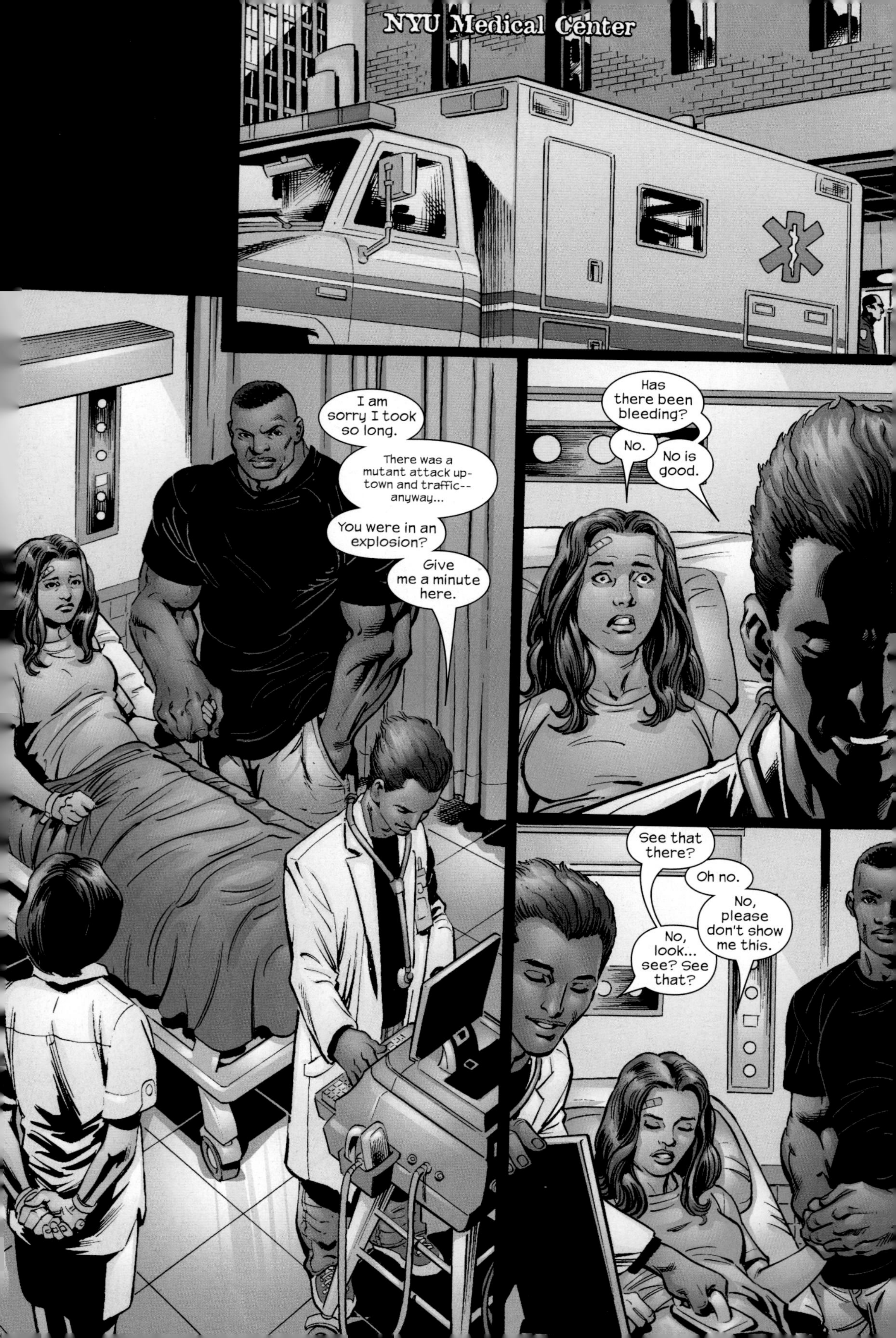
NYU Medical Center
I am sorry I took so long.
There was a mutant attack uptown and traffic--anyway...
You were in an explosion?
Give me a minute here.
Has there been bleeding?
No.
No is good.
See that there?
Oh no.
No, please don't show me this.
No, look... see? See that?

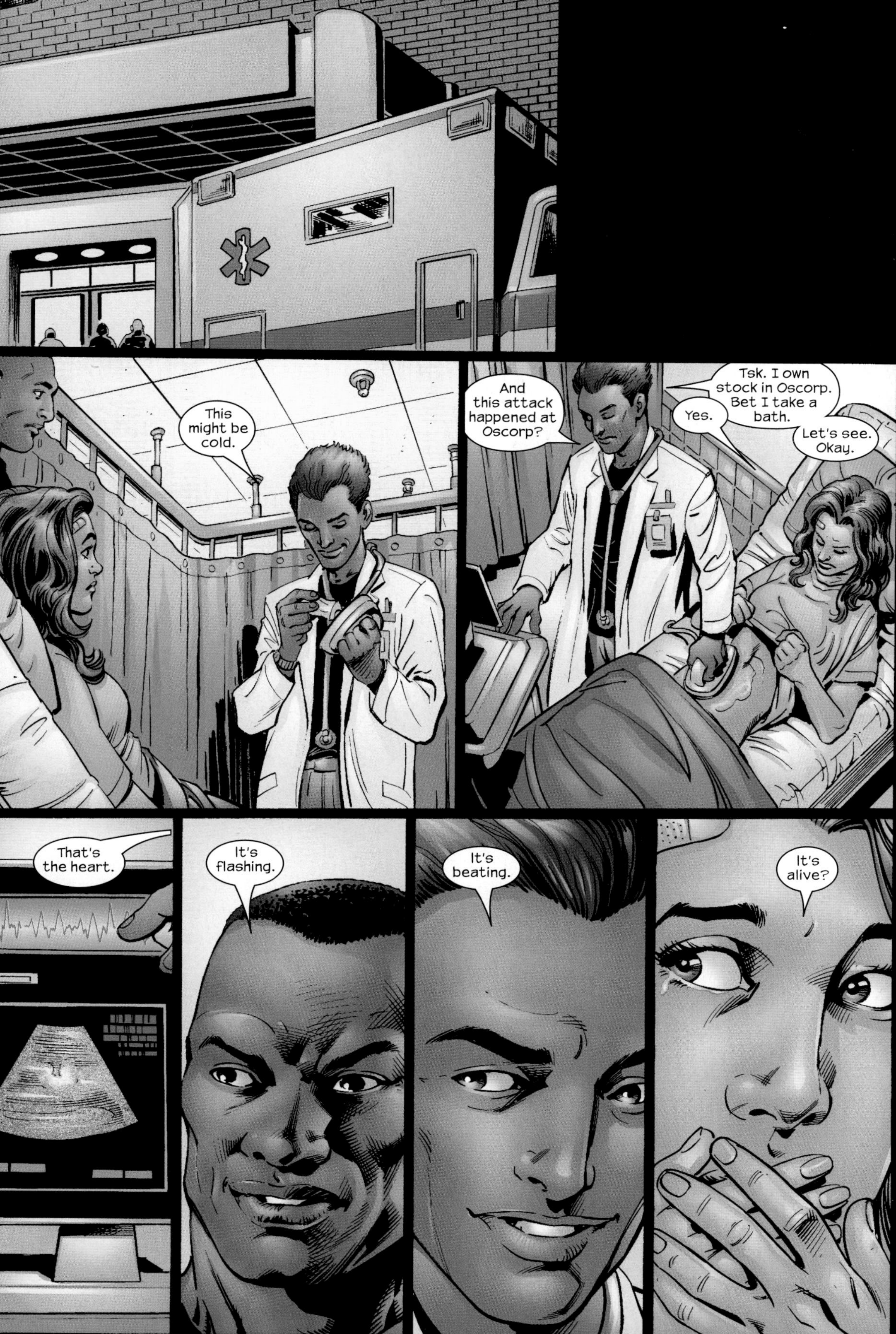
This might be cold.
And this attack happened at Oscorp?
Yes.
Tsk. I own stock in Oscorp. Bet I take a bath.
Let's see. Okay.
That's the heart.
It's flashing.
It's beating.
It's alive?

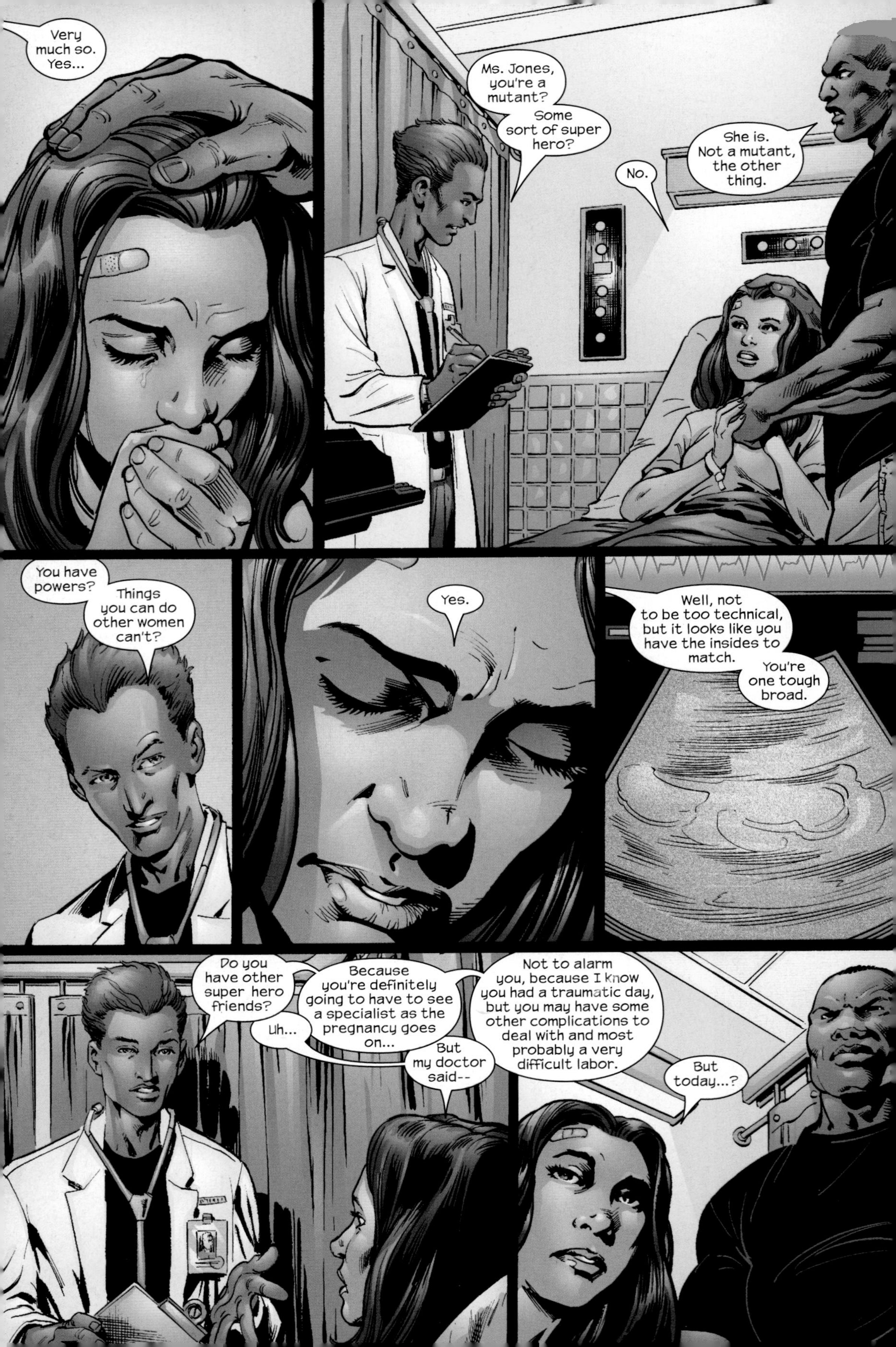
Very much so. Yes...
Ms. Jones, you're a mutant?
Some sort of super hero?
No.
She is. Not a mutant, the other thing.
You have powers?
Things you can do other women can't?
Yes.
Well, not to be too technical, but it looks like you have the insides to match.
You're one tough broad.
Do you have other super hero friends?
Uh...
Because you're definitely going to have to see a specialist as the pregnancy goes on...
But my doctor said--
Not to alarm you, because I know you had a traumatic day, but you may have some other complications to deal with and most probably a very difficult labor.
But today...?

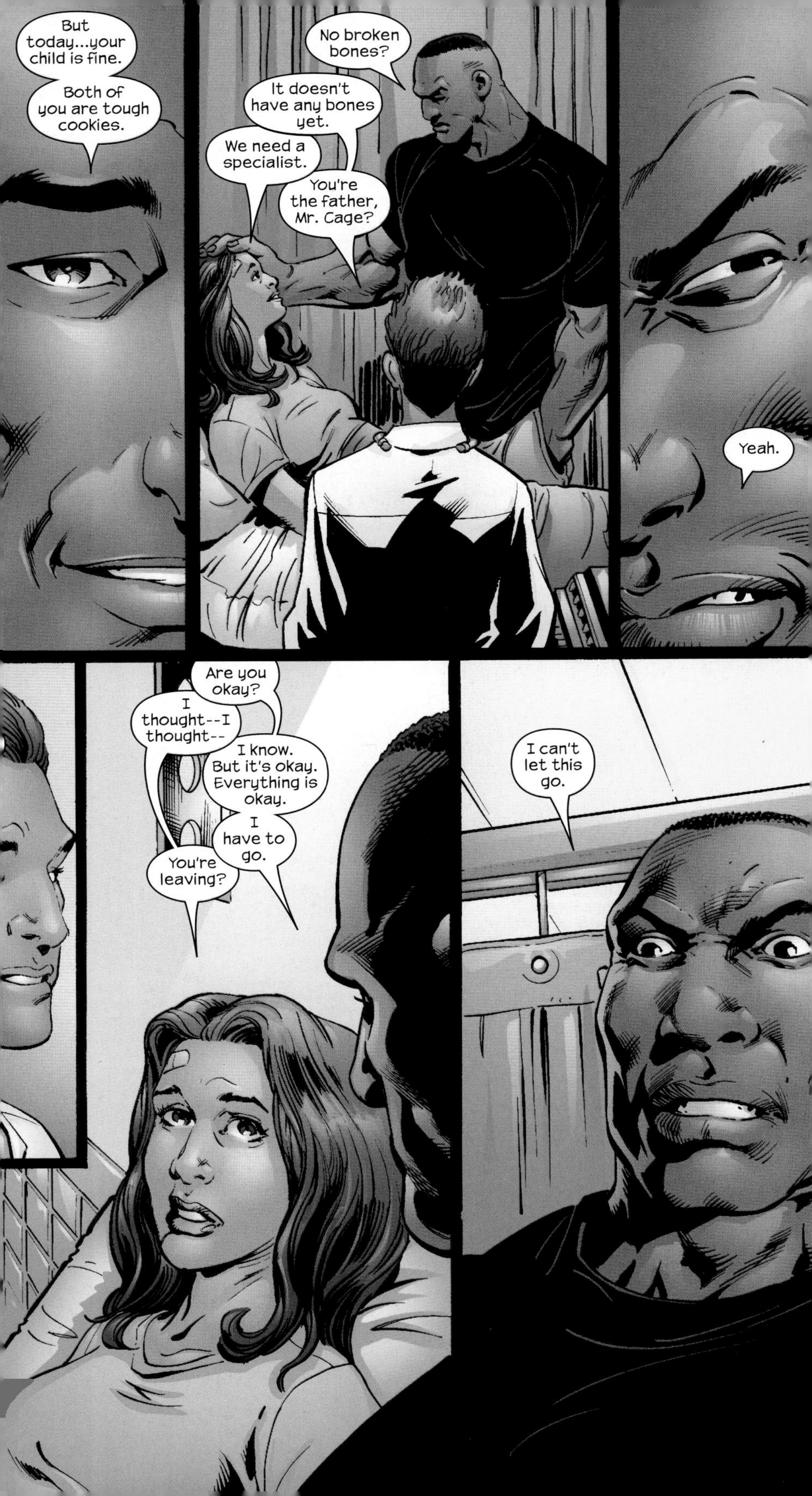
But today...your child is fine.
Both of you are tough cookies.
No broken bones?
It doesn't have any bones yet.
We need a specialist.
You're the father, Mr. Cage?
Yeah.
Are you okay?
I thought--I thought--
I know. But it's okay. Everything is okay.
I have to go.
You're leaving?
I can't let this go.

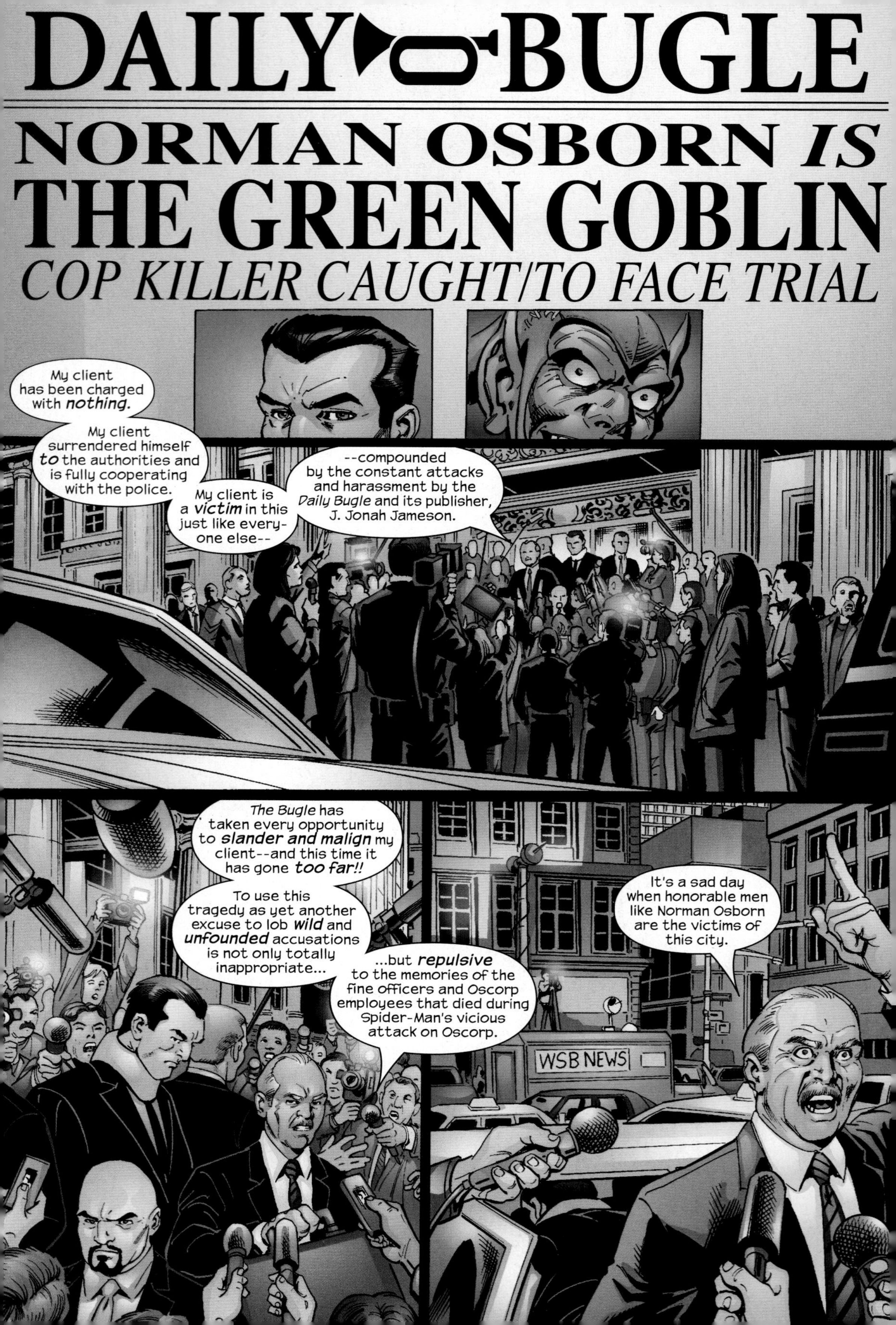
DAILY BUGLE
NORMAN OSBORN IS THE GREEN GOBLIN
COP KILLER CAUGHT/TO FACE TRIAL
My client has been charged with nothing.
My client surrendered himself to the authorities and is fully cooperating with the police.
My client is a victim in this just like every-one else--
--compounded by the constant attacks and harassment by the Daily Bugle and its publisher, J. Jonah Jameson.
The Bugle has taken every opportunity to slander and malign my client--and this time it has gone too far!!
To use this tragedy as yet another excuse to lob wild and unfounded accusations is not only totally inappropriate...
...but repulsive to the memories of the fine officers and Oscorp employees that died during Spider-Man's vicious attack on Oscorp.
WSB NEWS
It's a sad day when honorable men like Norman Osborn are the victims of this city.

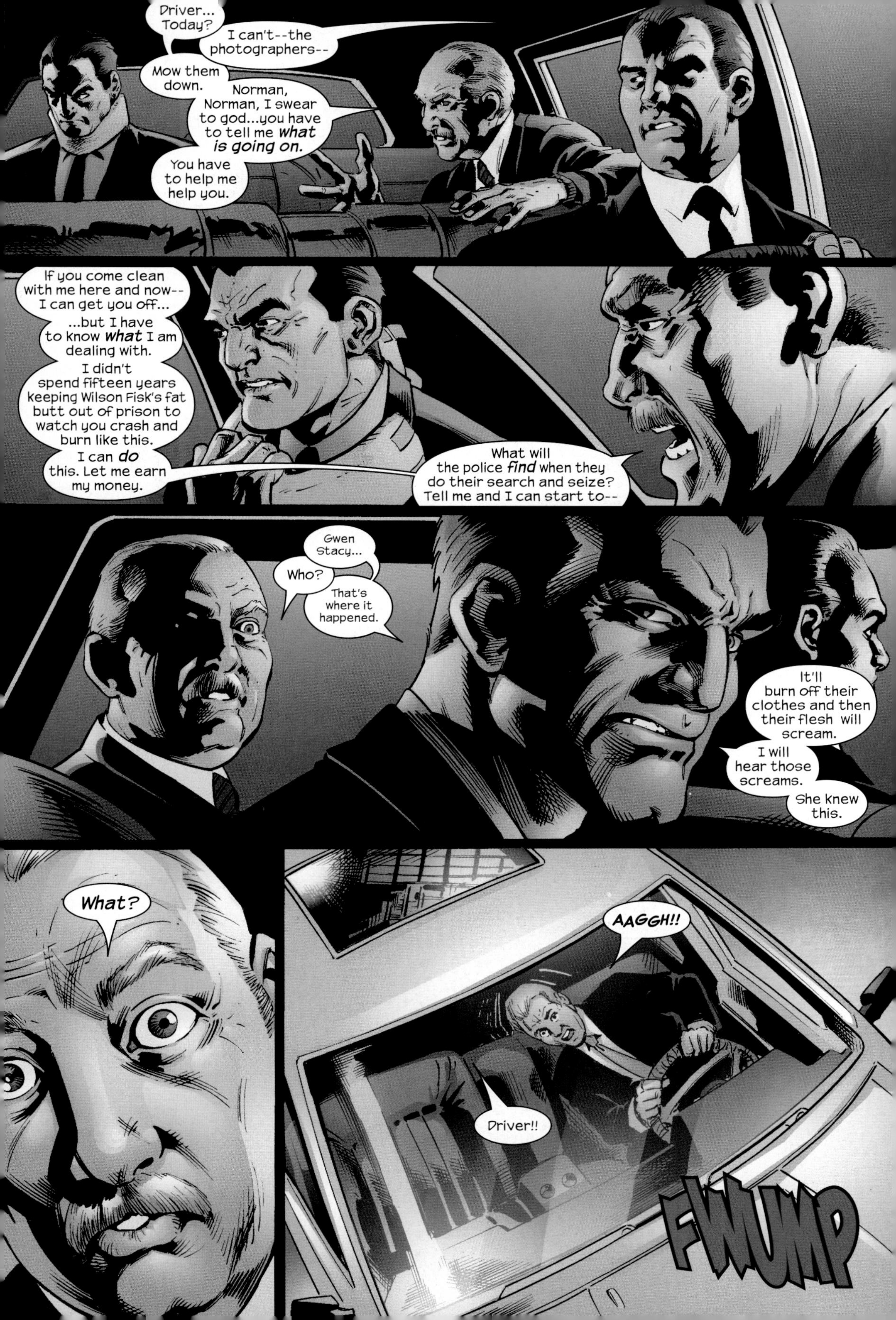
Driver... Today?
I can't--the photographers--
Mow them down.
Norman, Norman, I swear to god...you have to tell me *what is going on.*
You have to help me help you.
If you come clean with me here and now--I can get you off...
...but I have to know *what* I am dealing with.
I didn't spend fifteen years keeping Wilson Fisk's fat butt out of prison to watch you crash and burn like this.
I can *do* this. Let me earn my money.
What will the police *find* when they do their search and seize? Tell me and I can start to--
Gwen Stacy...
Who?
That's where it happened.
It'll burn off their clothes and then their flesh will scream.
I will hear those screams.
She knew this.
What?
AAGGH!!
Driver!!
FWUMP

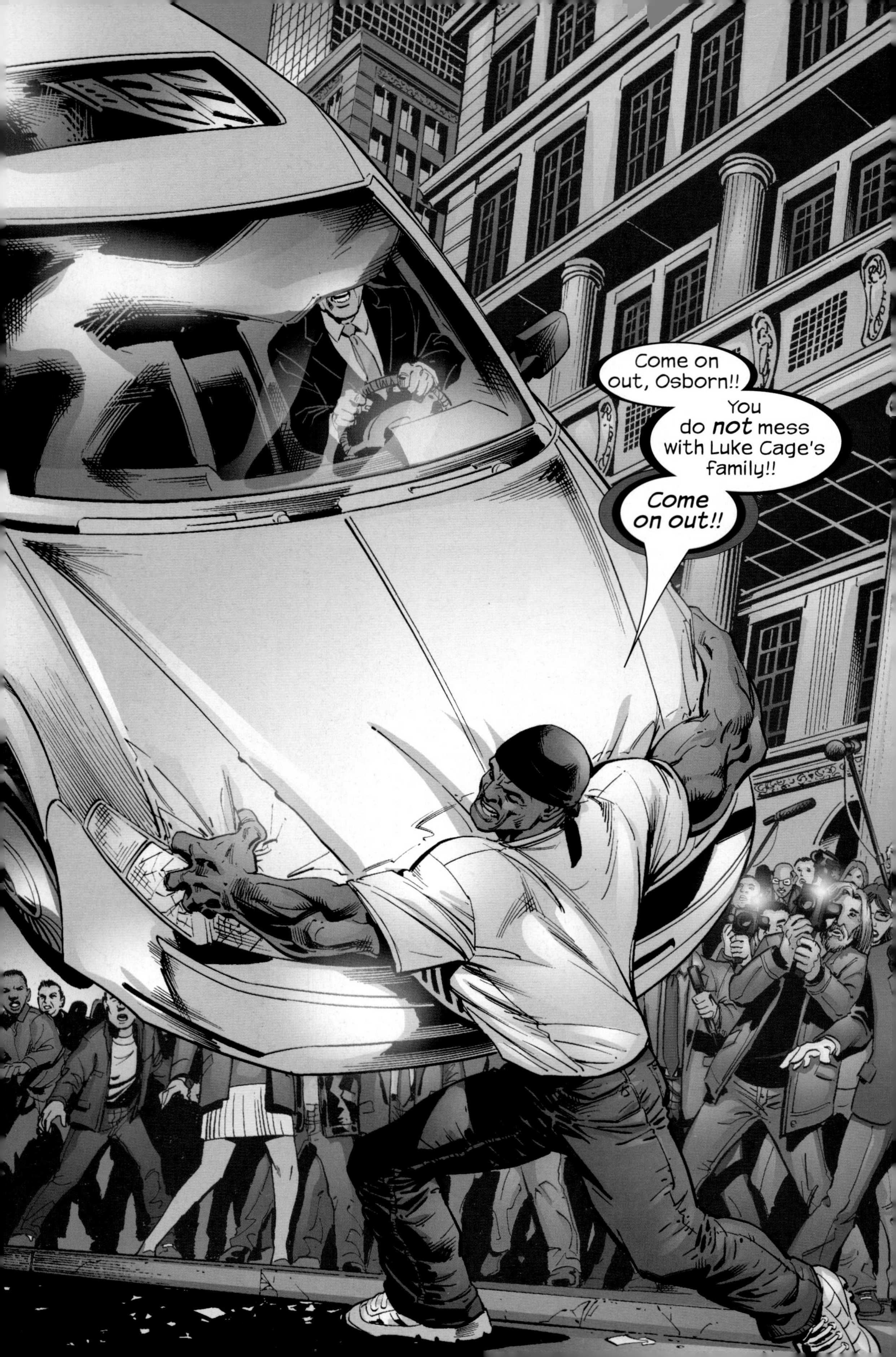
Come on out, Osborn!!
You do *not* mess with Luke Cage's family!!
Come on out!!

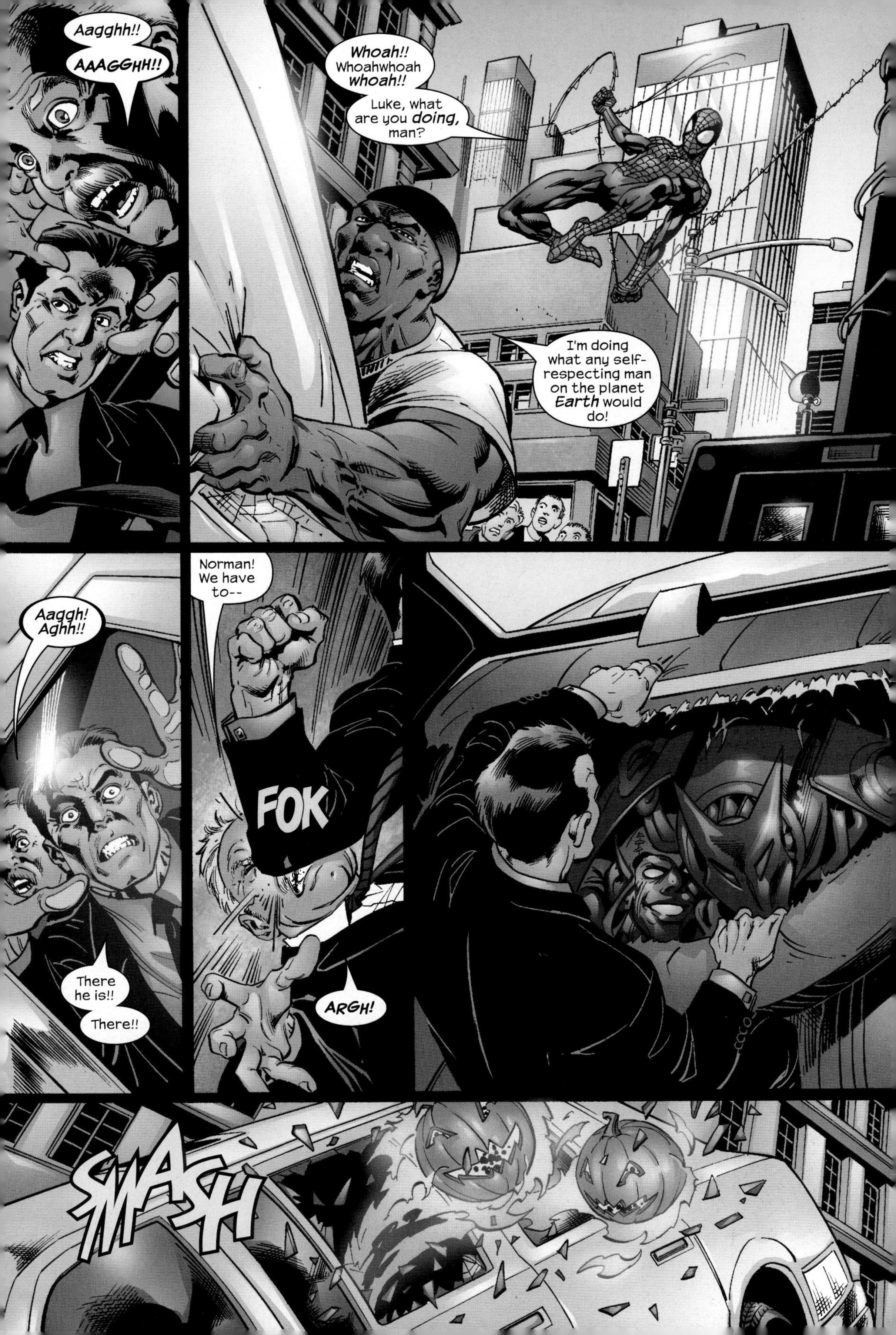
Aagghh!!
AAAGGHH!!
Whoah!! Whoahwhoah whoah!!
Luke, what are you doing, man?
I'm doing what any self-respecting man on the planet Earth would do!
Aaggh! Aghh!!
There he is!!
There!!
Norman! We have to--
FOK
ARGH!
SMASH

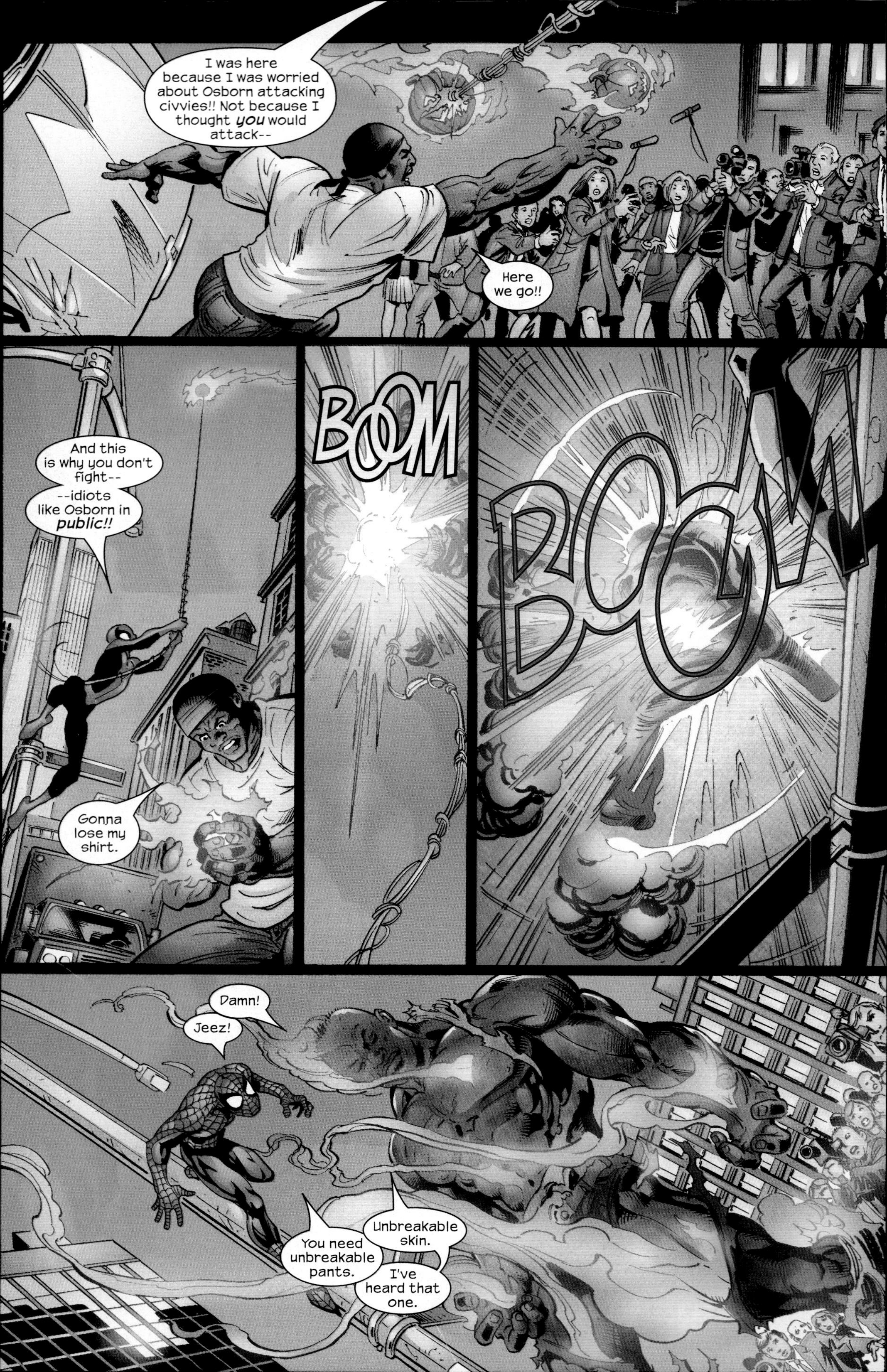
I was here because I was worried about Osborn attacking civvies!! Not because I thought *you* would attack--
Here we go!!
And this is why you don't fight--
--idiots like Osborn in *public!!*
Gonna lose my shirt.
BOOM
BOOM
Damn!
Jeez!
Unbreakable skin.
You need unbreakable pants.
I've heard that one.

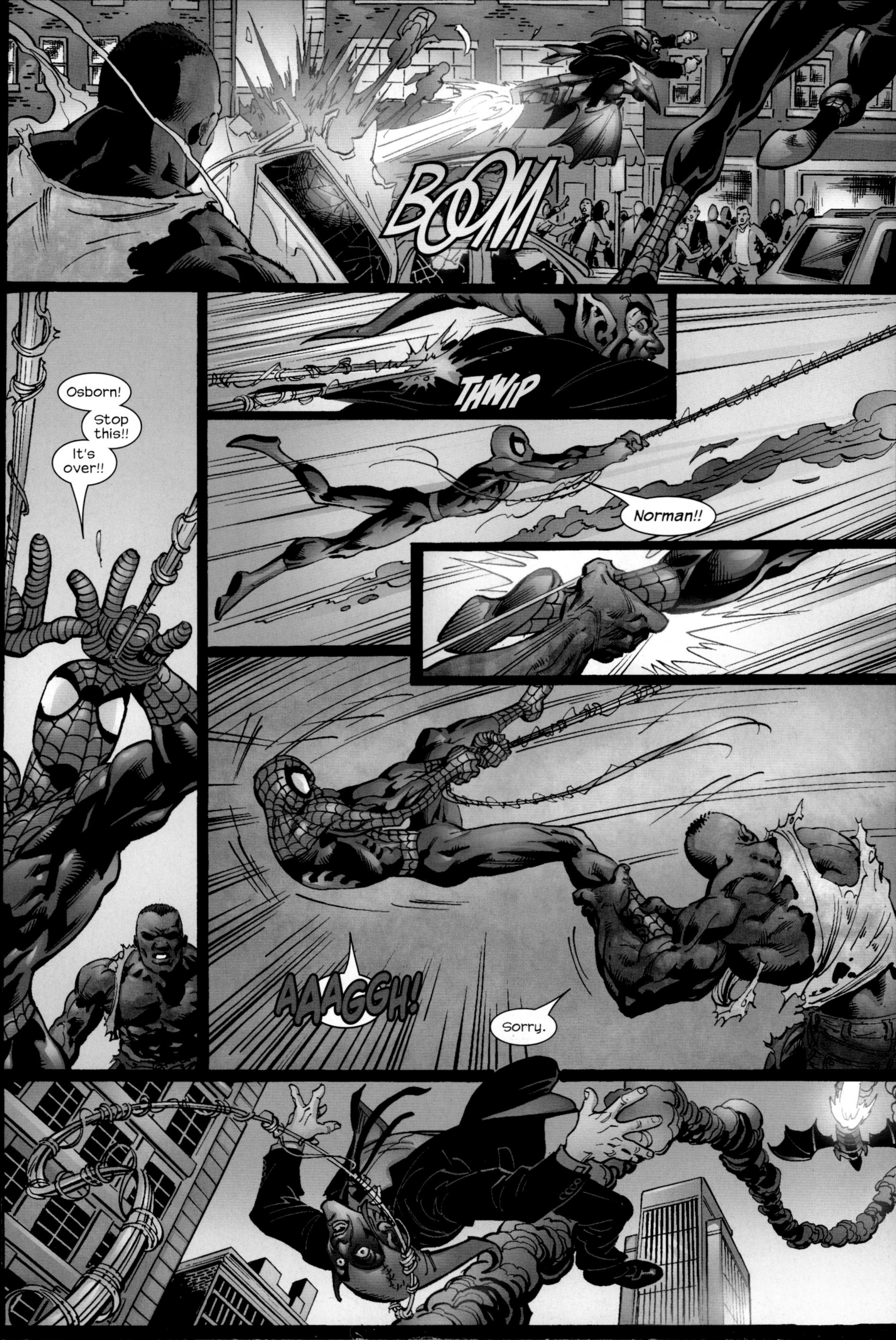
BOOM
Osborn!
Stop this!!
It's over!!
THWIP
Norman!!
AAAGGH!
Sorry.

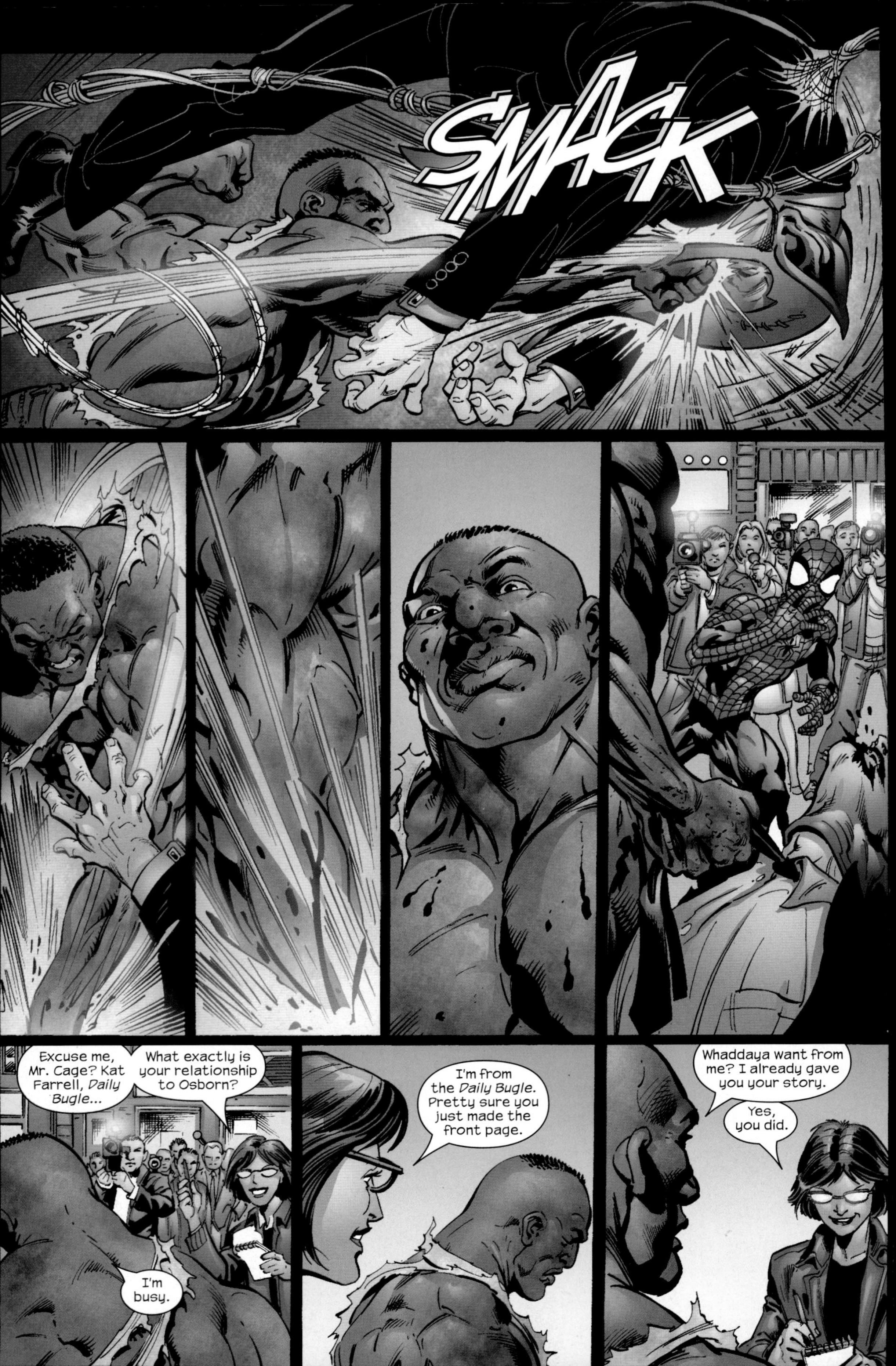
SMACK
Excuse me, Mr. Cage? Kat Farrell, *Daily Bugle*...
What exactly is your relationship to Osborn?
I'm busy.
I'm from the *Daily Bugle*. Pretty sure you just made the front page.
Whaddaya want from me? I already gave you your story.
Yes, you did.

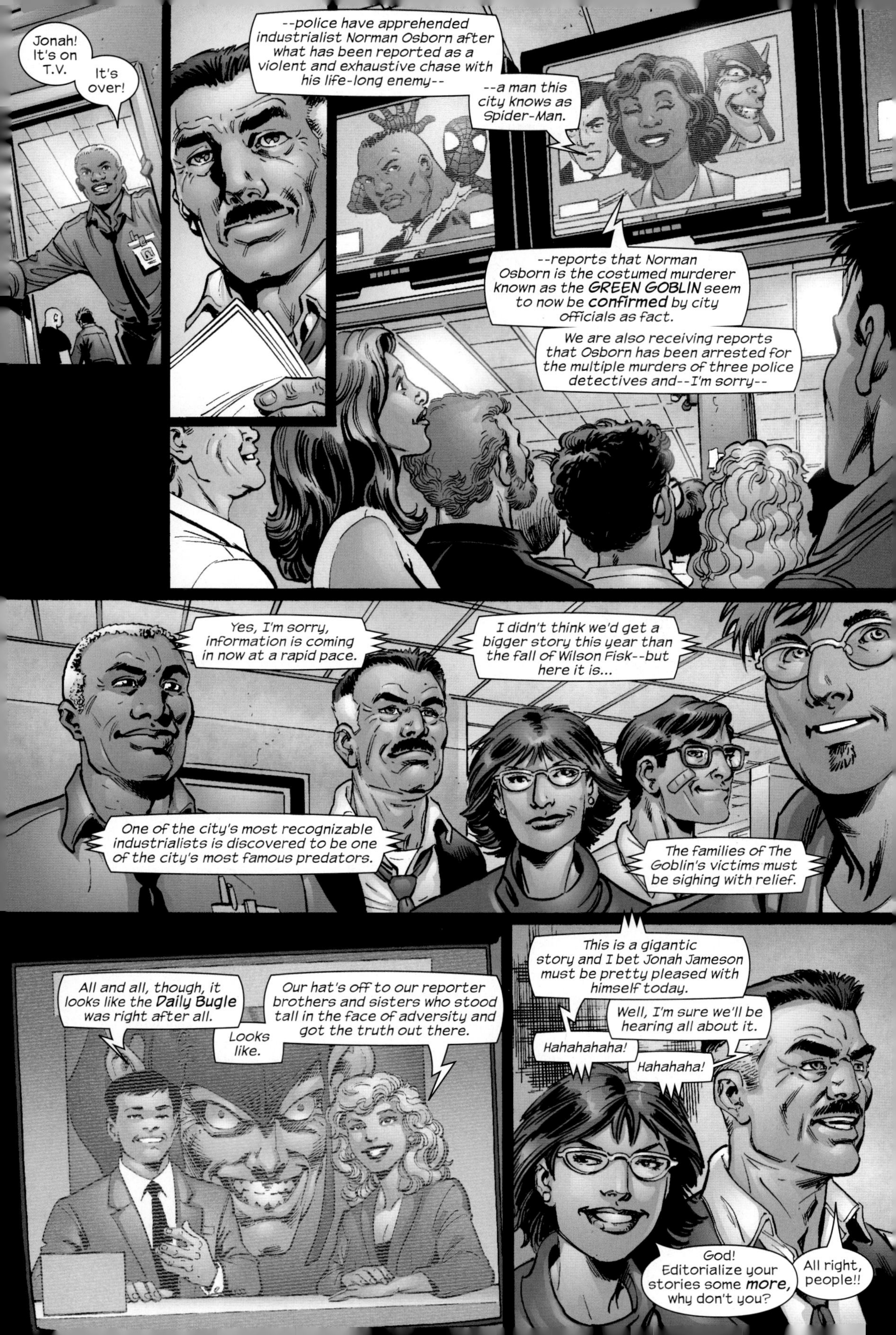
Jonah! It's on T.V.
It's over!
--police have apprehended industrialist Norman Osborn after what has been reported as a violent and exhaustive chase with his life-long enemy--
--a man this city knows as Spider-Man.
--reports that Norman Osborn is the costumed murderer known as the GREEN GOBLIN seem to now be confirmed by city officials as fact.
We are also receiving reports that Osborn has been arrested for the multiple murders of three police detectives and--I'm sorry--
Yes, I'm sorry, information is coming in now at a rapid pace.
I didn't think we'd get a bigger story this year than the fall of Wilson Fisk--but here it is...
One of the city's most recognizable industrialists is discovered to be one of the city's most famous predators.
The families of The Goblin's victims must be sighing with relief.
All and all, though, it looks like the Daily Bugle was right after all.
Looks like.
Our hat's off to our reporter brothers and sisters who stood tall in the face of adversity and got the truth out there.
This is a gigantic story and I bet Jonah Jameson must be pretty pleased with himself today.
Well, I'm sure we'll be hearing all about it.
Hahahahaha!
Hahahaha!
God! Editorialize your stories some more, why don't you?
All right, people!!

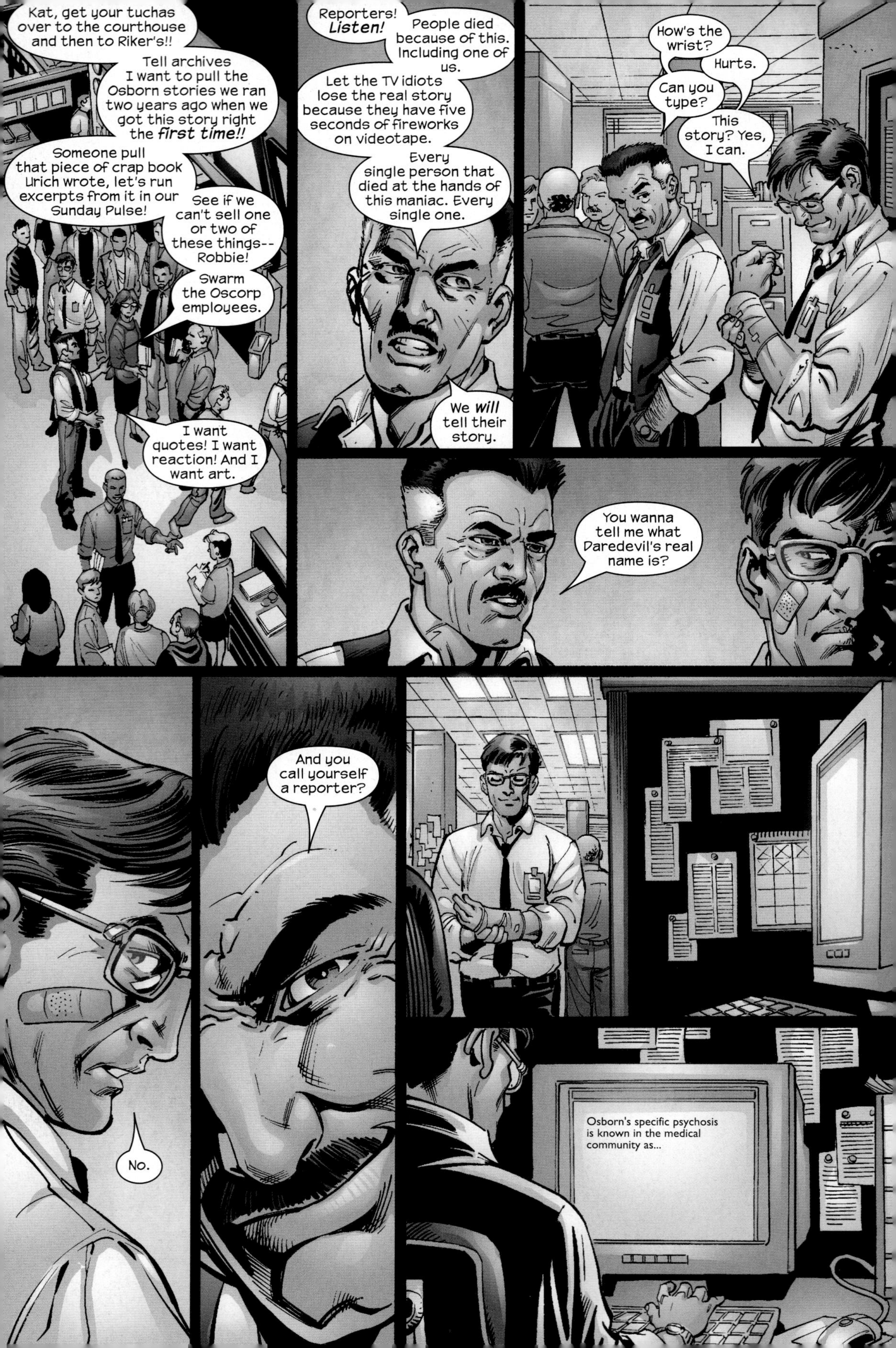
Kat, get your tuchas over to the courthouse and then to Riker's!!
Tell archives I want to pull the Osborn stories we ran two years ago when we got this story right the *first time!!*
Someone pull that piece of crap book Urich wrote, let's run excerpts from it in our Sunday Pulse!
See if we can't sell one or two of these things-- Robbie!
Swarm the Oscorp employees.
I want quotes! I want reaction! And I want art.
Reporters! *Listen!*
People died because of this. Including one of us.
Let the TV idiots lose the real story because they have five seconds of fireworks on videotape.
Every single person that died at the hands of this maniac. Every single one.
We *will* tell their story.
How's the wrist?
Hurts.
Can you type?
This story? Yes, I can.
You wanna tell me what Daredevil's real name is?
No.
And you call yourself a reporter?
Osborn's specific psychosis is known in the medical community as...

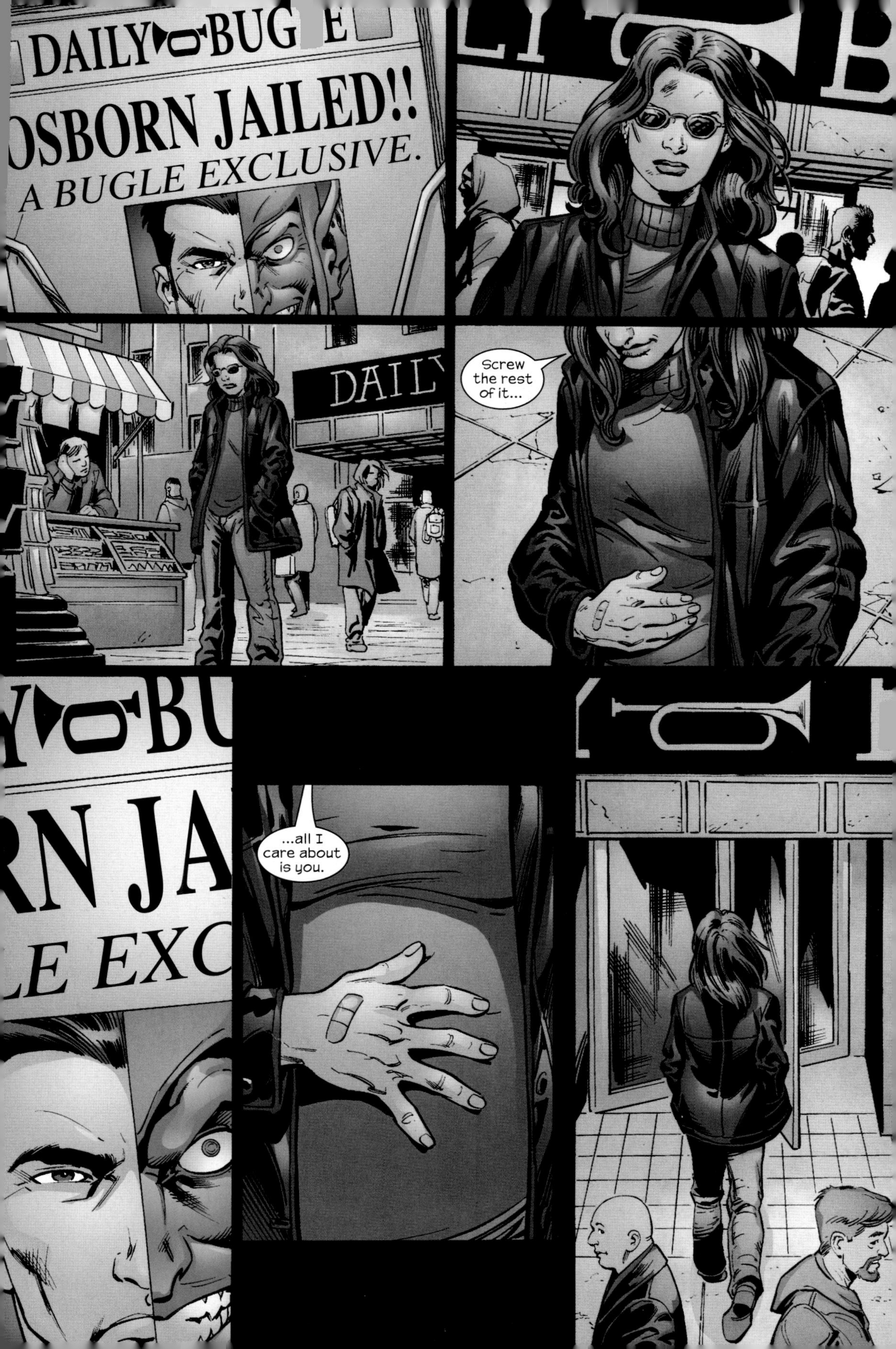

DAILY BUGLE
OSBORN JAILED!!
A BUGLE EXCLUSIVE.
DAILY
Screw the rest of it...
...all I care about is you.

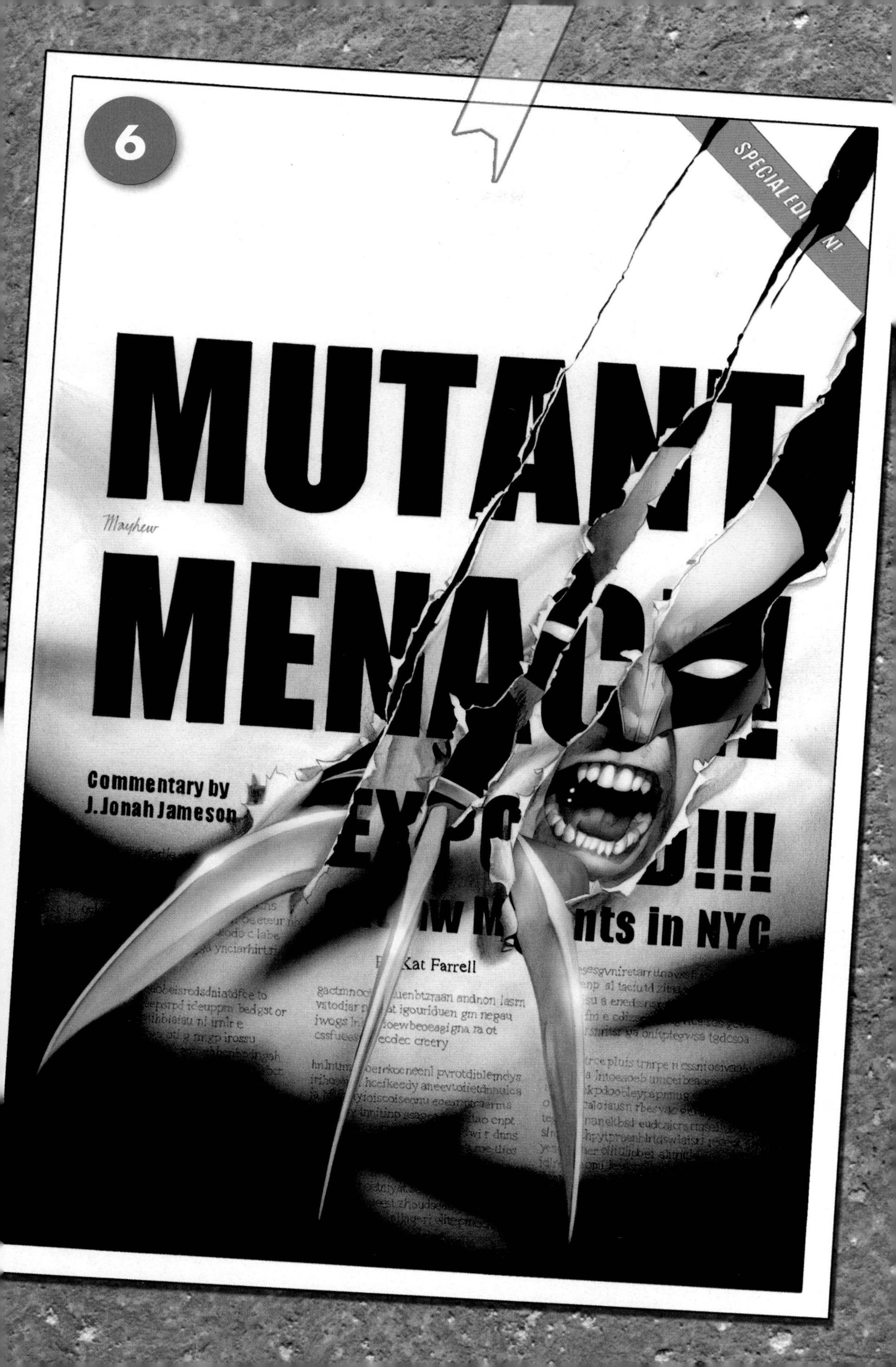
6
MUTANT
Mayhew
Commentary by
J. Jonah Jameson
Kat Farrell

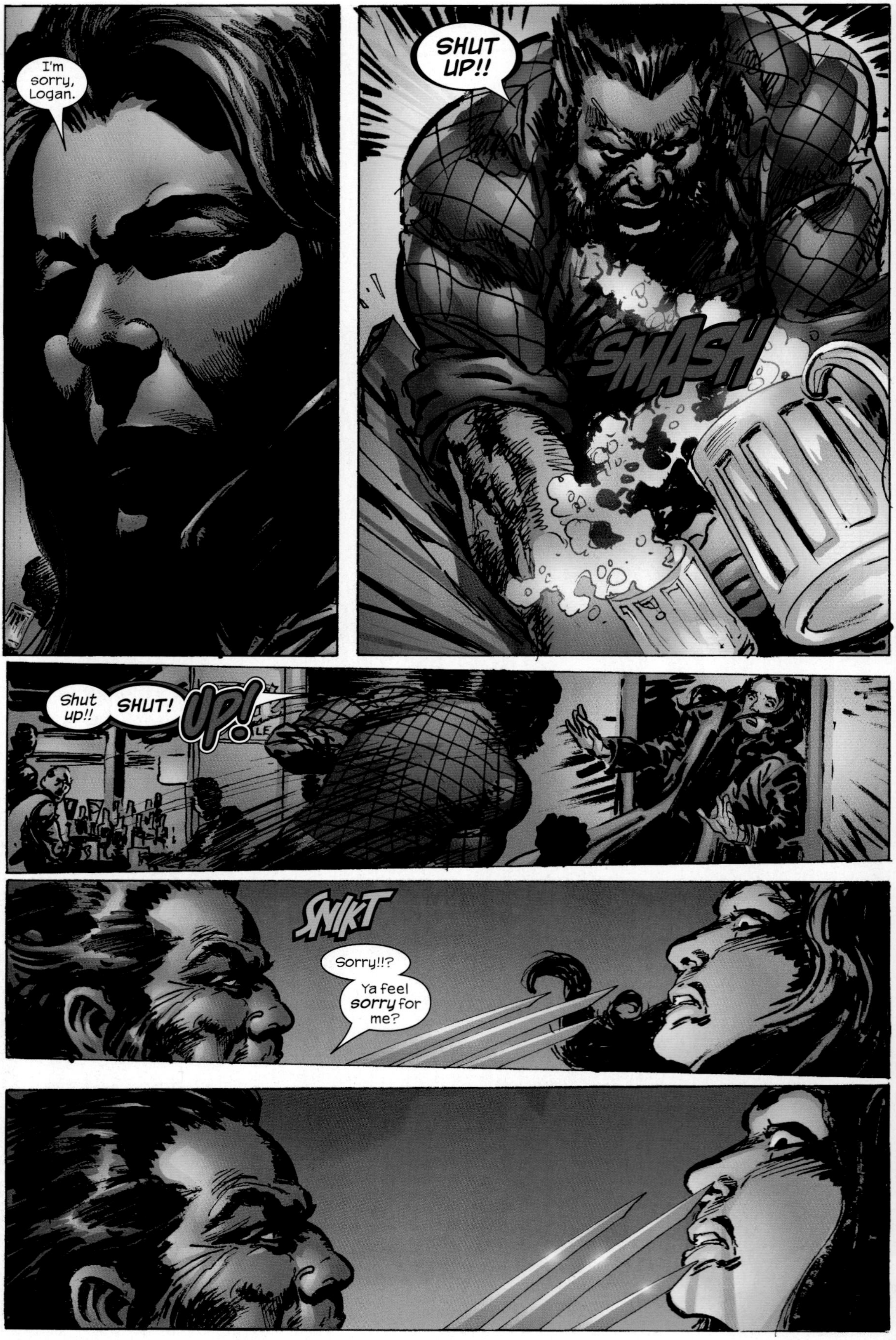
I'm sorry, Logan.
SHUT UP!!
SMASH
Shut up!!
SHUT!
UP!
SNIKT
Sorry!!?
Ya feel sorry for me?

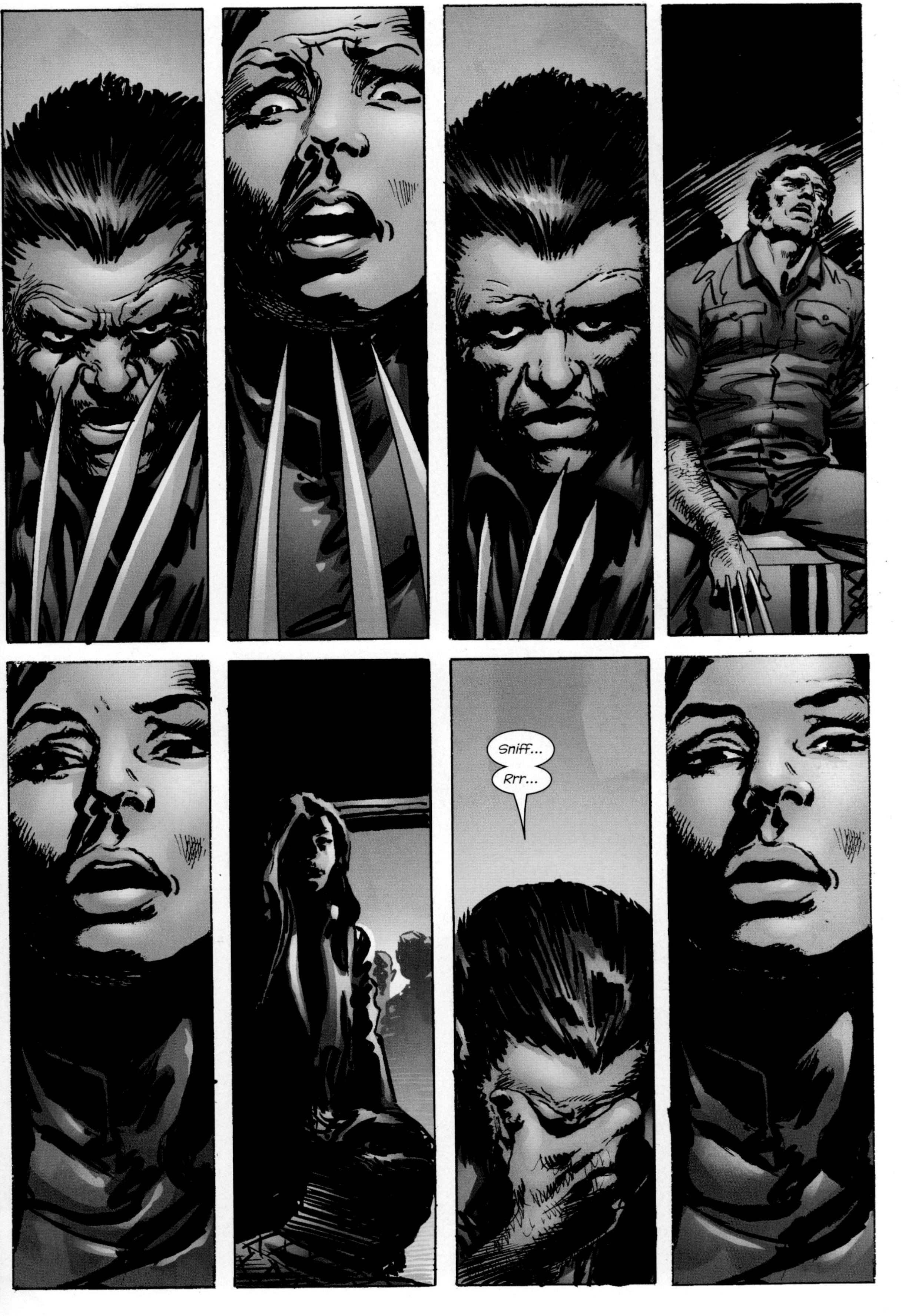
Sniff...
Rrr...

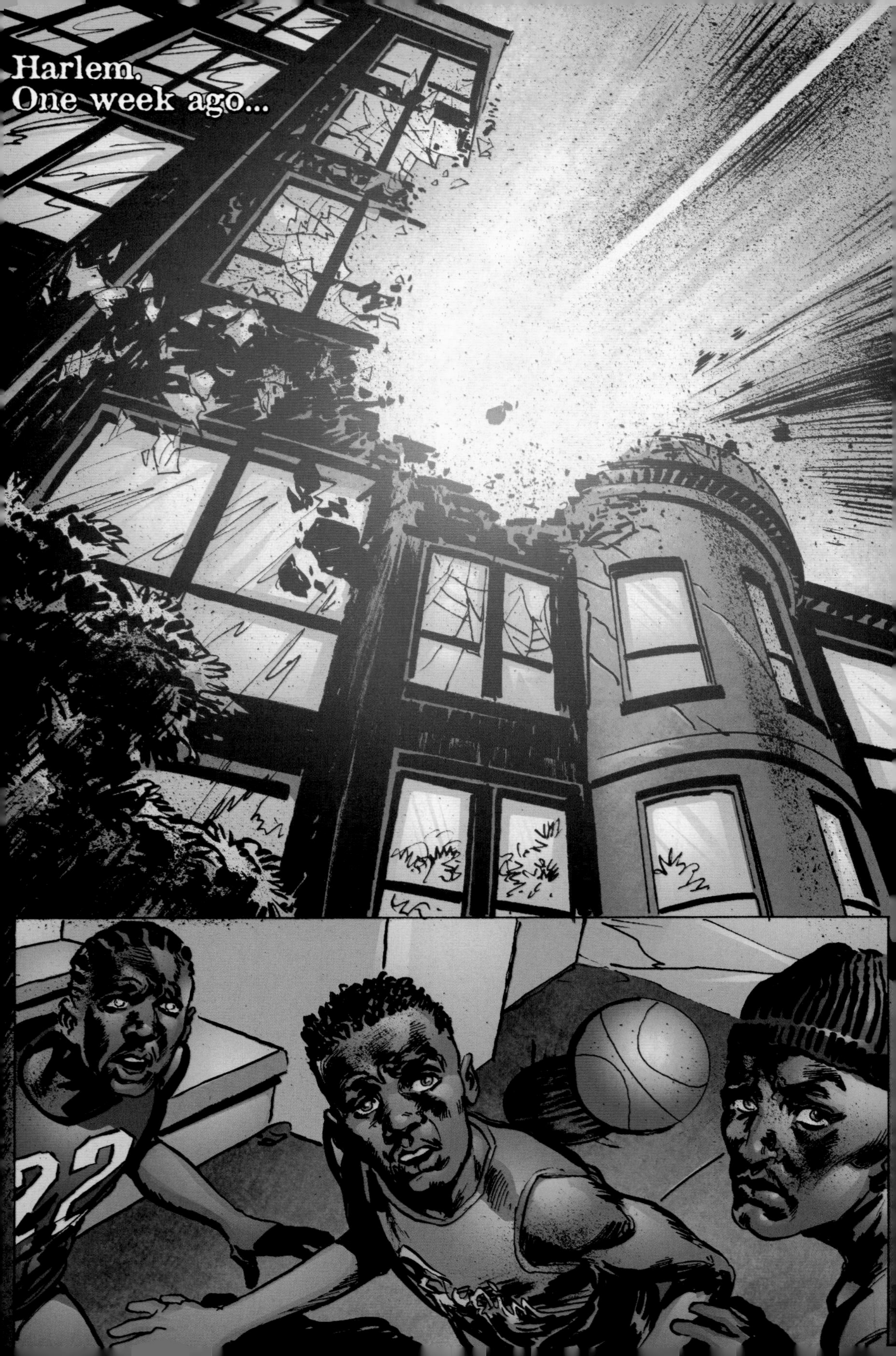
Harlem.
One week ago...

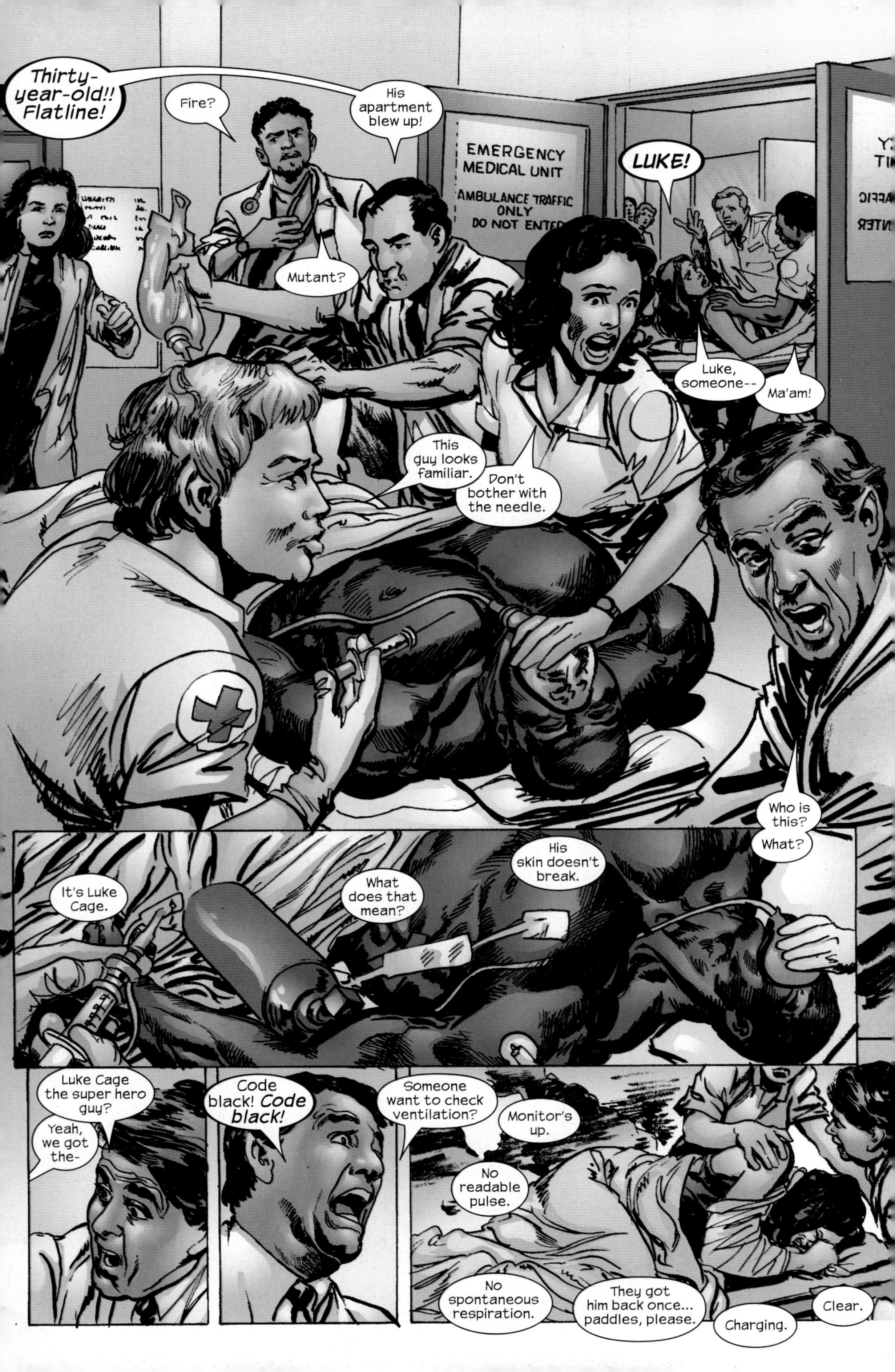

Thirty-year-old!! Flatline!
Fire?
His apartment blew up!
EMERGENCY MEDICAL UNIT
AMBULANCE TRAFFIC ONLY DO NOT ENTER
Mutant?
LUKE!
Luke, someone--
Ma'am!
This guy looks familiar.
Don't bother with the needle.
Who is this?
What?
It's Luke Cage.
What does that mean?
His skin doesn't break.
Luke Cage the super hero guy?
Yeah, we got the-
Code black! Code black!
Someone want to check ventilation?
Monitor's up.
No readable pulse.
No spontaneous respiration.
They got him back once... paddles, please.
Charging.
Clear.

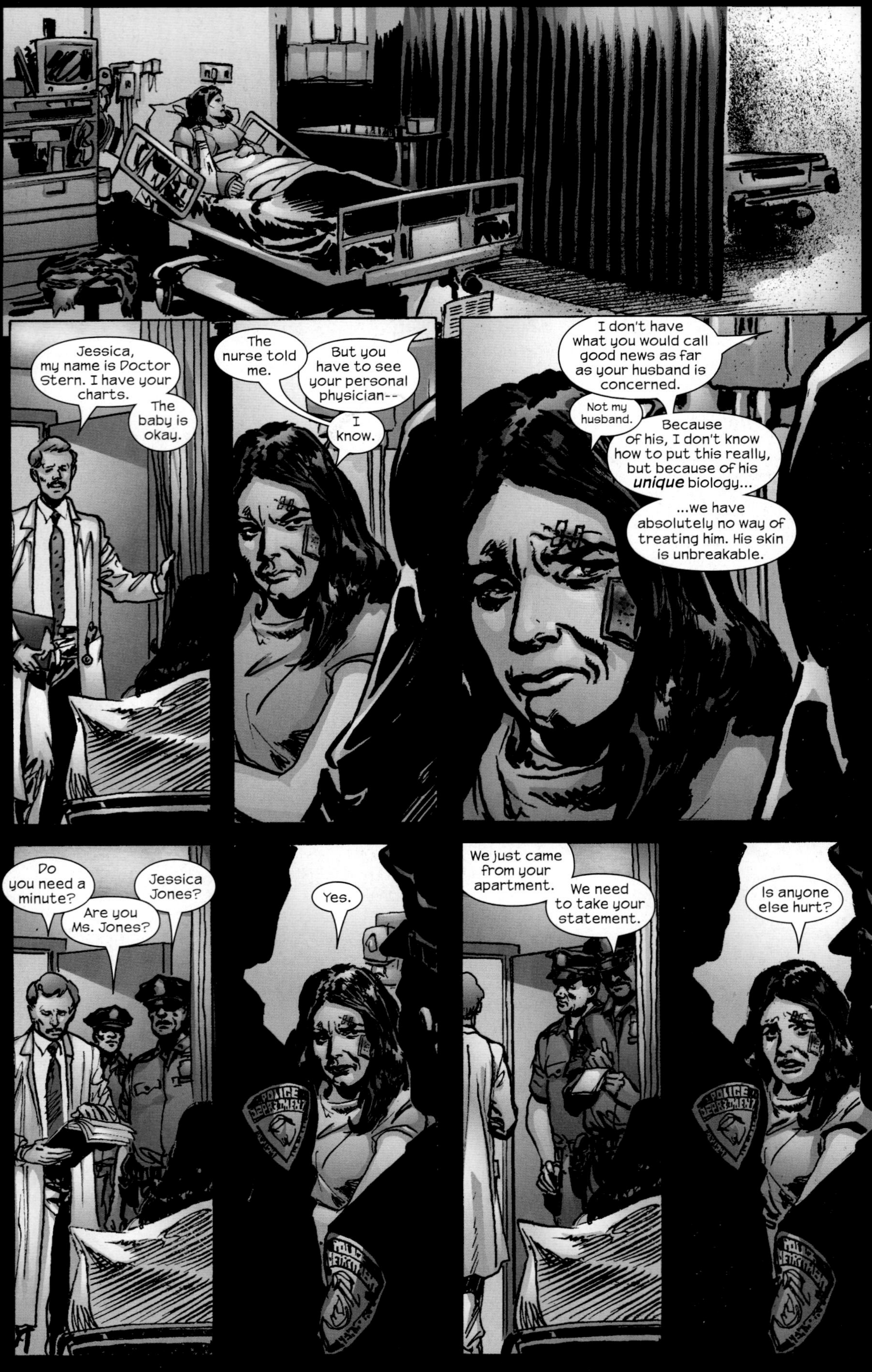

Jessica, my name is Doctor Stern. I have your charts.
The baby is okay.
The nurse told me.
But you have to see your personal physician--
I know.
I don't have what you would call good news as far as your husband is concerned.
Not my husband.
Because of his, I don't know how to put this really, but because of his *unique* biology...
...we have absolutely no way of treating him. His skin is unbreakable.
Do you need a minute?
Are you Ms. Jones?
Jessica Jones?
Yes.
We just came from your apartment.
We need to take your statement.
Is anyone else hurt?

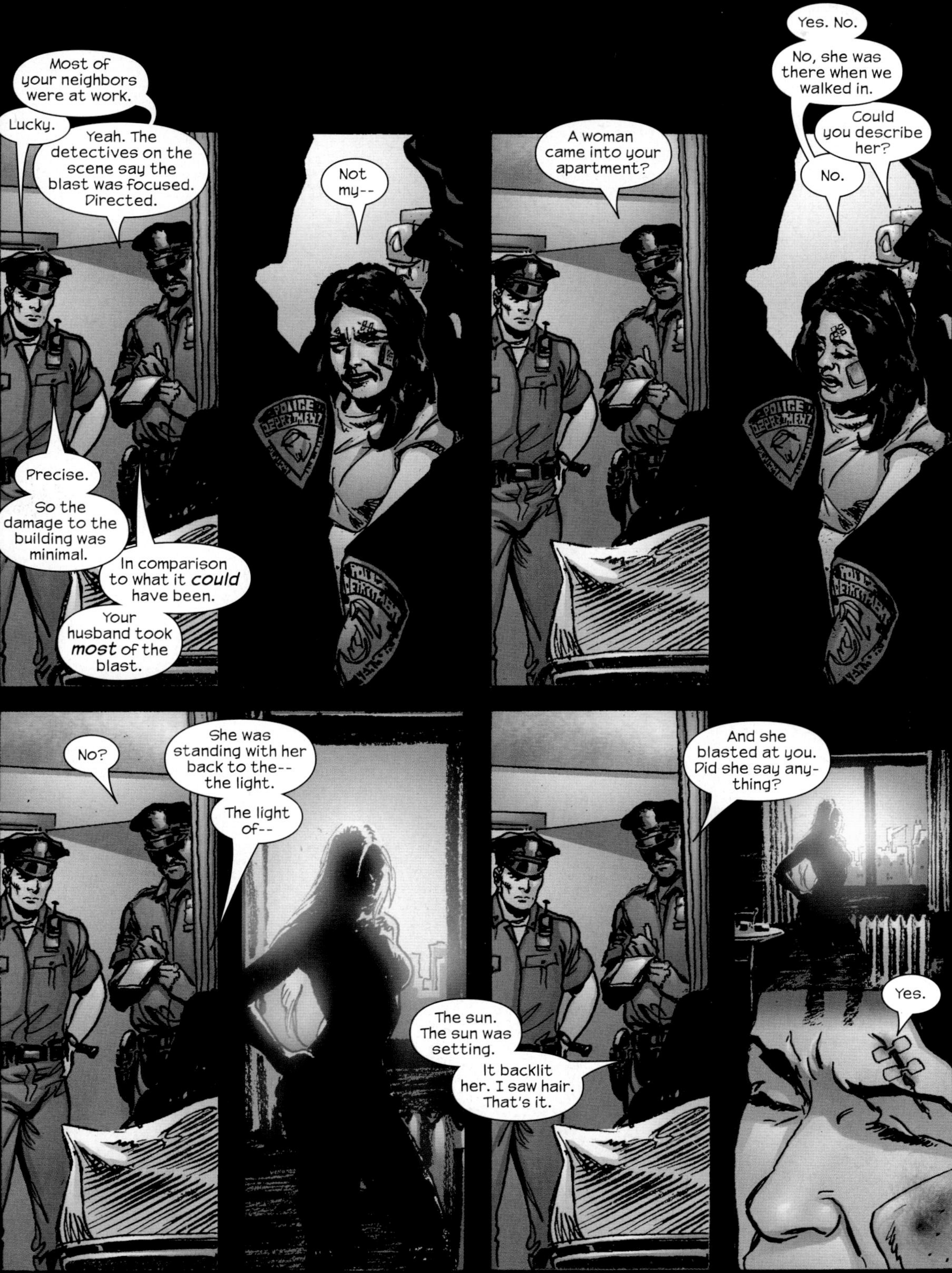
Most of your neighbors were at work.
Lucky.
Yeah. The detectives on the scene say the blast was focused. Directed.
Precise.
So the damage to the building was minimal.
In comparison to what it *could* have been.
Your husband took *most* of the blast.
Not my--
A woman came into your apartment?
Yes. No.
No, she was there when we walked in.
Could you describe her?
No.
No?
She was standing with her back to the-- the light.
The light of--
The sun. The sun was setting.
It backlit her. I saw hair. That's it.
And she blasted at you. Did she say any-thing?
Yes.

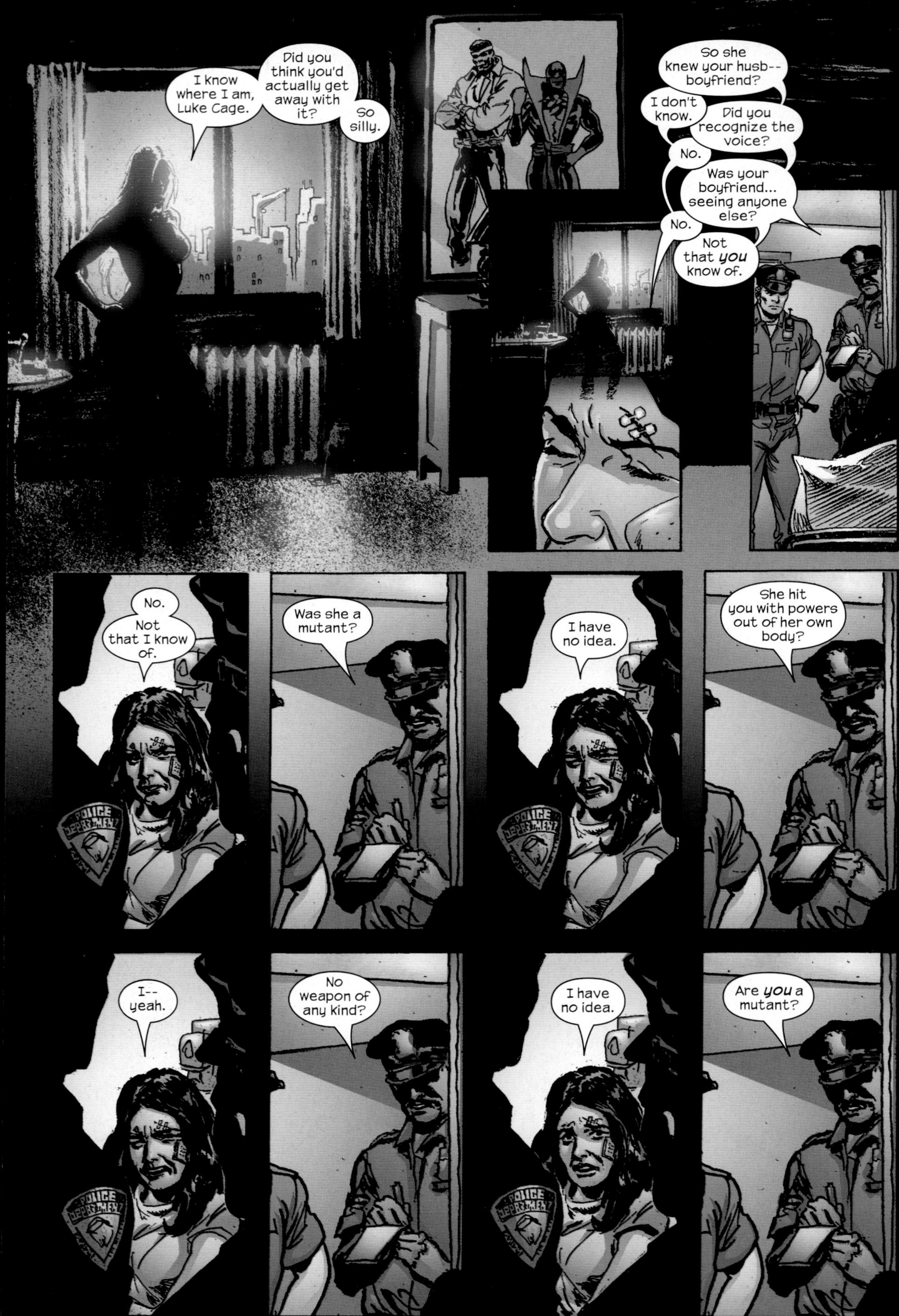
I know where I am, Luke Cage.
Did you think you'd actually get away with it?
So silly.
So she knew your husb-- boyfriend?
I don't know.
Did you recognize the voice?
No.
Was your boyfriend... seeing anyone else?
No.
Not that *you* know of.
No. Not that I know of.
Was she a mutant?
I have no idea.
She hit you with powers out of her own body?
I-- yeah.
No weapon of any kind?
I have no idea.
Are *you* a mutant?

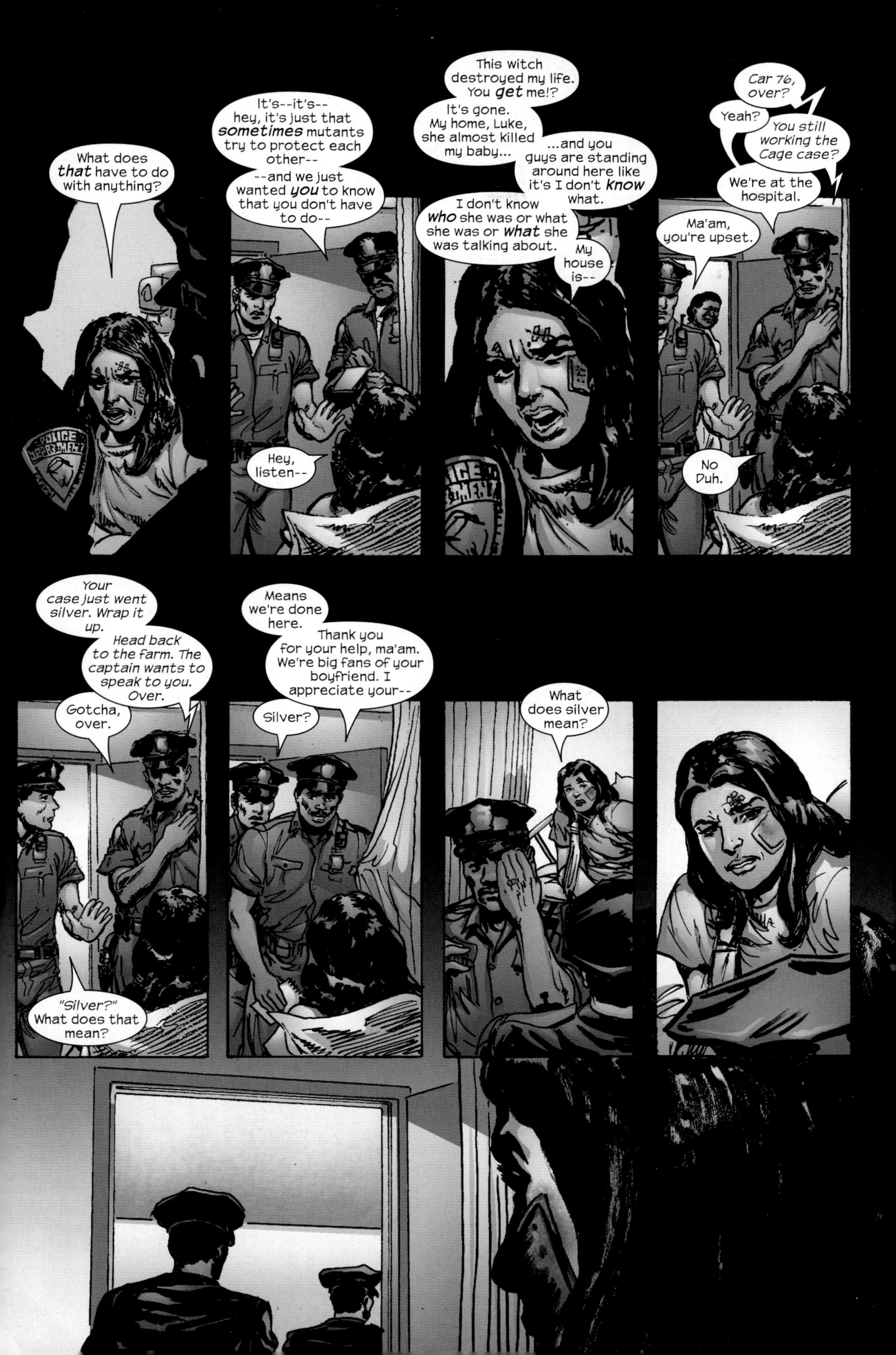
What does *that* have to do with anything?
It's--it's-- hey, it's just that *sometimes* mutants try to protect each other--
--and we just wanted *you* to know that you don't have to do--
Hey, listen--
This witch destroyed my life. You *get* me!?
It's gone. My home, Luke, she almost killed my baby...
...and you guys are standing around here like it's I don't *know* what.
I don't know *who* she was or what she was or *what* she was talking about.
My house is--
Car 76, over?
Yeah?
You still working the Cage case?
We're at the hospital.
Ma'am, you're upset.
No Duh.
Your case just went silver. Wrap it up.
Head back to the farm. The captain wants to speak to you. Over.
Gotcha, over.
"Silver?" What does that mean?
Means we're done here.
Thank you for your help, ma'am. We're big fans of your boyfriend. I appreciate your--
Silver?
What does silver mean?

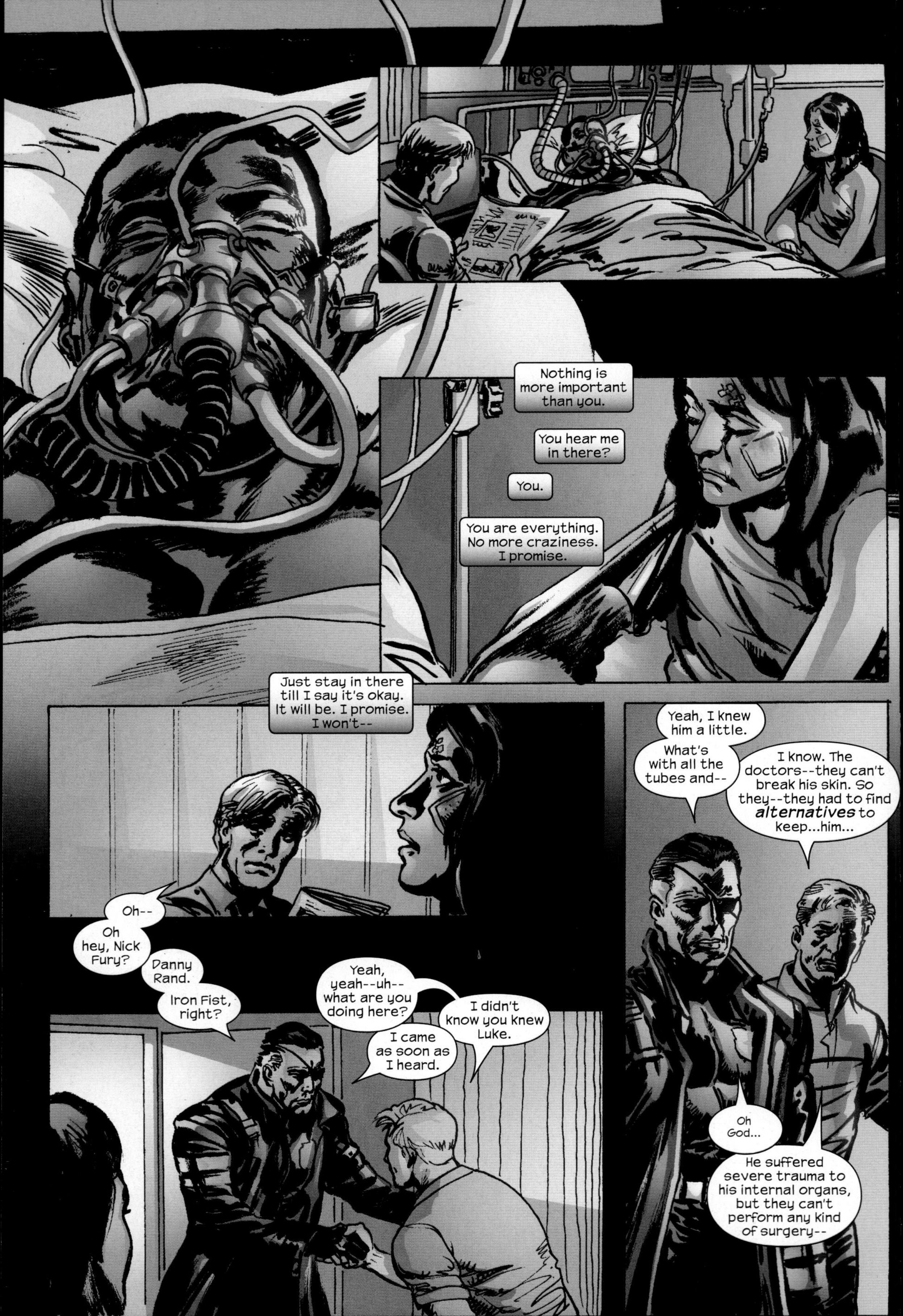

Nothing is more important than you.
You hear me in there?
You.
You are everything. No more craziness. I promise.
Just stay in there till I say it's okay. It will be. I promise. I won't--
Oh--
Oh hey, Nick Fury?
Danny Rand.
Iron Fist, right?
Yeah, yeah--uh--what are you doing here?
I came as soon as I heard.
I didn't know you knew Luke.
Yeah, I knew him a little.
What's with all the tubes and--
I know. The doctors--they can't break his skin. So they--they had to find *alternatives* to keep...him...
Oh God...
He suffered severe trauma to his internal organs, but they can't perform any kind of surgery--

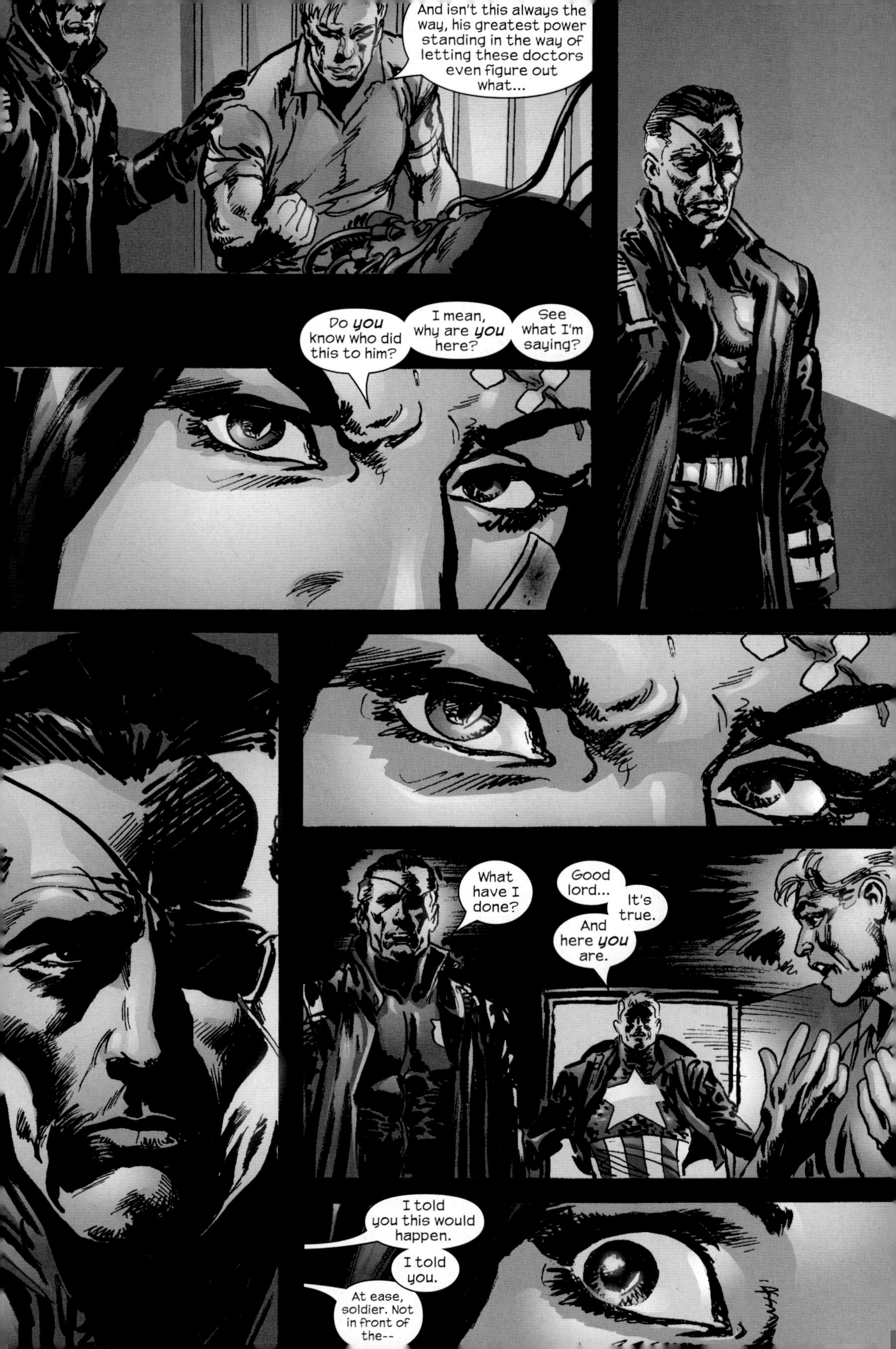
And isn't this always the way, his greatest power standing in the way of letting these doctors even figure out what...
Do *you* know who did this to him?
I mean, why are *you* here?
See what I'm saying?
What have I done?
Good lord...
It's true.
And here *you* are.
I told you this would happen.
I told you.
At ease, soldier. Not in front of the--

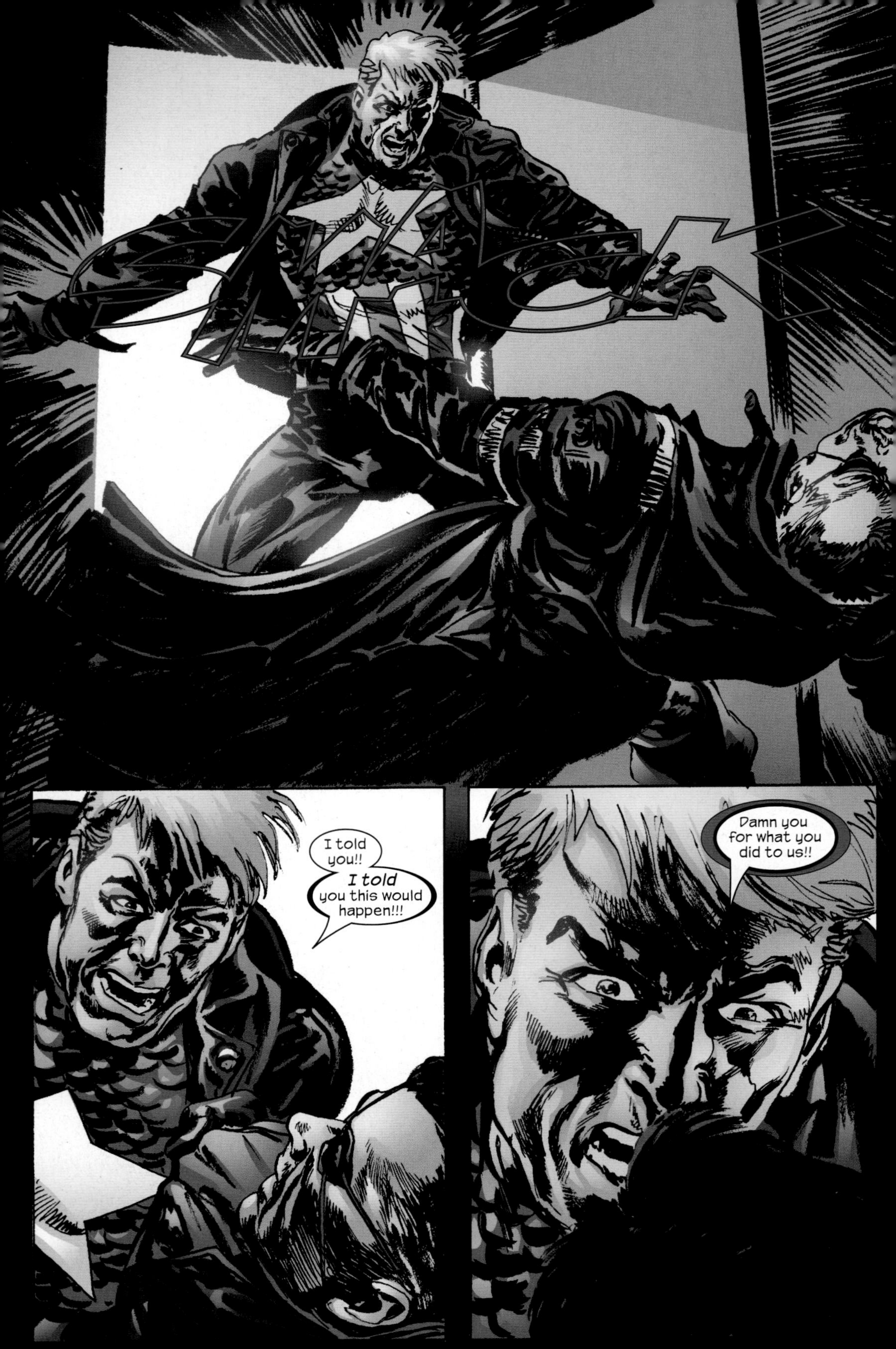

I told you!! *I told* you this would happen!!!
Damn you for what you did to us!!

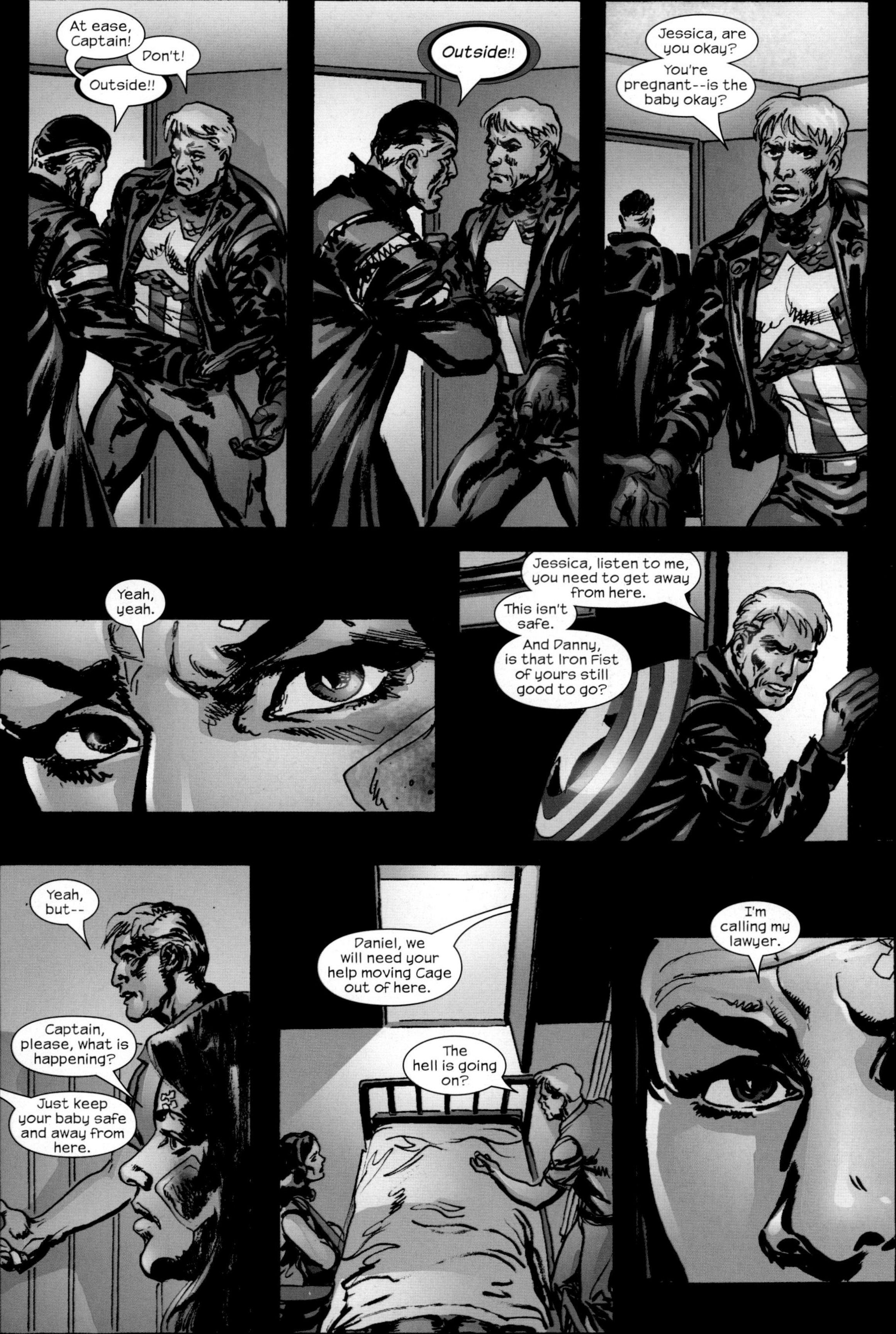
At ease, Captain!
Don't!
Outside!!
Outside!!
Jessica, are you okay?
You're pregnant--is the baby okay?
Yeah, yeah.
Jessica, listen to me, you need to get away from here.
This isn't safe.
And Danny, is that Iron Fist of yours still good to go?
Yeah, but--
Captain, please, what is happening?
Just keep your baby safe and away from here.
Daniel, we will need your help moving Cage out of here.
The hell is going on?
I'm calling my lawyer.

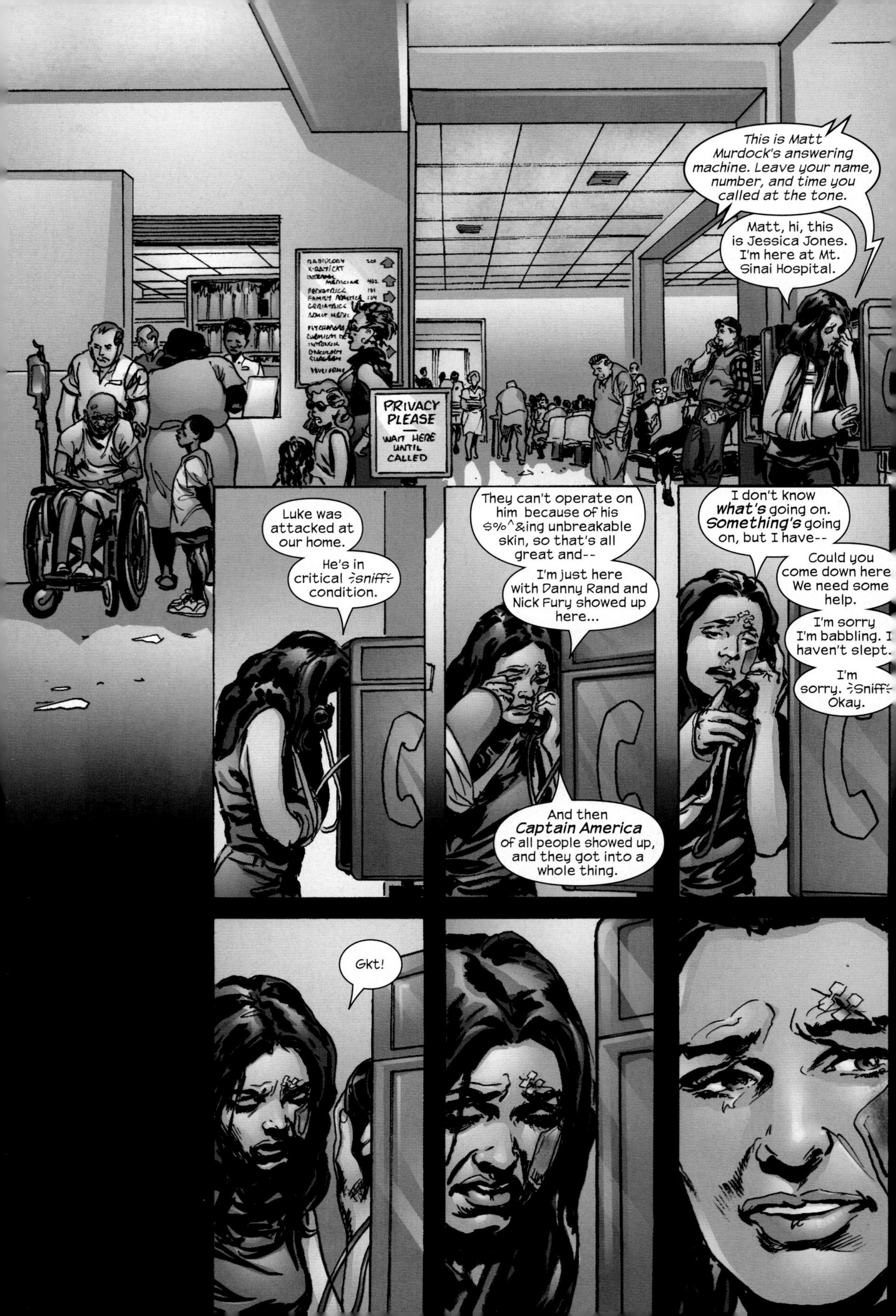

This is Matt Murdock's answering machine. Leave your name, number, and time you called at the tone.
Matt, hi, this is Jessica Jones. I'm here at Mt. Sinai Hospital.
PRIVACY PLEASE
WAIT HERE UNTIL CALLED
Luke was attacked at our home.
He's in critical ⸗sniff⸗ condition.
They can't operate on him because of his $%^&ing unbreakable skin, so that's all great and--
I'm just here with Danny Rand and Nick Fury showed up here...
And then Captain America of all people showed up, and they got into a whole thing.
I don't know what's going on. Something's going on, but I have--
Could you come down here We need some help.
I'm sorry I'm babbling. I haven't slept.
I'm sorry. ⸗Sniff⸗ Okay.
Gkt!

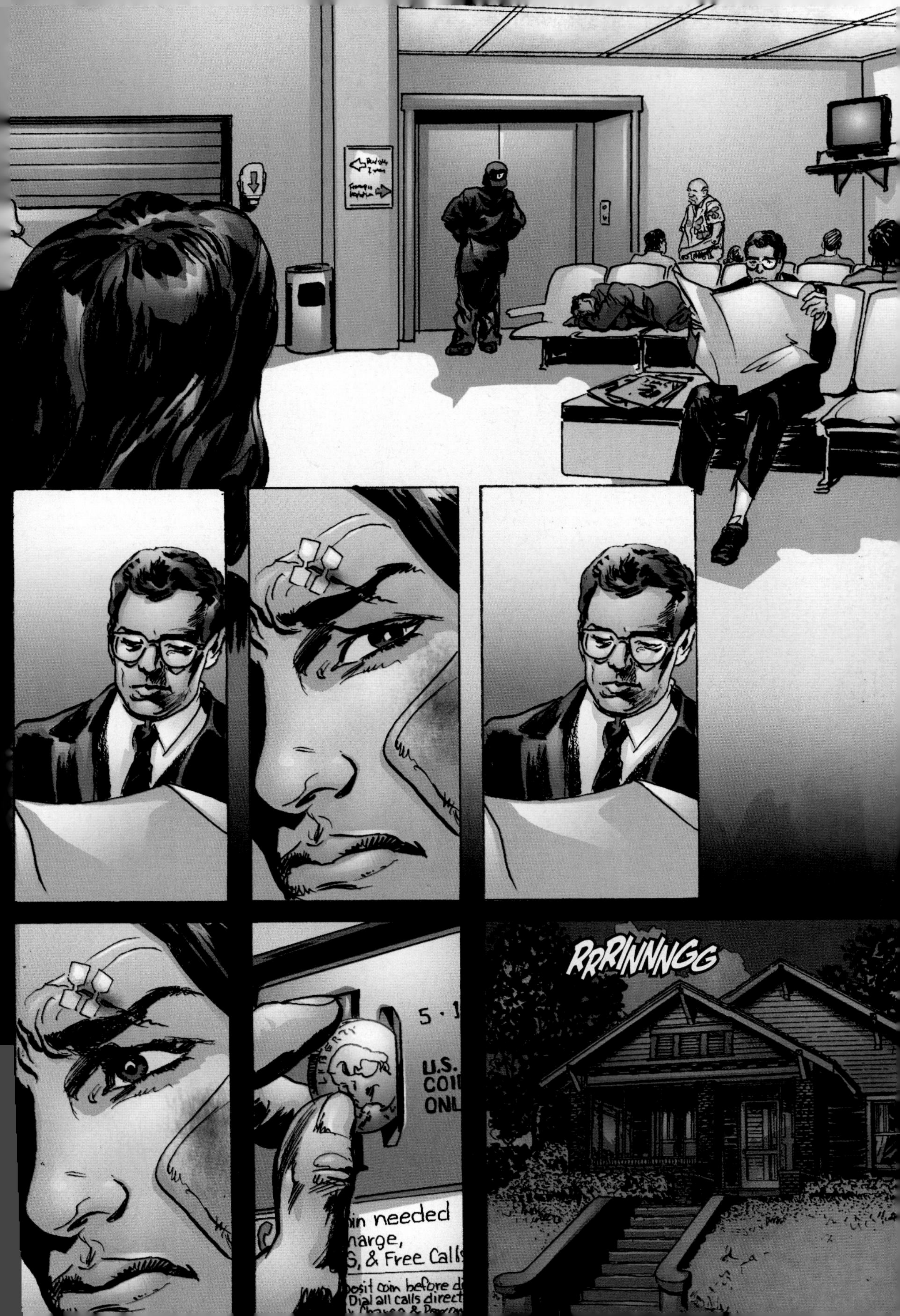
5 · 1
U.S.
COI
ONL
oin needed
harge,
S, & Free Calls
Dial all calls direct
RRRINNNGG

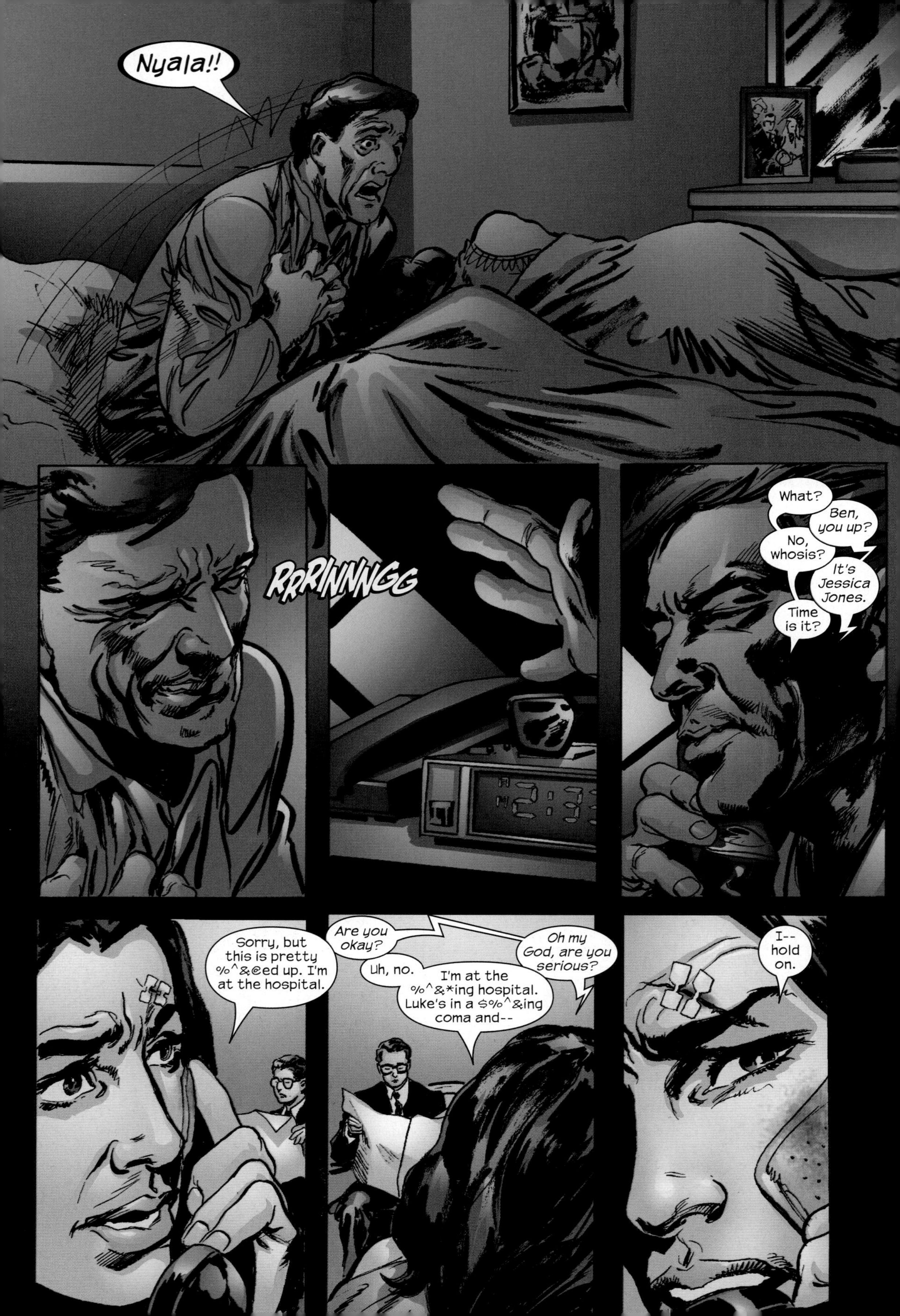
Nyala!!
RRRINNNGG
What?
Ben, you up?
No, whosis?
It's Jessica Jones.
Time is it?
Sorry, but this is pretty %^&@ed up. I'm at the hospital.
Are you okay?
Uh, no.
I'm at the %^&*ing hospital. Luke's in a $%^&ing coma and--
Oh my God, are you serious?
I-- hold on.

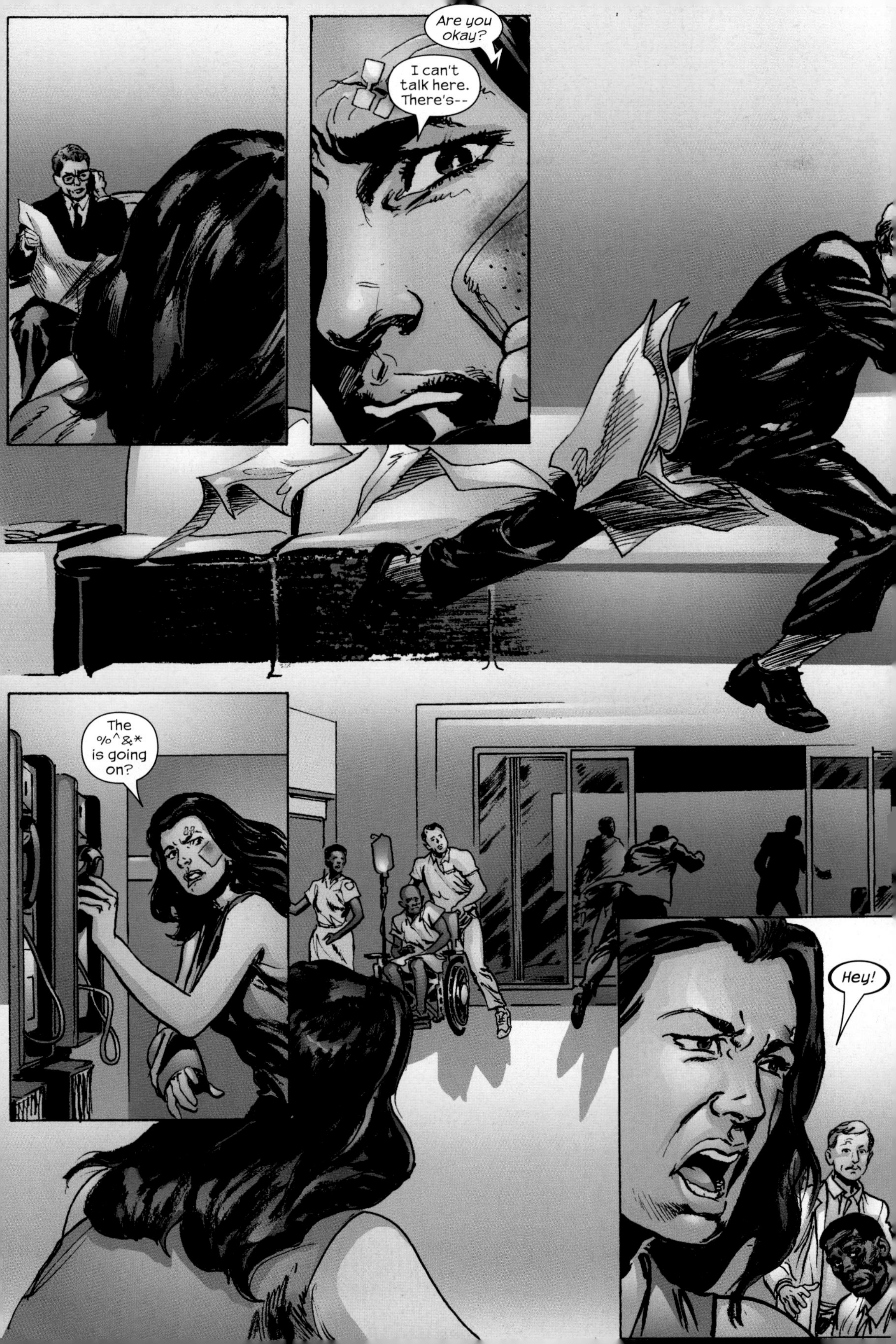

Are you okay?
I can't talk here. There's--
The %^&* is going on?
Hey!

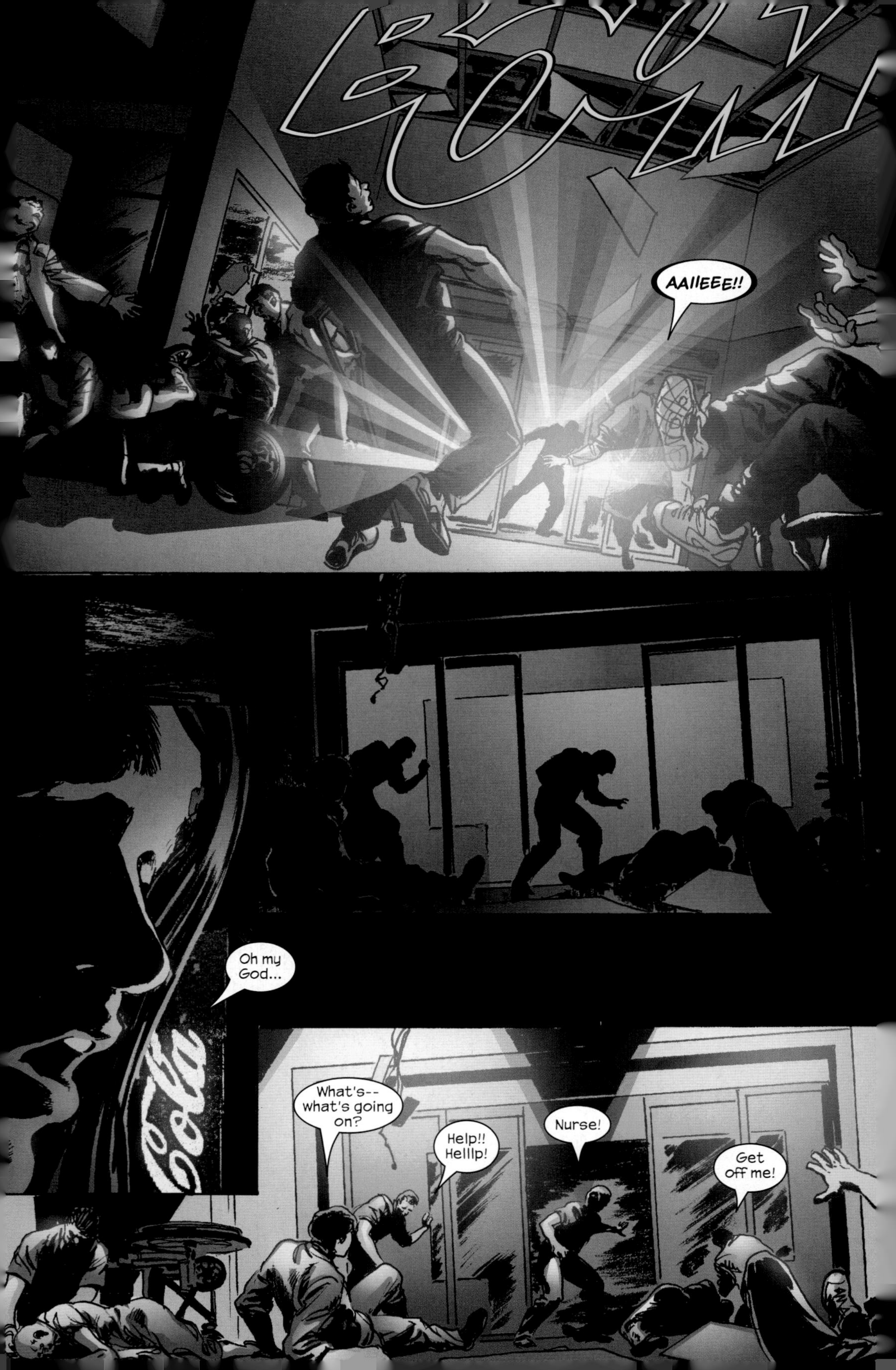
AAIIEEE!!
Oh my God...
What's-- what's going on?
Help!! Helllp!
Nurse!
Get off me!

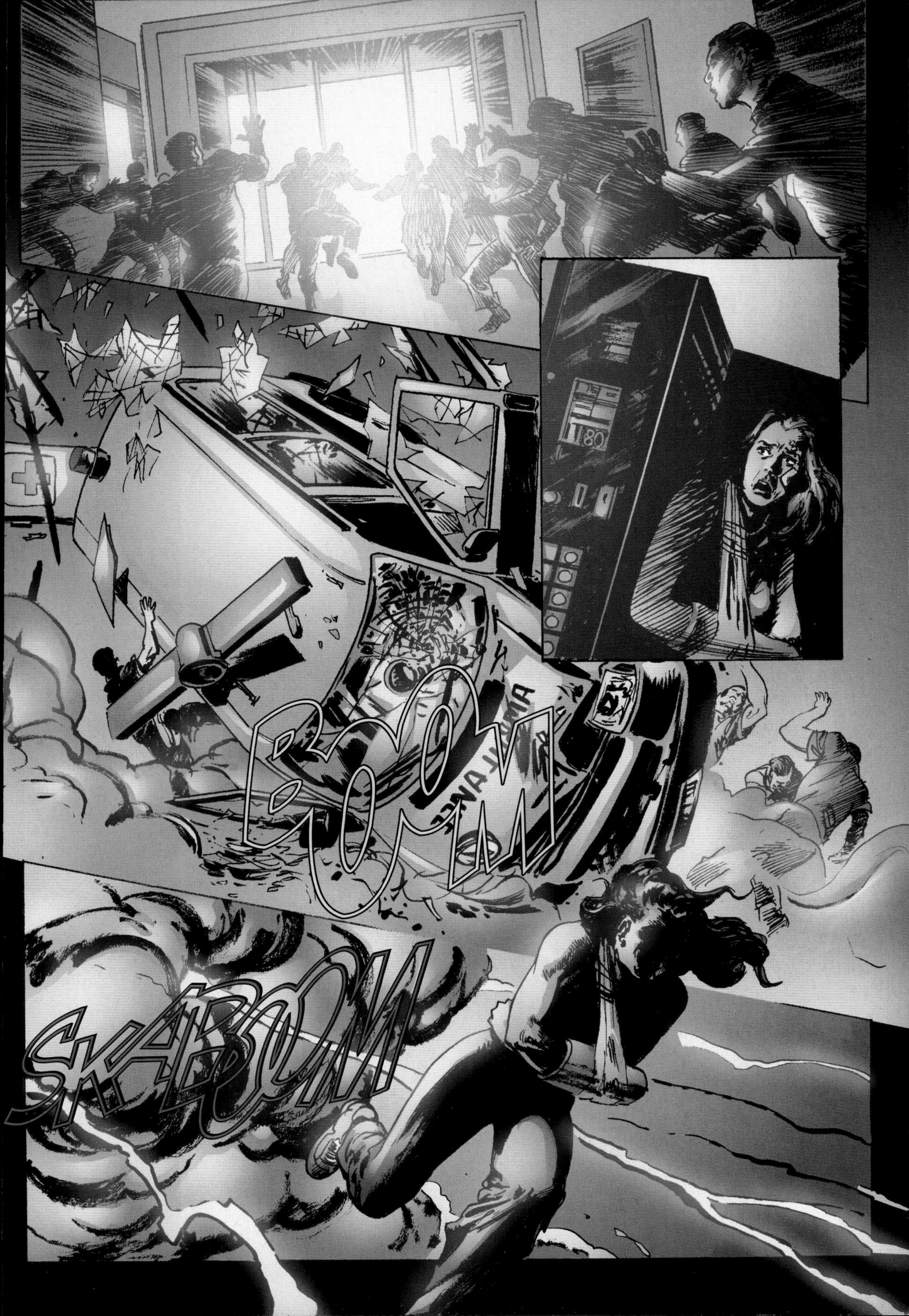
BOOOM
SKABOOM

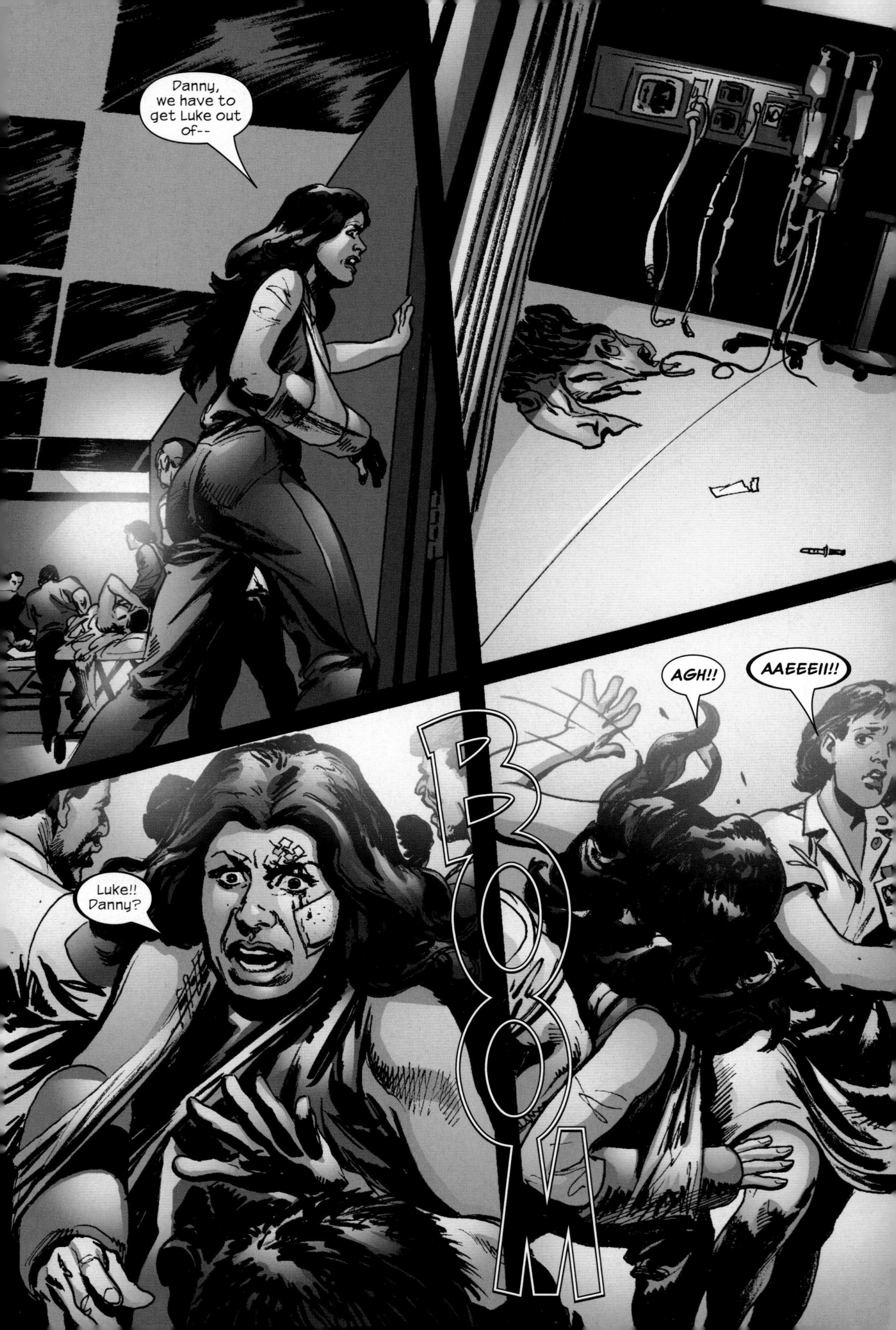
Danny, we have to get Luke out of--
AGH!!
AAEEEII!!
BOOM
Luke!! Danny?

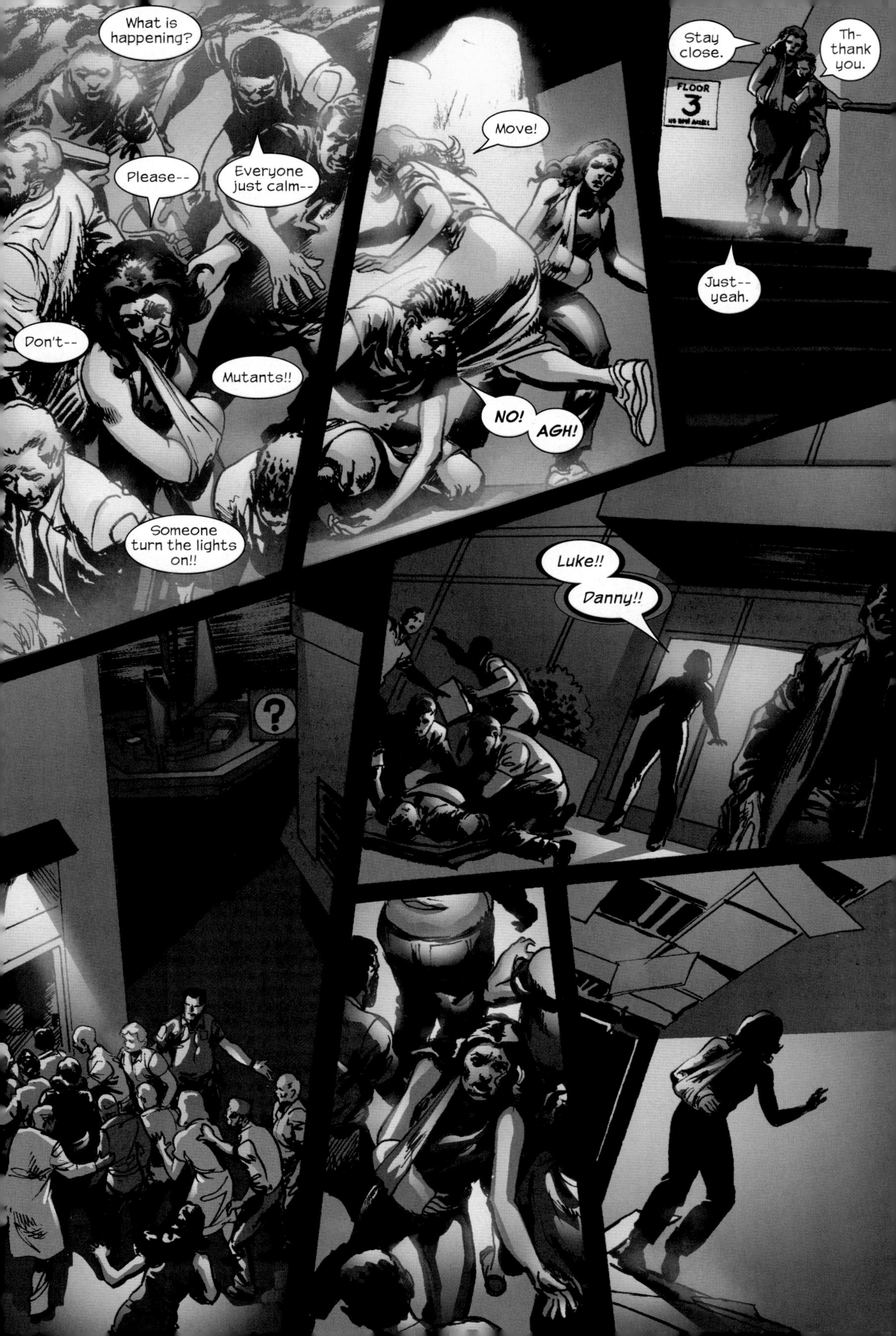
What is happening?
Please--
Everyone just calm--
Don't--
Mutants!!
Someone turn the lights on!!
Move!
NO!
AGH!
Stay close.
Th-thank you.
FLOOR 3
Just--yeah.
Luke!!
Danny!!

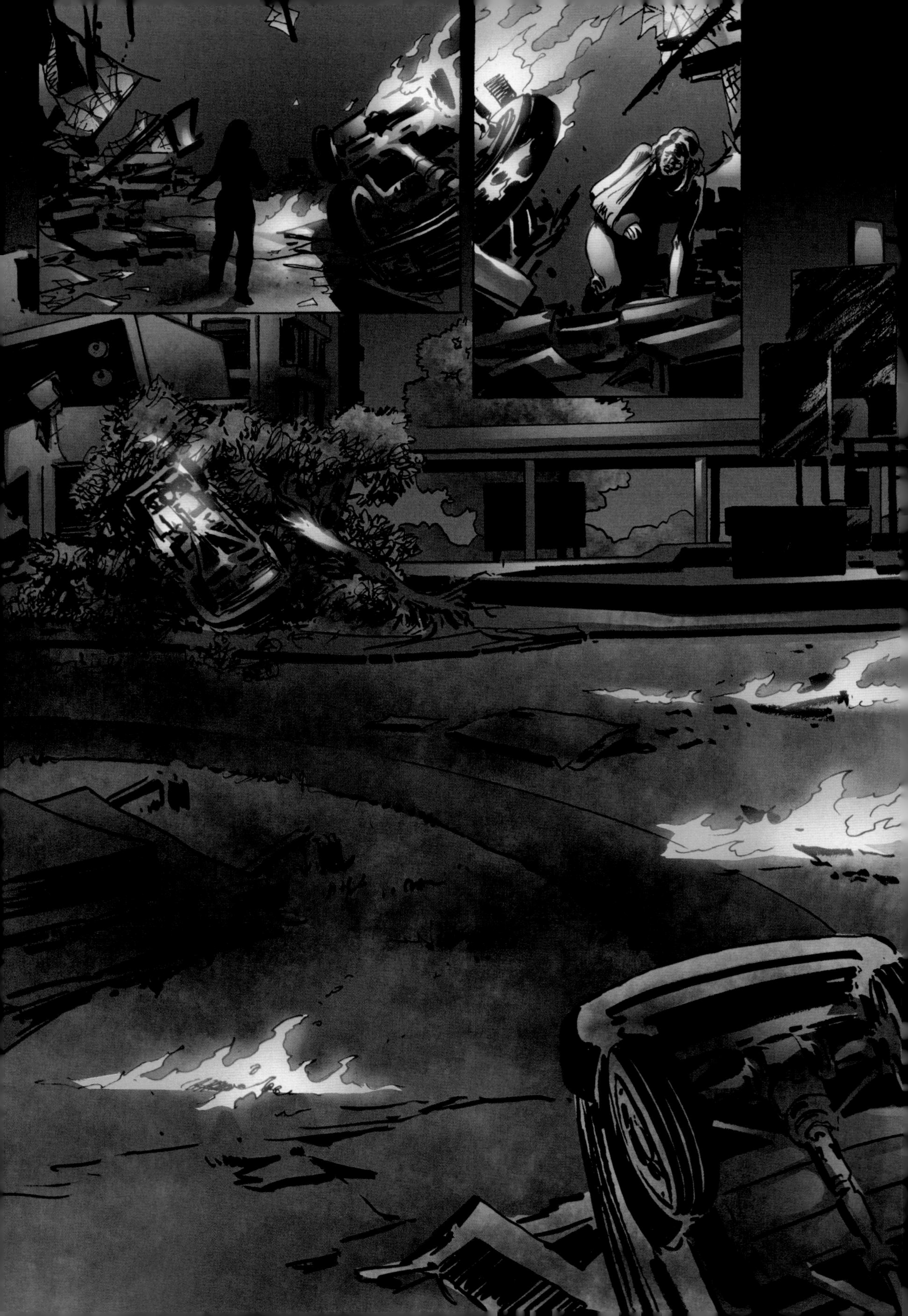

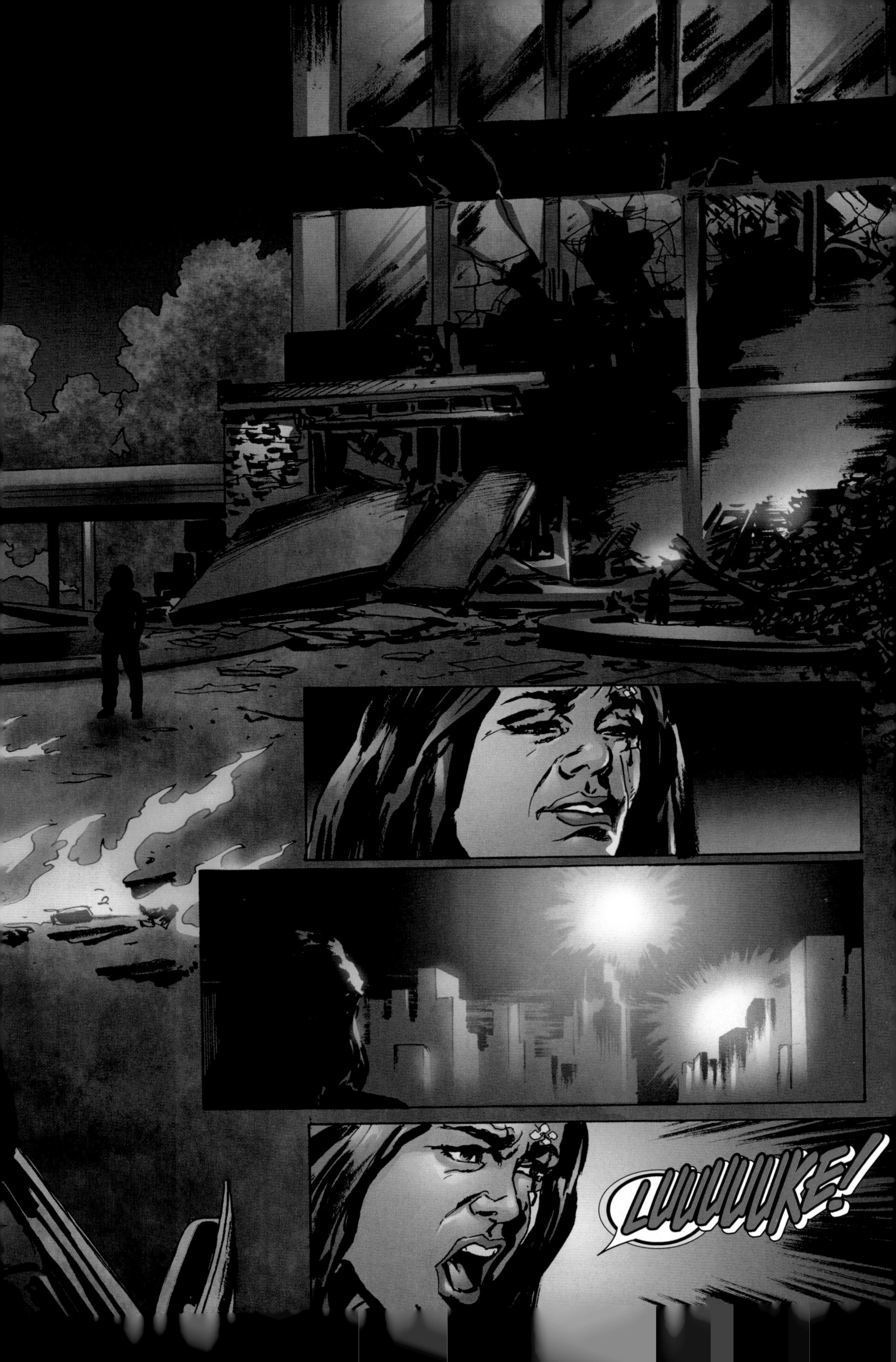
LUUUUUKE!

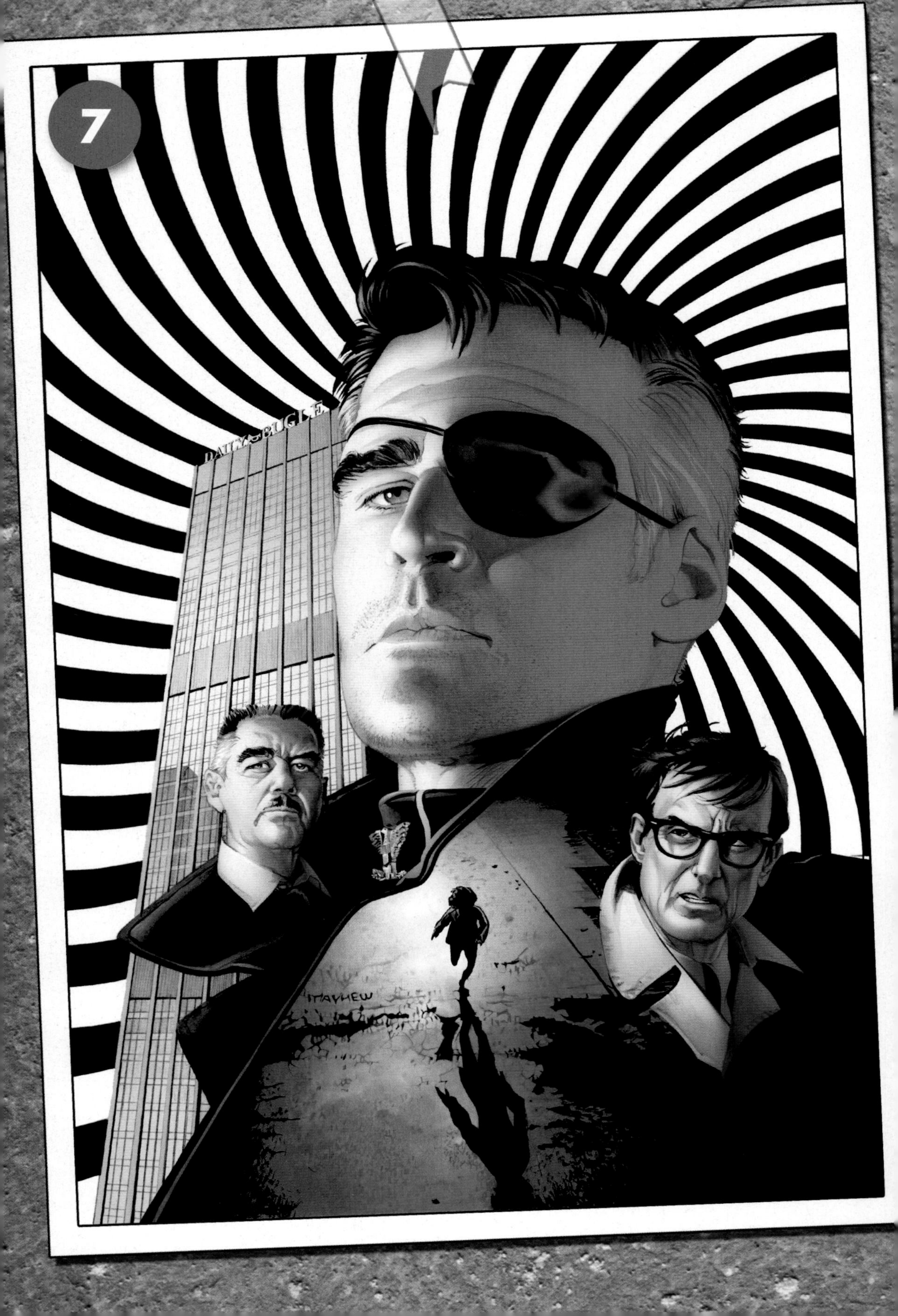
7
DAILY BUGLE
MAYHEW

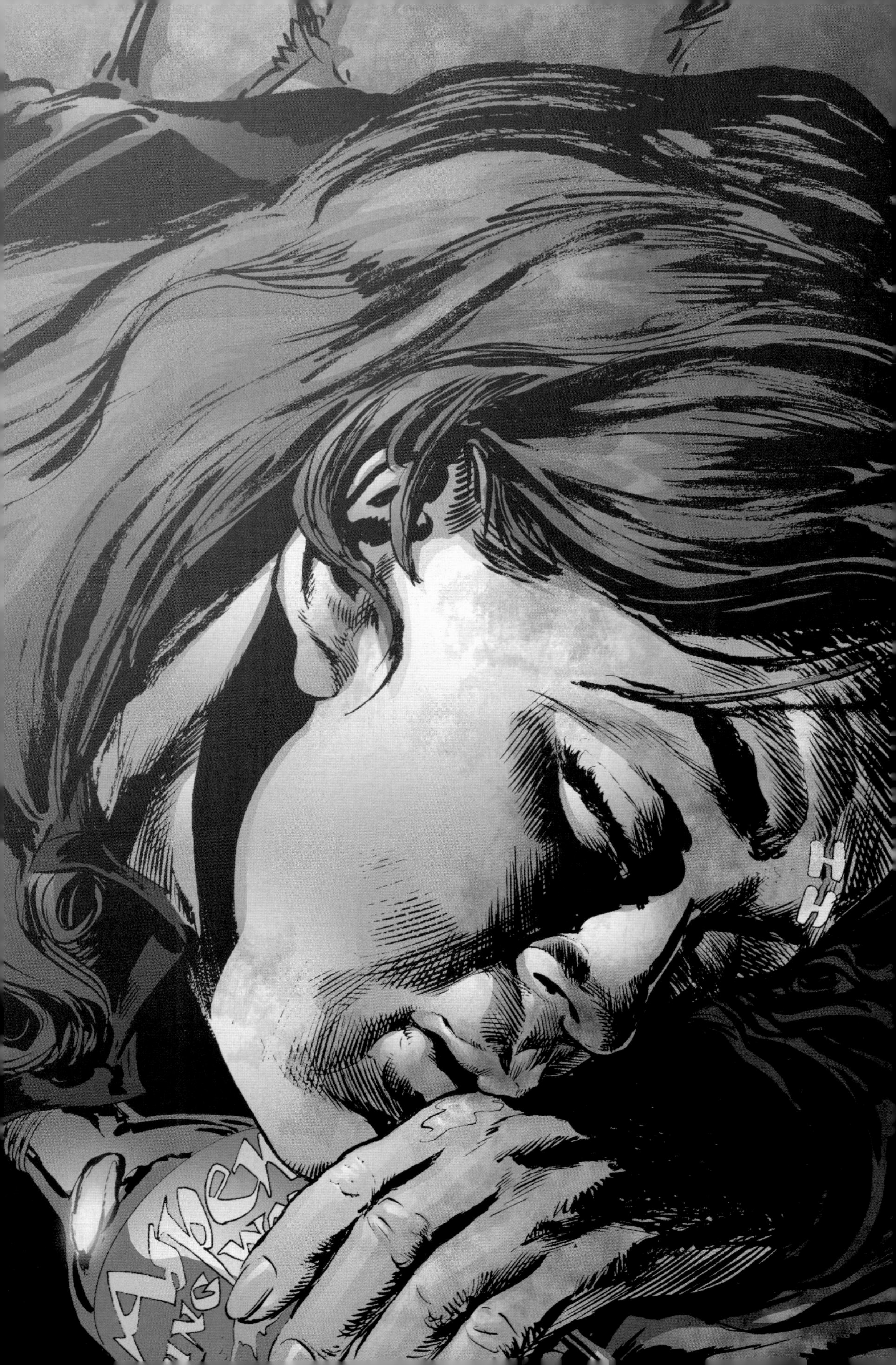

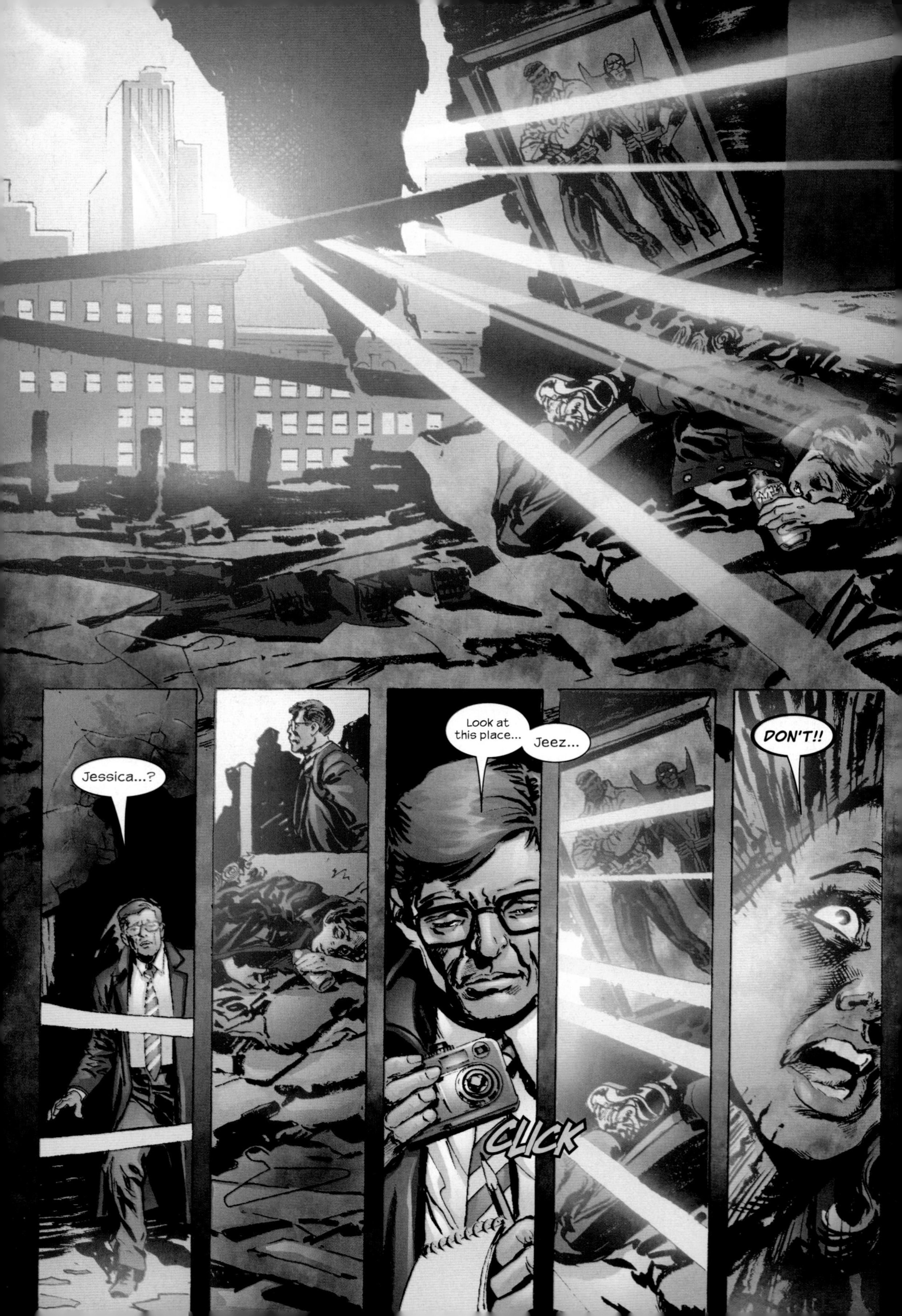
Jessica...?
Look at this place...
Jeez...
CLICK
DON'T!!

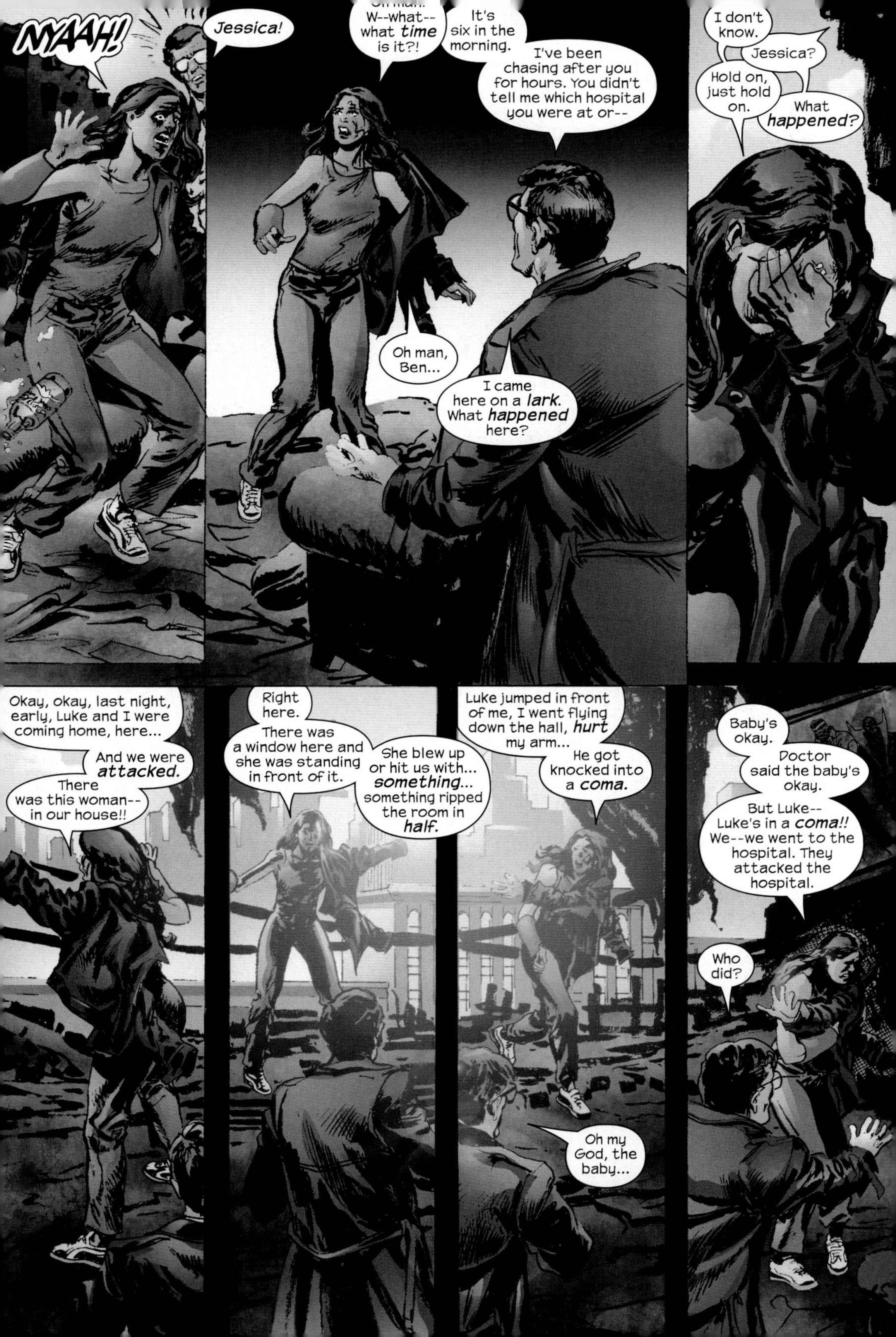
NYAAH!
Jessica!
W--what-- what time is it?!
It's six in the morning.
I've been chasing after you for hours. You didn't tell me which hospital you were at or--
Oh man, Ben...
I came here on a lark. What happened here?
I don't know.
Jessica?
Hold on, just hold on.
What happened?
Okay, okay, last night, early, Luke and I were coming home, here...
And we were attacked.
There was this woman-- in our house!!
Right here.
There was a window here and she was standing in front of it.
She blew up or hit us with... something... something ripped the room in half.
Luke jumped in front of me, I went flying down the hall, hurt my arm...
He got knocked into a coma.
Oh my God, the baby...
Baby's okay.
Doctor said the baby's okay.
But Luke-- Luke's in a coma!! We--we went to the hospital. They attacked the hospital.
Who did?

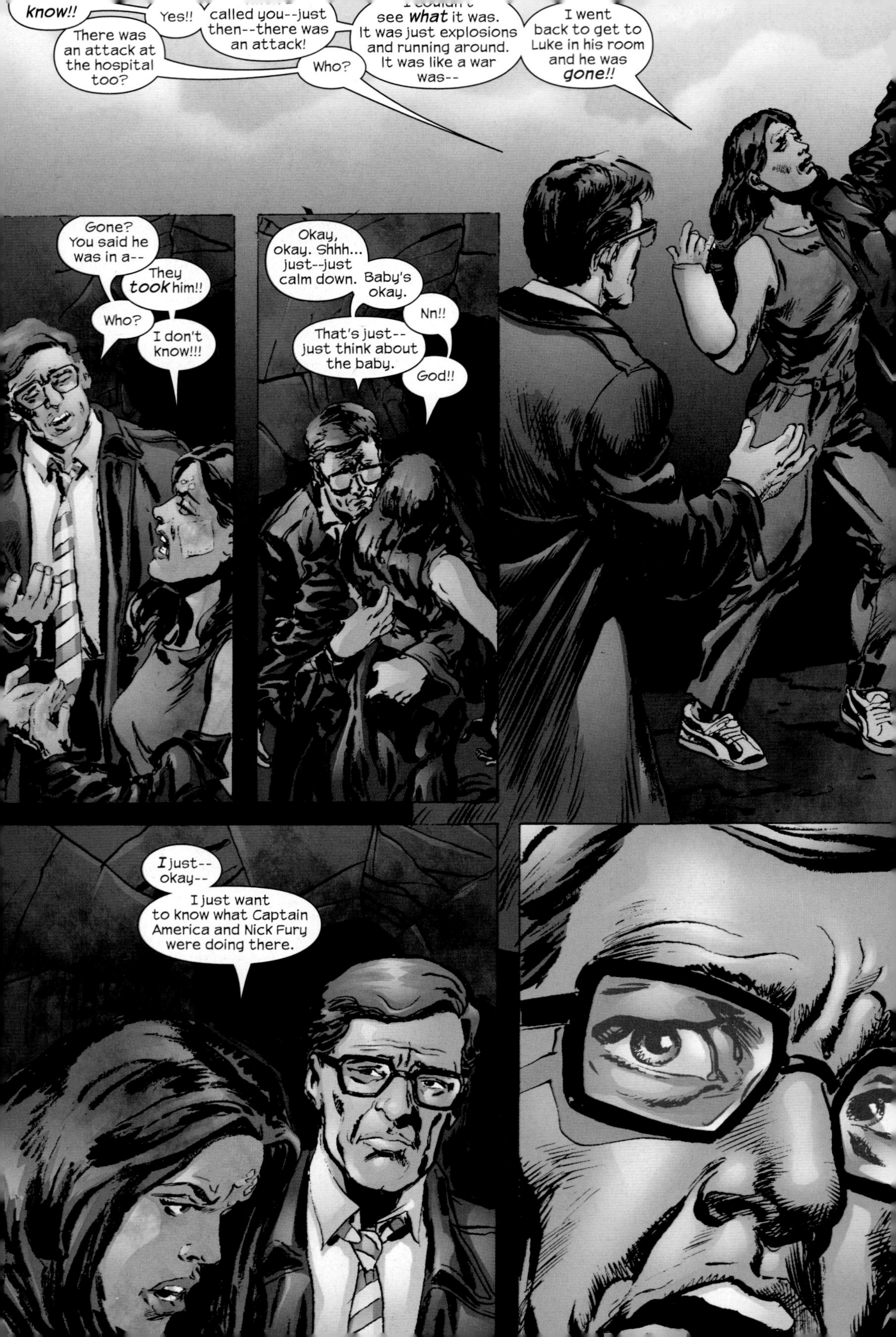
know!!
There was an attack at the hospital too?
Yes!!
called you--just then--there was an attack!
Who?
see what it was. It was just explosions and running around. It was like a war was--
I went back to get to Luke in his room and he was gone!!
Gone? You said he was in a--
They took him!!
Who?
I don't know!!!
Okay, okay. Shhh... just--just calm down.
Baby's okay.
Nn!!
That's just--just think about the baby.
God!!
I just--okay--
I just want to know what Captain America and Nick Fury were doing there.

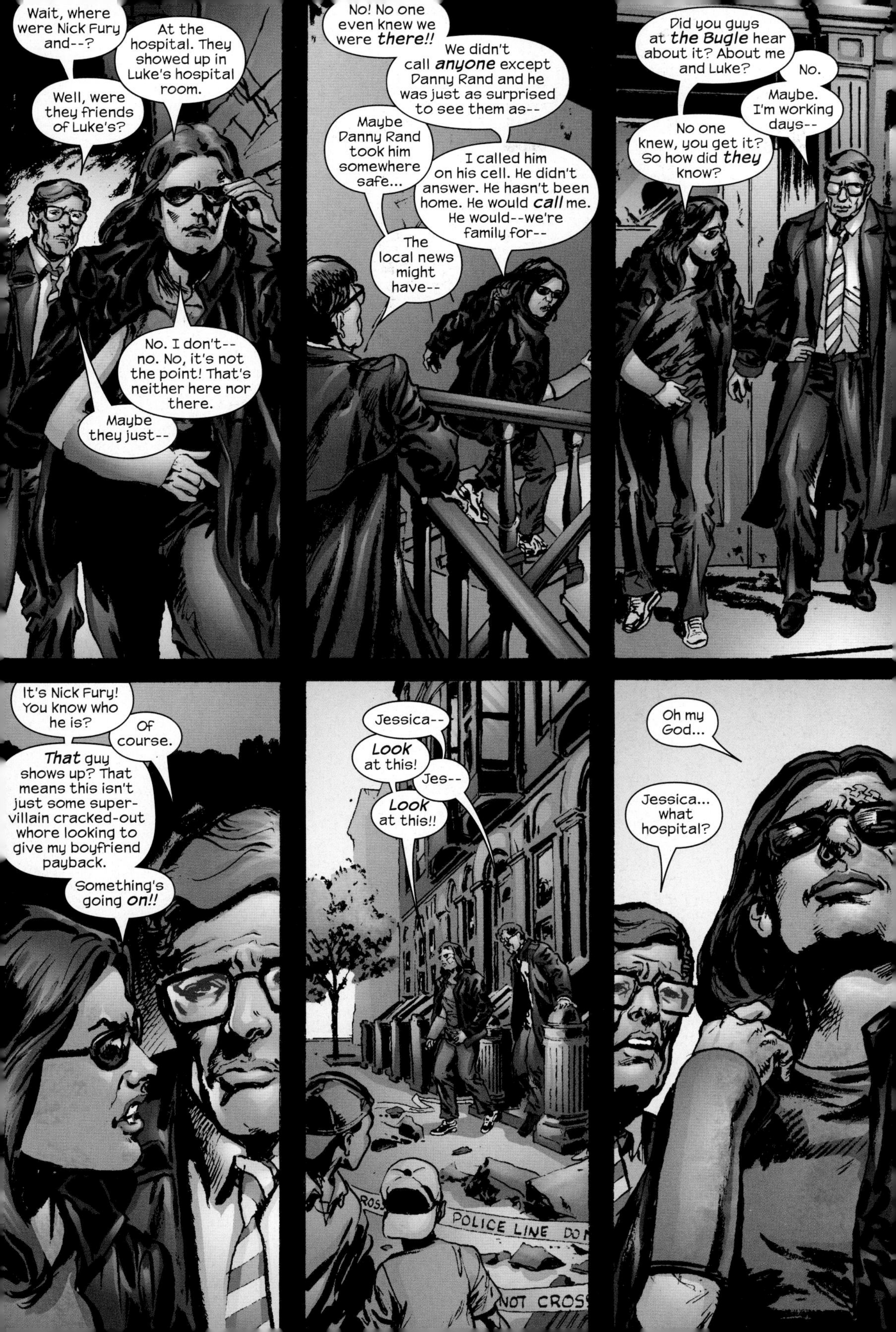

Wait, where were Nick Fury and--?
At the hospital. They showed up in Luke's hospital room.
Well, were they friends of Luke's?
No. I don't-- no. No, it's not the point! That's neither here nor there.
Maybe they just--
No! No one even knew we were *there!!*
We didn't call ***anyone*** except Danny Rand and he was just as surprised to see them as--
Maybe Danny Rand took him somewhere safe...
I called him on his cell. He didn't answer. He hasn't been home. He would ***call*** me. He would--we're family for--
The local news might have--
Did you guys at ***the Bugle*** hear about it? About me and Luke?
No.
Maybe. I'm working days--
No one knew, you get it? So how did ***they*** know?
It's Nick Fury! You know who he is?
Of course.
That guy shows up? That means this isn't just some super-villain cracked-out whore looking to give my boyfriend payback.
Something's going ***on!!***
Jessica--
Look at this!
Jes--
Look at this!!
POLICE LINE DO N
NOT CROSS
Oh my God...
Jessica... what hospital?

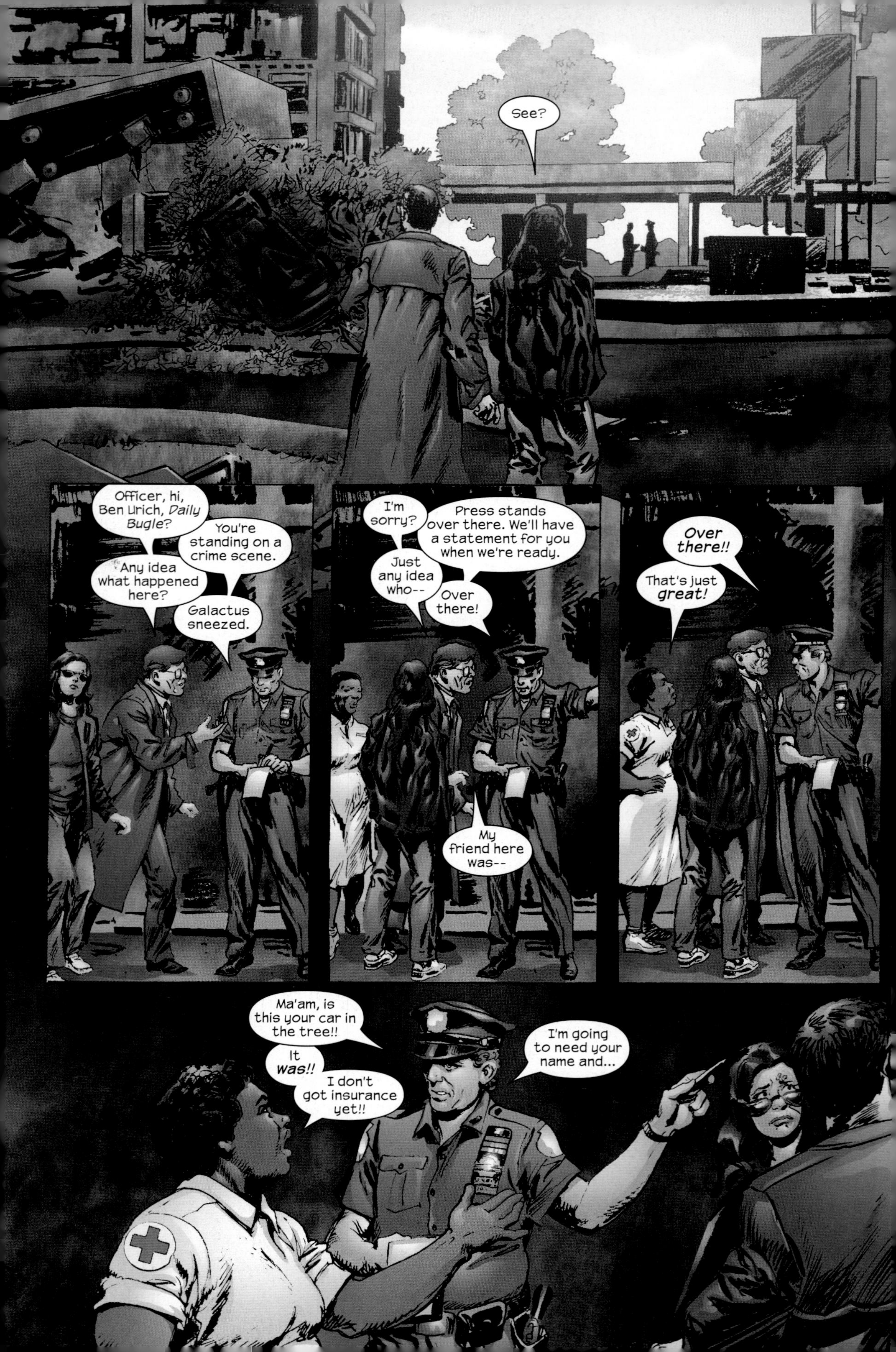
See?
Officer, hi, Ben Urich, *Daily Bugle*?
You're standing on a crime scene.
Any idea what happened here?
Galactus sneezed.
I'm sorry?
Press stands over there. We'll have a statement for you when we're ready.
Just any idea who--
Over there!
My friend here was--
Over there!!
That's just ***great!***
Ma'am, is this your car in the tree!!
It ***was!!***
I don't got insurance yet!!
I'm going to need your name and...

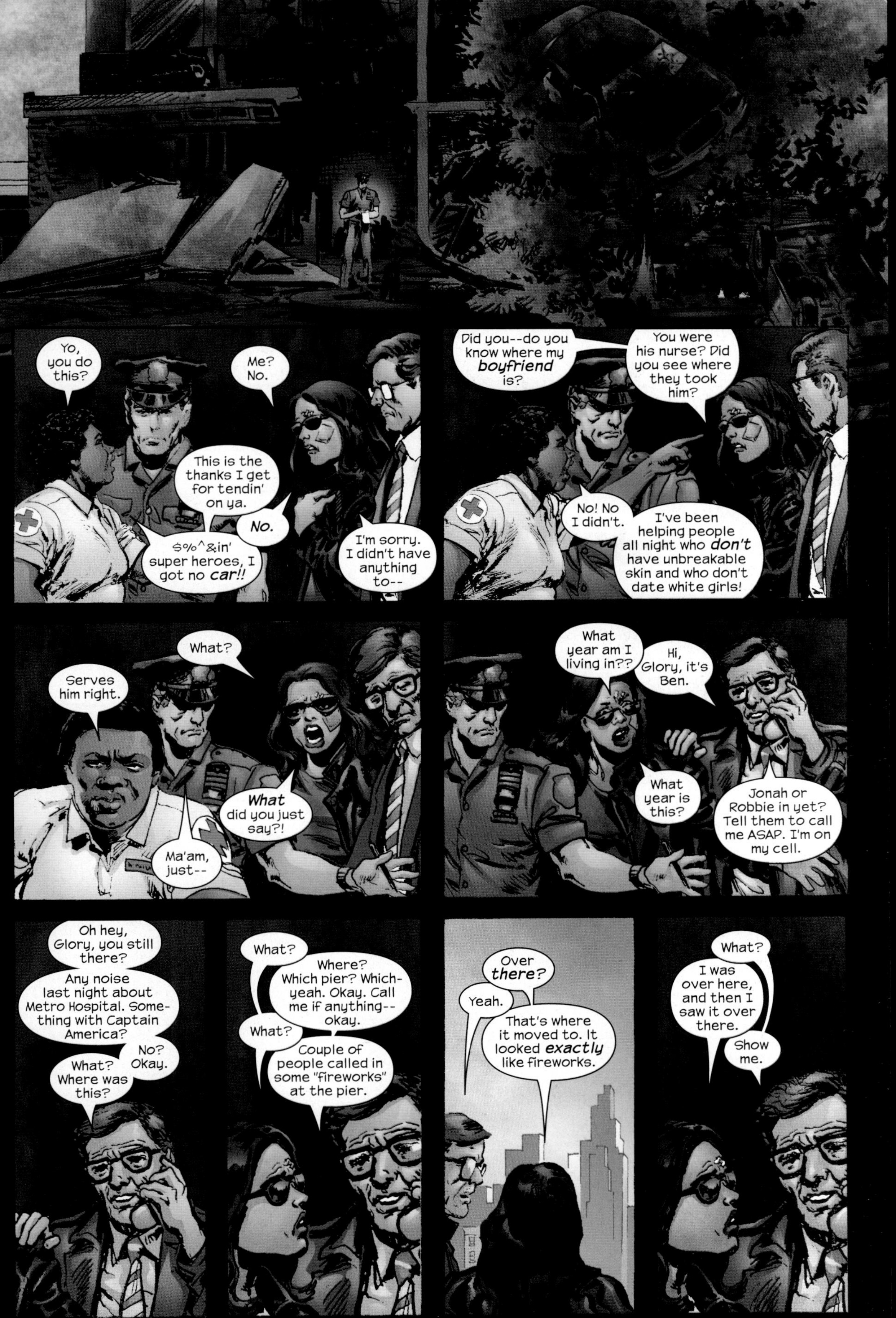
Yo, you do this?
Me? No.
This is the thanks I get for tendin' on ya.
No.
$%^&in' super heroes, I got no car!!
I'm sorry. I didn't have anything to--
Did you--do you know where my boyfriend is?
You were his nurse? Did you see where they took him?
No! No I didn't.
I've been helping people all night who don't have unbreakable skin and who don't date white girls!
Serves him right.
What?
What did you just say?!
Ma'am, just--
What year am I living in??
Hi, Glory, it's Ben.
What year is this?
Jonah or Robbie in yet? Tell them to call me ASAP. I'm on my cell.
Oh hey, Glory, you still there?
Any noise last night about Metro Hospital. Something with Captain America?
No? Okay.
What? Where was this?
What?
Where? Which pier? Which- yeah. Okay. Call me if anything-- okay.
What?
Couple of people called in some "fireworks" at the pier.
Over there?
Yeah.
That's where it moved to. It looked exactly like fireworks.
What?
I was over here, and then I saw it over there.
Show me.

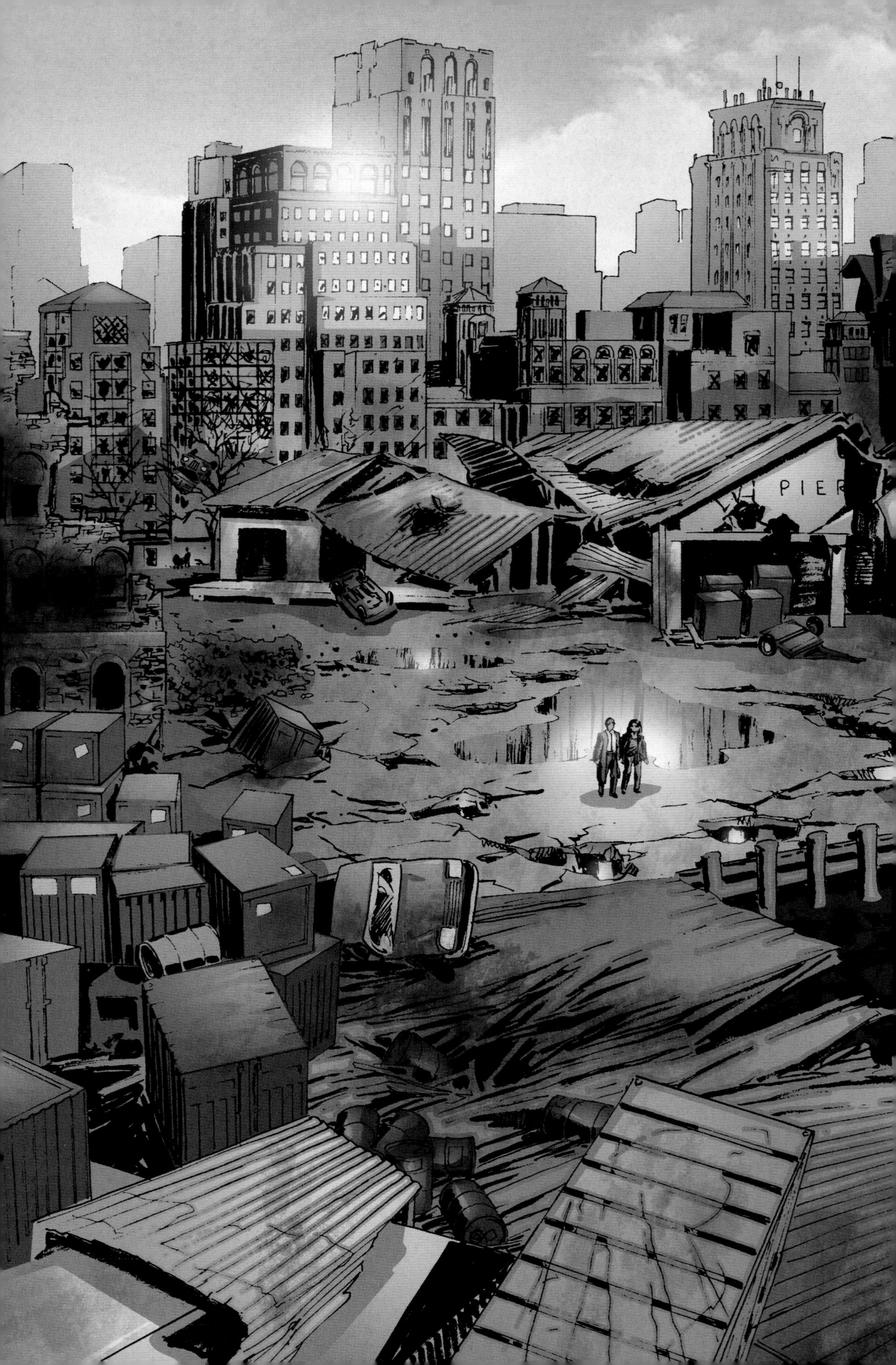
PIER

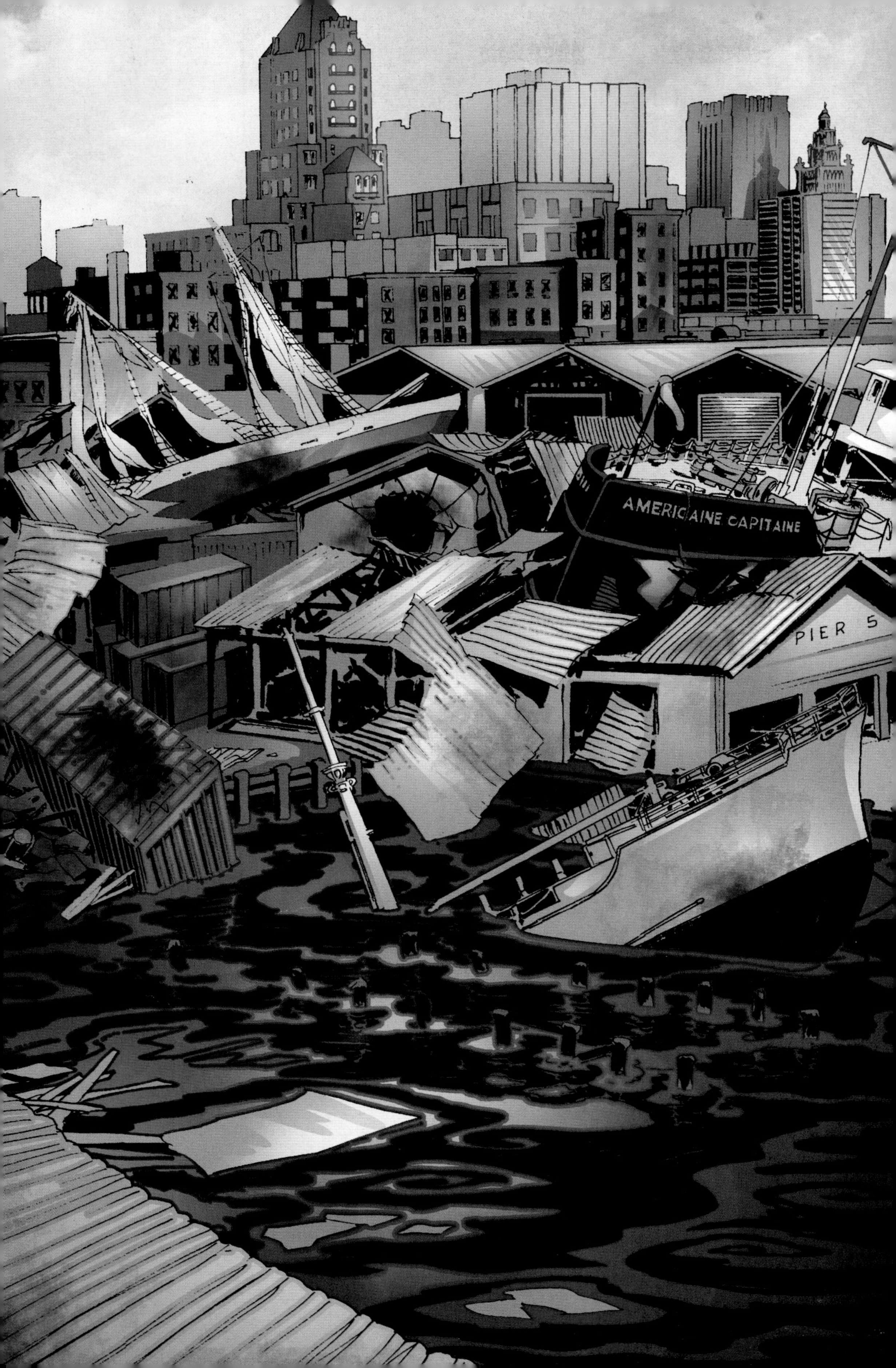
AMERICAINE CAPITAINE
PIER 5

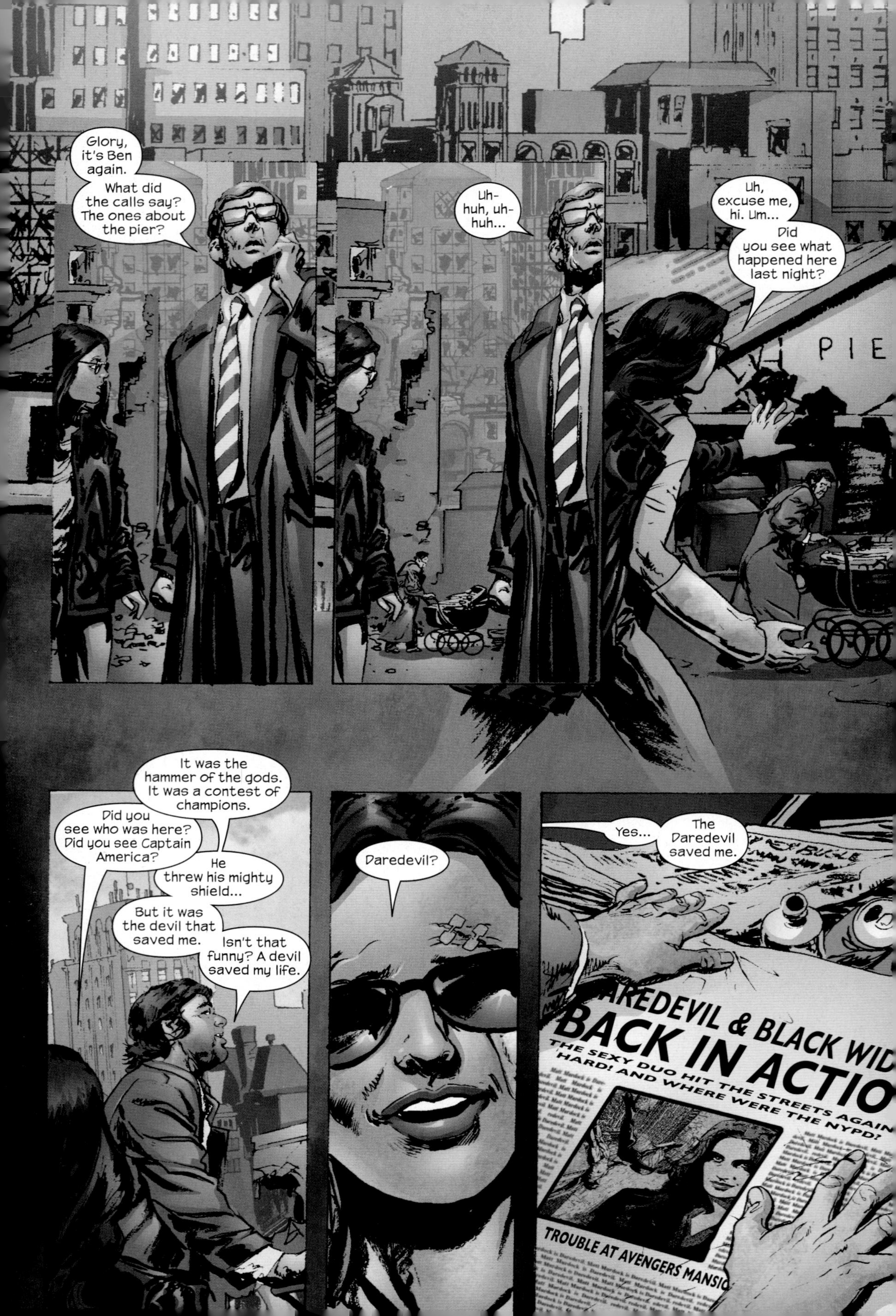

Glory, it's Ben again.
What did the calls say? The ones about the pier?
Uh-huh, uh-huh...
Uh, excuse me, hi. Um...
Did you see what happened here last night?
PIE
It was the hammer of the gods. It was a contest of champions.
Did you see who was here? Did you see Captain America?
He threw his mighty shield...
But it was the devil that saved me.
Isn't that funny? A devil saved my life.
Daredevil?
Yes...
The Daredevil saved me.
AREDEVIL & BLACK WID
BACK IN ACTIO
THE SEXY DUO HIT THE STREETS AGAIN HARD! AND WHERE WERE THE NYPD?
TROUBLE AT AVENGERS MANSIO

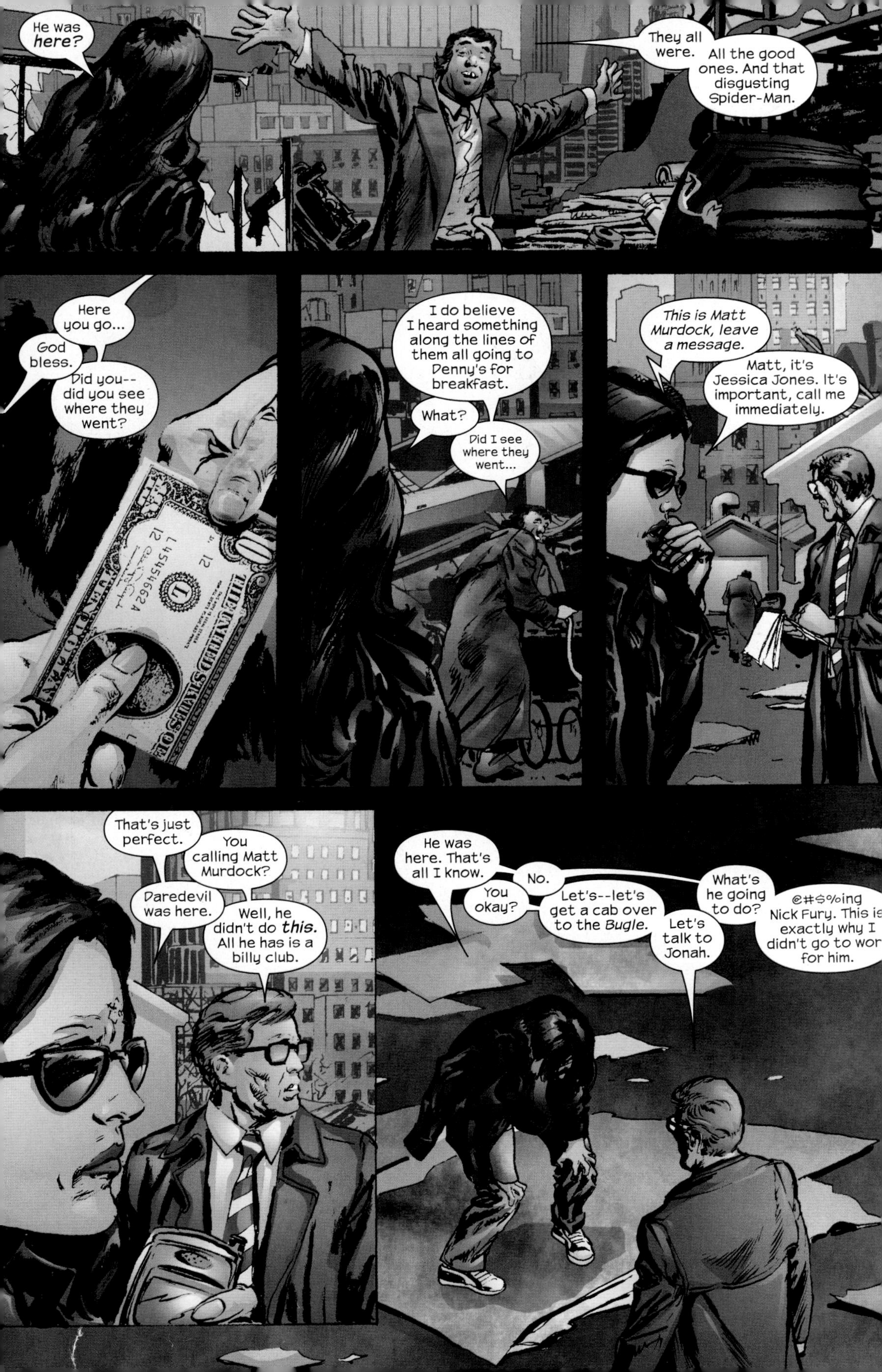

He was *here?*
They all were.
All the good ones. And that disgusting Spider-Man.
Here you go...
God bless.
Did you-- did you see where they went?
I do believe I heard something along the lines of them all going to Denny's for breakfast.
What?
Did I see where they went...
This is Matt Murdock, leave a message.
Matt, it's Jessica Jones. It's important, call me immediately.
That's just perfect.
You calling Matt Murdock?
Daredevil was here.
Well, he didn't do *this.* All he has is a billy club.
He was here. That's all I know.
No.
You okay?
Let's--let's get a cab over to the *Bugle.*
What's he going to do?
Let's talk to Jonah.
@#$%ing Nick Fury. This is exactly why I didn't go to work for him.

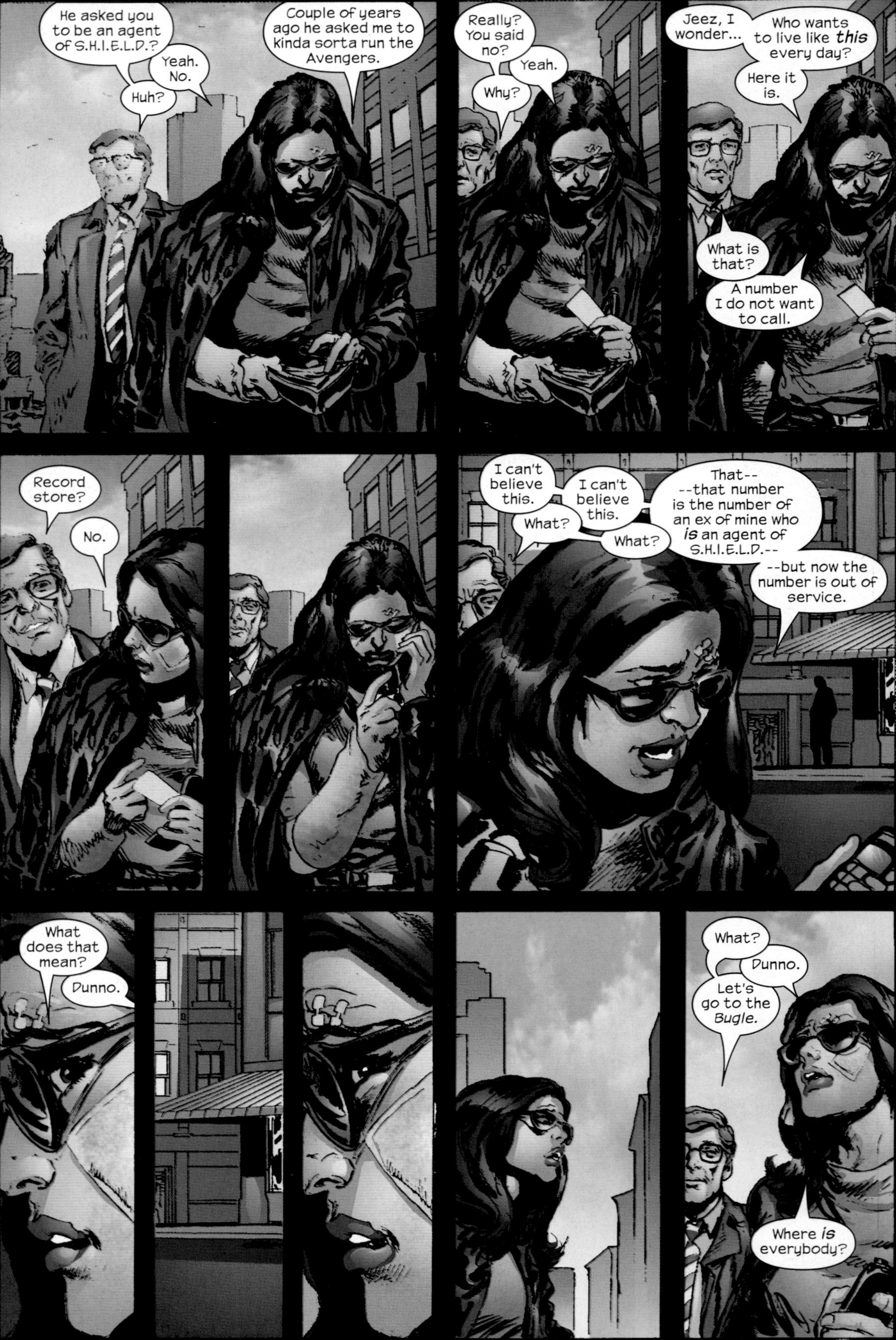
He asked you to be an agent of S.H.I.E.L.D.?
Yeah. No.
Huh?
Couple of years ago he asked me to kinda sorta run the Avengers.
Really? You said no?
Yeah.
Why?
Jeez, I wonder...
Who wants to live like *this* every day?
Here it is.
What is that?
A number I do not want to call.
Record store?
No.
I can't believe this.
I can't believe this.
What?
What?
That--
--that number is the number of an ex of mine who *is* an agent of S.H.I.E.L.D.--
--but now the number is out of service.
What does that mean?
Dunno.
What?
Dunno.
Let's go to the *Bugle*.
Where *is* everybody?

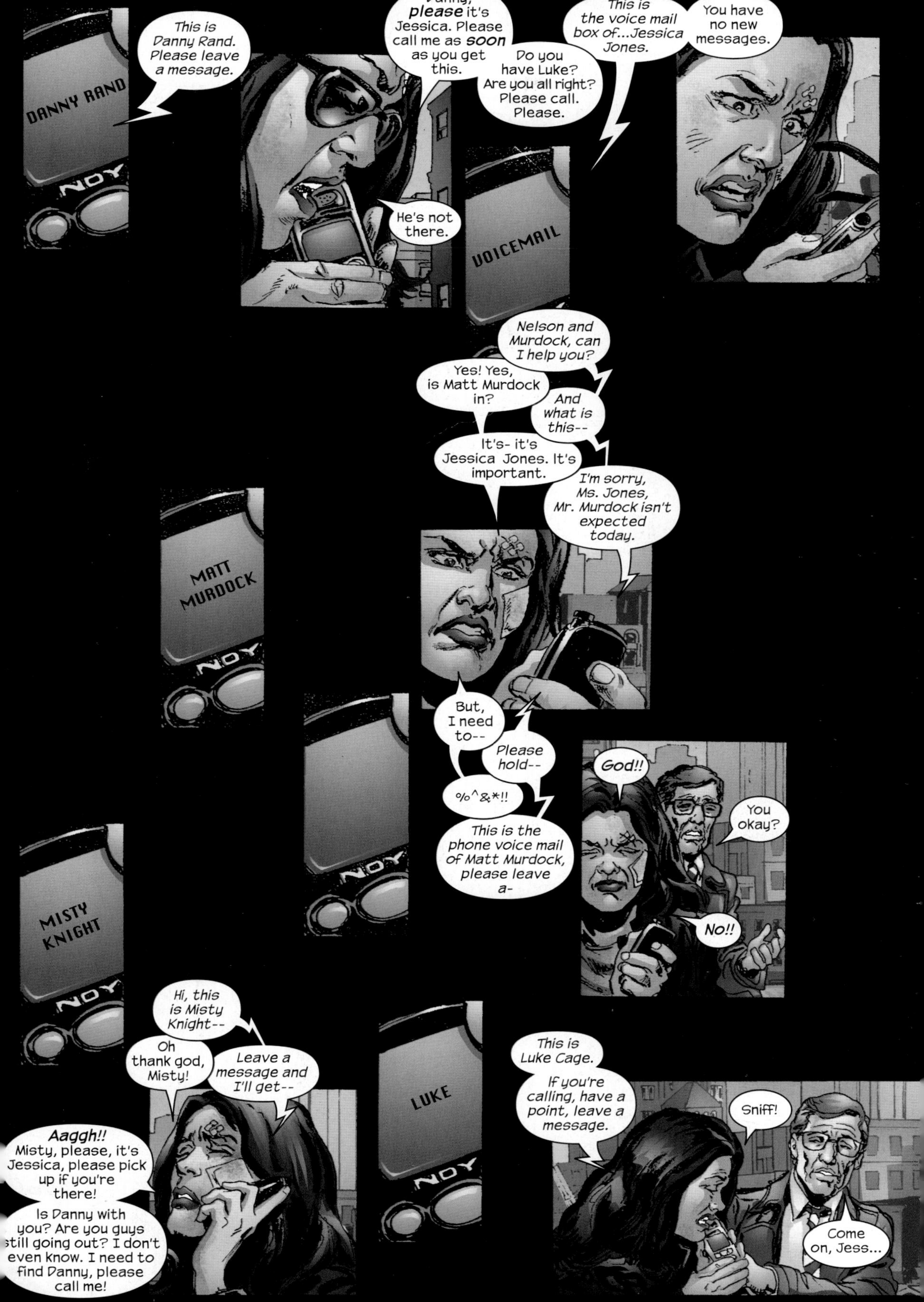
This is Danny Rand. Please leave a message.
DANNY RAND
NOY
Danny, please it's Jessica. Please call me as soon as you get this.
He's not there.
Do you have Luke? Are you all right? Please call. Please.
VOICEMAIL
This is the voice mail box of...Jessica Jones.
You have no new messages.
Nelson and Murdock, can I help you?
Yes! Yes, is Matt Murdock in?
And what is this--
It's- it's Jessica Jones. It's important.
I'm sorry, Ms. Jones, Mr. Murdock isn't expected today.
MATT MURDOCK
NOY
But, I need to--
Please hold--
%^&*!!
This is the phone voice mail of Matt Murdock, please leave a-
NOY
God!!
You okay?
No!!
MISTY KNIGHT
NOY
Hi, this is Misty Knight--
Oh thank god, Misty!
Leave a message and I'll get--
Aaggh!! Misty, please, it's Jessica, please pick up if you're there!
Is Danny with you? Are you guys still going out? I don't even know. I need to find Danny, please call me!
LUKE
NOY
This is Luke Cage.
If you're calling, have a point, leave a message.
Sniff!
Come on, Jess...

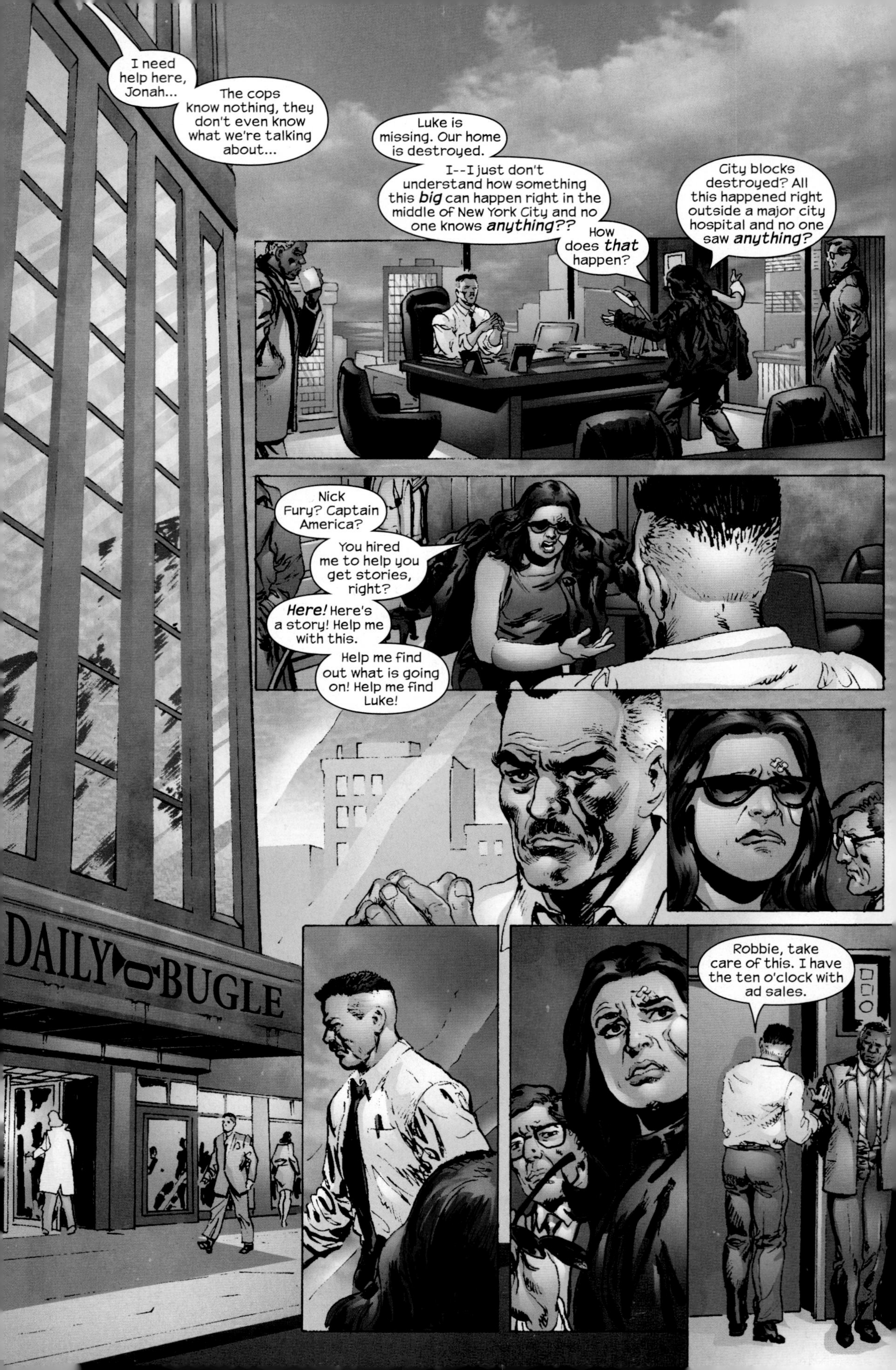
I need help here, Jonah...
The cops know nothing, they don't even know what we're talking about...
Luke is missing. Our home is destroyed.
I--I just don't understand how something this *big* can happen right in the middle of New York City and no one knows *anything*??
How does *that* happen?
City blocks destroyed? All this happened right outside a major city hospital and no one saw *anything*?
Nick Fury? Captain America?
You hired me to help you get stories, right?
Here! Here's a story! Help me with this.
Help me find out what is going on! Help me find Luke!
DAILY BUGLE
Robbie, take care of this. I have the ten o'clock with ad sales.

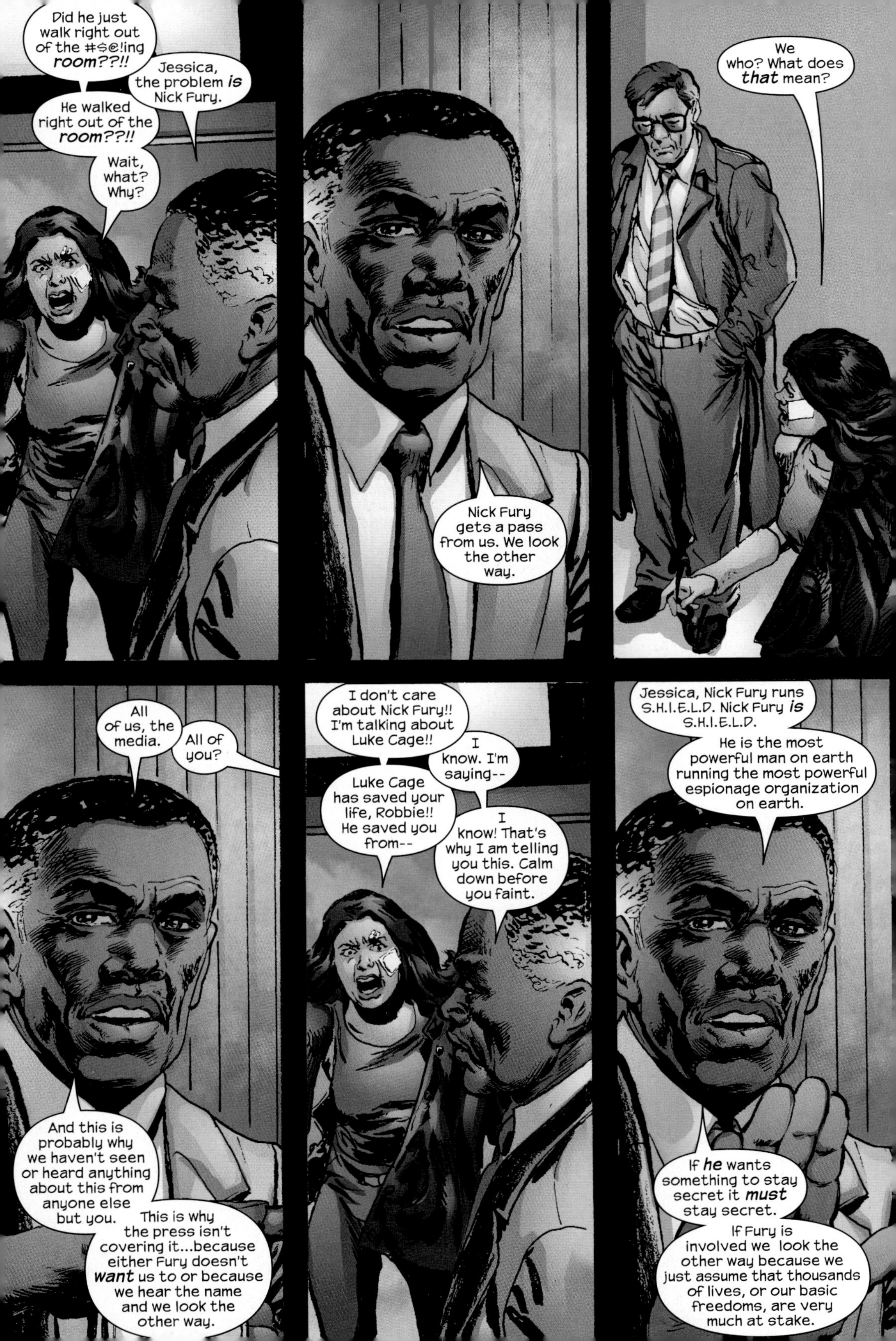

Did he just walk right out of the #$@!ing room??!!
Jessica, the problem is Nick Fury.
He walked right out of the room??!!
Wait, what? Why?
Nick Fury gets a pass from us. We look the other way.
We who? What does that mean?
All of us, the media.
All of you?
And this is probably why we haven't seen or heard anything about this from anyone else but you.
This is why the press isn't covering it...because either Fury doesn't want us to or because we hear the name and we look the other way.
I don't care about Nick Fury!! I'm talking about Luke Cage!!
I know. I'm saying--
Luke Cage has saved your life, Robbie!! He saved you from--
I know! That's why I am telling you this. Calm down before you faint.
Jessica, Nick Fury runs S.H.I.E.L.D. Nick Fury is S.H.I.E.L.D.
He is the most powerful man on earth running the most powerful espionage organization on earth.
If he wants something to stay secret it must stay secret.
If Fury is involved we look the other way because we just assume that thousands of lives, or our basic freedoms, are very much at stake.

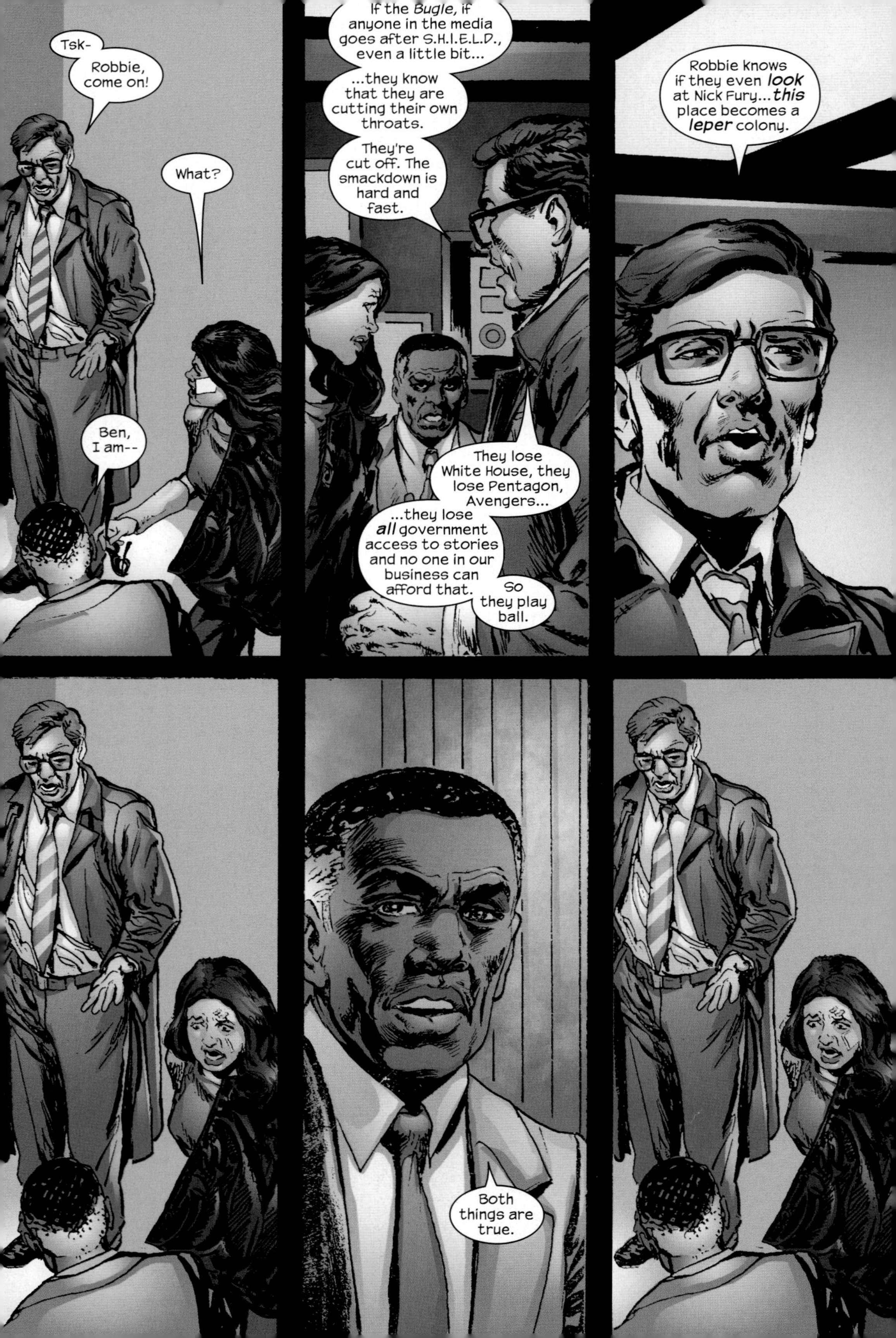
Tsk-
Robbie, come on!
What?
Ben, I am--
If the *Bugle,* if anyone in the media goes after S.H.I.E.L.D., even a little bit...
...they know that they are cutting their own throats.
They're cut off. The smackdown is hard and fast.
They lose White House, they lose Pentagon, Avengers...
...they lose *all* government access to stories and no one in our business can afford that.
So they play ball.
Robbie knows if they even *look* at Nick Fury...*this* place becomes a *leper* colony.
Both things are true.

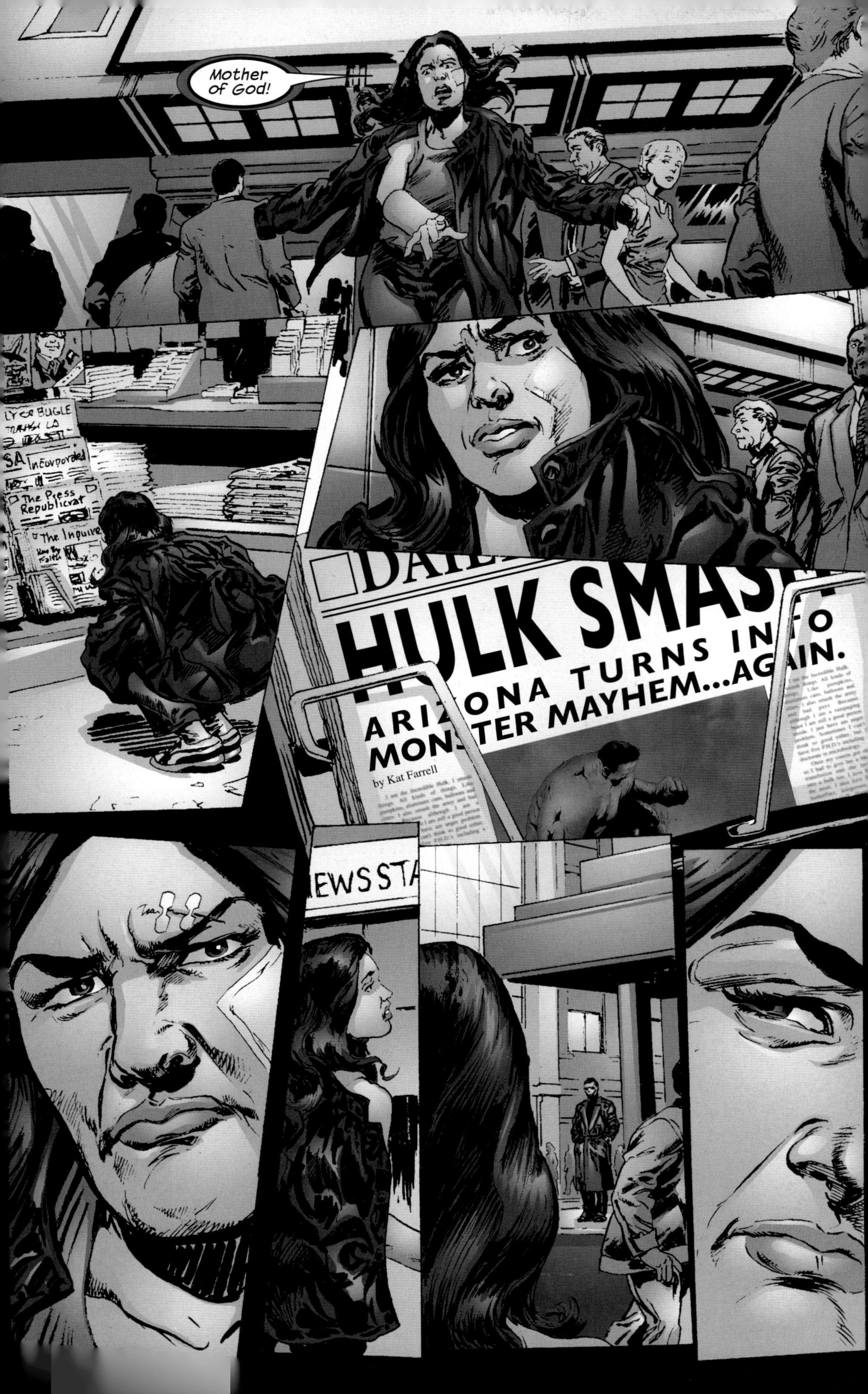

Mother of God!
BUGLE
The Press Republicrat
The Inquire
DAIL
HULK SMAS
ARIZONA TURNS INTO MONSTER MAYHEM...AGAIN.
by Kat Farrell
EWS STA

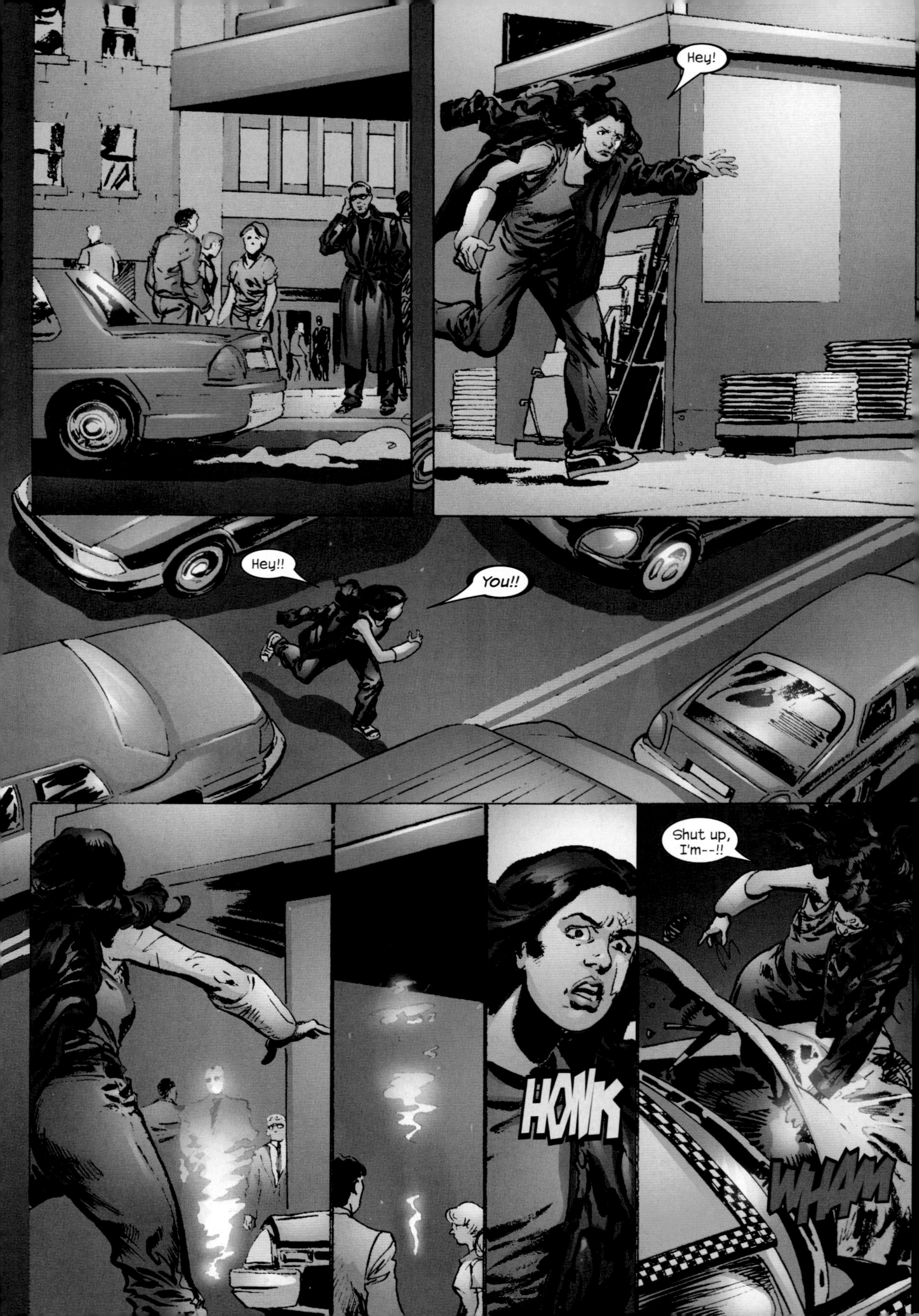
Hey!
Hey!!
You!!
Shut up, I'm--!!
HONK
WHAM

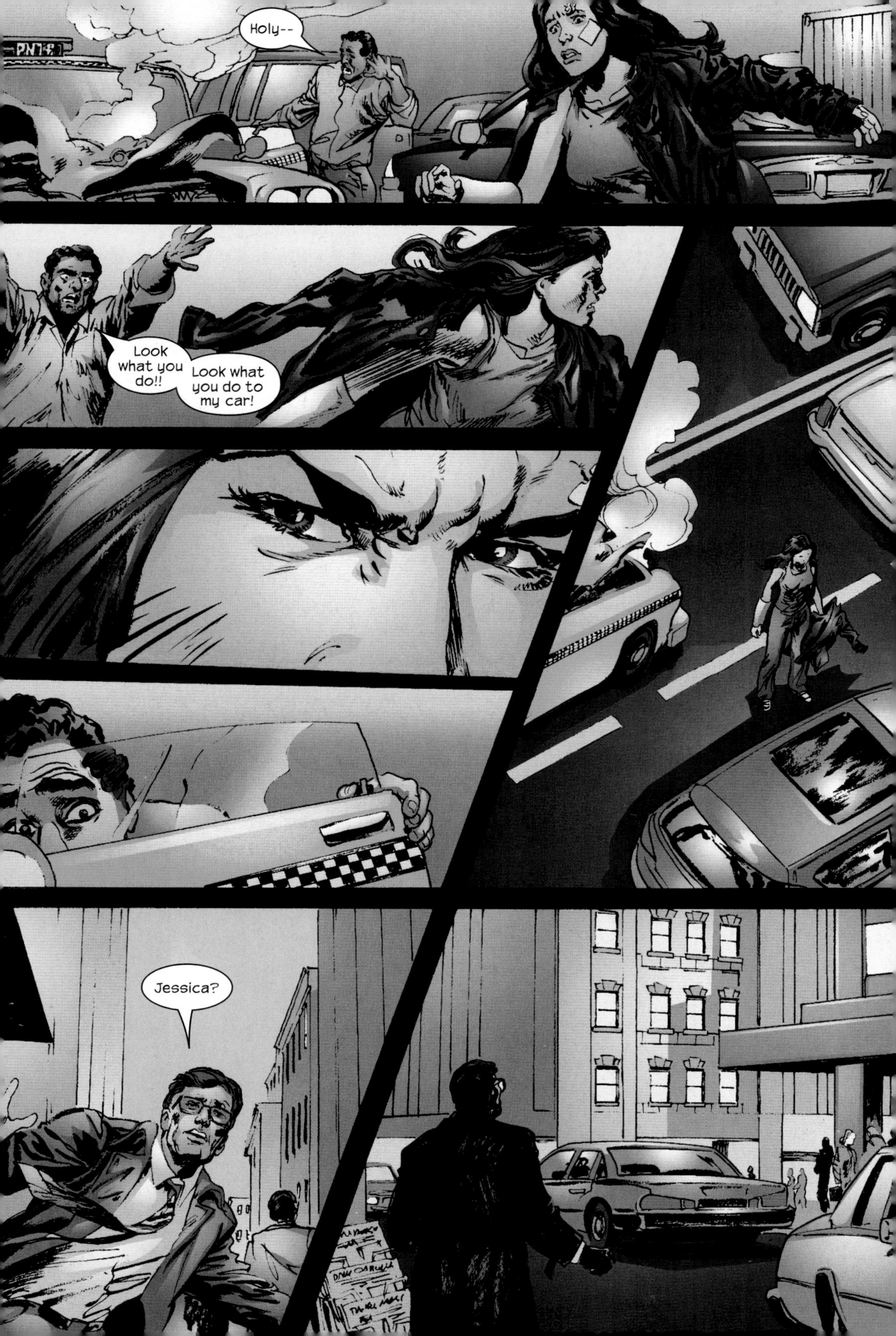
Holy--
Look what you do!!
Look what you do to my car!
Jessica?

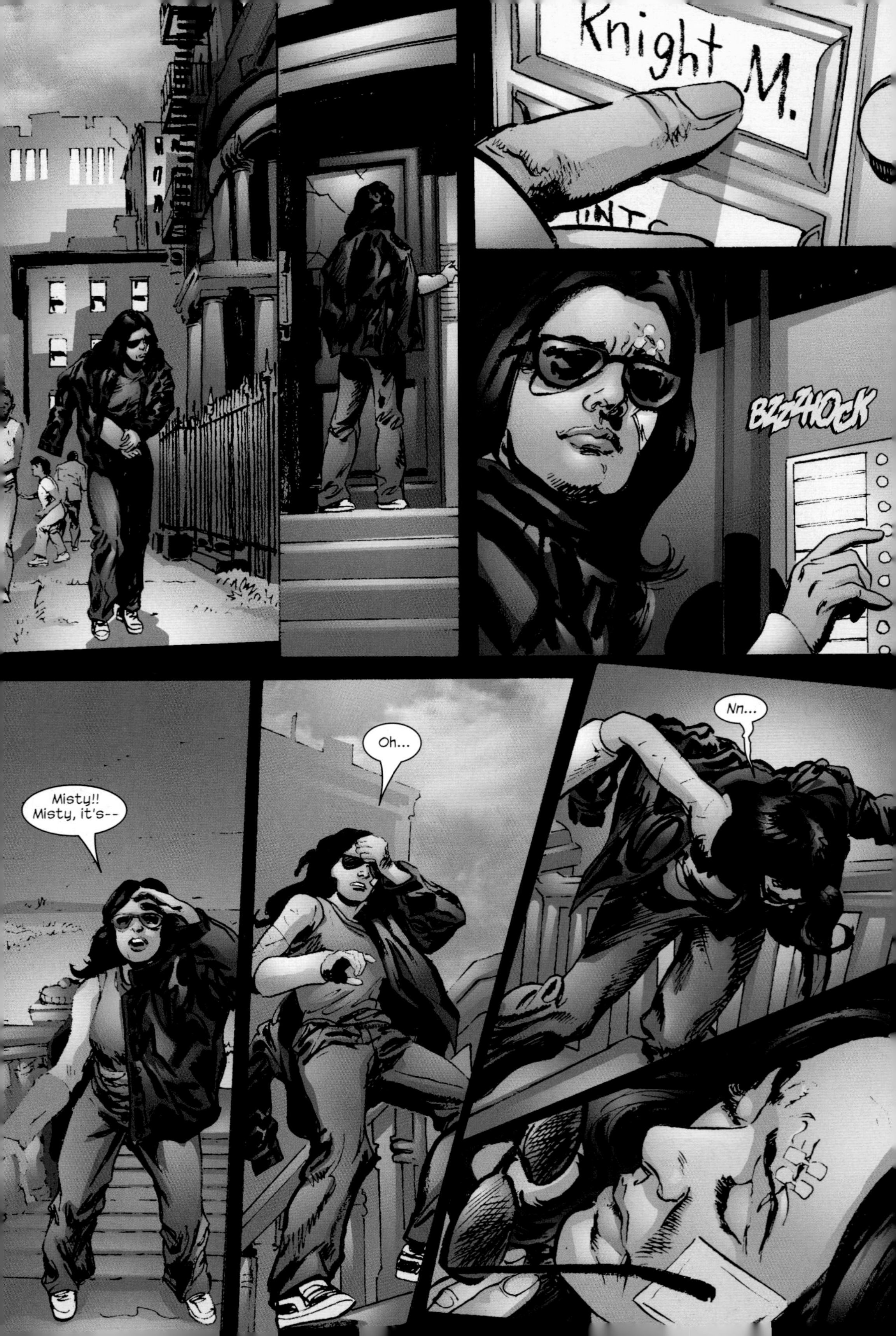
Knight M.
BZZHOCK
Misty!! Misty, it's--
Oh...
Nn...

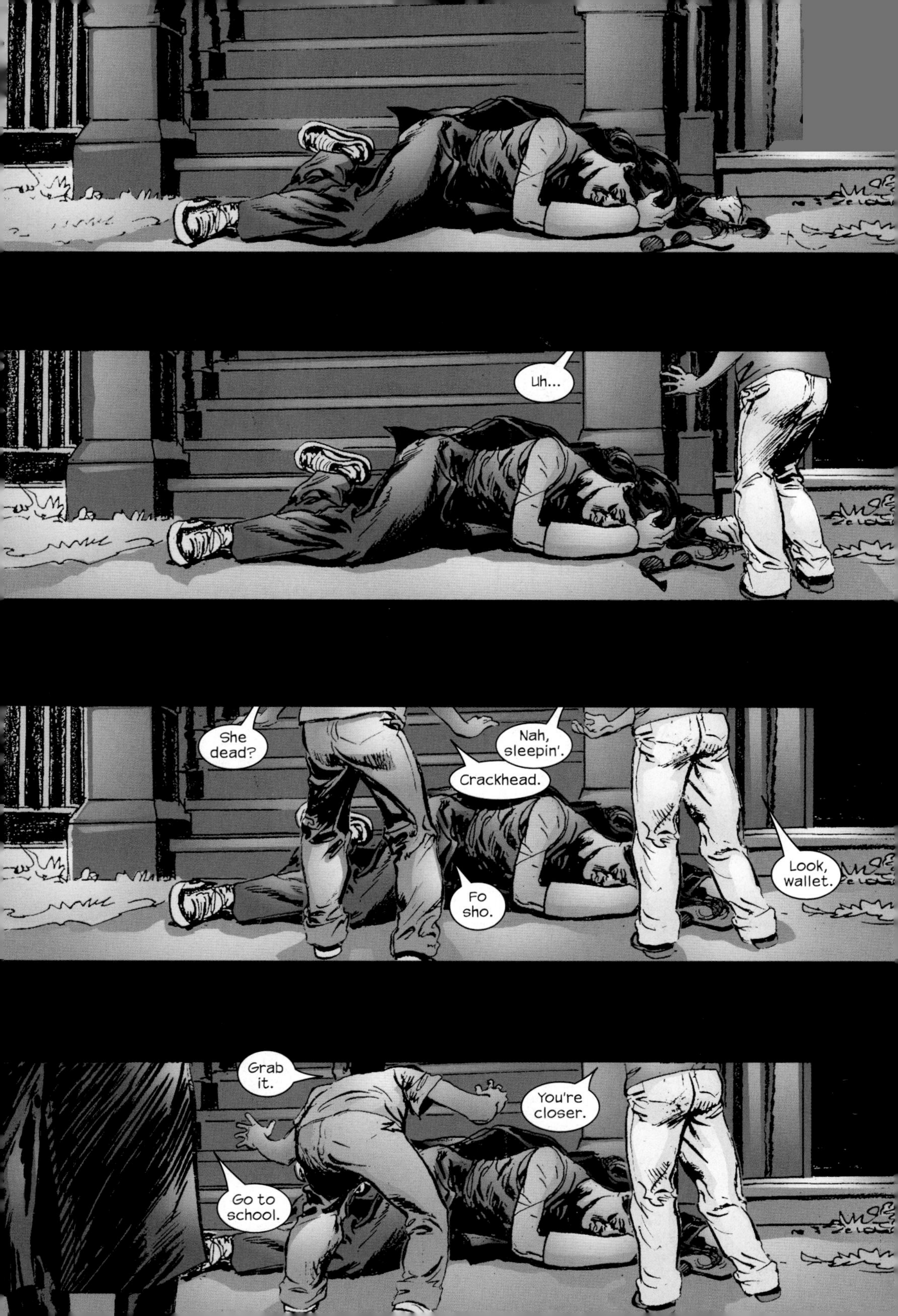
Uh...
She dead?
Nah, sleepin'.
Crackhead.
Fo sho.
Look, wallet.
Grab it.
You're closer.
Go to school.

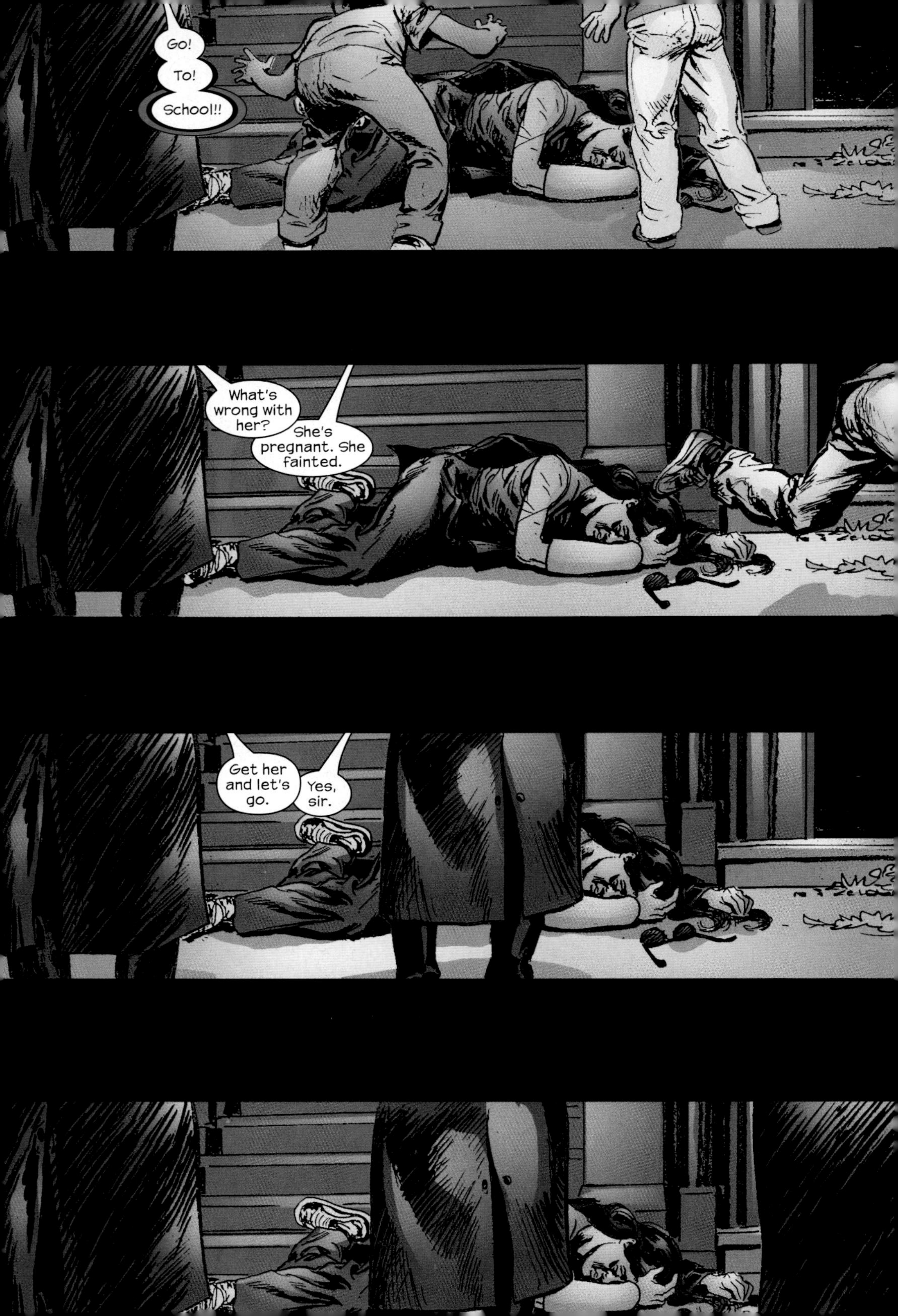
Go!
To!
School!!
What's wrong with her?
She's pregnant. She fainted.
Get her and let's go.
Yes, sir.

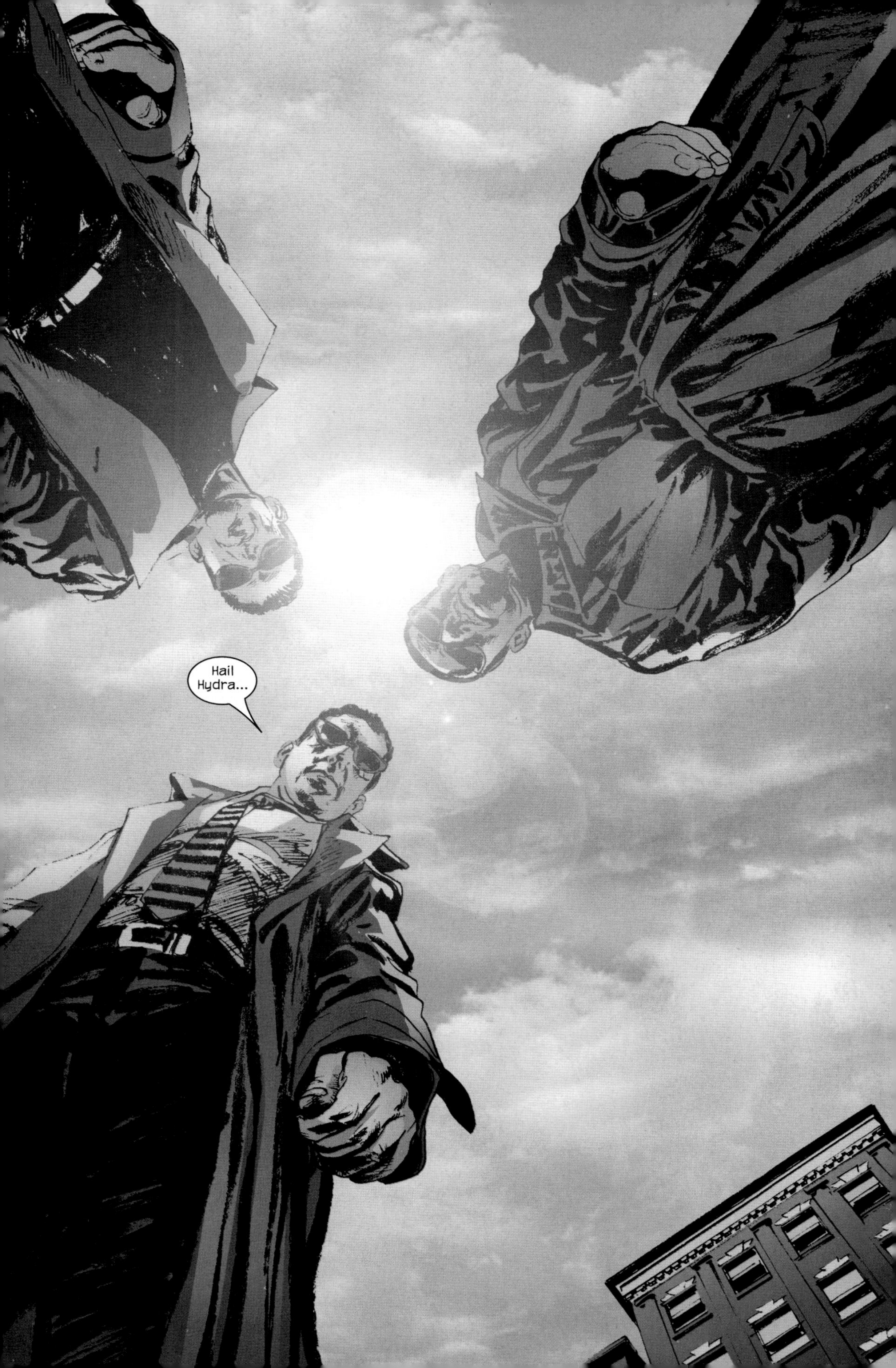
Hail Hydra...

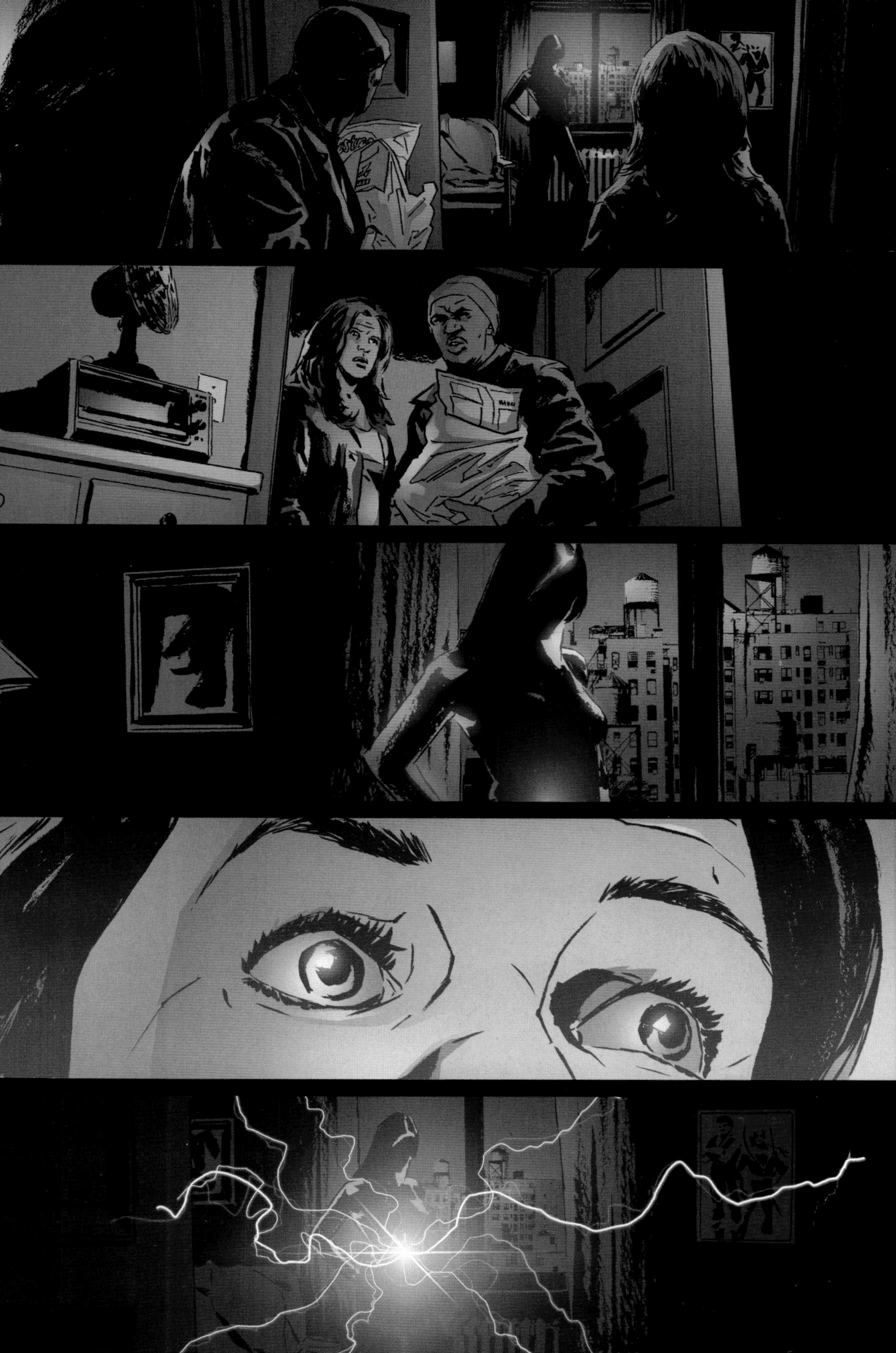

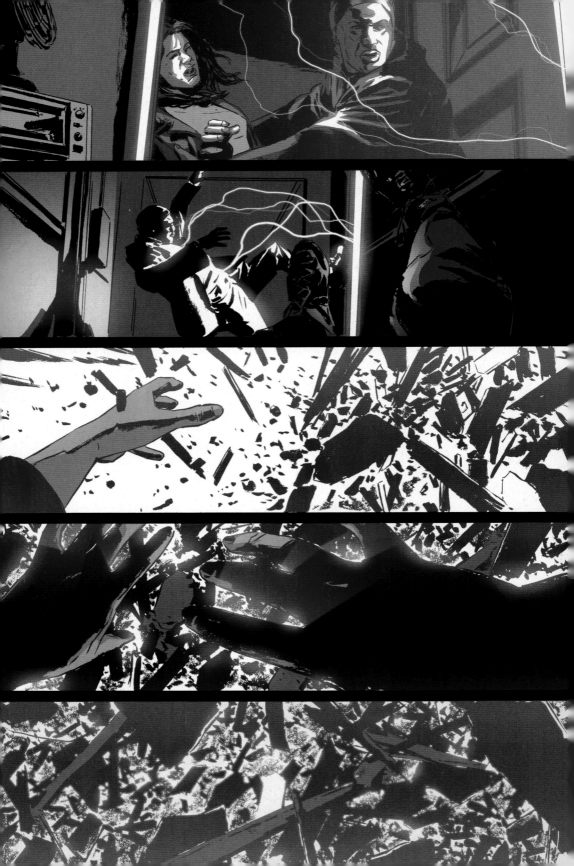

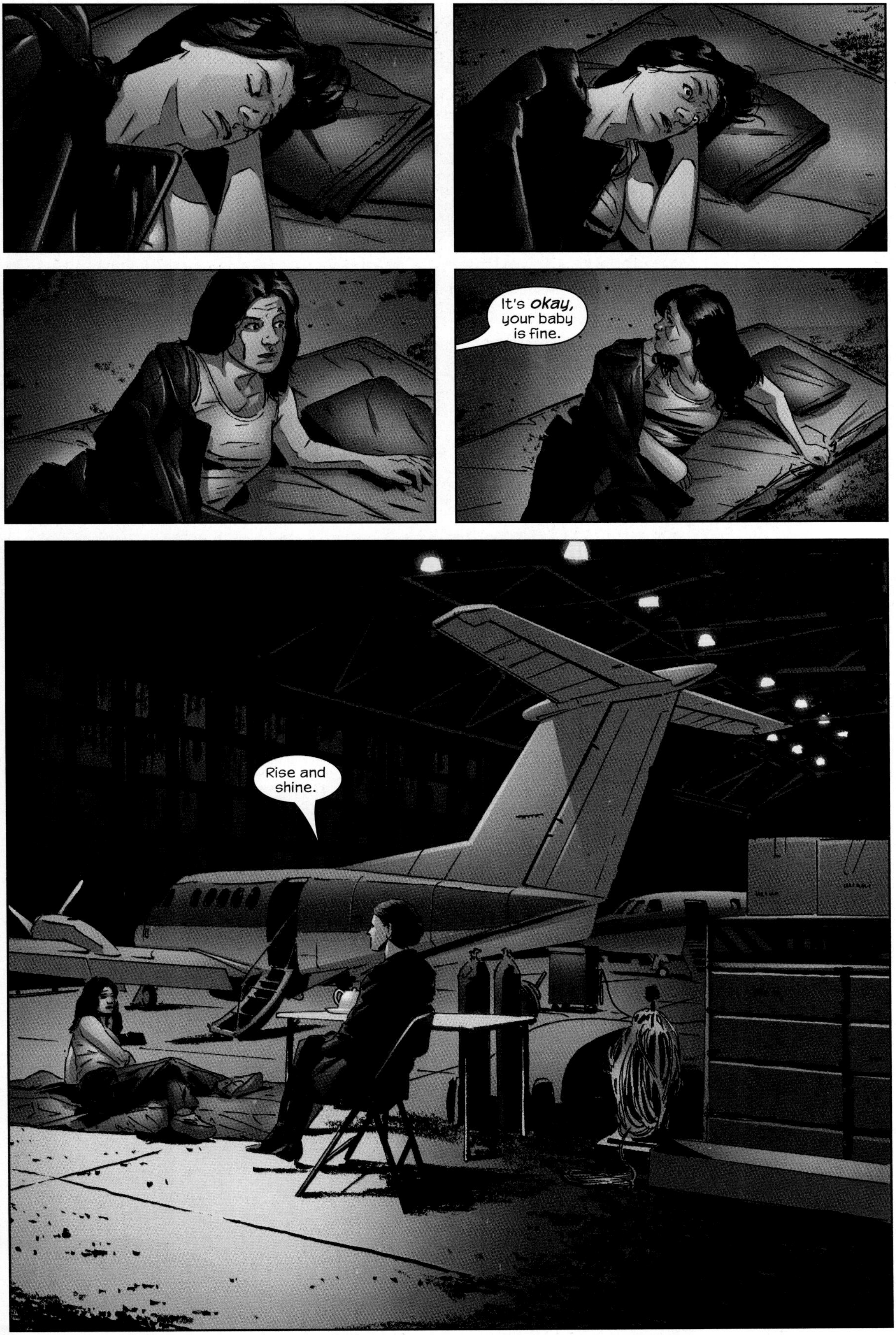
It's *okay,* your baby is fine.
Rise and shine.

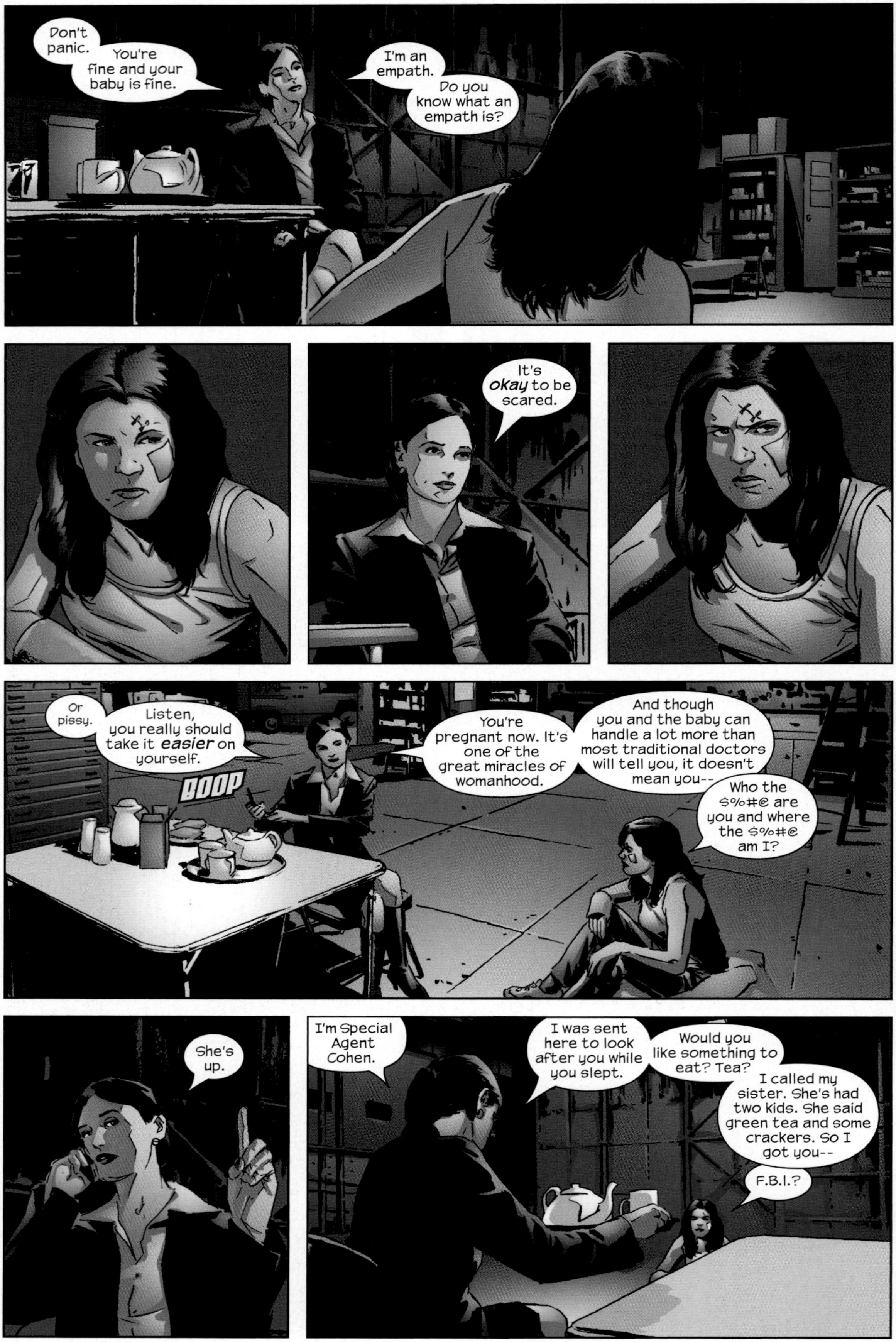

Don't panic.
You're fine and your baby is fine.
I'm an empath.
Do you know what an empath is?
It's *okay* to be scared.
Or pissy.
Listen, you really should take it *easier* on yourself.
BOOP
You're pregnant now. It's one of the great miracles of womanhood.
And though you and the baby can handle a lot more than most traditional doctors will tell you, it doesn't mean you--
Who the $%#@ are you and where the $%#@ am I?
She's up.
I'm Special Agent Cohen.
I was sent here to look after you while you slept.
Would you like something to eat? Tea?
I called my sister. She's had two kids. She said green tea and some crackers. So I got you--
F.B.I.?

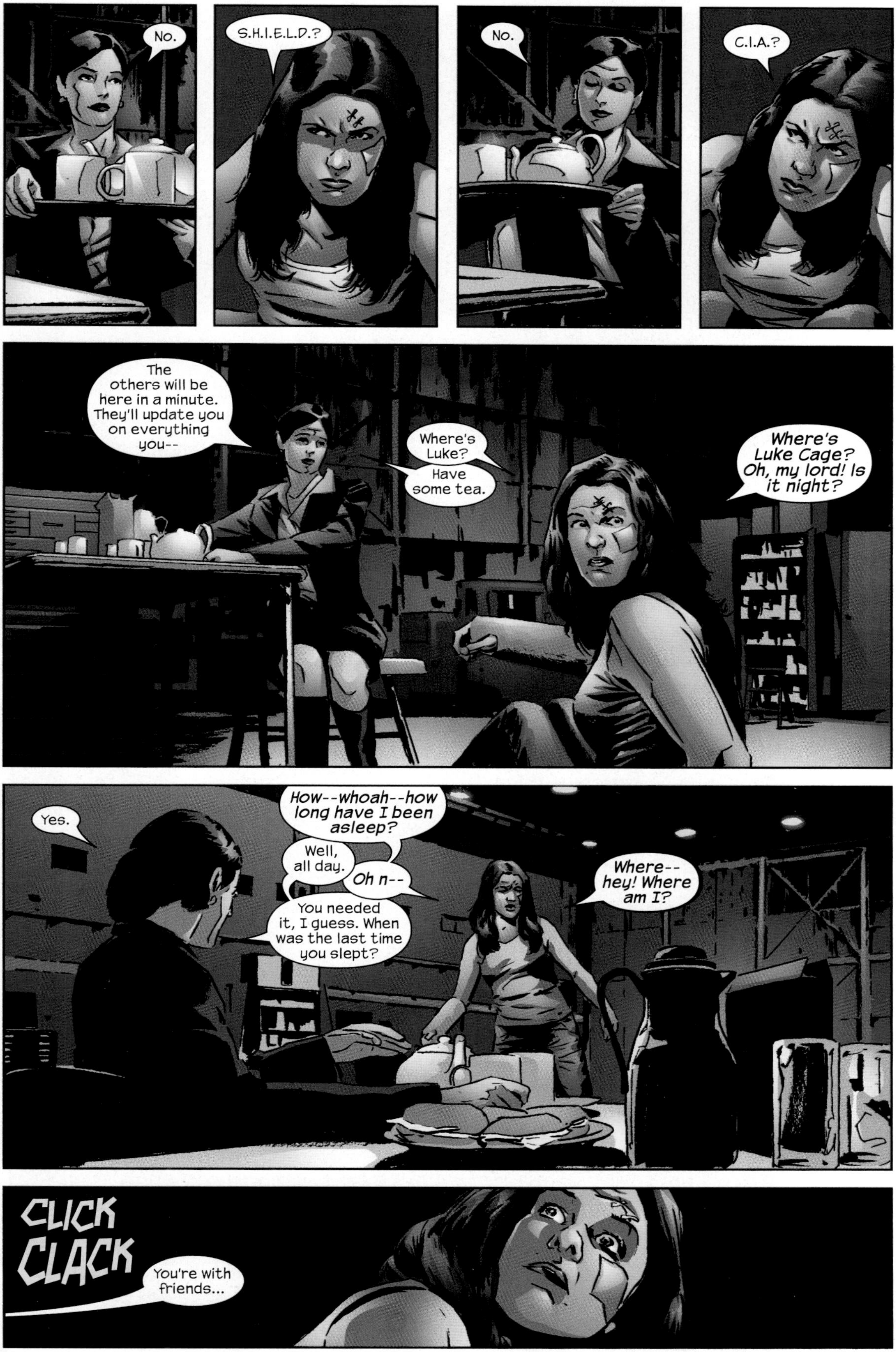

No.
S.H.I.E.L.D.?
No.
C.I.A.?
The others will be here in a minute. They'll update you on everything you--
Where's Luke?
Have some tea.
Where's Luke Cage? Oh, my lord! Is it night?
Yes.
How--whoah--how long have I been asleep?
Well, all day.
Oh n--
You needed it, I guess. When was the last time you slept?
Where--hey! Where am I?
CLICK
CLACK
You're with friends...

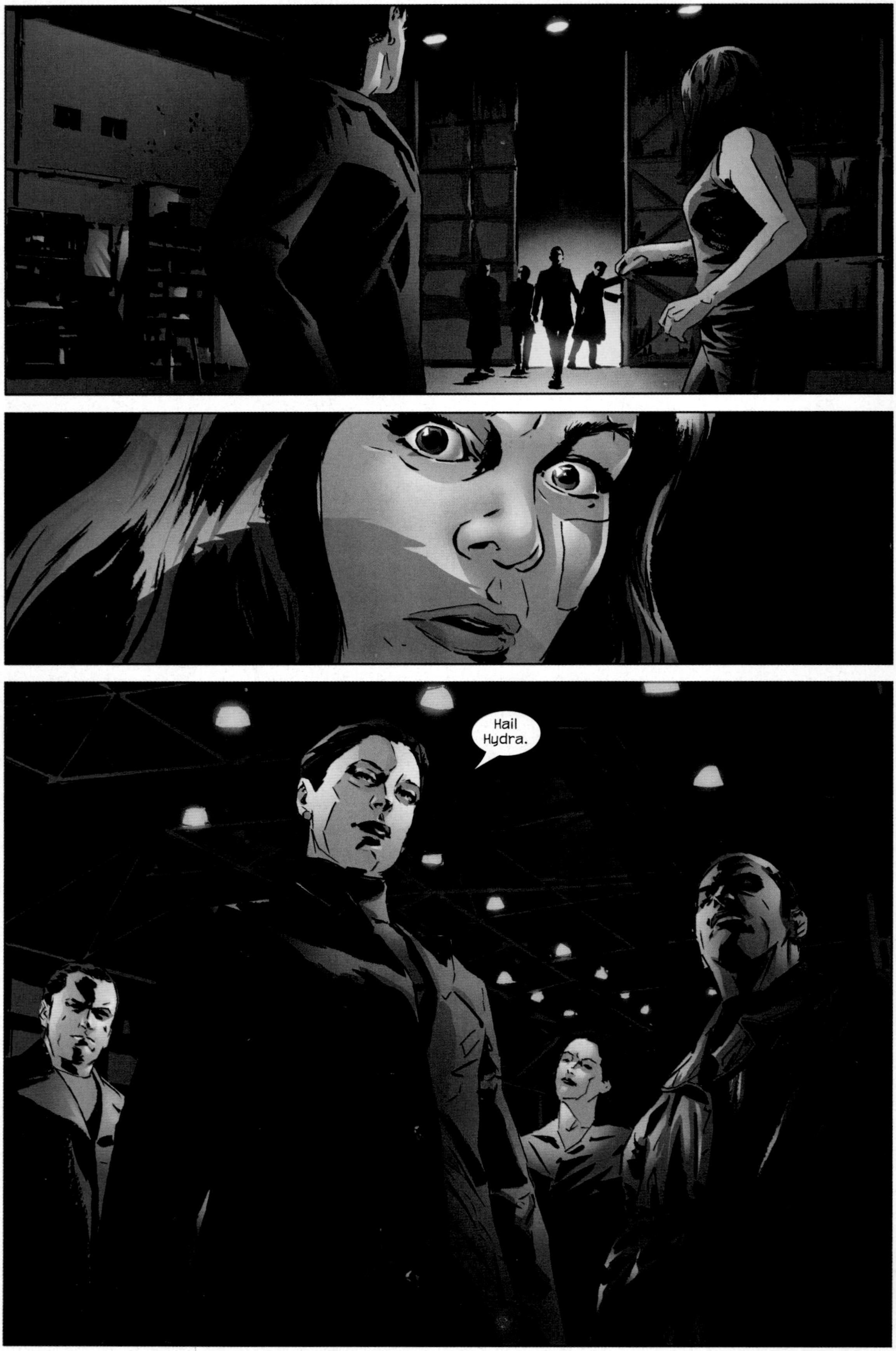
Hail Hydra.

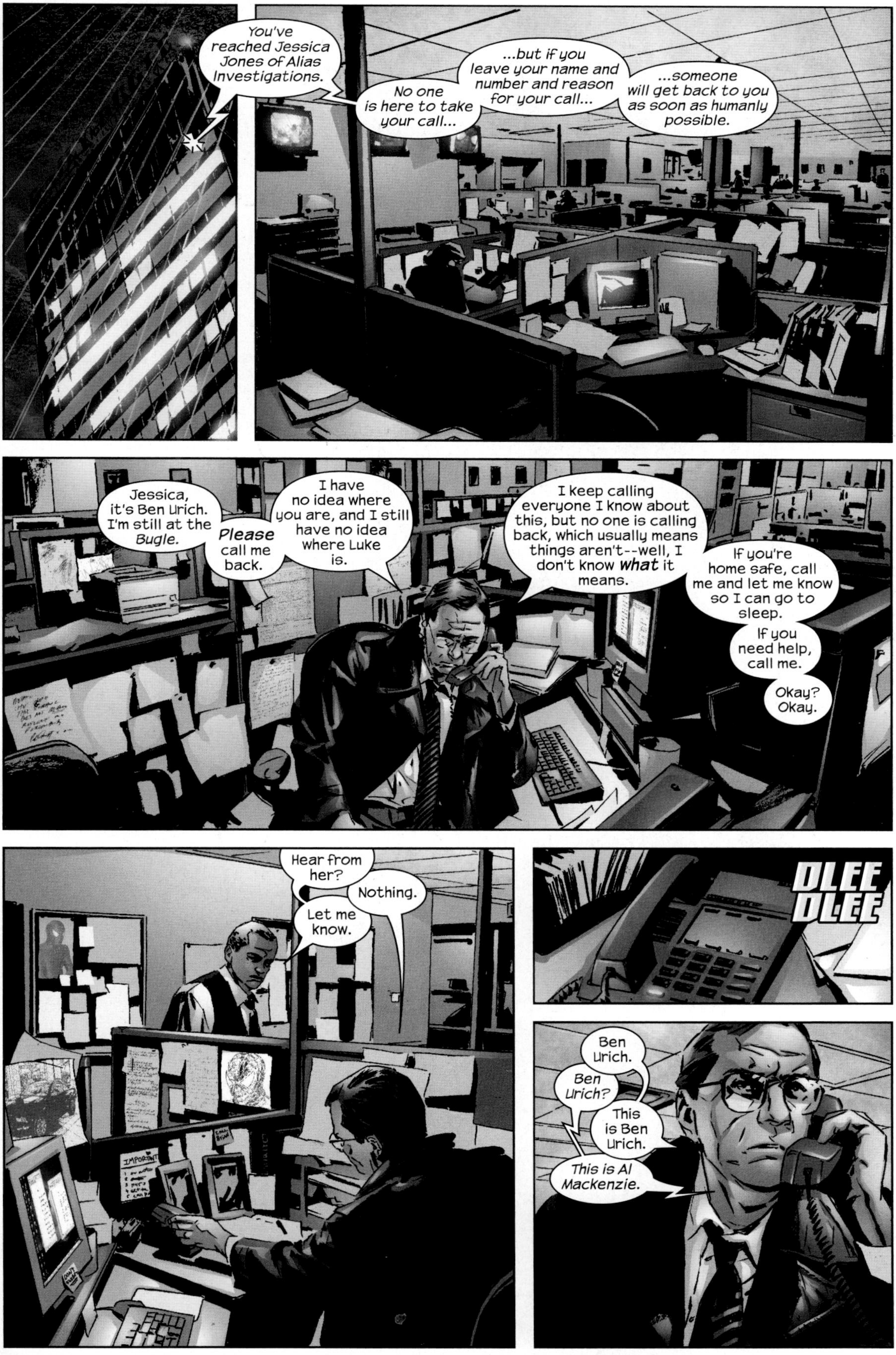
You've reached Jessica Jones of Alias Investigations.
No one is here to take your call...
...but if you leave your name and number and reason for your call...
...someone will get back to you as soon as humanly possible.
Jessica, it's Ben Urich. I'm still at the Bugle.
Please call me back.
I have no idea where you are, and I still have no idea where Luke is.
I keep calling everyone I know about this, but no one is calling back, which usually means things aren't--well, I don't know what it means.
If you're home safe, call me and let me know so I can go to sleep.
If you need help, call me.
Okay? Okay.
Hear from her?
Nothing.
Let me know.
DLEE DLEE
Ben Urich.
Ben Urich?
This is Ben Urich.
This is Al Mackenzie.

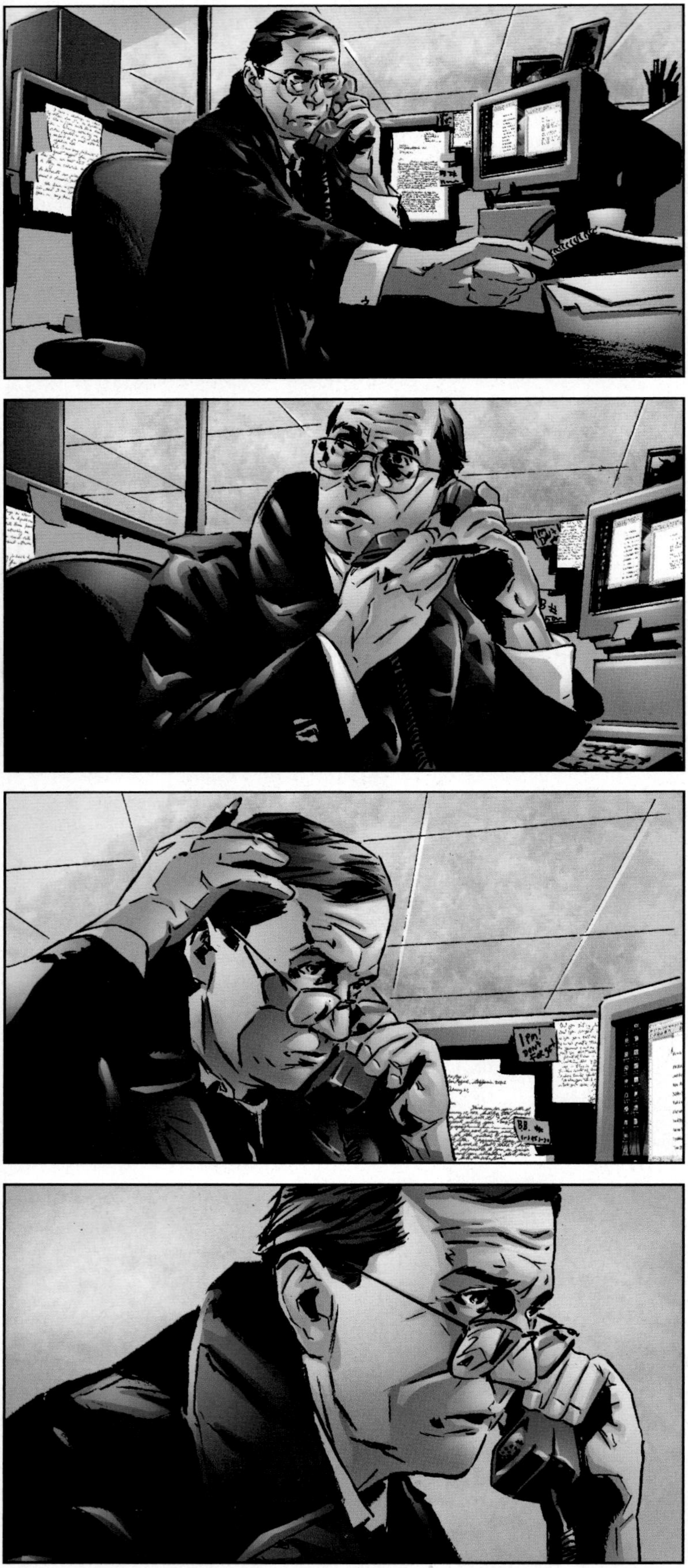

Ben: I'm sorry, I don't--

Al: Hmm, don't know how best to put this...

Al: ...but you helped me out a while back with something our friend...

Al: ...with the eye patch...

Ben: Ni--

Al: Don't! Don't say his name. If you say his name, it triggers a digital tap at the S.H.I.E.L.D. mainframe.

Ben: We're being bugged?

Al: No. No, don't be silly. You're being **monitored.** *You* **are** *a major media outlet.*

Ben: Monitored?

Al: Listen, I never thanked you for that thing you did for me that time.

Ben: Um. It wasn't me. It was my publisher.

Al: Don't be modest. I know it was you that went to him.

Ben: What can I do for you, Agent Mackenzie?

Al: What have you heard about something going down around your neck of the woods?

Ben: In New York?

Al: Yeah.

Ben: It's a big place.

Al: In some ways.

Ben: Like what?

Al: You'd know if you heard about it.

Ben: There's something that went on at a hospital.

Al: **That's** *the one.*

Ben: What happened?

Al: What did you hear?

Ben: Something that involved a guy we both know.

Al: With an eye patch.

Ben: Yes.

Al: Yeah.

Ben: Anything you want to tell me about it?

Al: Let's just say the patch $%#@ed up really bad.

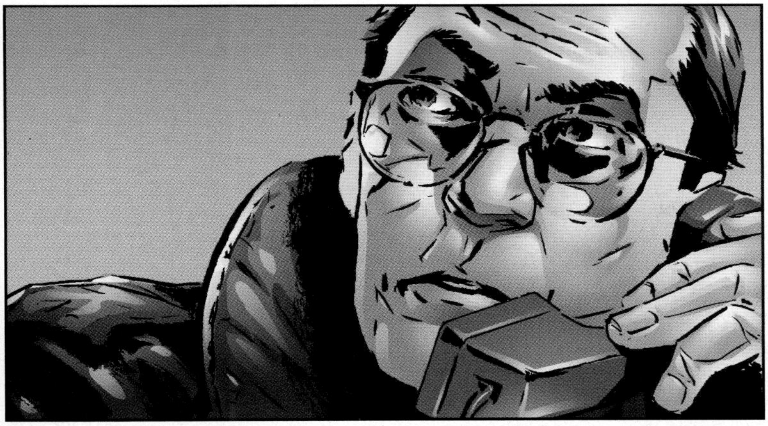

Ben: How?

Al: He did something he wasn't supposed to do and it came back to bite him on the ass.

Ben: What did he do?

Al: Something bad.

Ben: Something illegal?

Al: Even for him.

Ben: Really?

Al: If you wanted to report it, I'd say, go ahead.

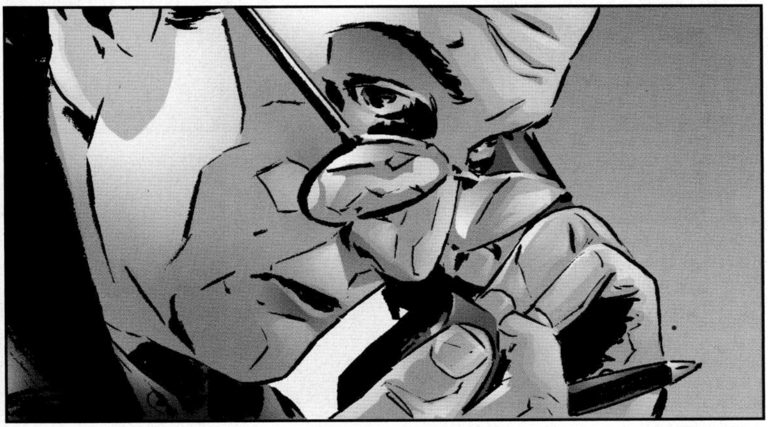

Ben: Report what?

Al: What happened.

Ben: We don't ***know*** what happened.

Al: You know that a major city hospital was attacked by a big load of tech-themed terrorists in retaliation for something someone did without the permission of the United States government or the United Nations.

Ben: Nick Fu--he--are you saying he attacked someone he wasn't supposed to and they attacked back? On American soil?

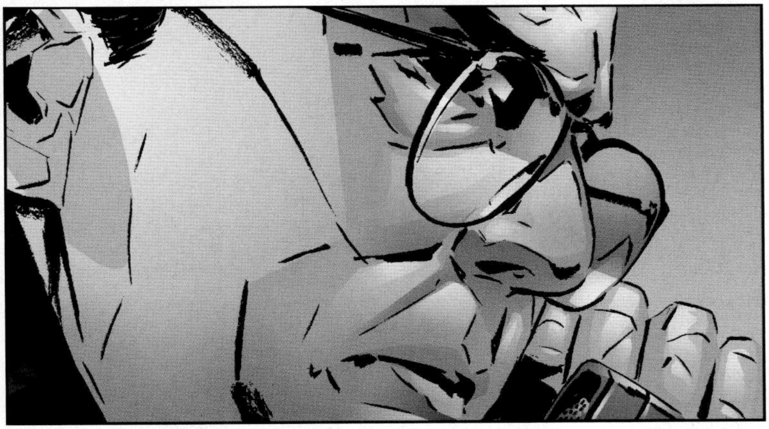

Al: You know that a lot of super heroes around the city were targeted for execution.

Ben: Is ***that*** what happened to Luke Cage?

*Al: See, you **do** have a story.*

Ben: Why is it ***okay*** to print this? Usually they put a blanket on us in the name of national security.

Al: I'm going to have to go now and call you maybe another time. We can get some lunch or something.

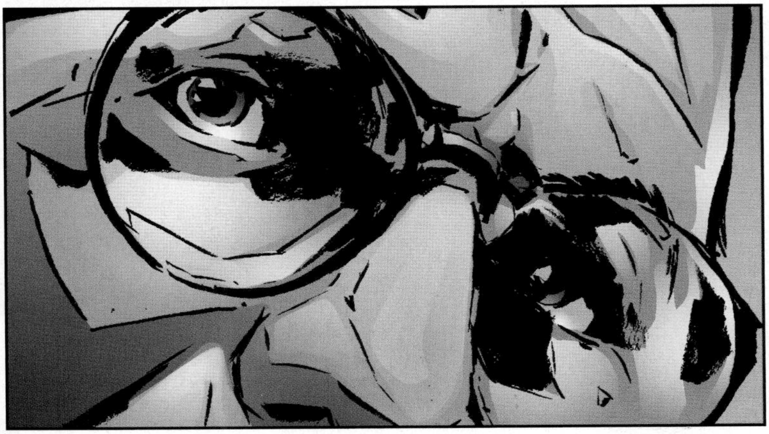

Ben: Answer me. Why is it okay to print this? Won't he--

Al: I wouldn't worry about the patch.

Ben: Did something happen to him?

Al: Not yet. But he's not going to be in a position to do anything to you if you do print this. Clearly, I can only be quoted as "an inside source."

Ben: Then tell me who attacked the hospital?

Al: You're not hearing me. It isn't "who", babe, it's "why"?

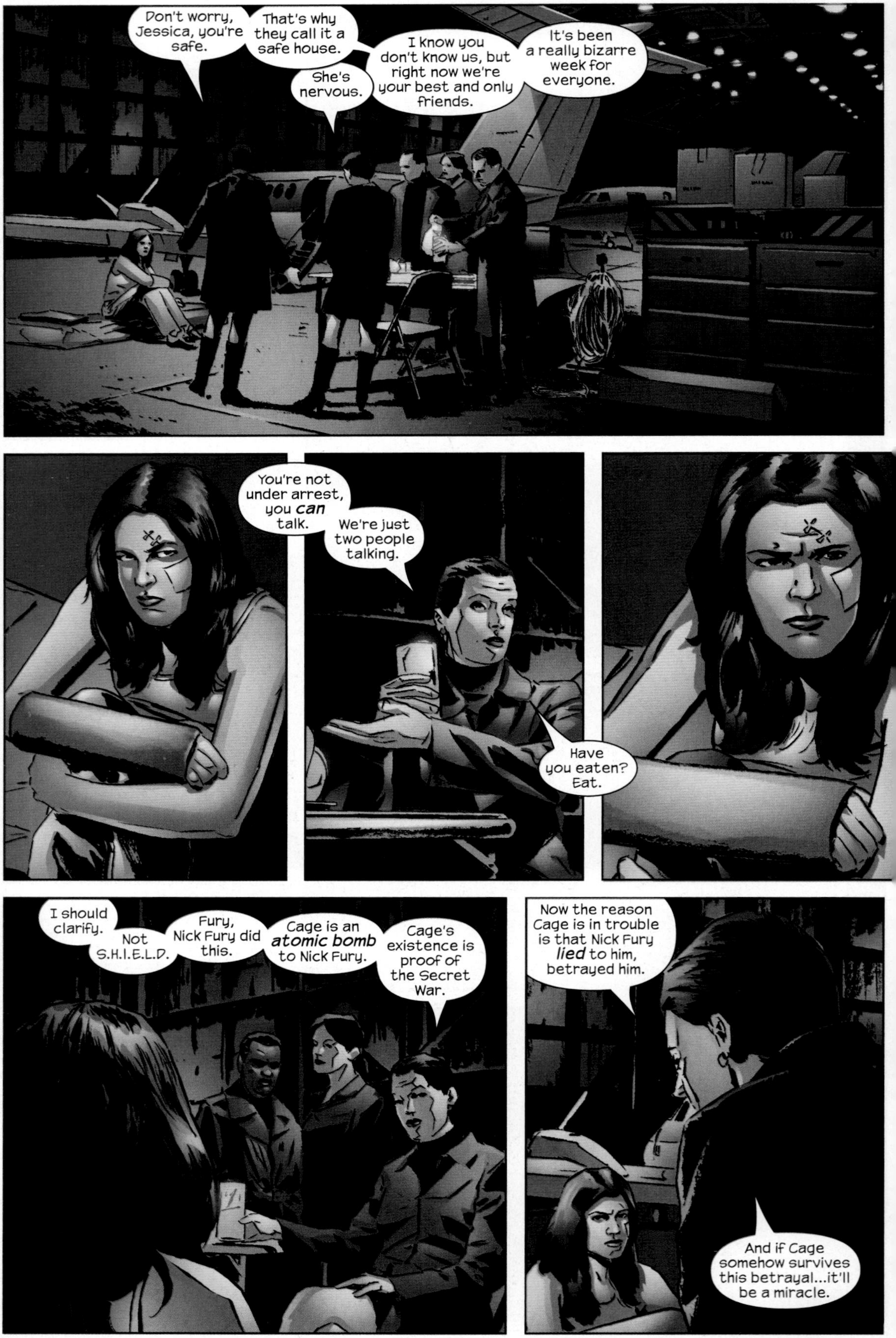
Don't worry, Jessica, you're safe.
That's why they call it a safe house.
She's nervous.
I know you don't know us, but right now we're your best and only friends.
It's been a really bizarre week for everyone.
You're not under arrest, you *can* talk.
We're just two people talking.
Have you eaten? Eat.
I should clarify.
Not S.H.I.E.L.D.
Fury, Nick Fury did this.
Cage is an *atomic bomb* to Nick Fury.
Cage's existence is proof of the Secret War.
Now the reason Cage is in trouble is that Nick Fury *lied* to him, betrayed him.
And if Cage somehow survives this betrayal...it'll be a miracle.

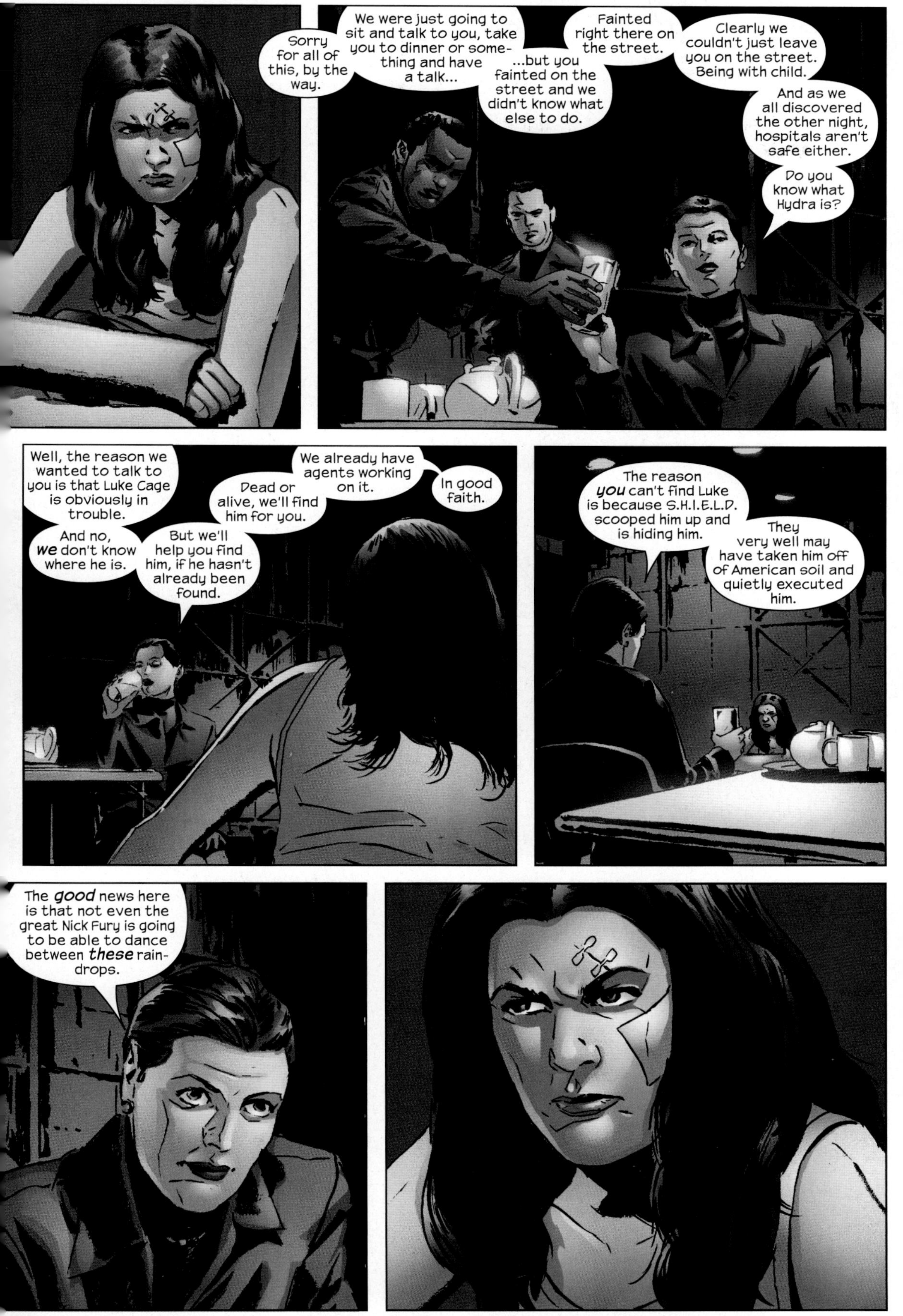
Sorry for all of this, by the way.
We were just going to sit and talk to you, take you to dinner or something and have a talk...
...but you fainted on the street and we didn't know what else to do.
Fainted right there on the street.
Clearly we couldn't just leave you on the street. Being with child.
And as we all discovered the other night, hospitals aren't safe either.
Do you know what Hydra is?
Well, the reason we wanted to talk to you is that Luke Cage is obviously in trouble.
And no, *we* don't know where he is.
But we'll help you find him, if he hasn't already been found.
Dead or alive, we'll find him for you.
We already have agents working on it.
In good faith.
The reason *you* can't find Luke is because S.H.I.E.L.D. scooped him up and is hiding him.
They very well may have taken him off of American soil and quietly executed him.
The *good* news here is that not even the great Nick Fury is going to be able to dance between *these* rain-drops.

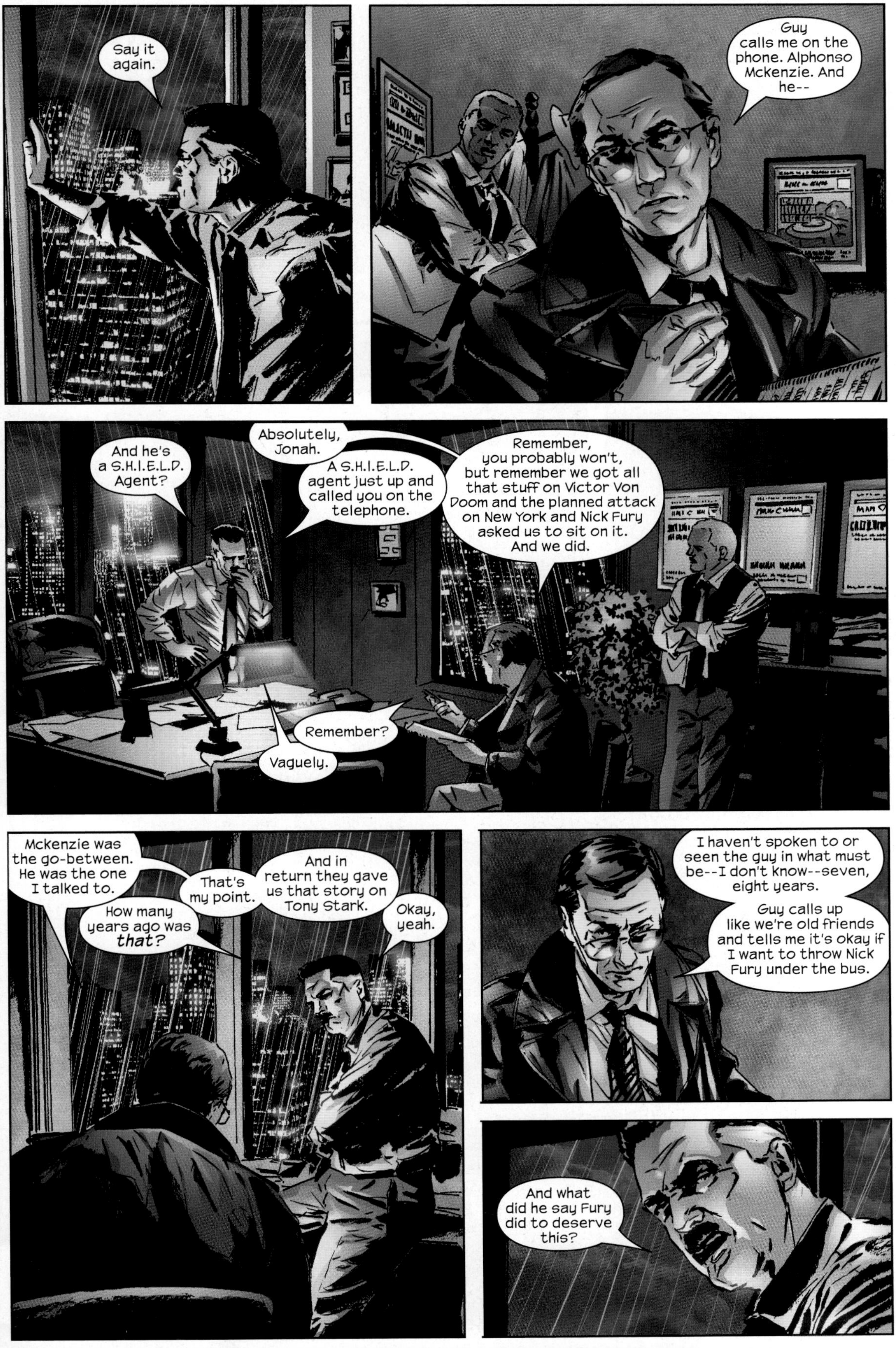

Say it again.
Guy calls me on the phone. Alphonso Mckenzie. And he--
And he's a S.H.I.E.L.D. Agent?
Absolutely, Jonah.
A S.H.I.E.L.D. agent just up and called you on the telephone.
Remember, you probably won't, but remember we got all that stuff on Victor Von Doom and the planned attack on New York and Nick Fury asked us to sit on it. And we did.
Remember?
Vaguely.
Mckenzie was the go-between. He was the one I talked to.
That's my point.
And in return they gave us that story on Tony Stark.
How many years ago was *that*?
Okay, yeah.
I haven't spoken to or seen the guy in what must be--I don't know--seven, eight years.
Guy calls up like we're old friends and tells me it's okay if I want to throw Nick Fury under the bus.
And what did he say Fury did to deserve this?

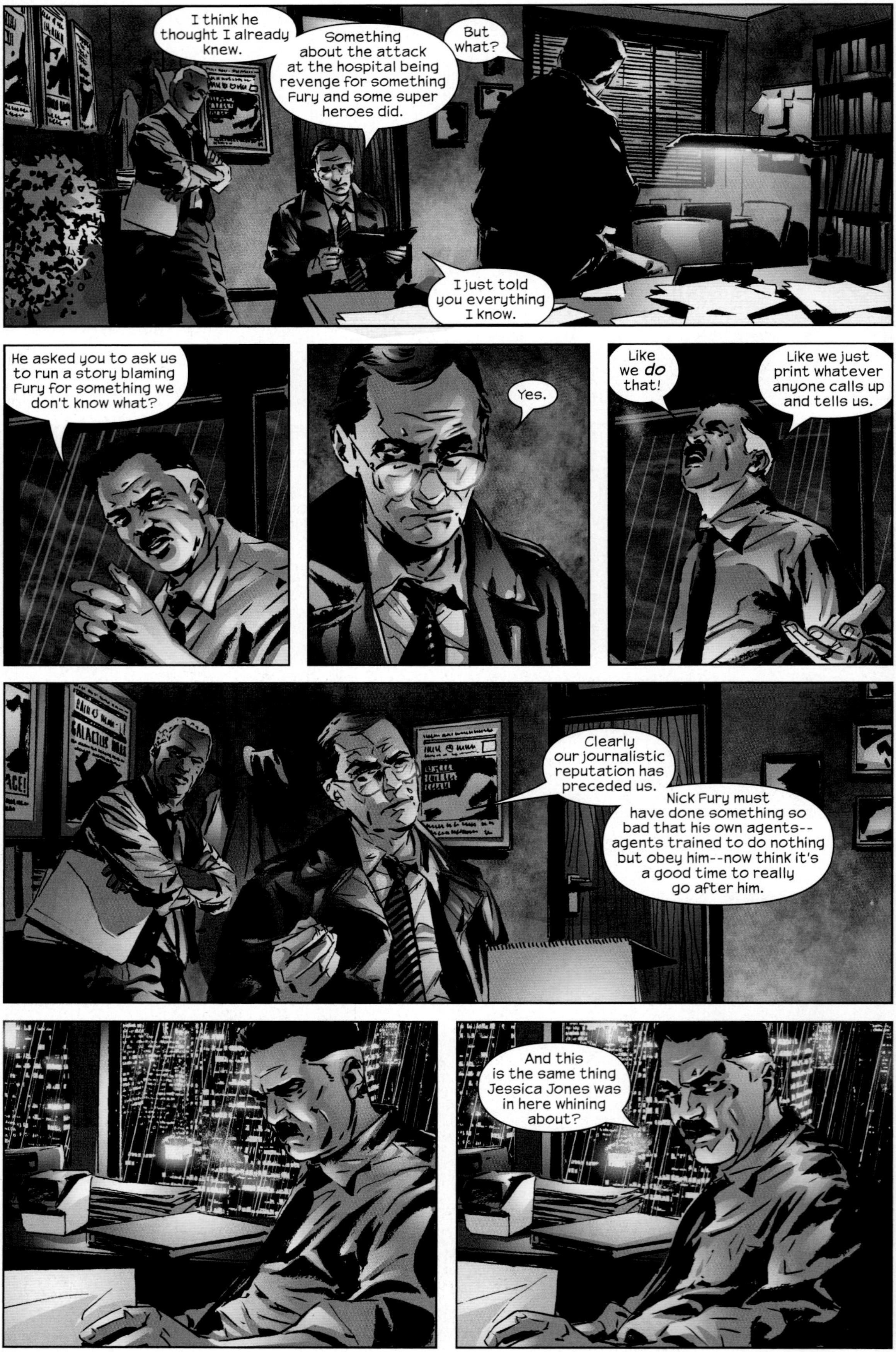
I think he thought I already knew.
Something about the attack at the hospital being revenge for something Fury and some super heroes did.
But what?
I just told you everything I know.
He asked you to ask us to run a story blaming Fury for something we don't know what?
Yes.
Like we *do* that!
Like we just print whatever anyone calls up and tells us.
Clearly our journalistic reputation has preceded us.
Nick Fury must have done something so bad that his own agents-- agents trained to do nothing but obey him--now think it's a good time to really go after him.
And this is the same thing Jessica Jones was in here whining about?

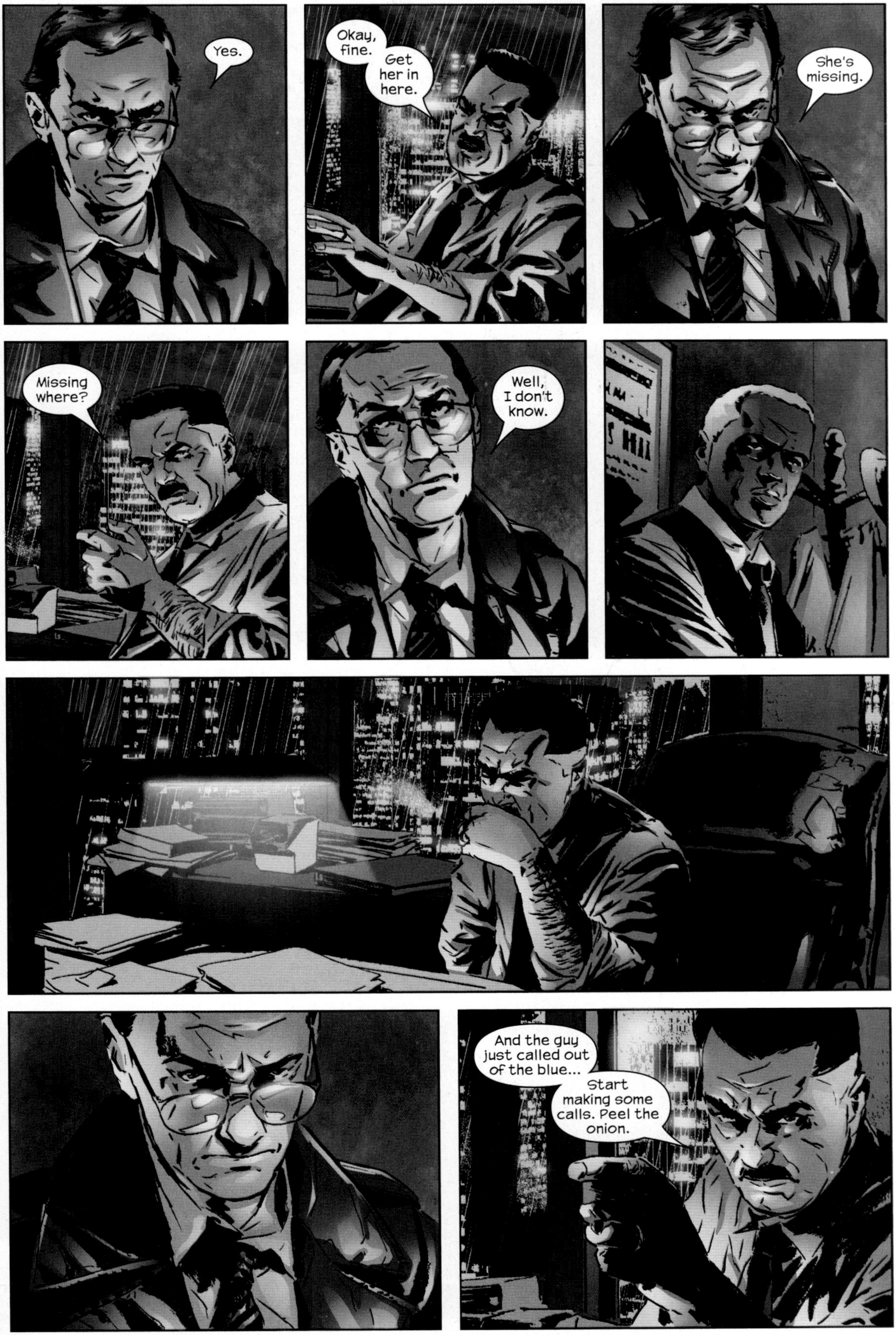
Yes.
Okay, fine.
Get her in here.
She's missing.
Missing where?
Well, I don't know.
And the guy just called out of the blue...
Start making some calls. Peel the onion.

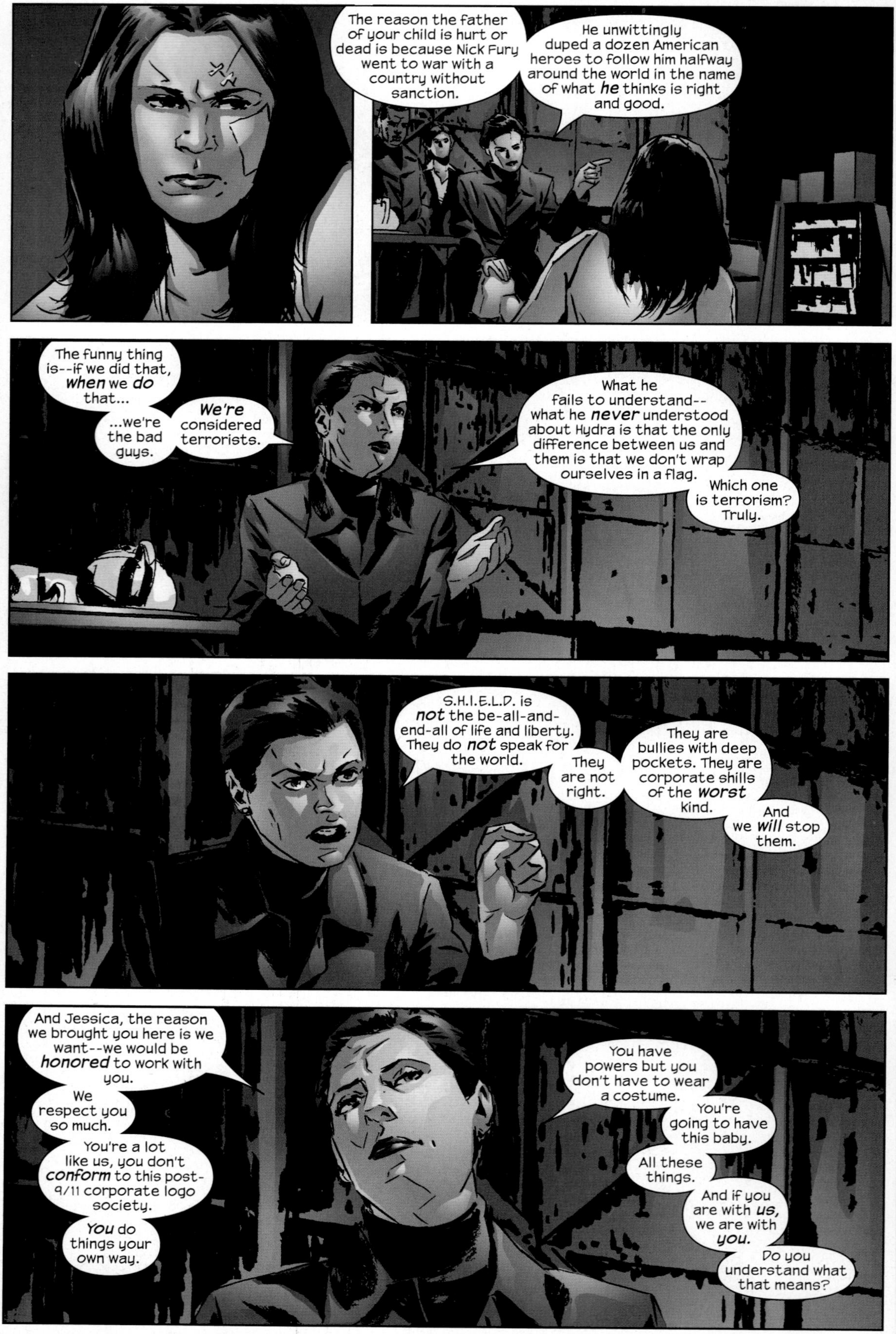

The reason the father of your child is hurt or dead is because Nick Fury went to war with a country without sanction.
He unwittingly duped a dozen American heroes to follow him halfway around the world in the name of what *he* thinks is right and good.
The funny thing is--if we did that, *when* we *do* that...
...we're the bad guys.
We're considered terrorists.
What he fails to understand--what he *never* understood about Hydra is that the only difference between us and them is that we don't wrap ourselves in a flag.
Which one is terrorism? Truly.
S.H.I.E.L.D. is *not* the be-all-and-end-all of life and liberty. They do *not* speak for the world.
They are not right.
They are bullies with deep pockets. They are corporate shills of the *worst* kind.
And we *will* stop them.
And Jessica, the reason we brought you here is we want--we would be *honored* to work with you.
We respect you so much.
You're a lot like us, you don't *conform* to this post-9/11 corporate logo society.
You do things your own way.
You have powers but you don't have to wear a costume.
You're going to have this baby.
All these things.
And if you are with *us,* we are with *you.*
Do you understand what that means?

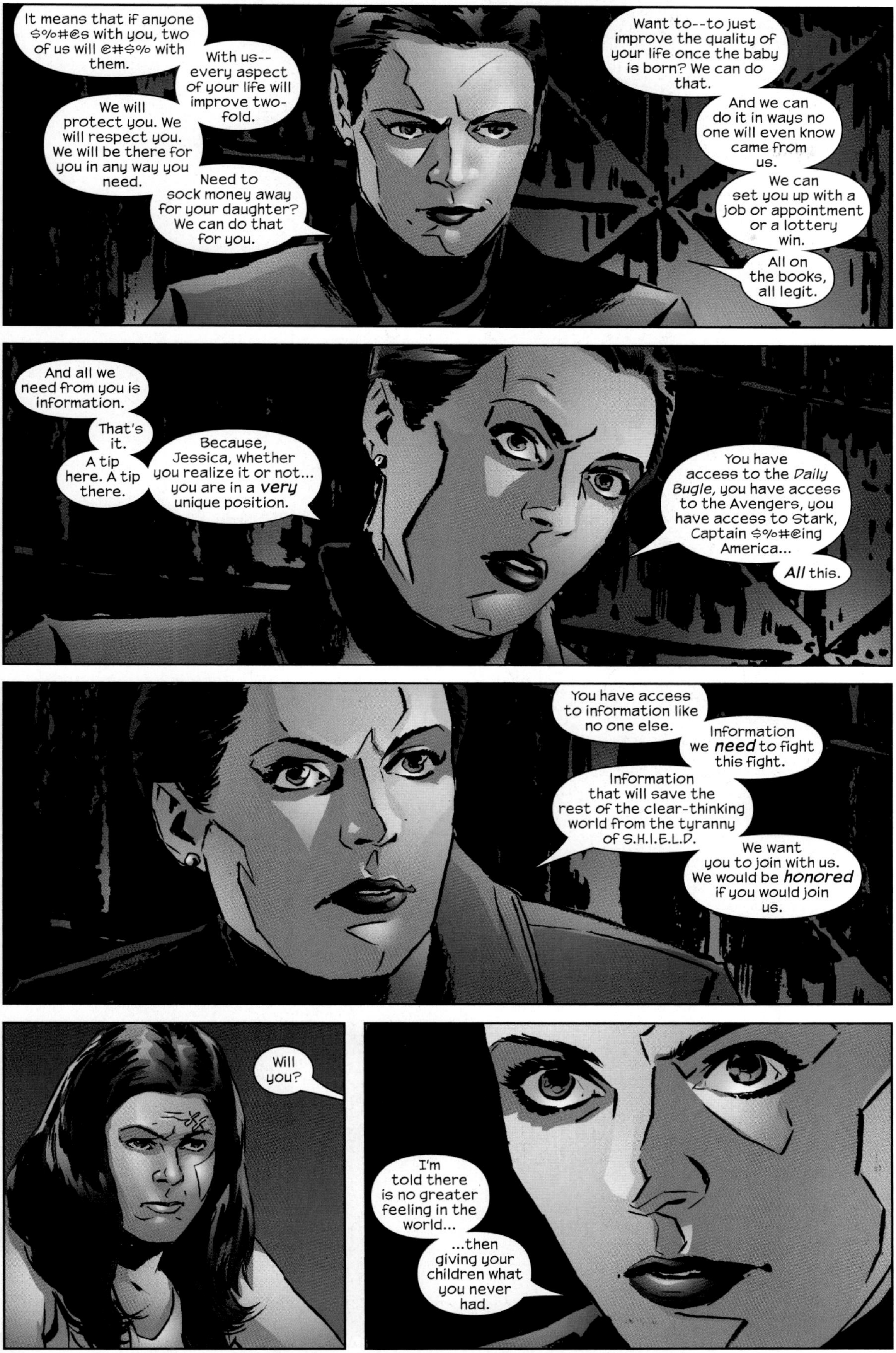
It means that if anyone $%#@s with you, two of us will @#$% with them.
With us-- every aspect of your life will improve two-fold.
We will protect you. We will respect you. We will be there for you in any way you need.
Need to sock money away for your daughter? We can do that for you.
Want to--to just improve the quality of your life once the baby is born? We can do that.
And we can do it in ways no one will even know came from us.
We can set you up with a job or appointment or a lottery win.
All on the books, all legit.
And all we need from you is information.
That's it.
A tip here. A tip there.
Because, Jessica, whether you realize it or not... you are in a *very* unique position.
You have access to the *Daily Bugle*, you have access to the Avengers, you have access to Stark, Captain $%#@ing America...
All this.
You have access to information like no one else.
Information we *need* to fight this fight.
Information that will save the rest of the clear-thinking world from the tyranny of S.H.I.E.L.D.
We want you to join with us. We would be *honored* if you would join us.
Will you?
I'm told there is no greater feeling in the world...
...then giving your children what you never had.

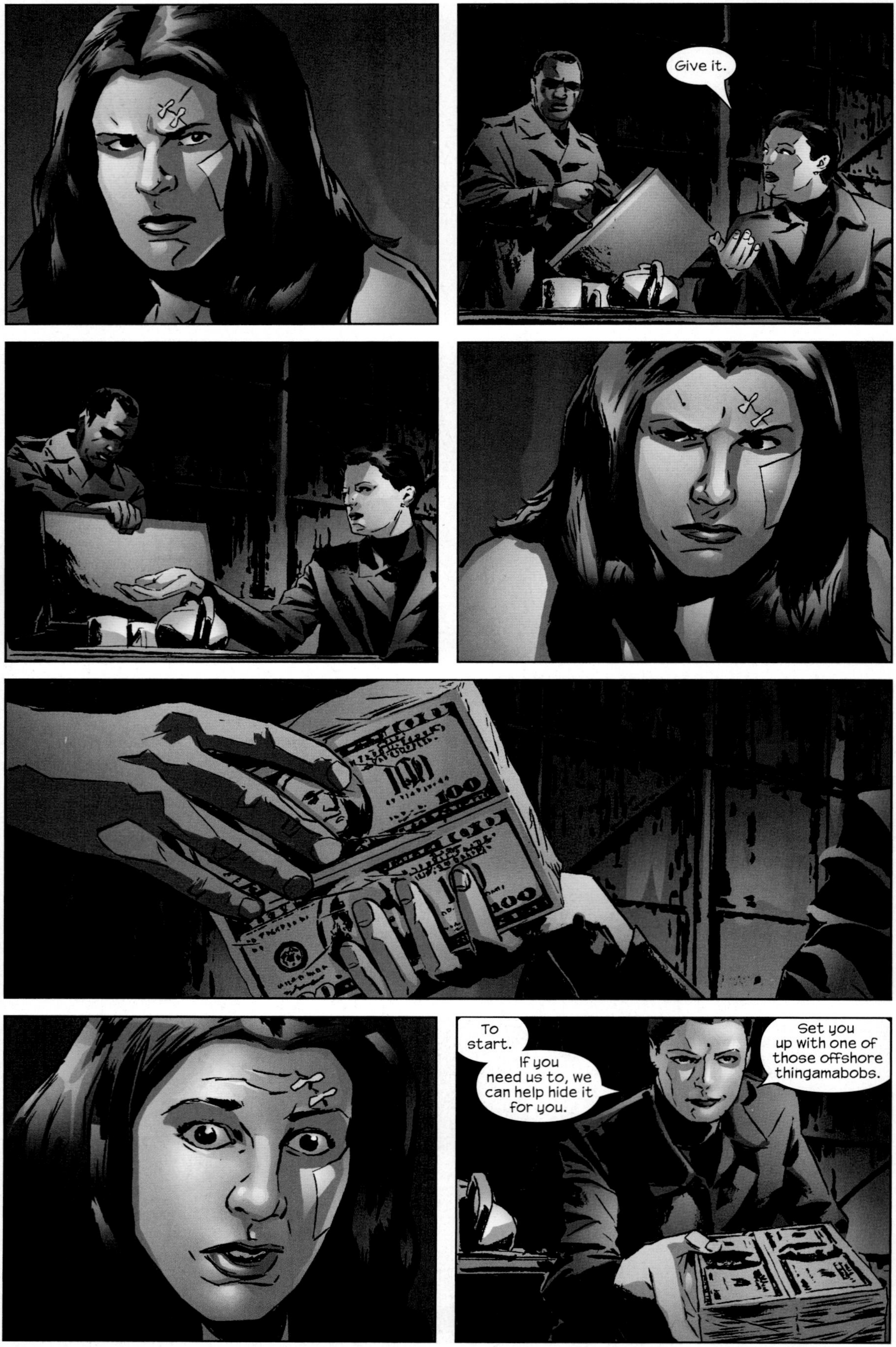

Give it.
To start.
If you need us to, we can help hide it for you.
Set you up with one of those offshore thingamabobs.

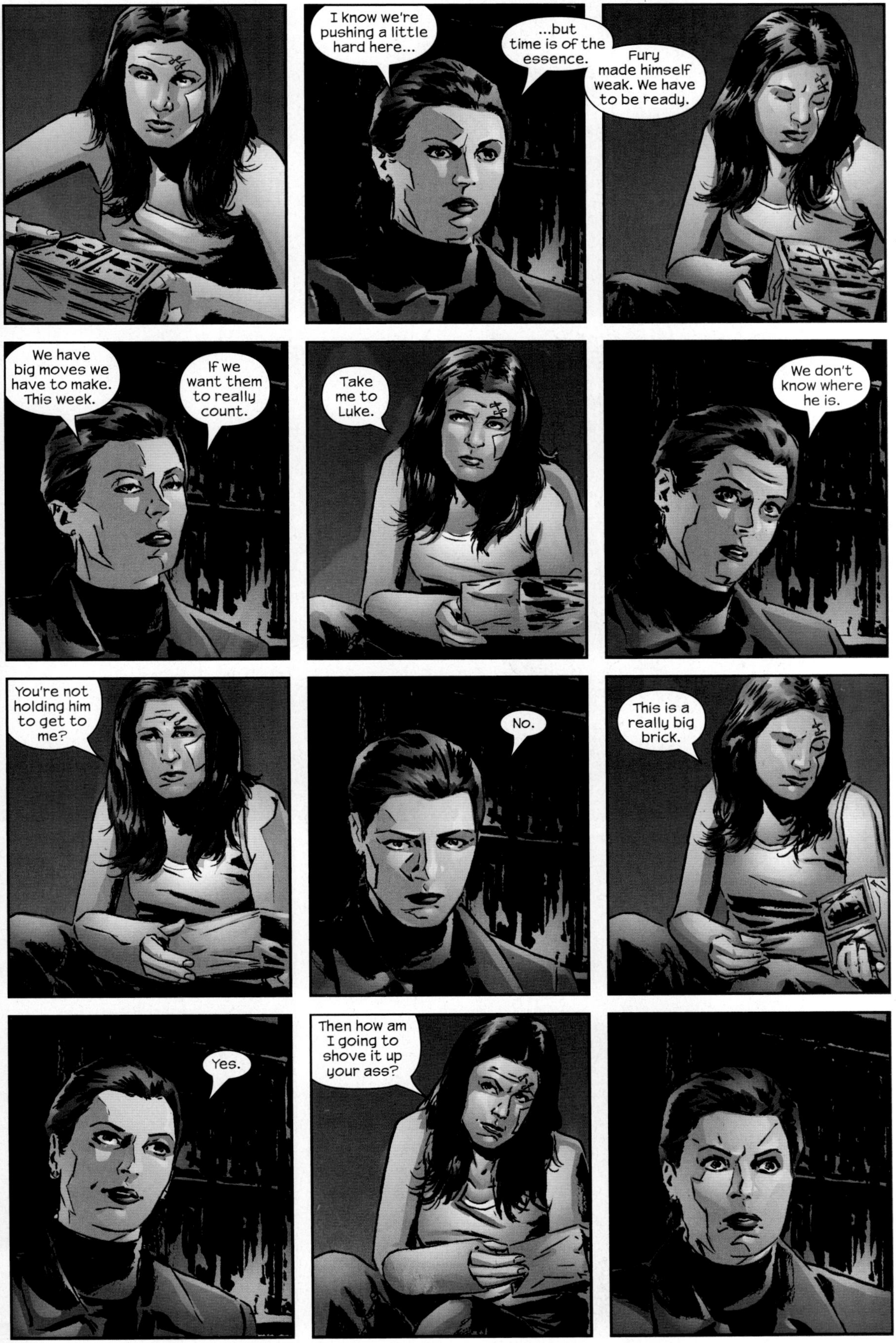
I know we're pushing a little hard here...
...but time is of the essence.
Fury made himself weak. We have to be ready.
We have big moves we have to make. This week.
If we want them to really count.
Take me to Luke.
We don't know where he is.
You're not holding him to get to me?
No.
This is a really big brick.
Yes.
Then how am I going to shove it up your ass?

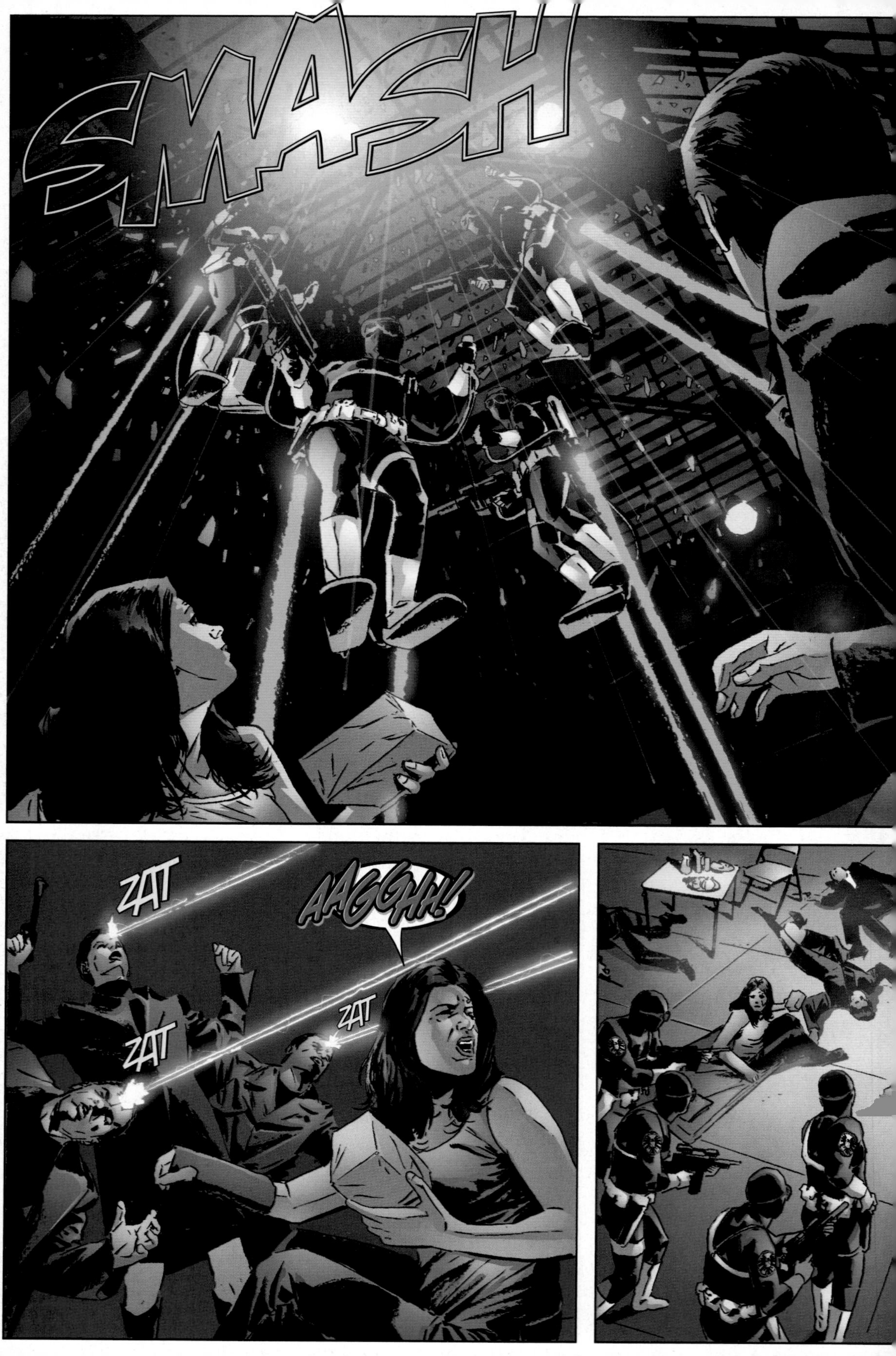
SMASH
ZAT
AAGGHH!
ZAT
ZAT

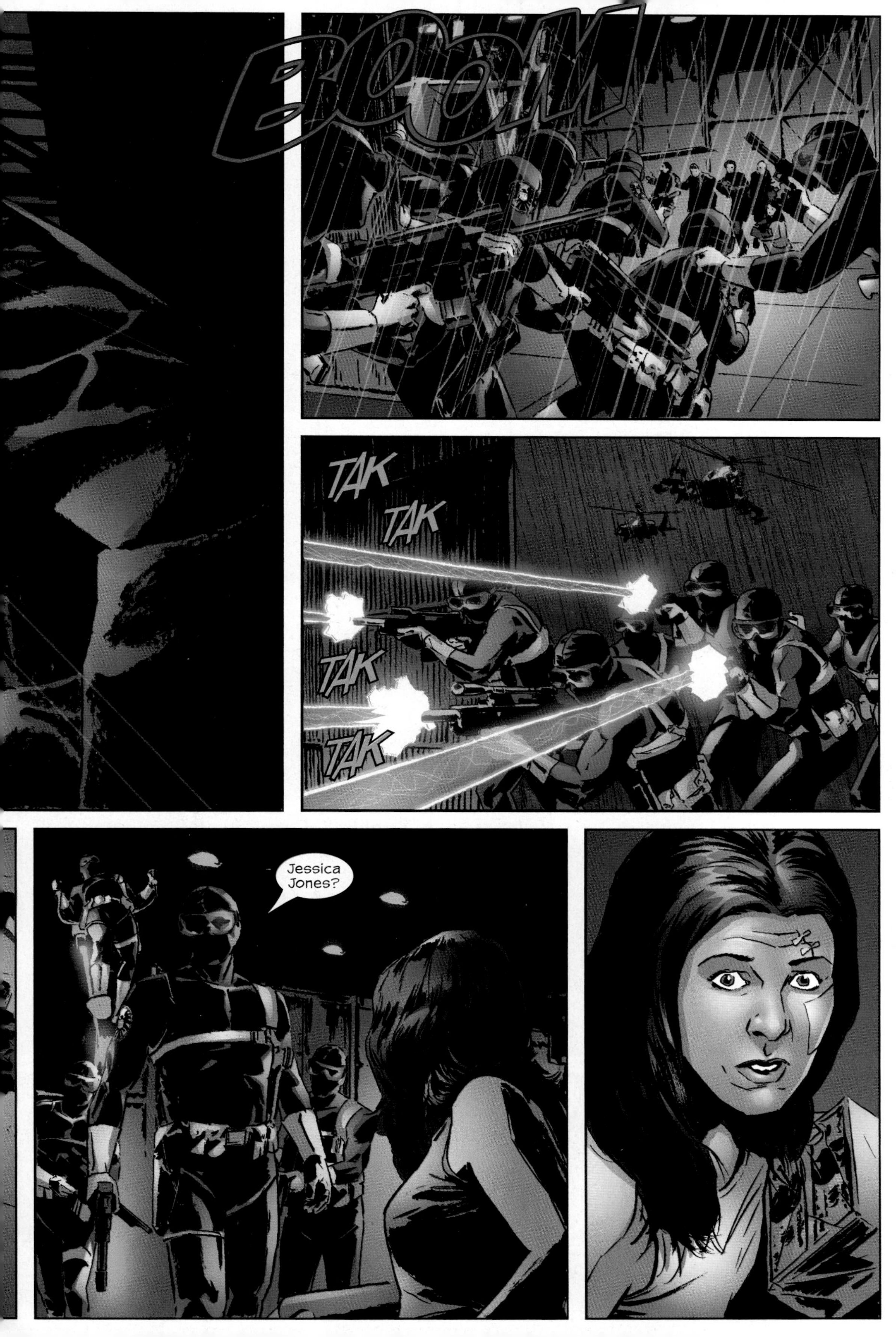
BOOM
TAK
TAK
TAK
TAK
Jessica Jones?

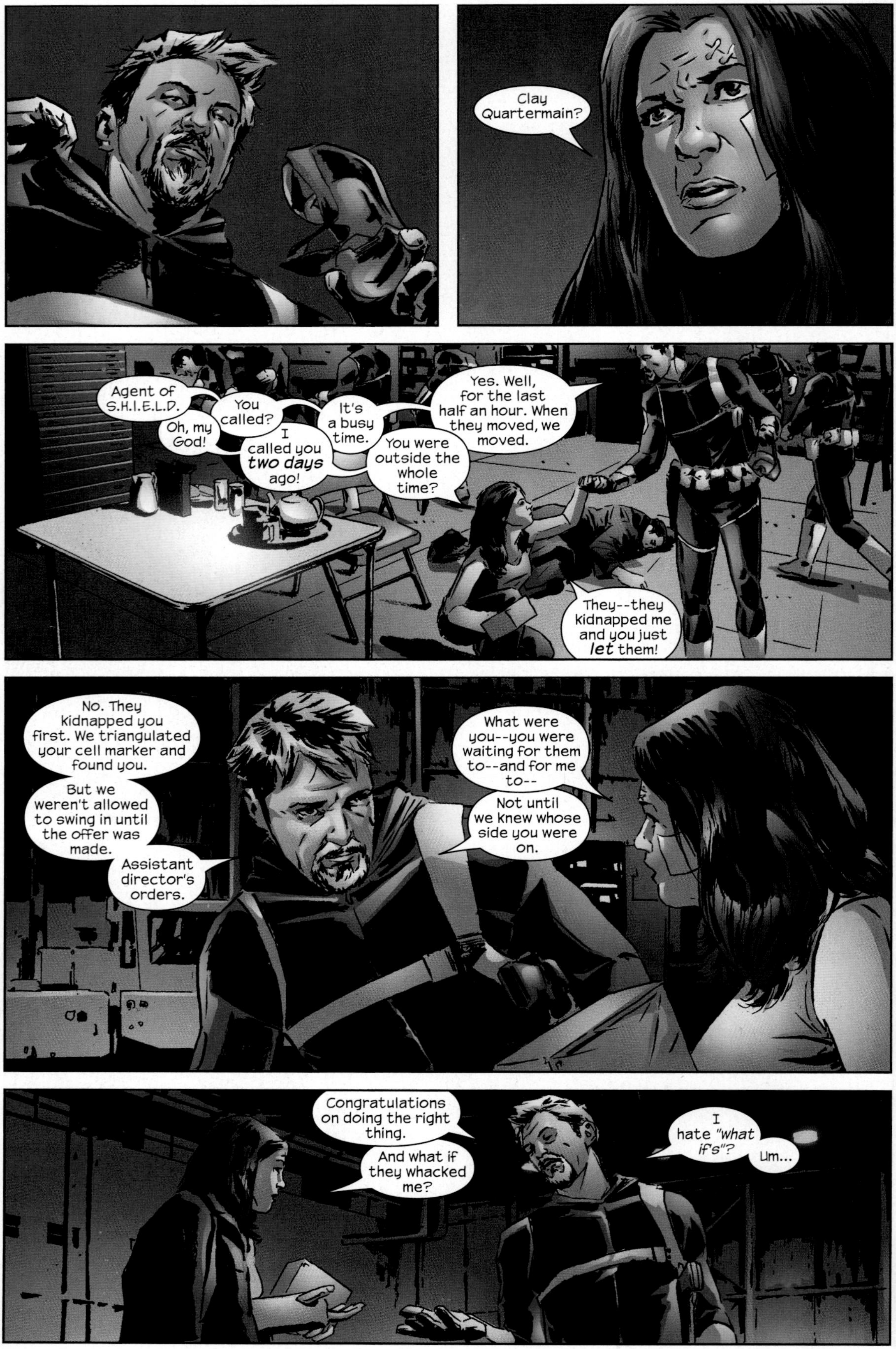

Clay Quartermain?
Agent of S.H.I.E.L.D.
Oh, my God!
You called?
I called you *two days* ago!
It's a busy time.
Yes. Well, for the last half an hour. When they moved, we moved.
You were outside the whole time?
They--they kidnapped me and you just *let* them!
No. They kidnapped you first. We triangulated your cell marker and found you.
But we weren't allowed to swing in until the offer was made.
Assistant director's orders.
What were you--you were waiting for them to--and for me to--
Not until we knew whose side you were on.
Congratulations on doing the right thing.
And what if they whacked me?
I hate "what if's"?
Um...

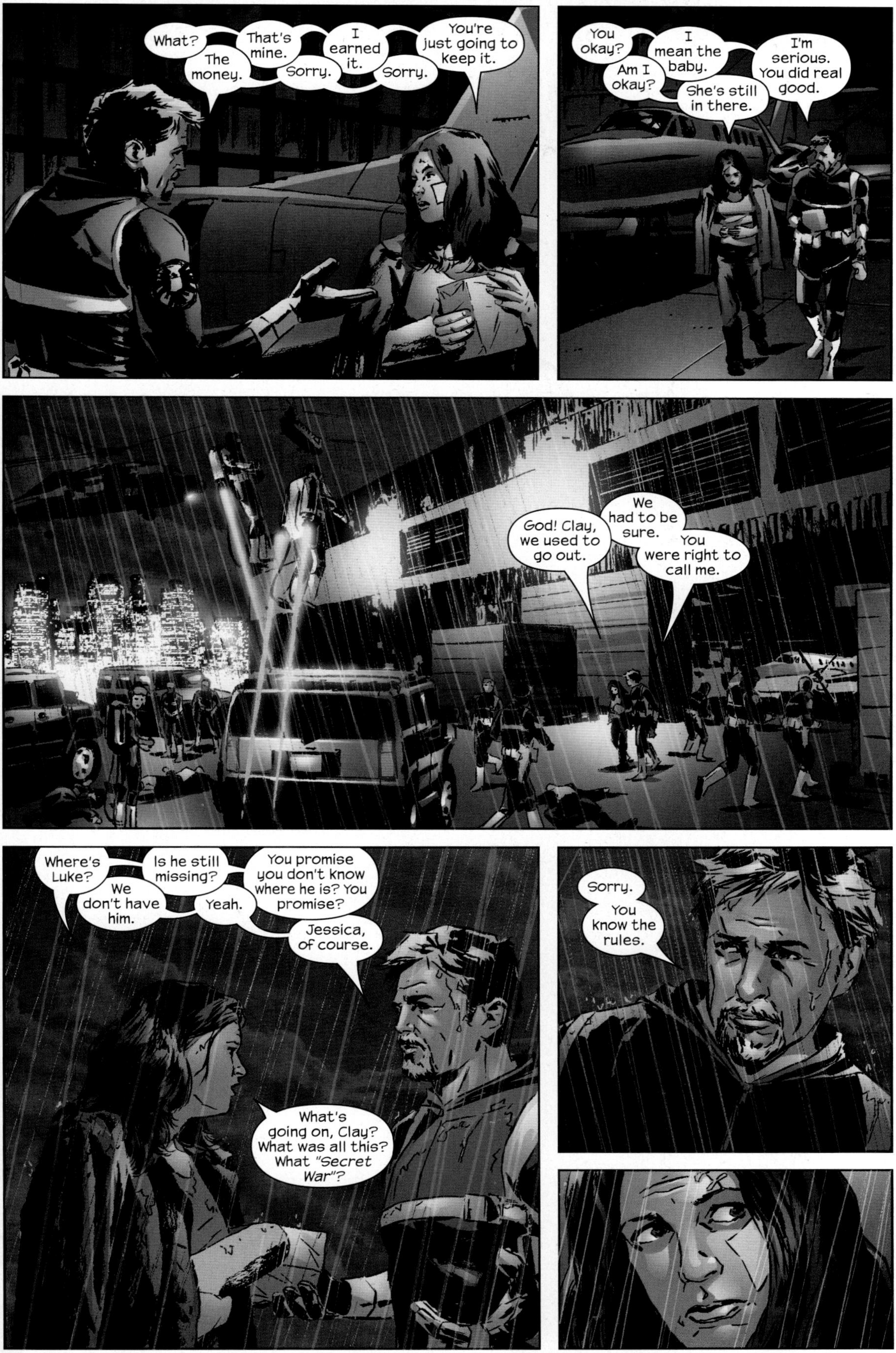
What?
The money.
That's mine.
Sorry.
I earned it.
Sorry.
You're just going to keep it.
You okay?
Am I okay?
I mean the baby.
She's still in there.
I'm serious. You did real good.
God! Clay, we used to go out.
We had to be sure.
You were right to call me.
Where's Luke?
We don't have him.
Is he still missing?
Yeah.
You promise you don't know where he is? You promise?
Jessica, of course.
What's going on, Clay? What was all this? What "Secret War"?
Sorry.
You know the rules.

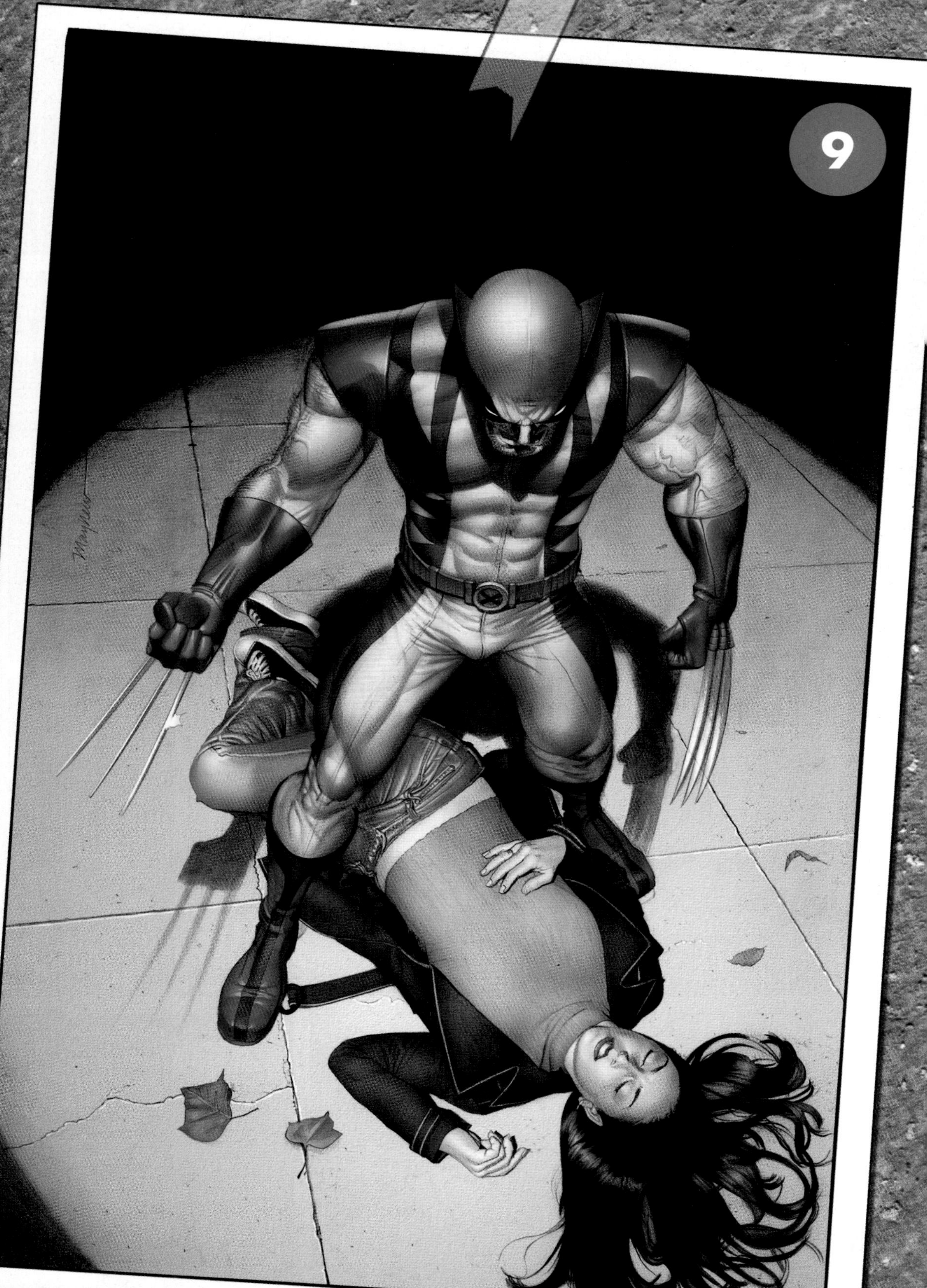
9

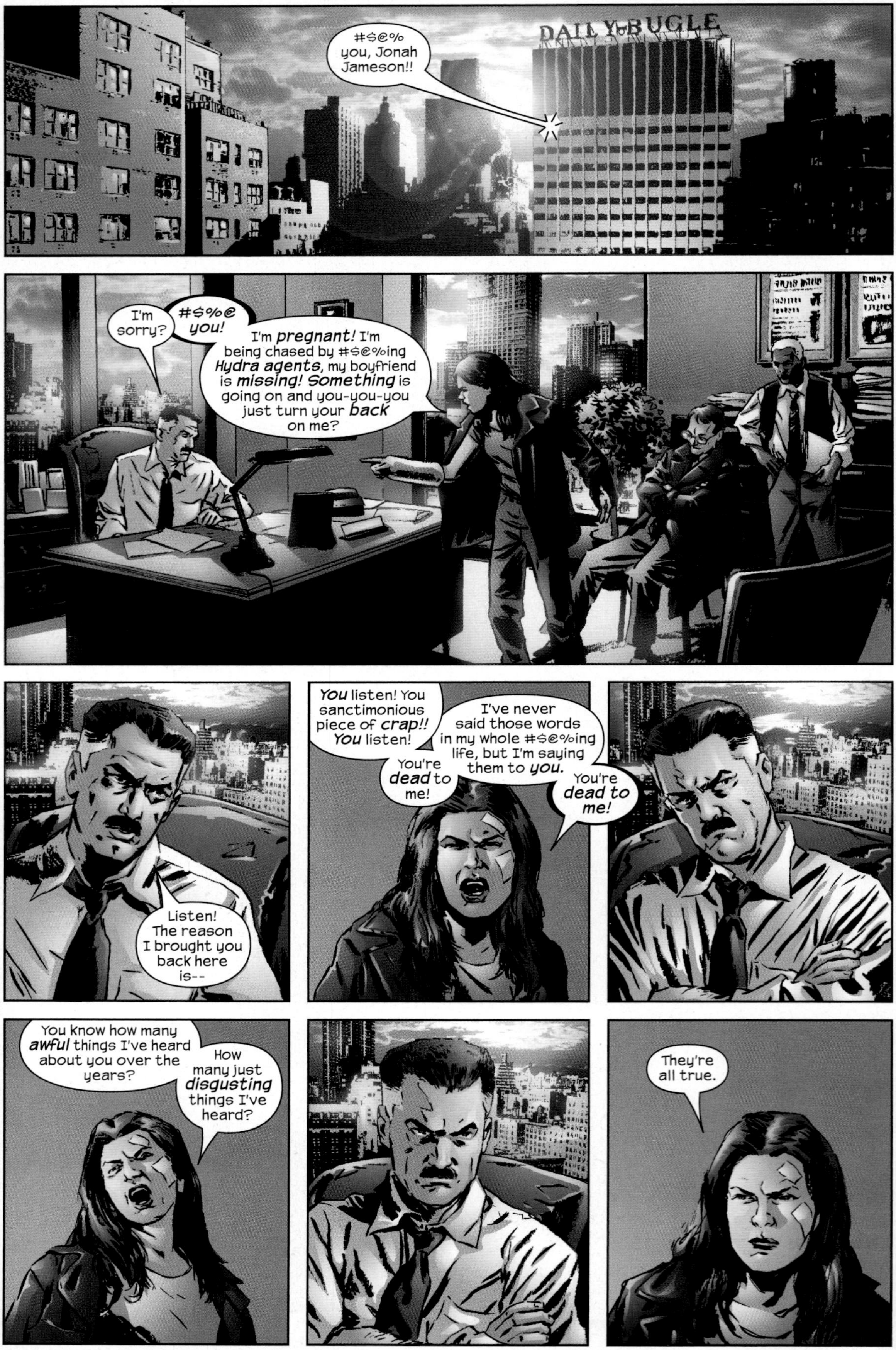

DAILY BUGLE
#$@% you, Jonah Jameson!!
I'm sorry?
#$%@ you!
I'm pregnant! I'm being chased by #$@%ing Hydra agents, my boyfriend is missing! Something is going on and you-you-you just turn your back on me?
Listen! The reason I brought you back here is--
You listen! You sanctimonious piece of crap!! You listen!
You're dead to me!
I've never said those words in my whole #$@%ing life, but I'm saying them to you.
You're dead to me!
You know how many awful things I've heard about you over the years?
How many just disgusting things I've heard?
They're all true.

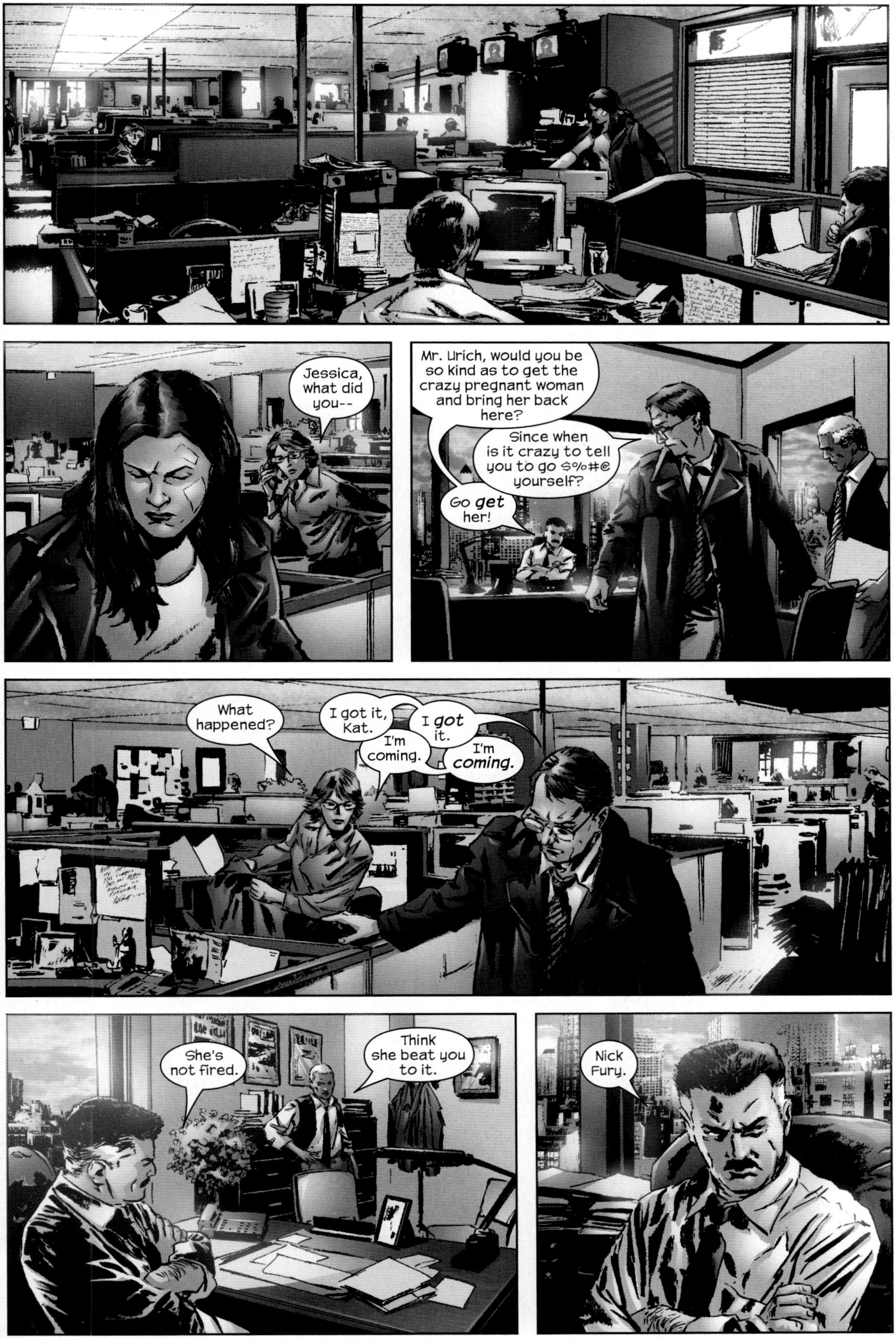

Jessica, what did you--
Mr. Urich, would you be so kind as to get the crazy pregnant woman and bring her back here?
Since when is it crazy to tell you to go $%#@ yourself?
Go get her!
What happened?
I got it, Kat.
I'm coming.
I got it.
I'm coming.
She's not fired.
Think she beat you to it.
Nick Fury.

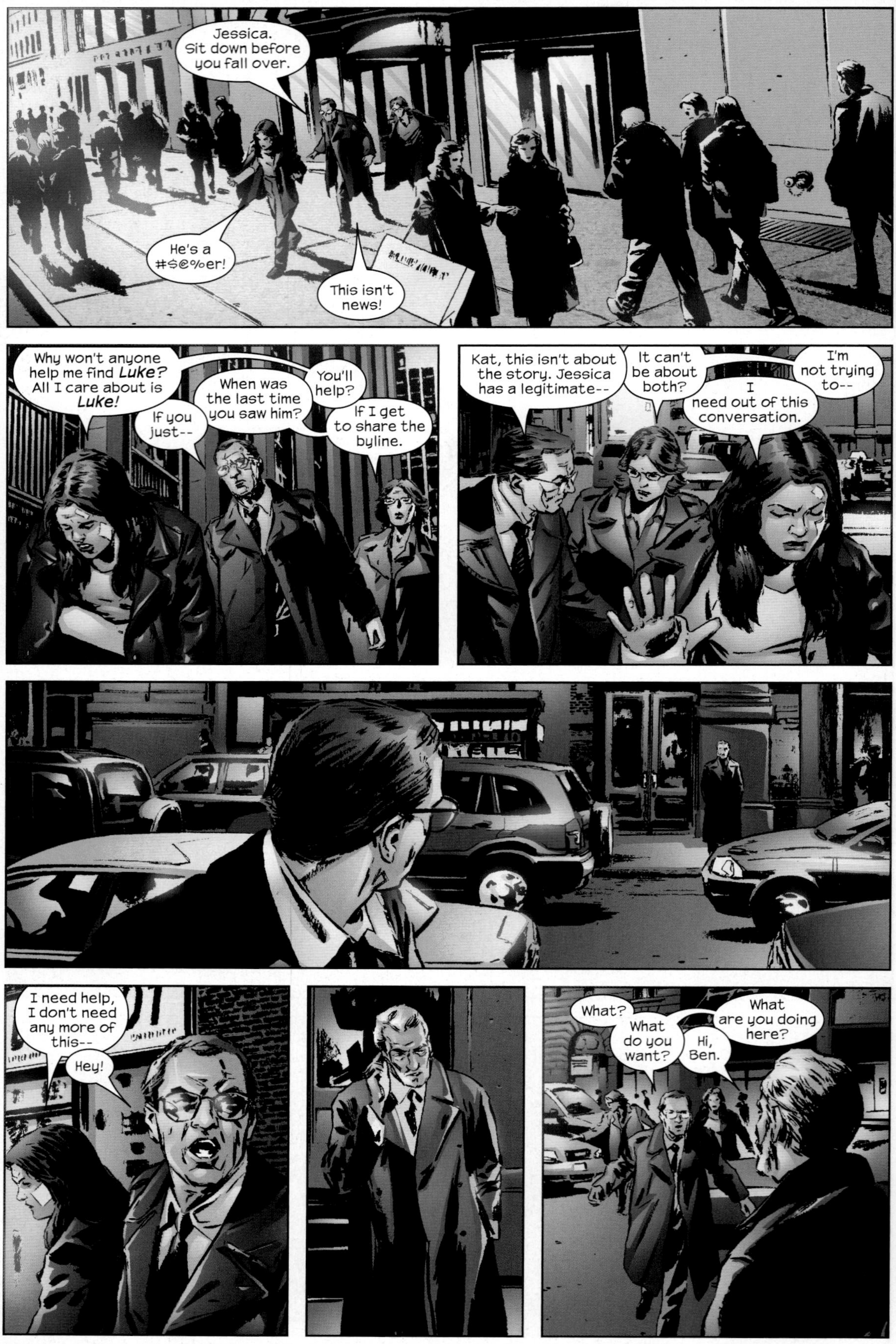
Jessica. Sit down before you fall over.
He's a #$@%er!
This isn't news!
Why won't anyone help me find *Luke?* All I care about is *Luke!*
If you just--
When was the last time you saw him?
You'll help?
If I get to share the byline.
Kat, this isn't about the story. Jessica has a legitimate--
It can't be about both?
I'm not trying to--
I need out of this conversation.
I need help, I don't need any more of this--
Hey!
What?
What do you want?
Hi, Ben.
What are you doing here?

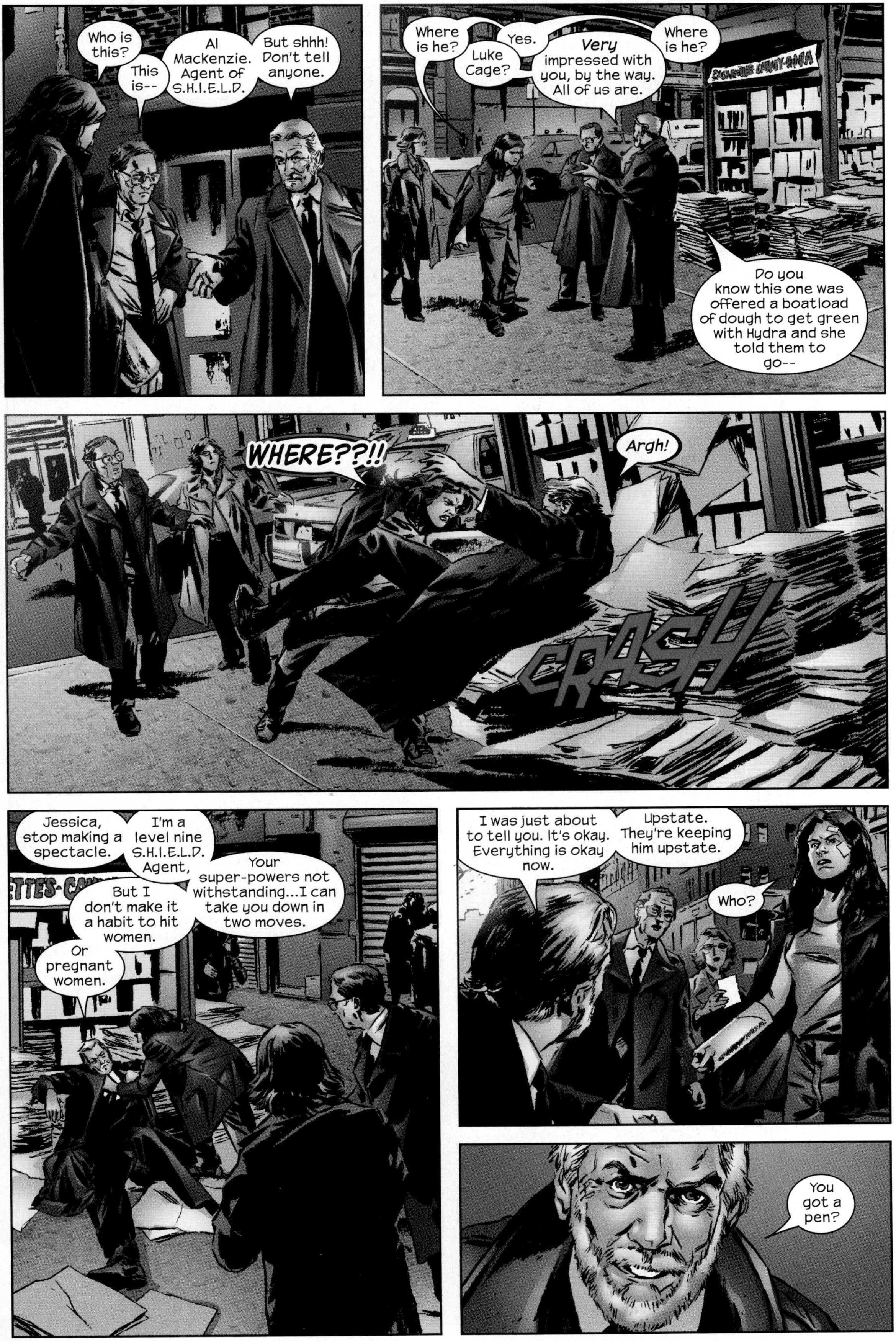

Who is this?
This is--
Al Mackenzie. Agent of S.H.I.E.L.D.
But shhh! Don't tell anyone.
Where is he?
Luke Cage?
Yes.
Very impressed with you, by the way. All of us are.
Where is he?
Do you know this one was offered a boatload of dough to get green with Hydra and she told them to go--
WHERE??!!
Argh!
CRASH
Jessica, stop making a spectacle.
I'm a level nine S.H.I.E.L.D. Agent,
Your super-powers not withstanding...I can take you down in two moves.
But I don't make it a habit to hit women.
Or pregnant women.
I was just about to tell you. It's okay. Everything is okay now.
Upstate. They're keeping him upstate.
Who?
You got a pen?

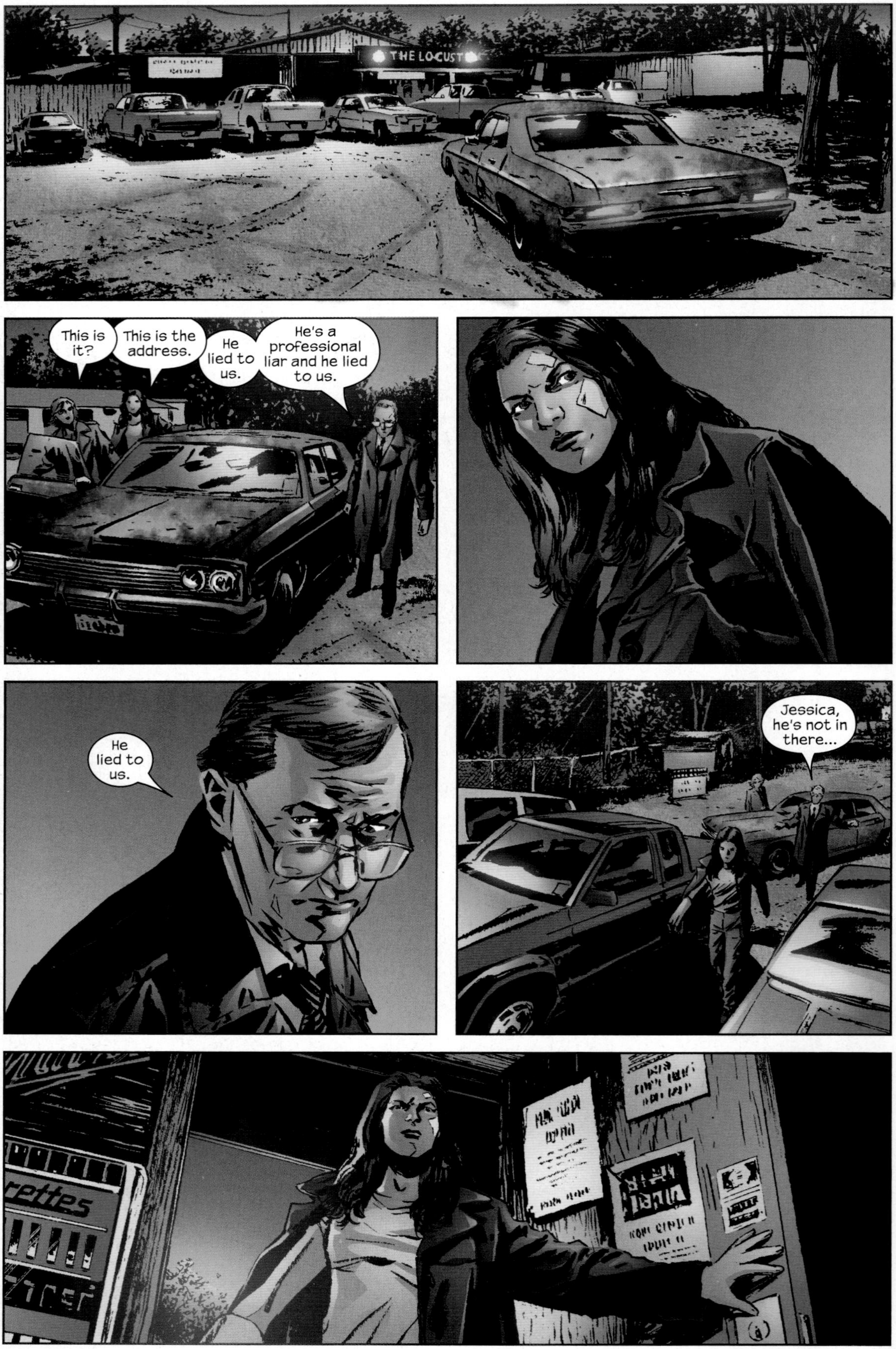
THE LOCUST
This is it?
This is the address.
He lied to us.
He's a professional liar and he lied to us.
He lied to us.
Jessica, he's not in there...

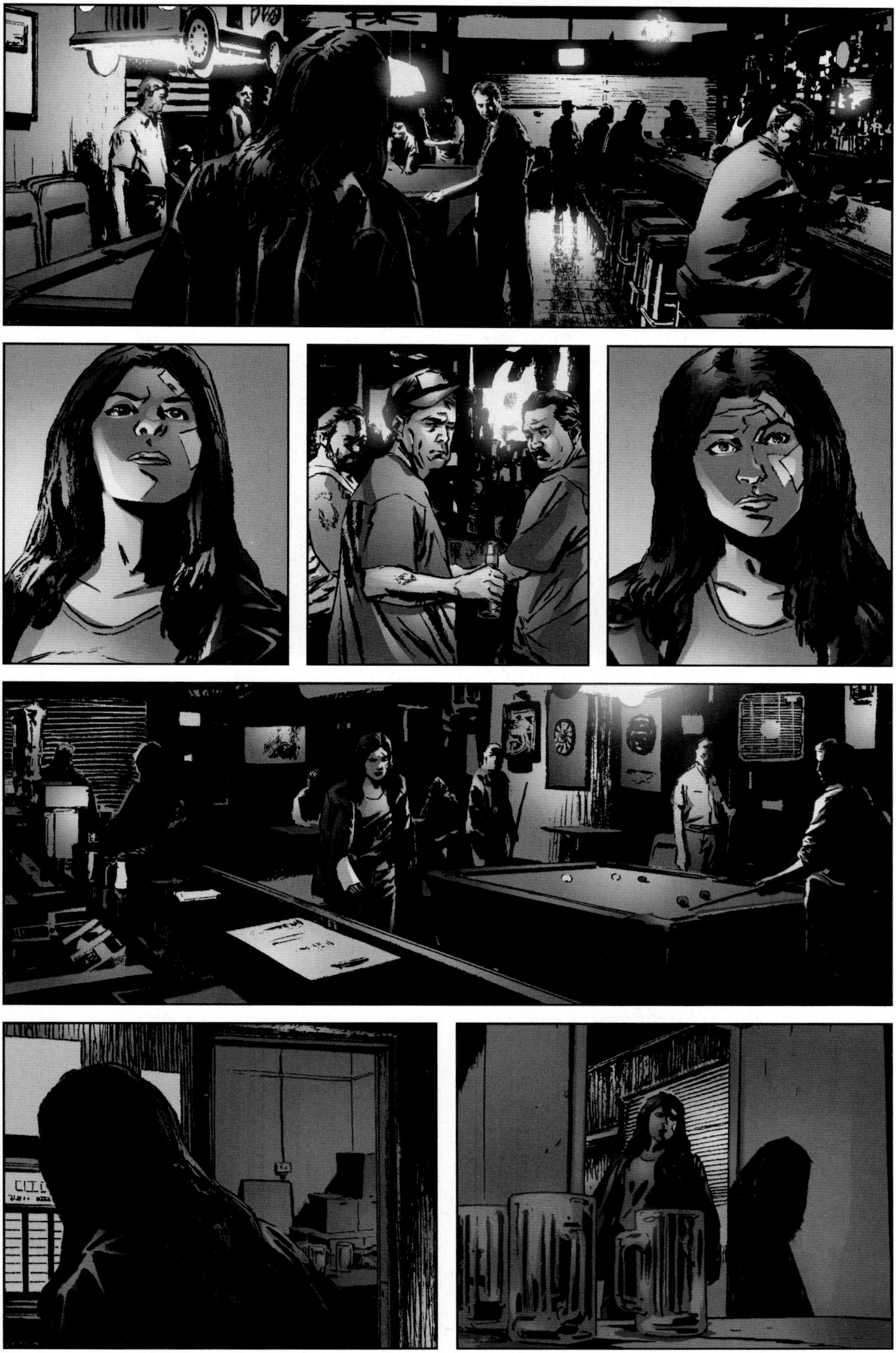

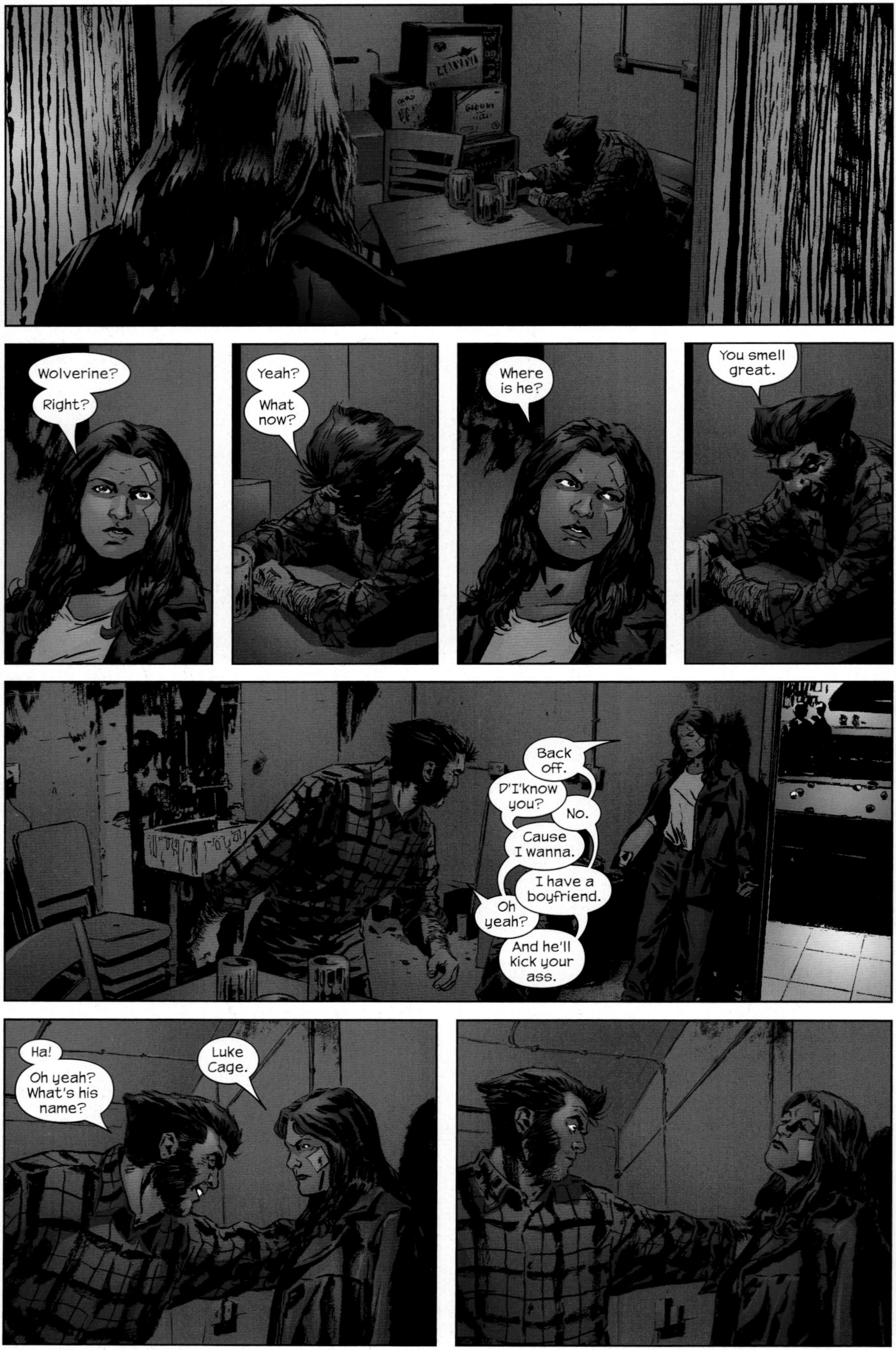
Wolverine?
Right?
Yeah?
What now?
Where is he?
You smell great.
Back off.
D'I'know you?
No.
Cause I wanna.
I have a boyfriend.
Oh yeah?
And he'll kick your ass.
Ha!
Oh yeah? What's his name?
Luke Cage.

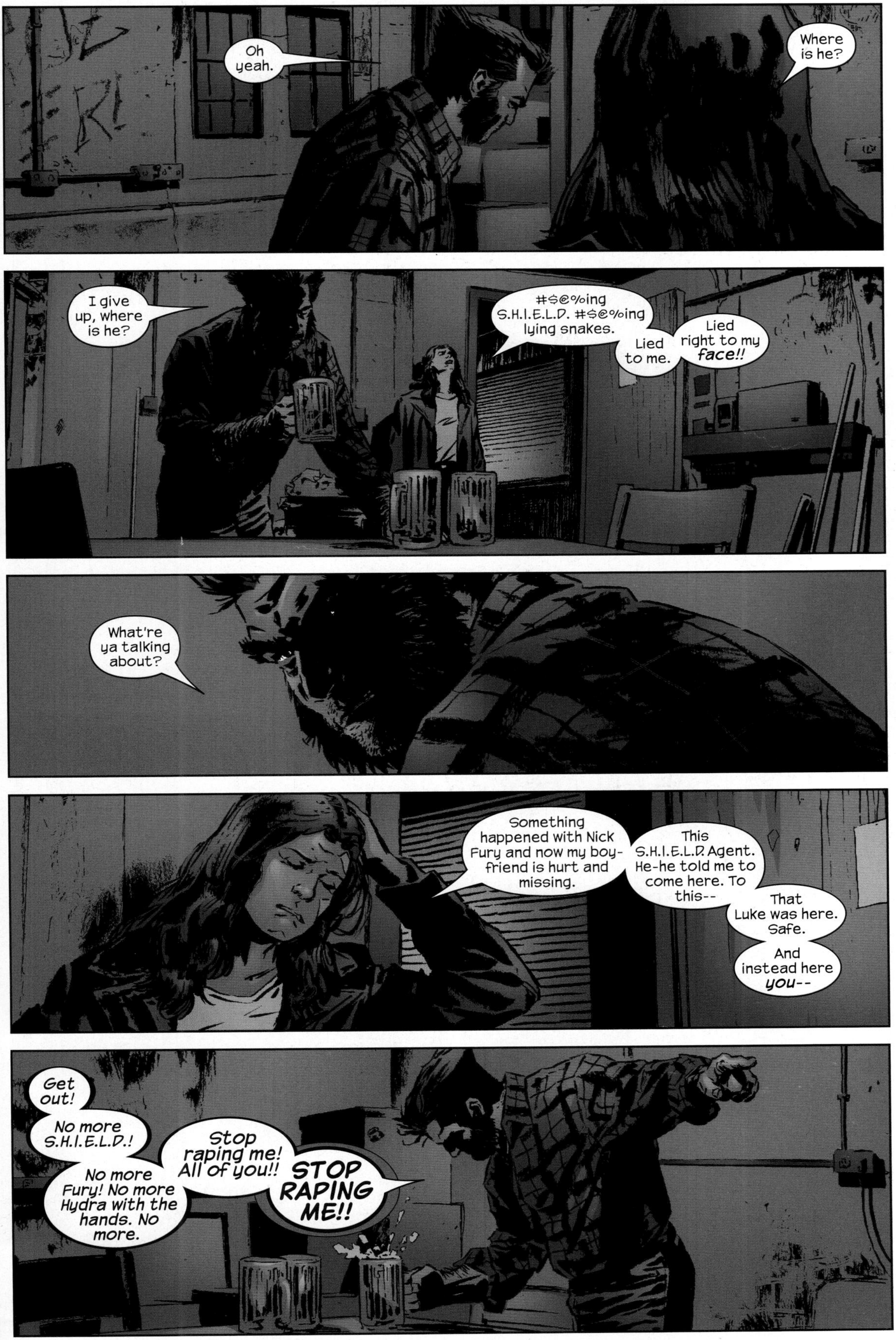

Oh yeah.
Where is he?
I give up, where is he?
#$@%ing S.H.I.E.L.D. #$@%ing lying snakes.
Lied to me.
Lied right to my *face!!*
What're ya talking about?
Something happened with Nick Fury and now my boy-friend is hurt and missing.
This S.H.I.E.L.D. Agent. He-he told me to come here. To this--
That Luke was here. Safe.
And instead here *you*--
Get out!
No more S.H.I.E.L.D.!
No more Fury! No more Hydra with the hands. No more.
Stop raping me! All of you!!
STOP RAPING ME!!

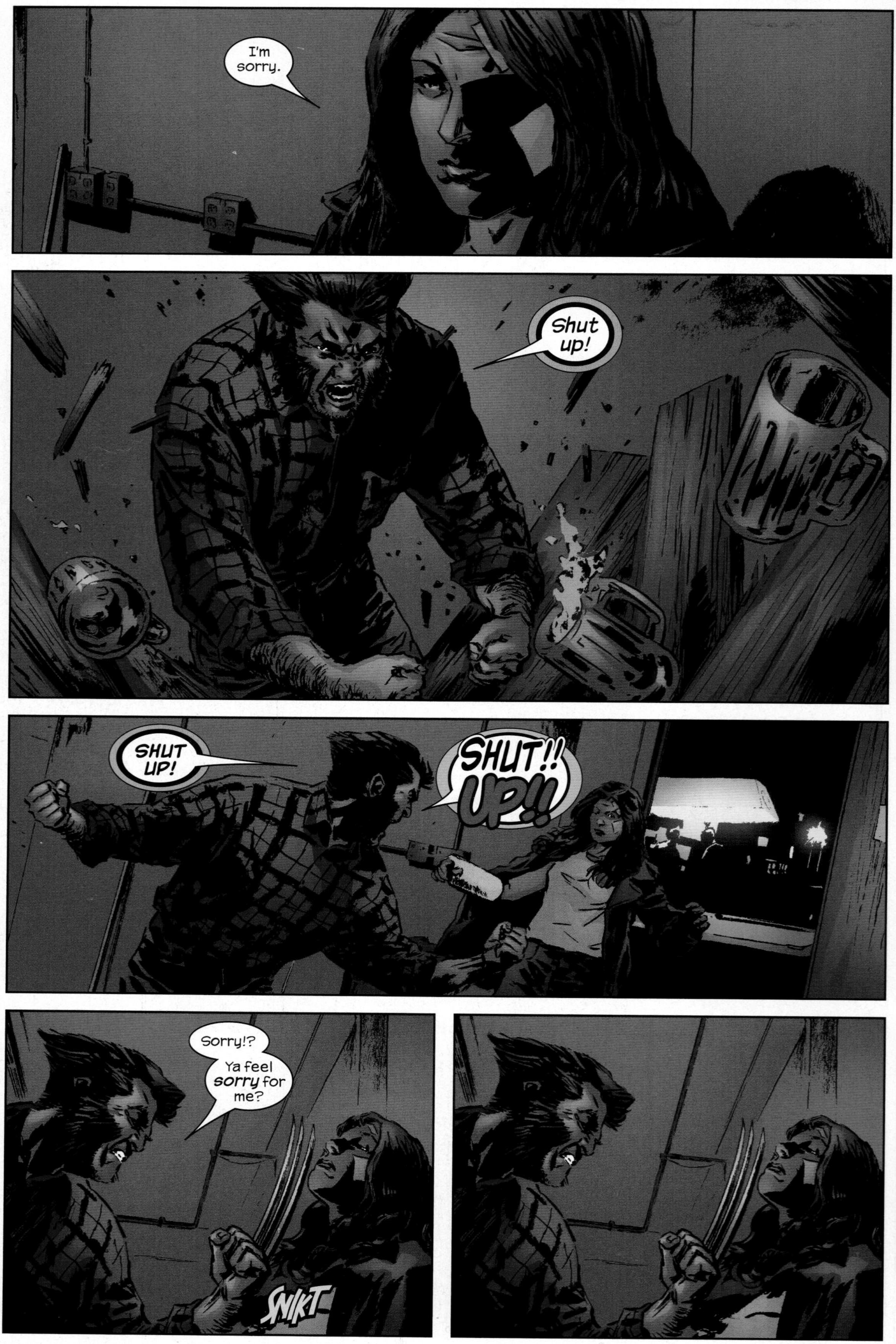

I'm sorry.
Shut up!
SHUT UP!
SHUT!! UP!!
Sorry!? Ya feel sorry for me?
SNIKT

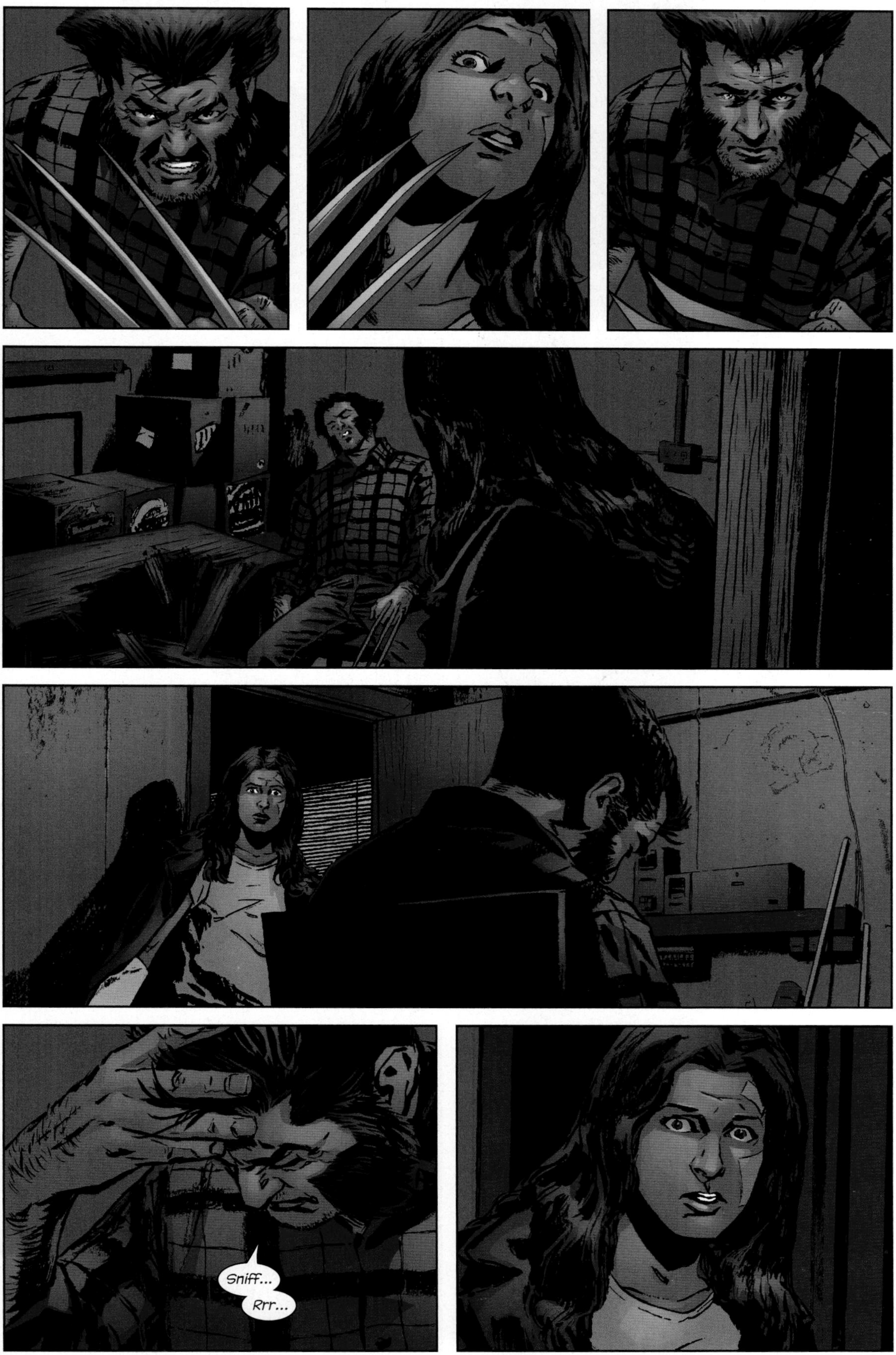
Sniff...
Rrr...

Every day of my life...

...my mind... or my body. There's no other word for it. They rape me.

Try ta get me to do somethin' I don't wanna do.

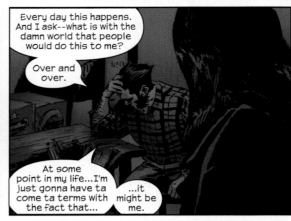

Every day this happens. And I ask--what is with the damn world that people would do this to me?

Over and over.

At some point in my life...I'm just gonna have ta come ta terms with the fact that...

...it might be me.

Know you can't tell from lookin' at me...

...but I'm usually not the self-pityin' type.

What is this? Why are we here?

I told you in the car-- that S.H.I.E.L.D. Agent has been trying to get me to throw Nick Fury under the bus. In print.

Screwing with me.

I don't *know* why he sent us here.

Let's go.

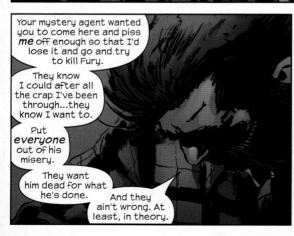

Your mystery agent wanted you to come here and piss *me* off enough so that I'd lose it and go and try to kill Fury.

They know I could after all the crap I've been through...they know I want to.

Put *everyone* out of his misery.

They want him dead for what he's done.

And they ain't wrong. At least, in theory.

What did he do?

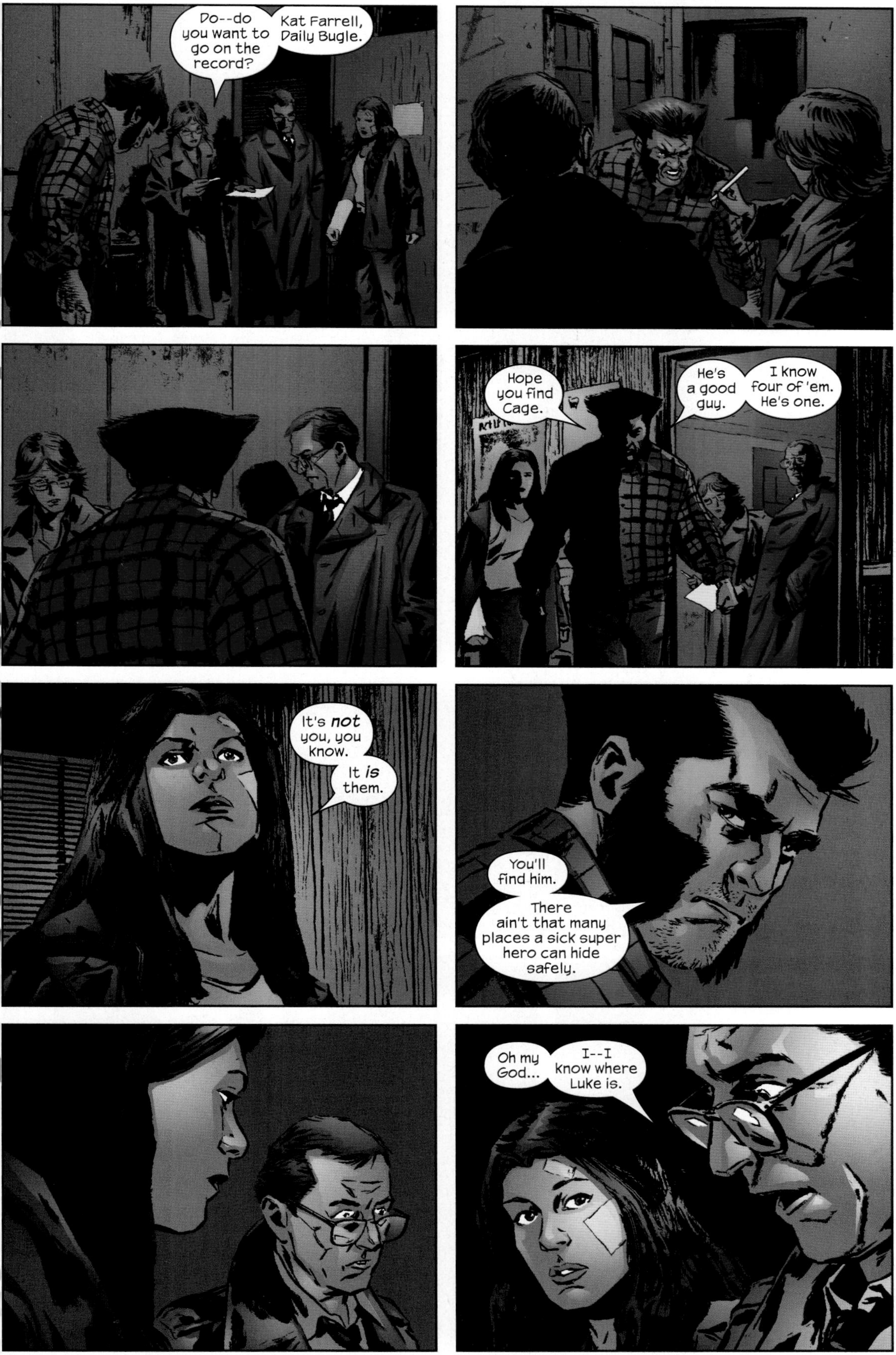
Do--do you want to go on the record?
Kat Farrell, Daily Bugle.
Hope you find Cage.
He's a good guy.
I know four of 'em. He's one.
It's *not* you, you know.
It *is* them.
You'll find him.
There ain't that many places a sick super hero can hide safely.
Oh my God...
I--I know where Luke is.

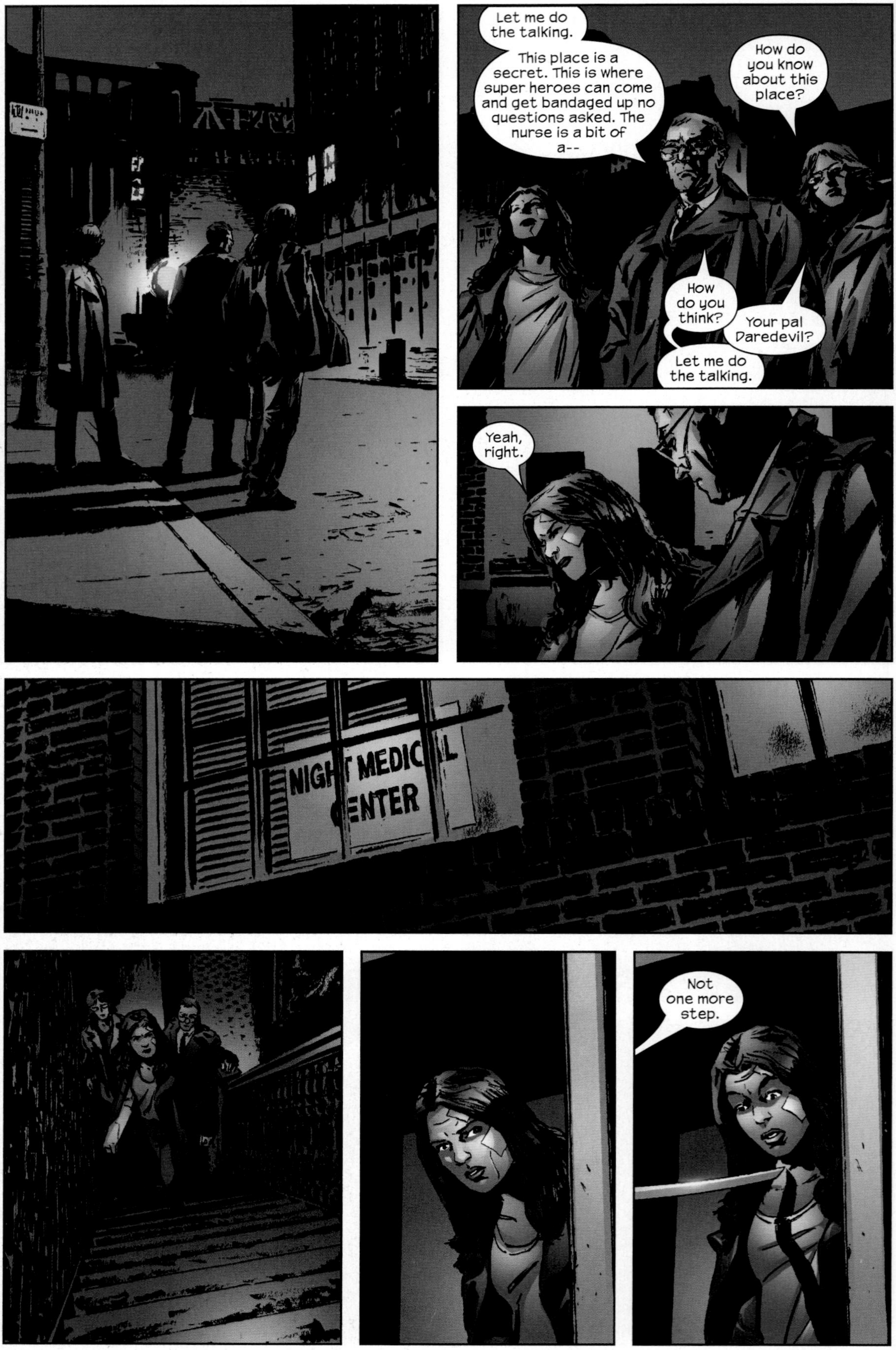
Let me do the talking.
This place is a secret. This is where super heroes can come and get bandaged up no questions asked. The nurse is a bit of a--
How do you know about this place?
How do you think?
Let me do the talking.
Your pal Daredevil?
Yeah, right.
NIGHT MEDIC L
ENTER
Not one more step.

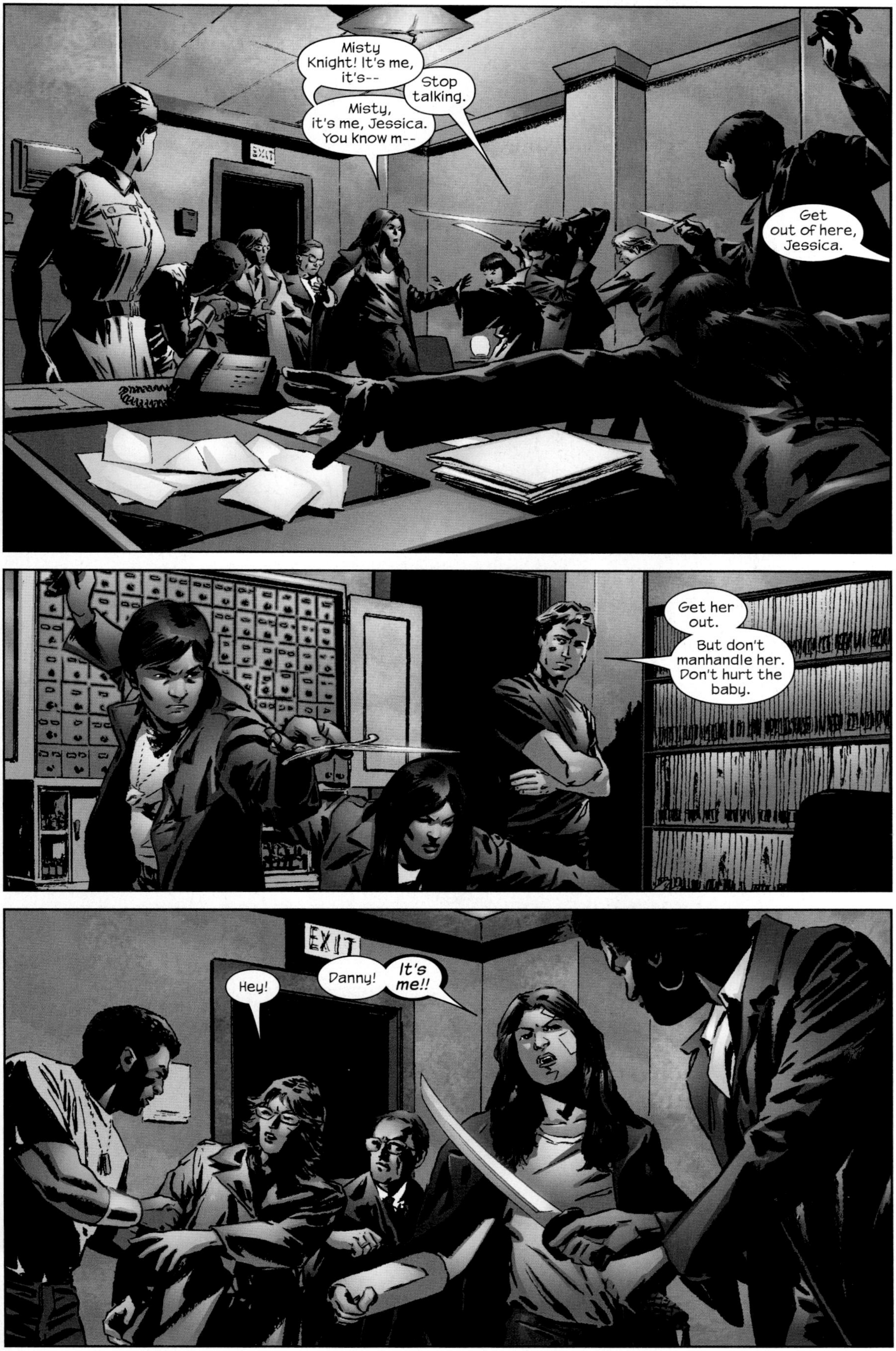

Misty Knight! It's me, it's--
Misty, it's me, Jessica. You know m--
Stop talking.
Get out of here, Jessica.
EXIT
Get her out.
But don't manhandle her. Don't hurt the baby.
EXIT
Hey!
Danny!
It's me!!

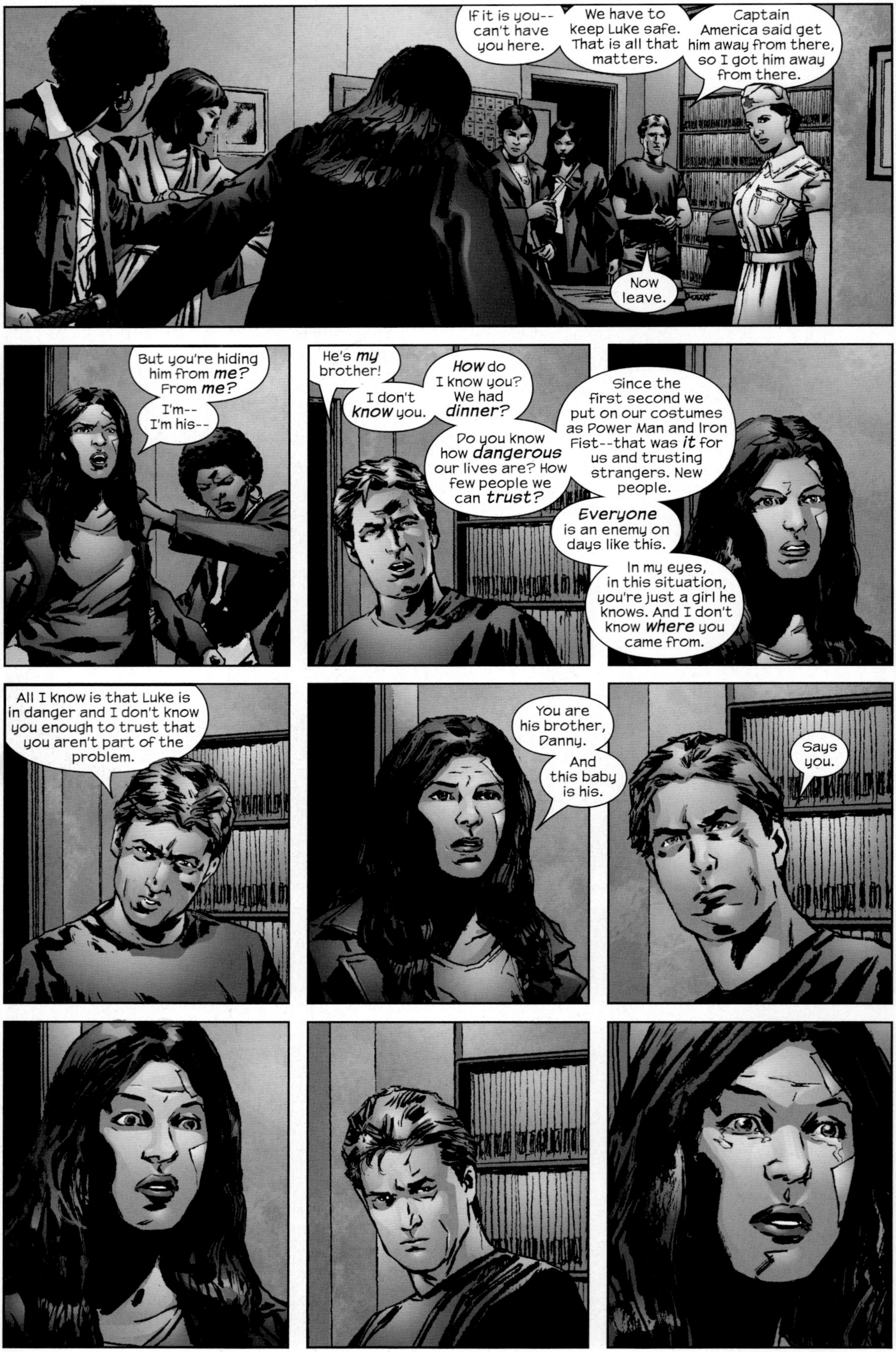
If it is you-- can't have you here.
We have to keep Luke safe. That is all that matters.
Captain America said get him away from there, so I got him away from there.
Now leave.
But you're hiding him from me? From me?
I'm-- I'm his--
He's my brother!
I don't know you.
How do I know you? We had dinner?
Do you know how dangerous our lives are? How few people we can trust?
Since the first second we put on our costumes as Power Man and Iron Fist--that was it for us and trusting strangers. New people.
Everyone is an enemy on days like this.
In my eyes, in this situation, you're just a girl he knows. And I don't know where you came from.
All I know is that Luke is in danger and I don't know you enough to trust that you aren't part of the problem.
You are his brother, Danny.
And this baby is his.
Says you.

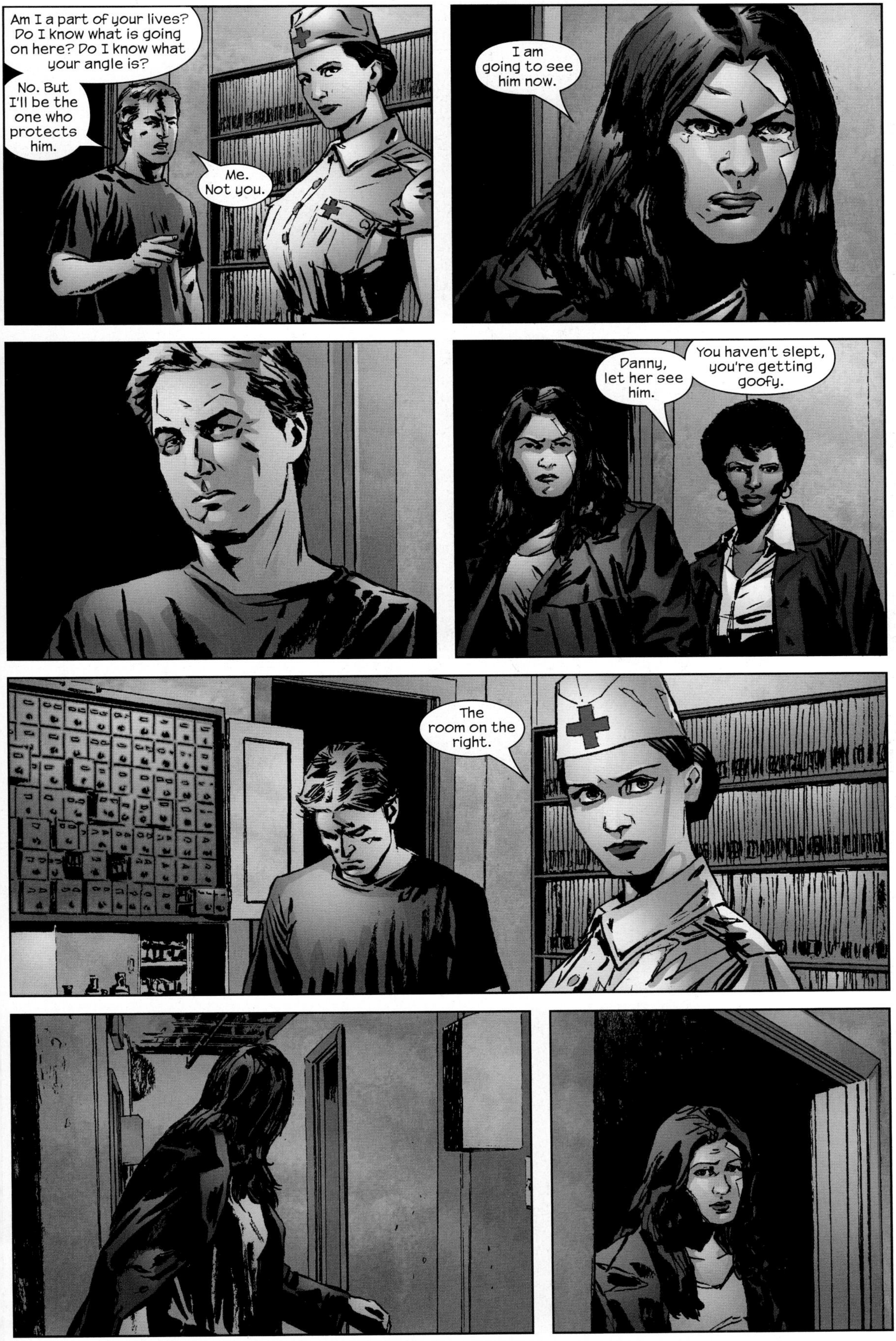
Am I a part of your lives? Do I know what is going on here? Do I know what your angle is?
No. But I'll be the one who protects him.
Me. Not you.
I am going to see him now.
Danny, let her see him.
You haven't slept, you're getting goofy.
The room on the right.

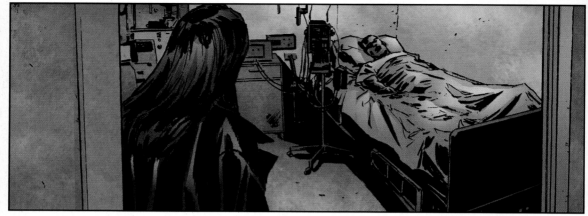

Hey...

Oh, thank God.

You okay?

Yes.

Baby?

She's in there.

That's all... ...that matters.

Hey... Didn't you used to be a tougher broad?

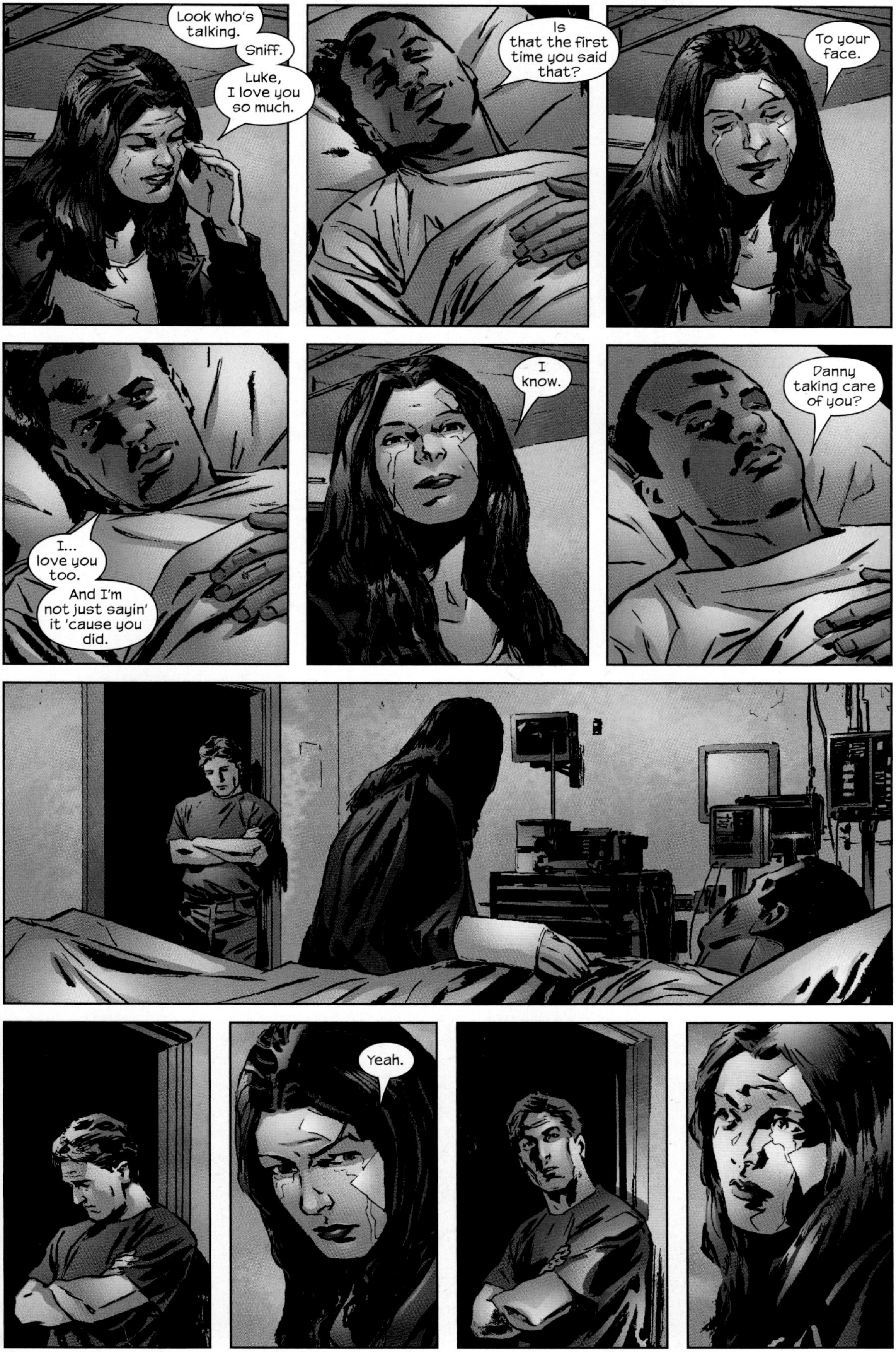
Look who's talking.
Sniff.
Luke, I love you so much.
Is that the first time you said that?
To your face.
I... love you too.
And I'm not just sayin' it 'cause you did.
I know.
Danny taking care of you?
Yeah.

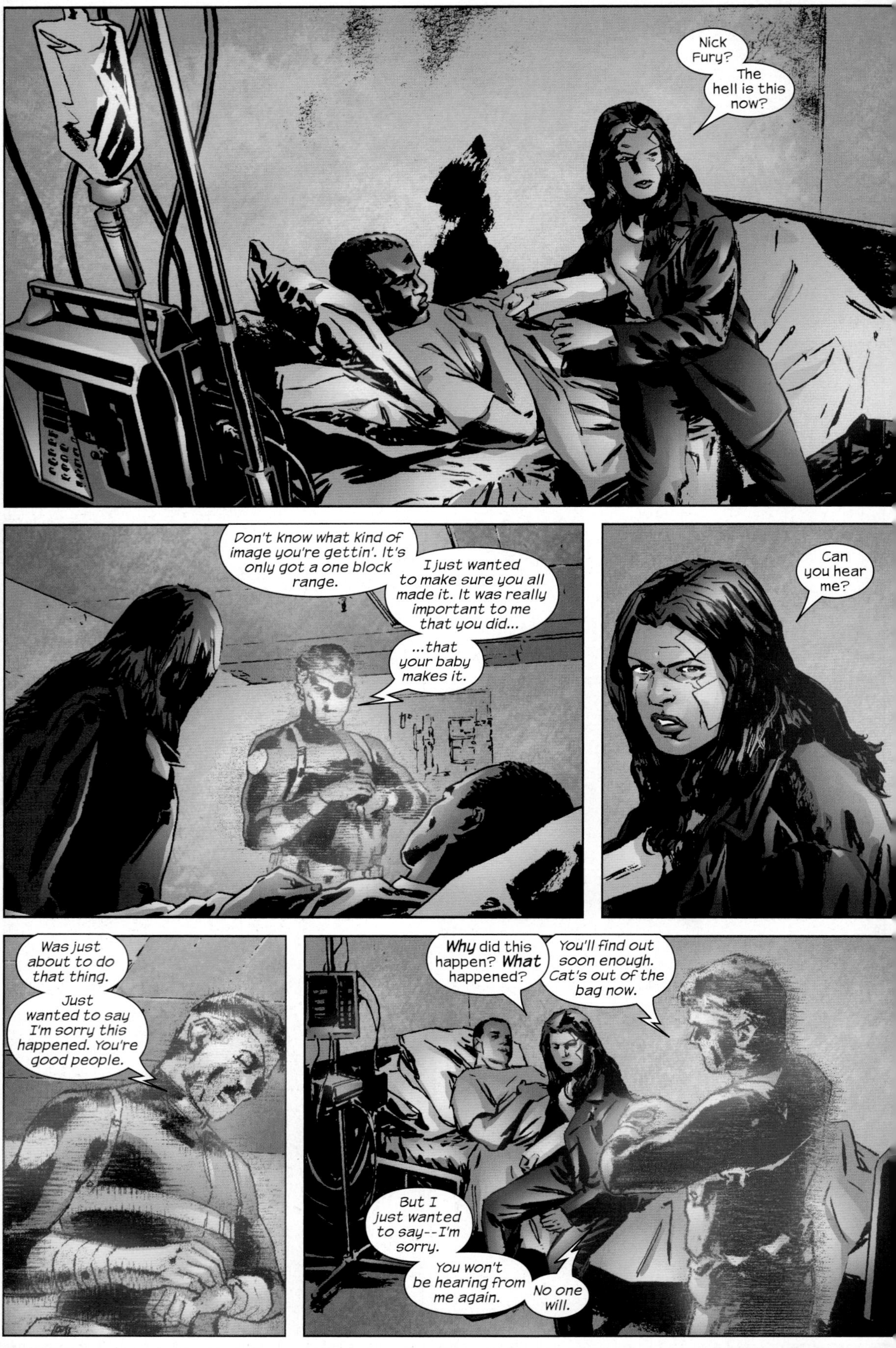
Nick Fury?
The hell is this now?
Don't know what kind of image you're gettin'. It's only got a one block range.
I just wanted to make sure you all made it. It was really important to me that you did...
...that your baby makes it.
Can you hear me?
Was just about to do that thing.
Just wanted to say I'm sorry this happened. You're good people.
Why did this happen? *What* happened?
You'll find out soon enough. Cat's out of the bag now.
But I just wanted to say--I'm sorry.
You won't be hearing from me again.
No one will.

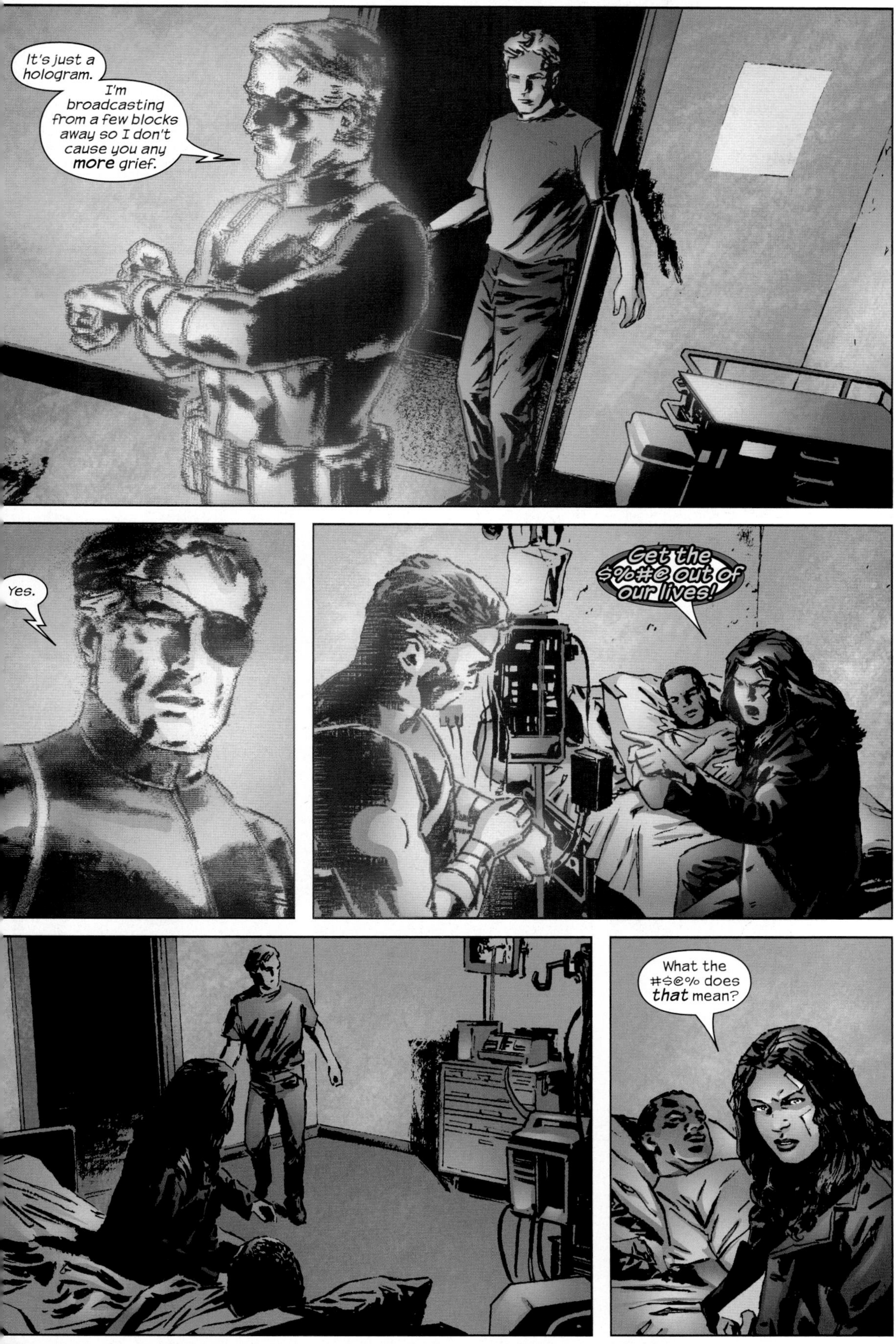
It's just a hologram.
I'm broadcasting from a few blocks away so I don't cause you any **more** grief.
Yes.
Get the $%#@ out of our lives!
What the #$@% does *that* mean?

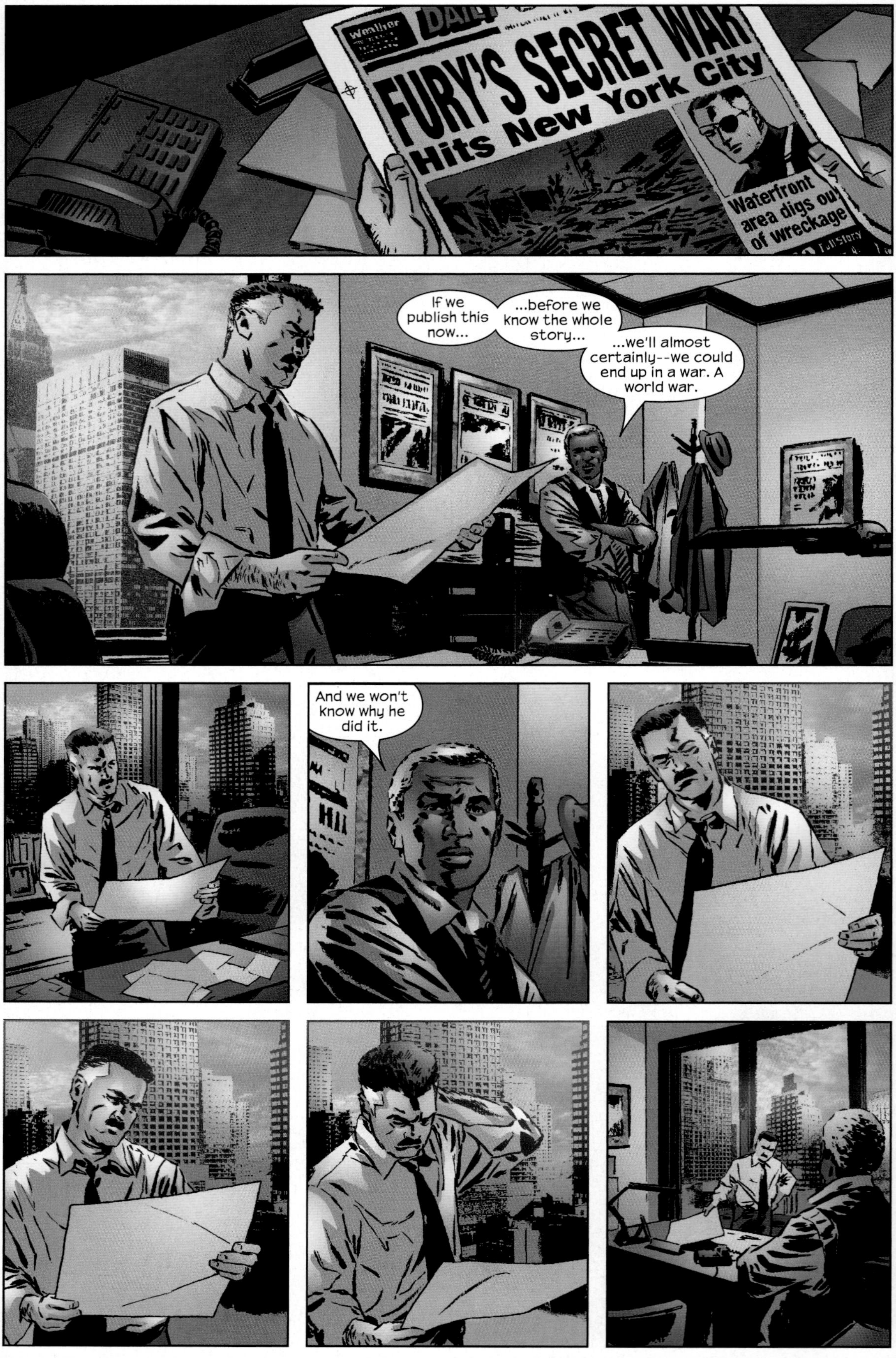
FURY'S SECRET WAR
Hits New York City
Waterfront area digs out of wreckage
If we publish this now...
...before we know the whole story...
...we'll almost certainly--we could end up in a war. A world war.
And we won't know why he did it.

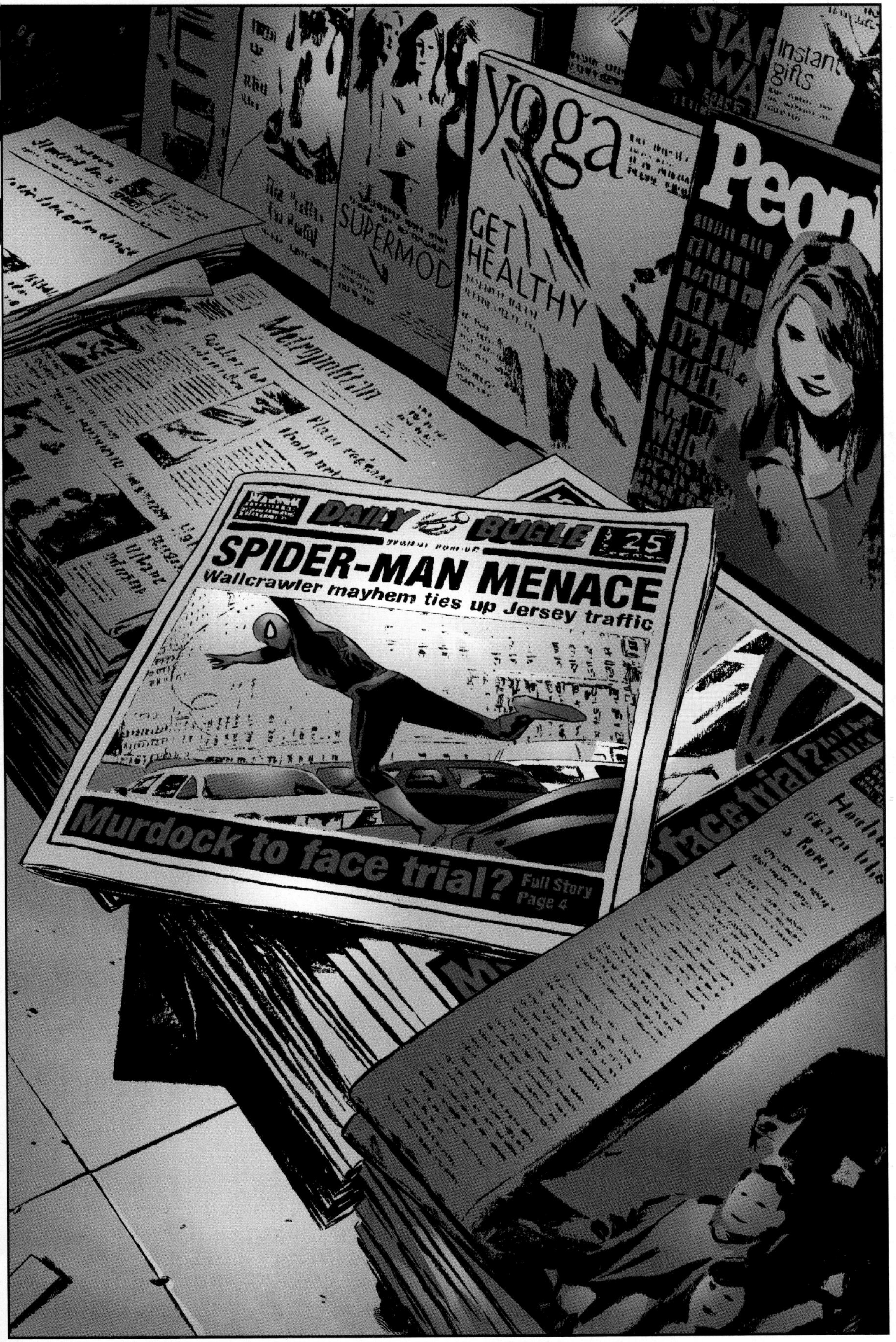

yoga
GET HEALTHY
SUPERMOD
Instant gifts
People
DAILY BUGLE
25
SPIDER-MAN MENACE
Wallcrawler mayhem ties up Jersey traffic
Murdock to face trial? Full Story Page 4

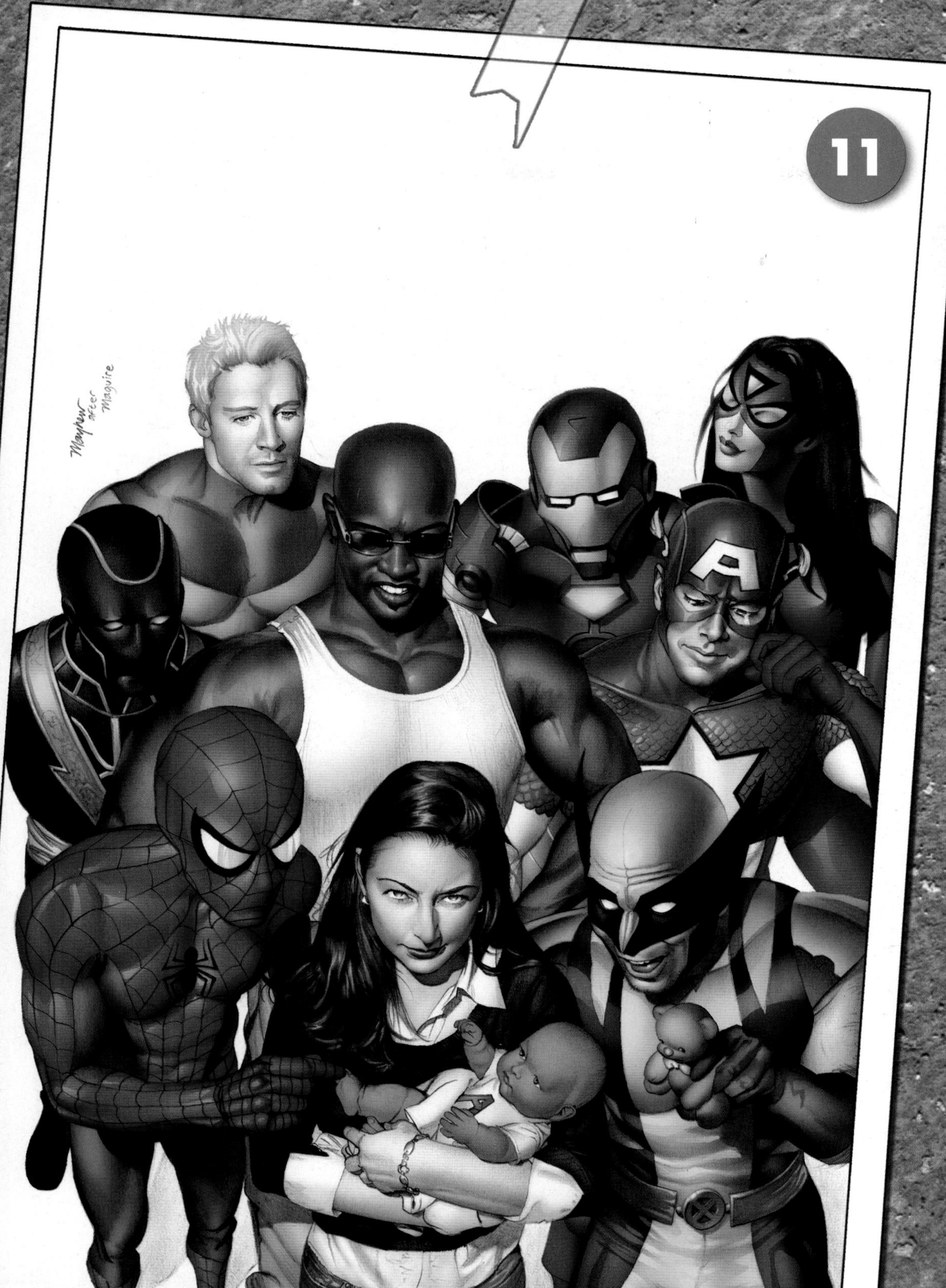
11

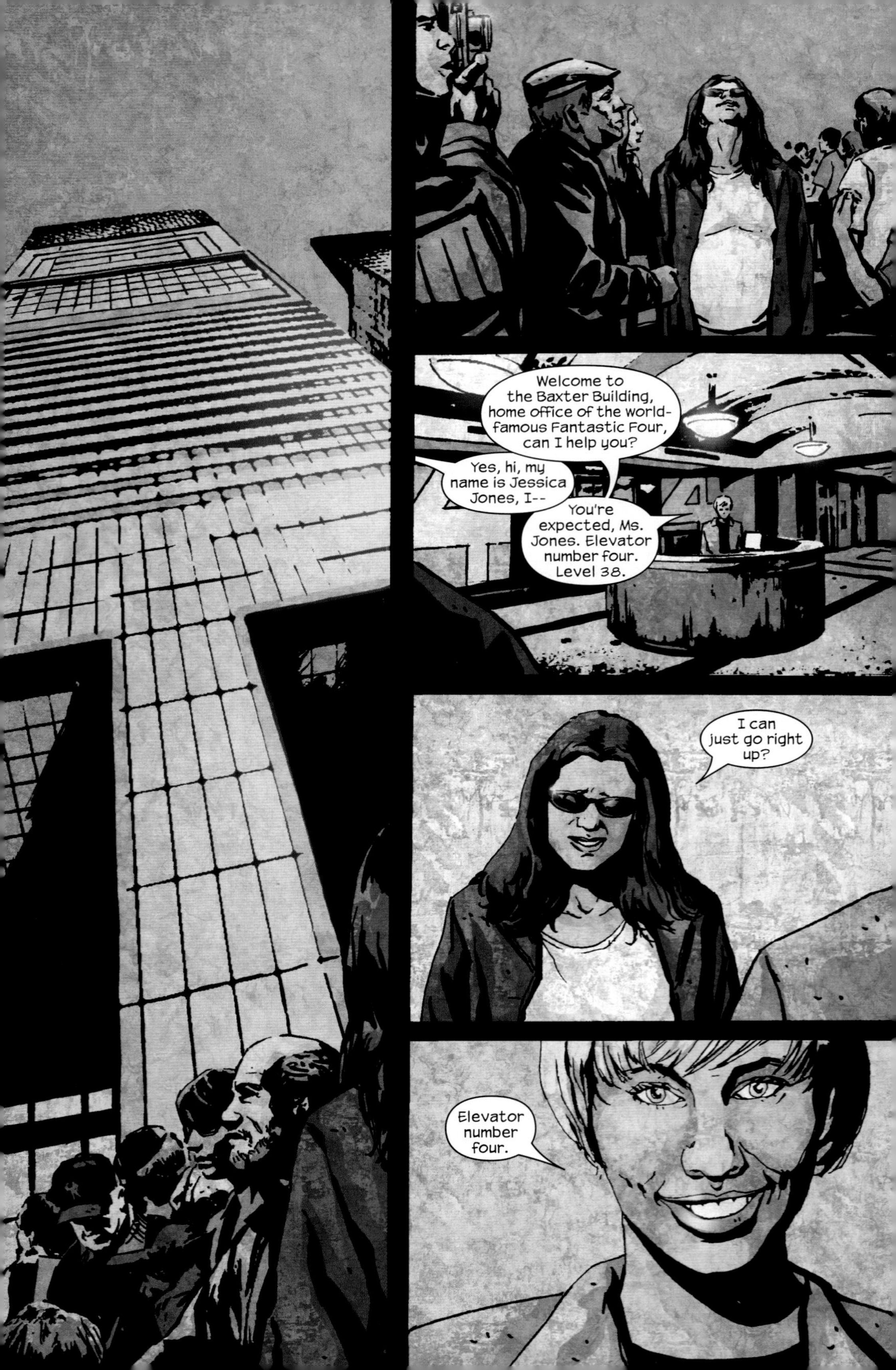
Welcome to the Baxter Building, home office of the world-famous Fantastic Four, can I help you?
Yes, hi, my name is Jessica Jones, I--
You're expected, Ms. Jones. Elevator number four. Level 38.
I can just go right up?
Elevator number four.

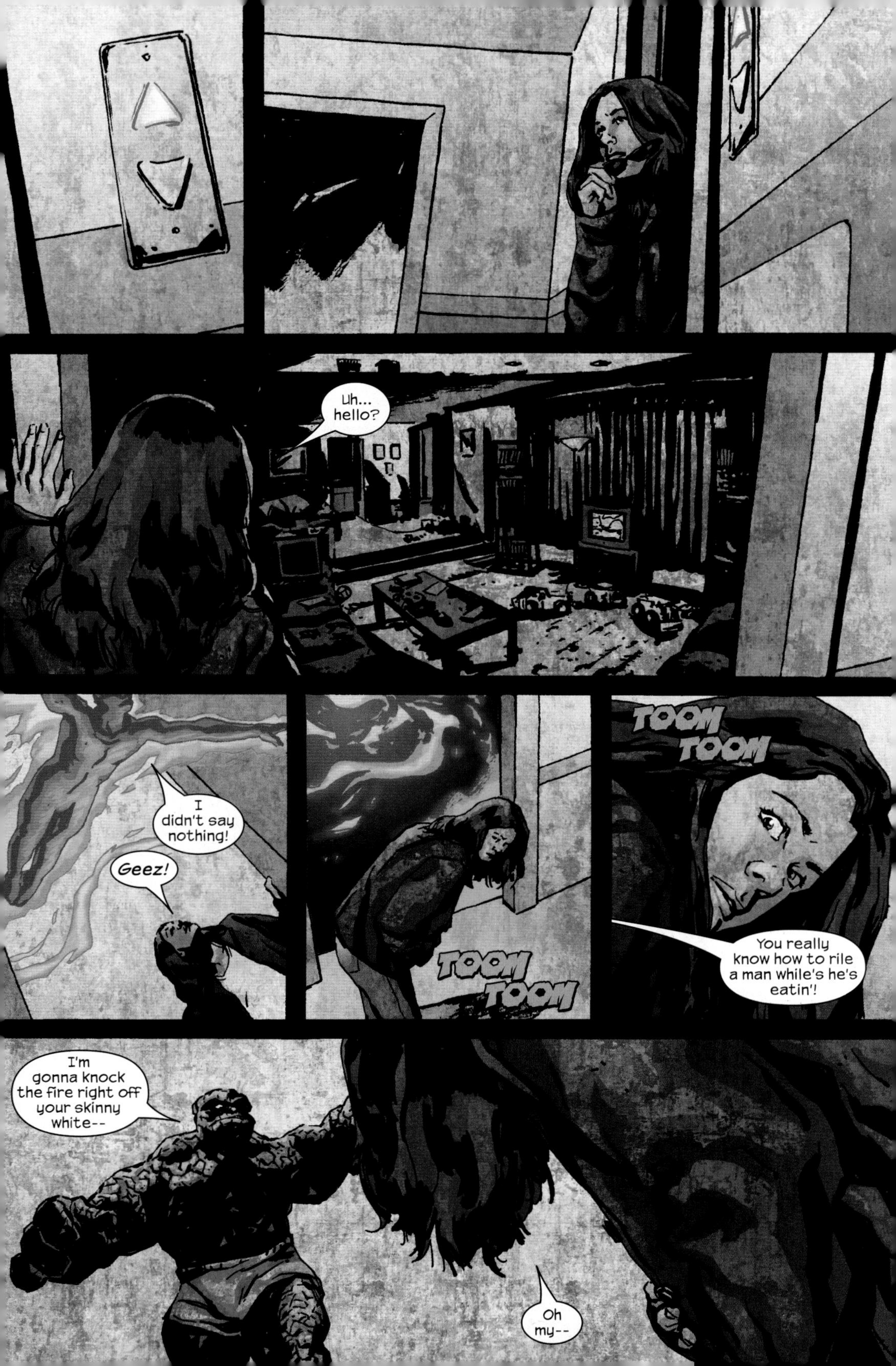
Uh... hello?
I didn't say nothing!
Geez!
TOOM TOOM
TOOM TOOM
You really know how to rile a man while's he's eatin'!
I'm gonna knock the fire right off your skinny white--
Oh my--

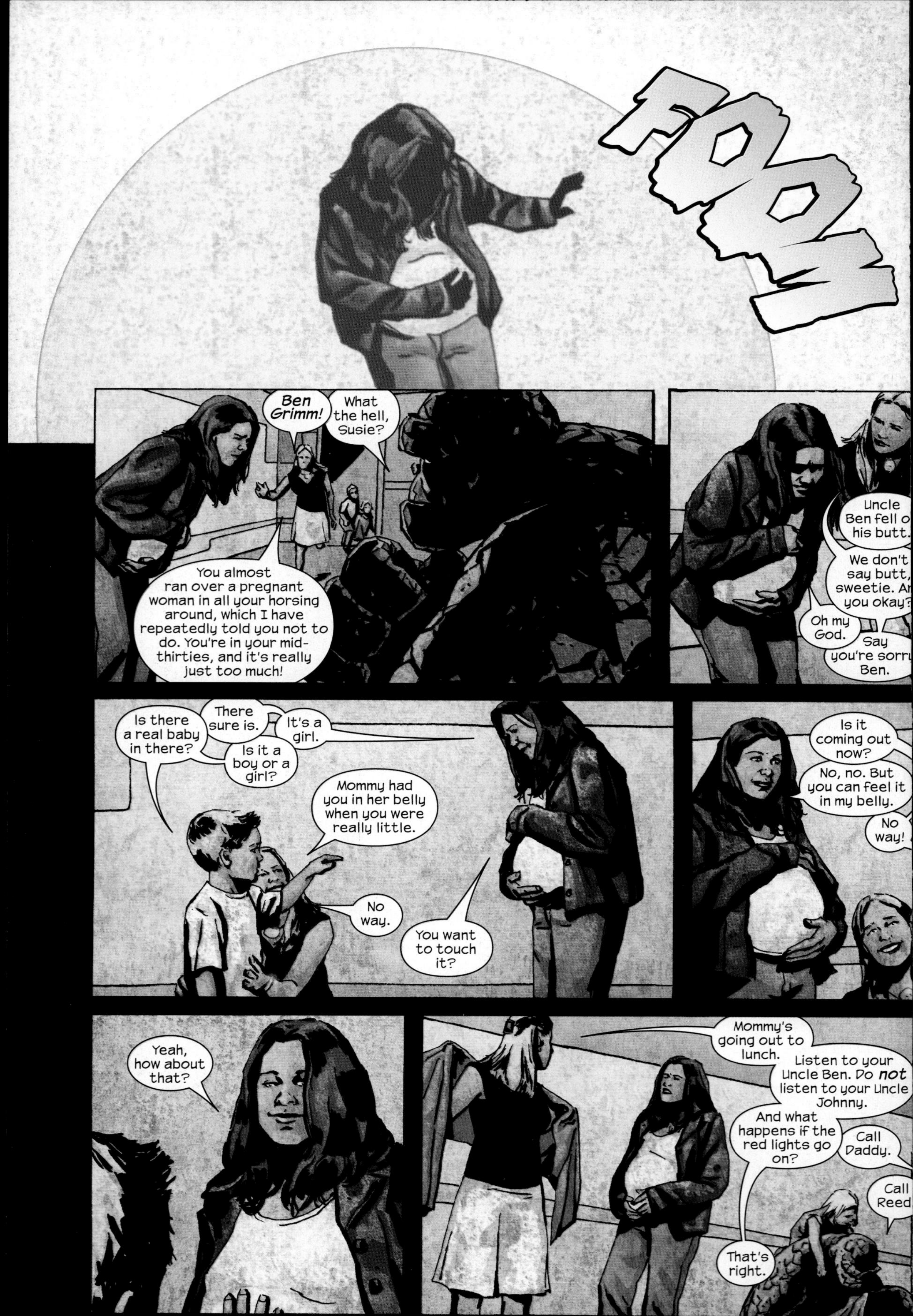
FOOM
Ben Grimm!
What the hell, Susie?
You almost ran over a pregnant woman in all your horsing around, which I have repeatedly told you not to do. You're in your mid-thirties, and it's really just too much!
Uncle Ben fell o his butt.
We don't say butt, sweetie. A you okay?
Oh my God.
Say you're sorr Ben.
Is there a real baby in there?
There sure is.
Is it a boy or a girl?
It's a girl.
Mommy had you in her belly when you were really little.
No way.
You want to touch it?
Is it coming out now?
No, no. But you can feel it in my belly.
No way!
Yeah, how about that?
Mommy's going out to lunch.
Listen to your Uncle Ben. Do not listen to your Uncle Johnny.
And what happens if the red lights go on?
Call Daddy.
Call Reed
That's right.

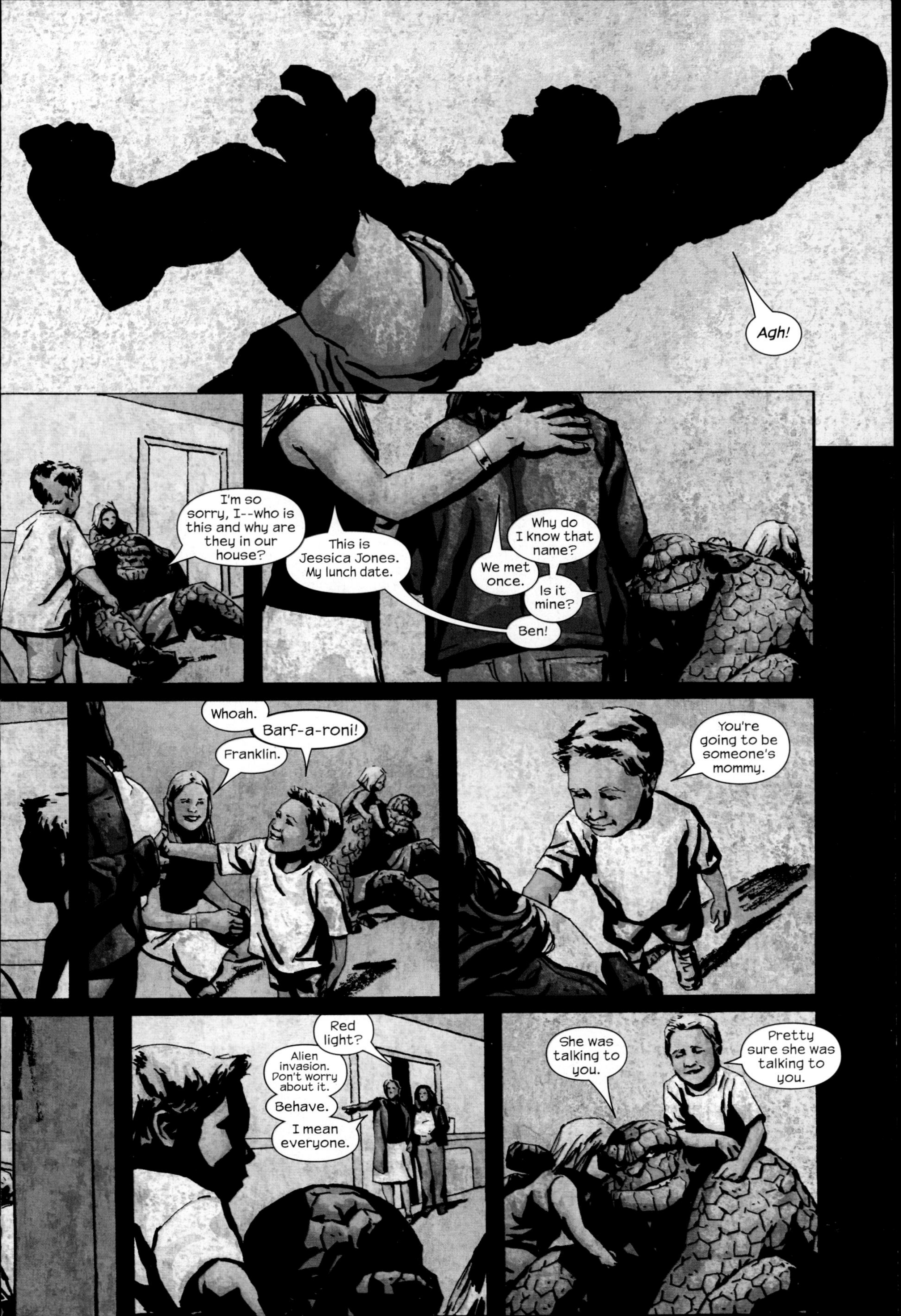
Agh!
I'm so sorry, I--who is this and why are they in our house?
This is Jessica Jones. My lunch date.
Why do I know that name?
We met once.
Is it mine?
Ben!
Whoah.
Barf-a-roni!
Franklin.
You're going to be someone's mommy.
Red light?
Alien invasion. Don't worry about it.
Behave.
I mean everyone.
She was talking to you.
Pretty sure she was talking to you.

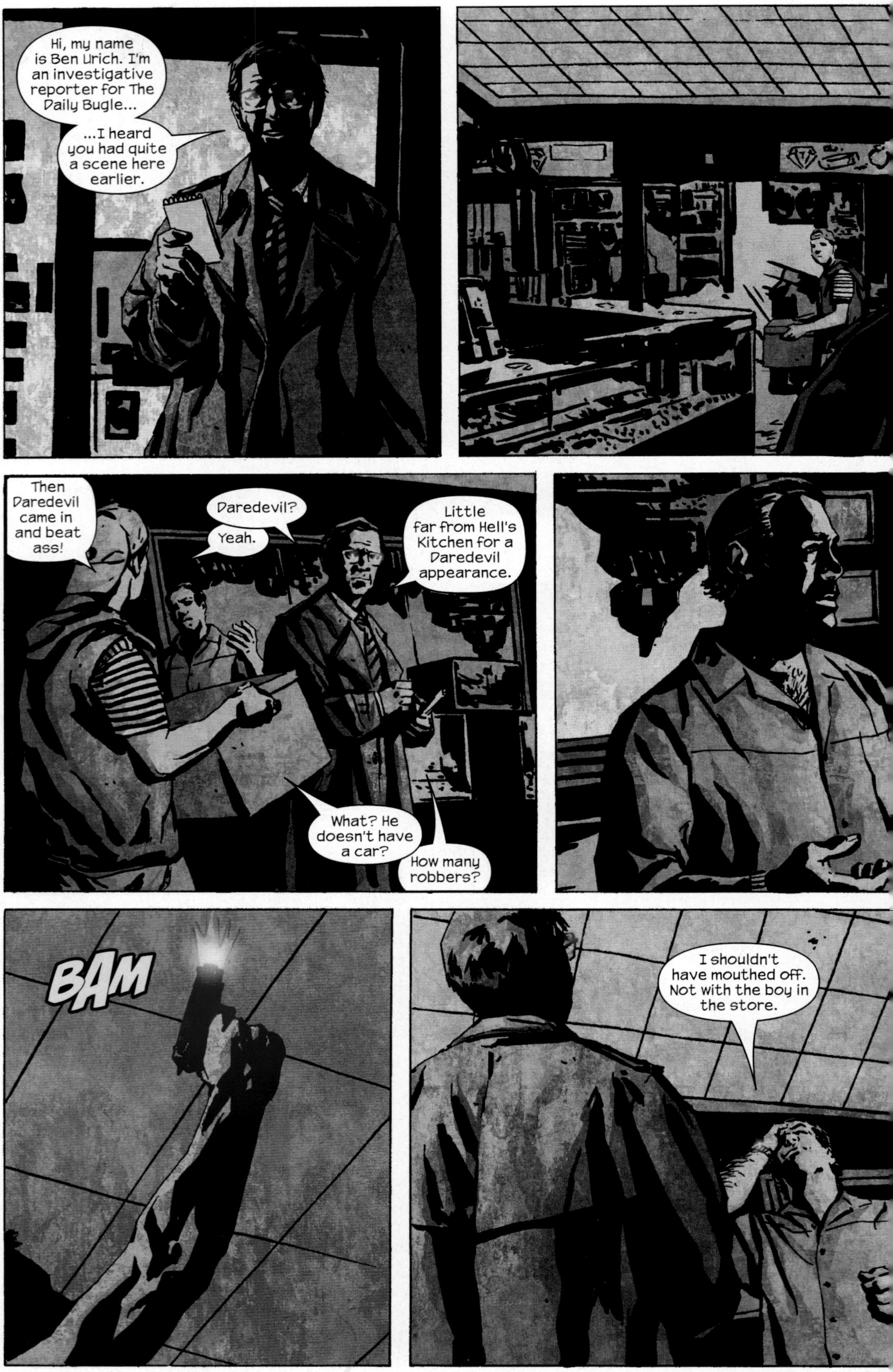

Hi, my name is Ben Urich. I'm an investigative reporter for The Daily Bugle...
...I heard you had quite a scene here earlier.
Then Daredevil came in and beat ass!
Daredevil?
Yeah.
Little far from Hell's Kitchen for a Daredevil appearance.
What? He doesn't have a car?
How many robbers?
BAM
I shouldn't have mouthed off. Not with the boy in the store.

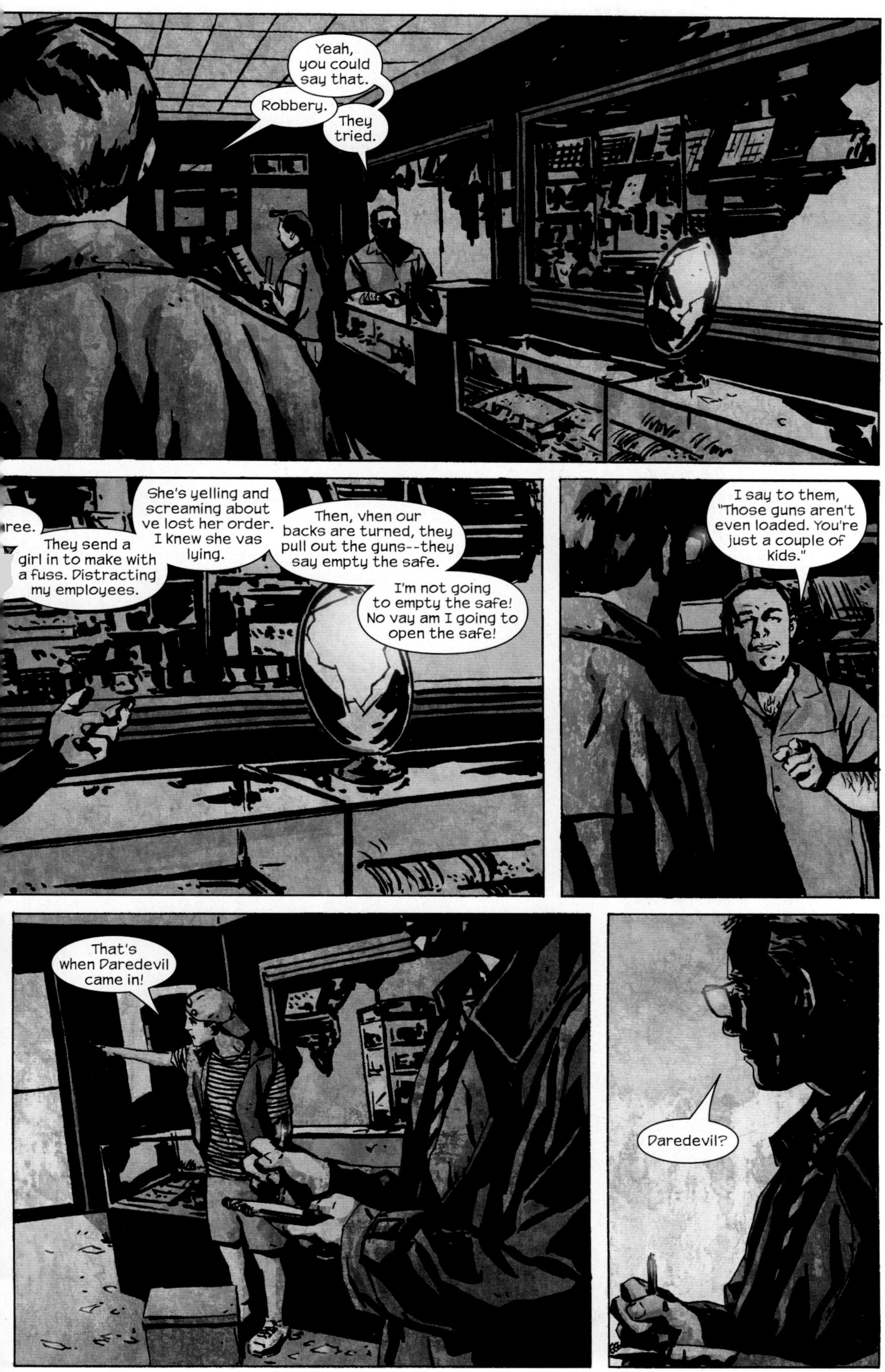
Yeah, you could say that.
Robbery.
They tried.
ree.
They send a girl in to make with a fuss. Distracting my employees.
She's yelling and screaming about ve lost her order. I knew she vas lying.
Then, vhen our backs are turned, they pull out the guns--they say empty the safe.
I'm not going to empty the safe! No vay am I going to open the safe!
I say to them, "Those guns aren't even loaded. You're just a couple of kids."
That's when Daredevil came in!
Daredevil?

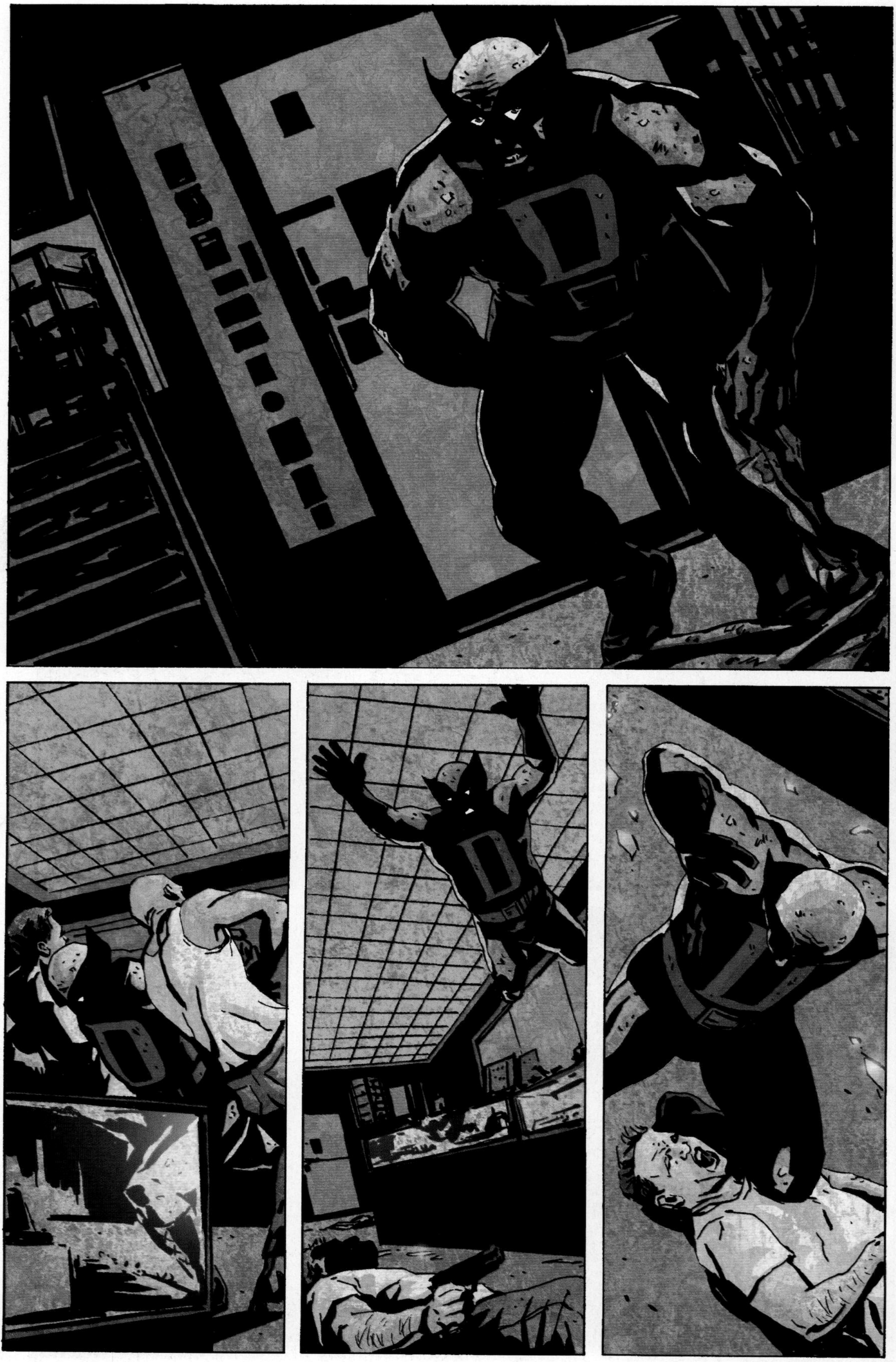

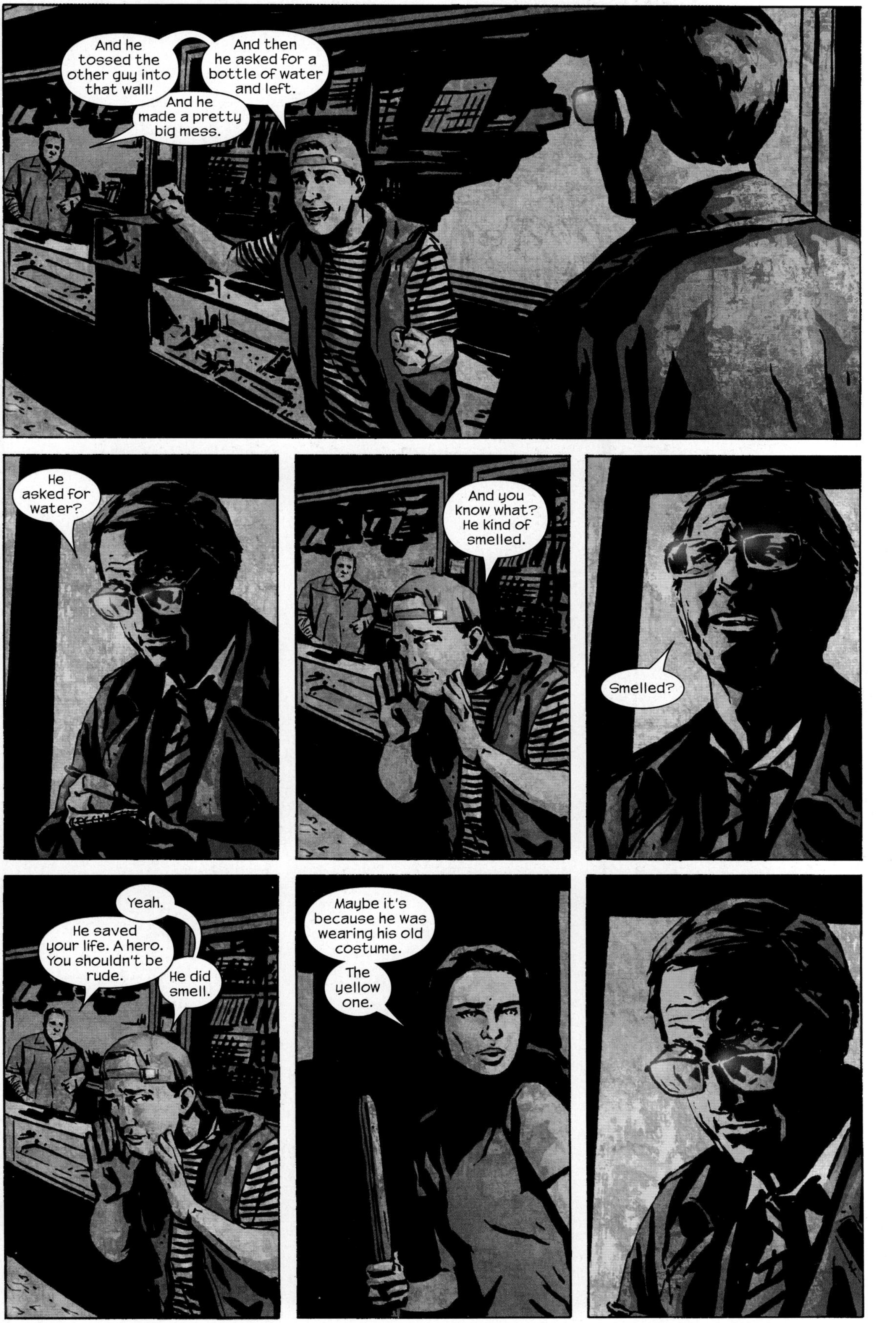
And he tossed the other guy into that wall!
And then he asked for a bottle of water and left.
And he made a pretty big mess.
He asked for water?
And you know what? He kind of smelled.
Smelled?
Yeah.
He saved your life. A hero. You shouldn't be rude.
He did smell.
Maybe it's because he was wearing his old costume.
The yellow one.

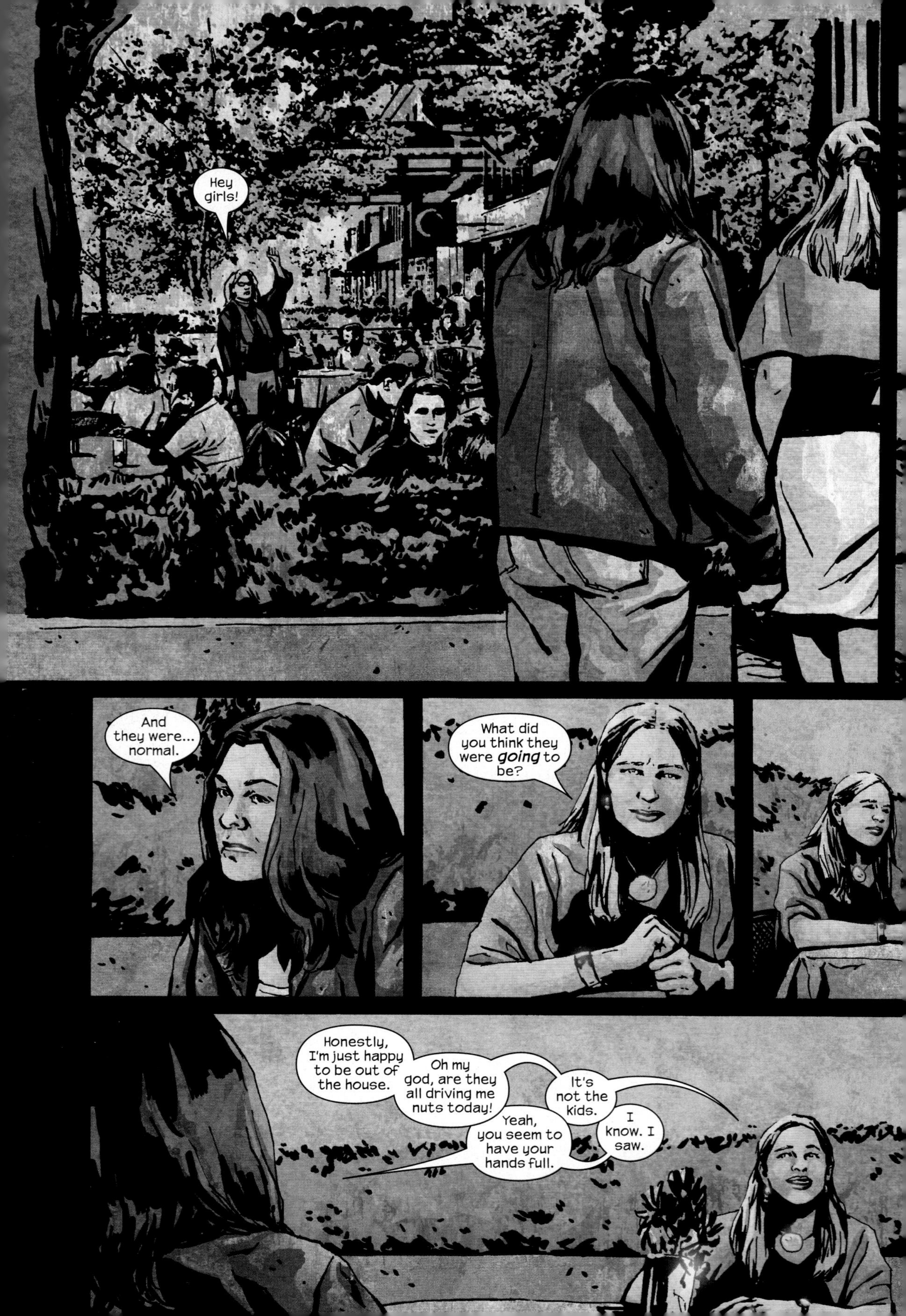
Hey girls!
And they were... normal.
What did you think they were *going* to be?
Honestly, I'm just happy to be out of the house.
Oh my god, are they all driving me nuts today!
It's not the kids.
Yeah, you seem to have your hands full.
I know. I saw.

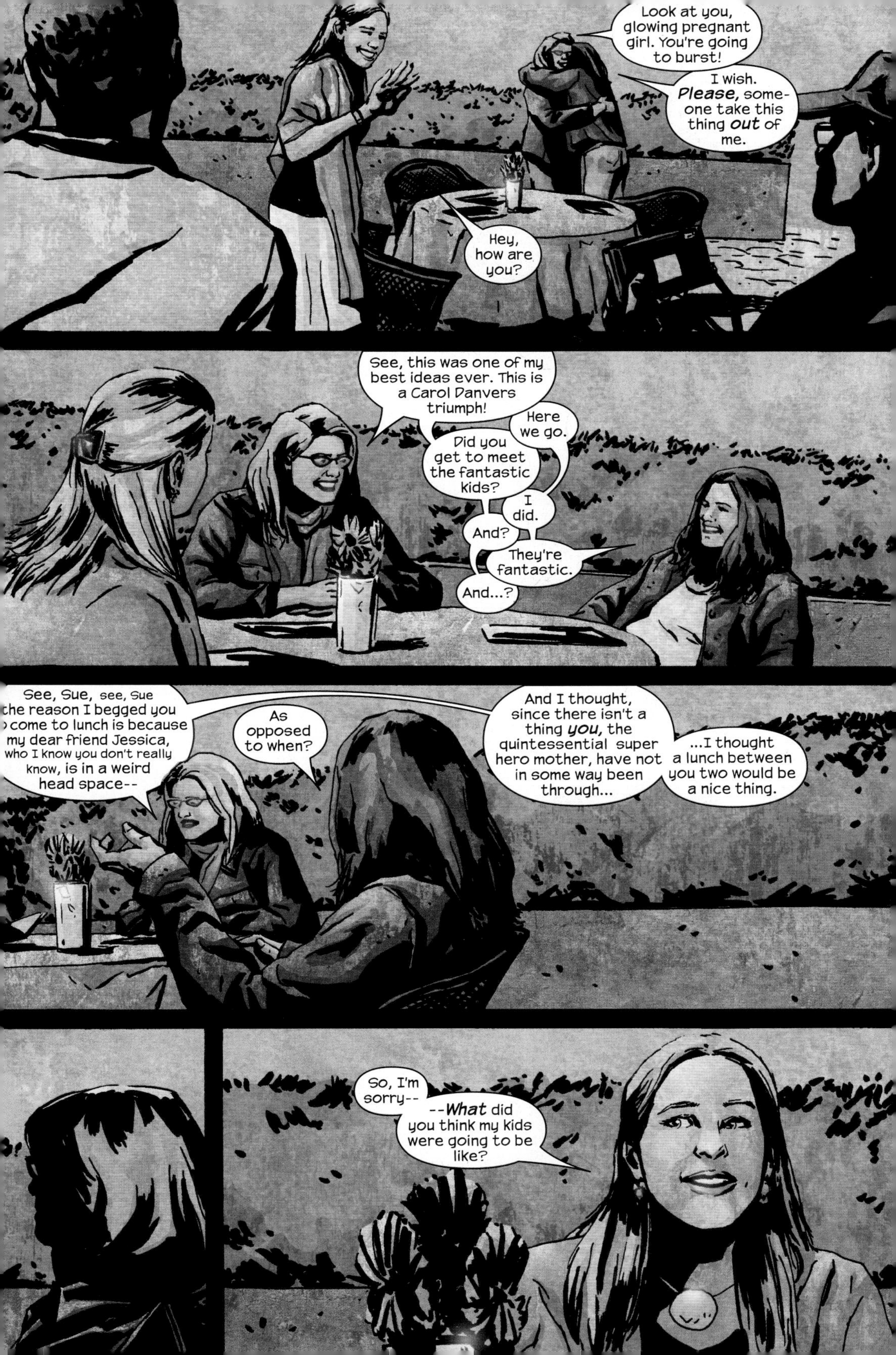
Look at you, glowing pregnant girl. You're going to burst!
I wish. Please, some-one take this thing out of me.
Hey, how are you?
See, this was one of my best ideas ever. This is a Carol Danvers triumph!
Here we go.
Did you get to meet the fantastic kids?
I did.
And?
They're fantastic.
And...?
See, Sue, see, Sue the reason I begged you to come to lunch is because my dear friend Jessica, who I know you don't really know, is in a weird head space--
As opposed to when?
And I thought, since there isn't a thing you, the quintessential super hero mother, have not in some way been through...
...I thought a lunch between you two would be a nice thing.
So, I'm sorry--
--What did you think my kids were going to be like?

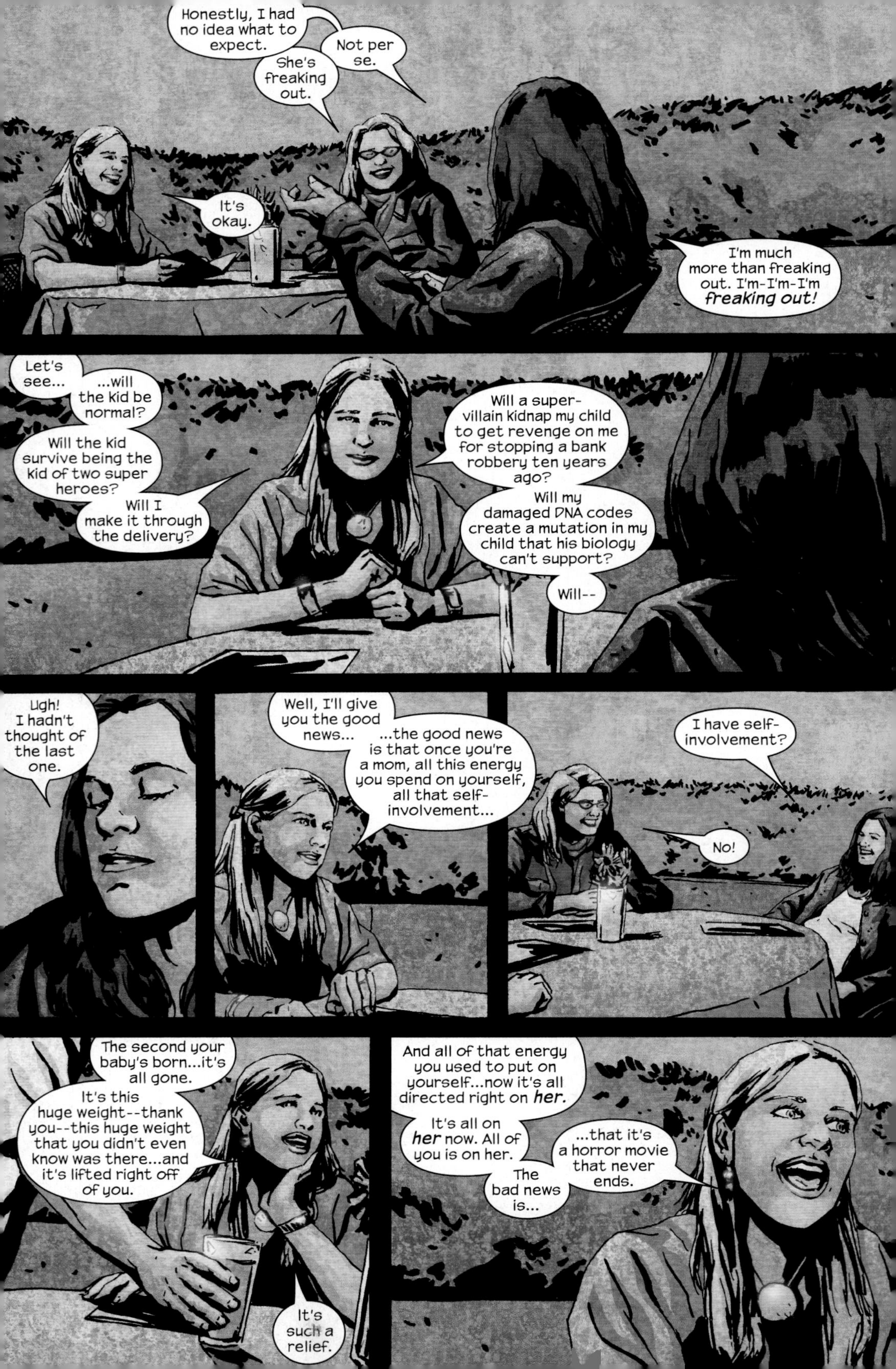

Honestly, I had no idea what to expect.
Not per se.
She's freaking out.
It's okay.
I'm much more than freaking out. I'm-I'm-I'm *freaking out!*
Let's see...
...will the kid be normal?
Will the kid survive being the kid of two super heroes?
Will I make it through the delivery?
Will a super-villain kidnap my child to get revenge on me for stopping a bank robbery ten years ago?
Will my damaged DNA codes create a mutation in my child that his biology can't support?
Will--
Ugh! I hadn't thought of the last one.
Well, I'll give you the good news...
...the good news is that once you're a mom, all this energy you spend on yourself, all that self-involvement...
I have self-involvement?
No!
The second your baby's born...it's all gone.
It's this huge weight--thank you--this huge weight that you didn't even know was there...and it's lifted right off of you.
It's such a relief.
And all of that energy you used to put on yourself...now it's all directed right on ***her.***
It's all on ***her*** now. All of you is on her.
The bad news is...
...that it's a horror movie that never ends.

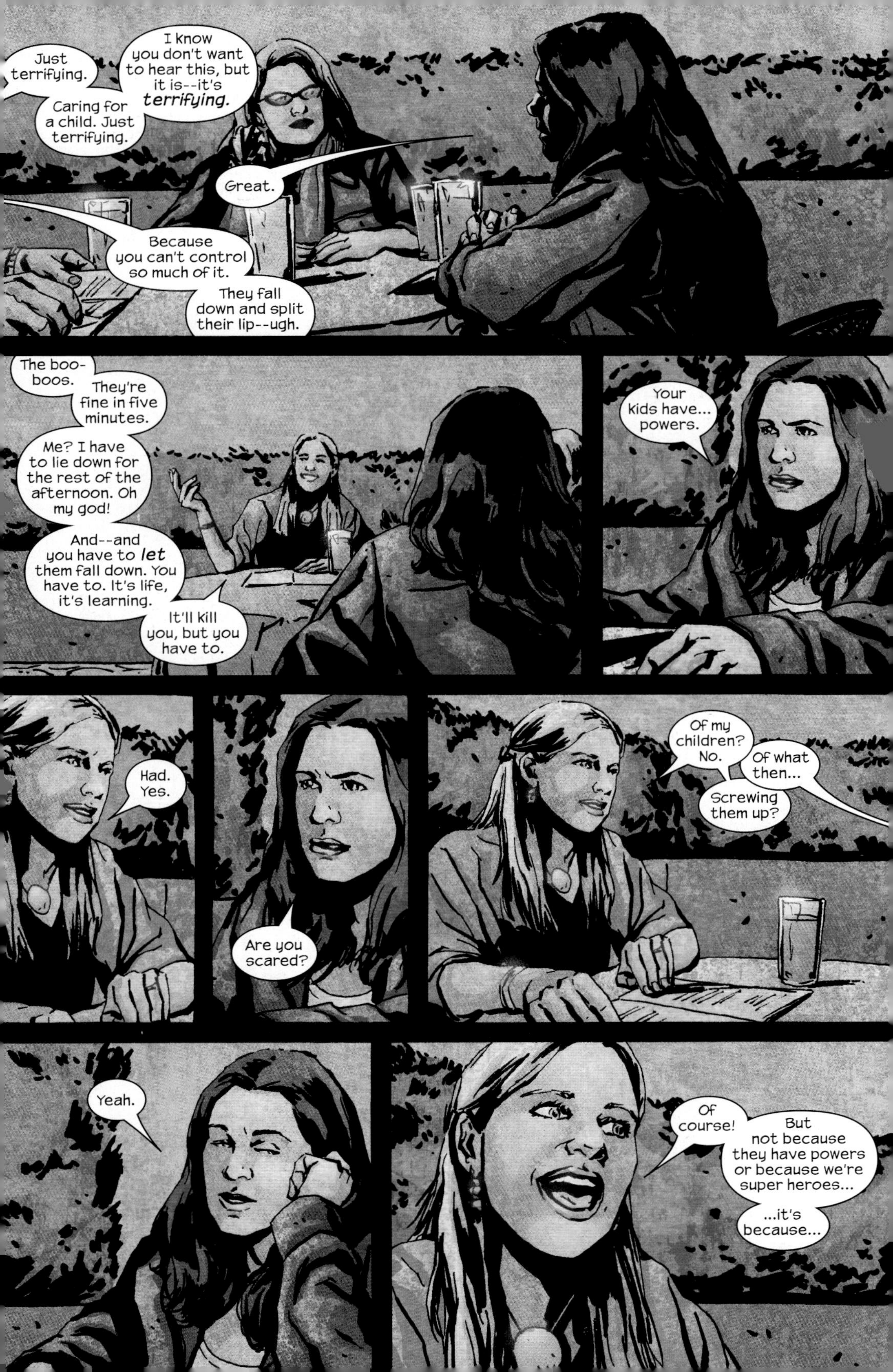

Just terrifying.
I know you don't want to hear this, but it is--it's *terrifying.*
Caring for a child. Just terrifying.
Great.
Because you can't control so much of it.
They fall down and split their lip--ugh.
The boo-boos.
They're fine in five minutes.
Me? I have to lie down for the rest of the afternoon. Oh my god!
And--and you have to *let* them fall down. You have to. It's life, it's learning.
It'll kill you, but you have to.
Your kids have... powers.
Had. Yes.
Are you scared?
Of my children? No.
Of what then...
Screwing them up?
Yeah.
Of course!
But not because they have powers or because we're super heroes...
...it's because...

Listen, you *are* talking to someone who has read every baby book written on this planet, and a few from other ones... no joke.

And all I have learned is this: There is no right. There is no wrong.

There is only love and--and guidance and kissing the boo-boos.

And you can do everything right...

...and they might *still* grow up to put on a big frog costume and jump around the city.

Can I ask you--I heard your kids were kidnapped once.

Yes.

Do I blame myself for being a super hero with enemies that would use my child to get to me and my husband?

Yes.

And no. I didn't-- listen--it's really hard to get my head around it sometimes, but when my head is clear...

...I know It's not my fault.

I didn't kidnap my children or *use* my children or put my children in harm's way...

...all I can do is protect them and--point out that evil man and say to my children that the man who did this is a disturbed, selfish, weak man and show them what being a selfish bastard leads to: nothing

Aren't you worried... about how it'll all affect them...

...You know, in the long run?

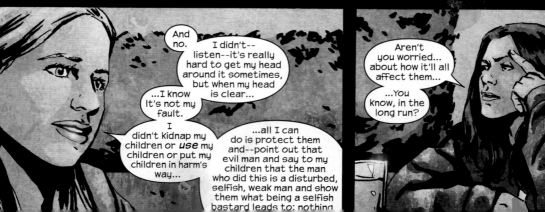

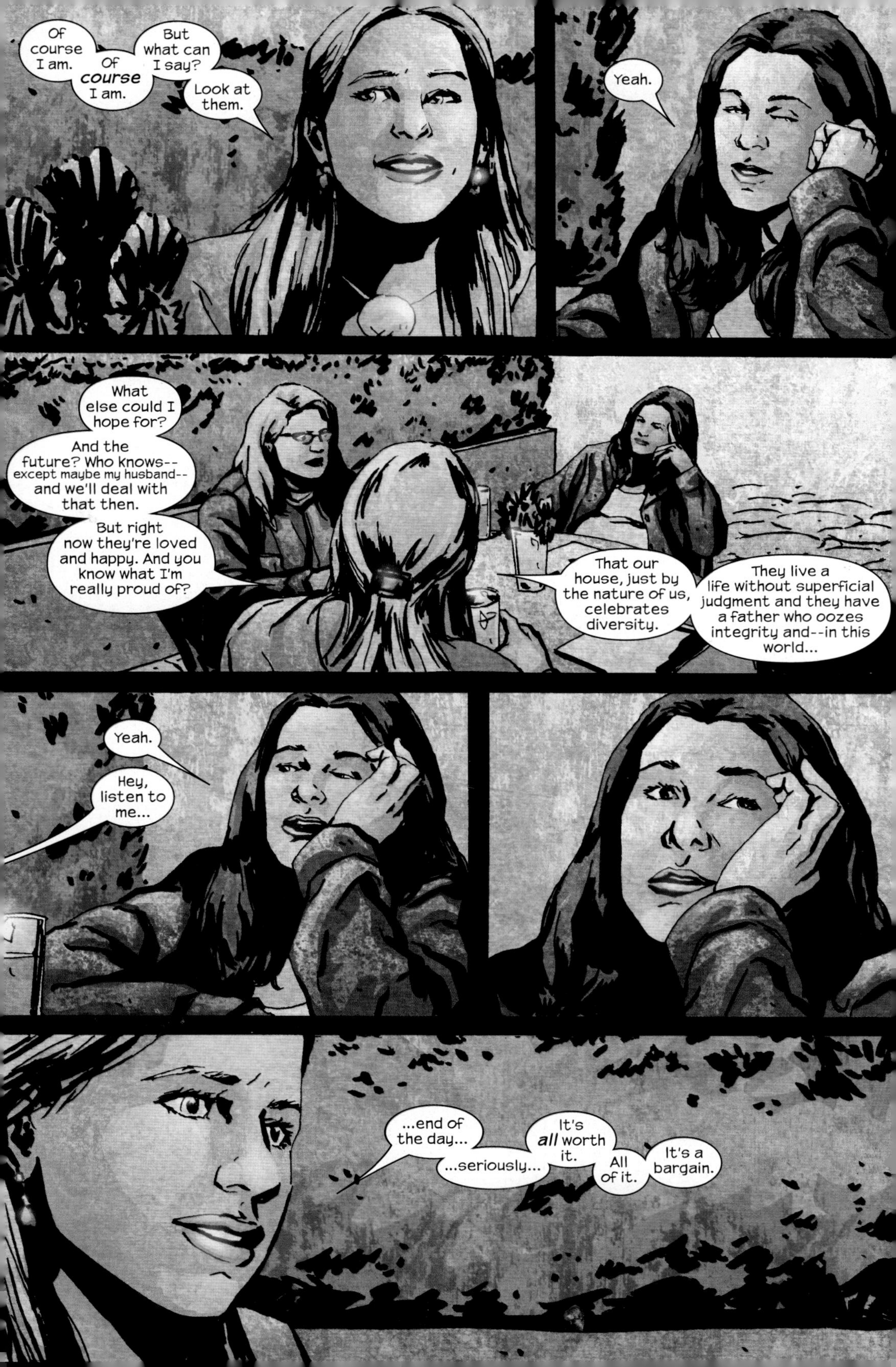
Of course I am.
Of *course* I am.
But what can I say?
Look at them.
Yeah.
What else could I hope for?
And the future? Who knows-- except maybe my husband-- and we'll deal with that then.
But right now they're loved and happy. And you know what I'm really proud of?
That our house, just by the nature of us, celebrates diversity.
They live a life without superficial judgment and they have a father who oozes integrity and--in this world...
Yeah.
Hey, listen to me...
...end of the day...
...seriously...
It's *all* worth it.
All of it.
It's a bargain.

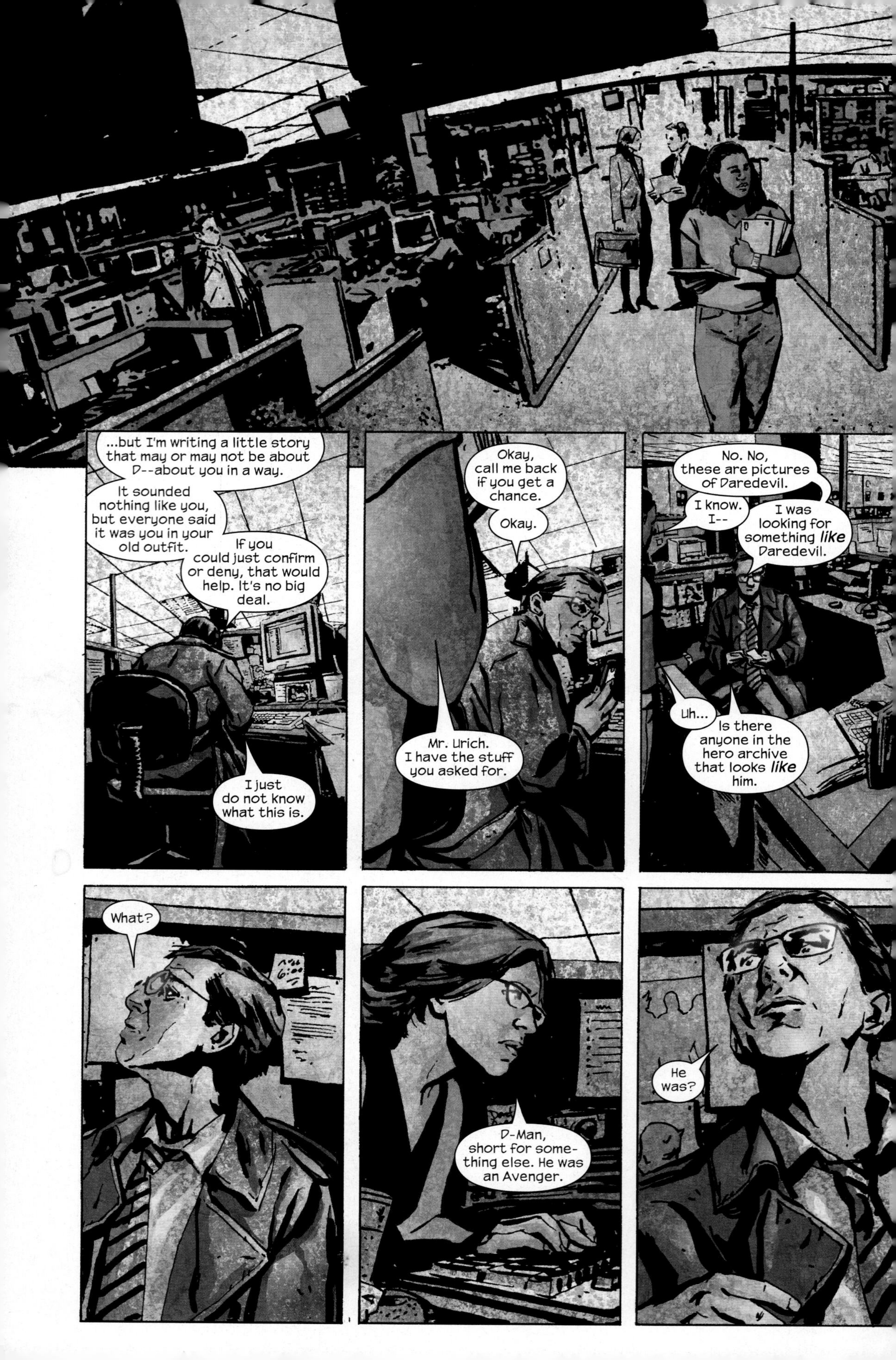
...but I'm writing a little story that may or may not be about D--about you in a way.
It sounded nothing like you, but everyone said it was you in your old outfit.
If you could just confirm or deny, that would help. It's no big deal.
I just do not know what this is.
Okay, call me back if you get a chance.
Okay.
Mr. Urich. I have the stuff you asked for.
No. No, these are pictures of Daredevil.
I know. I--
I was looking for something *like* Daredevil.
Uh...
Is there anyone in the hero archive that looks *like* him.
What?
D-Man, short for something else. He was an Avenger.
He was?

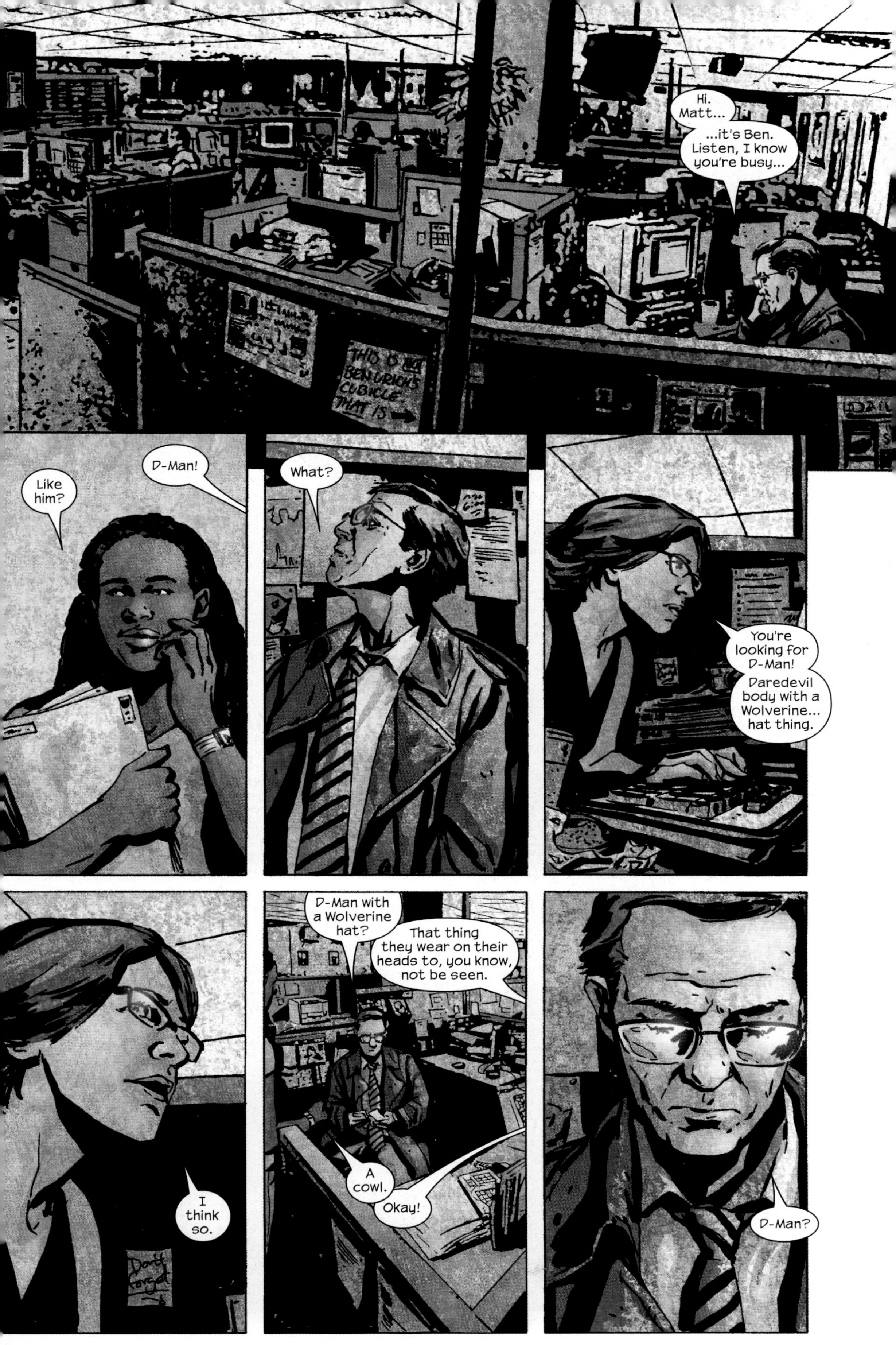
Hi. Matt...
...it's Ben. Listen, I know you're busy...
THIS IS NOT BEN URICH'S CUBICLE THAT IS →
D-Man!
Like him?
What?
You're looking for D-Man!
Daredevil body with a Wolverine... hat thing.
I think so.
D-Man with a Wolverine hat?
That thing they wear on their heads to, you know, not be seen.
A cowl.
Okay!
D-Man?

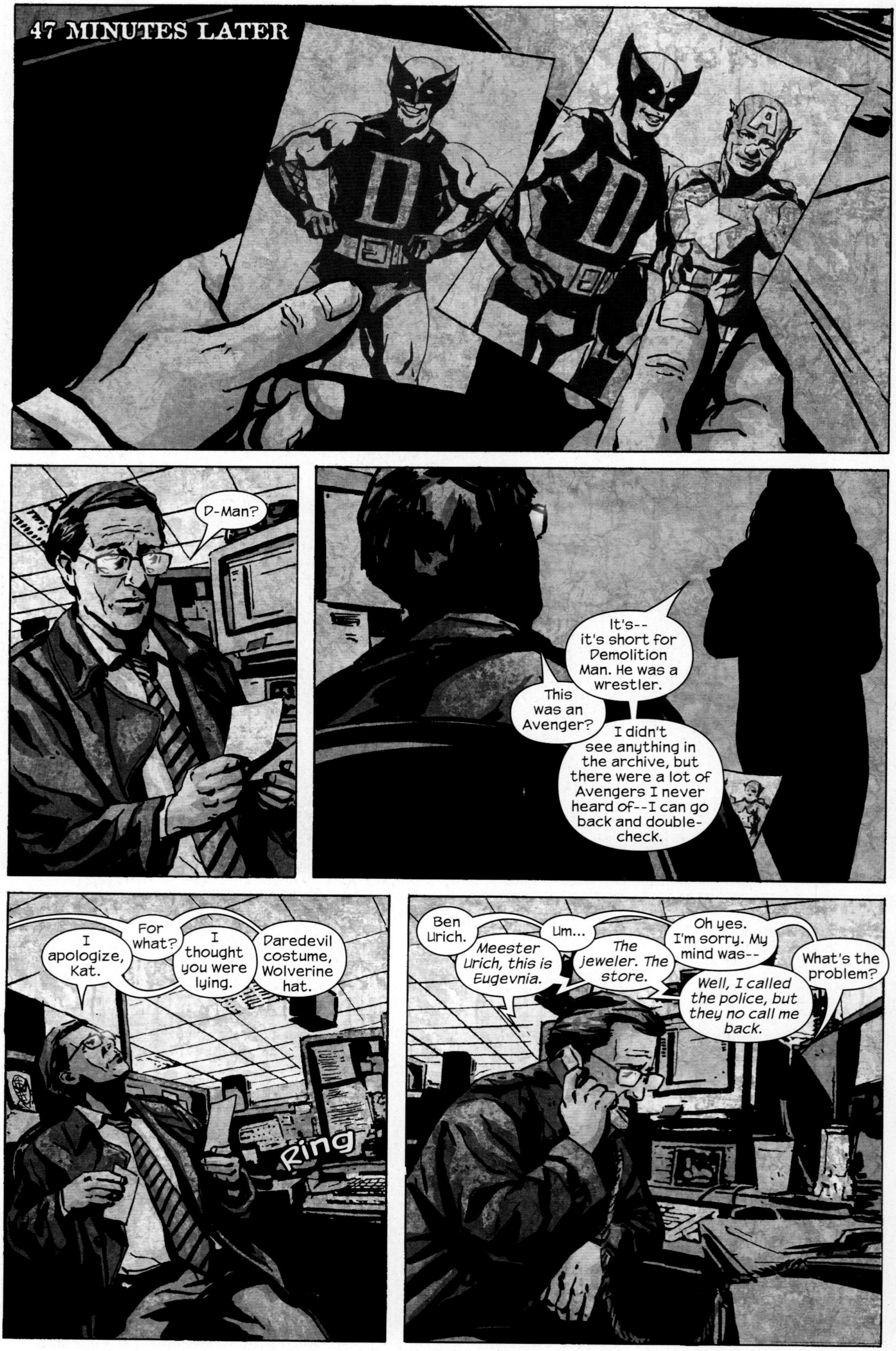
47 MINUTES LATER
D-Man?
It's--
it's short for Demolition Man. He was a wrestler.
This was an Avenger?
I didn't see anything in the archive, but there were a lot of Avengers I never heard of--I can go back and double-check.
I apologize, Kat.
For what?
I thought you were lying.
Daredevil costume, Wolverine hat.
Ring
Ben Urich.
Meester Urich, this is Eugevnia.
Um...
The jeweler. The store.
Oh yes. I'm sorry. My mind was--
Well, I called the police, but they no call me back.
What's the problem?

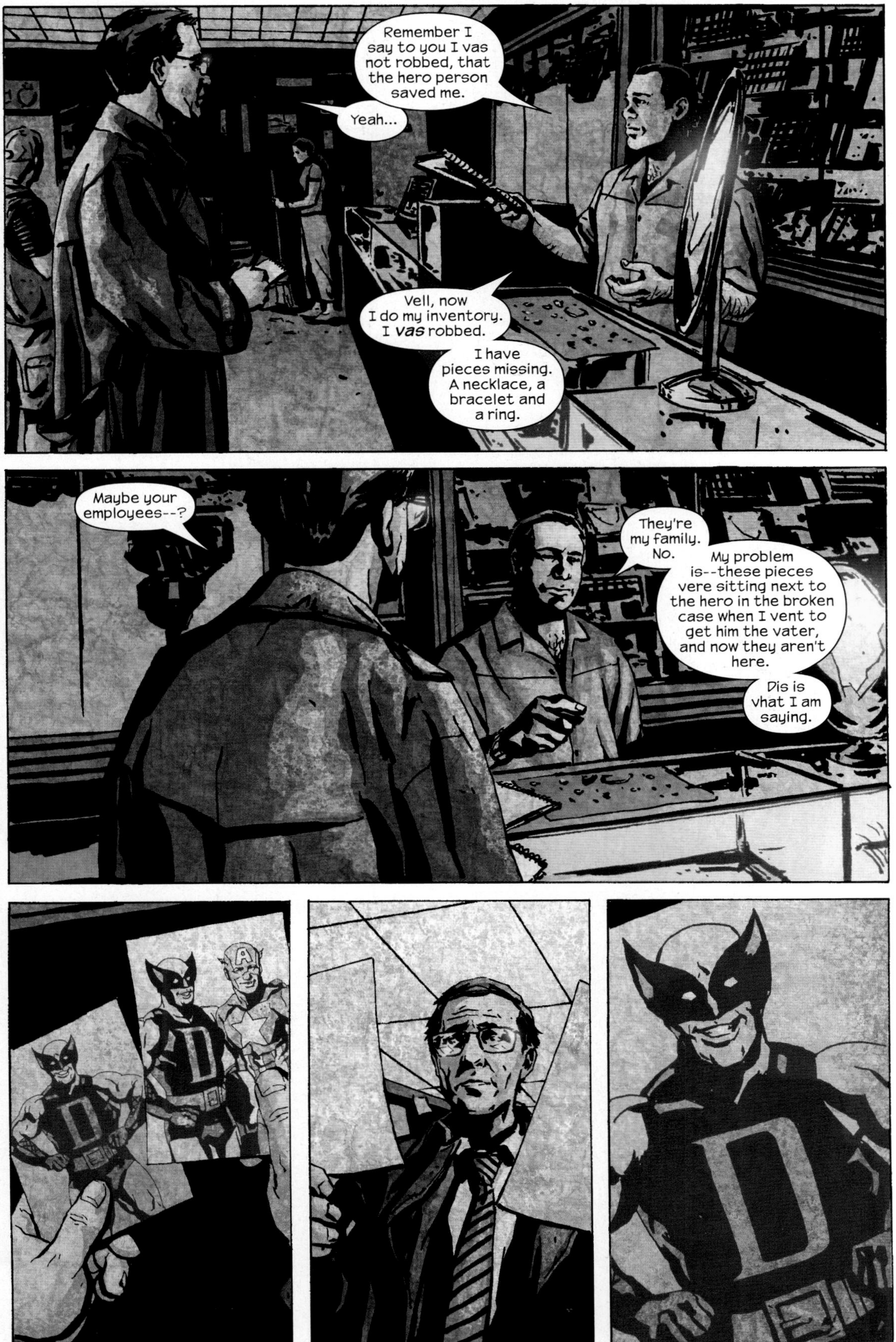
Remember I say to you I vas not robbed, that the hero person saved me.
Yeah...
Vell, now I do my inventory. I *vas* robbed.
I have pieces missing. A necklace, a bracelet and a ring.
Maybe your employees--?
They're my family. No.
My problem is--these pieces vere sitting next to the hero in the broken case when I vent to get him the vater, and now they aren't here.
Dis is vhat I am saying.

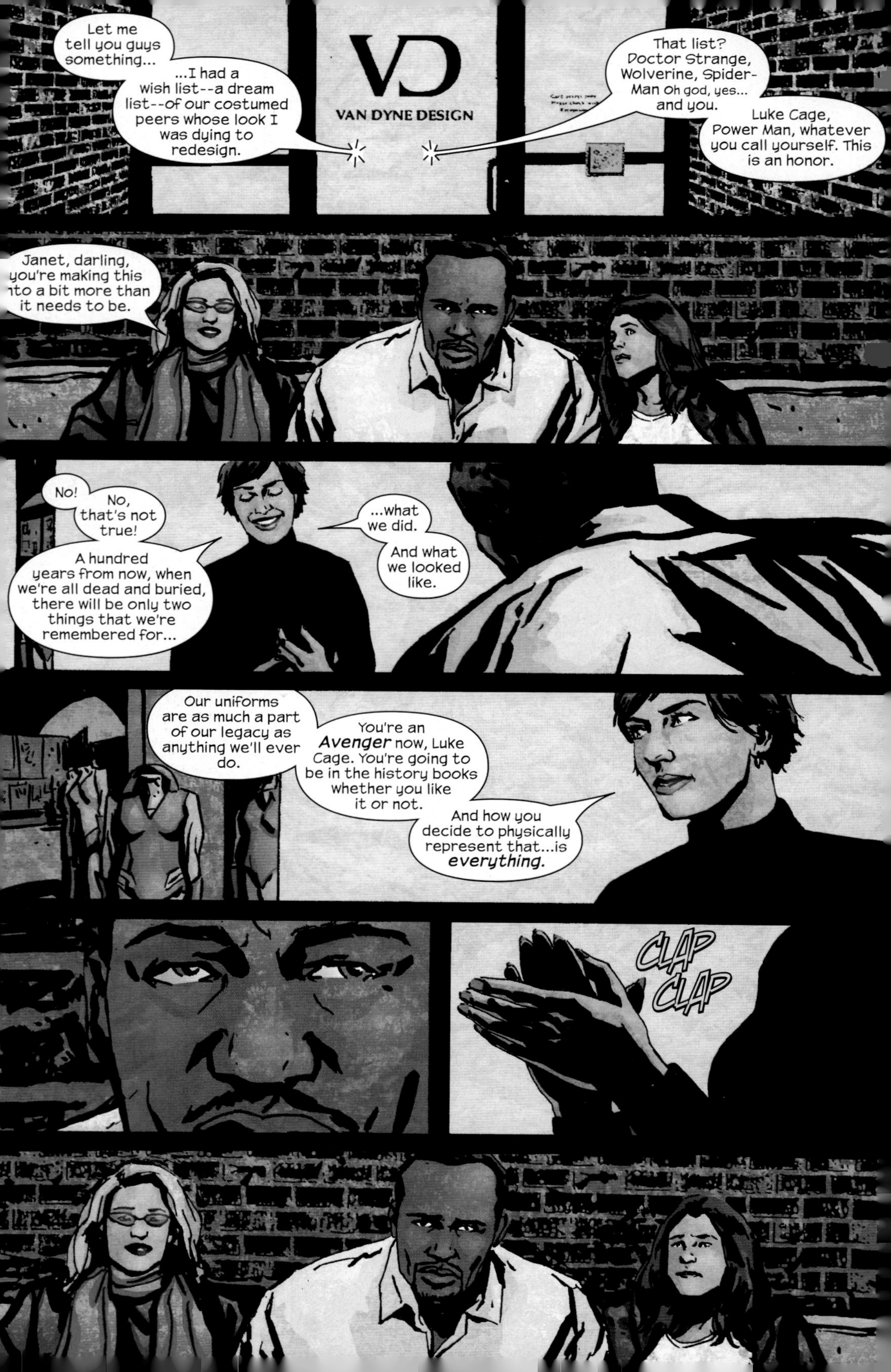
Let me tell you guys something...
...I had a wish list--a dream list--of our costumed peers whose look I was dying to redesign.
VD
VAN DYNE DESIGN
That list? Doctor Strange, Wolverine, Spider-Man Oh god, yes... and you.
Luke Cage, Power Man, whatever you call yourself. This is an honor.
Janet, darling, you're making this into a bit more than it needs to be.
No!
No, that's not true!
A hundred years from now, when we're all dead and buried, there will be only two things that we're remembered for...
...what we did.
And what we looked like.
Our uniforms are as much a part of our legacy as anything we'll ever do.
You're an Avenger now, Luke Cage. You're going to be in the history books whether you like it or not.
And how you decide to physically represent that...is everything.
CLAP
CLAP

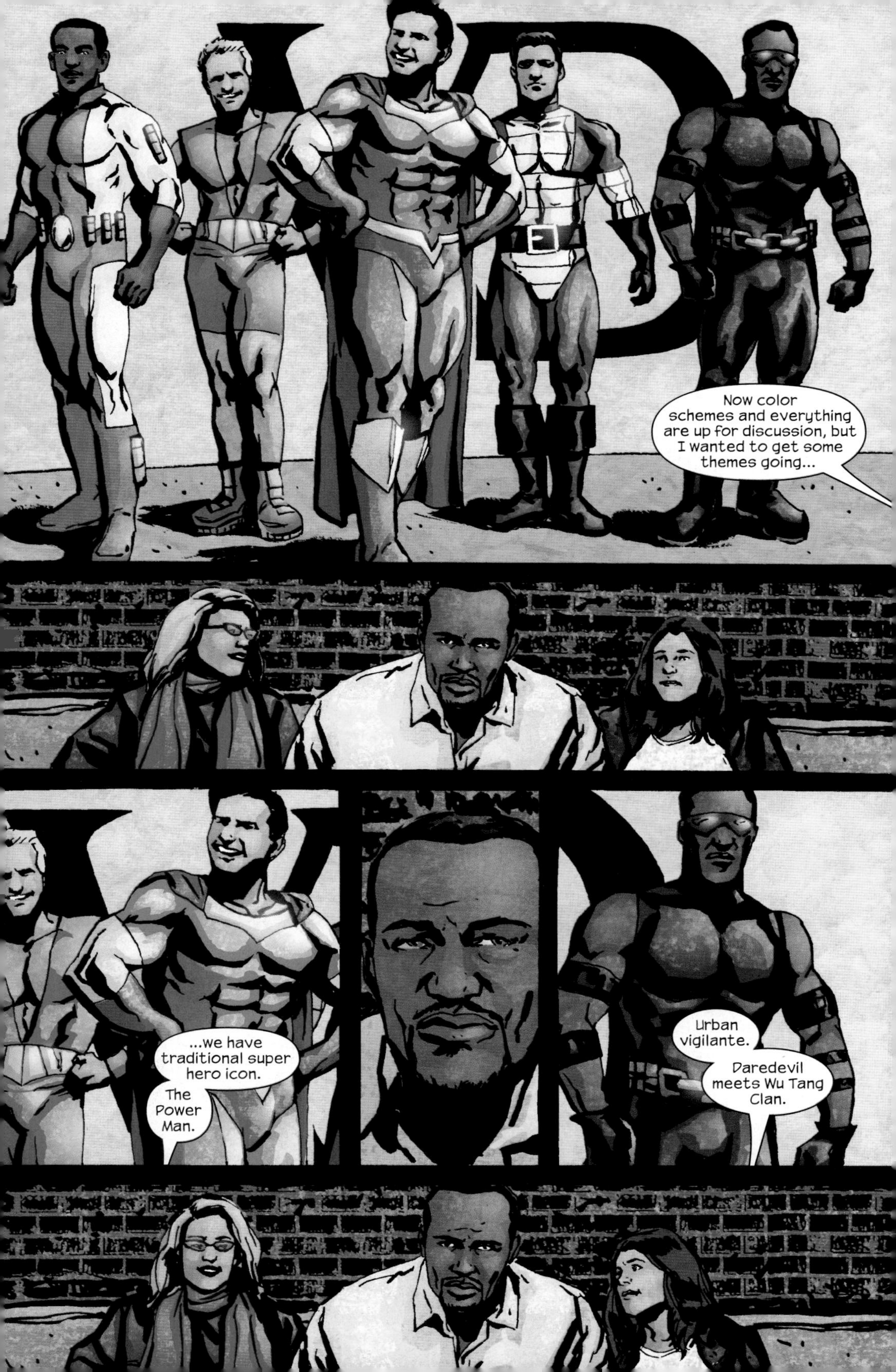
Now color schemes and everything are up for discussion, but I wanted to get some themes going...
...we have traditional super hero icon.
The Power Man.
Urban vigilante.
Daredevil meets Wu Tang Clan.

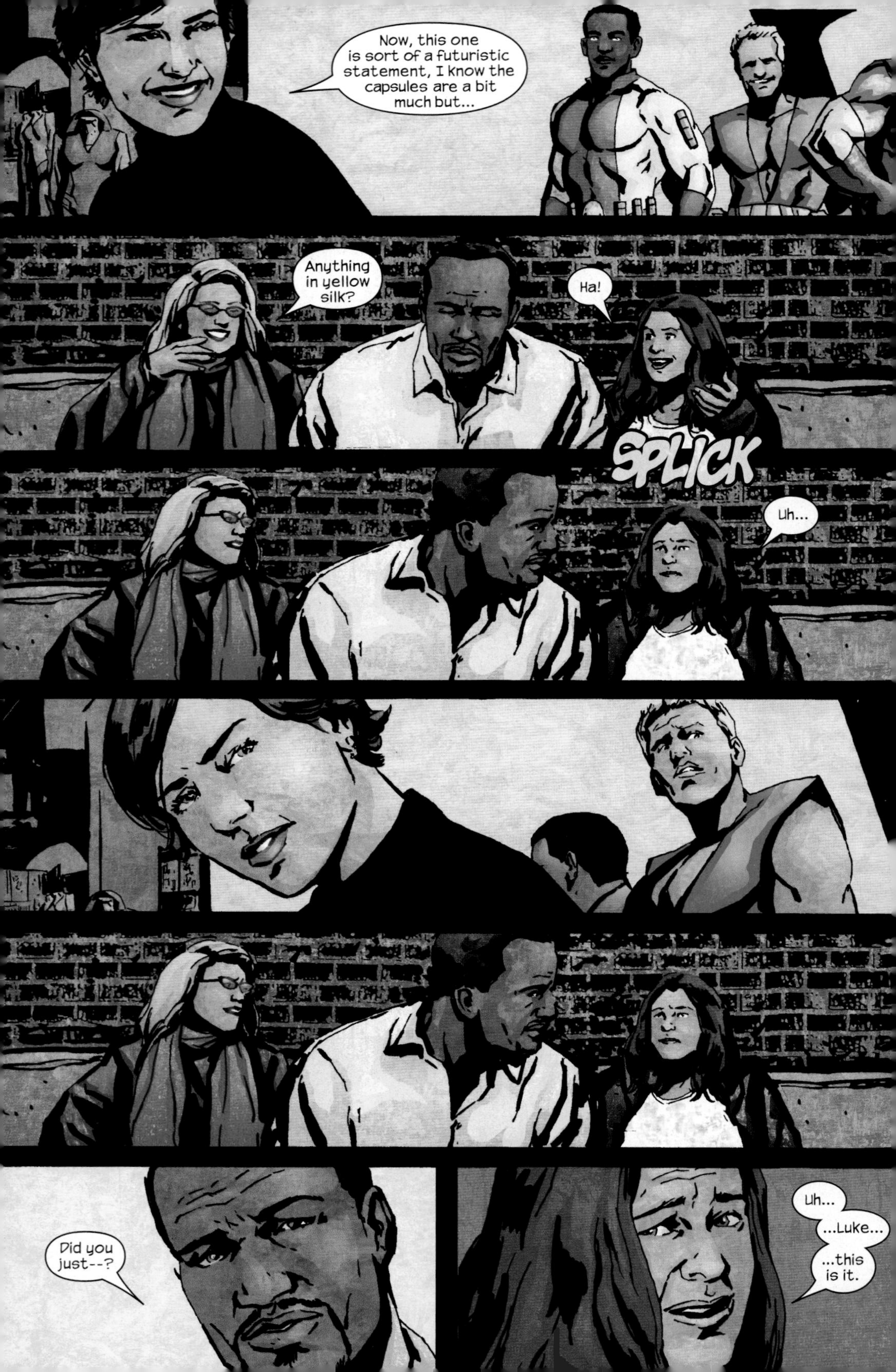
Now, this one is sort of a futuristic statement, I know the capsules are a bit much but...
Anything in yellow silk?
Ha!
SPLICK
Uh...
Did you just--?
Uh...
...Luke...
...this is it.

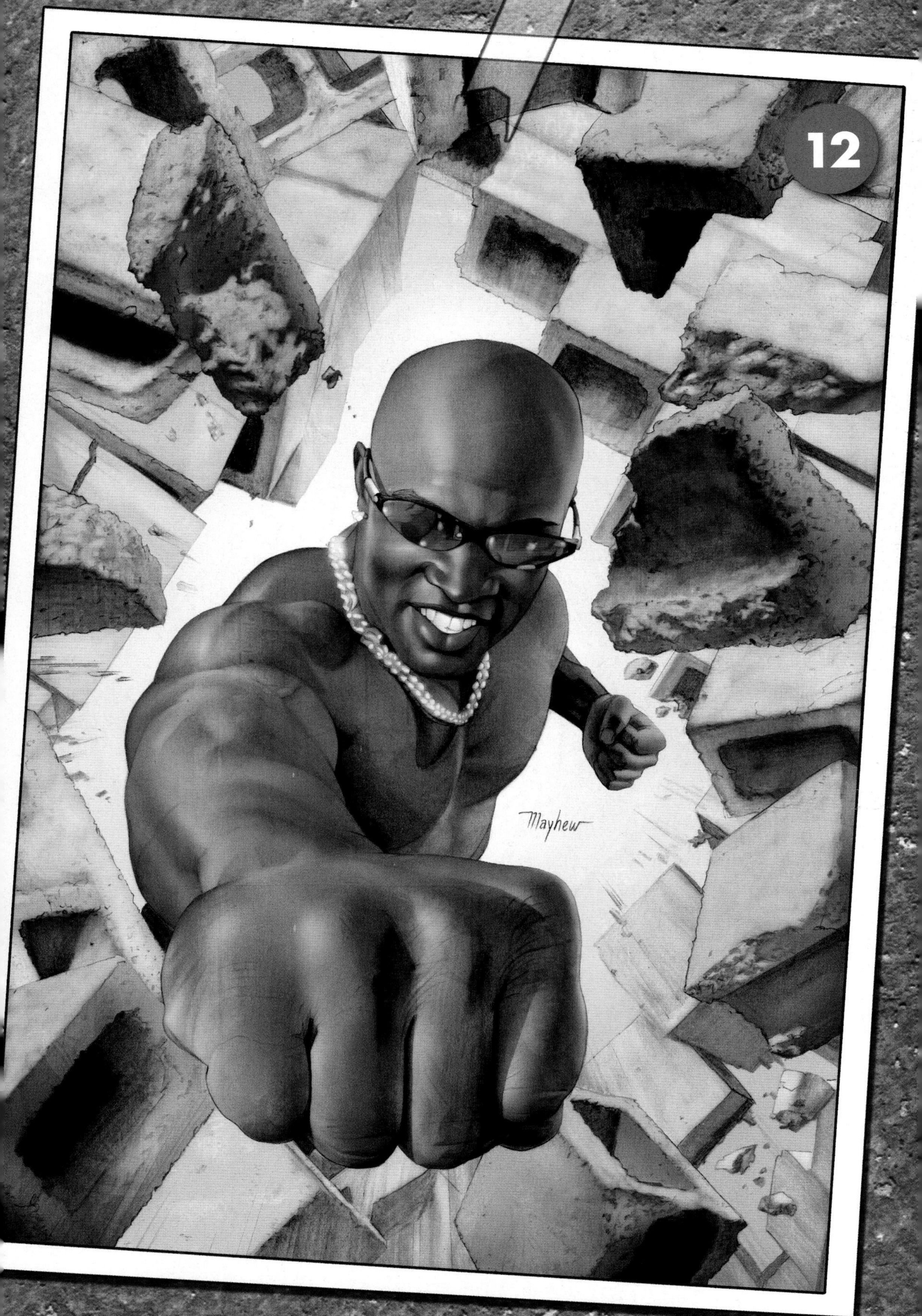
12
Mayhew

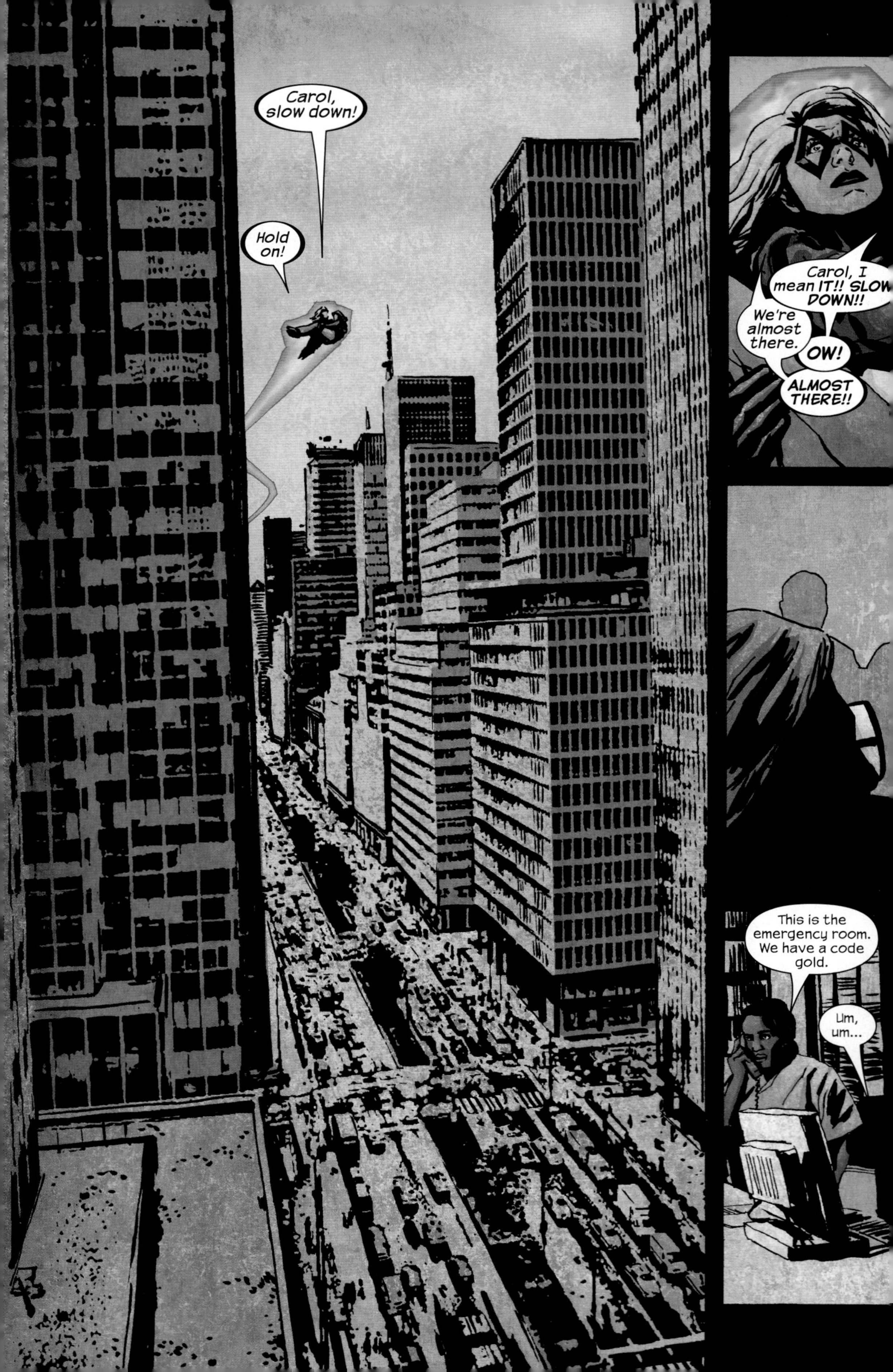
Carol, slow down!
Hold on!
Carol, I mean IT!! SLOW DOWN!!
We're almost there.
OW!
ALMOST THERE!!
This is the emergency room. We have a code gold.
Um, um...

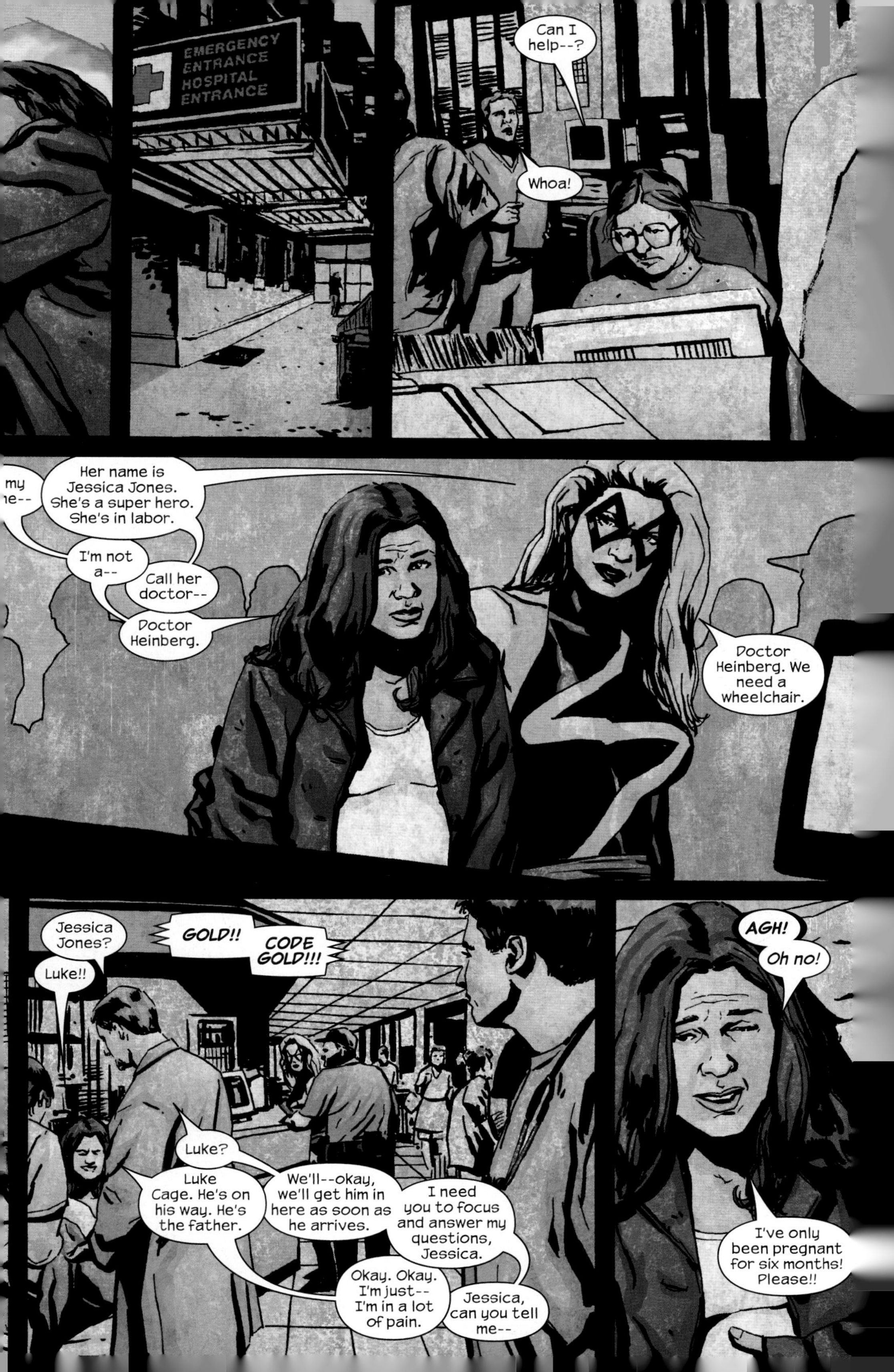
EMERGENCY ENTRANCE HOSPITAL ENTRANCE
Can I help--?
Whoa!
my
ne--
Her name is Jessica Jones. She's a super hero. She's in labor.
I'm not a--
Call her doctor--
Doctor Heinberg.
Doctor Heinberg. We need a wheelchair.
Jessica Jones?
GOLD!!
CODE GOLD!!!
Luke!!
Luke?
Luke Cage. He's on his way. He's the father.
We'll--okay, we'll get him in here as soon as he arrives.
I need you to focus and answer my questions, Jessica.
Okay. Okay. I'm just-- I'm in a lot of pain.
Jessica, can you tell me--
AGH!
Oh no!
I've only been pregnant for six months! Please!!

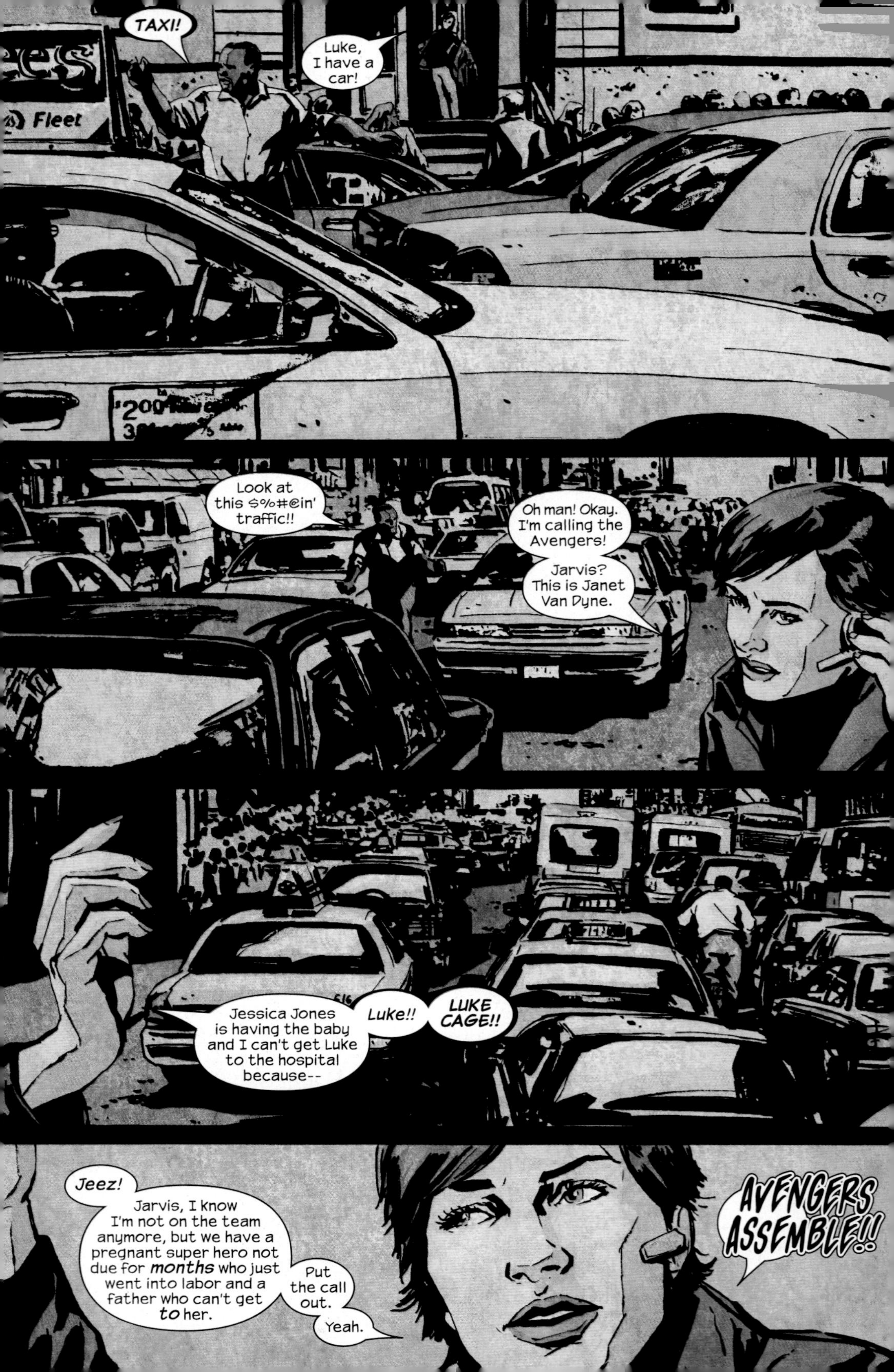
TAXI!
Luke, I have a car!
Fleet
Look at this $%#@in' traffic!!
Oh man! Okay. I'm calling the Avengers!
Jarvis? This is Janet Van Dyne.
Jessica Jones is having the baby and I can't get Luke to the hospital because--
Luke!!
LUKE CAGE!!
Jeez!
Jarvis, I know I'm not on the team anymore, but we have a pregnant super hero not due for *months* who just went into labor and a father who can't get *to* her.
Put the call out.
Yeah.
AVENGERS ASSEMBLE!!

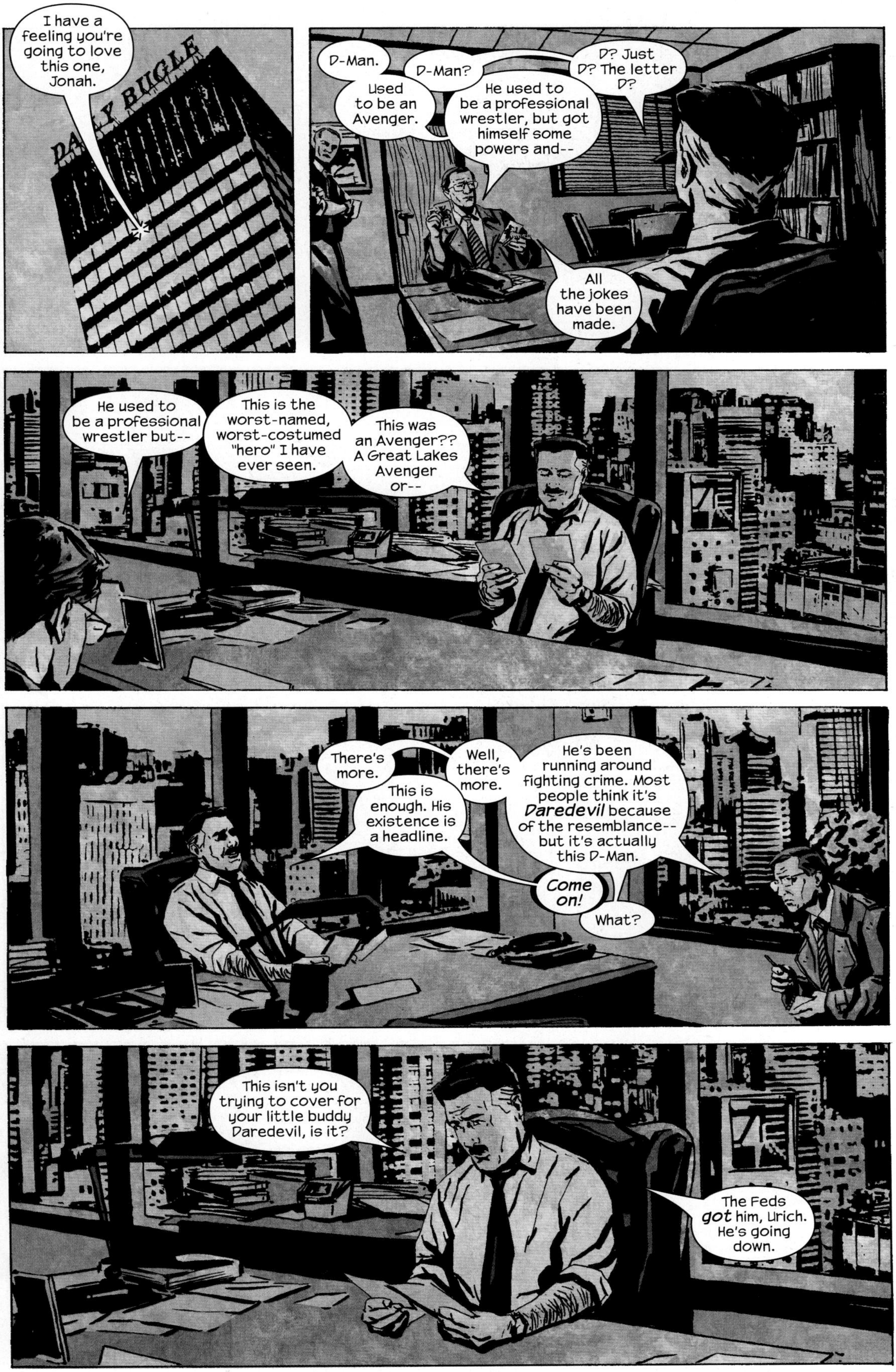

I have a feeling you're going to love this one, Jonah.
DAILY BUGLE
D-Man.
Used to be an Avenger.
D-Man?
He used to be a professional wrestler, but got himself some powers and--
D? Just D? The letter D?
All the jokes have been made.
He used to be a professional wrestler but--
This is the worst-named, worst-costumed "hero" I have ever seen.
This was an Avenger?? A Great Lakes Avenger or--
There's more.
Well, there's more.
This is enough. His existence is a headline.
He's been running around fighting crime. Most people think it's *Daredevil* because of the resemblance-- but it's actually this D-Man.
Come on!
What?
This isn't you trying to cover for your little buddy Daredevil, is it?
The Feds *got* him, Urich. He's going down.

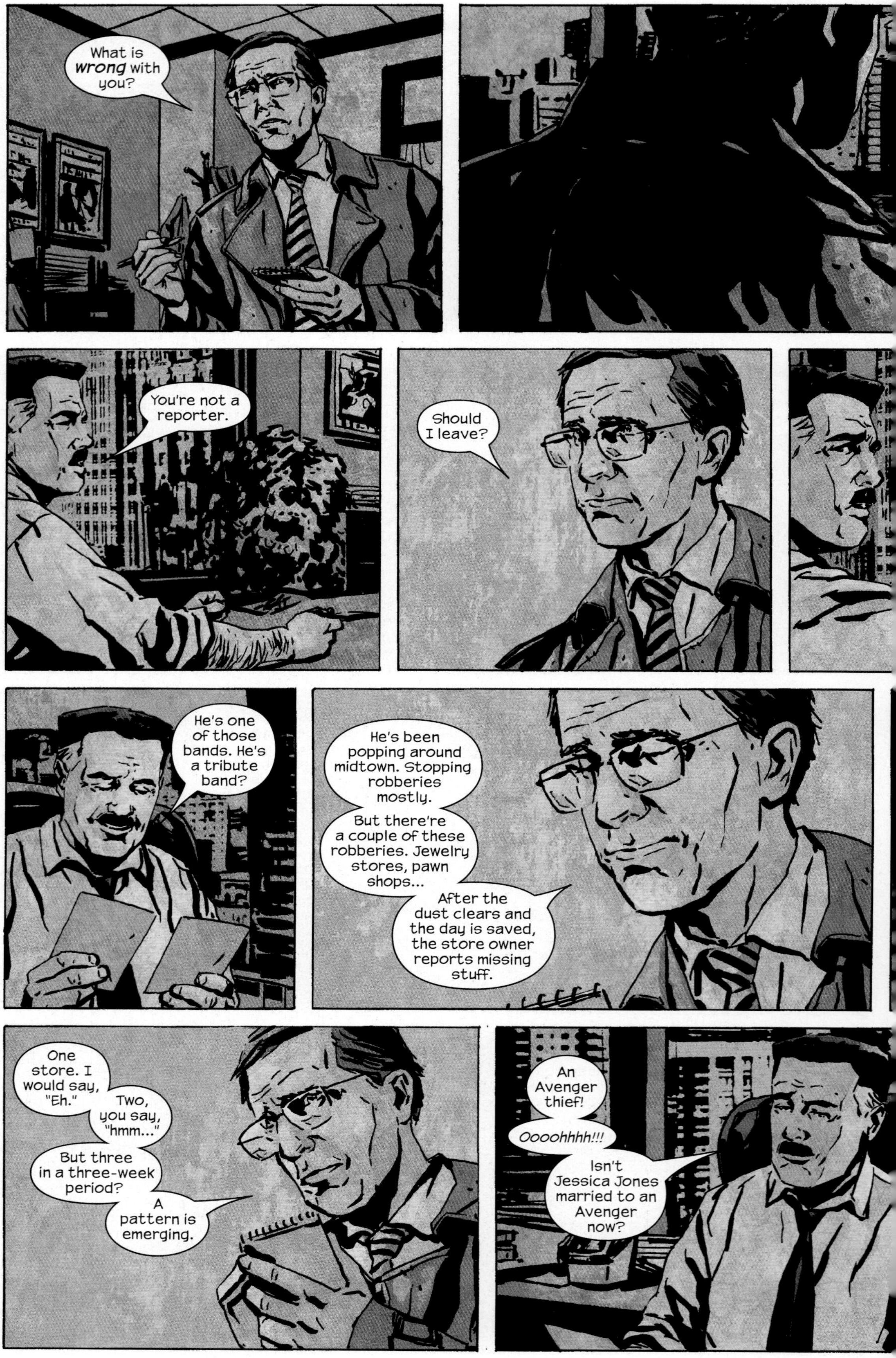
What is *wrong* with you?
You're not a reporter.
Should I leave?
He's one of those bands. He's a tribute band?
He's been popping around midtown. Stopping robberies mostly.
But there're a couple of these robberies. Jewelry stores, pawn shops...
After the dust clears and the day is saved, the store owner reports missing stuff.
One store. I would say, "Eh."
Two, you say, "hmm..."
But three in a three-week period?
A pattern is emerging.
An Avenger thief!
Ooooohhhh!!!
Isn't Jessica Jones married to an Avenger now?

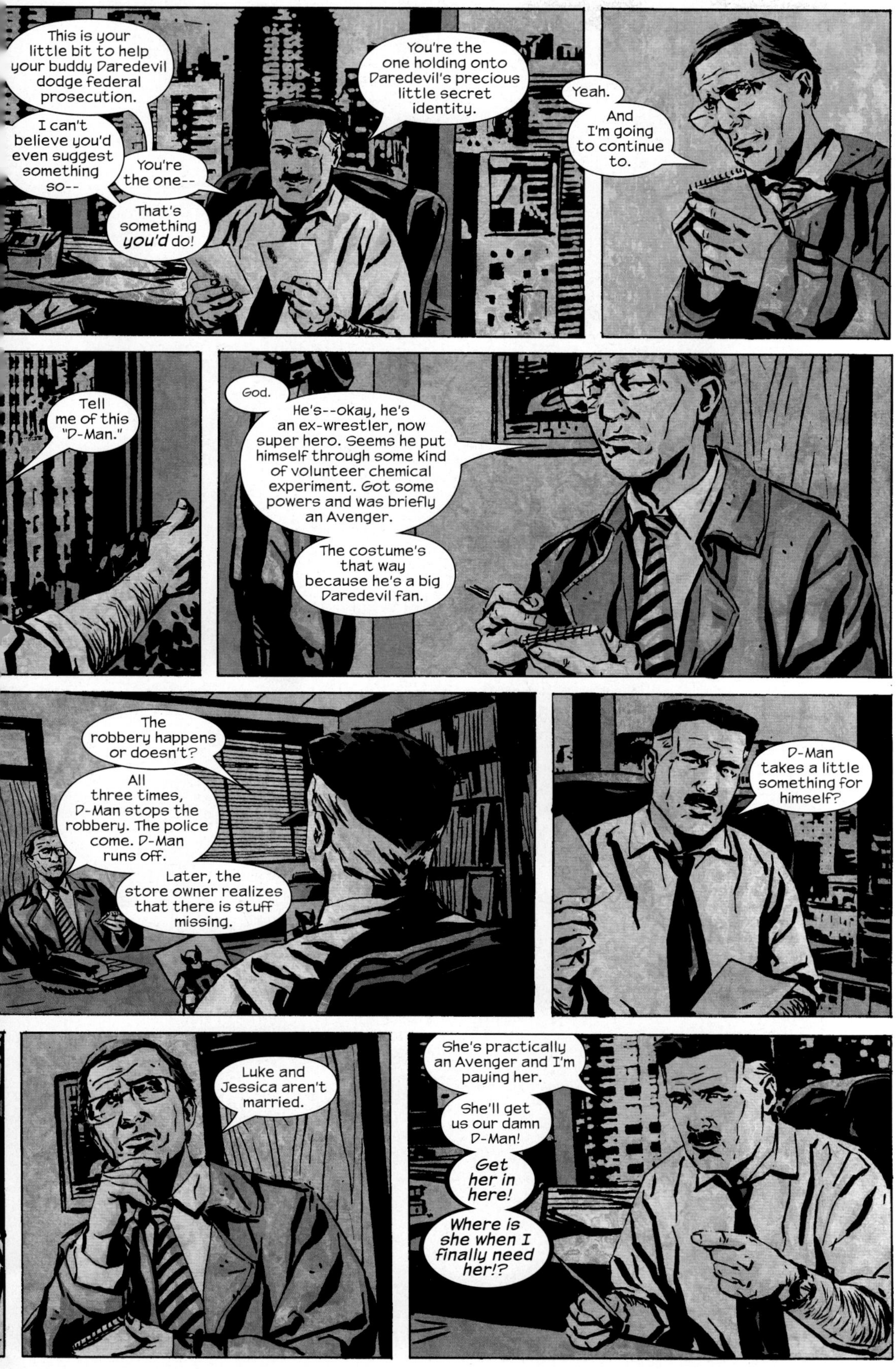
This is your little bit to help your buddy Daredevil dodge federal prosecution.
I can't believe you'd even suggest something so--
You're the one--
That's something *you'd* do!
You're the one holding onto Daredevil's precious little secret identity.
Yeah.
And I'm going to continue to.
Tell me of this "D-Man."
God.
He's--okay, he's an ex-wrestler, now super hero. Seems he put himself through some kind of volunteer chemical experiment. Got some powers and was briefly an Avenger.
The costume's that way because he's a big Daredevil fan.
The robbery happens or doesn't?
All three times, D-Man stops the robbery. The police come. D-Man runs off.
Later, the store owner realizes that there is stuff missing.
D-Man takes a little something for himself?
Luke and Jessica aren't married.
She's practically an Avenger and I'm paying her.
She'll get us our damn D-Man!
Get her in here!
Where is she when I finally need her!?

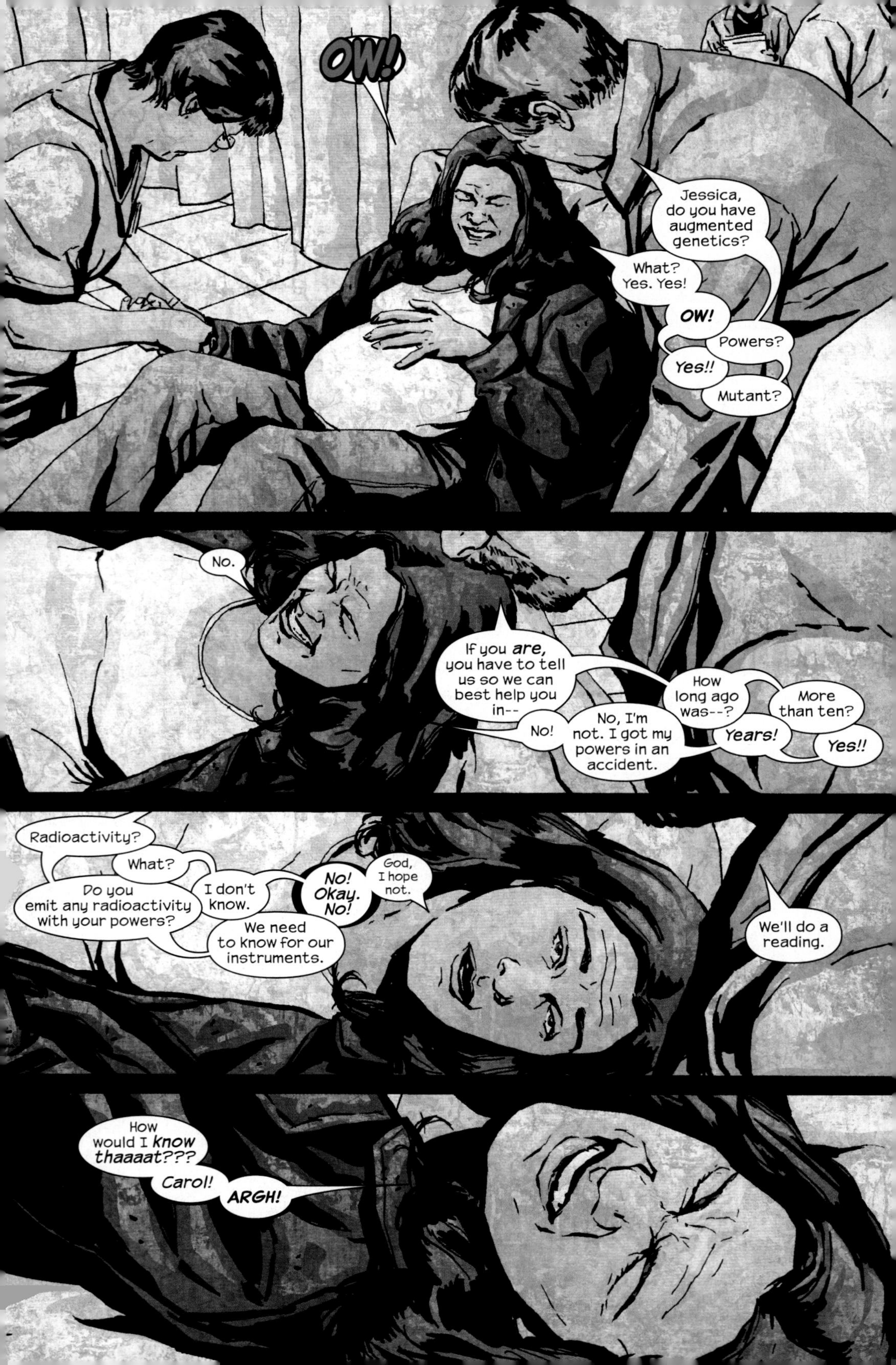
OW!
Jessica, do you have augmented genetics?
What? Yes. Yes!
OW!
Powers?
Yes!!
Mutant?
No.
If you *are,* you have to tell us so we can best help you in--
No!
No, I'm not. I got my powers in an accident.
How long ago was--?
Years!
More than ten?
Yes!!
Radioactivity?
What?
Do you emit any radioactivity with your powers?
I don't know.
We need to know for our instruments.
No! Okay. No!
God, I hope not.
We'll do a reading.
How would I *know thaaaat???*
Carol!
ARGH!

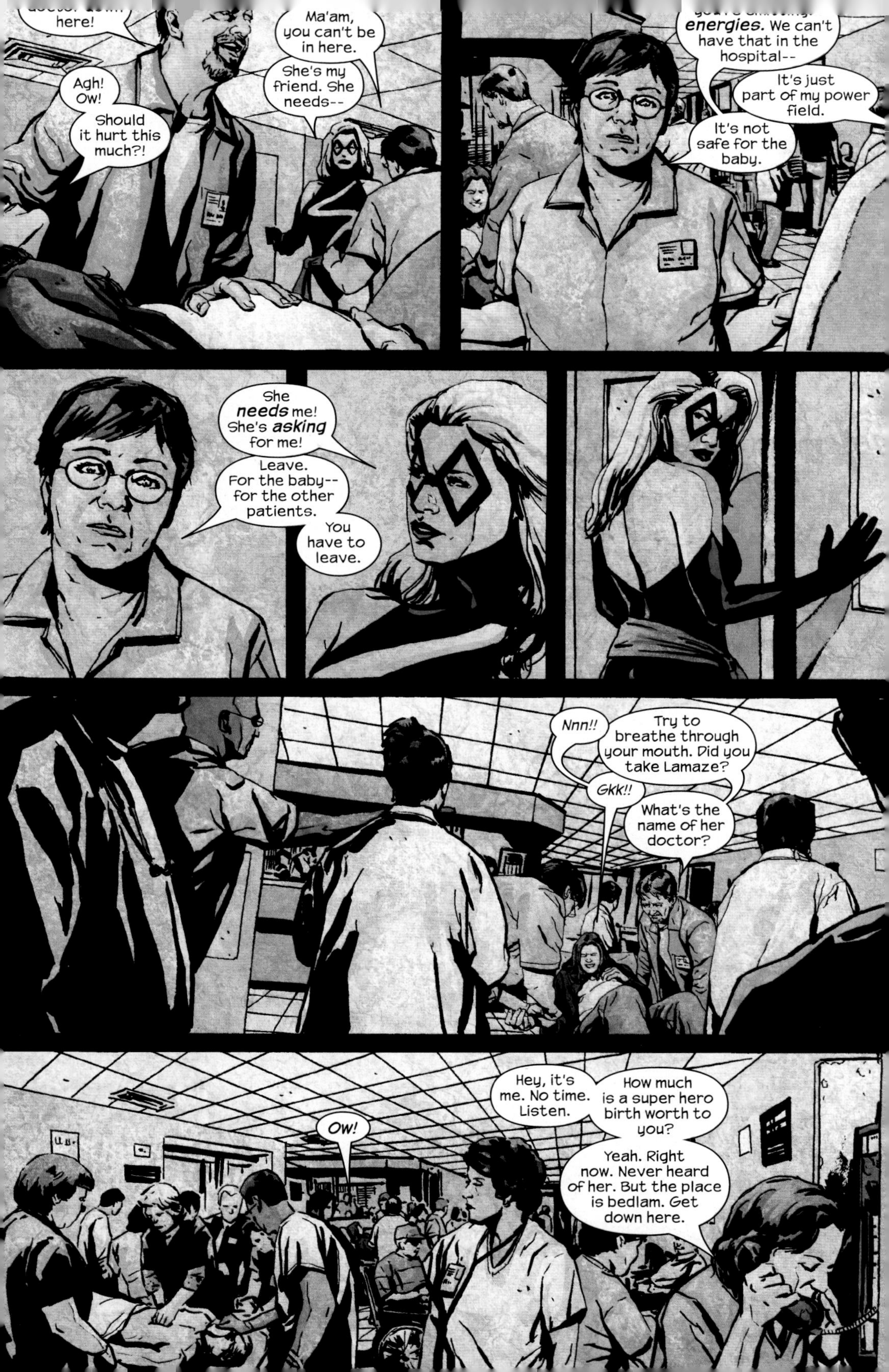
here!
Ma'am, you can't be in here.
Agh! Ow!
Should it hurt this much?!
She's my friend. She needs--
energies. We can't have that in the hospital--
It's just part of my power field.
It's not safe for the baby.
She needs me! She's asking for me!
Leave. For the baby-- for the other patients.
You have to leave.
Nnn!!
Try to breathe through your mouth. Did you take Lamaze?
Gkk!!
What's the name of her doctor?
OW!
Hey, it's me. No time. Listen.
How much is a super hero birth worth to you?
Yeah. Right now. Never heard of her. But the place is bedlam. Get down here.

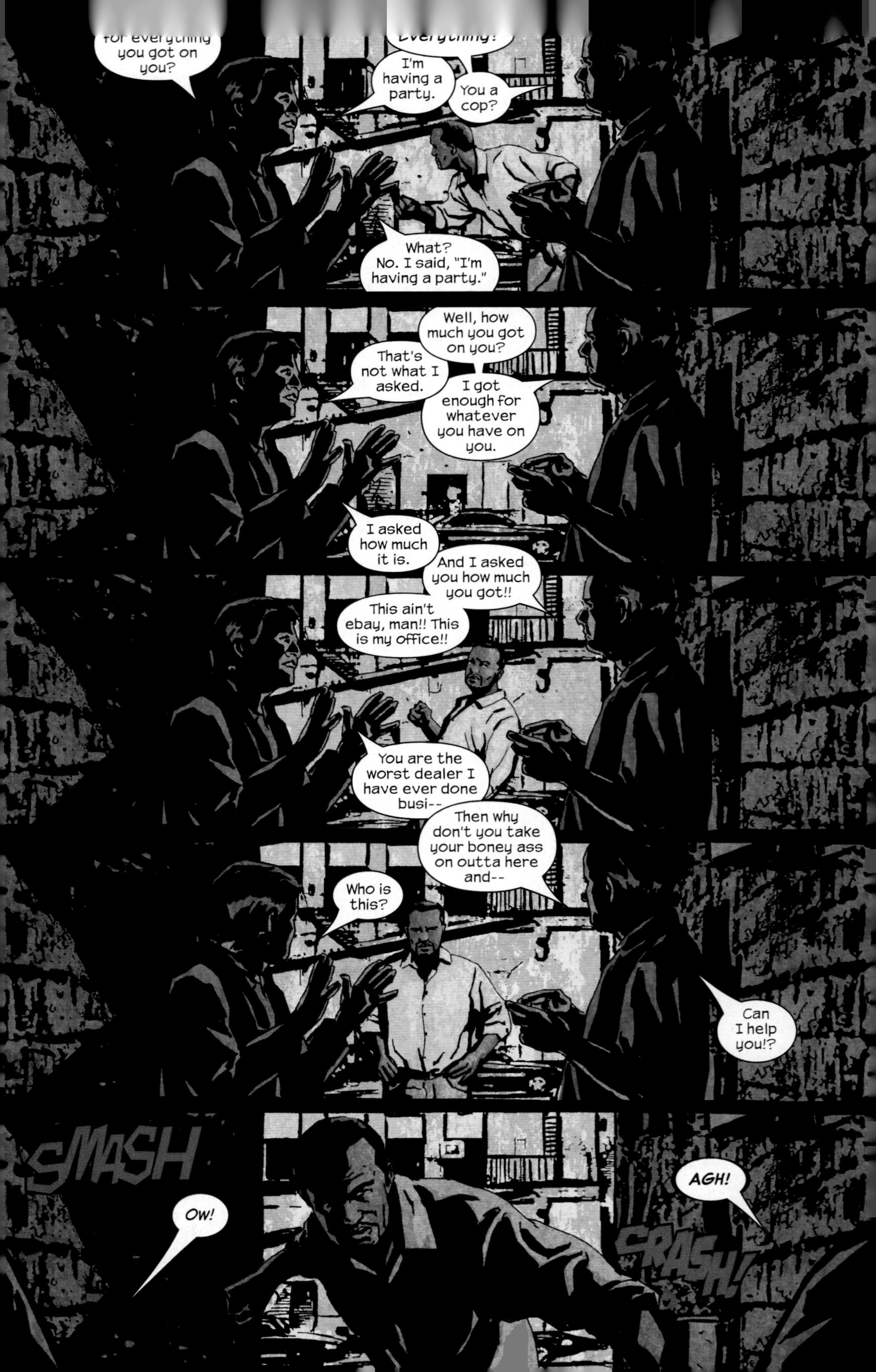

for everything you got on you?
Everything!
I'm having a party.
You a cop?
What? No. I said, "I'm having a party."
Well, how much you got on you?
That's not what I asked.
I got enough for whatever you have on you.
I asked how much it is.
And I asked you how much you got!!
This ain't ebay, man!! This is my office!!
You are the worst dealer I have ever done busi--
Then why don't you take your boney ass on outta here and--
Who is this?
Can I help you!?
SMASH
Ow!
AGH!
CRASH!

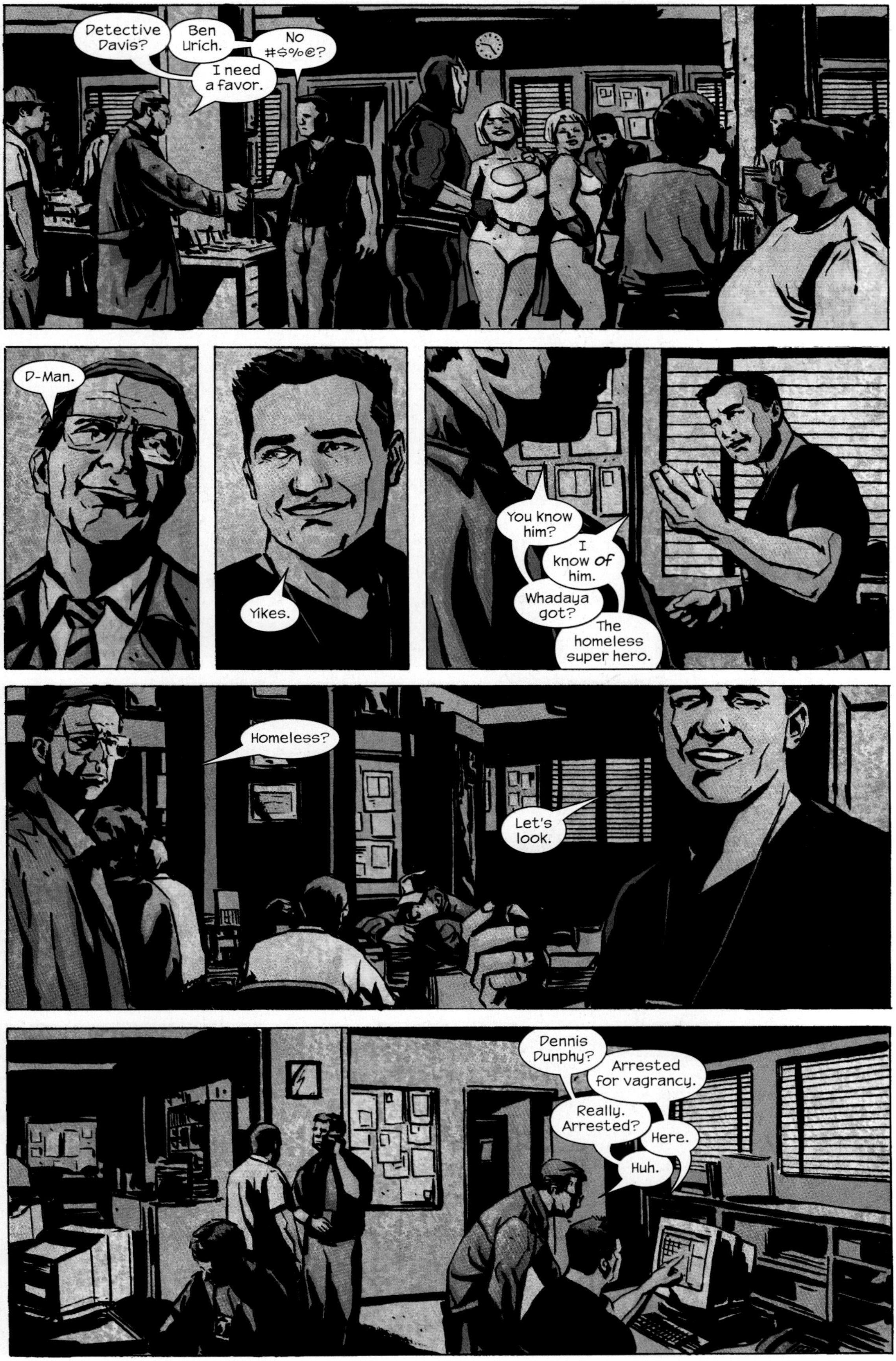

Detective Davis?
Ben Urich.
I need a favor.
No #$%@?
D-Man.
Yikes.
You know him?
I know of him.
Whadaya got?
The homeless super hero.
Homeless?
Let's look.
Dennis Dunphy?
Arrested for vagrancy.
Really. Arrested?
Here.
Huh.

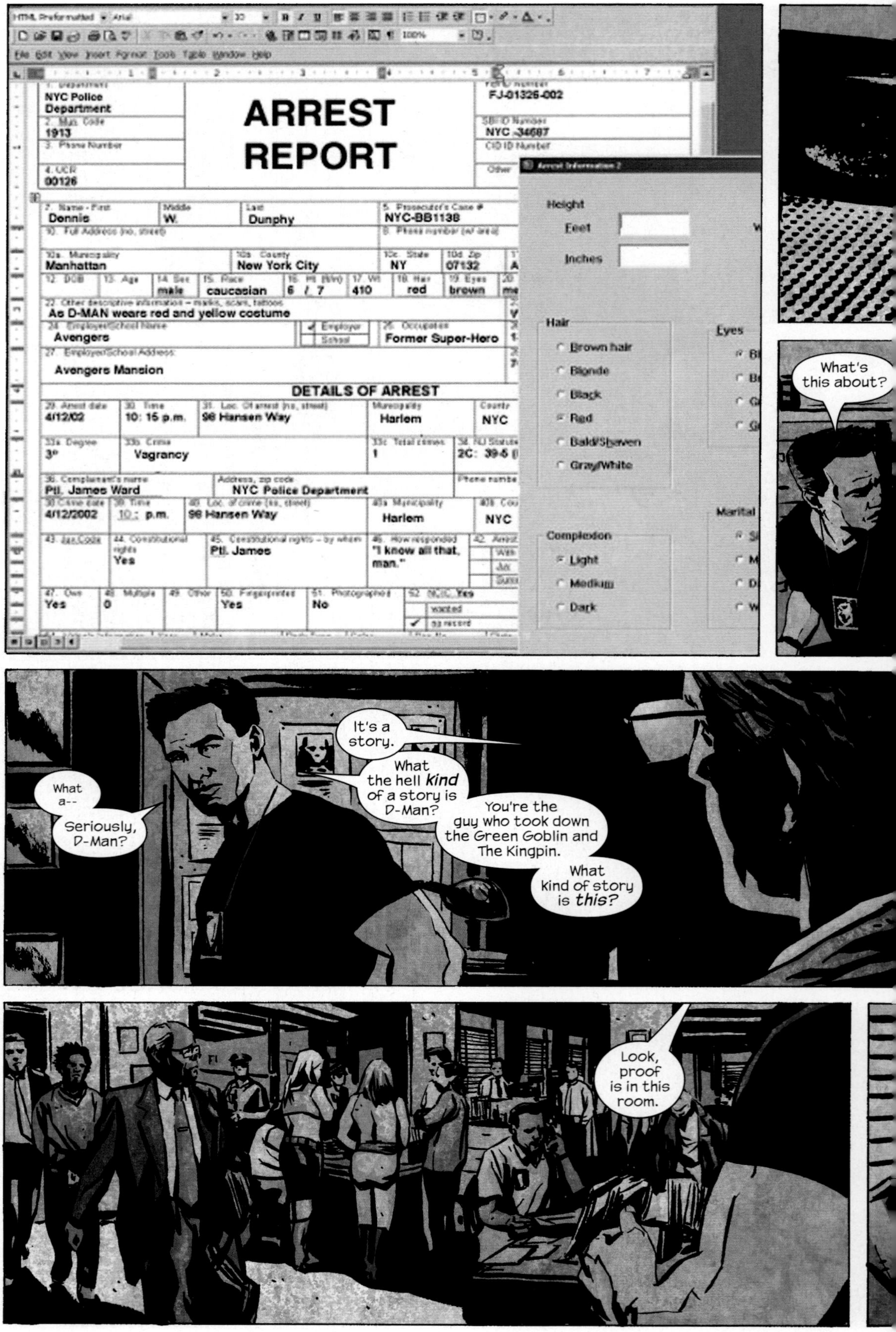
ARREST REPORT
NYC Police Department
1913
00126
FJ-01326-002
NYC 34687
Dennis
W.
Dunphy
NYC-BB1138
Manhattan
New York City
NY
07132
male
caucasian
6 / 7
410
red
brown
As D-MAN wears red and yellow costume
Avengers
Former Super-Hero
Avengers Mansion
DETAILS OF ARREST
4/12/02
10: 15 p.m.
98 Hansen Way
Harlem
NYC
3°
Vagrancy
1
Ptl. James Ward
NYC Police Department
4/12/2002
10 : p.m.
98 Hansen Way
Harlem
NYC
Yes
Ptl. James
"I know all that, man."
Yes
0
Yes
No
Height
Feet
Inches
Hair
Brown hair
Blonde
Black
Red
Bald/Shaven
Gray/White
Eyes
Complexion
Light
Medium
Dark
Marital
What's this about?
What a--
Seriously, D-Man?
It's a story.
What the hell kind of a story is D-Man?
You're the guy who took down the Green Goblin and The Kingpin.
What kind of story is this?
Look, proof is in this room.

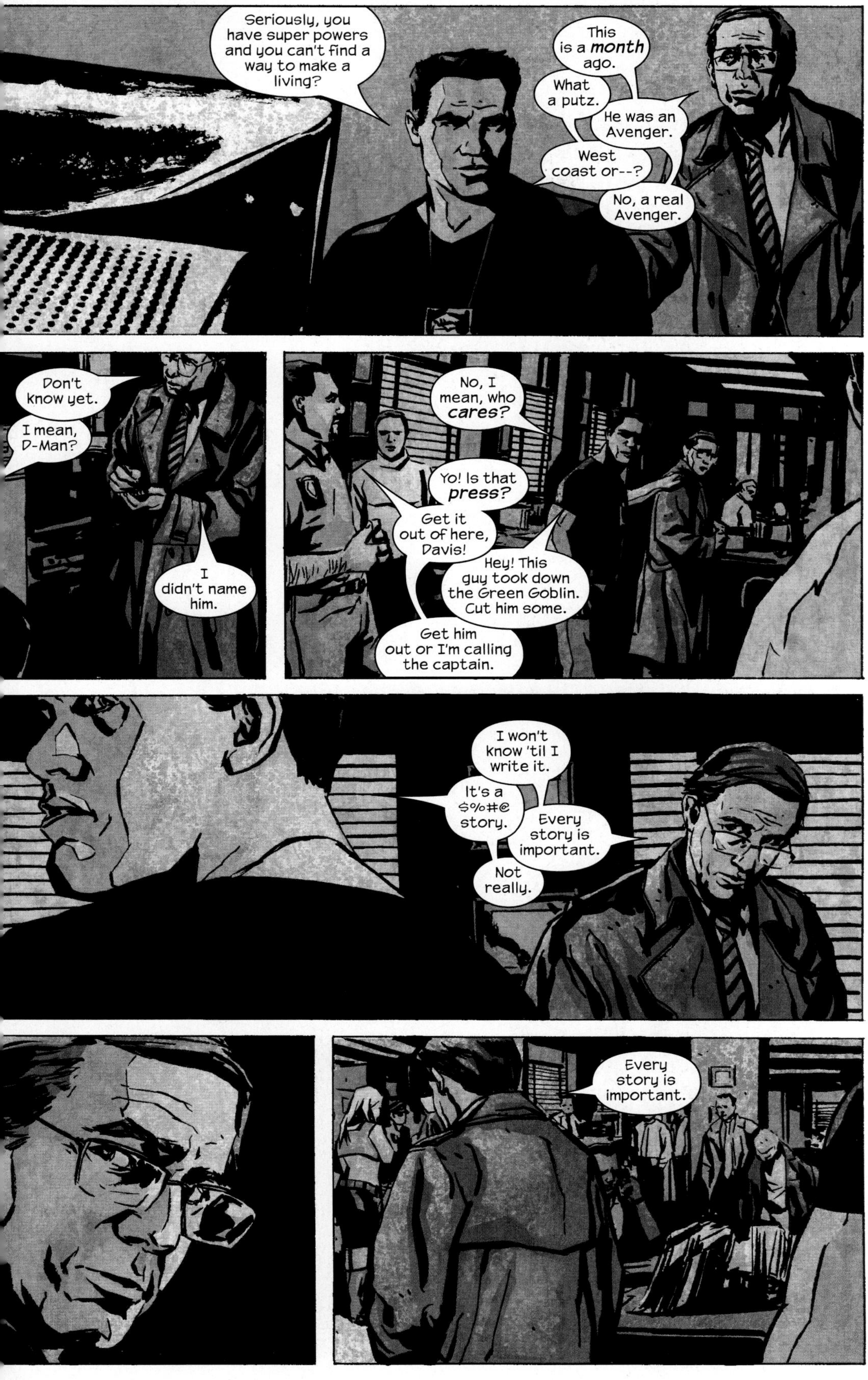
Seriously, you have super powers and you can't find a way to make a living?
This is a month ago.
What a putz.
He was an Avenger.
West coast or--?
No, a real Avenger.
Don't know yet.
I mean, D-Man?
I didn't name him.
No, I mean, who cares?
Yo! Is that press?
Get it out of here, Davis!
Hey! This guy took down the Green Goblin. Cut him some.
Get him out or I'm calling the captain.
I won't know 'til I write it.
It's a $%#@ story.
Every story is important.
Not really.
Every story is important.

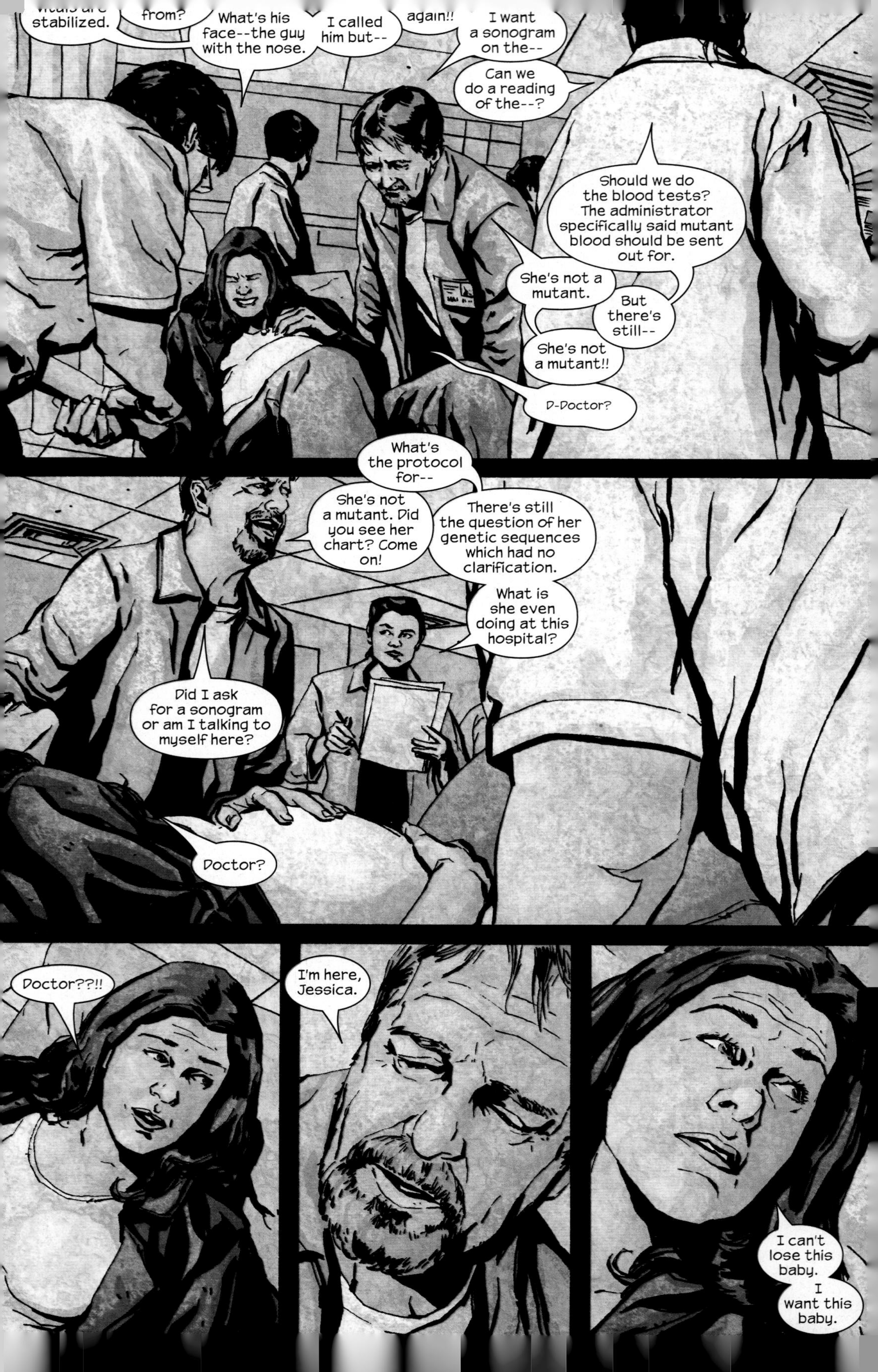
stabilized.
from?
What's his face--the guy with the nose.
I called him but--
again!!
I want a sonogram on the--
Can we do a reading of the--?
Should we do the blood tests? The administrator specifically said mutant blood should be sent out for.
She's not a mutant.
But there's still--
She's not a mutant!!
D-Doctor?
What's the protocol for--
She's not a mutant. Did you see her chart? Come on!
There's still the question of her genetic sequences which had no clarification.
What is she even doing at this hospital?
Did I ask for a sonogram or am I talking to myself here?
Doctor?
Doctor??!!
I'm here, Jessica.
I can't lose this baby.
I want this baby.

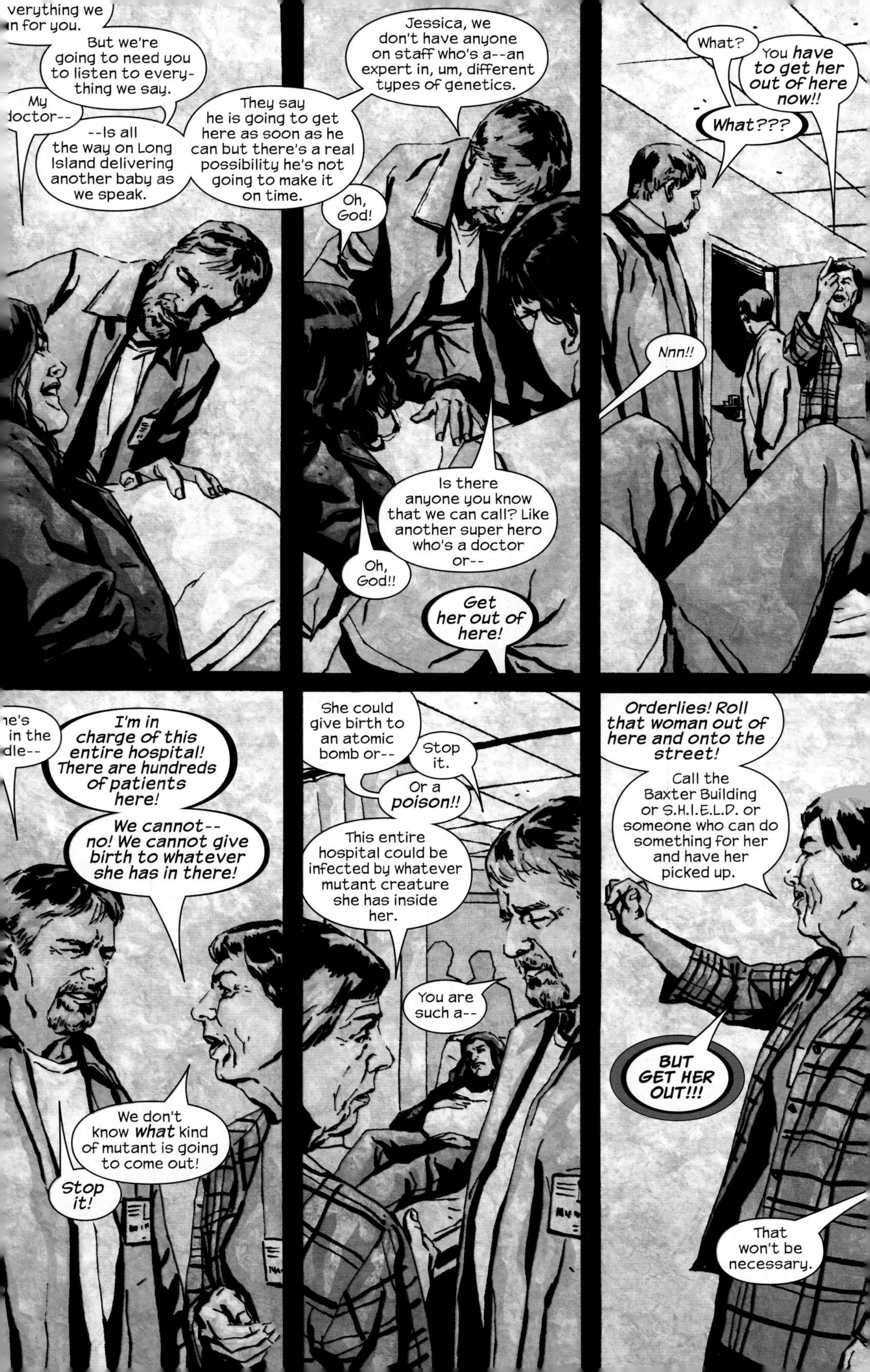

verything we
n for you.
But we're going to need you to listen to everything we say.
My doctor--
--Is all the way on Long Island delivering another baby as we speak.
They say he is going to get here as soon as he can but there's a real possibility he's not going to make it on time.
Jessica, we don't have anyone on staff who's a--an expert in, um, different types of genetics.
Oh, God!
Is there anyone you know that we can call? Like another super hero who's a doctor or--
Oh, God!!
Get her out of here!
What?
You have to get her out of here now!!
What???
Nnn!!
ne's
in the
dle--
I'm in charge of this entire hospital! There are hundreds of patients here!
We cannot-- no! We cannot give birth to whatever she has in there!
We don't know what kind of mutant is going to come out!
Stop it!
She could give birth to an atomic bomb or--
Stop it.
Or a poison!!
This entire hospital could be infected by whatever mutant creature she has inside her.
You are such a--
Orderlies! Roll that woman out of here and onto the street!
Call the Baxter Building or S.H.I.E.L.D. or someone who can do something for her and have her picked up.
BUT GET HER OUT!!!
That won't be necessary.

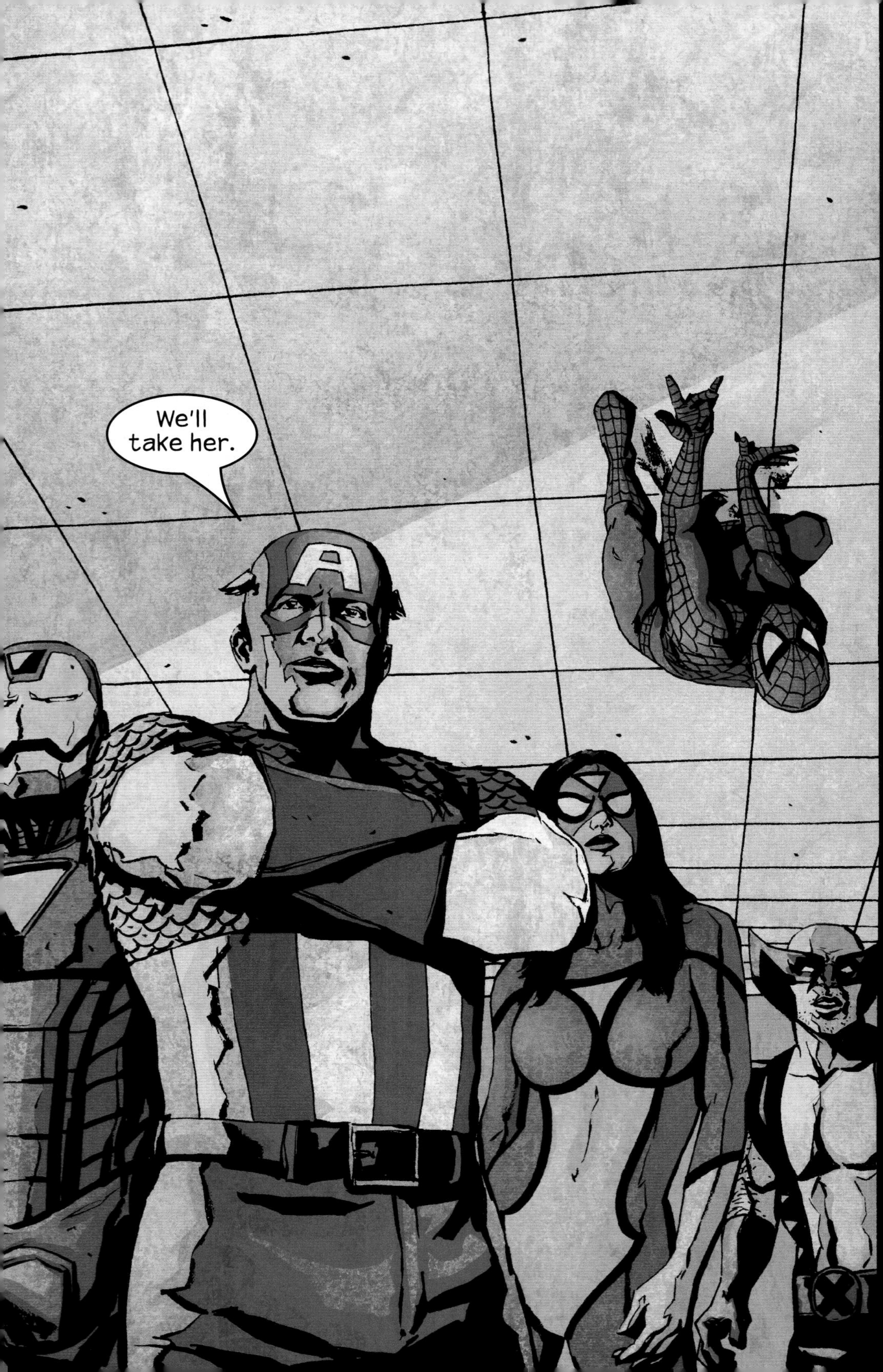
We'll take her.

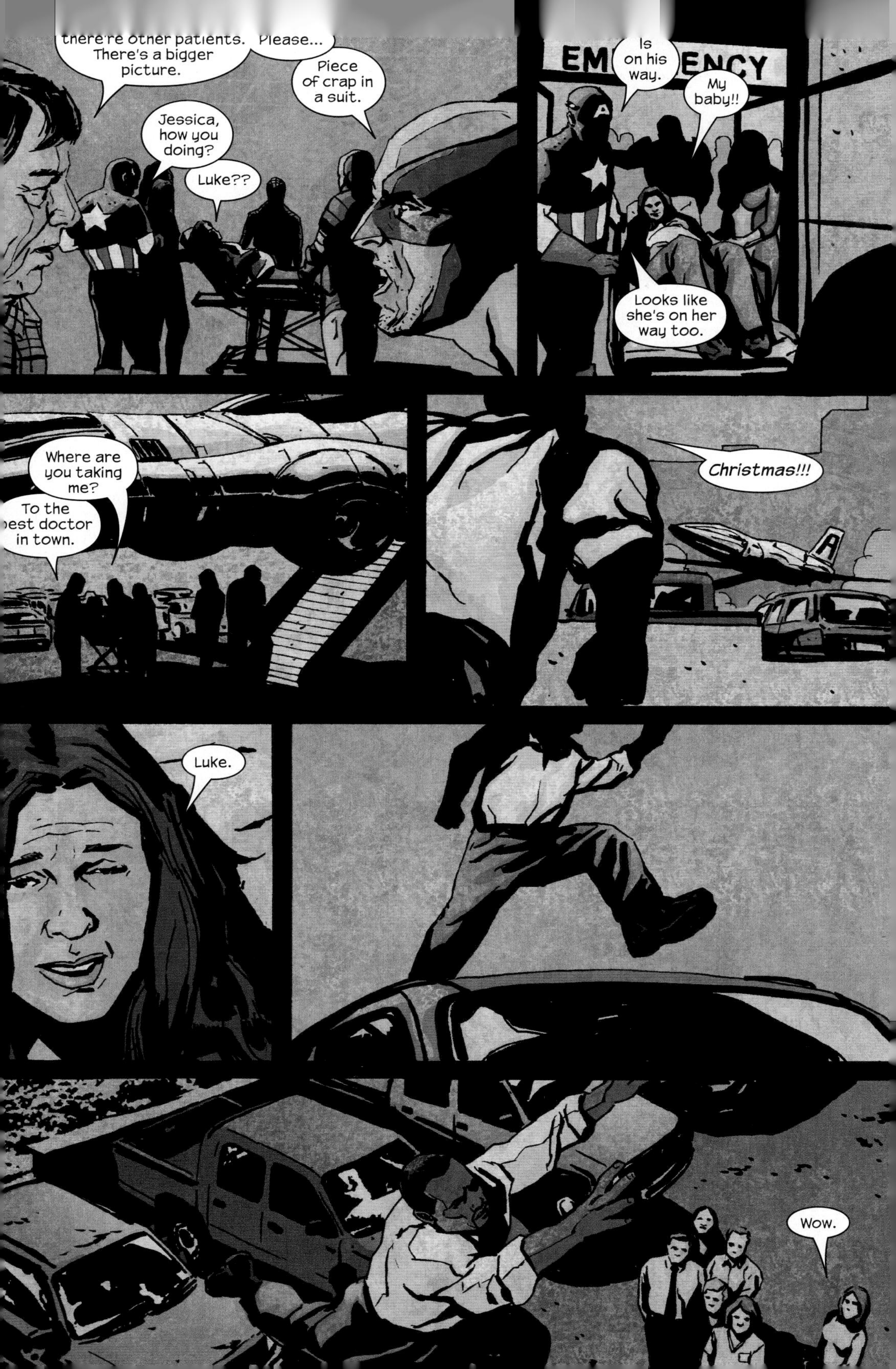
there're other patients. There's a bigger picture.
Please...
Piece of crap in a suit.
Jessica, how you doing?
Luke??
Is on his way.
My baby!!
Looks like she's on her way too.
Where are you taking me?
To the best doctor in town.
Christmas!!!
Luke.
Wow.

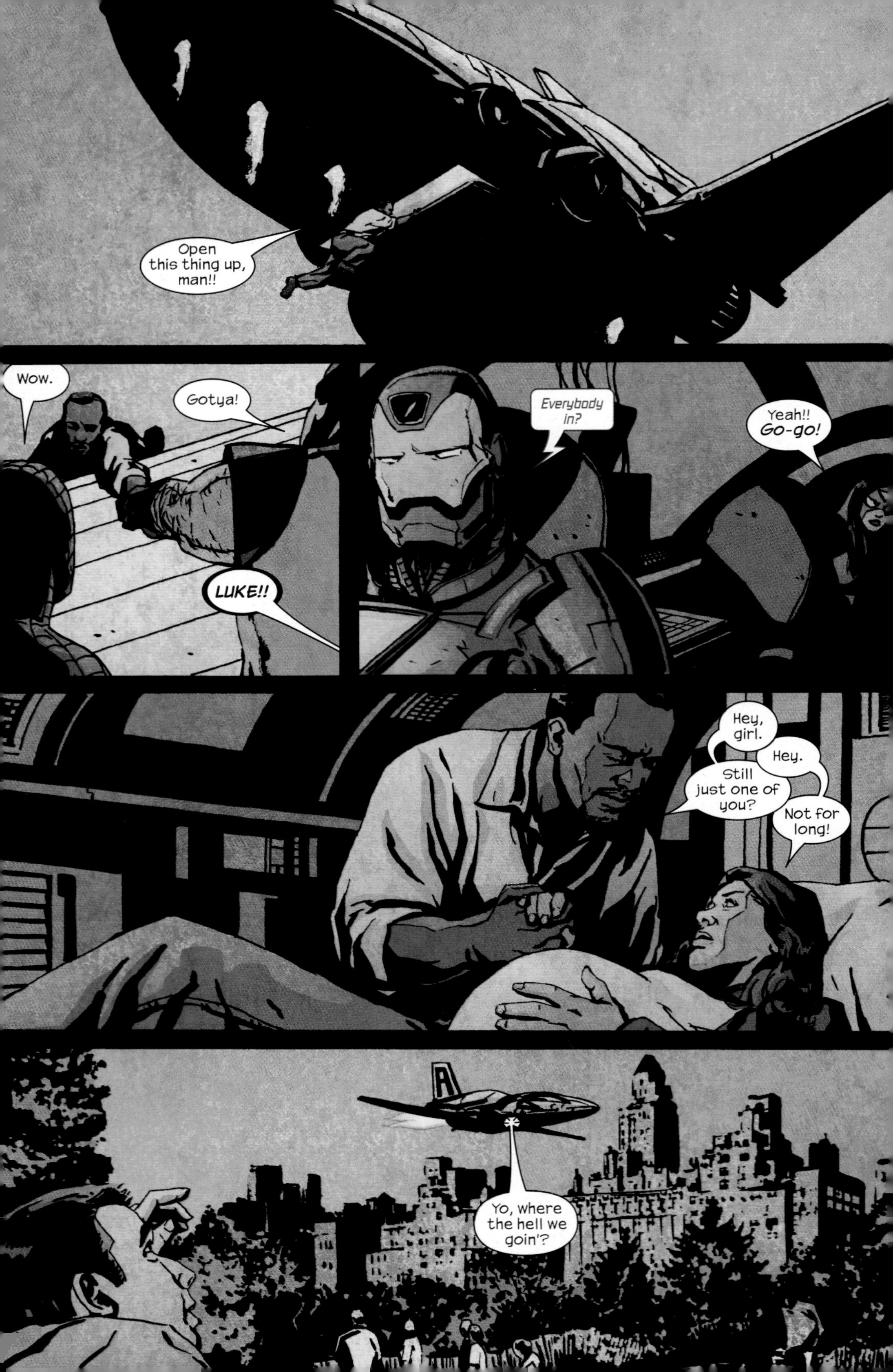
Open this thing up, man!!
Wow.
Gotya!
LUKE!!
Everybody in?
Yeah!! Go-go!
Hey, girl.
Hey.
Still just one of you?
Not for long!
Yo, where the hell we goin'?

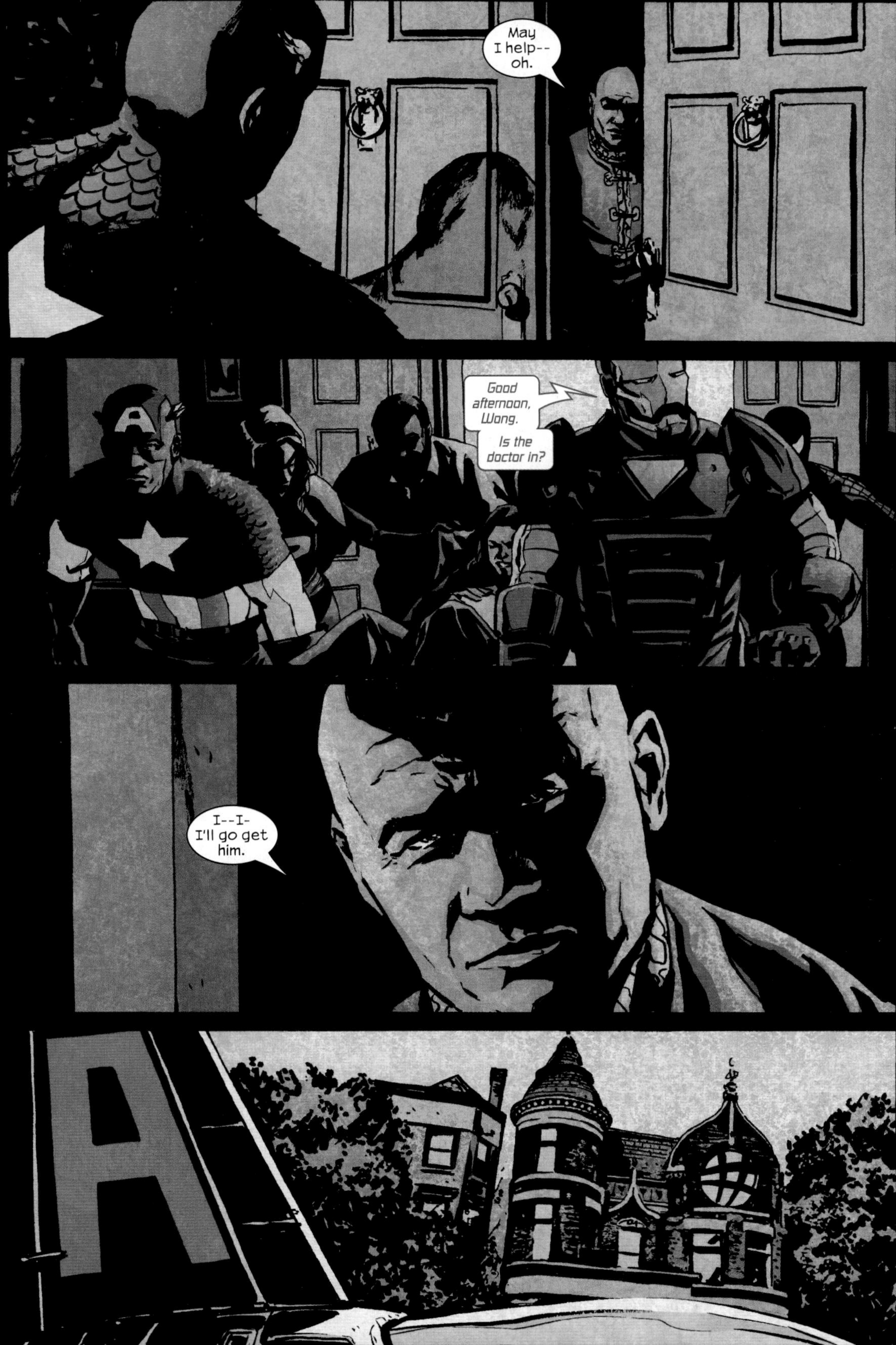
May I help-- oh.
Good afternoon, Wong.
Is the doctor in?
I--I- I'll go get him.

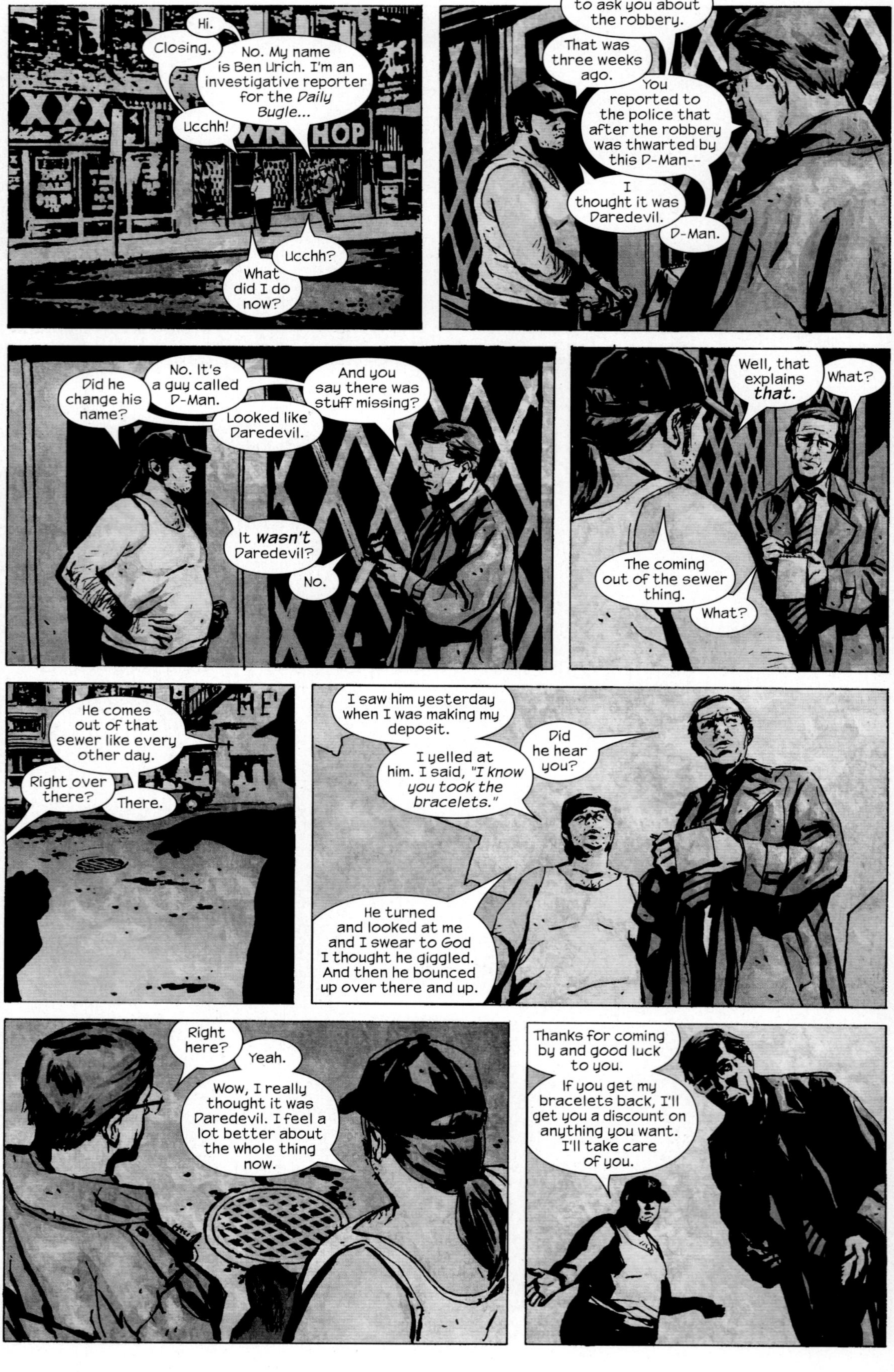
Hi.
Closing.
No. My name is Ben Urich. I'm an investigative reporter for the *Daily Bugle*...
Ucchh!
Ucchh?
What did I do now?
XXX
WN HOP
Um, I was going to ask you about the robbery.
That was three weeks ago.
You reported to the police that after the robbery was thwarted by this D-Man--
I thought it was Daredevil.
D-Man.
Did he change his name?
No. It's a guy called D-Man.
Looked like Daredevil.
And you say there was stuff missing?
It *wasn't* Daredevil?
No.
Well, that explains ***that.***
What?
The coming out of the sewer thing.
What?
He comes out of that sewer like every other day.
Right over there?
There.
I saw him yesterday when I was making my deposit.
I yelled at him. I said, *"I know you took the bracelets."*
Did he hear you?
He turned and looked at me and I swear to God I thought he giggled. And then he bounced up over there and up.
Right here?
Yeah.
Wow, I really thought it was Daredevil. I feel a lot better about the whole thing now.
Thanks for coming by and good luck to you.
If you get my bracelets back, I'll get you a discount on anything you want. I'll take care of you.

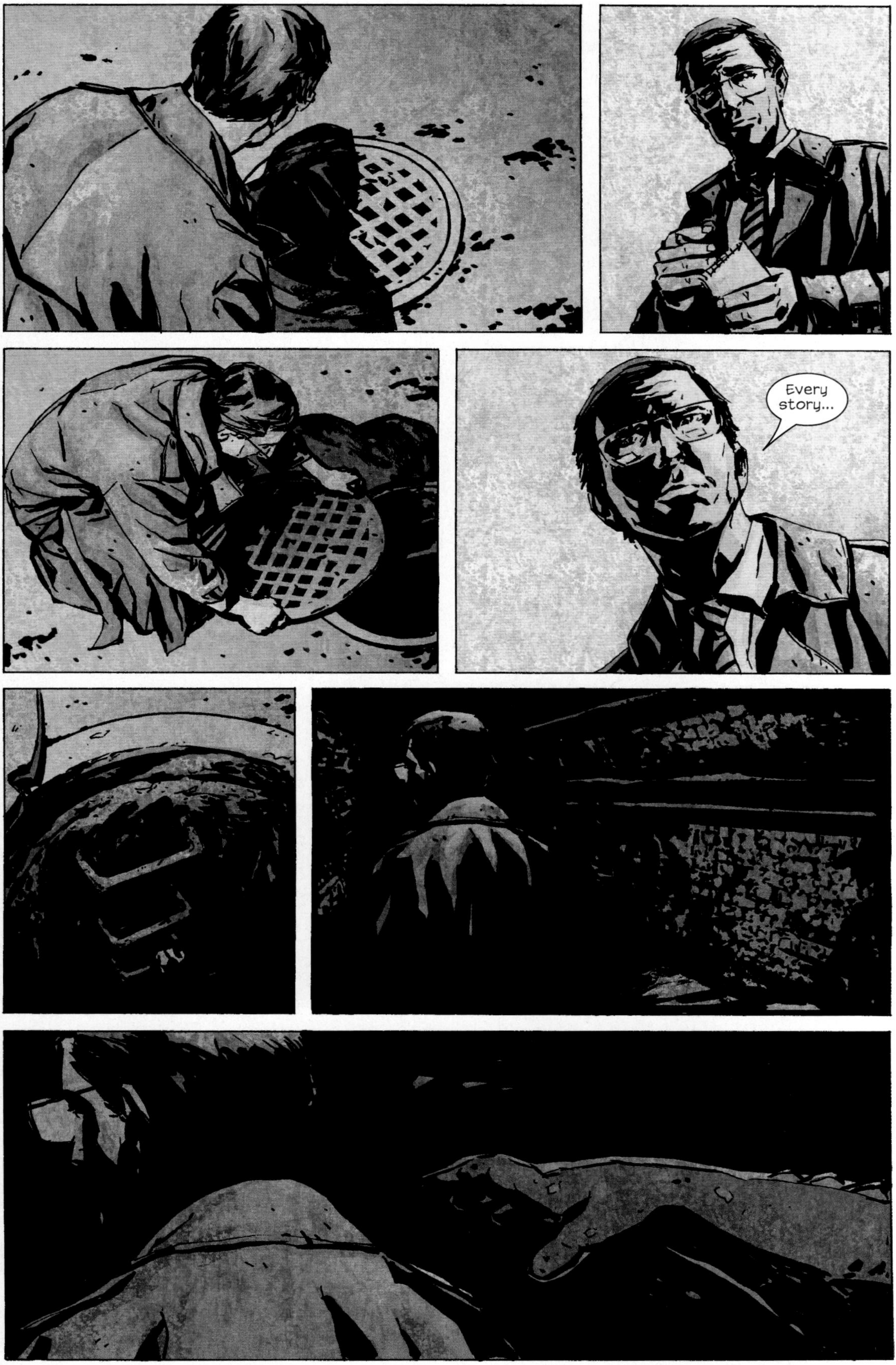
Every story...

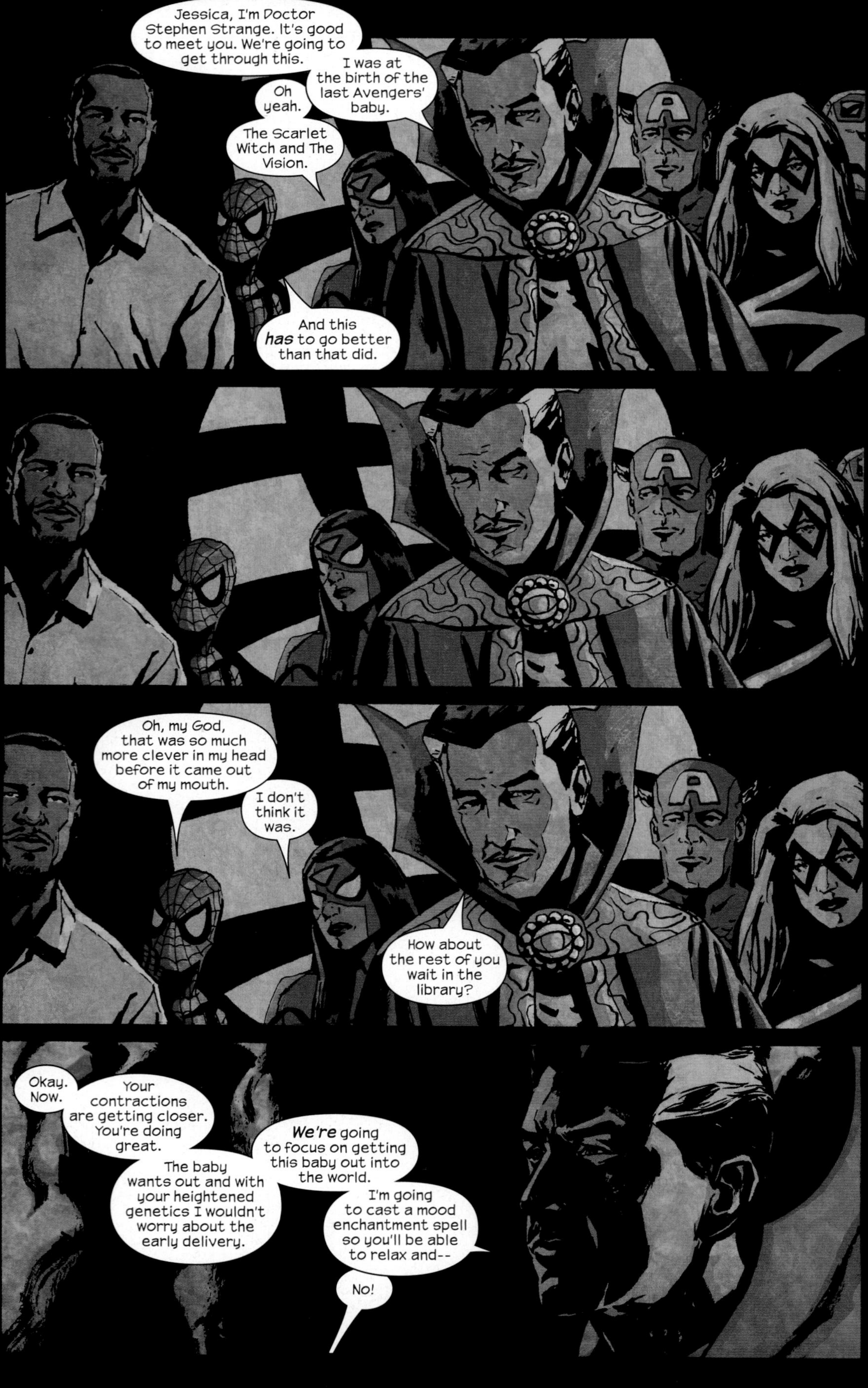

Jessica, I'm Doctor Stephen Strange. It's good to meet you. We're going to get through this.
I was at the birth of the last Avengers' baby.
Oh yeah.
The Scarlet Witch and The Vision.
And this *has* to go better than that did.
Oh, my God, that was so much more clever in my head before it came out of my mouth.
I don't think it was.
How about the rest of you wait in the library?
Okay. Now.
Your contractions are getting closer. You're doing great.
The baby wants out and with your heightened genetics I wouldn't worry about the early delivery.
We're going to focus on getting this baby out into the world.
I'm going to cast a mood enchantment spell so you'll be able to relax and--
No!

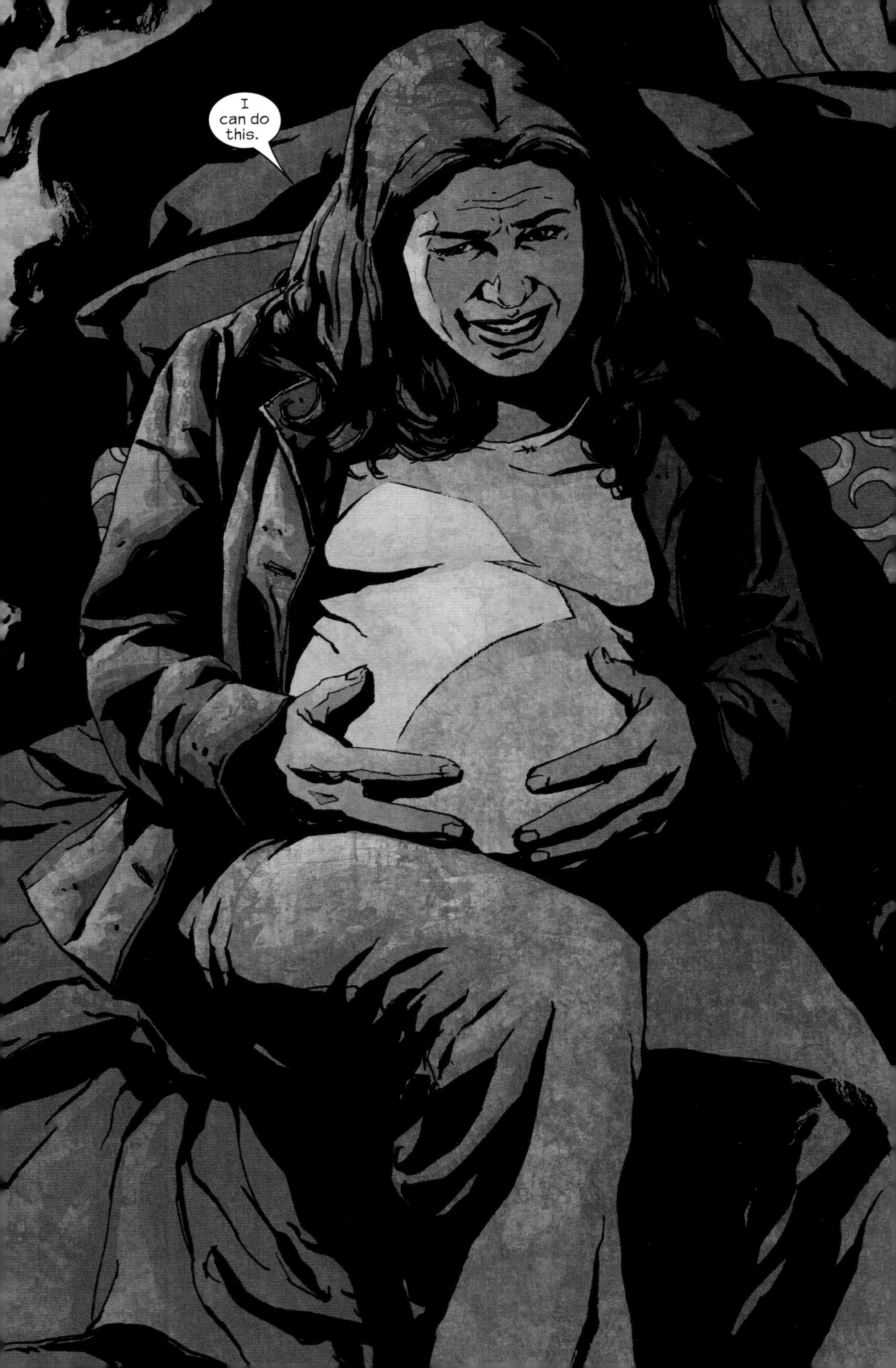
I can do this.

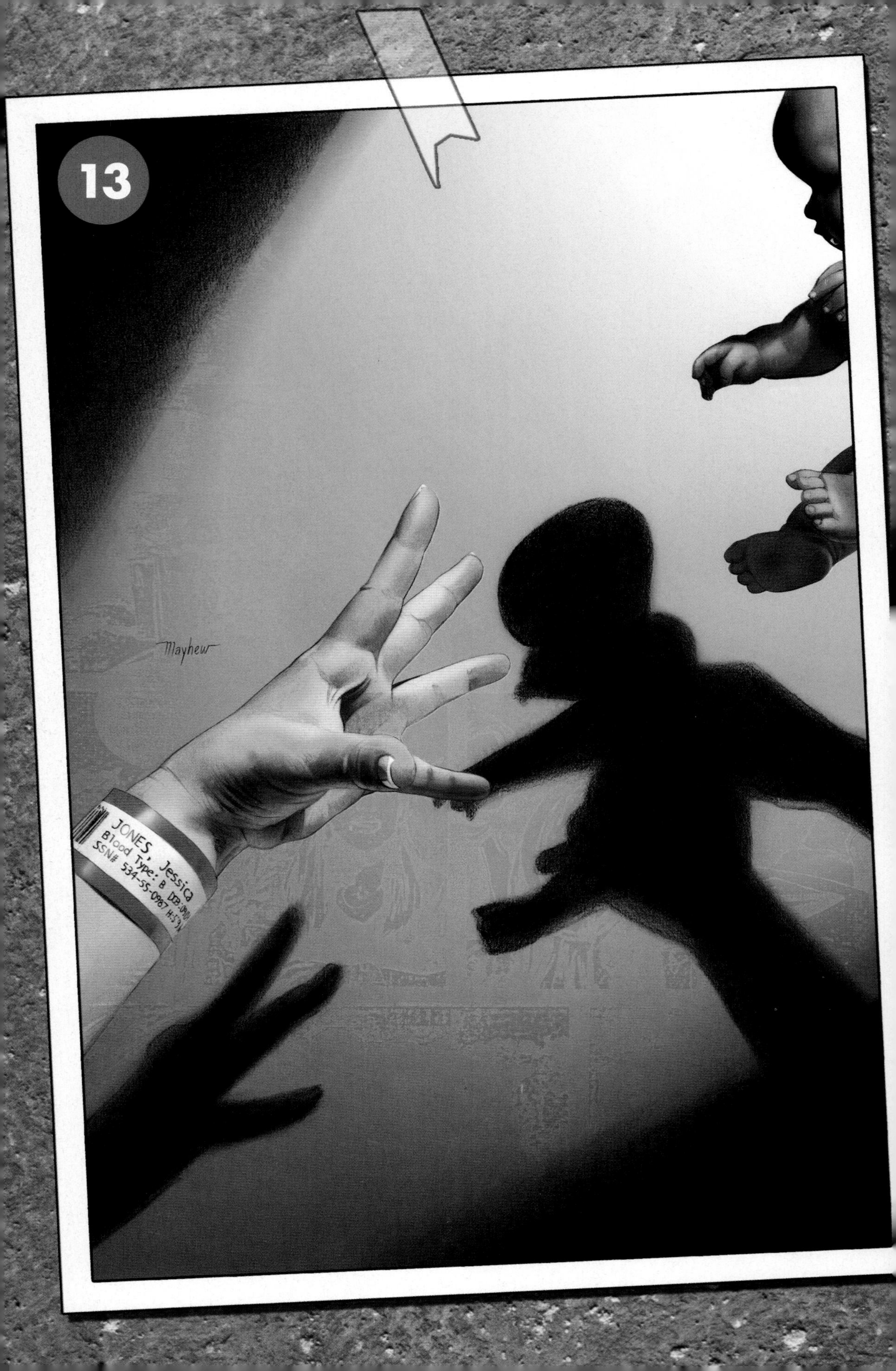
13
Mayhew
JONES, Jessica
Blood Type: B
SSN# 534-55-0987

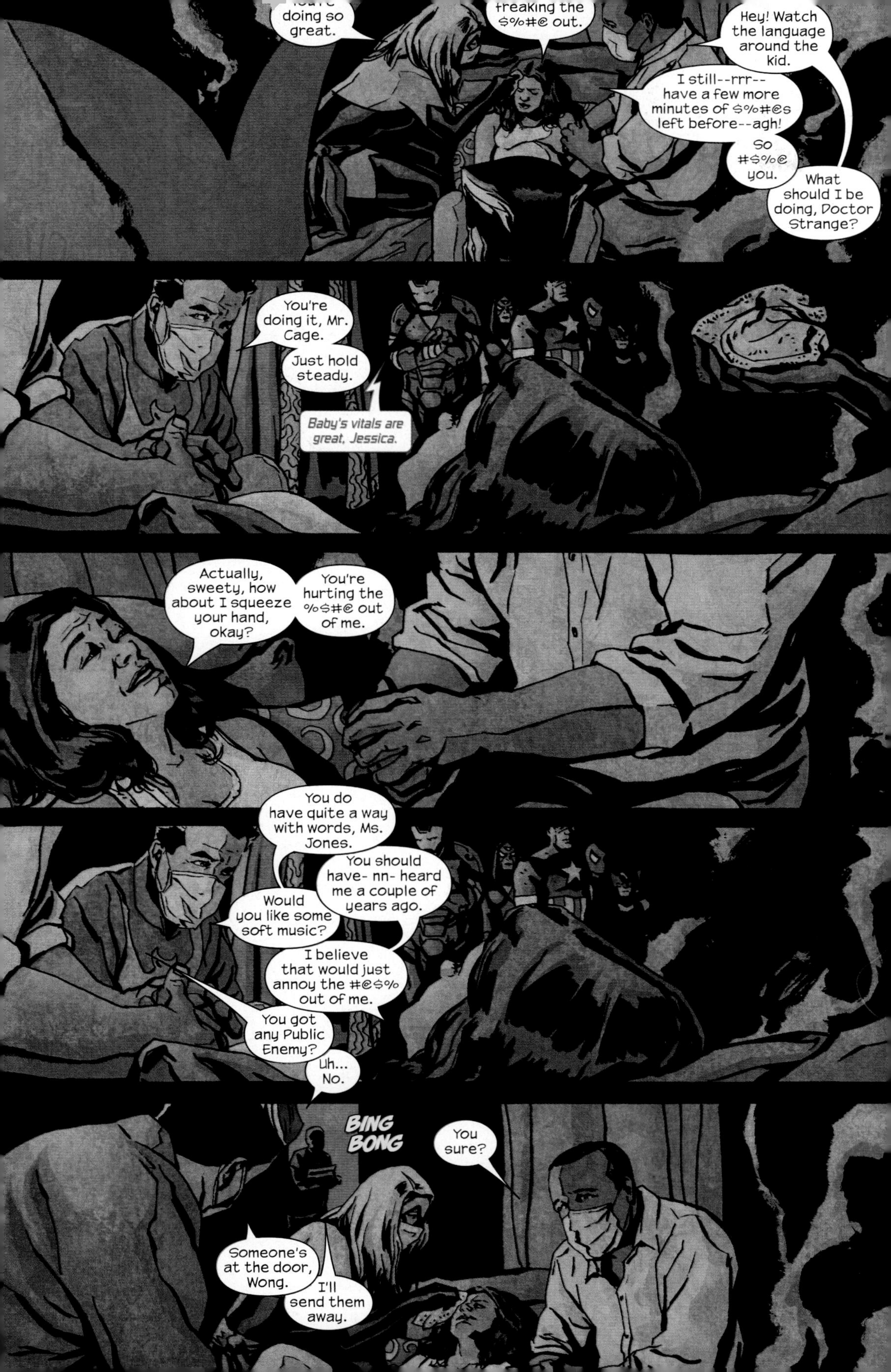

doing so great.
freaking the $%#@ out.
Hey! Watch the language around the kid.
I still--rrr--have a few more minutes of $%#@s left before--agh!
So #$%@ you.
What should I be doing, Doctor Strange?
You're doing it, Mr. Cage.
Just hold steady.
Baby's vitals are great, Jessica.
Actually, sweety, how about I squeeze your hand, okay?
You're hurting the %$#@ out of me.
You do have quite a way with words, Ms. Jones.
You should have- nn- heard me a couple of years ago.
Would you like some soft music?
I believe that would just annoy the #@$% out of me.
You got any Public Enemy?
Uh... No.
BING BONG
You sure?
Someone's at the door, Wong.
I'll send them away.

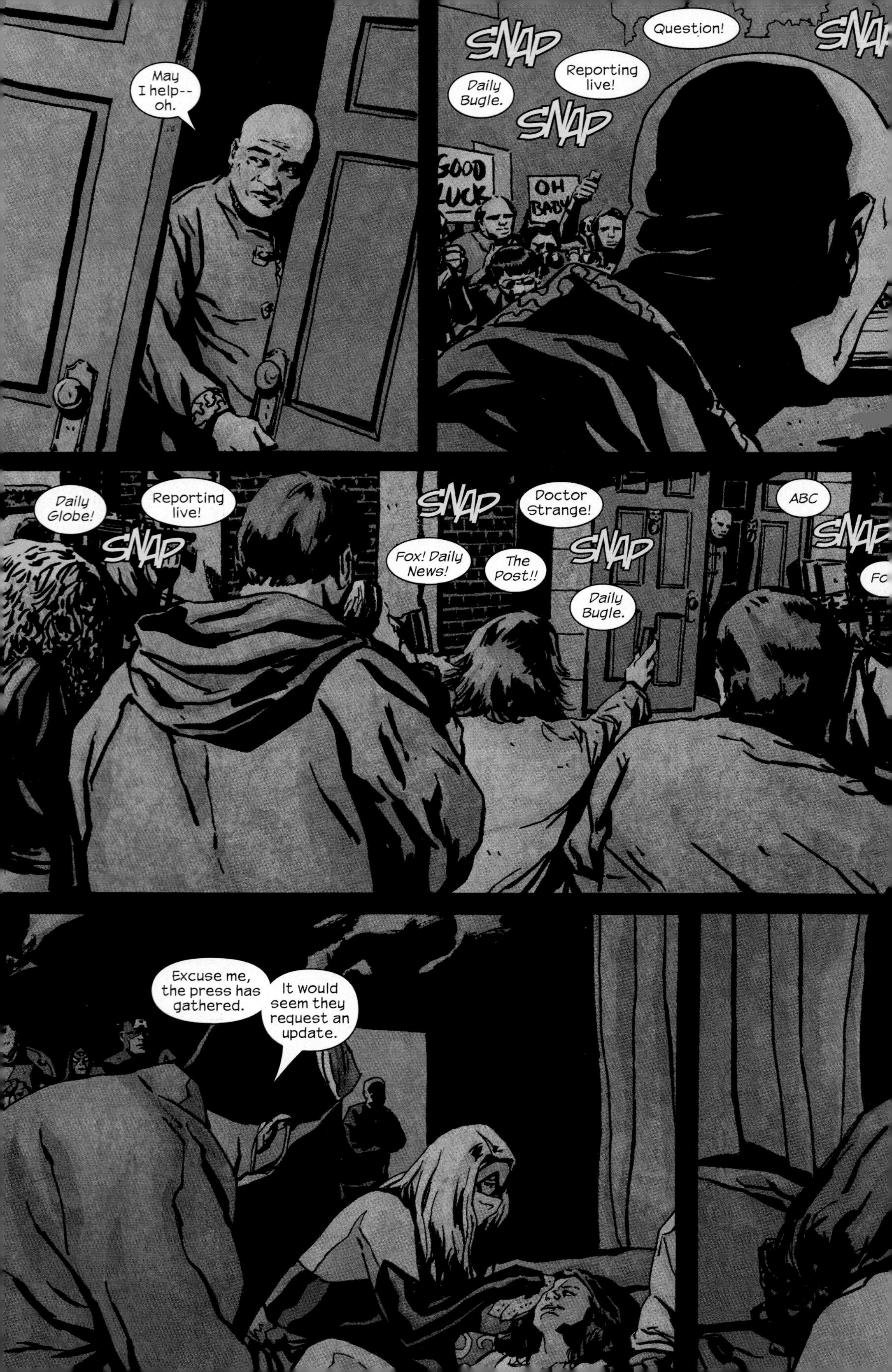
May I help-- oh.
SNAP
Question!
Daily Bugle.
Reporting live!
SNAP
GOOD LUCK
OH BABY
Daily Globe!
Reporting live!
SNAP
SNAP
Doctor Strange!
Fox! Daily News!
The Post!!
SNAP
Daily Bugle.
ABC
Excuse me, the press has gathered.
It would seem they request an update.

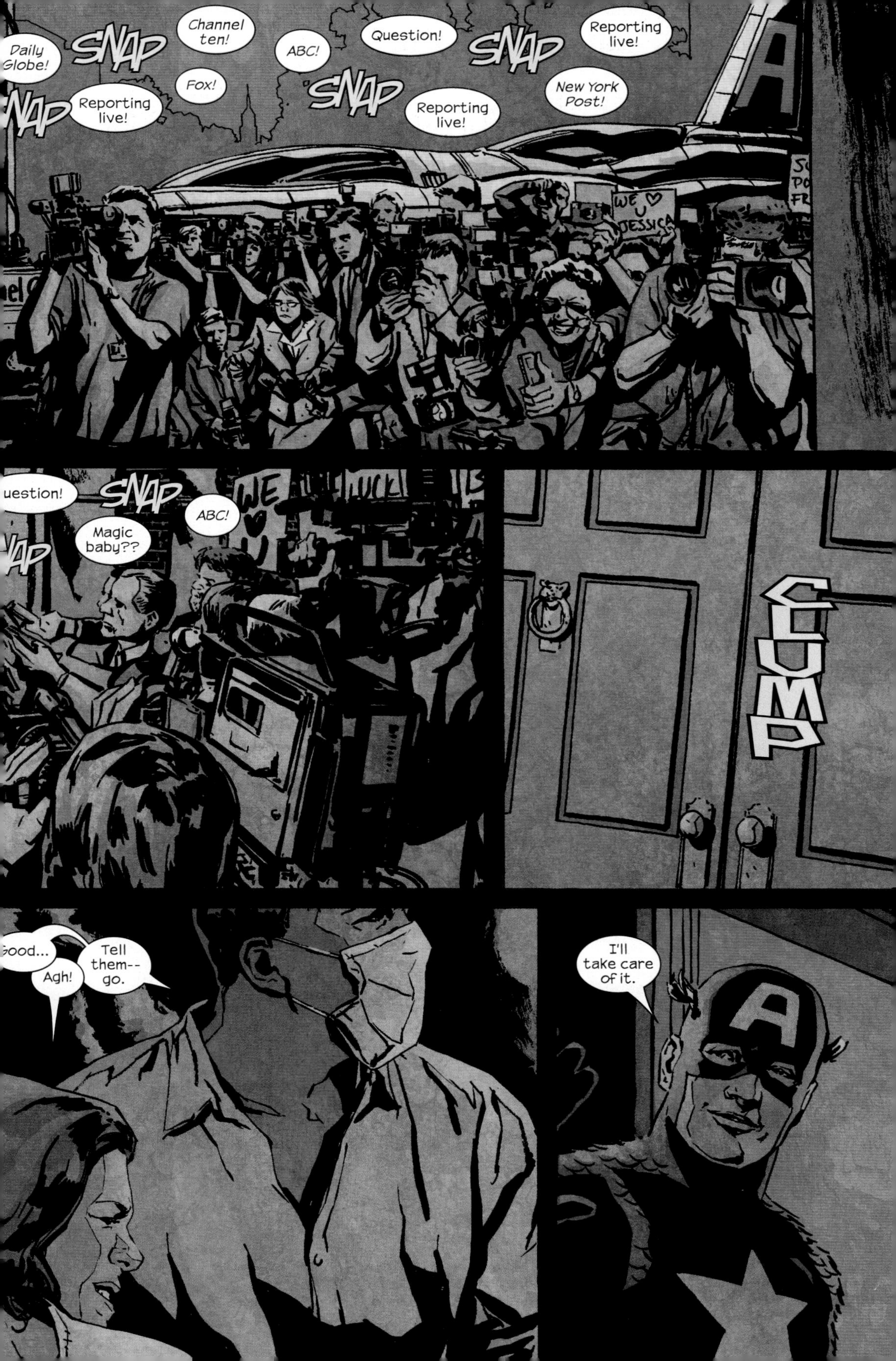
Daily Globe!
SNAP
Channel ten!
ABC!
Question!
SNAP
Reporting live!
NAP
Reporting live!
Fox!
SNAP
Reporting live!
New York Post!
WE ♡ U JESSICA
uestion!
SNAP
ABC!
Magic baby??
NAP
CLUMP
Good...
Agh!
Tell them-- go.
I'll take care of it.

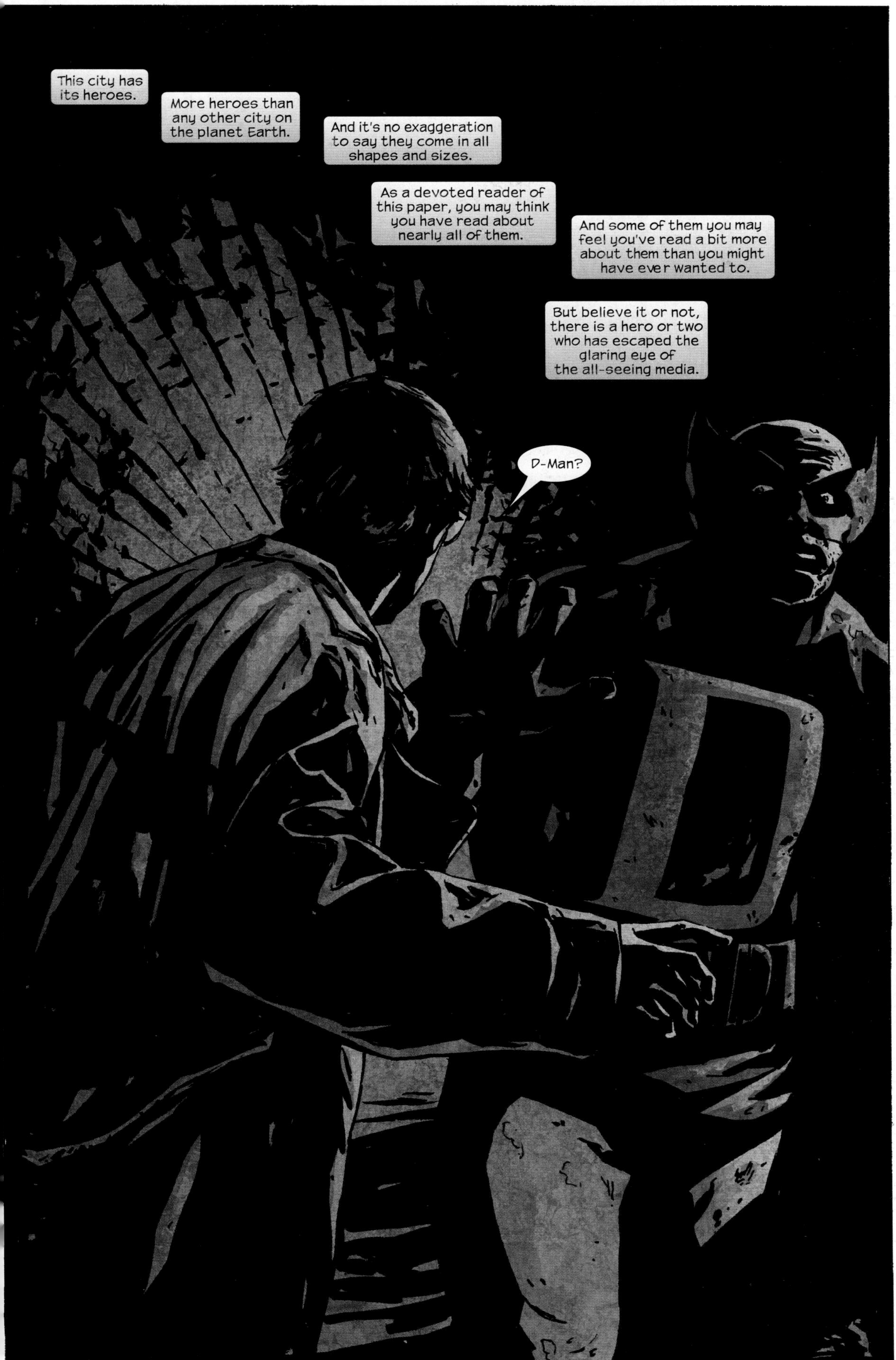
This city has its heroes.
More heroes than any other city on the planet Earth.
And it's no exaggeration to say they come in all shapes and sizes.
As a devoted reader of this paper, you may think you have read about nearly all of them.
And some of them you may feel you've read a bit more about them than you might have ever wanted to.
But believe it or not, there is a hero or two who has escaped the glaring eye of the all-seeing media.
D-Man?

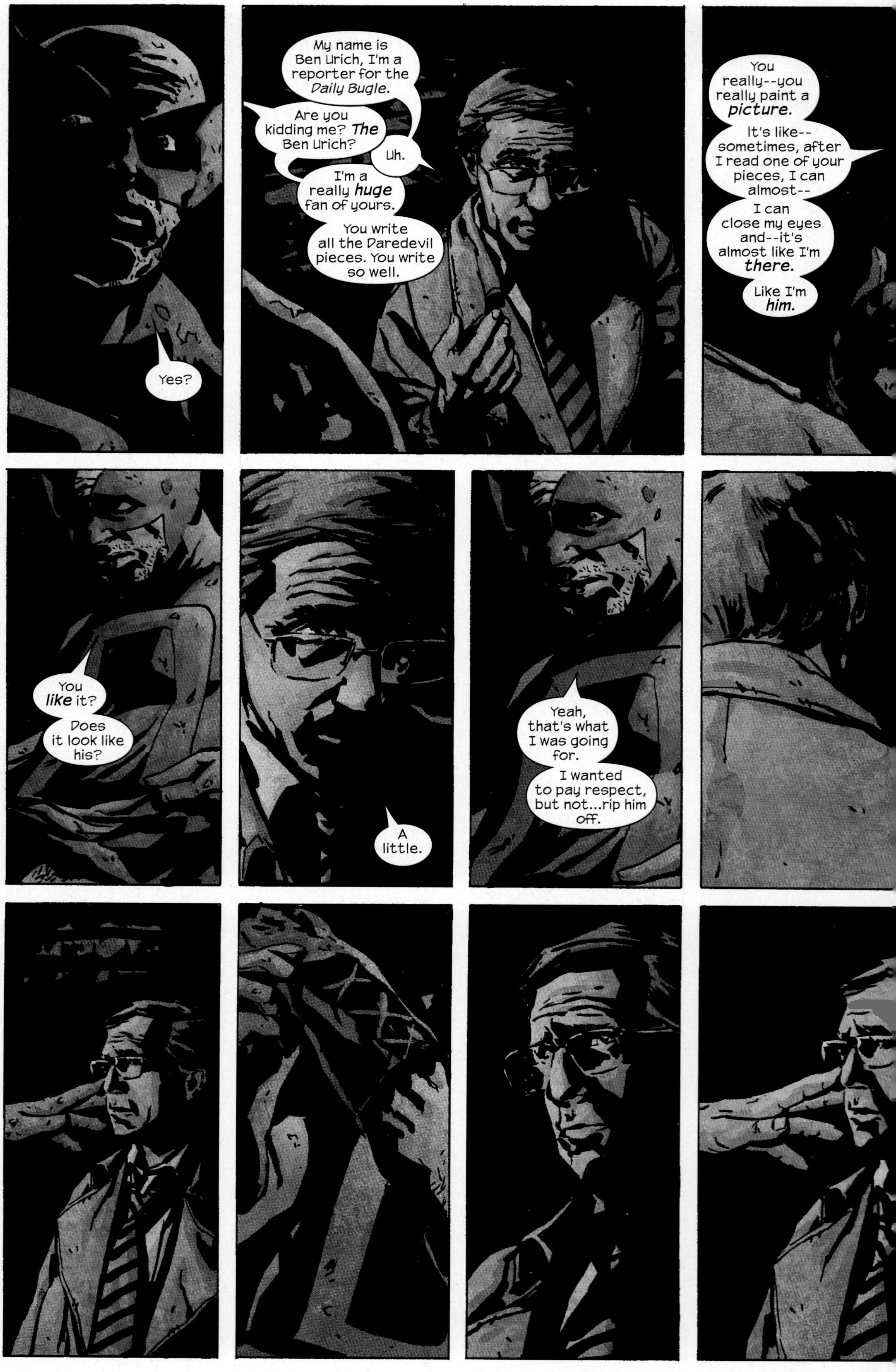
Yes?
My name is Ben Urich, I'm a reporter for the *Daily Bugle*.
Are you kidding me? ***The*** Ben Urich?
Uh.
I'm a really ***huge*** fan of yours.
You write all the Daredevil pieces. You write so well.
You really--you really paint a ***picture.***
It's like--sometimes, after I read one of your pieces, I can almost--
I can close my eyes and--it's almost like I'm ***there.***
Like I'm ***him.***
You ***like*** it?
Does it look like his?
A little.
Yeah, that's what I was going for.
I wanted to pay respect, but not...rip him off.

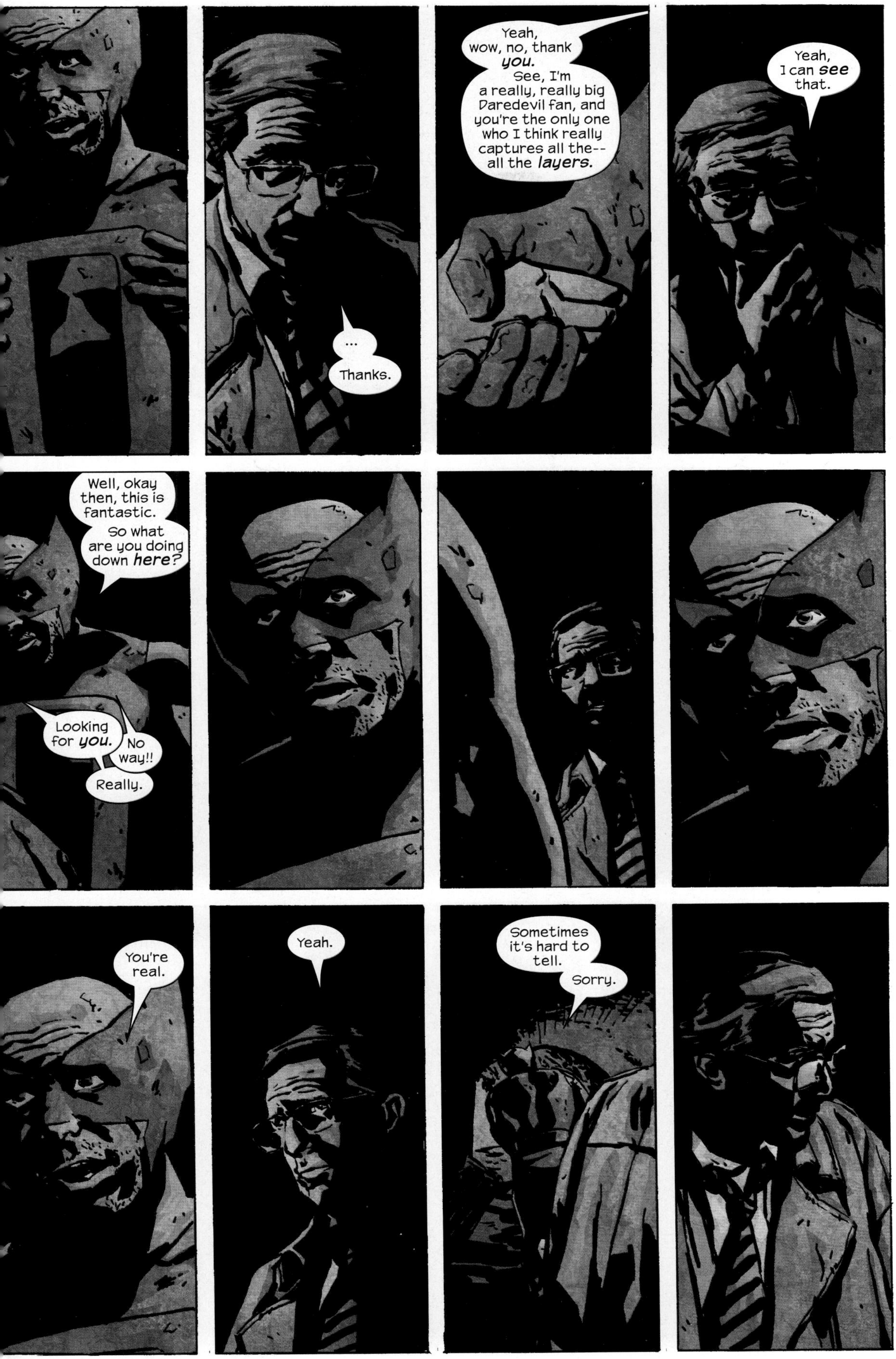
...
Thanks.
Yeah, wow, no, thank you.
See, I'm a really, really big Daredevil fan, and you're the only one who I think really captures all the-- all the layers.
Yeah, I can see that.
Well, okay then, this is fantastic.
So what are you doing down here?
Looking for you.
No way!!
Really.
You're real.
Yeah.
Sometimes it's hard to tell.
Sorry.

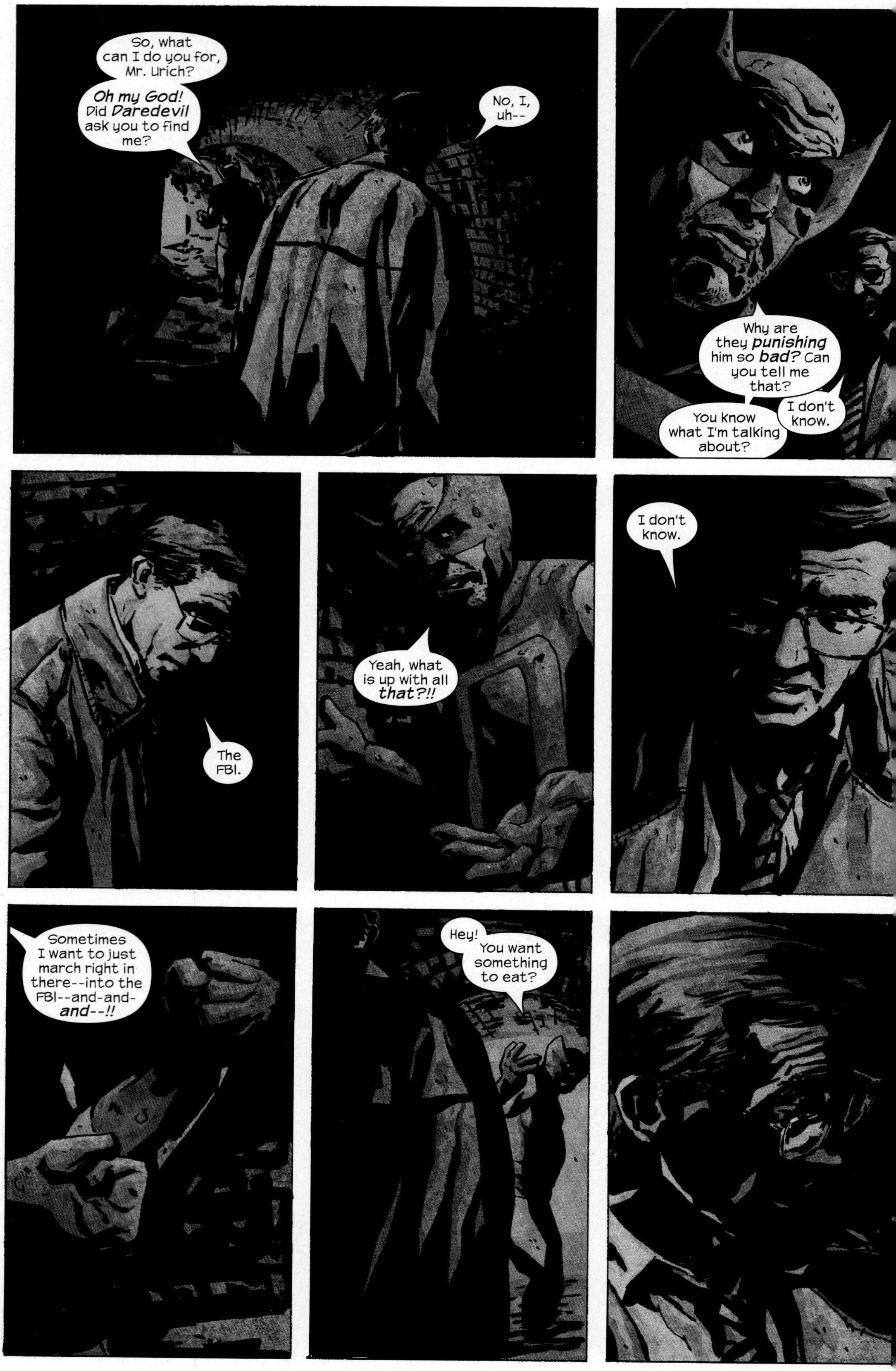
So, what can I do you for, Mr. Urich?
Oh my God! Did *Daredevil* ask you to find me?
No, I, uh--
Why are they *punishing* him so *bad?* Can you tell me that?
You know what I'm talking about?
I don't know.
The FBI.
Yeah, what is up with all *that?!!*
I don't know.
Sometimes I want to just march right in there--into the FBI--and-and- *and--!!*
Hey! You want something to eat?

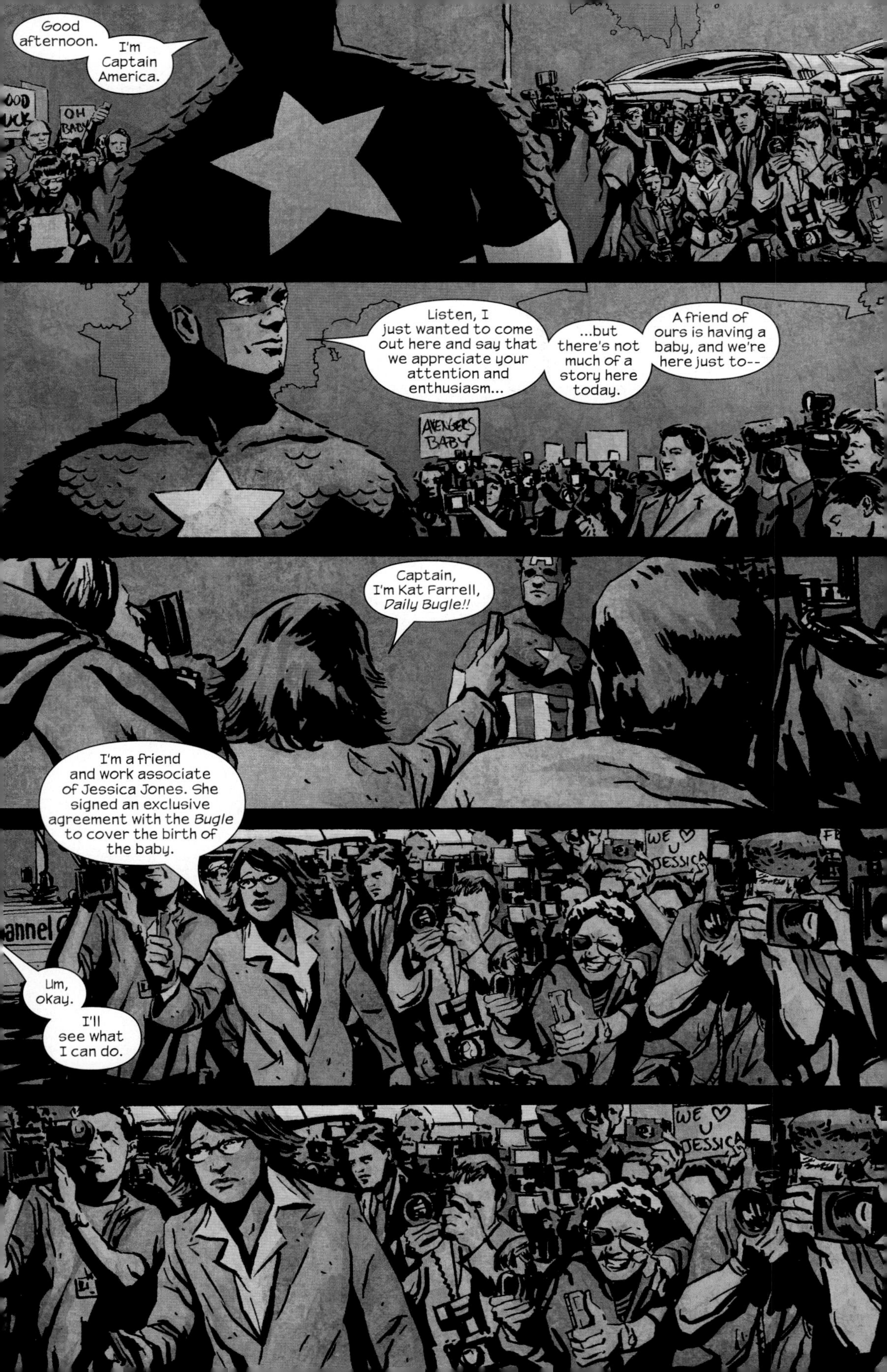
Good afternoon.
I'm Captain America.
OOD UCK
OH BABY
Listen, I just wanted to come out here and say that we appreciate your attention and enthusiasm...
...but there's not much of a story here today.
A friend of ours is having a baby, and we're here just to--
AVENGERS BABY
Captain, I'm Kat Farrell, *Daily Bugle!!*
I'm a friend and work associate of Jessica Jones. She signed an exclusive agreement with the *Bugle* to cover the birth of the baby.
WE ♡ U JESSICA
Um, okay.
I'll see what I can do.
WE ♡ U JESSICA

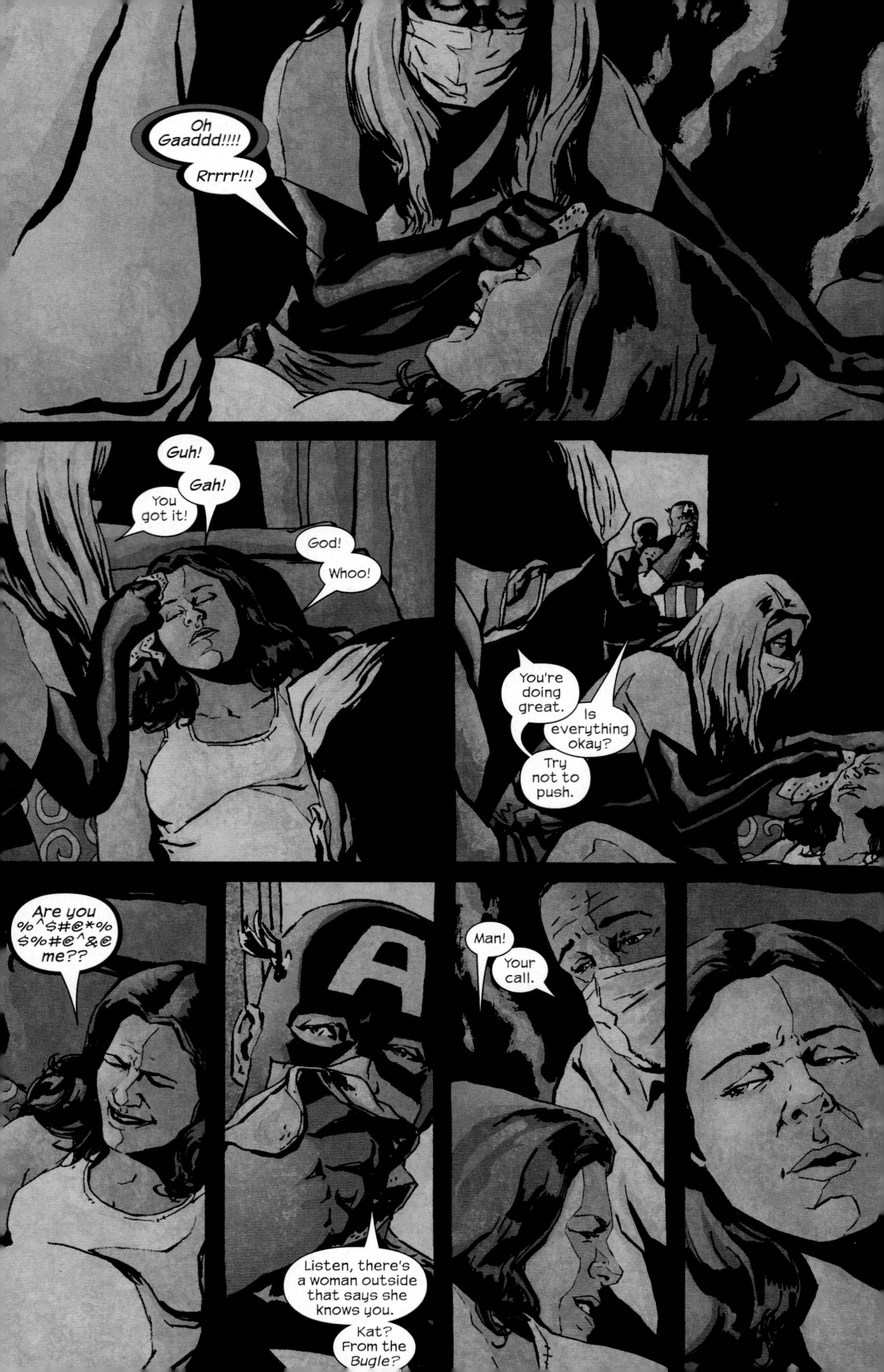

Oh Gaaddd!!!!
Rrrrr!!!
Guh!
Gah!
You got it!
God!
Whoo!
You're doing great.
Is everything okay?
Try not to push.
Are you %^$#@*% $%#@^&@ me??
Man!
Your call.
Listen, there's a woman outside that says she knows you.
Kat? From the *Bugle*?

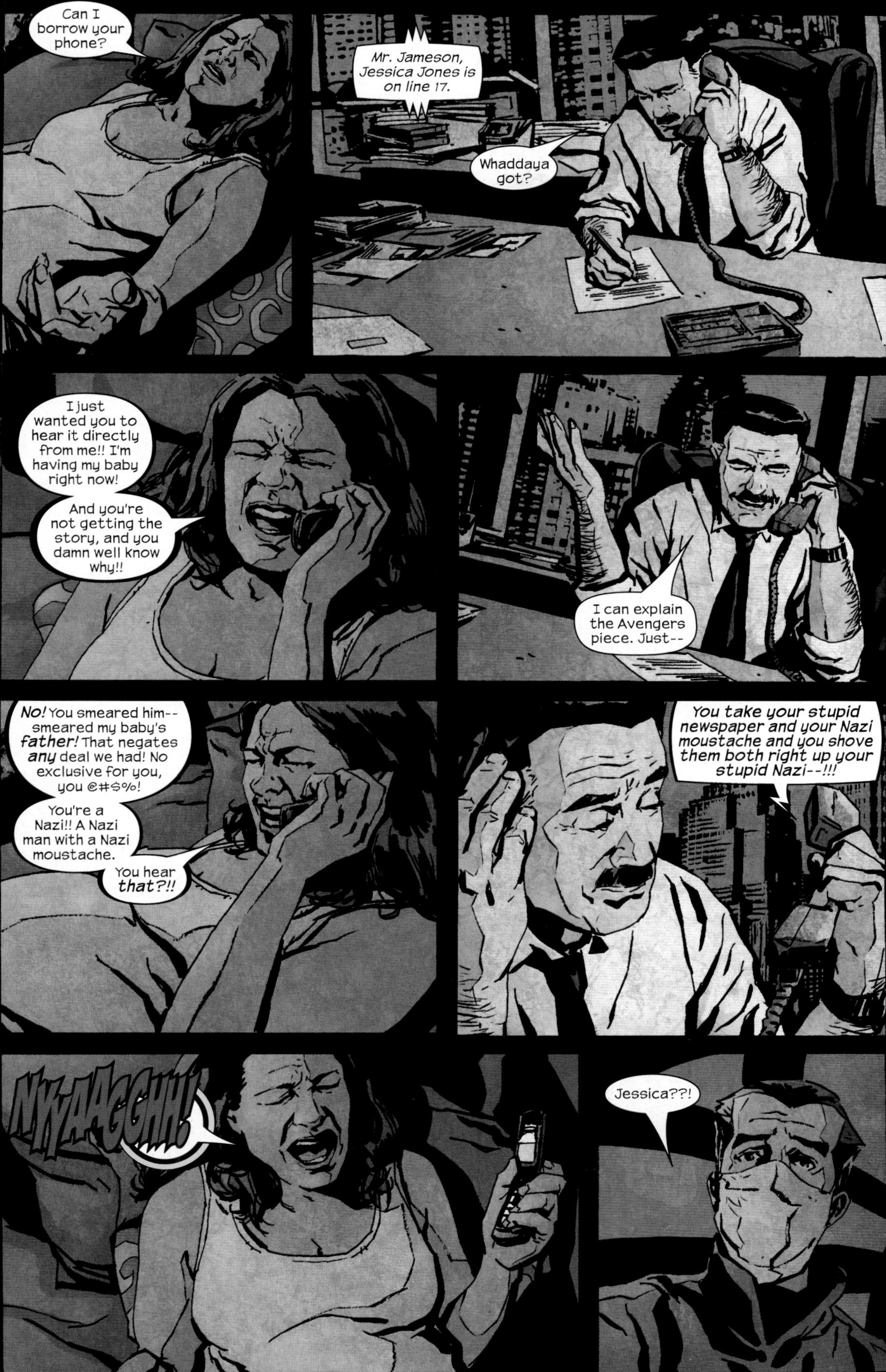

Can I borrow your phone?
Mr. Jameson, Jessica Jones is on line 17.
Whaddaya got?
I just wanted you to hear it directly from me!! I'm having my baby right now!
And you're not getting the story, and you damn well know why!!
I can explain the Avengers piece. Just--
No! You smeared him-- smeared my baby's father! That negates any deal we had! No exclusive for you, you @#$%!
You're a Nazi!! A Nazi man with a Nazi moustache.
You hear that?!!
You take your stupid newspaper and your Nazi moustache and you shove them both right up your stupid Nazi--!!!
NYAAGGHH!
Jessica??!

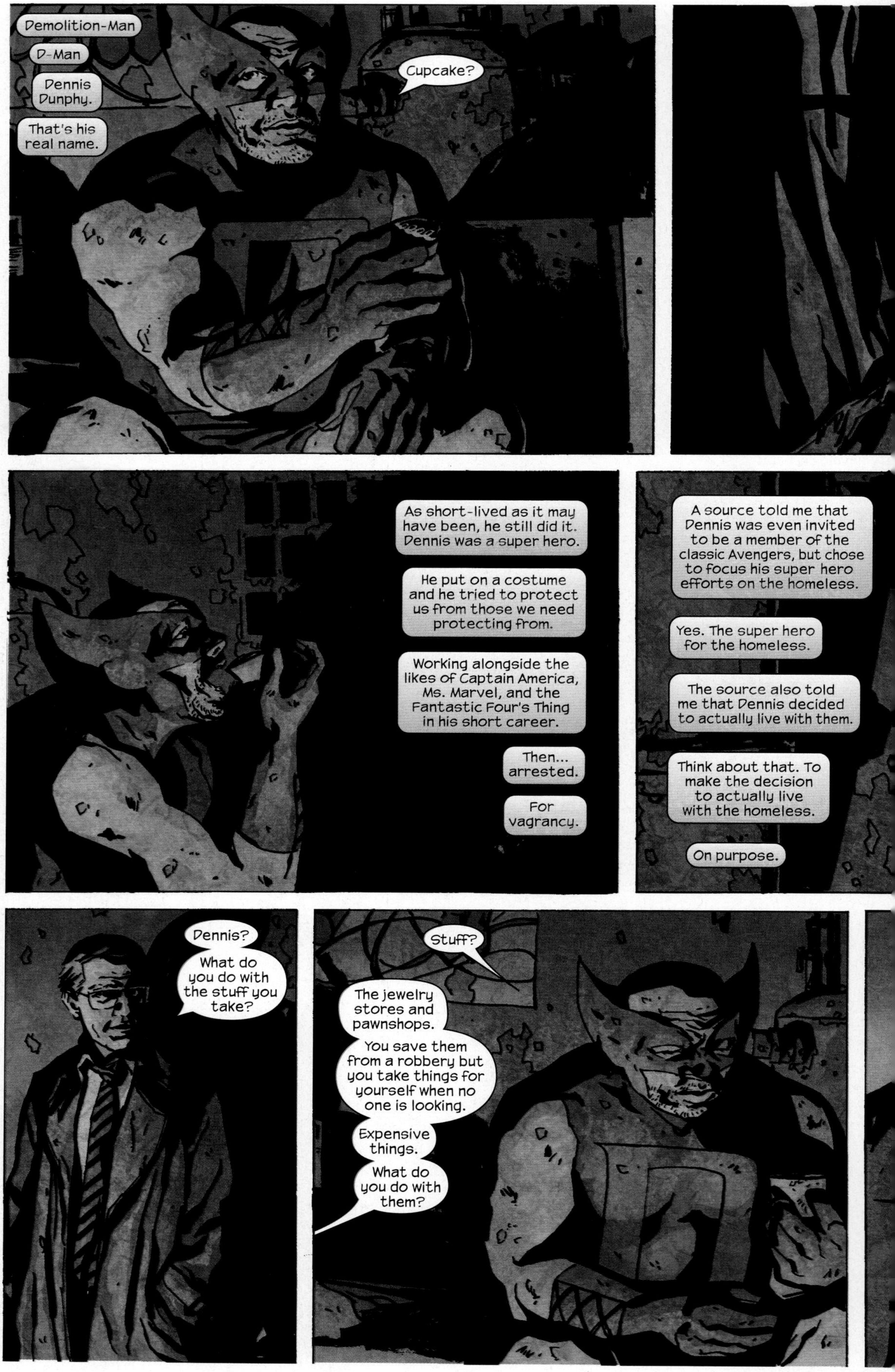

Demolition-Man
D-Man
Dennis Dunphy.
That's his real name.
Cupcake?
As short-lived as it may have been, he still did it. Dennis was a super hero.
He put on a costume and he tried to protect us from those we need protecting from.
Working alongside the likes of Captain America, Ms. Marvel, and the Fantastic Four's Thing in his short career.
Then... arrested.
For vagrancy.
A source told me that Dennis was even invited to be a member of the classic Avengers, but chose to focus his super hero efforts on the homeless.
Yes. The super hero for the homeless.
The source also told me that Dennis decided to actually live with them.
Think about that. To make the decision to actually live with the homeless.
On purpose.
Dennis?
What do you do with the stuff you take?
Stuff?
The jewelry stores and pawnshops.
You save them from a robbery but you take things for yourself when no one is looking.
Expensive things.
What do you do with them?

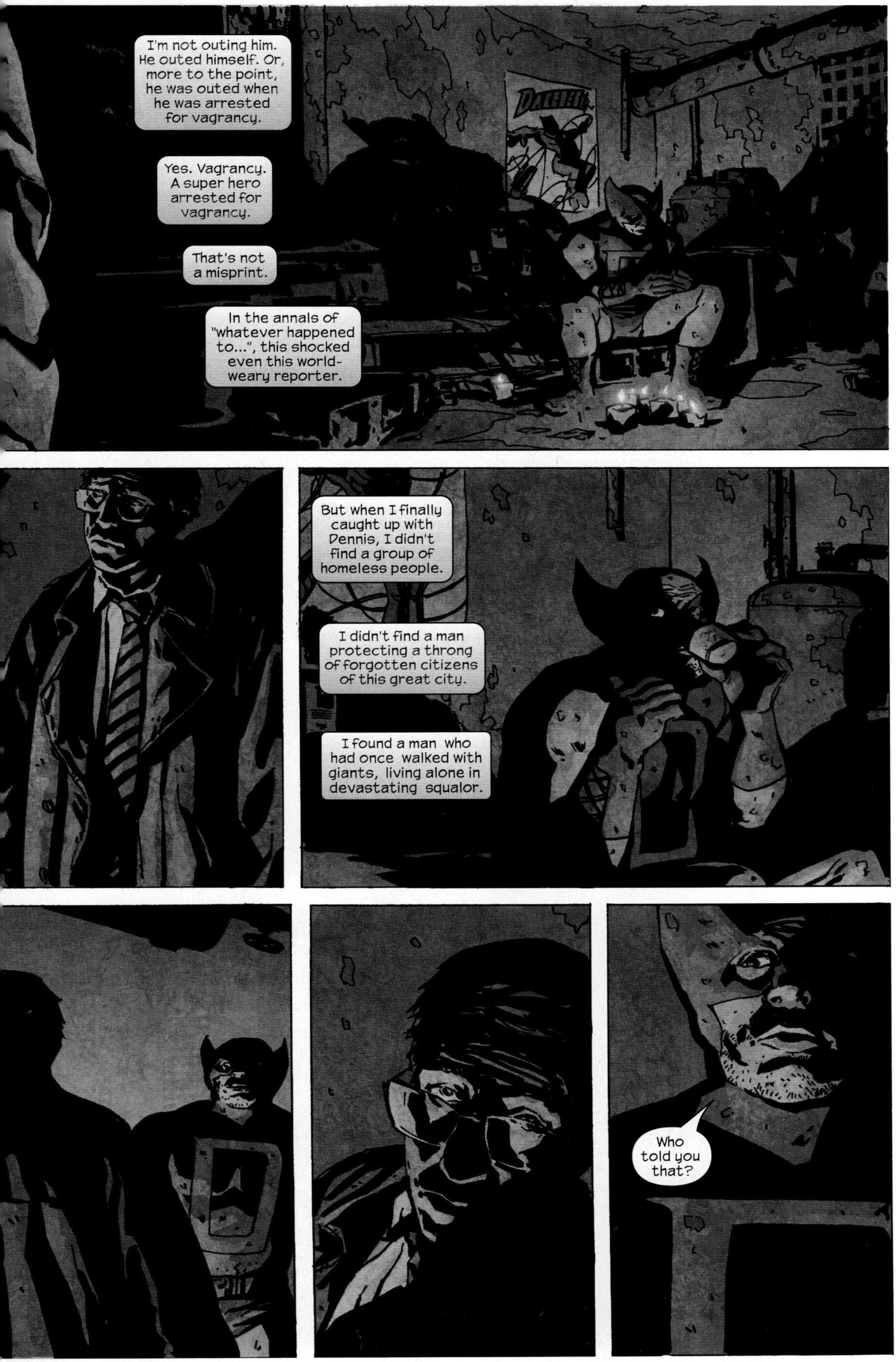
I'm not outing him. He outed himself. Or, more to the point, he was outed when he was arrested for vagrancy.
Yes. Vagrancy. A super hero arrested for vagrancy.
That's not a misprint.
In the annals of "whatever happened to...", this shocked even this world-weary reporter.
But when I finally caught up with Dennis, I didn't find a group of homeless people.
I didn't find a man protecting a throng of forgotten citizens of this great city.
I found a man who had once walked with giants, living alone in devastating squalor.
Who told you that?

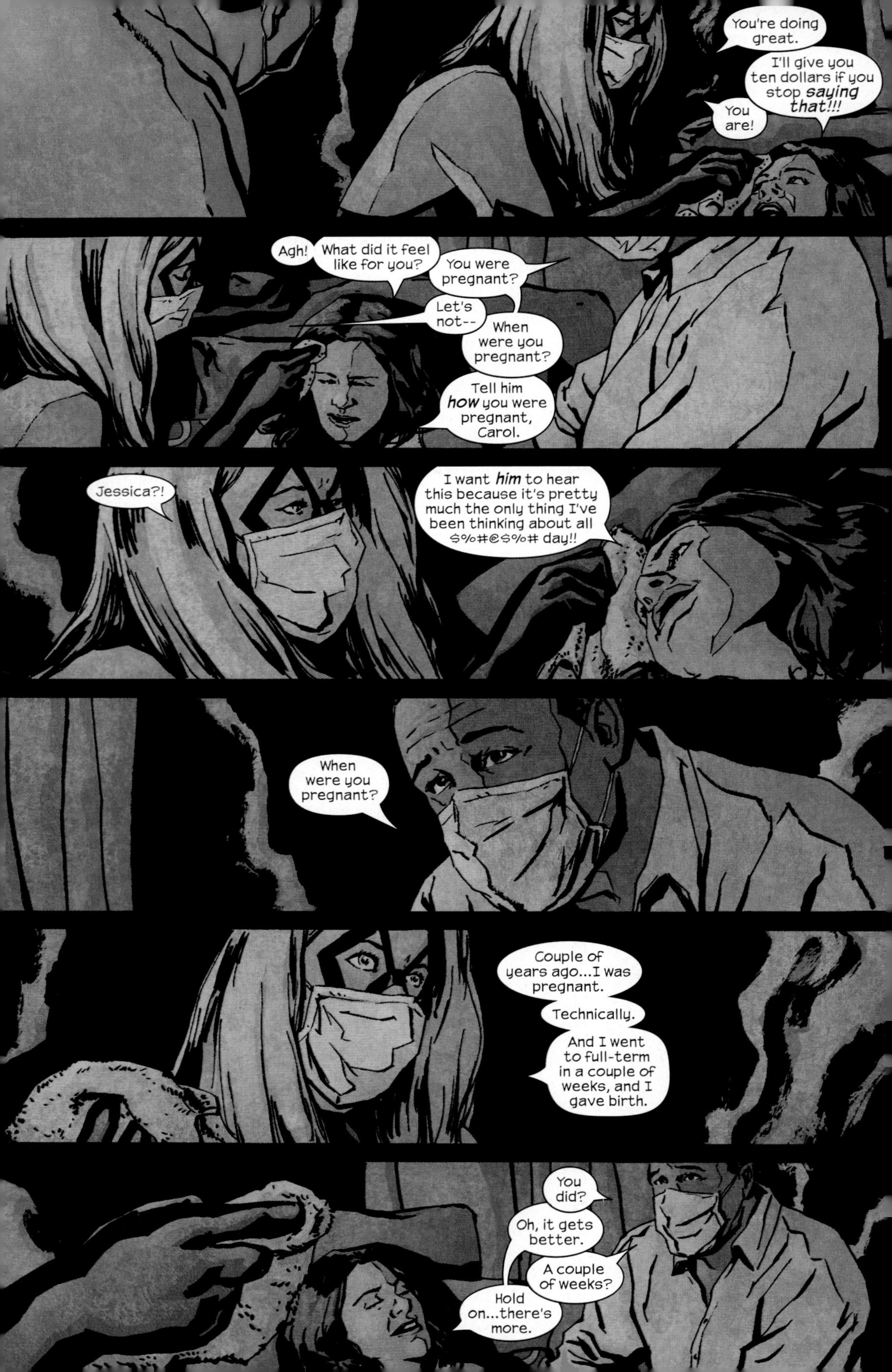

You're doing great.
I'll give you ten dollars if you stop *saying that*!!!
You are!
Agh!
What did it feel like for you?
You were pregnant?
Let's not--
When were you pregnant?
Tell him *how* you were pregnant, Carol.
Jessica?!
I want *him* to hear this because it's pretty much the only thing I've been thinking about all $%#@$%# day!!
When were you pregnant?
Couple of years ago...I was pregnant.
Technically.
And I went to full-term in a couple of weeks, and I gave birth.
You did?
Oh, it gets better.
A couple of weeks?
Hold on...there's more.

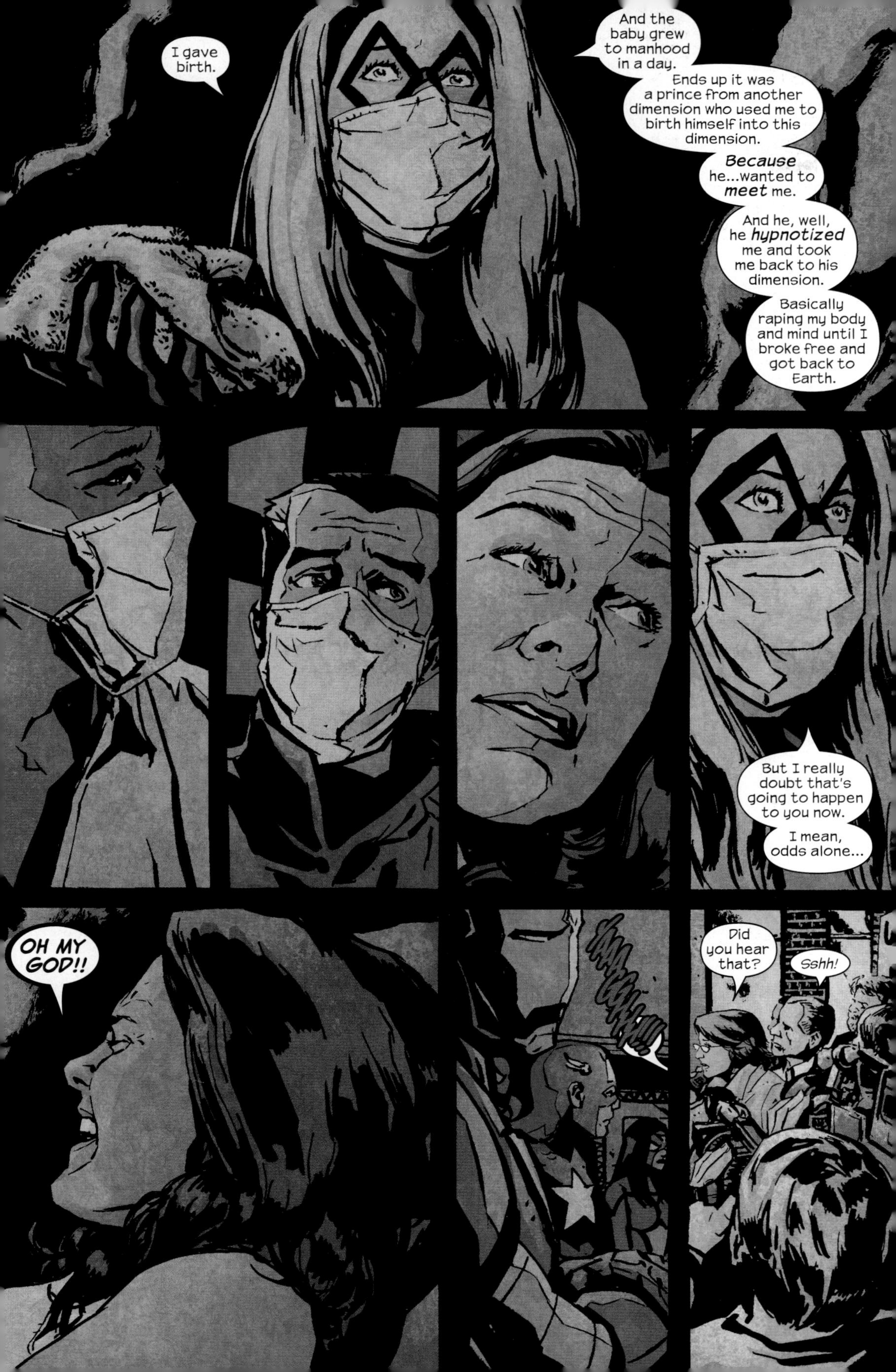
I gave birth.
And the baby grew to manhood in a day.
Ends up it was a prince from another dimension who used me to birth himself into this dimension.
Because he...wanted to *meet* me.
And he, well, he *hypnotized* me and took me back to his dimension.
Basically raping my body and mind until I broke free and got back to Earth.
But I really doubt that's going to happen to you now.
I mean, odds alone...
OH MY GOD!!
Did you hear that?
Sshh!

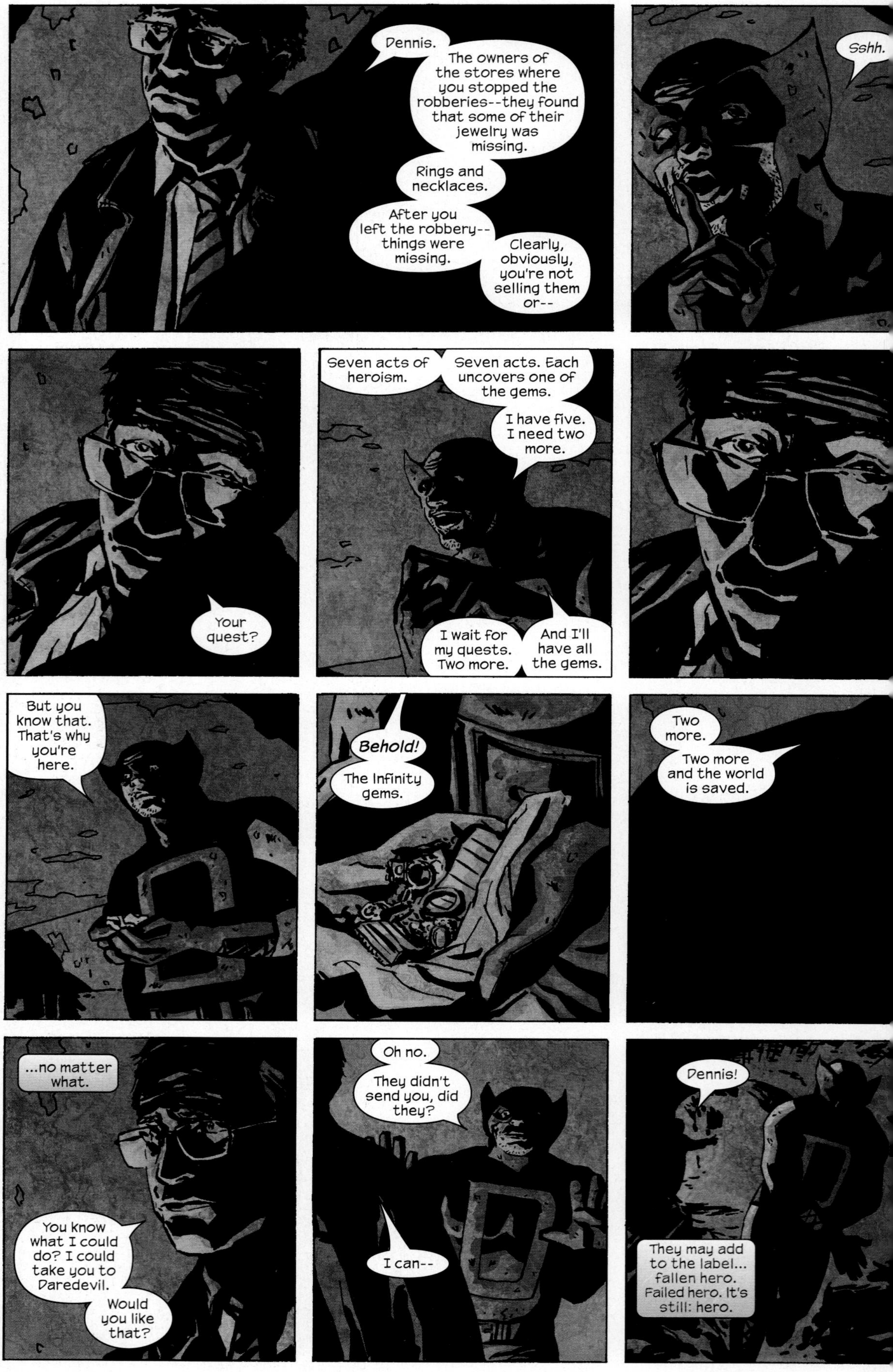
Dennis.
The owners of the stores where you stopped the robberies--they found that some of their jewelry was missing.
Rings and necklaces.
After you left the robbery--things were missing.
Clearly, obviously, you're not selling them or--
Sshh.
Your quest?
Seven acts of heroism.
Seven acts. Each uncovers one of the gems.
I have five. I need two more.
I wait for my quests. Two more.
And I'll have all the gems.
But you know that. That's why you're here.
Behold!
The Infinity gems.
Two more.
Two more and the world is saved.
...no matter what.
You know what I could do? I could take you to Daredevil.
Would you like that?
Oh no.
They didn't send you, did they?
I can--
Dennis!
They may add to the label... fallen hero. Failed hero. It's still: hero.

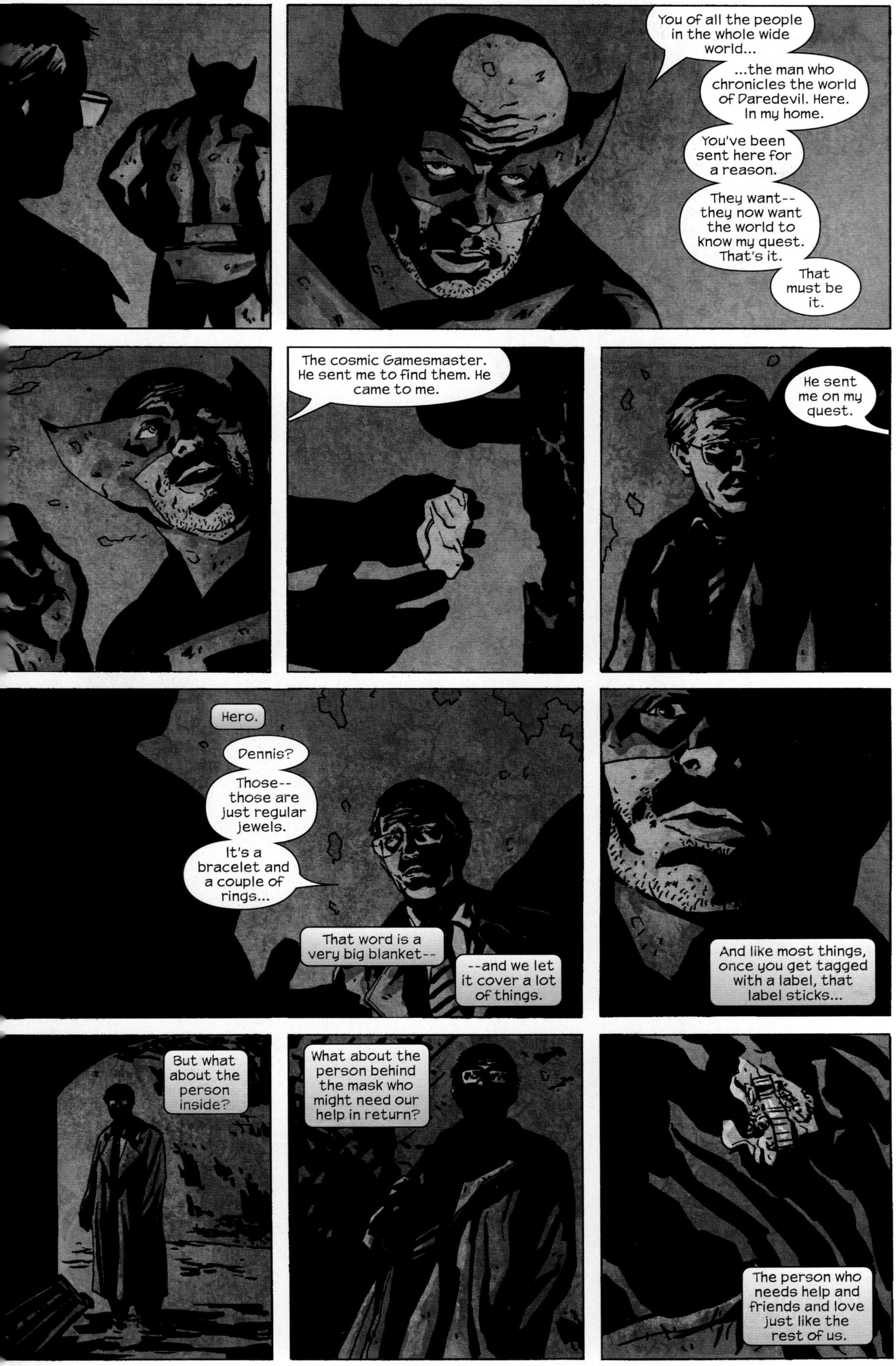
You of all the people in the whole wide world...
...the man who chronicles the world of Daredevil. Here. In my home.
You've been sent here for a reason.
They want--they now want the world to know my quest. That's it.
That must be it.
The cosmic Gamesmaster. He sent me to find them. He came to me.
He sent me on my quest.
Hero.
Dennis?
Those--those are just regular jewels.
It's a bracelet and a couple of rings...
That word is a very big blanket--
--and we let it cover a lot of things.
And like most things, once you get tagged with a label, that label sticks...
But what about the person inside?
What about the person behind the mask who might need our help in return?
The person who needs help and friends and love just like the rest of us.

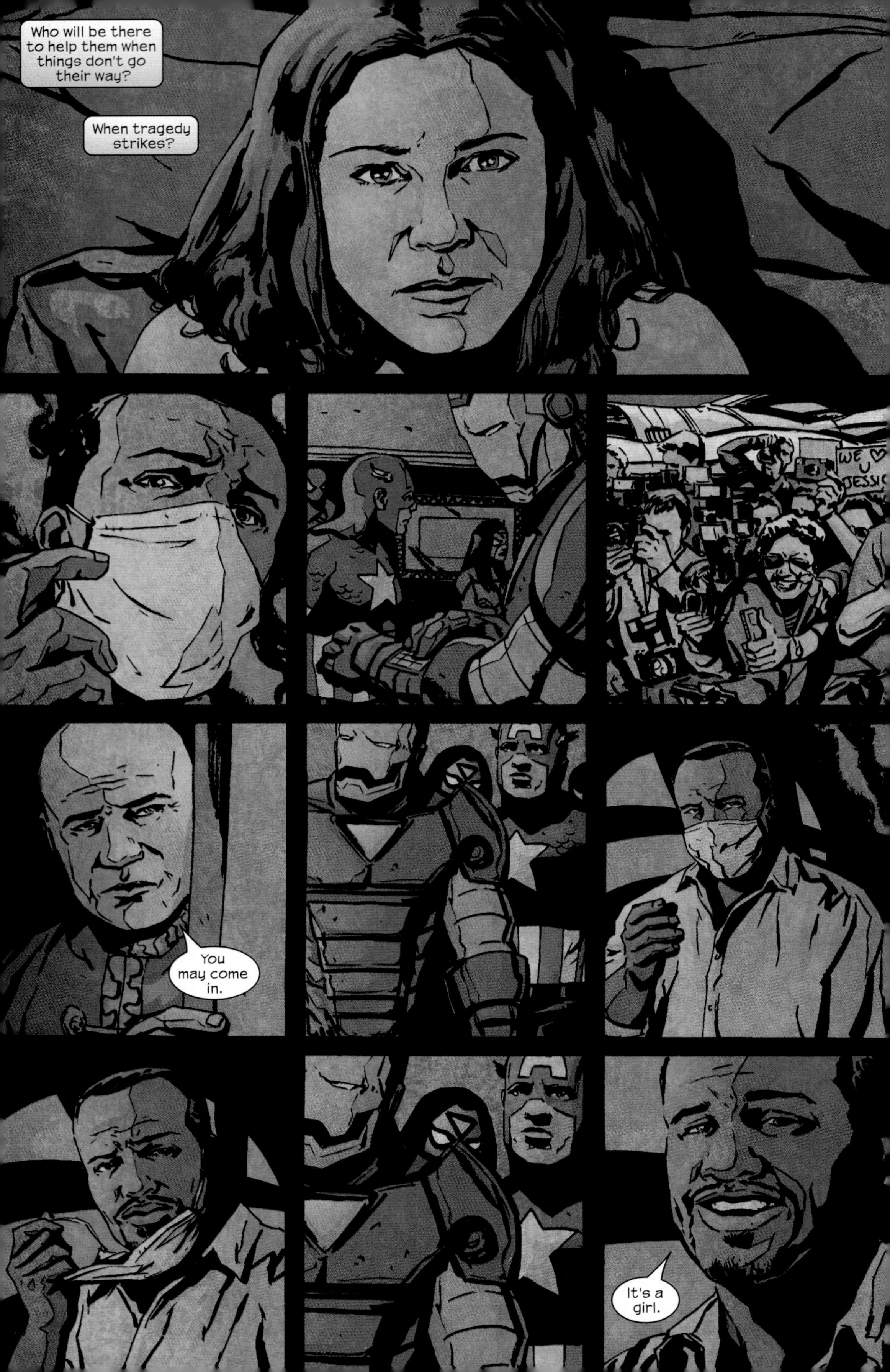
Who will be there to help them when things don't go their way?
When tragedy strikes?
WE ♥ U JESSIC
You may come in.
It's a girl.

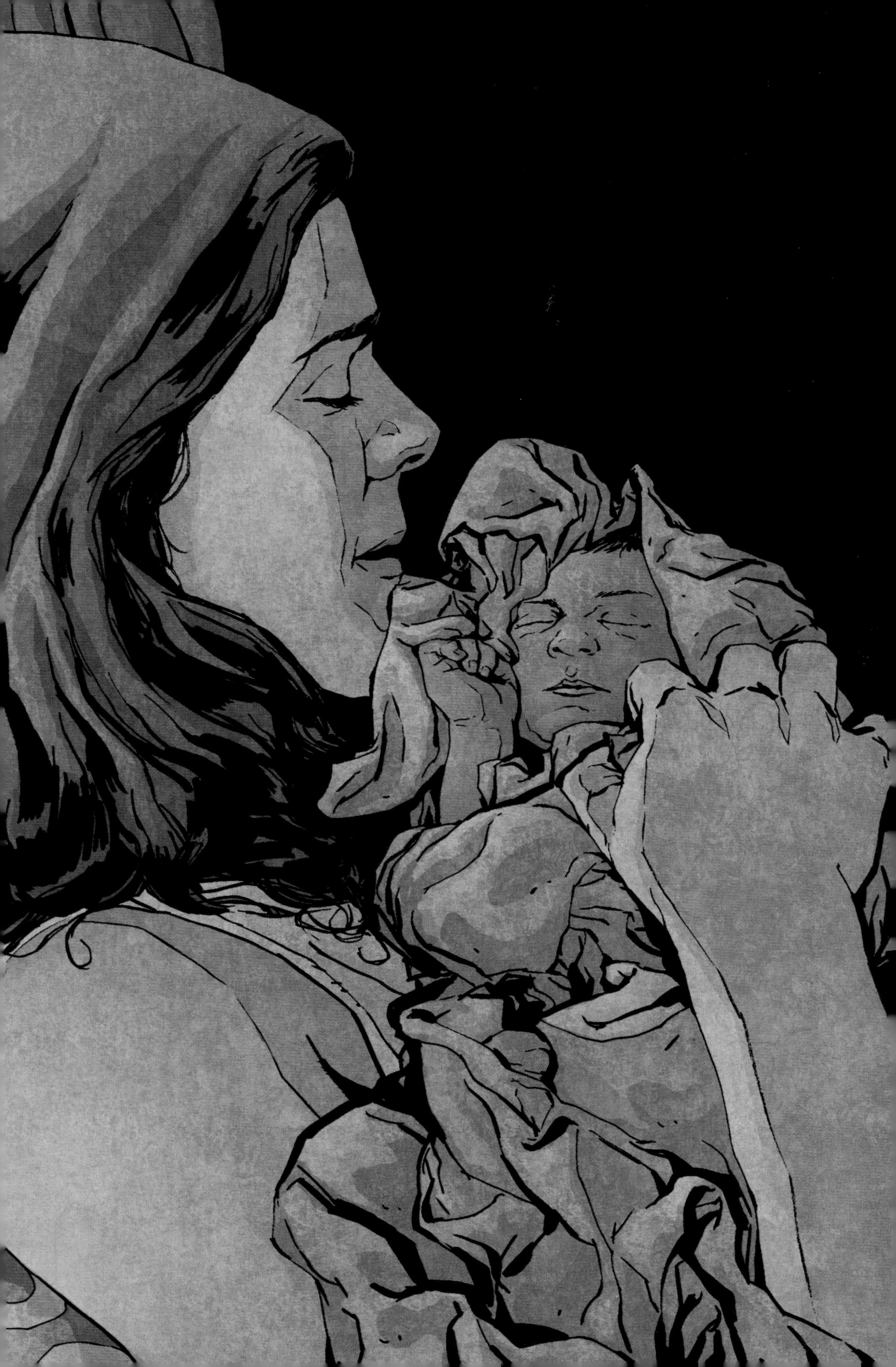

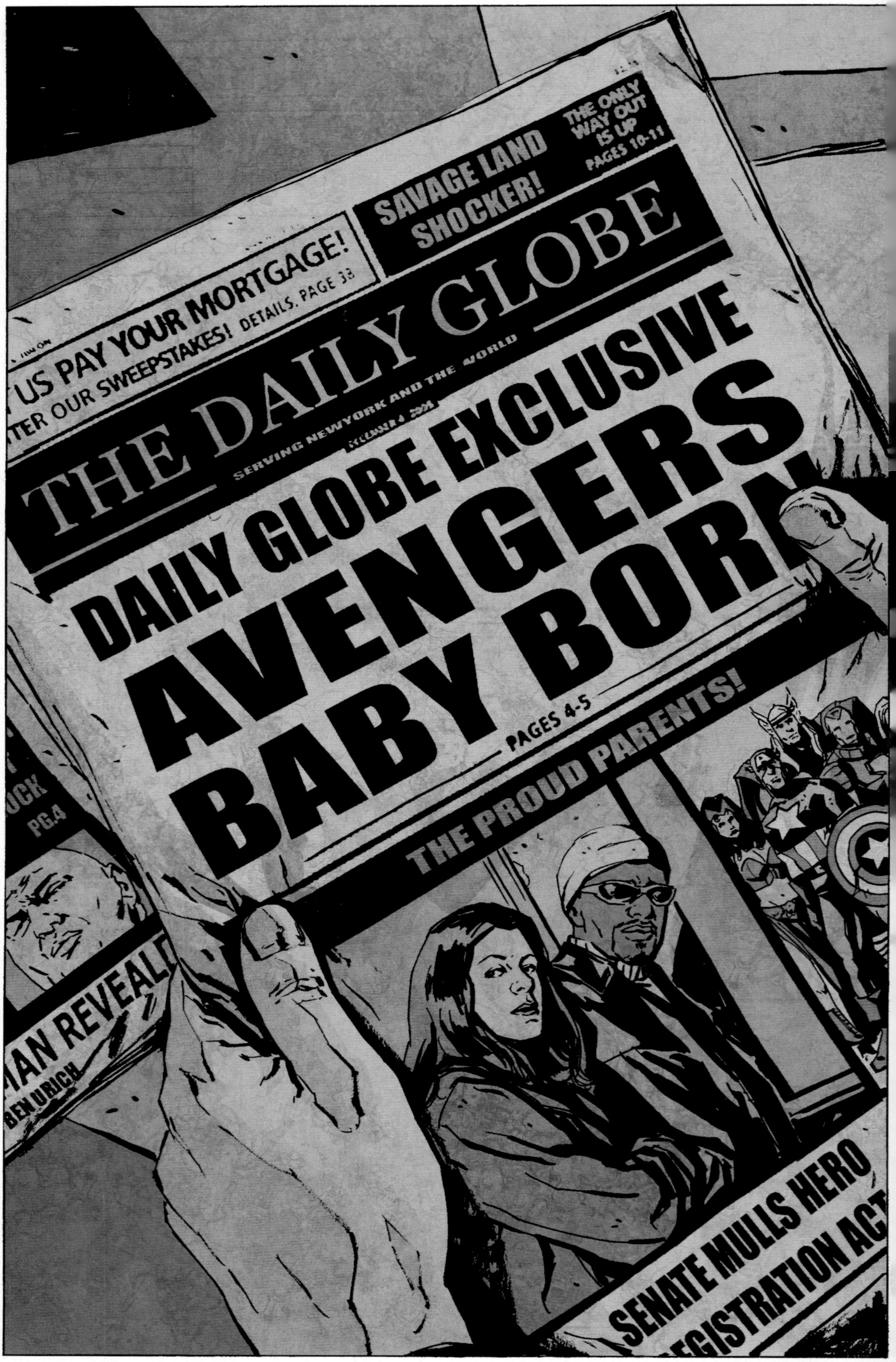

US PAY YOUR MORTGAGE!
TER OUR SWEEPSTAKES! DETAILS, PAGE 33
SAVAGE LAND SHOCKER!
THE ONLY WAY OUT IS UP
PAGES 10-11
THE DAILY GLOBE
SERVING NEW YORK AND THE WORLD
DAILY GLOBE EXCLUSIVE
AVENGERS BABY BOR
PAGES 4-5
THE PROUD PARENTS!
PG.4
MAN REVEAL
BEN URICH
SENATE MULLS HERO
EGISTRATION AC

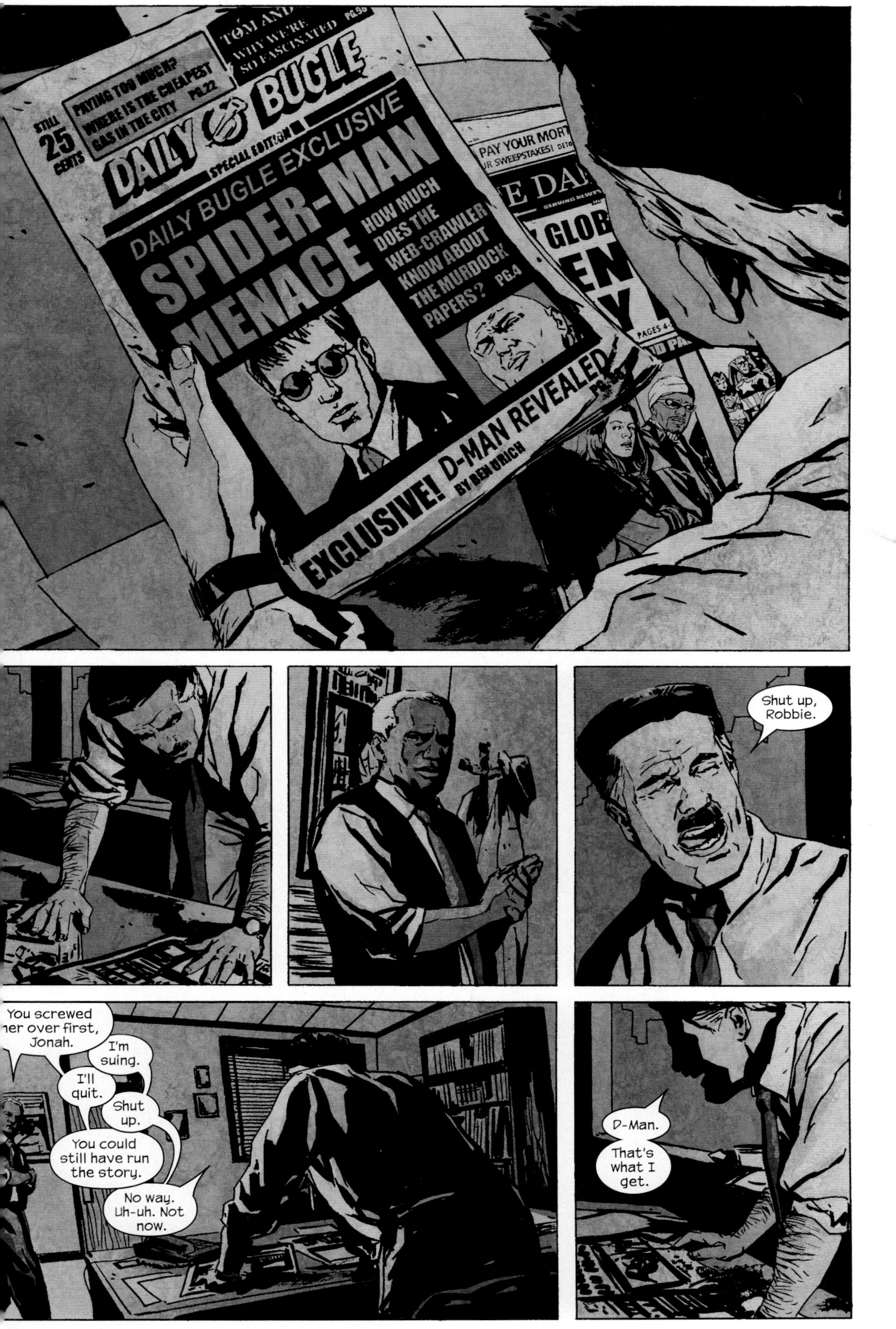

TOM AND
WHY WE'RE SO FASCINATED
PG.96
PAYING TOO MUCH? WHERE IS THE CHEAPEST GAS IN THE CITY PG.22
STILL 25 CENTS
DAILY BUGLE
SPECIAL EDITION
DAILY BUGLE EXCLUSIVE
SPIDER-MAN MENACE
HOW MUCH DOES THE WEB-CRAWLER KNOW ABOUT THE MURDOCK PAPERS? PG.4
EXCLUSIVE! D-MAN REVEALED
BY BEN URICH
PAY YOUR MORT
Shut up, Robbie.
You screwed her over first, Jonah.
I'm suing.
I'll quit.
Shut up.
You could still have run the story.
No way. Uh-uh. Not now.
D-Man.
That's what I get.

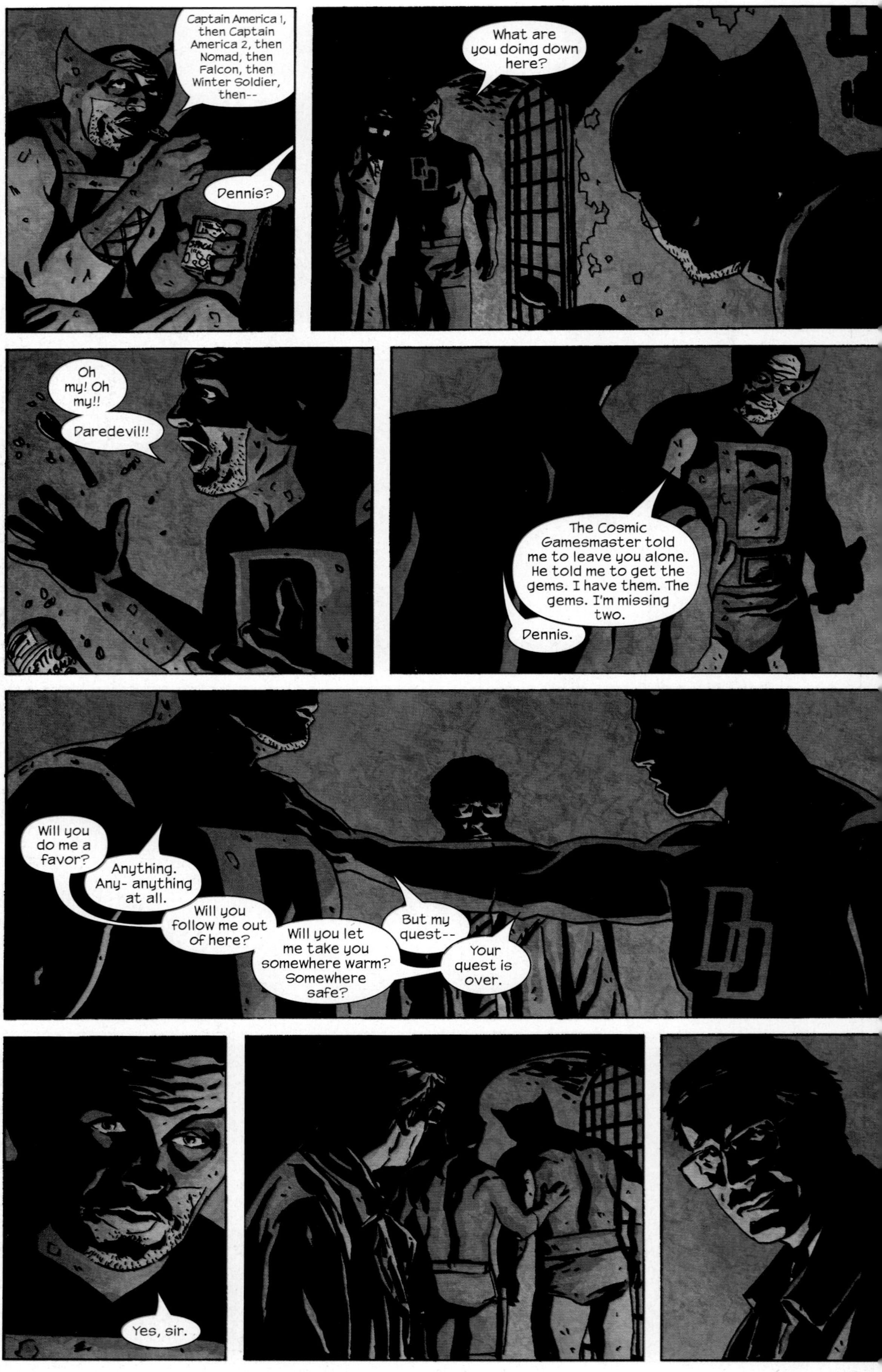
Captain America 1, then Captain America 2, then Nomad, then Falcon, then Winter Soldier, then--
Dennis?
What are you doing down here?
Oh my! Oh my!!
Daredevil!!
The Cosmic Gamesmaster told me to leave you alone. He told me to get the gems. I have them. The gems. I'm missing two.
Dennis.
Will you do me a favor?
Anything. Any- anything at all.
Will you follow me out of here?
Will you let me take you somewhere warm? Somewhere safe?
But my quest--
Your quest is over.
Yes, sir.

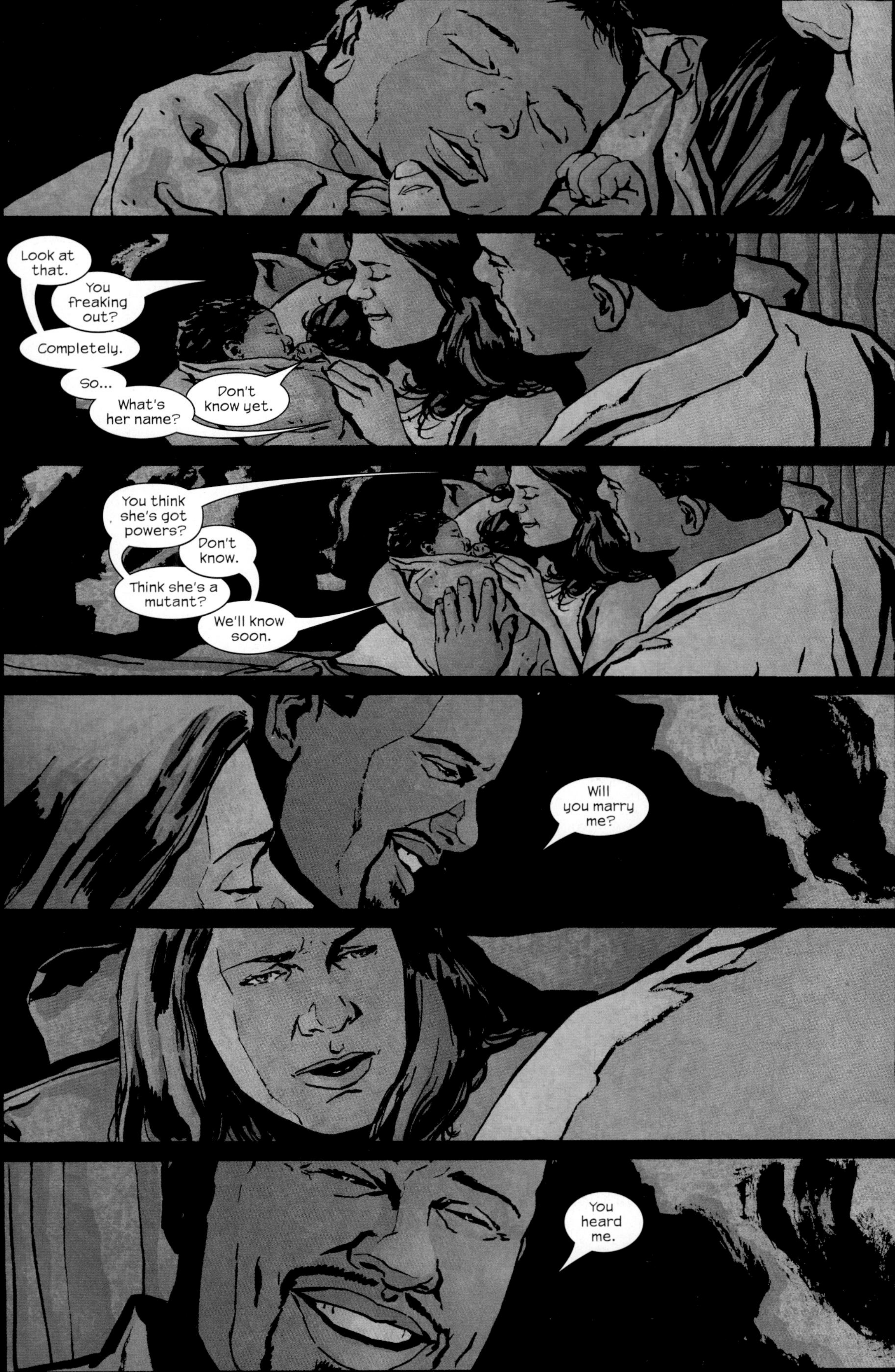
Look at that.
You freaking out?
Completely.
So... What's her name?
Don't know yet.
You think she's got powers?
Don't know.
Think she's a mutant?
We'll know soon.
Will you marry me?
You heard me.

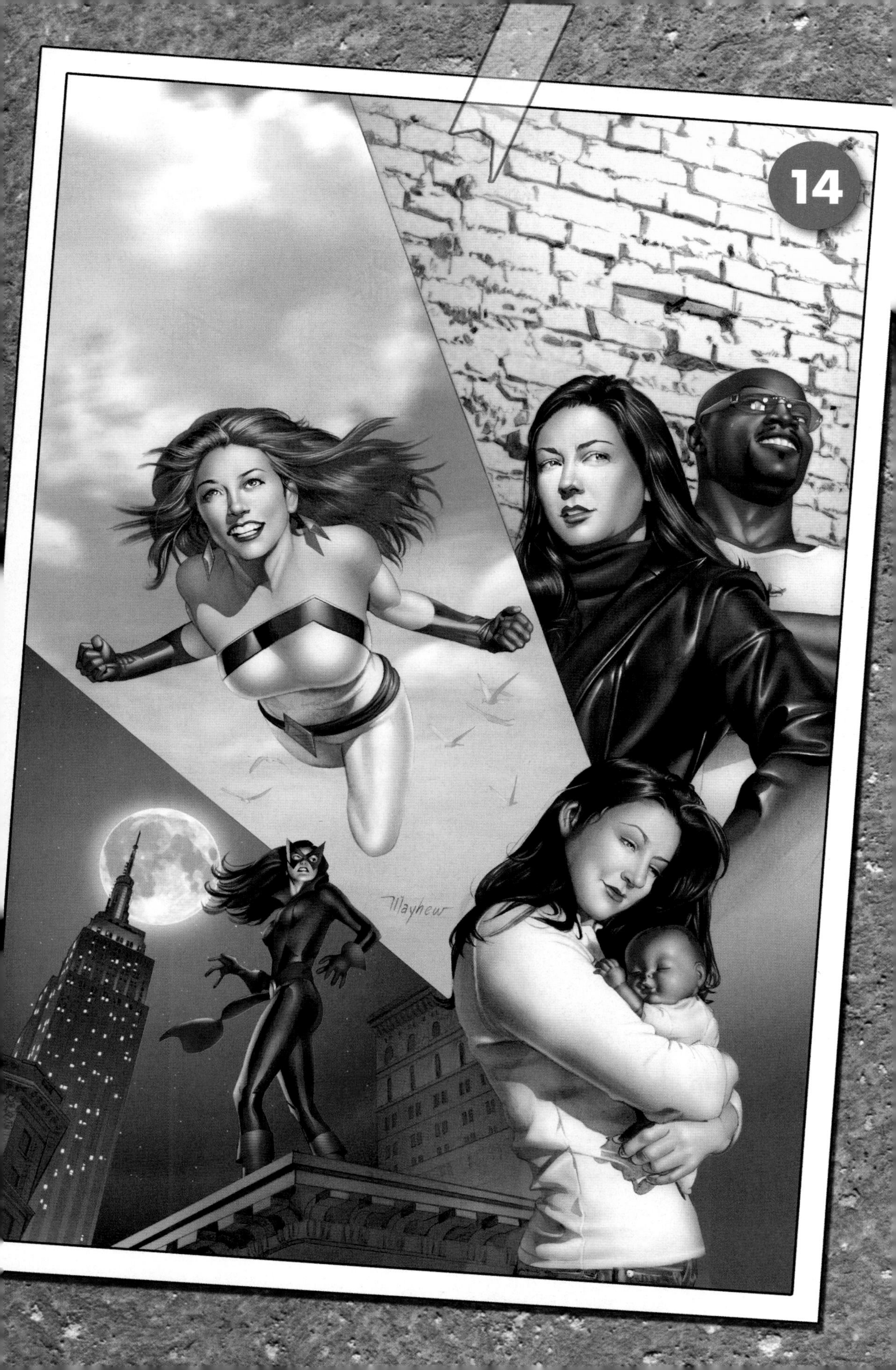
14
Mayhew

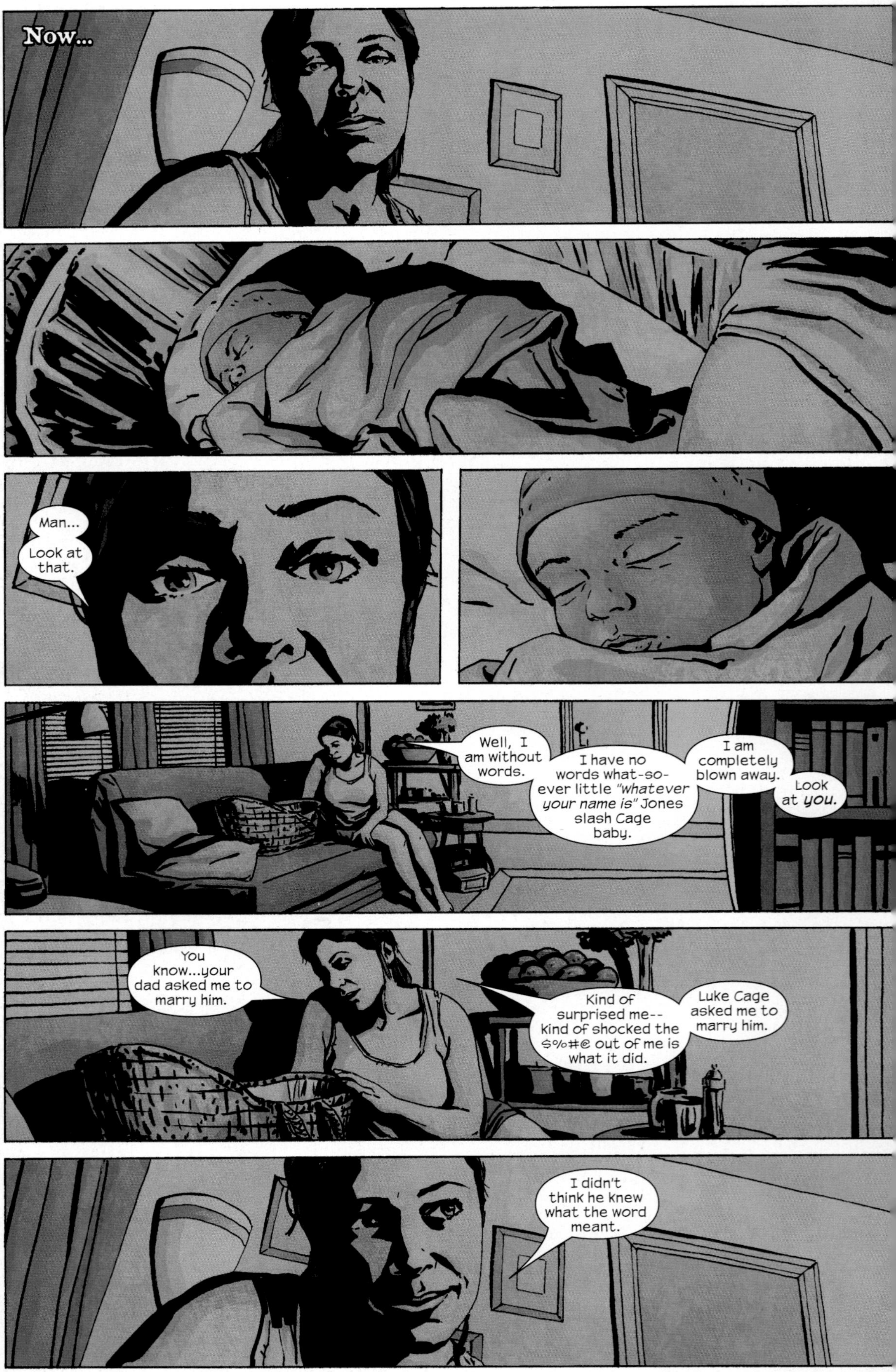
Now...
Man...
Look at that.
Well, I am without words.
I have no words what-so-ever little "whatever your name is" Jones slash Cage baby.
I am completely blown away.
Look at *you.*
You know...your dad asked me to marry him.
Kind of surprised me-- kind of shocked the $%#@ out of me is what it did.
Luke Cage asked me to marry him.
I didn't think he knew what the word meant.

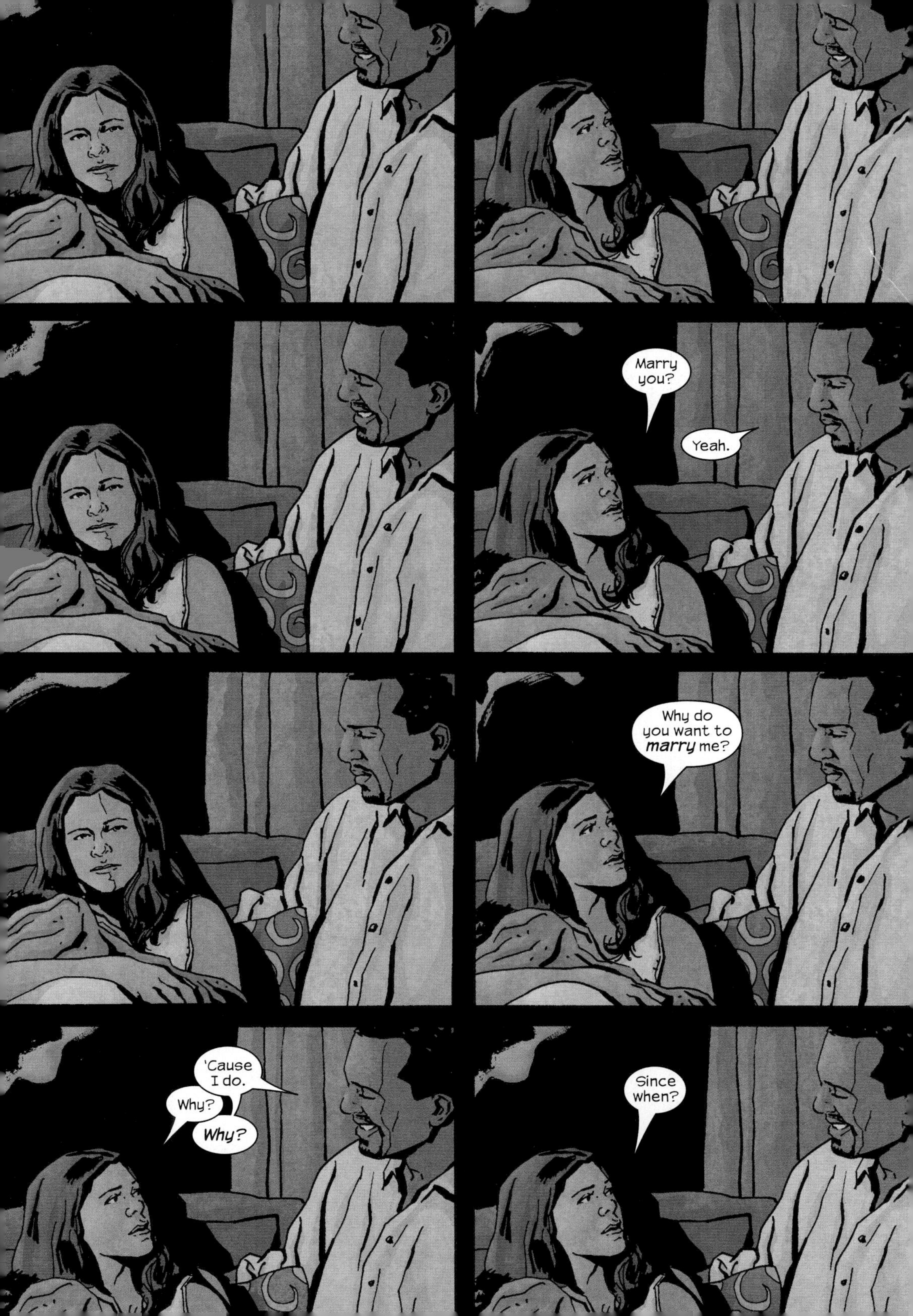
Marry you?
Yeah.
Why do you want to *marry* me?
'Cause I do.
Why?
Why?
Since when?

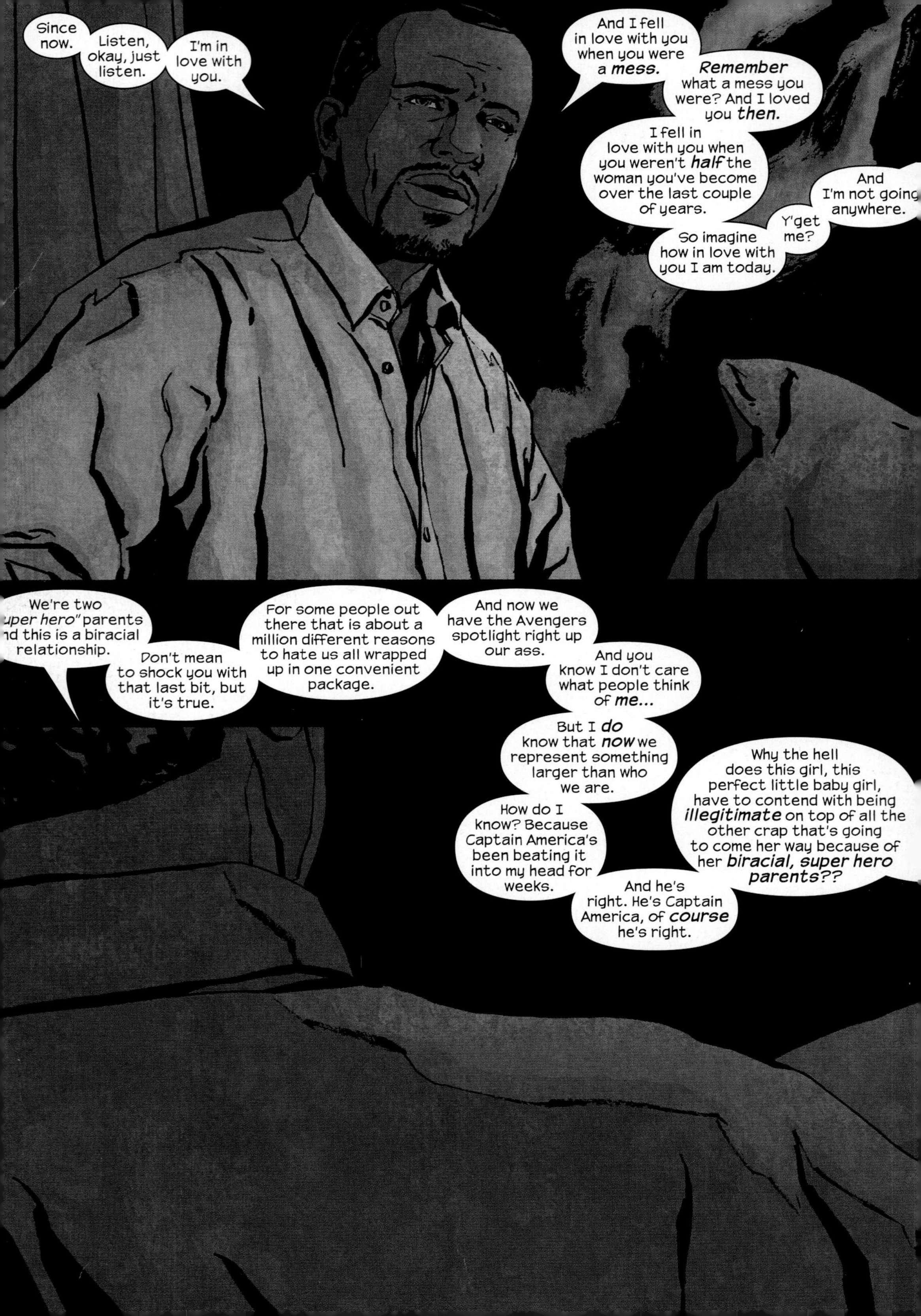
Since now.
Listen, okay, just listen.
I'm in love with you.
And I fell in love with you when you were a *mess.*
Remember what a mess you were? And I loved you *then.*
I fell in love with you when you weren't *half* the woman you've become over the last couple of years.
So imagine how in love with you I am today.
Y'get me?
And I'm not going anywhere.
We're two "super hero" parents and this is a biracial relationship.
Don't mean to shock you with that last bit, but it's true.
For some people out there that is about a million different reasons to hate us all wrapped up in one convenient package.
And now we have the Avengers spotlight right up our ass.
And you know I don't care what people think of *me...*
But I *do* know that *now* we represent something larger than who we are.
How do I know? Because Captain America's been beating it into my head for weeks.
And he's right. He's Captain America, of *course* he's right.
Why the hell does this girl, this perfect little baby girl, have to contend with being *illegitimate* on top of all the other crap that's going to come her way because of her *biracial, super hero parents??*

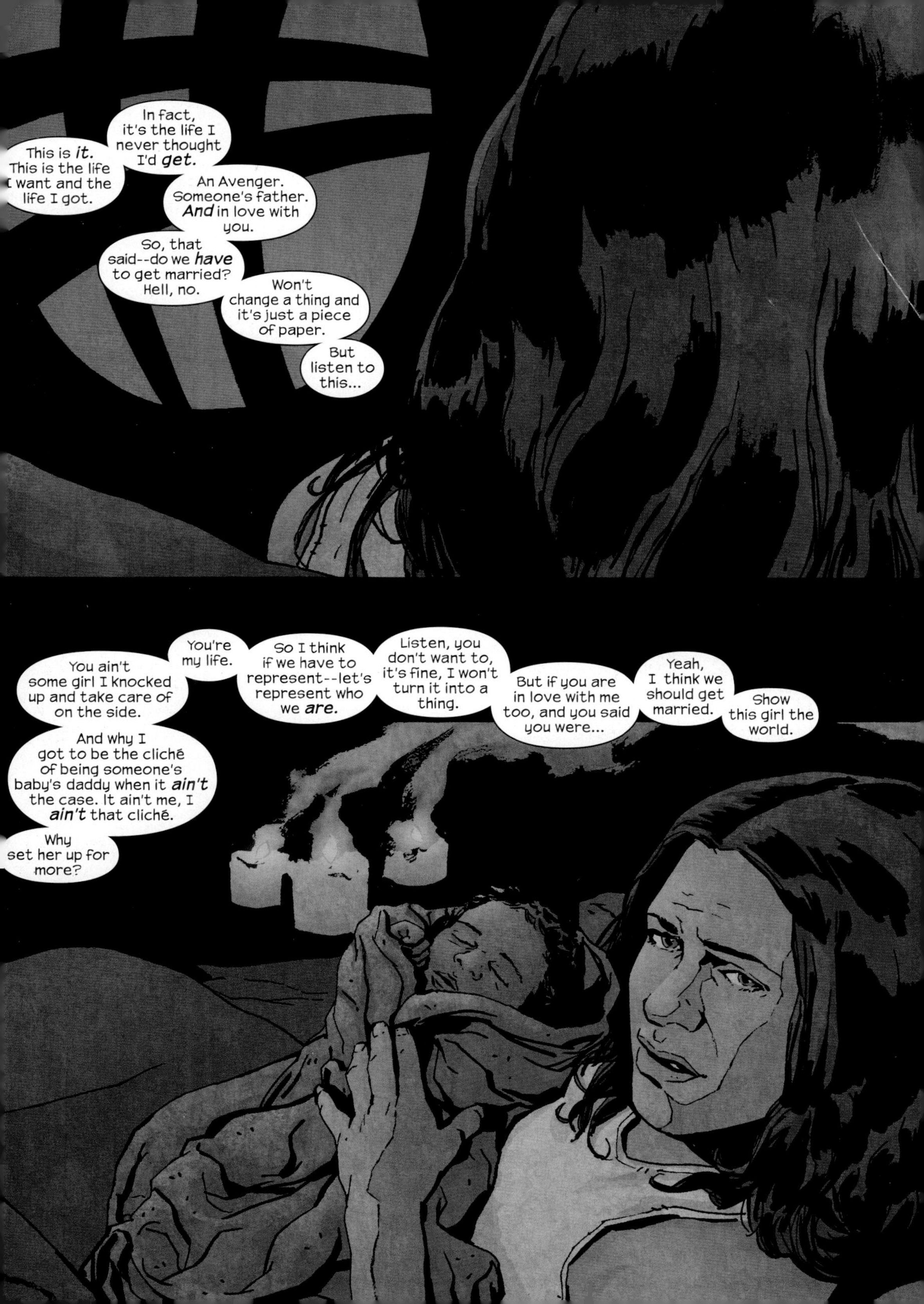
This is it. This is the life I want and the life I got.
In fact, it's the life I never thought I'd get.
An Avenger. Someone's father. And in love with you.
So, that said--do we have to get married? Hell, no.
Won't change a thing and it's just a piece of paper.
But listen to this...
You ain't some girl I knocked up and take care of on the side.
You're my life.
And why I got to be the cliché of being someone's baby's daddy when it ain't the case. It ain't me, I ain't that cliché.
Why set her up for more?
So I think if we have to represent--let's represent who we are.
Listen, you don't want to, it's fine, I won't turn it into a thing.
But if you are in love with me too, and you said you were...
Yeah, I think we should get married.
Show this girl the world.

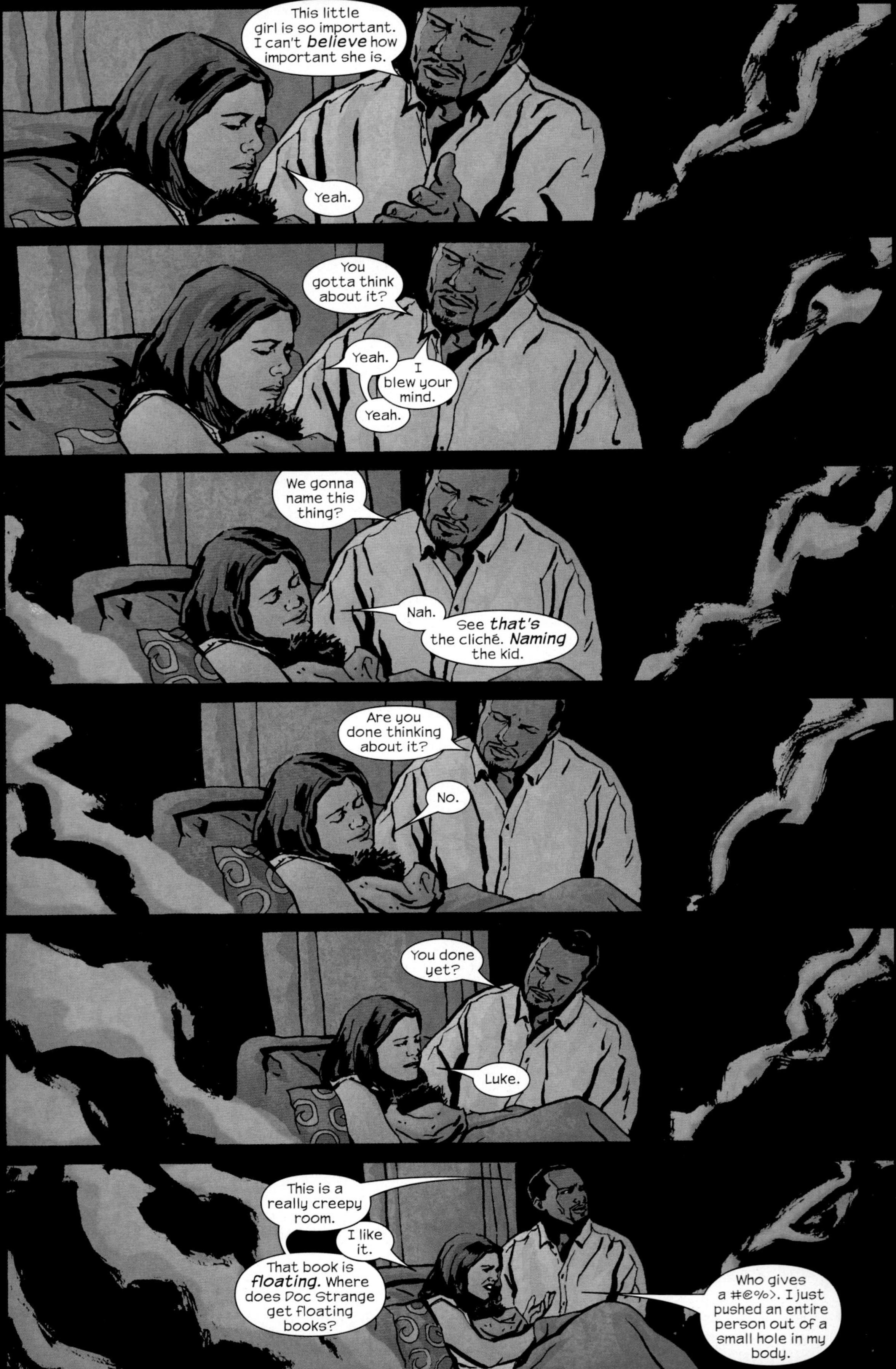

This little girl is so important. I can't *believe* how important she is.
Yeah.
You gotta think about it?
Yeah.
I blew your mind.
Yeah.
We gonna name this thing?
Nah.
See *that's* the cliché. *Naming* the kid.
Are you done thinking about it?
No.
You done yet?
Luke.
This is a really creepy room.
I like it.
That book is *floating.* Where does Doc Strange get floating books?
Who gives a #@%>. I just pushed an entire person out of a small hole in my body.

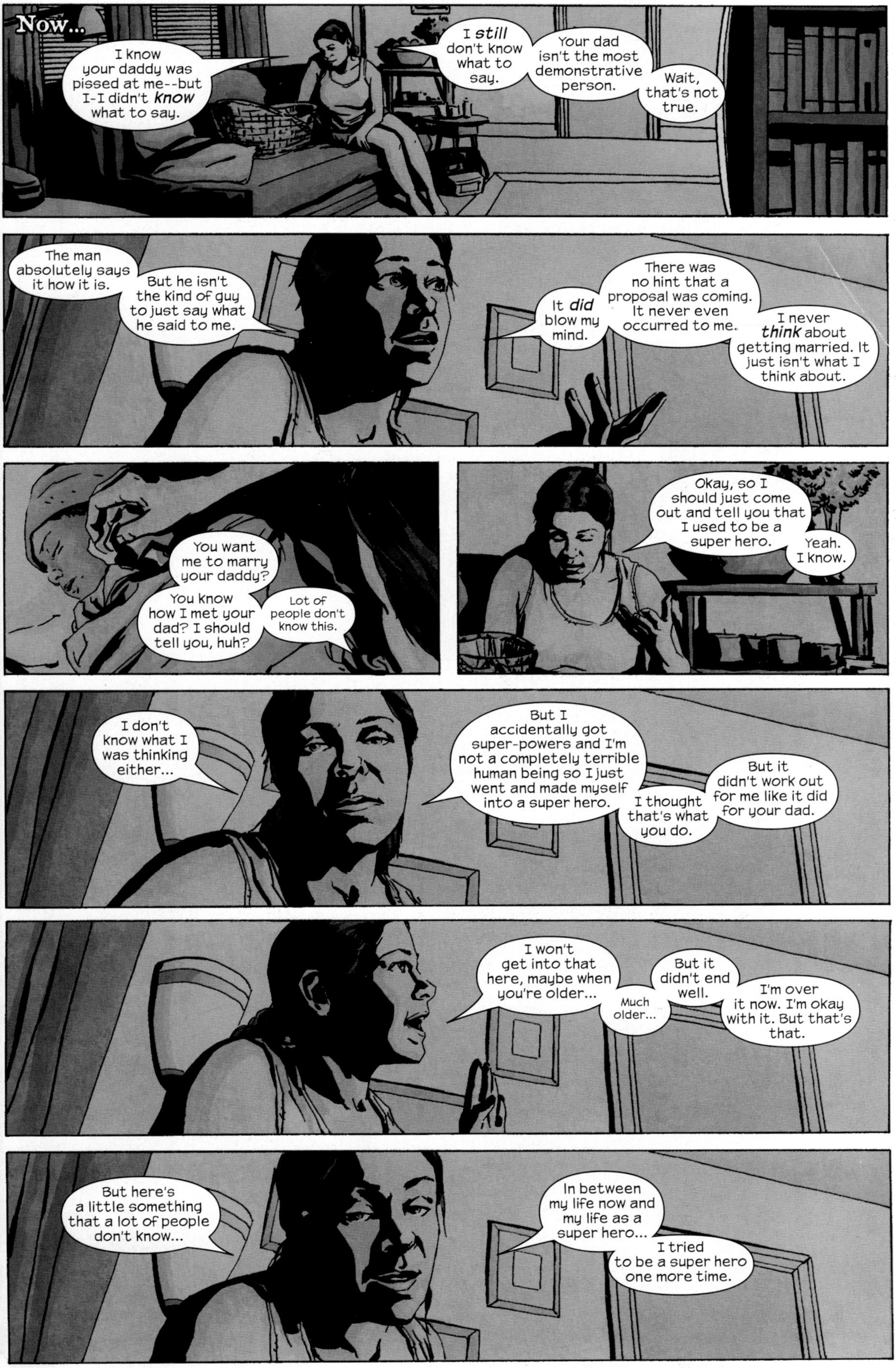
Now...
I know your daddy was pissed at me--but I-I didn't *know* what to say.
I *still* don't know what to say.
Your dad isn't the most demonstrative person.
Wait, that's not true.
The man absolutely says it how it is.
But he isn't the kind of guy to just say what he said to me.
It *did* blow my mind.
There was no hint that a proposal was coming. It never even occurred to me.
I never *think* about getting married. It just isn't what I think about.
You want me to marry your daddy?
You know how I met your dad? I should tell you, huh?
Lot of people don't know this.
Okay, so I should just come out and tell you that I used to be a super hero.
Yeah. I know.
I don't know what I was thinking either...
But I accidentally got super-powers and I'm not a completely terrible human being so I just went and made myself into a super hero.
I thought that's what you do.
But it didn't work out for me like it did for your dad.
I won't get into that here, maybe when you're older...
Much older...
But it didn't end well.
I'm over it now. I'm okay with it. But that's that.
But here's a little something that a lot of people don't know...
In between my life now and my life as a super hero...
I tried to be a super hero one more time.

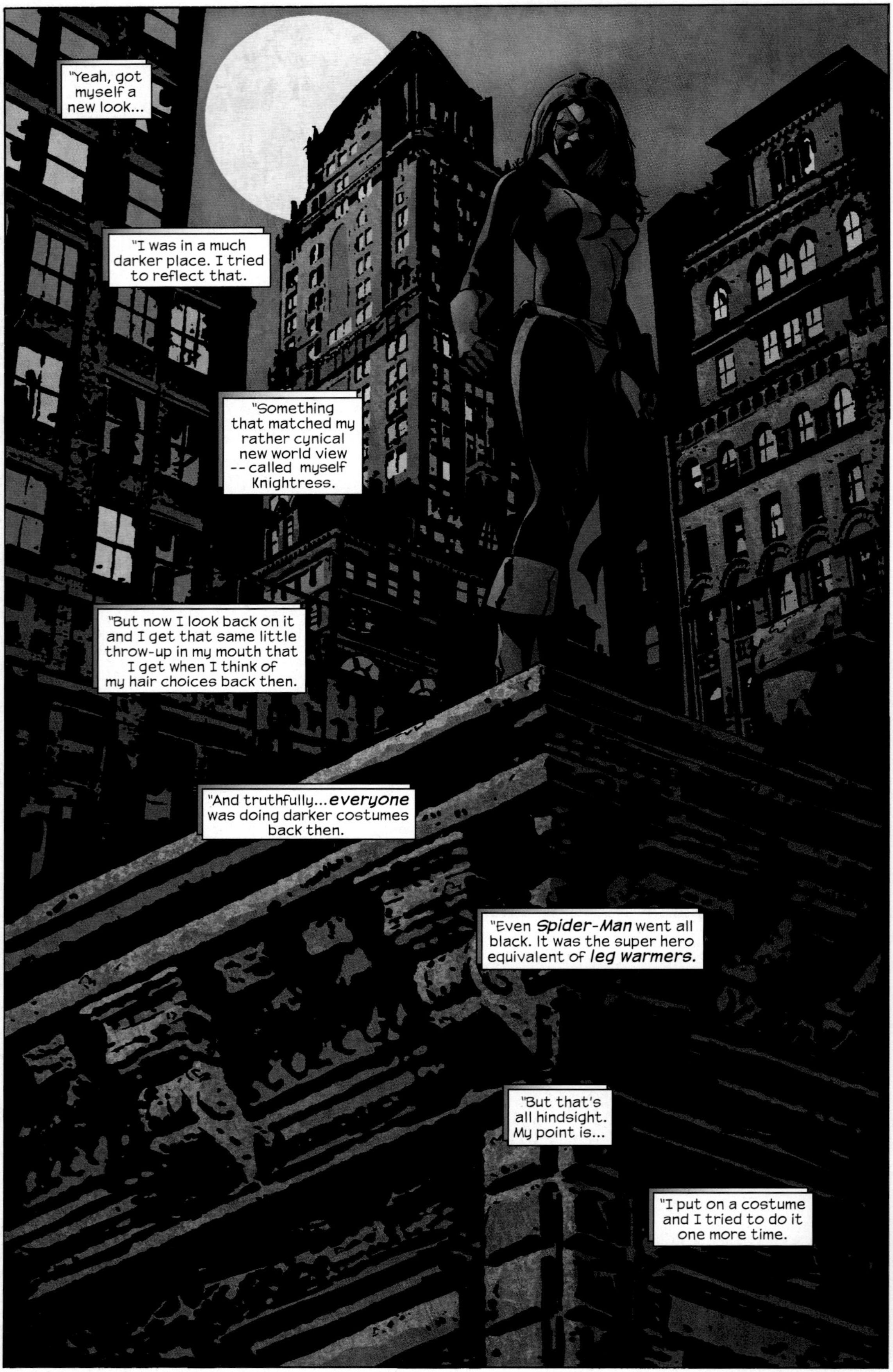
"Yeah, got myself a new look...
"I was in a much darker place. I tried to reflect that.
"Something that matched my rather cynical new world view -- called myself Knightress.
"But now I look back on it and I get that same little throw-up in my mouth that I get when I think of my hair choices back then.
"And truthfully... *everyone* was doing darker costumes back then.
"Even *Spider-Man* went all black. It was the super hero equivalent of *leg warmers.*
"But that's all hindsight. My point is...
"I put on a costume and I tried to do it one more time.

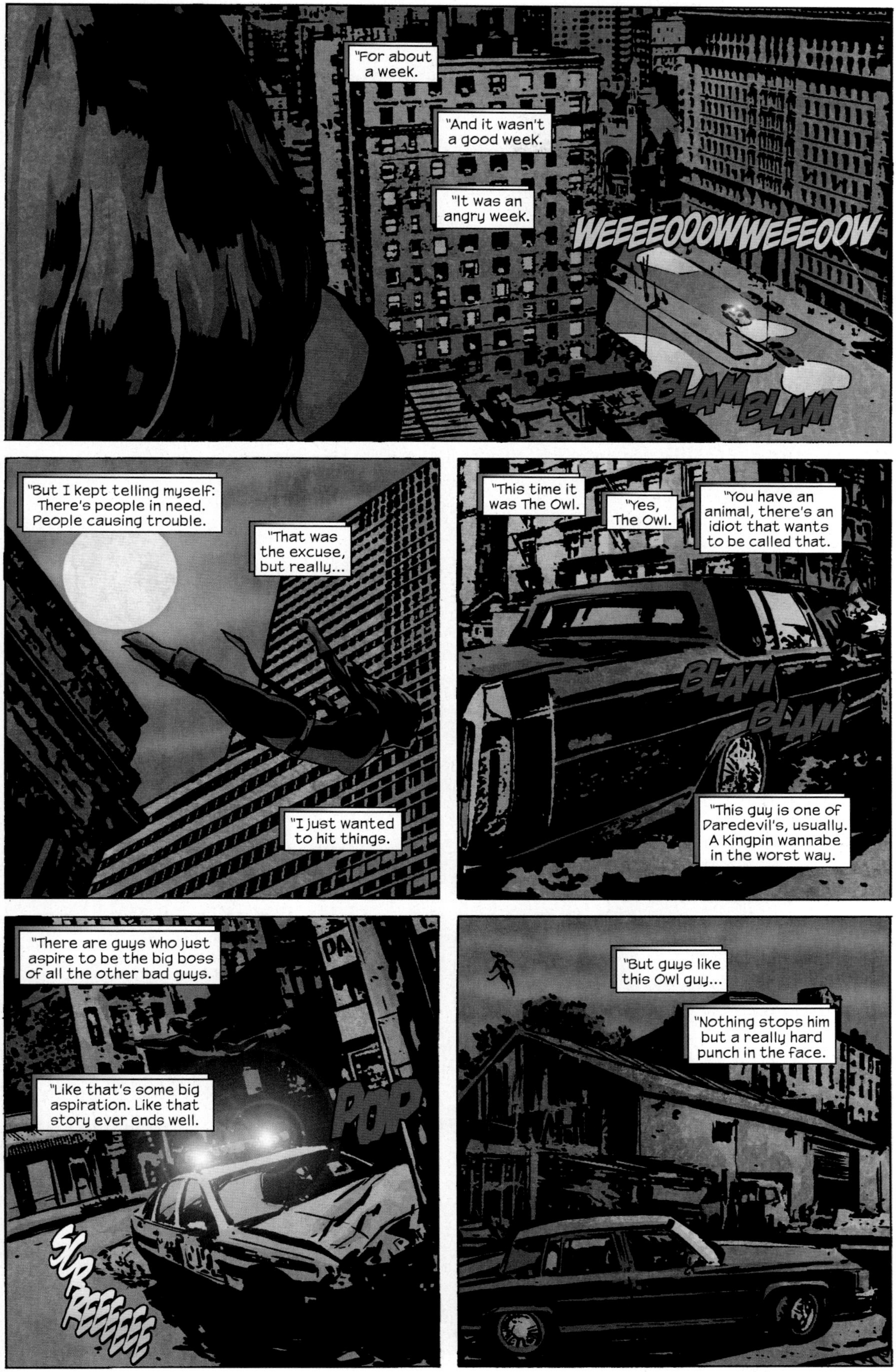
"For about a week.
"And it wasn't a good week.
"It was an angry week.
WEEEEOOOWWEEEOOW
BLAM BLAM
"But I kept telling myself: There's people in need. People causing trouble.
"That was the excuse, but really...
"I just wanted to hit things.
"This time it was The Owl.
"Yes, The Owl.
"You have an animal, there's an idiot that wants to be called that.
BLAM
BLAM
"This guy is one of Daredevil's, usually. A Kingpin wannabe in the worst way.
"There are guys who just aspire to be the big boss of all the other bad guys.
PA
"Like that's some big aspiration. Like that story ever ends well.
POP
SCREEEEEE
"But guys like this Owl guy...
"Nothing stops him but a really hard punch in the face.

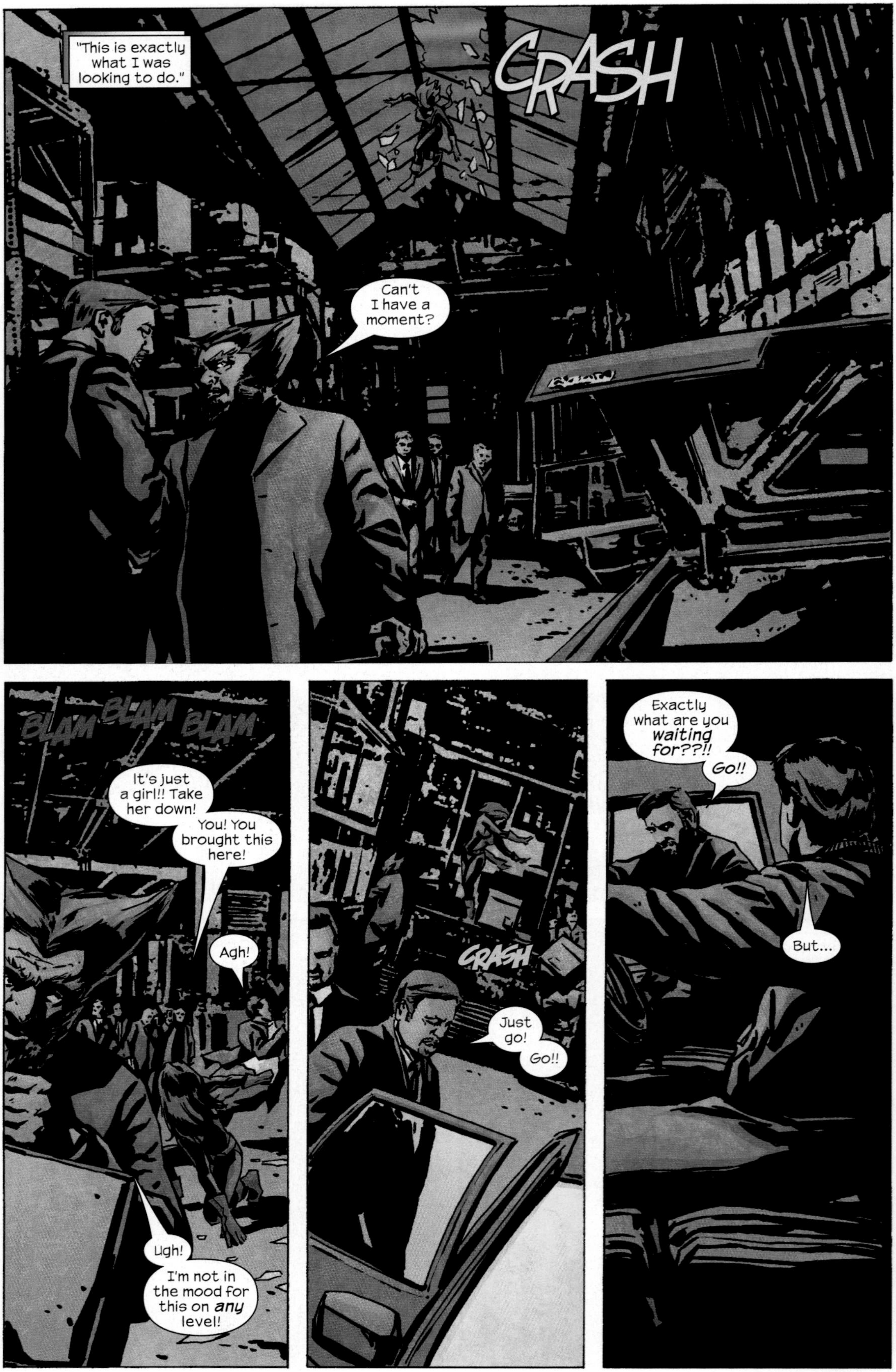
"This is exactly what I was looking to do."
CRASH
Can't I have a moment?
BLAM BLAM BLAM
It's just a girl!! Take her down!
You! You brought this here!
Agh!
Ugh!
I'm not in the mood for this on *any* level!
CRASH
Just go!
Go!!
Exactly what are you *waiting for??!!*
Go!!
But...

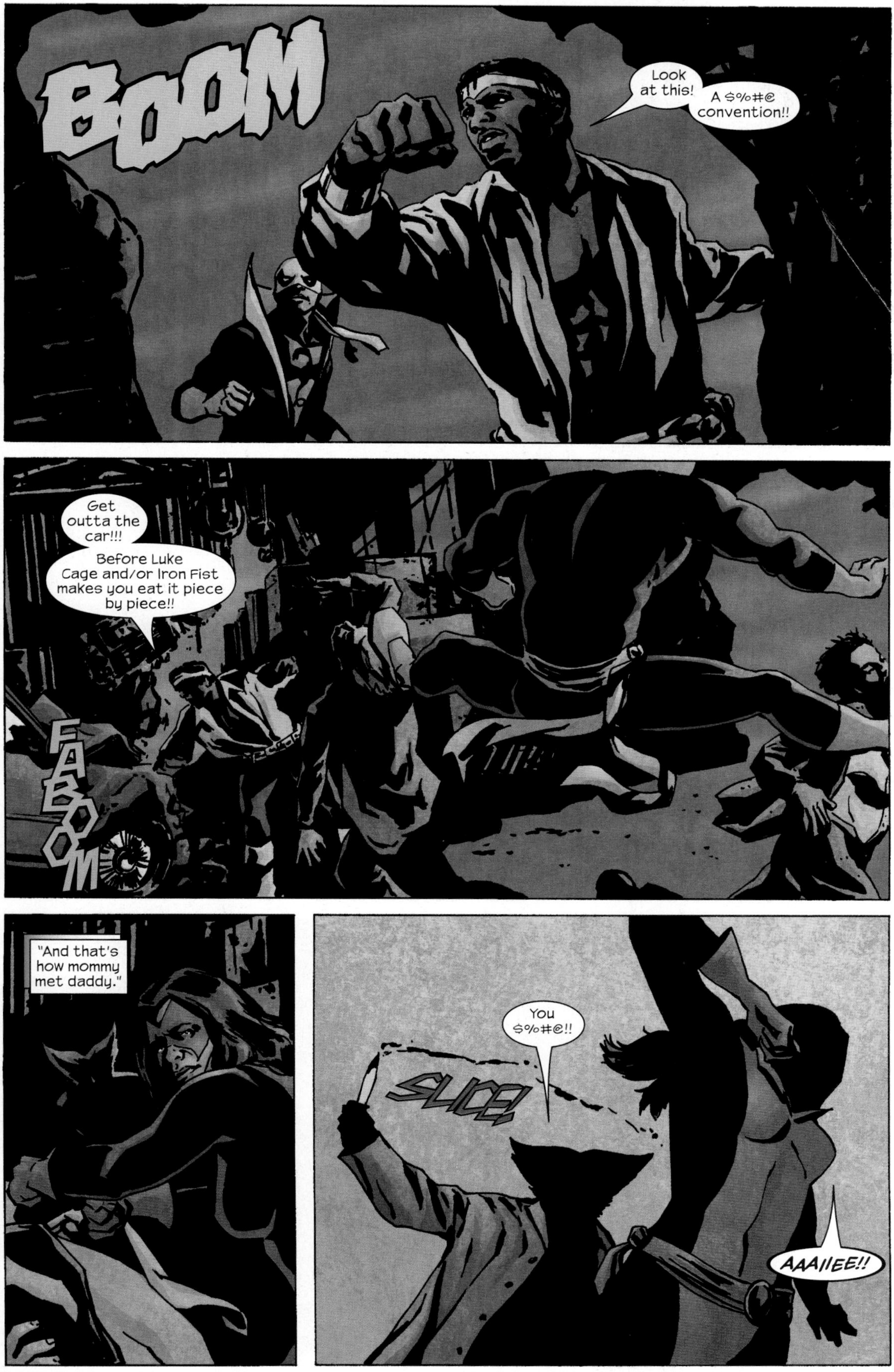

BOOM
Look at this!
A $%#@ convention!!
Get outta the car!!!
Before Luke Cage and/or Iron Fist makes you eat it piece by piece!!
FABOOM
"And that's how mommy met daddy."
You $%#@!!
SLICE!
AAAIIEE!!

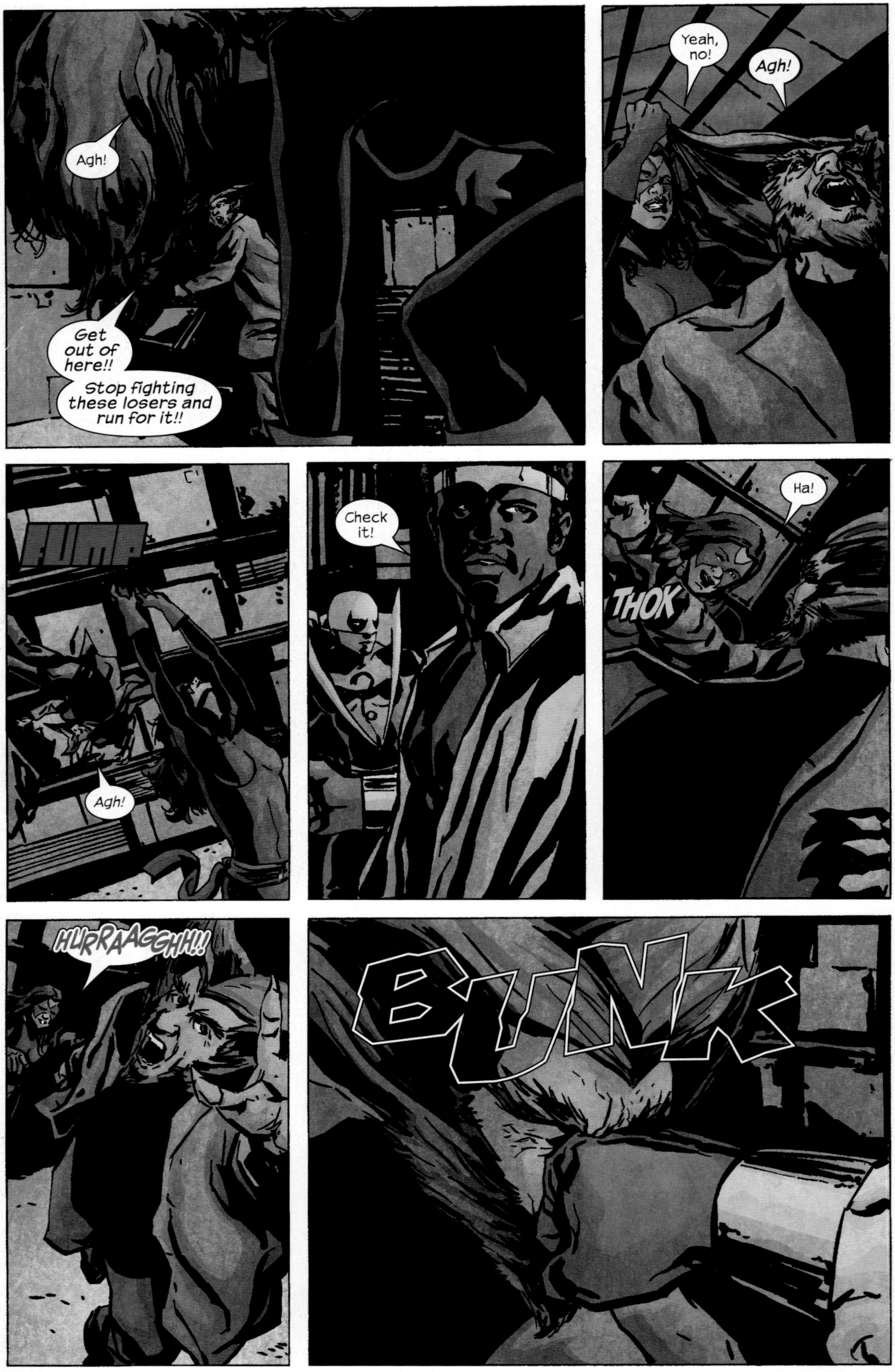
Agh!
Get out of here!!
Stop fighting these losers and run for it!!
Yeah, no!
Agh!
FUMP
Agh!
Check it!
Ha!
THOK
HURRAAGGHH!!
BUNK

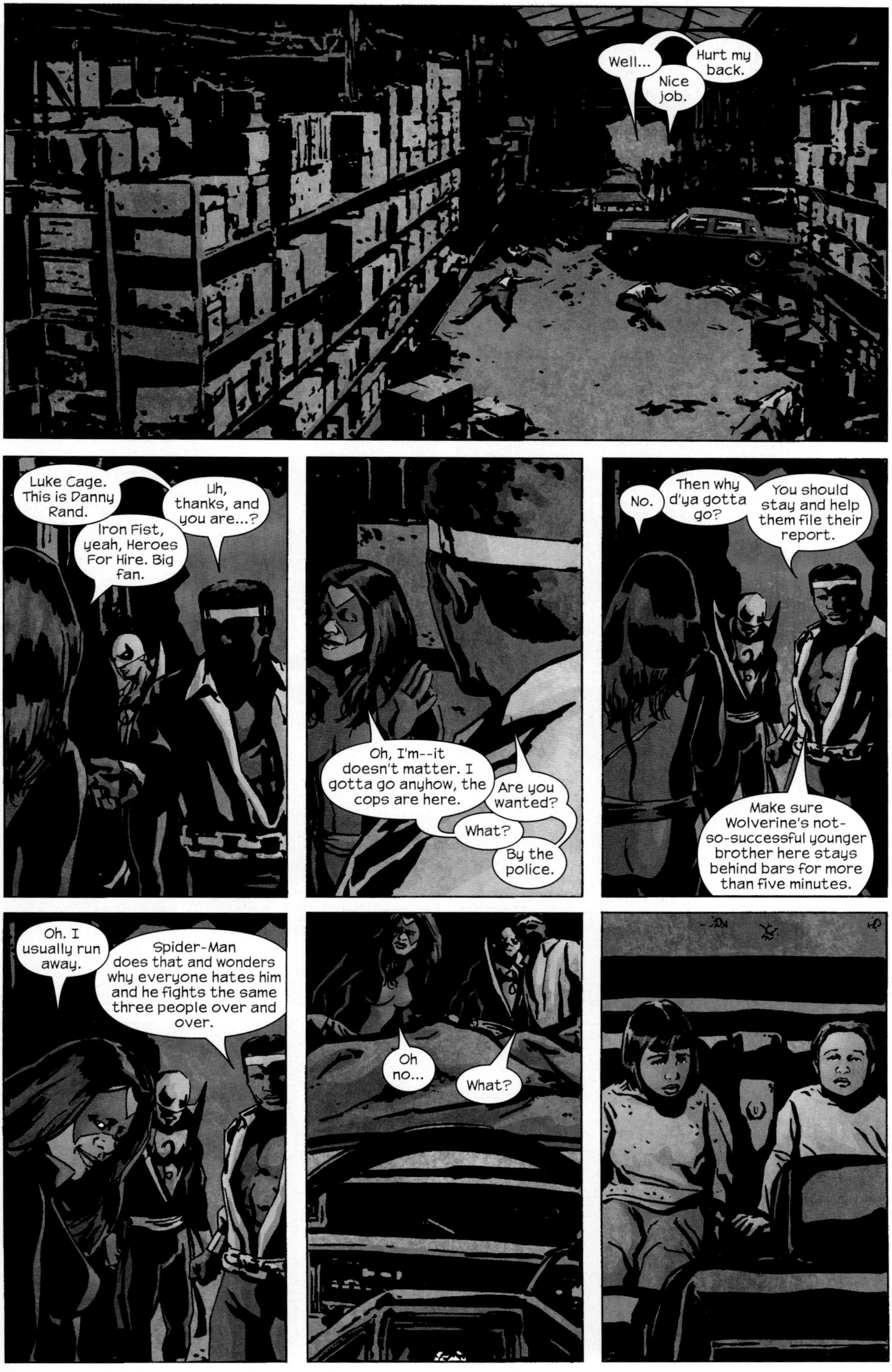
Well...
Hurt my back.
Nice job.
Luke Cage. This is Danny Rand.
Uh, thanks, and you are...?
Iron Fist, yeah, Heroes For Hire. Big fan.
Oh, I'm--it doesn't matter. I gotta go anyhow, the cops are here.
Are you wanted?
What?
By the police.
No.
Then why d'ya gotta go?
You should stay and help them file their report.
Make sure Wolverine's not-so-successful younger brother here stays behind bars for more than five minutes.
Oh. I usually run away.
Spider-Man does that and wonders why everyone hates him and he fights the same three people over and over.
Oh no...
What?

So, yeah, from what we can gather, The Owl was hired to break into some science lab and stole some genetic formulas that he was supposed to hand over to the Russian mob.

Wow, he did that *badly*.

That's not even interesting.

Tripped alarms. Shot at cops. Got beat up by super heroes.

Really I think these guys *want* to get caught. They just want the attention.

Yeah.

Well, we can't thank you enough.

What about the kids?

Guy brings his kids to a super-villian meet. Amazing.

What's going to happen to them?

Can't find the mom. We'll have social services take them in the morning.

Where do they go till then? It's nine at night.

We'll take them back to the station.

To jail?

Not in jail, but there's nothing else we can do till morning.

Can't you take them home?

We're actually not allowed. And I'm not off till morning anyhow. None of us are.

That's terrible.

Well, thanks for your help. Seriously.

Can *you* take them?

Take them where?

Can I take them?

Back to where? The bat cave?

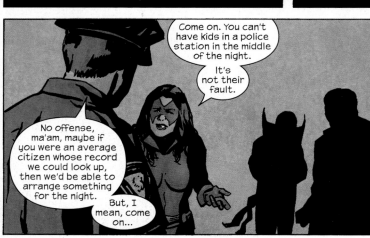

Come on. You can't have kids in a police station in the middle of the night.

It's not their fault.

No offense, ma'am, maybe if you were an average citizen whose record we could look up, then we'd be able to arrange something for the night.

But, I mean, come on...

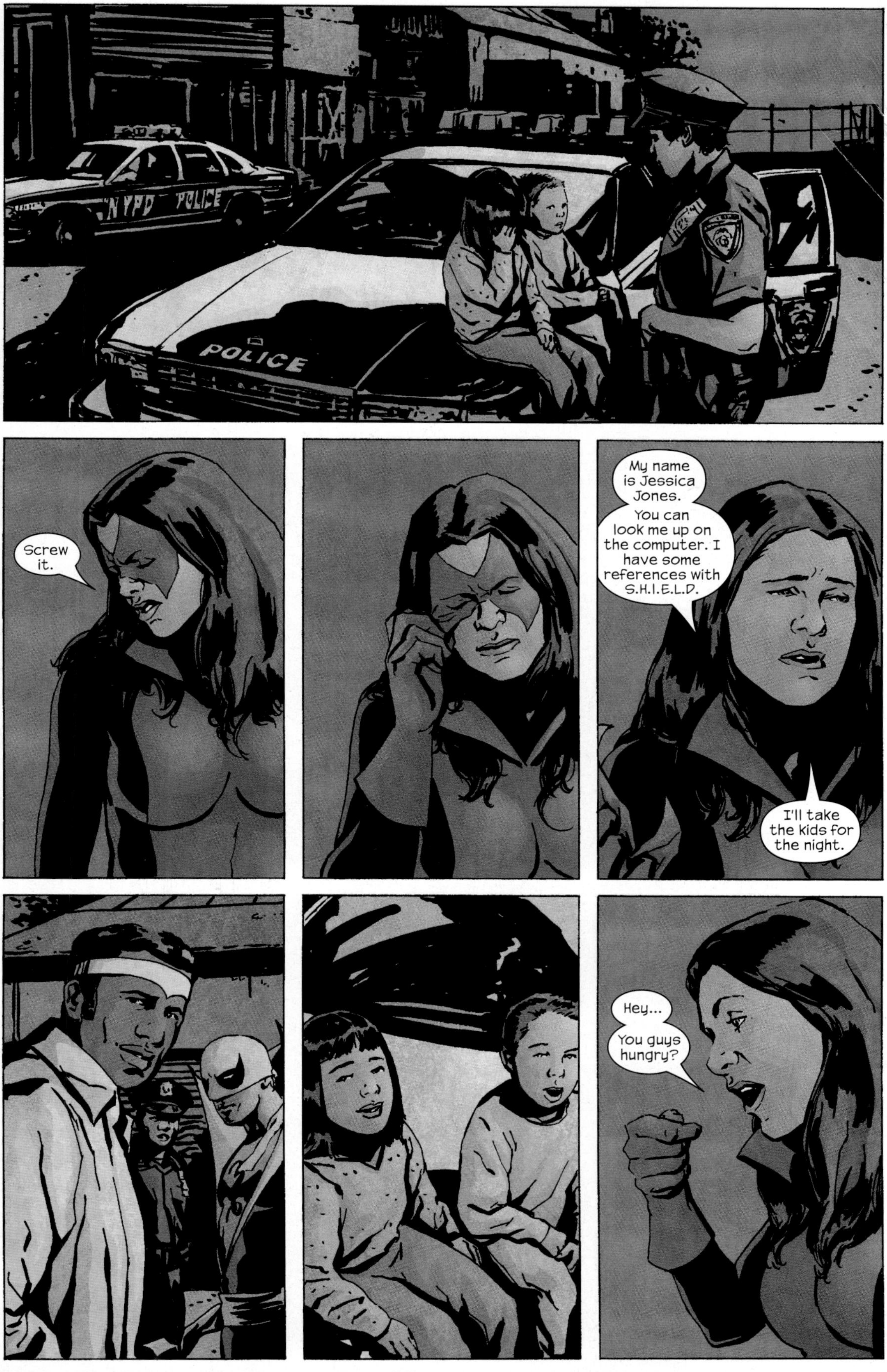
NYPD POLICE
POLICE
Screw it.
My name is Jessica Jones.
You can look me up on the computer. I have some references with S.H.I.E.L.D.
I'll take the kids for the night.
Hey...
You guys hungry?

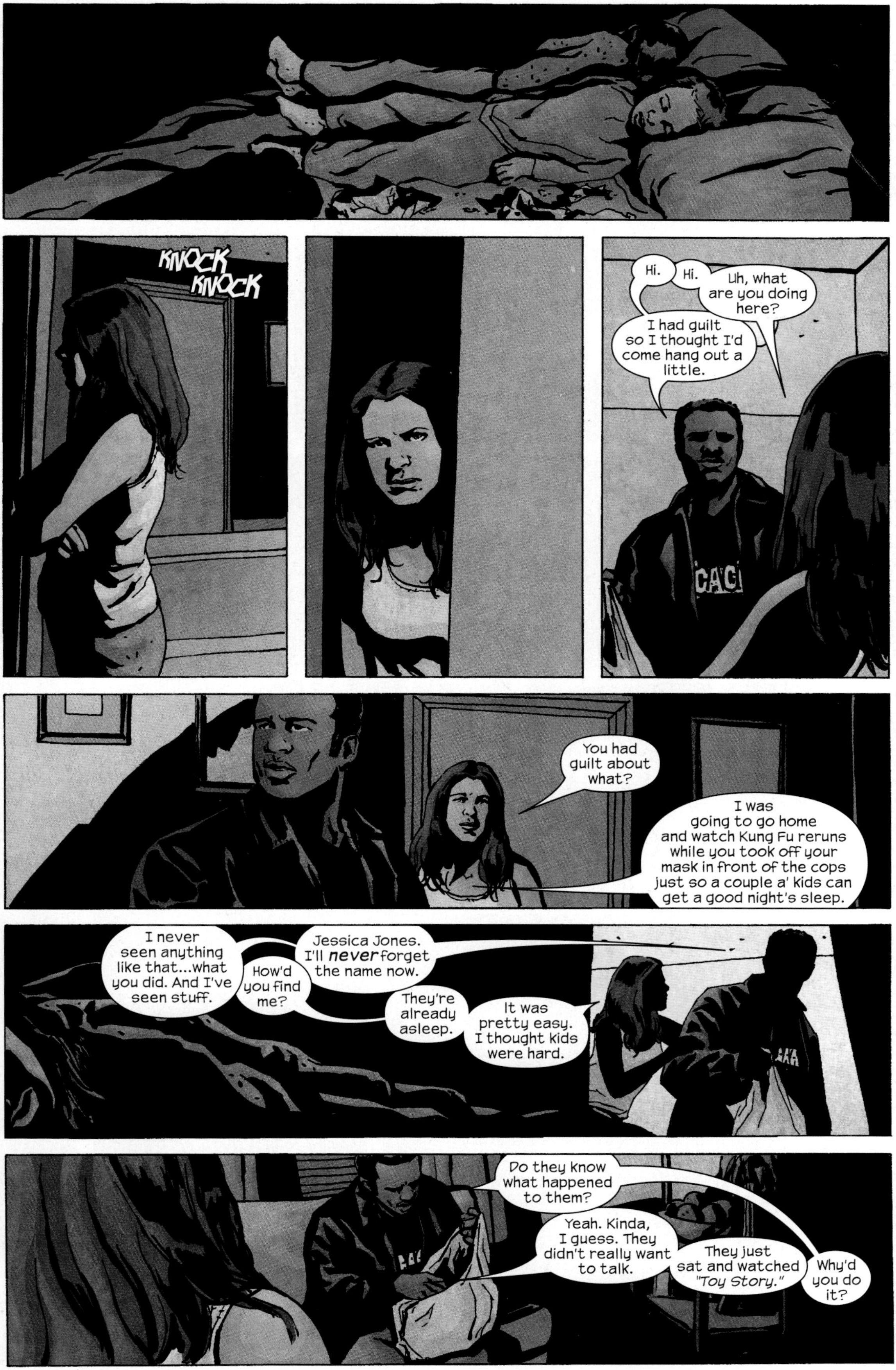
KNOCK KNOCK
Hi.
Hi.
Uh, what are you doing here?
I had guilt so I thought I'd come hang out a little.
You had guilt about what?
I was going to go home and watch Kung Fu reruns while you took off your mask in front of the cops just so a couple a' kids can get a good night's sleep.
I never seen anything like that...what you did. And I've seen stuff.
Jessica Jones. I'll *never* forget the name now.
How'd you find me?
It was pretty easy.
They're already asleep.
I thought kids were hard.
Do they know what happened to them?
Yeah. Kinda, I guess. They didn't really want to talk.
They just sat and watched "Toy Story."
Why'd you do it?

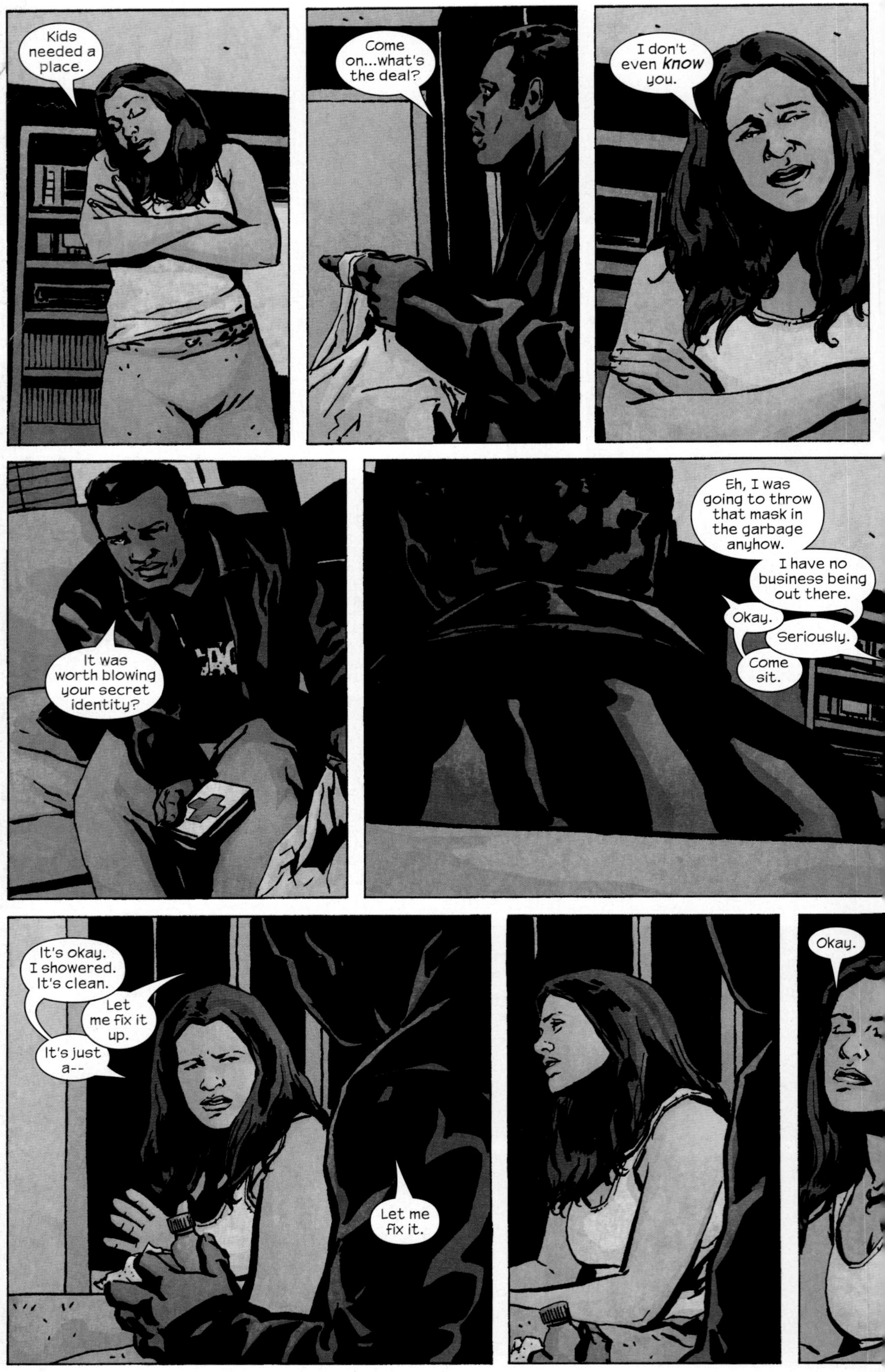
Kids needed a place.
Come on...what's the deal?
I don't even *know* you.
It was worth blowing your secret identity?
Eh, I was going to throw that mask in the garbage anyhow.
I have no business being out there.
Okay.
Seriously.
Come sit.
It's okay. I showered. It's clean.
Let me fix it up.
It's just a--
Let me fix it.
Okay.

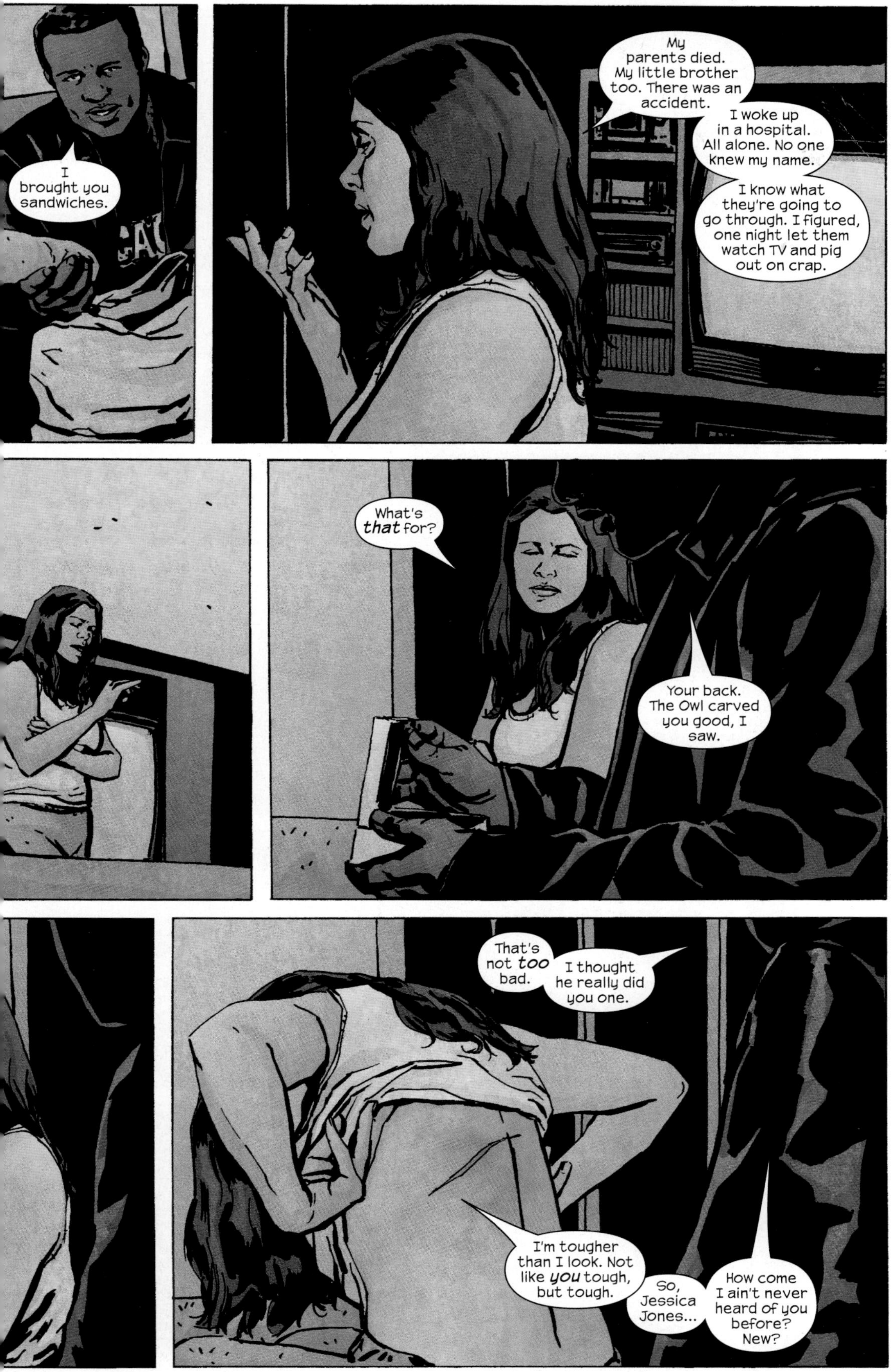
I brought you sandwiches.
My parents died. My little brother too. There was an accident.
I woke up in a hospital. All alone. No one knew my name.
I know what they're going to go through. I figured, one night let them watch TV and pig out on crap.
What's *that* for?
Your back. The Owl carved you good, I saw.
That's not *too* bad.
I thought he really did you one.
I'm tougher than I look. Not like *you* tough, but tough.
So, Jessica Jones...
How come I ain't never heard of you before? New?

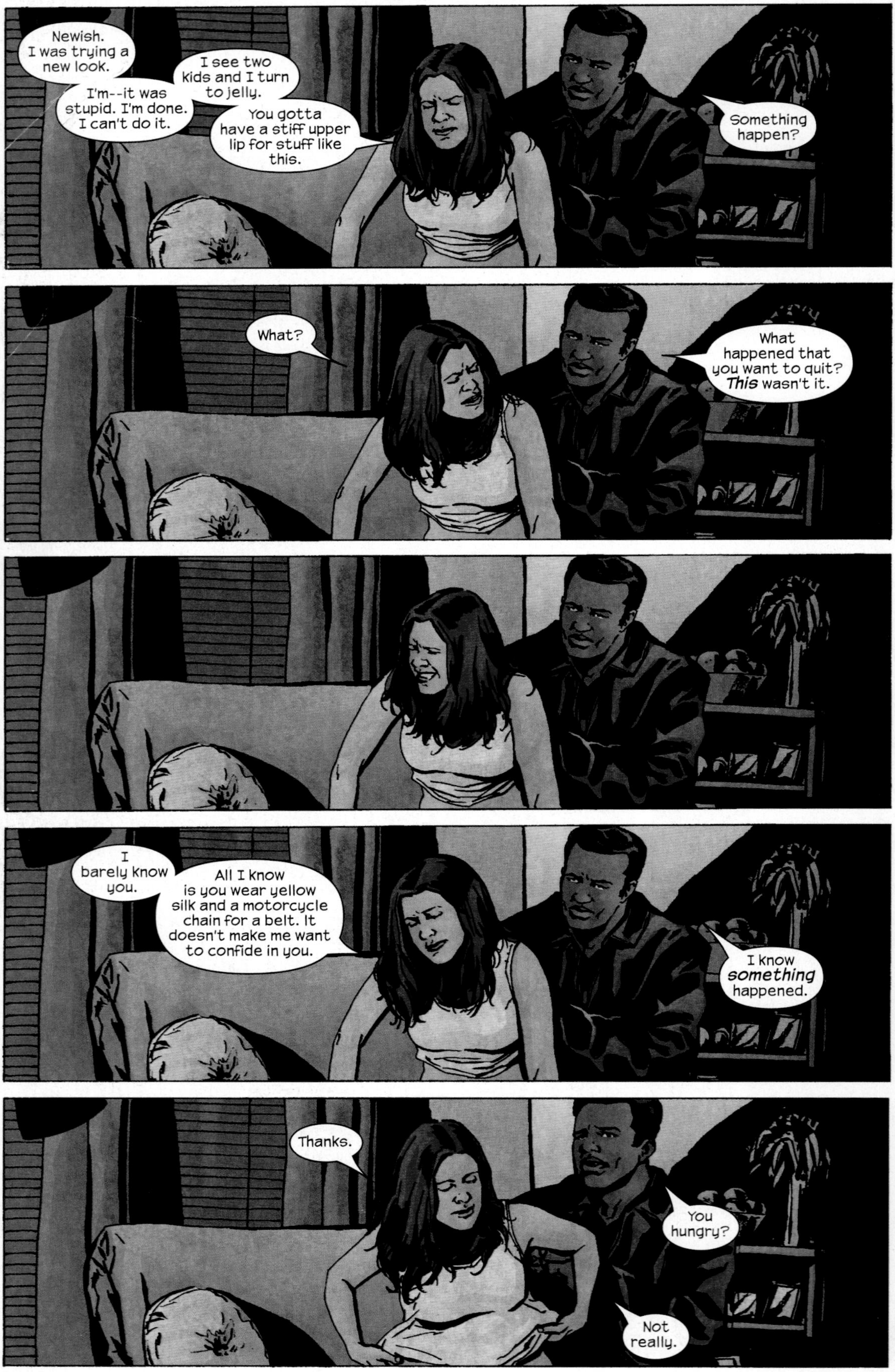
Newish. I was trying a new look.
I see two kids and I turn to jelly.
I'm--it was stupid. I'm done. I can't do it.
You gotta have a stiff upper lip for stuff like this.
Something happen?
What?
What happened that you want to quit? *This* wasn't it.
I barely know you.
All I know is you wear yellow silk and a motorcycle chain for a belt. It doesn't make me want to confide in you.
I know *something* happened.
Thanks.
You hungry?
Not really.

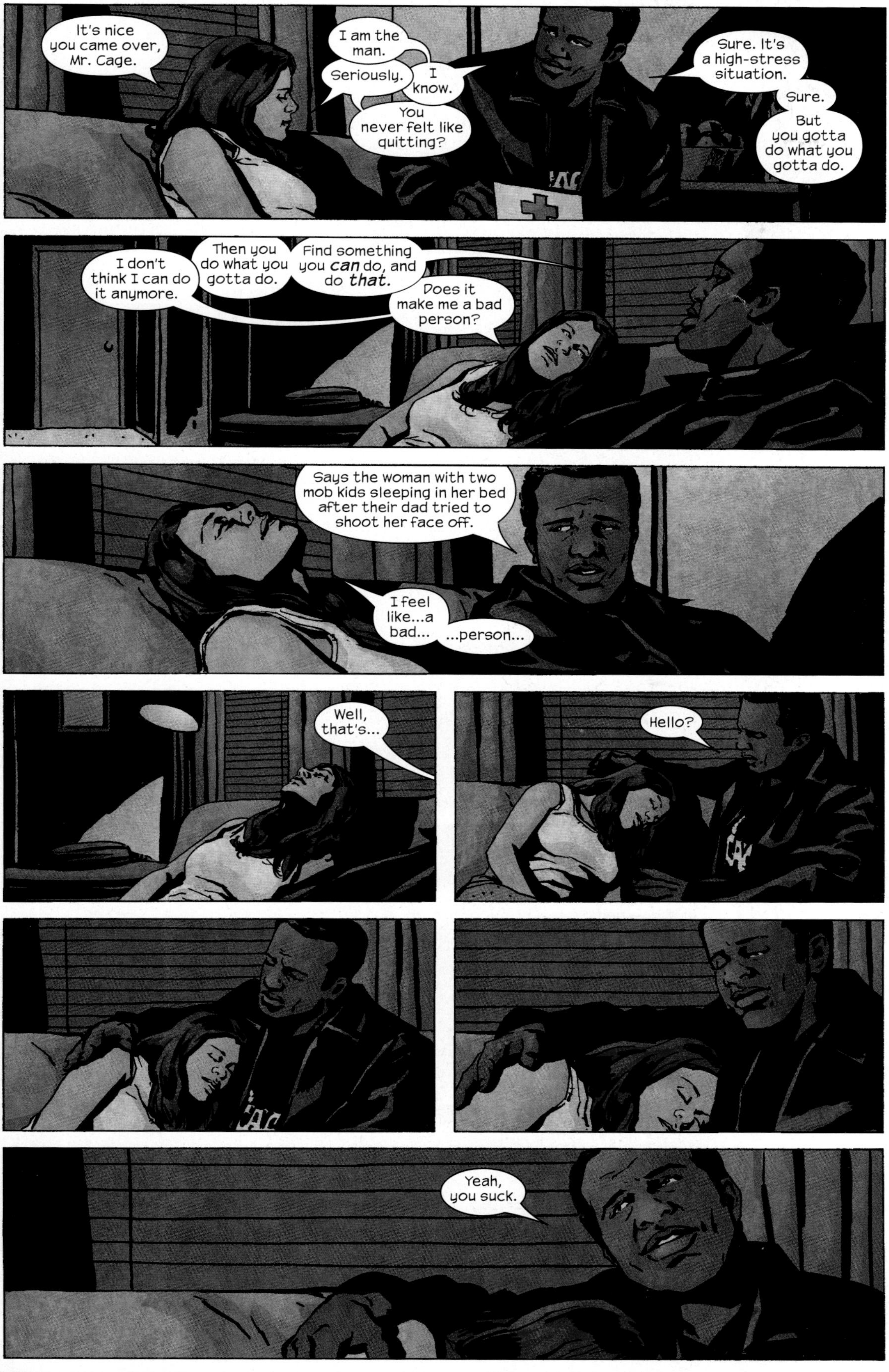
It's nice you came over, Mr. Cage.
I am the man.
Seriously.
I know.
You never felt like quitting?
Sure. It's a high-stress situation.
Sure.
But you gotta do what you gotta do.
I don't think I can do it anymore.
Then you do what you gotta do.
Find something you *can* do, and do *that.*
Does it make me a bad person?
Says the woman with two mob kids sleeping in her bed after their dad tried to shoot her face off.
I feel like...a bad...
...person...
Well, that's...
Hello?
Yeah, you suck.

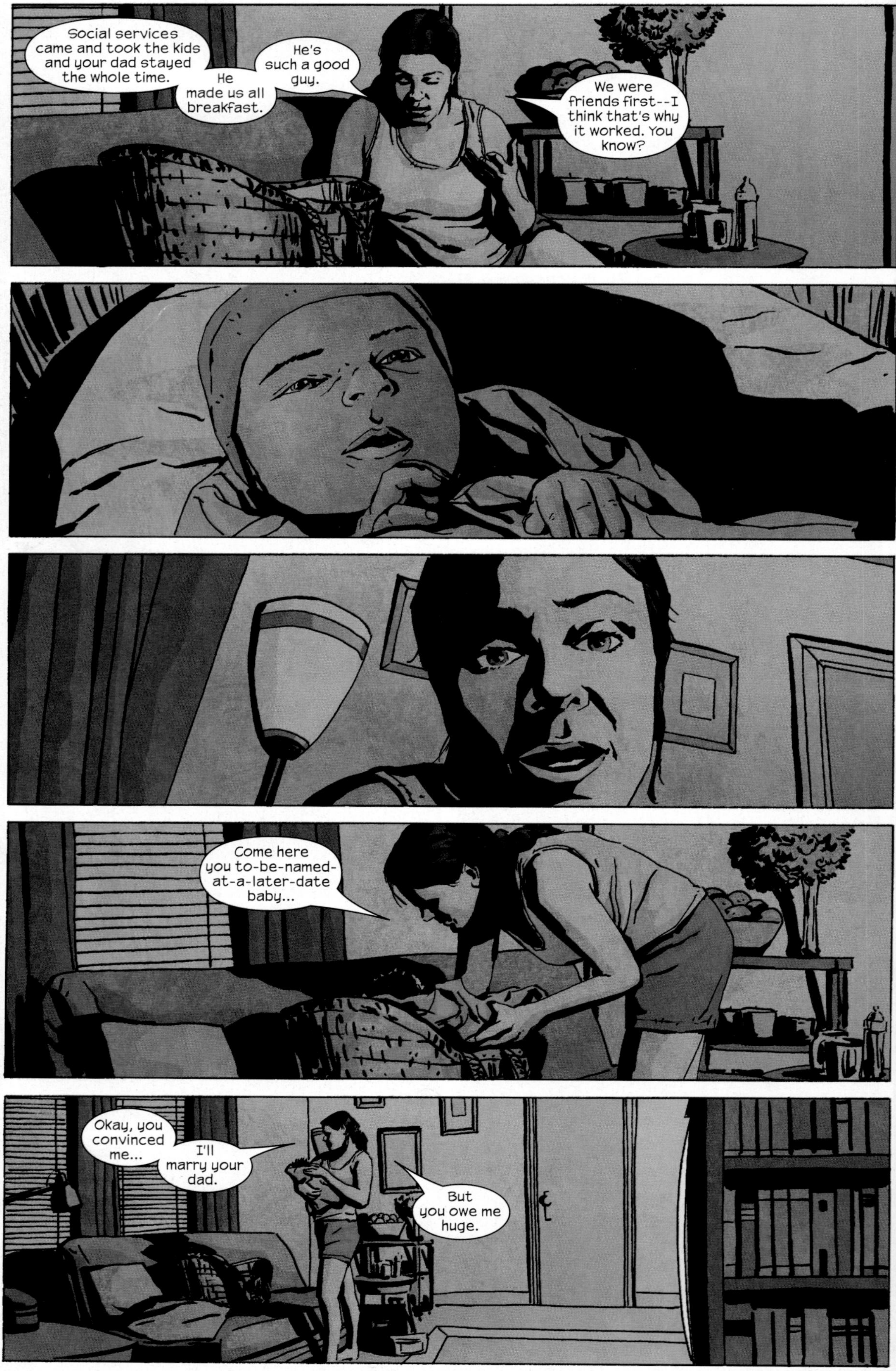
Social services came and took the kids and your dad stayed the whole time.
He made us all breakfast.
He's such a good guy.
We were friends first--I think that's why it worked. You know?
Come here you to-be-named-at-a-later-date baby...
Okay, you convinced me...
I'll marry your dad.
But you owe me huge.

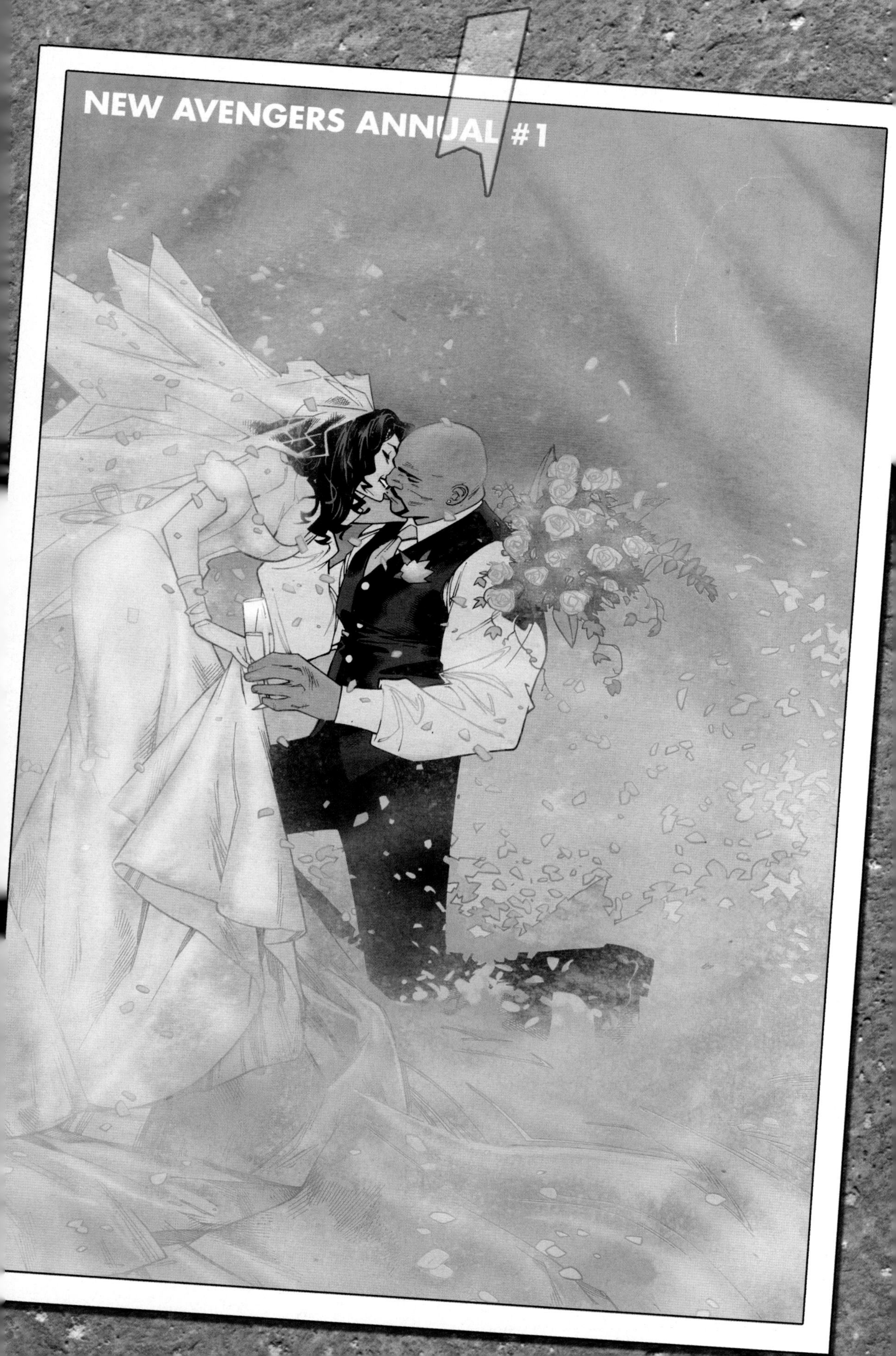
NEW AVENGERS ANNUAL #1

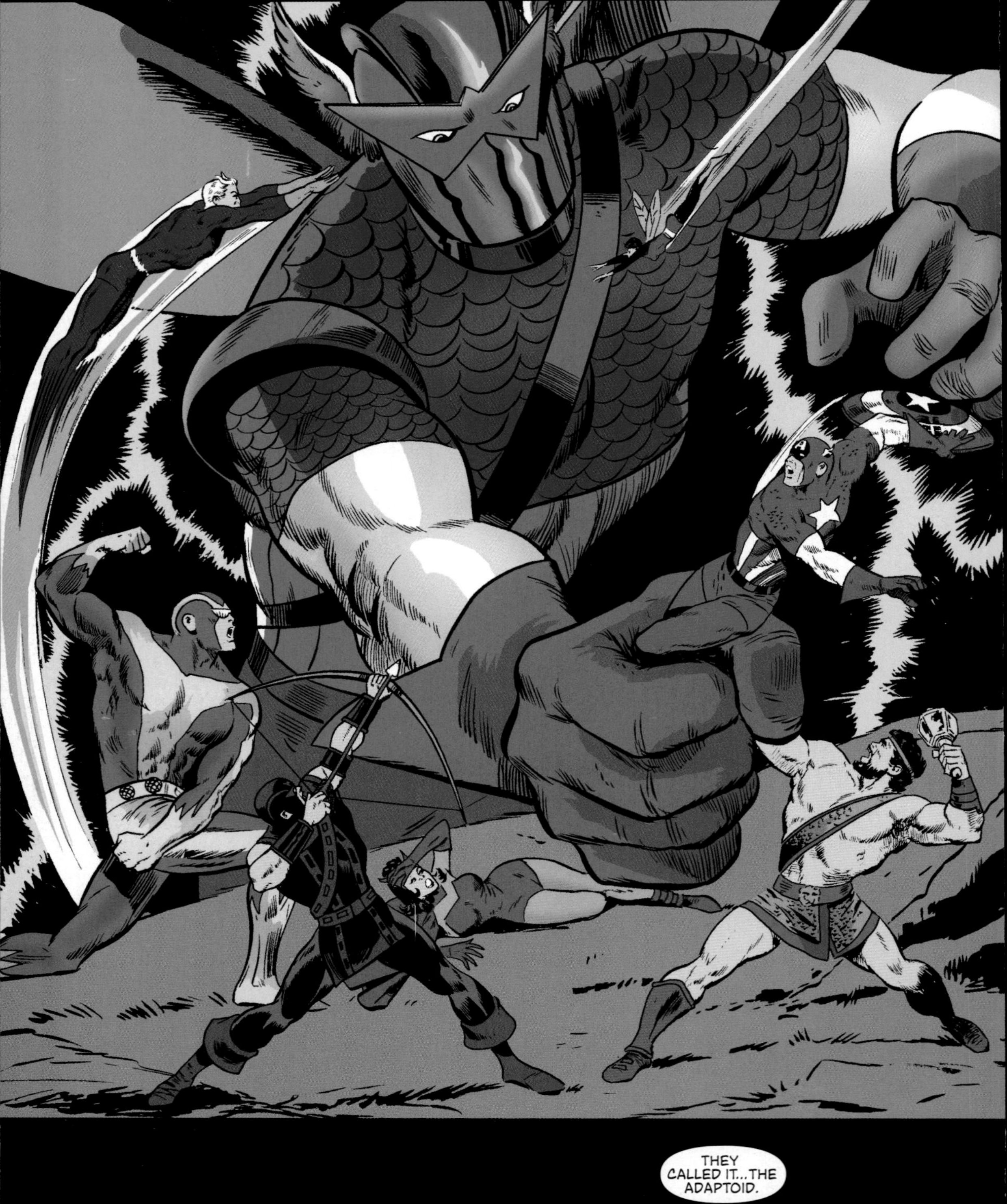
THEY CALLED IT... THE ADAPTOID.

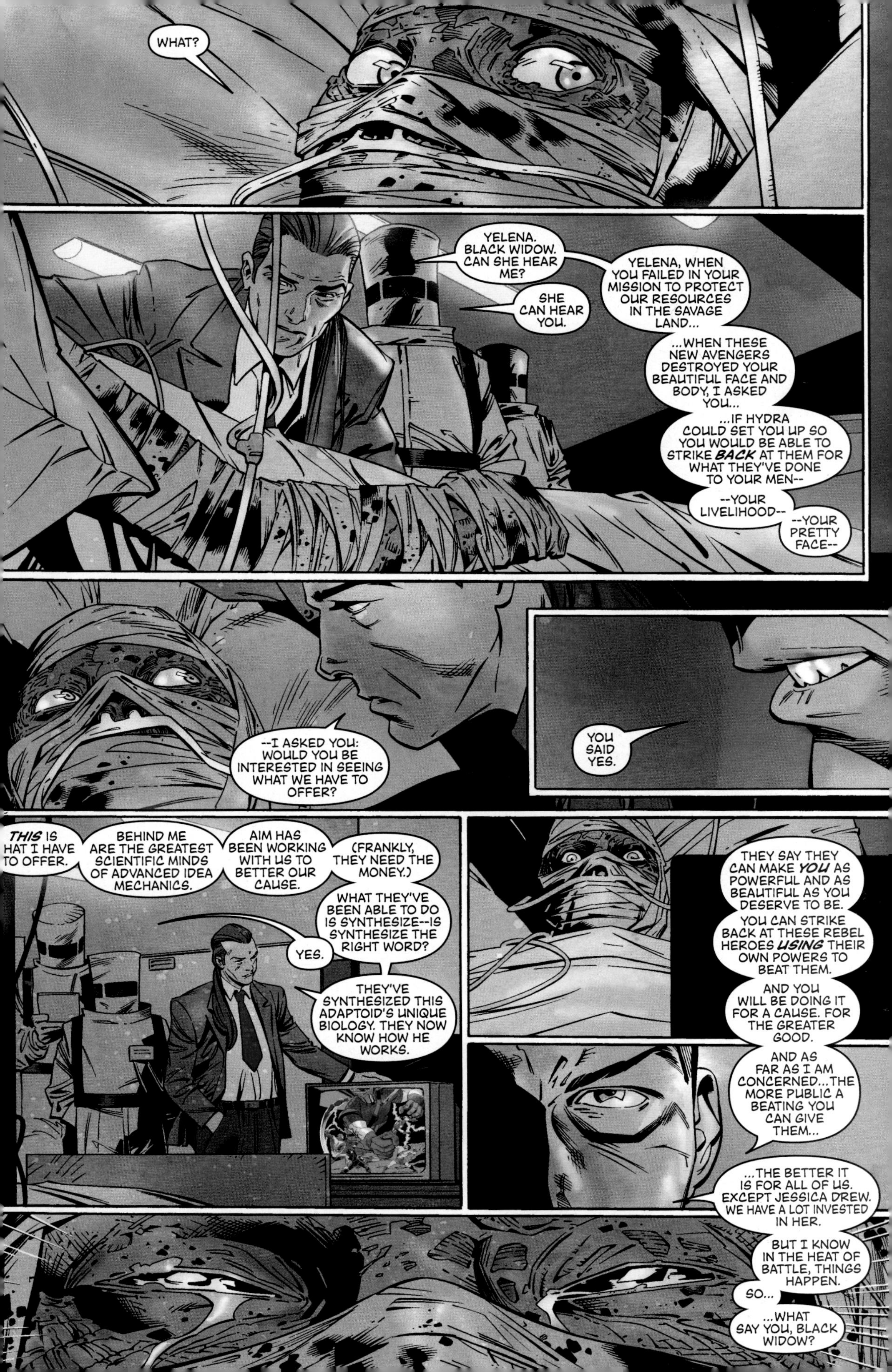
WHAT?
YELENA. BLACK WIDOW. CAN SHE HEAR ME?
SHE CAN HEAR YOU.
YELENA, WHEN YOU FAILED IN YOUR MISSION TO PROTECT OUR RESOURCES IN THE SAVAGE LAND...
...WHEN THESE NEW AVENGERS DESTROYED YOUR BEAUTIFUL FACE AND BODY, I ASKED YOU...
...IF HYDRA COULD SET YOU UP SO YOU WOULD BE ABLE TO STRIKE BACK AT THEM FOR WHAT THEY'VE DONE TO YOUR MEN--
--YOUR LIVELIHOOD--
--YOUR PRETTY FACE--
--I ASKED YOU: WOULD YOU BE INTERESTED IN SEEING WHAT WE HAVE TO OFFER?
YOU SAID YES.
THIS IS HAT I HAVE TO OFFER.
BEHIND ME ARE THE GREATEST SCIENTIFIC MINDS OF ADVANCED IDEA MECHANICS.
AIM HAS BEEN WORKING WITH US TO BETTER OUR CAUSE.
(FRANKLY, THEY NEED THE MONEY.)
WHAT THEY'VE BEEN ABLE TO DO IS SYNTHESIZE--IS SYNTHESIZE THE RIGHT WORD?
YES.
THEY'VE SYNTHESIZED THIS ADAPTOID'S UNIQUE BIOLOGY. THEY NOW KNOW HOW HE WORKS.
THEY SAY THEY CAN MAKE YOU AS POWERFUL AND AS BEAUTIFUL AS YOU DESERVE TO BE.
YOU CAN STRIKE BACK AT THESE REBEL HEROES USING THEIR OWN POWERS TO BEAT THEM.
AND YOU WILL BE DOING IT FOR A CAUSE. FOR THE GREATER GOOD.
AND AS FAR AS I AM CONCERNED...THE MORE PUBLIC A BEATING YOU CAN GIVE THEM...
...THE BETTER IT IS FOR ALL OF US. EXCEPT JESSICA DREW. WE HAVE A LOT INVESTED IN HER.
BUT I KNOW IN THE HEAT OF BATTLE, THINGS HAPPEN.
SO...
...WHAT SAY YOU, BLACK WIDOW?

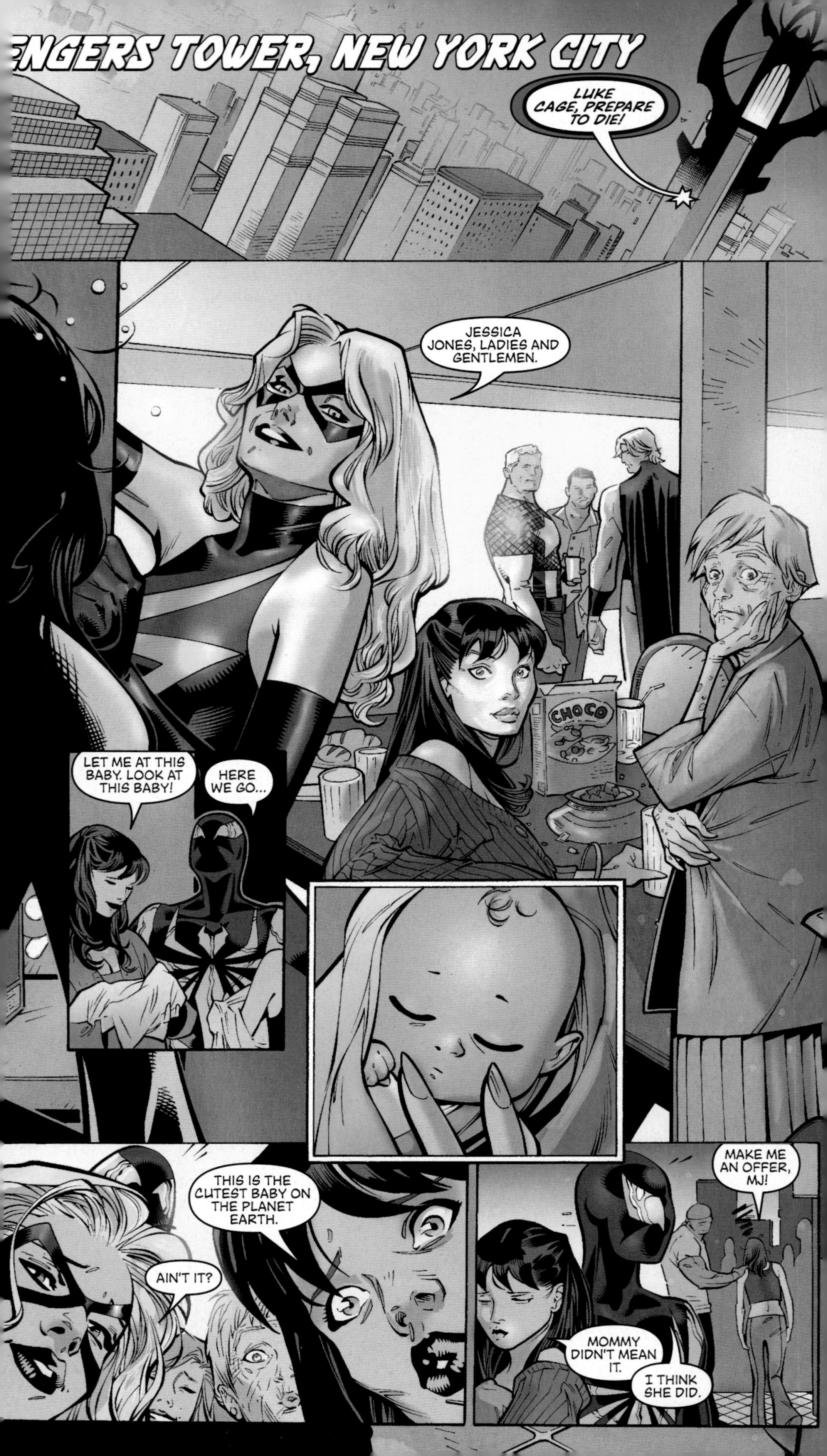
ENGERS TOWER, NEW YORK CITY
LUKE CAGE, PREPARE TO DIE!
JESSICA JONES, LADIES AND GENTLEMEN.
LET ME AT THIS BABY. LOOK AT THIS BABY!
HERE WE GO...
THIS IS THE CUTEST BABY ON THE PLANET EARTH.
AIN'T IT?
MAKE ME AN OFFER, MJ!
MOMMY DIDN'T MEAN IT.
I THINK SHE DID.

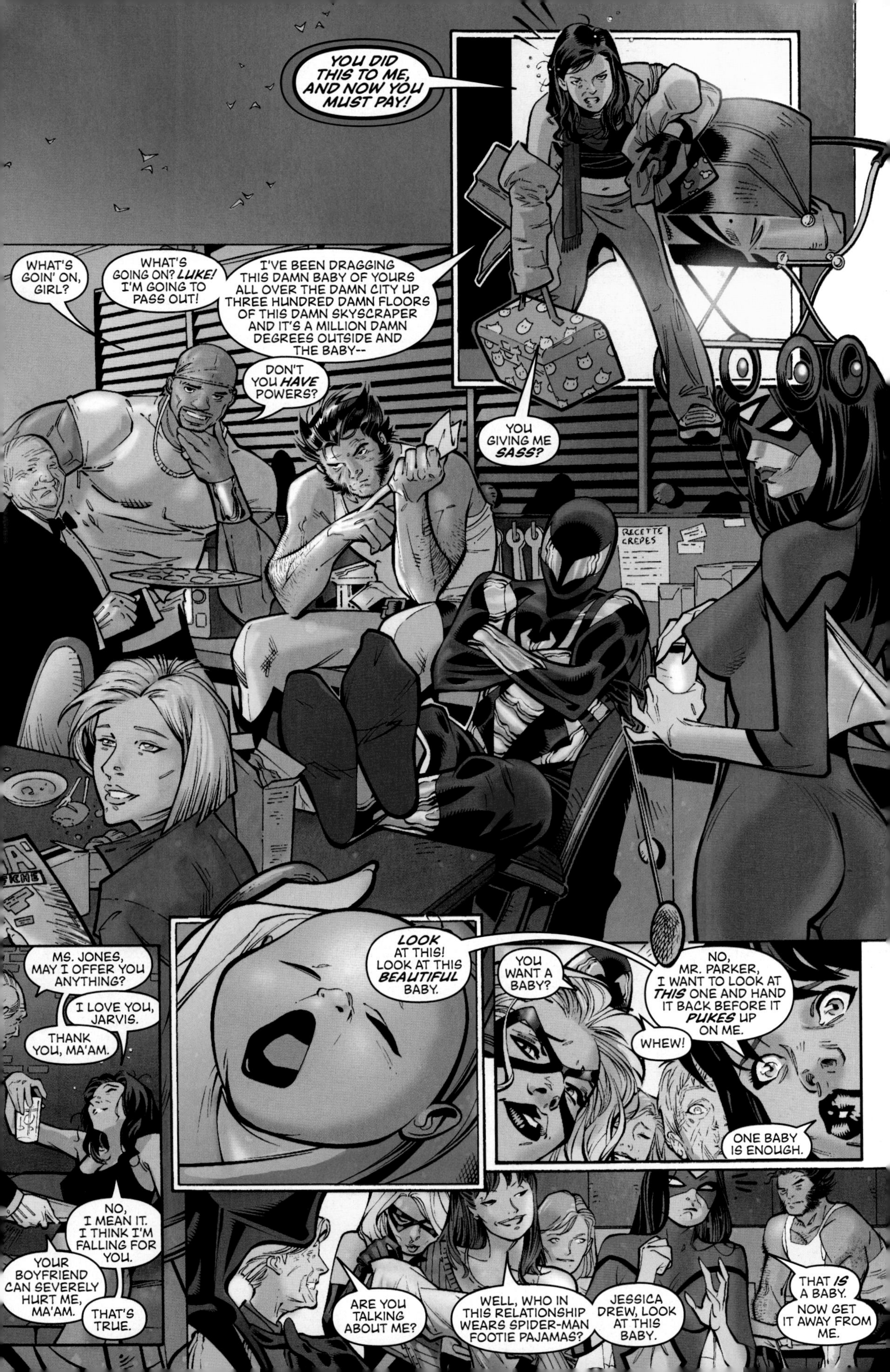

YOU DID THIS TO ME, AND NOW YOU MUST PAY!
WHAT'S GOIN' ON, GIRL?
WHAT'S GOING ON? LUKE! I'M GOING TO PASS OUT!
I'VE BEEN DRAGGING THIS DAMN BABY OF YOURS ALL OVER THE DAMN CITY UP THREE HUNDRED DAMN FLOORS OF THIS DAMN SKYSCRAPER AND IT'S A MILLION DAMN DEGREES OUTSIDE AND THE BABY--
DON'T YOU HAVE POWERS?
YOU GIVING ME SASS?
RECETTE CREPES
MS. JONES, MAY I OFFER YOU ANYTHING?
I LOVE YOU, JARVIS.
THANK YOU, MA'AM.
LOOK AT THIS! LOOK AT THIS BEAUTIFUL BABY.
YOU WANT A BABY?
NO, MR. PARKER, I WANT TO LOOK AT THIS ONE AND HAND IT BACK BEFORE IT PUKES UP ON ME.
WHEW!
ONE BABY IS ENOUGH.
NO, I MEAN IT. I THINK I'M FALLING FOR YOU.
YOUR BOYFRIEND CAN SEVERELY HURT ME, MA'AM.
THAT'S TRUE.
ARE YOU TALKING ABOUT ME?
WELL, WHO IN THIS RELATIONSHIP WEARS SPIDER-MAN FOOTIE PAJAMAS?
JESSICA DREW, LOOK AT THIS BABY.
THAT IS A BABY. NOW GET IT AWAY FROM ME.

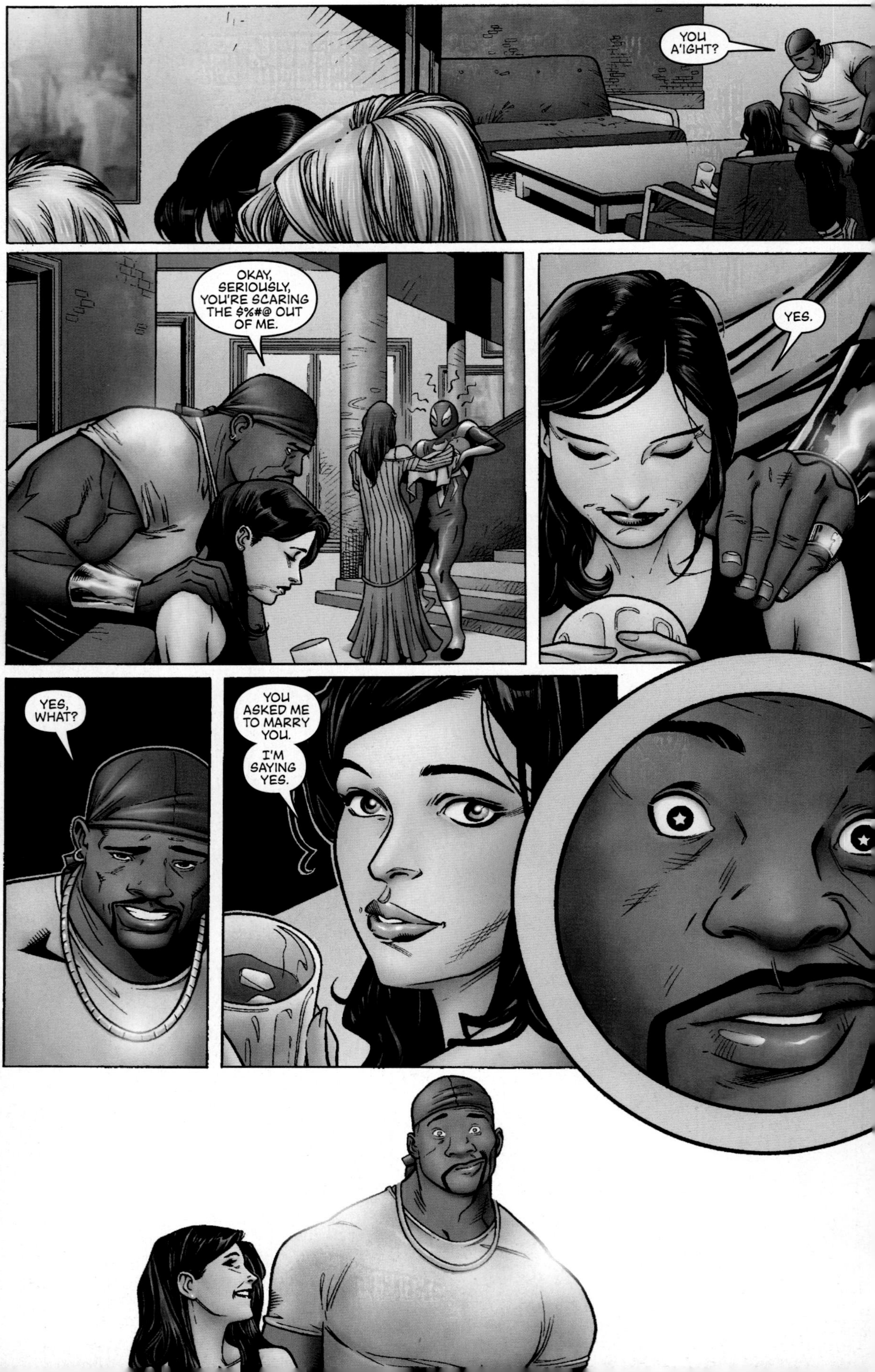
YOU A'IGHT?
OKAY, SERIOUSLY, YOU'RE SCARING THE $%#@ OUT OF ME.
YES.
YES, WHAT?
YOU ASKED ME TO MARRY YOU.
I'M SAYING YES.

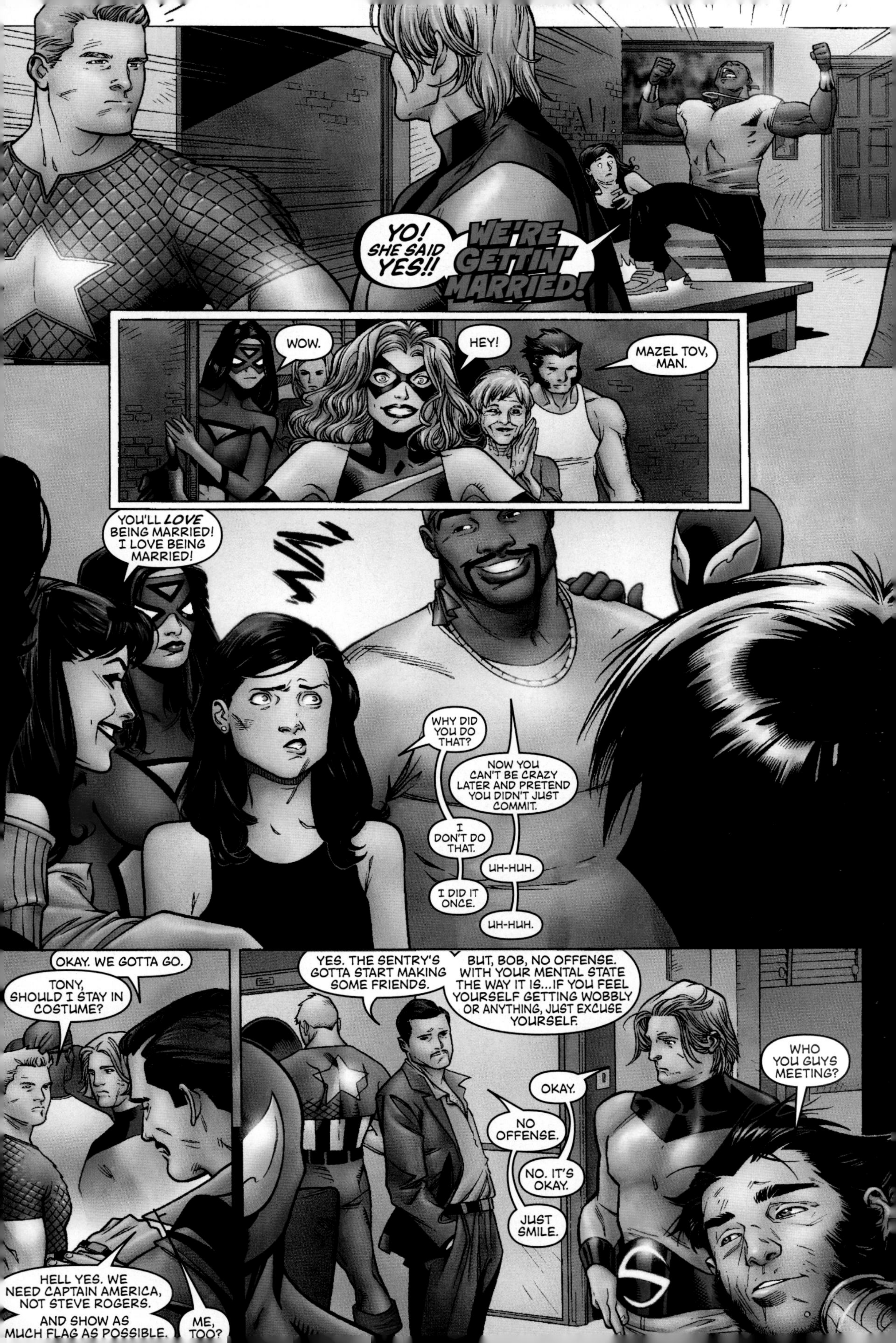
YO! SHE SAID YES!!
WE'RE GETTIN' MARRIED!
WOW.
HEY!
MAZEL TOV, MAN.
YOU'LL LOVE BEING MARRIED! I LOVE BEING MARRIED!
WHY DID YOU DO THAT?
NOW YOU CAN'T BE CRAZY LATER AND PRETEND YOU DIDN'T JUST COMMIT.
I DON'T DO THAT.
UH-HUH.
I DID IT ONCE.
UH-HUH.
OKAY. WE GOTTA GO.
TONY, SHOULD I STAY IN COSTUME?
HELL YES. WE NEED CAPTAIN AMERICA, NOT STEVE ROGERS.
AND SHOW AS MUCH FLAG AS POSSIBLE.
ME, TOO?
YES. THE SENTRY'S GOTTA START MAKING SOME FRIENDS.
BUT, BOB, NO OFFENSE. WITH YOUR MENTAL STATE THE WAY IT IS...IF YOU FEEL YOURSELF GETTING WOBBLY OR ANYTHING, JUST EXCUSE YOURSELF.
OKAY.
NO OFFENSE.
NO. IT'S OKAY.
JUST SMILE.
WHO YOU GUYS MEETING?

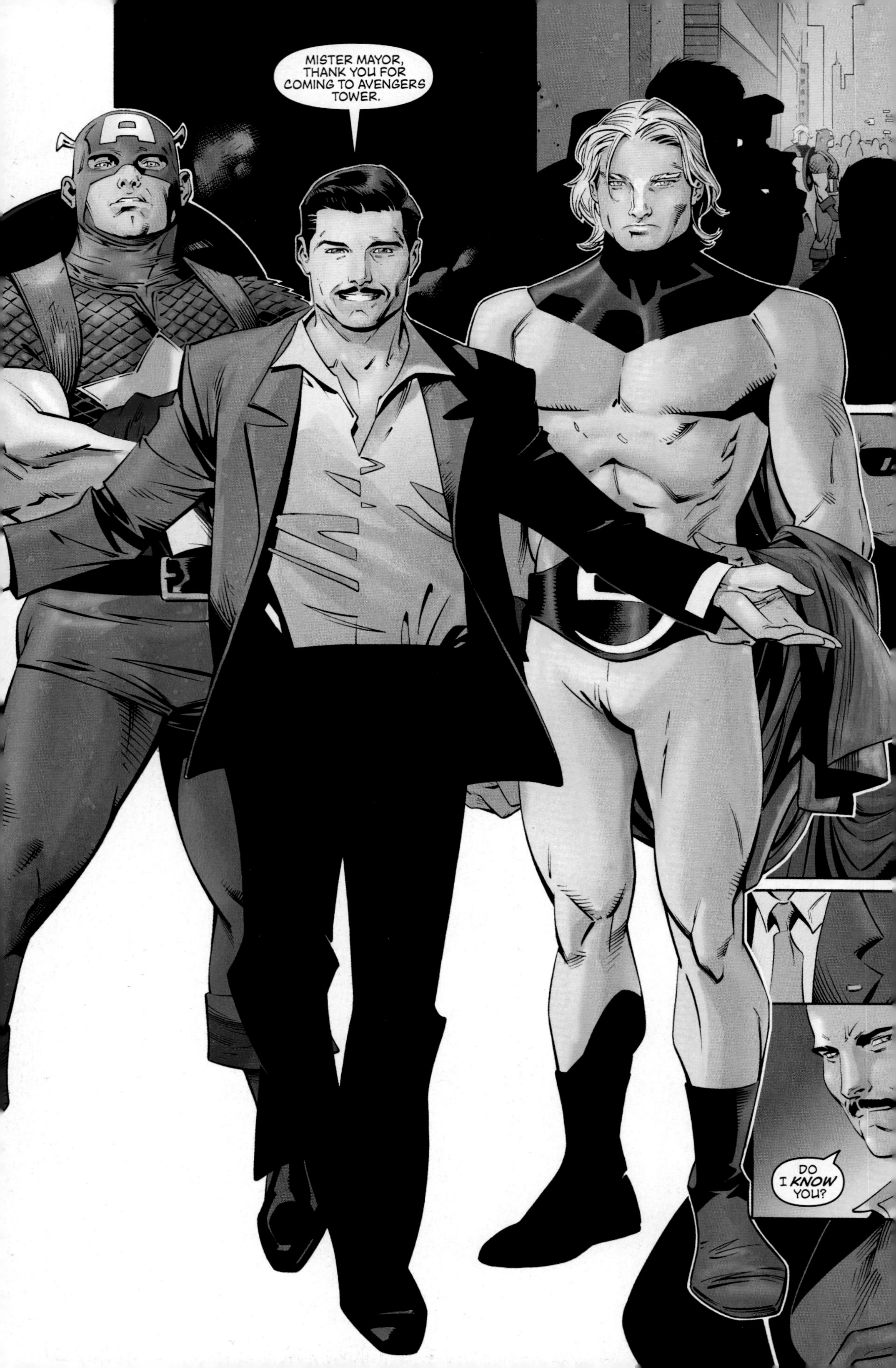
MISTER MAYOR, THANK YOU FOR COMING TO AVENGERS TOWER.
DO I *KNOW* YOU?

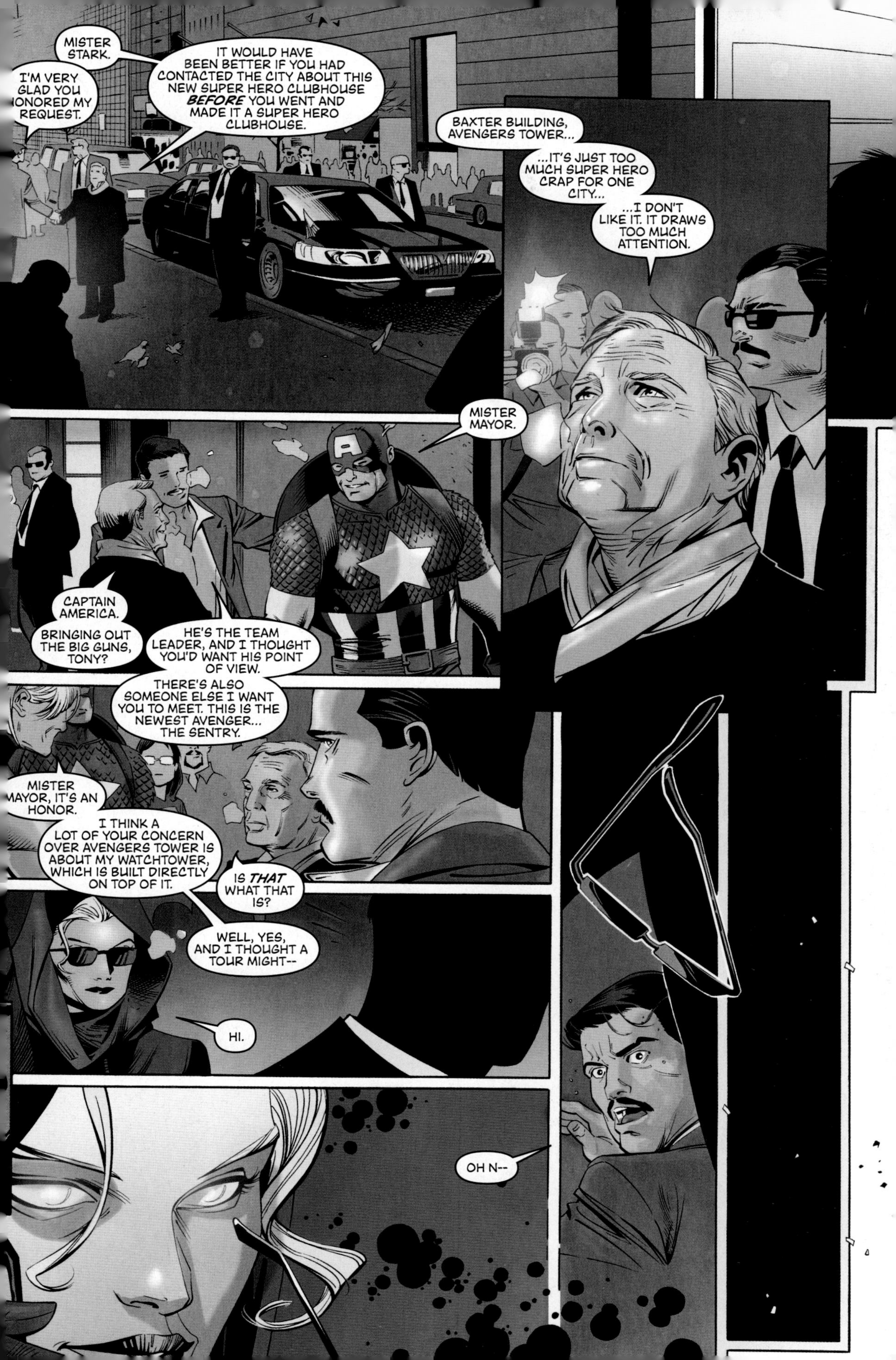
MISTER STARK.
I'M VERY GLAD YOU HONORED MY REQUEST.
IT WOULD HAVE BEEN BETTER IF YOU HAD CONTACTED THE CITY ABOUT THIS NEW SUPER HERO CLUBHOUSE BEFORE YOU WENT AND MADE IT A SUPER HERO CLUBHOUSE.
BAXTER BUILDING, AVENGERS TOWER...
...IT'S JUST TOO MUCH SUPER HERO CRAP FOR ONE CITY...
...I DON'T LIKE IT. IT DRAWS TOO MUCH ATTENTION.
MISTER MAYOR.
CAPTAIN AMERICA.
BRINGING OUT THE BIG GUNS, TONY?
HE'S THE TEAM LEADER, AND I THOUGHT YOU'D WANT HIS POINT OF VIEW.
THERE'S ALSO SOMEONE ELSE I WANT YOU TO MEET. THIS IS THE NEWEST AVENGER... THE SENTRY.
MISTER MAYOR, IT'S AN HONOR.
I THINK A LOT OF YOUR CONCERN OVER AVENGERS TOWER IS ABOUT MY WATCHTOWER, WHICH IS BUILT DIRECTLY ON TOP OF IT.
IS THAT WHAT THAT IS?
WELL, YES, AND I THOUGHT A TOUR MIGHT--
HI.
OH N--

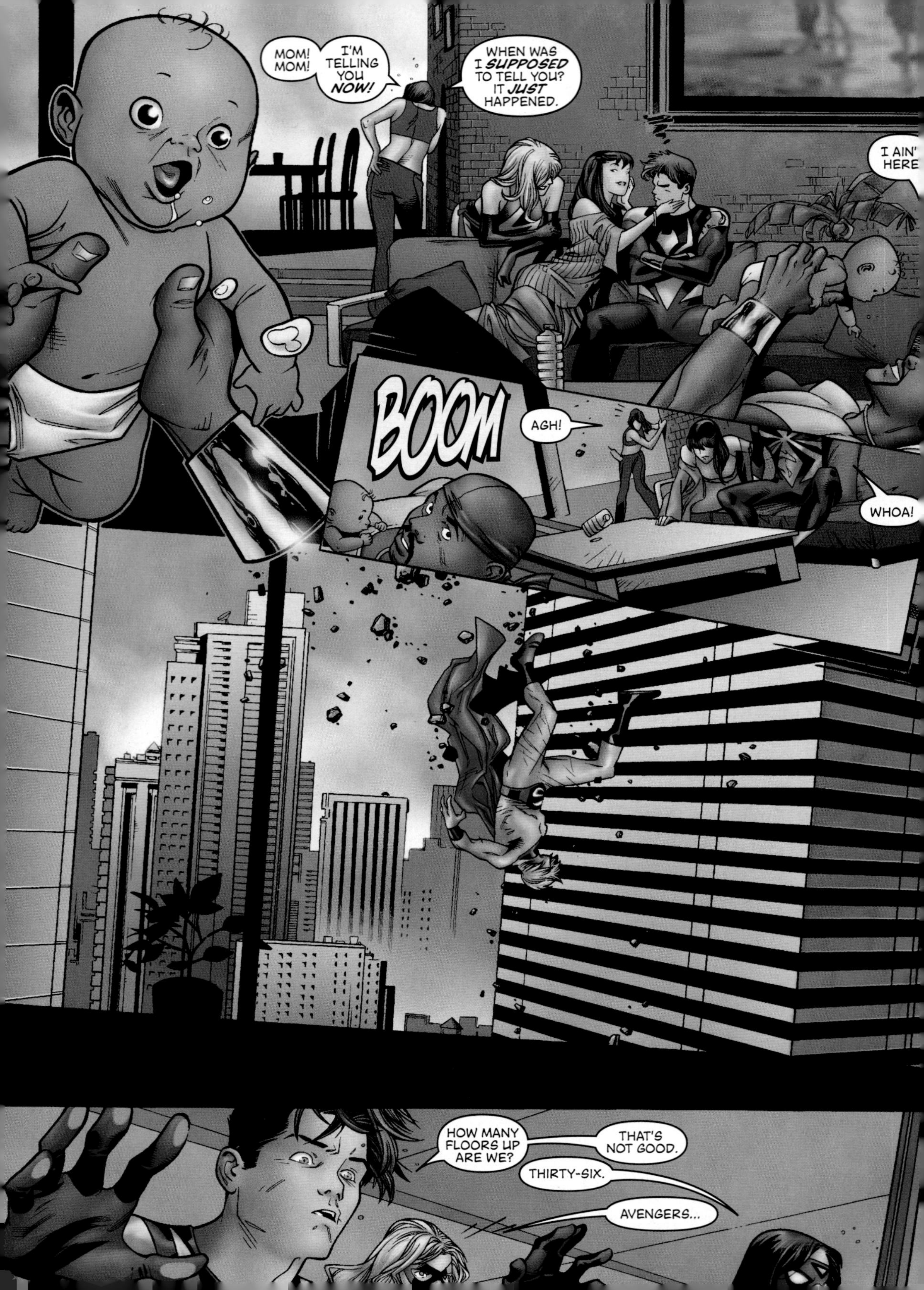
MOM! MOM!
I'M TELLING YOU NOW!
WHEN WAS I SUPPOSED TO TELL YOU? IT JUST HAPPENED.
I AIN' HERE
BOOM
AGH!
WHOA!
HOW MANY FLOORS UP ARE WE?
THAT'S NOT GOOD.
THIRTY-SIX.
AVENGERS...

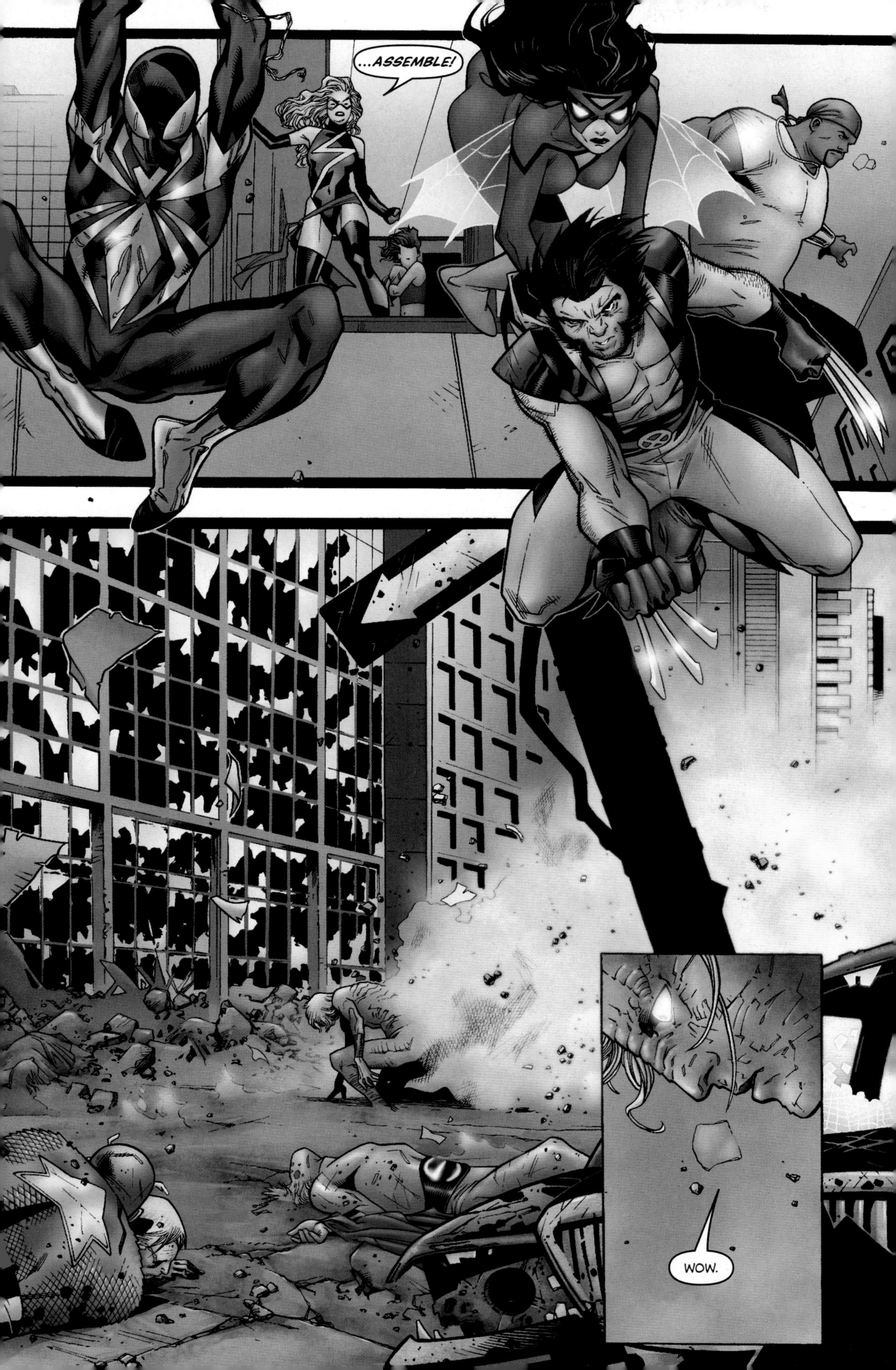
...ASSEMBLE!
WOW.

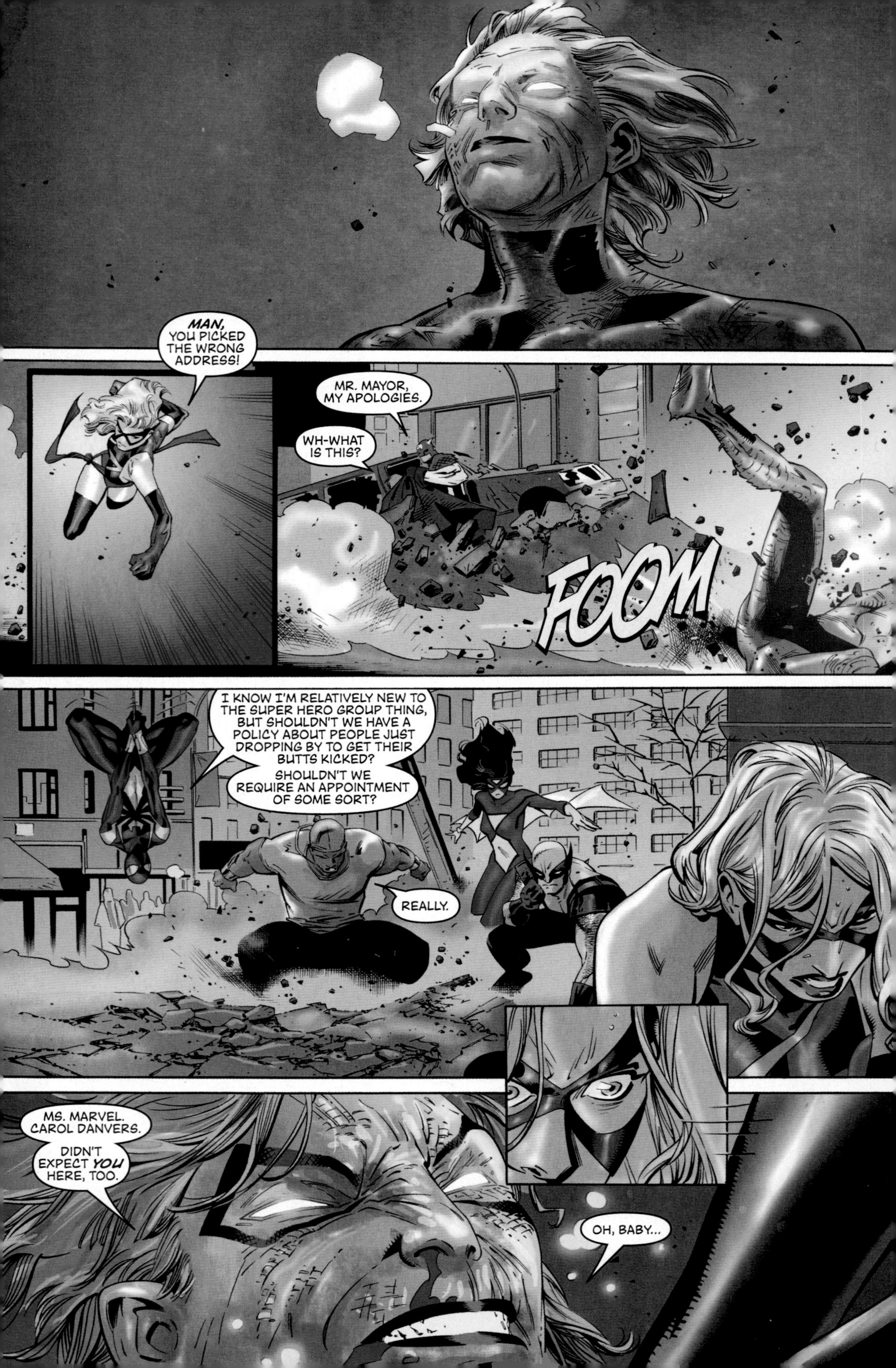
MAN, YOU PICKED THE WRONG ADDRESS!
MR. MAYOR, MY APOLOGIES.
WH-WHAT IS THIS?
FOOM
I KNOW I'M RELATIVELY NEW TO THE SUPER HERO GROUP THING, BUT SHOULDN'T WE HAVE A POLICY ABOUT PEOPLE JUST DROPPING BY TO GET THEIR BUTTS KICKED?
SHOULDN'T WE REQUIRE AN APPOINTMENT OF SOME SORT?
REALLY.
MS. MARVEL. CAROL DANVERS.
DIDN'T EXPECT YOU HERE, TOO.
OH, BABY...

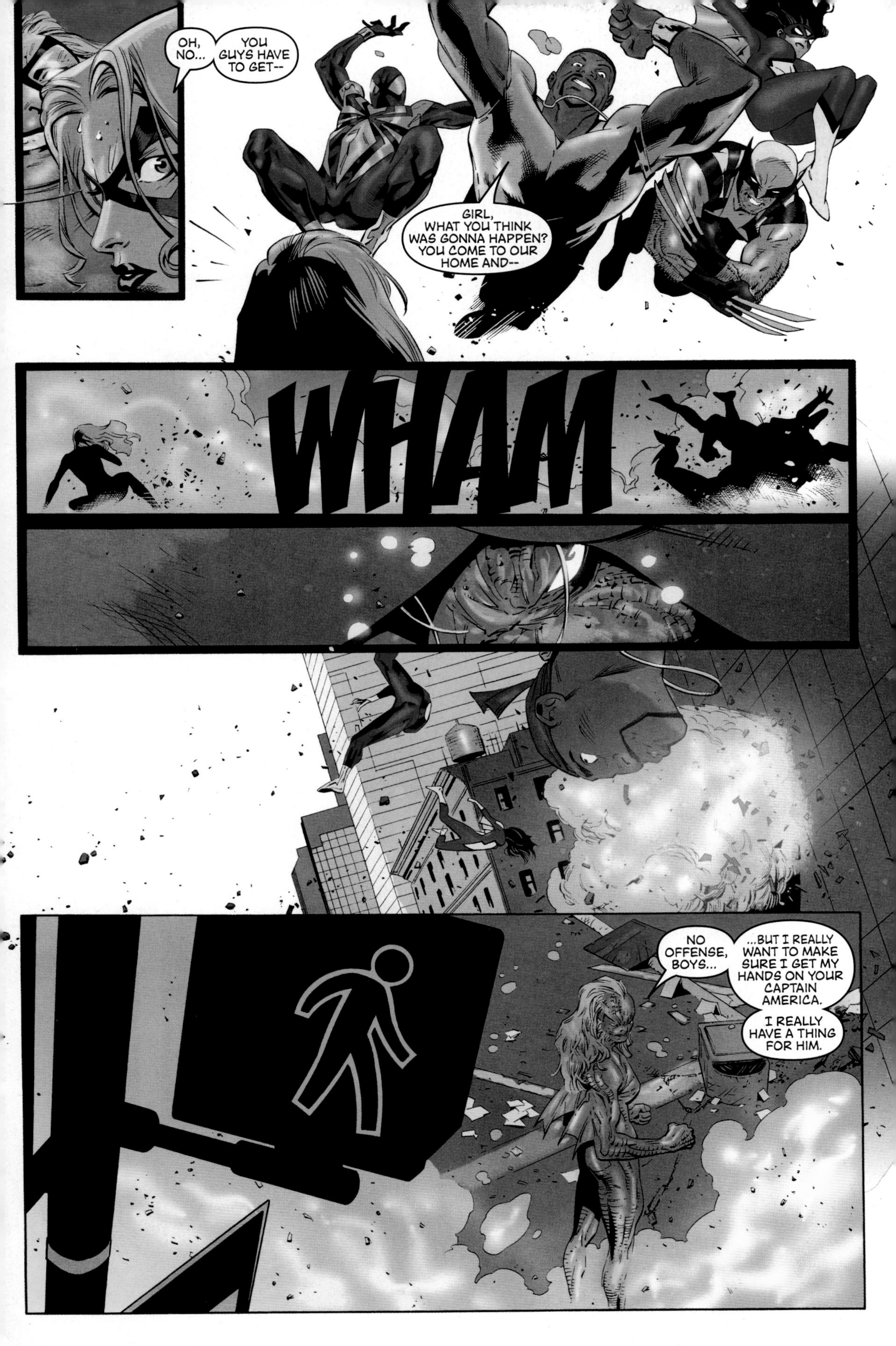
OH, NO...
YOU GUYS HAVE TO GET--
GIRL, WHAT YOU THINK WAS GONNA HAPPEN? YOU COME TO OUR HOME AND--
WHAM
NO OFFENSE, BOYS...
...BUT I REALLY WANT TO MAKE SURE I GET MY HANDS ON YOUR CAPTAIN AMERICA.
I REALLY HAVE A THING FOR HIM.

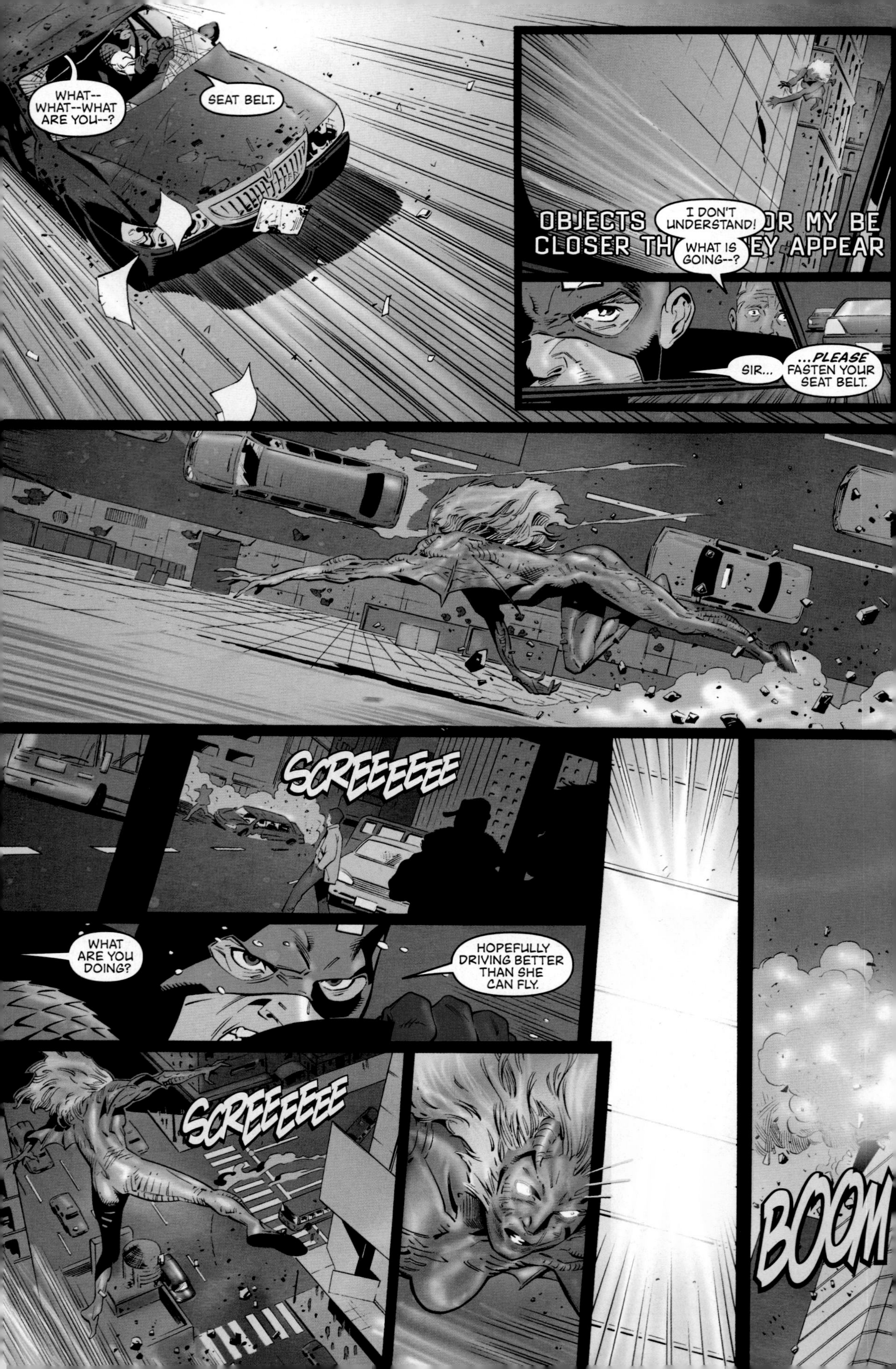
WHAT-- WHAT--WHAT ARE YOU--?
SEAT BELT.
OBJECTS IN MIRROR MAY BE CLOSER THAN THEY APPEAR
I DON'T UNDERSTAND!
WHAT IS GOING--?
SIR...
...PLEASE FASTEN YOUR SEAT BELT.
SCREEEEEE
WHAT ARE YOU DOING?
HOPEFULLY DRIVING BETTER THAN SHE CAN FLY.
SCREEEEEE
BOOM

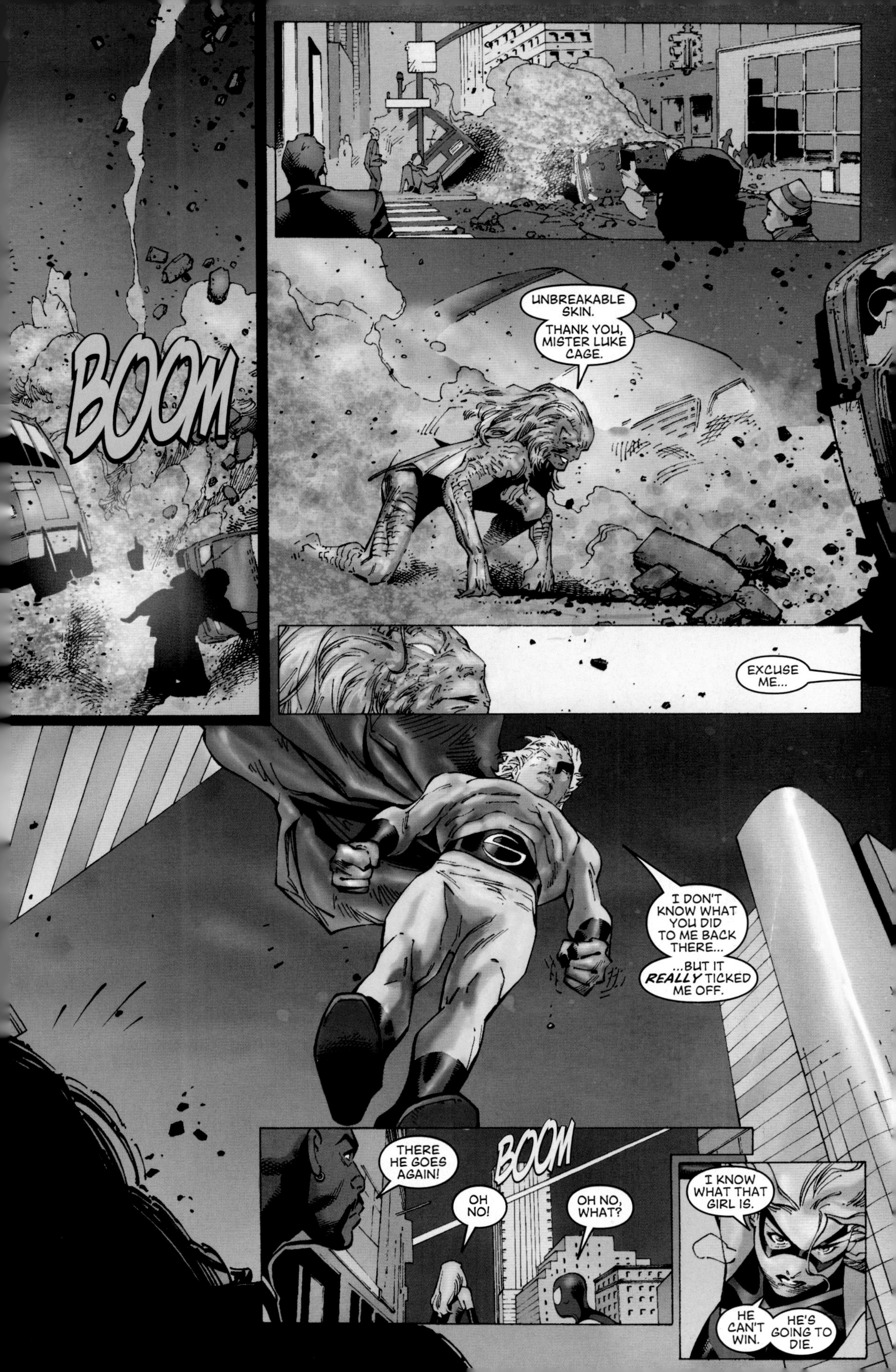
BOOM
UNBREAKABLE SKIN.
THANK YOU, MISTER LUKE CAGE.
EXCUSE ME...
I DON'T KNOW WHAT YOU DID TO ME BACK THERE...
...BUT IT REALLY TICKED ME OFF.
BOOM
THERE HE GOES AGAIN!
OH NO!
OH NO, WHAT?
I KNOW WHAT THAT GIRL IS.
HE CAN'T WIN.
HE'S GOING TO DIE.

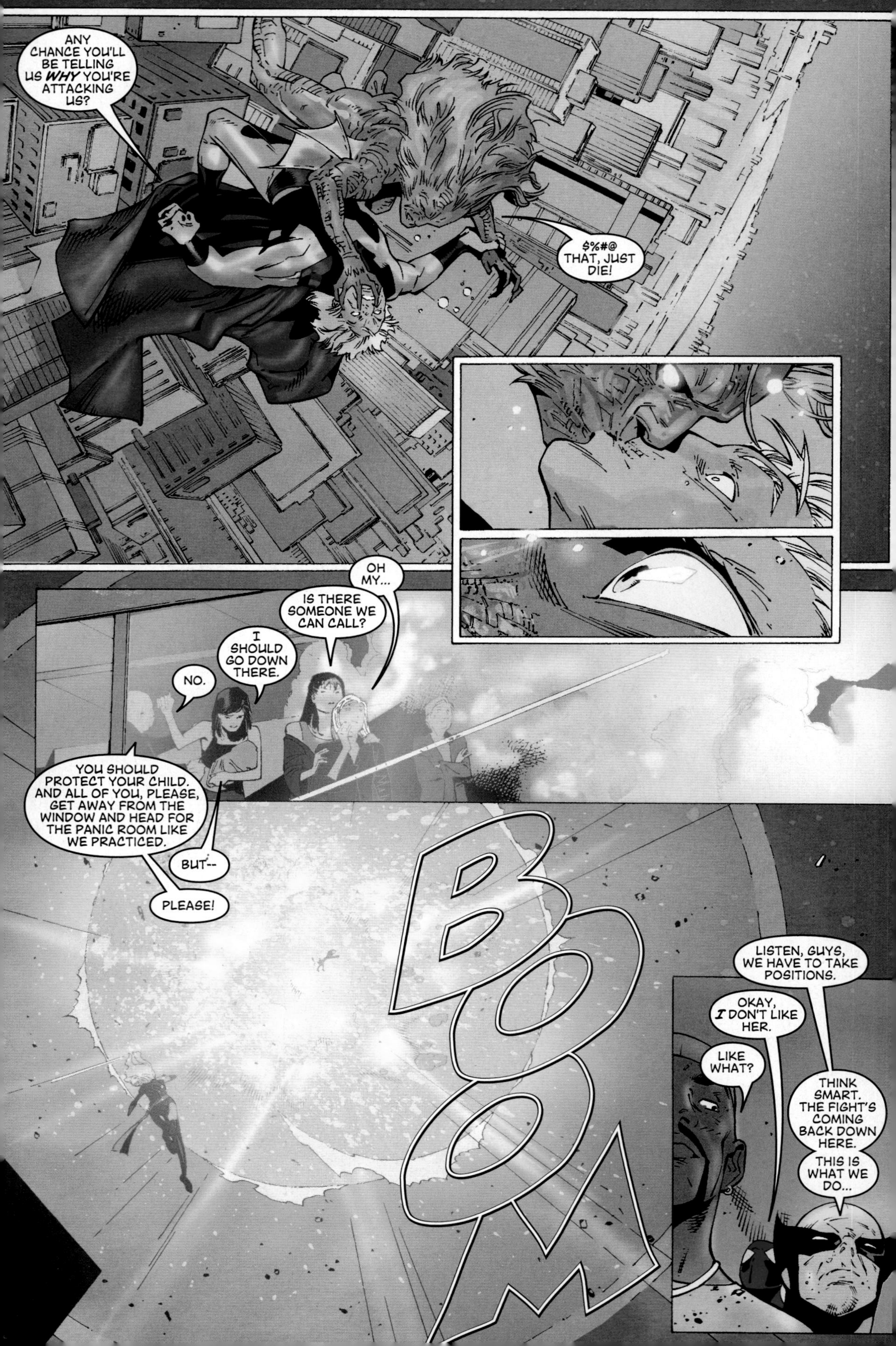

ANY CHANCE YOU'LL BE TELLING US *WHY* YOU'RE ATTACKING US?
$%#@ THAT, JUST DIE!
OH MY...
IS THERE SOMEONE WE CAN CALL?
I SHOULD GO DOWN THERE.
NO.
YOU SHOULD PROTECT YOUR CHILD. AND ALL OF YOU, PLEASE, GET AWAY FROM THE WINDOW AND HEAD FOR THE PANIC ROOM LIKE WE PRACTICED.
BUT--
PLEASE!
BOOM
LISTEN, GUYS, WE HAVE TO TAKE POSITIONS.
OKAY, *I* DON'T LIKE HER.
LIKE WHAT?
THINK SMART. THE FIGHT'S COMING BACK DOWN HERE.
THIS IS WHAT WE DO...

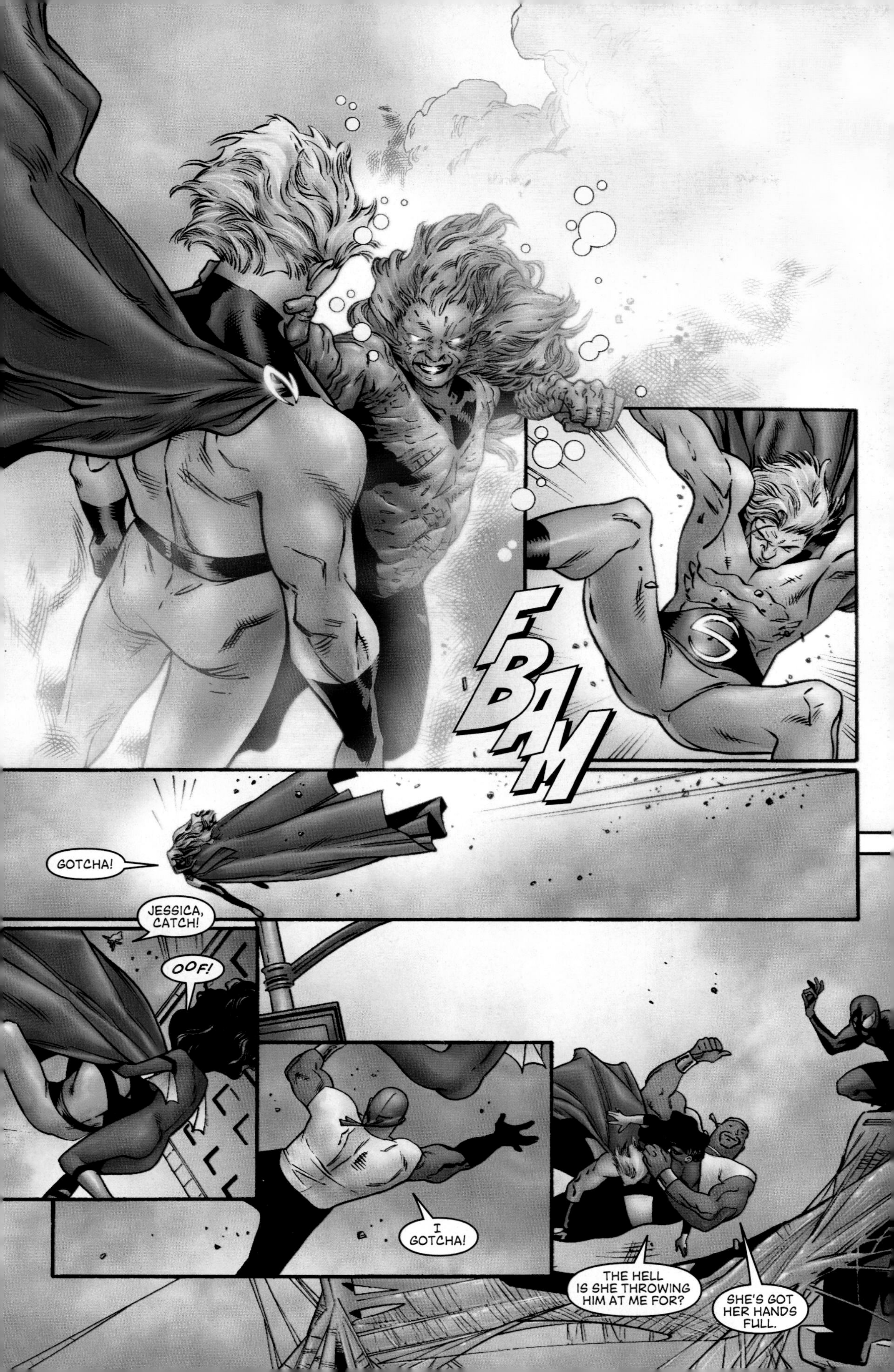
FBAM
GOTCHA!
JESSICA, CATCH!
OOF!
I GOTCHA!
THE HELL IS SHE THROWING HIM AT ME FOR?
SHE'S GOT HER HANDS FULL.

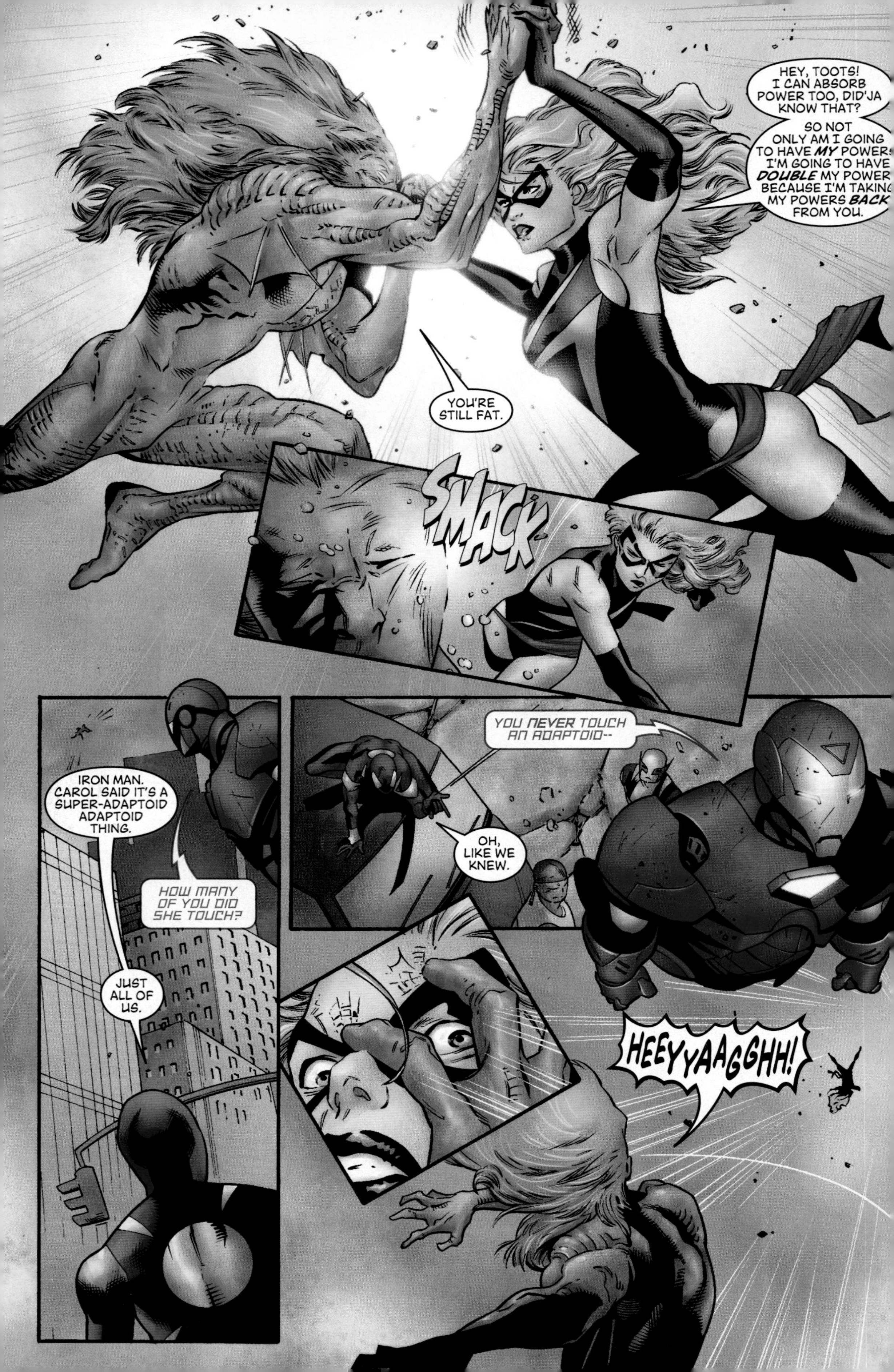
HEY, TOOTS! I CAN ABSORB POWER TOO, DID'JA KNOW THAT?
SO NOT ONLY AM I GOING TO HAVE MY POWERS I'M GOING TO HAVE DOUBLE MY POWERS BECAUSE I'M TAKING MY POWERS BACK FROM YOU.
YOU'RE STILL FAT.
SMACK
IRON MAN. CAROL SAID IT'S A SUPER-ADAPTOID ADAPTOID THING.
HOW MANY OF YOU DID SHE TOUCH?
JUST ALL OF US.
YOU NEVER TOUCH AN ADAPTOID--
OH, LIKE WE KNEW.
HEEYYAAGGHH!

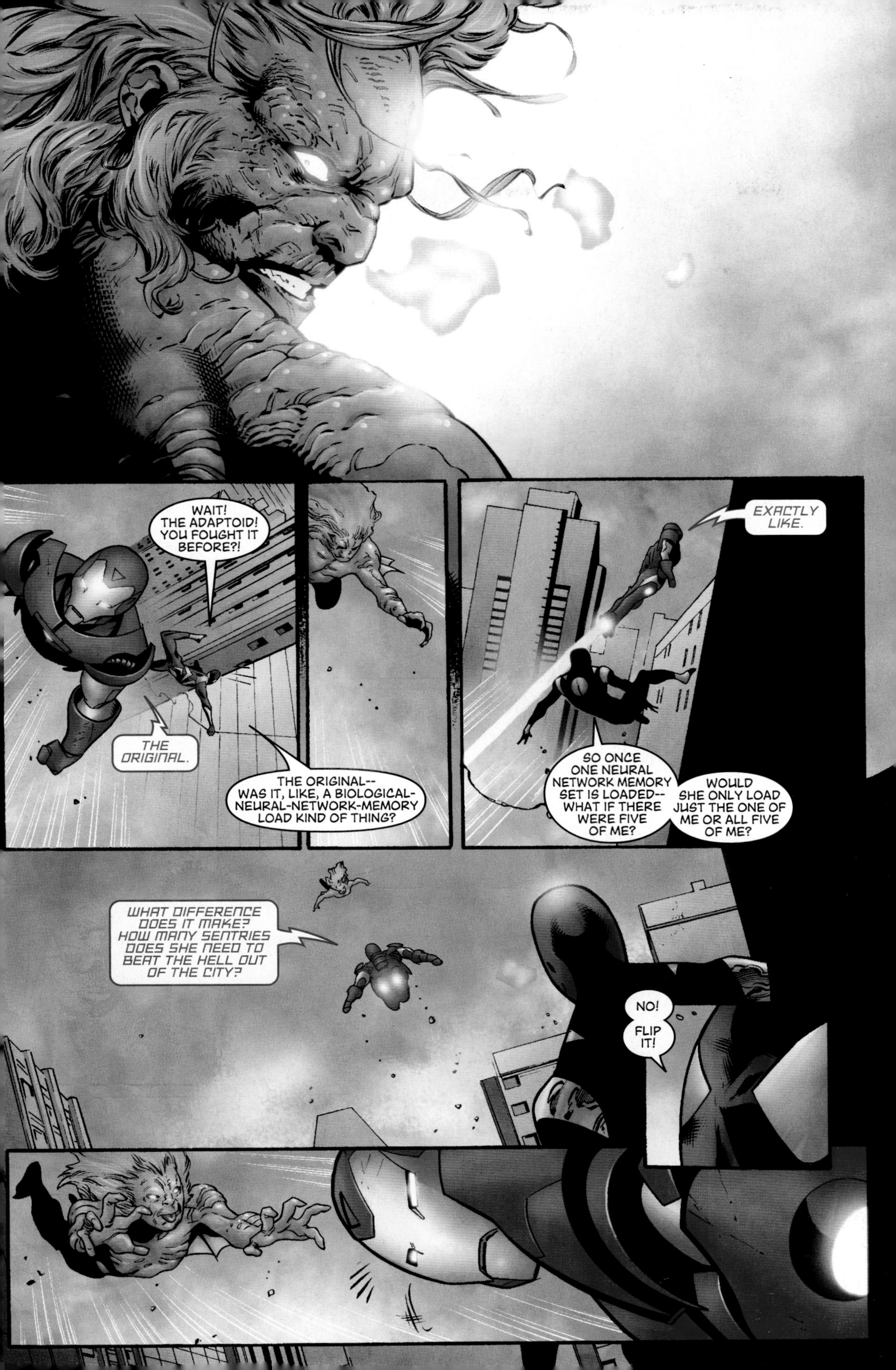
WAIT! THE ADAPTOID! YOU FOUGHT IT BEFORE?!
THE ORIGINAL.
THE ORIGINAL-- WAS IT, LIKE, A BIOLOGICAL-NEURAL-NETWORK-MEMORY LOAD KIND OF THING?
EXACTLY LIKE.
SO ONCE ONE NEURAL NETWORK MEMORY SET IS LOADED-- WHAT IF THERE WERE FIVE OF ME?
WOULD SHE ONLY LOAD JUST THE ONE OF ME OR ALL FIVE OF ME?
WHAT DIFFERENCE DOES IT MAKE? HOW MANY SENTRIES DOES SHE NEED TO BEAT THE HELL OUT OF THE CITY?
NO! FLIP IT!

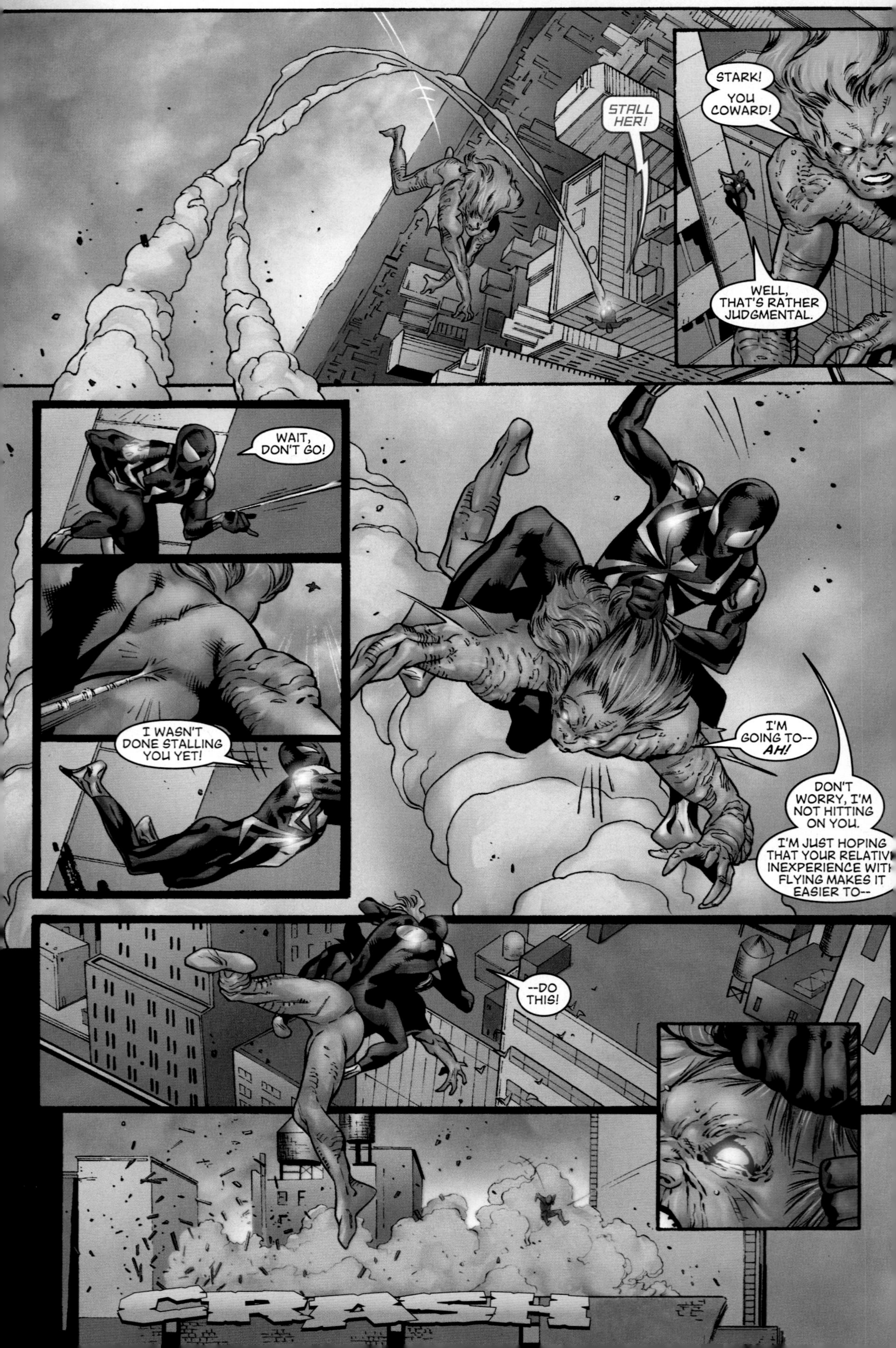
STALL HER!
STARK!
YOU COWARD!
WELL, THAT'S RATHER JUDGMENTAL.
WAIT, DON'T GO!
I WASN'T DONE STALLING YOU YET!
I'M GOING TO-- AH!
DON'T WORRY, I'M NOT HITTING ON YOU.
I'M JUST HOPING THAT YOUR RELATIVE INEXPERIENCE WITH FLYING MAKES IT EASIER TO--
--DO THIS!
CRASH

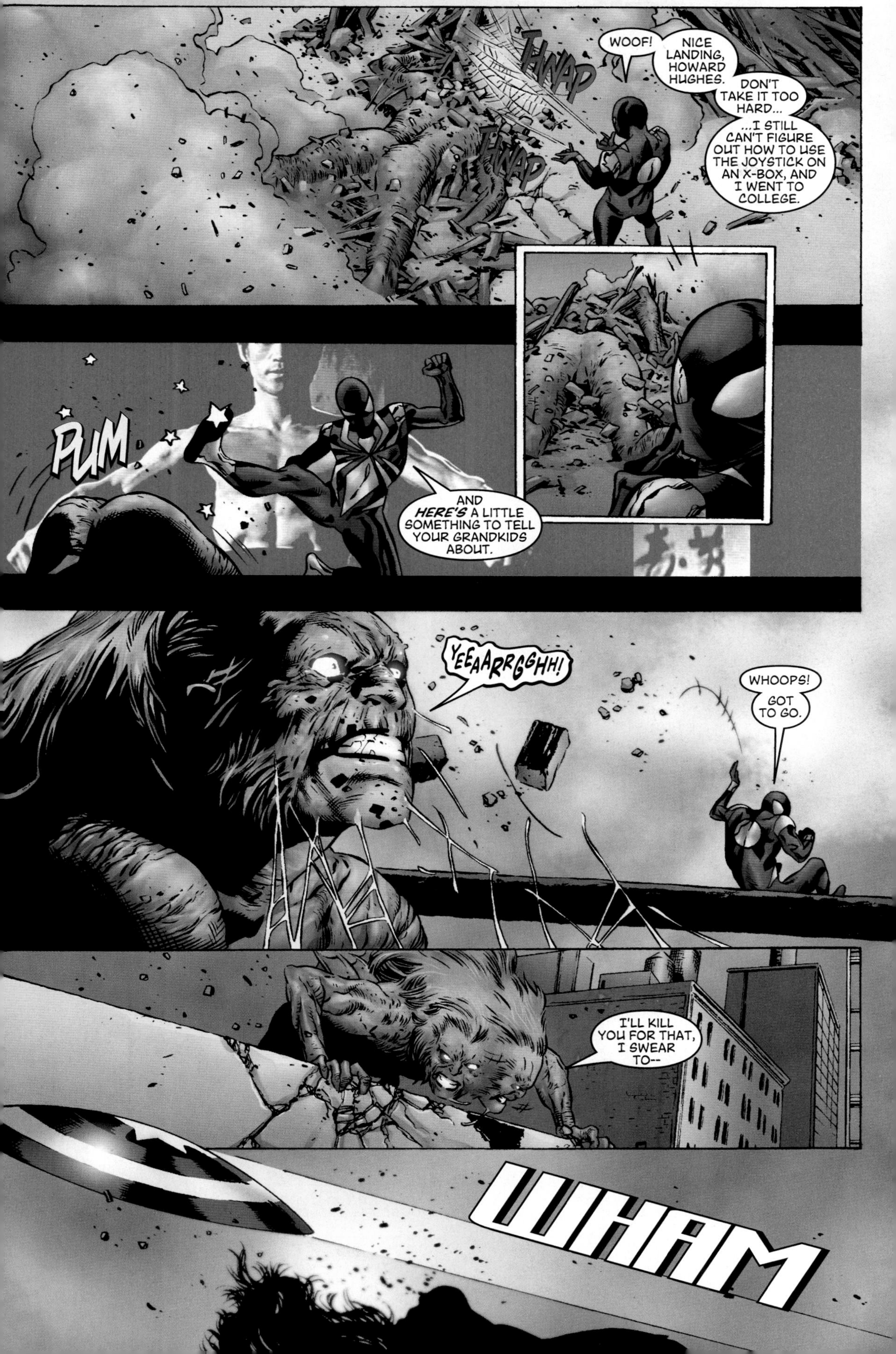
THWAP
THWAP
WOOF!
NICE LANDING, HOWARD HUGHES.
DON'T TAKE IT TOO HARD...
...I STILL CAN'T FIGURE OUT HOW TO USE THE JOYSTICK ON AN X-BOX, AND I WENT TO COLLEGE.
PUM
AND *HERE'S* A LITTLE SOMETHING TO TELL YOUR GRANDKIDS ABOUT.
YEEAARRGGHH!
WHOOPS!
GOT TO GO.
I'LL KILL YOU FOR THAT, I SWEAR TO--
WHAM

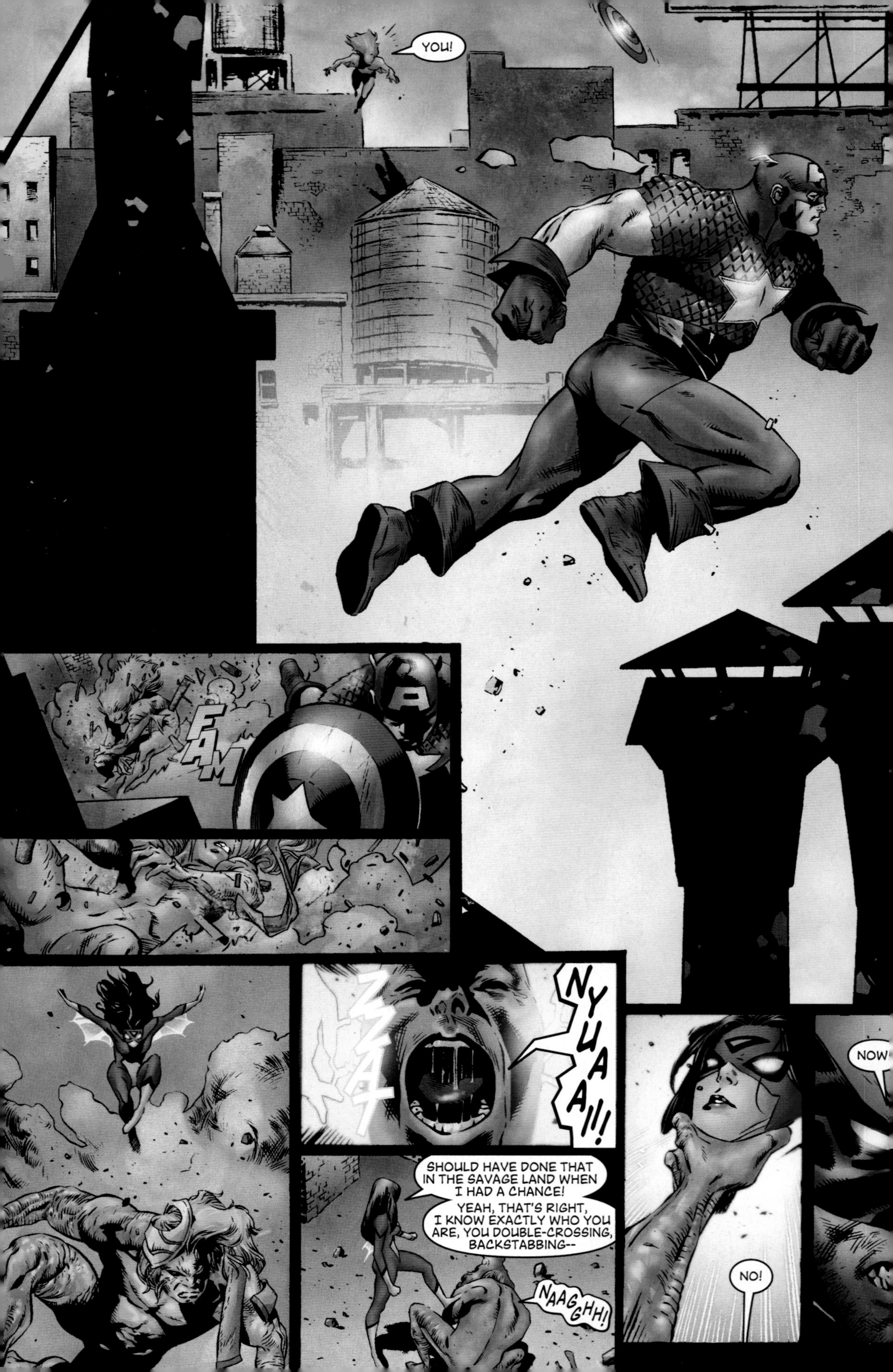

YOU!
FAM
NYUAAII!
ZZAT
NOW
SHOULD HAVE DONE THAT IN THE SAVAGE LAND WHEN I HAD A CHANCE!
YEAH, THAT'S RIGHT, I KNOW EXACTLY WHO YOU ARE, YOU DOUBLE-CROSSING, BACKSTABBING--
NAAGGHH!
NO!

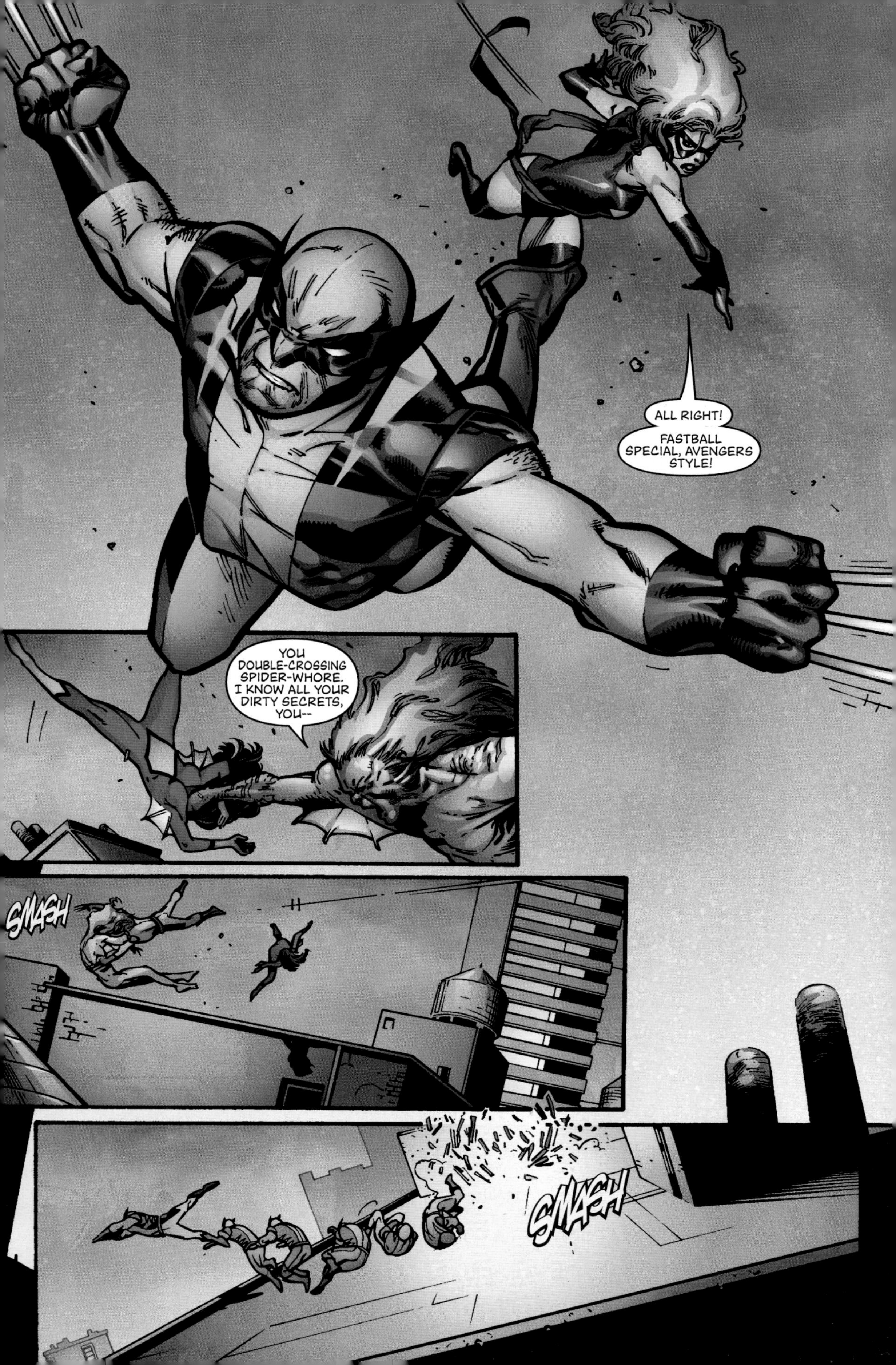
ALL RIGHT! FASTBALL SPECIAL, AVENGERS STYLE!
YOU DOUBLE-CROSSING SPIDER-WHORE. I KNOW ALL YOUR DIRTY SECRETS, YOU--
SMASH
SMASH

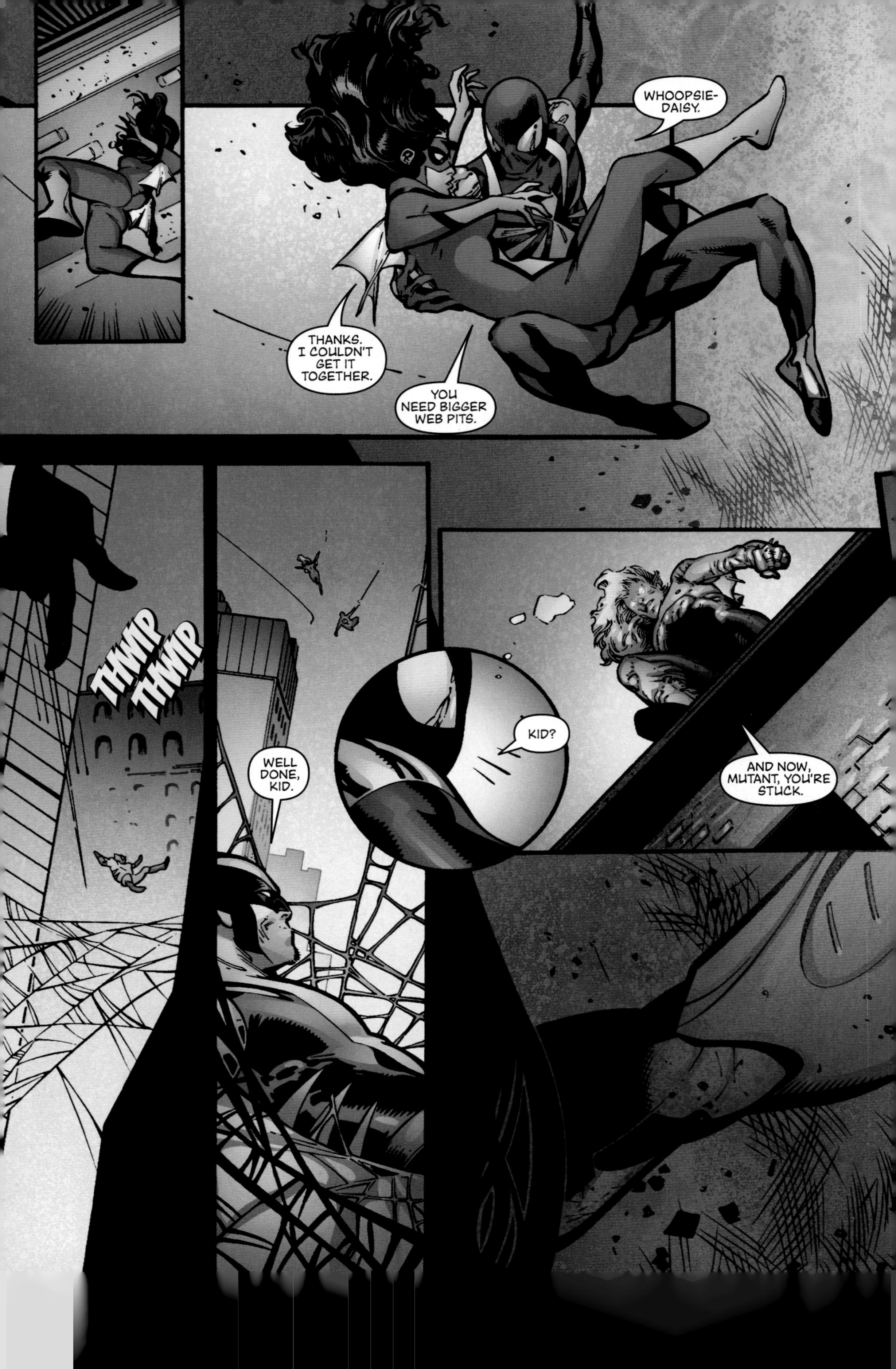
WHOOPSIE-DAISY.
THANKS. I COULDN'T GET IT TOGETHER.
YOU NEED BIGGER WEB PITS.
THWIP THWIP
WELL DONE, KID.
KID?
AND NOW, MUTANT, YOU'RE STUCK.

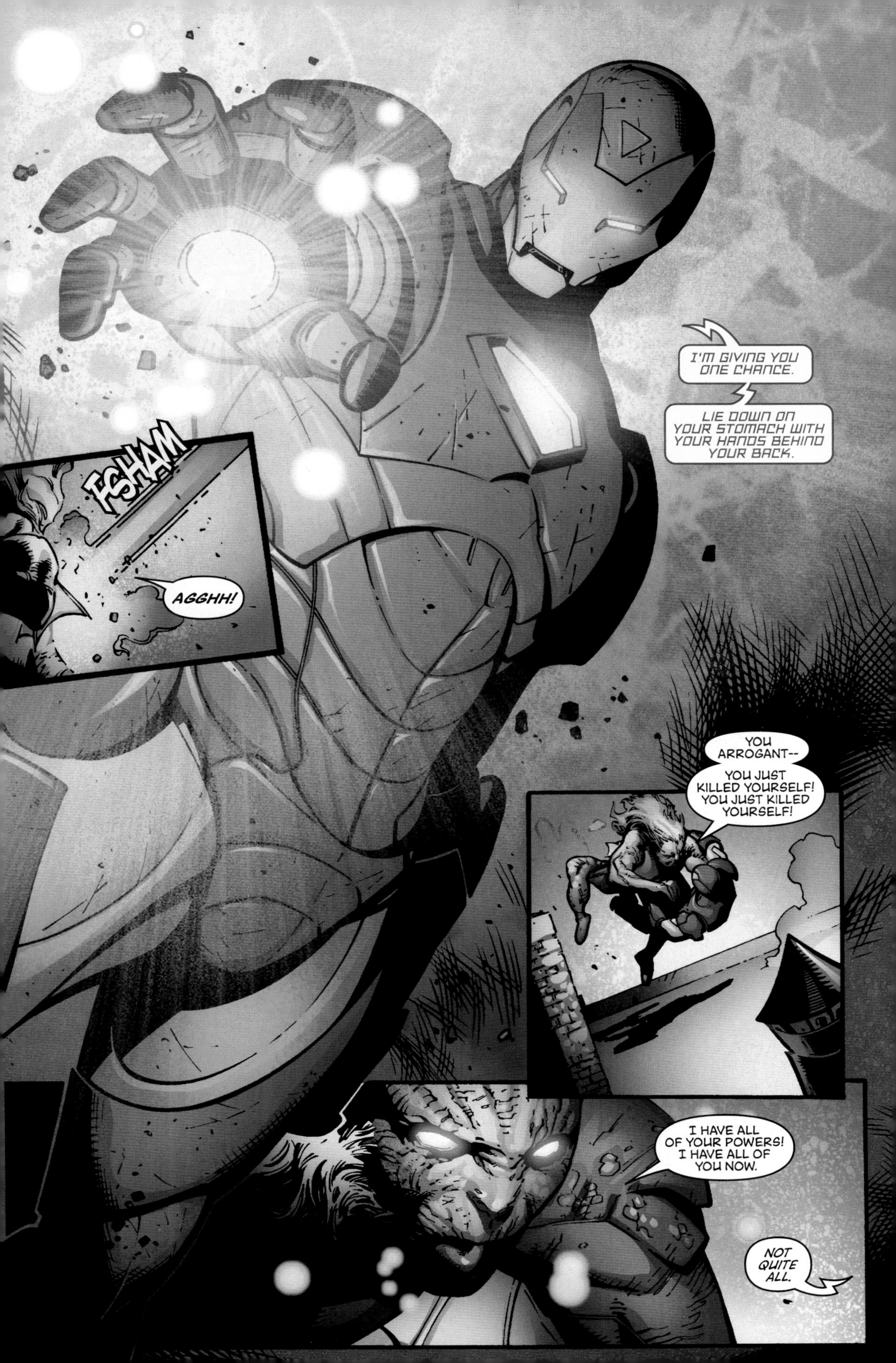

I'M GIVING YOU ONE CHANCE.
LIE DOWN ON YOUR STOMACH WITH YOUR HANDS BEHIND YOUR BACK.
FSHAM
AGGHH!
YOU ARROGANT--
YOU JUST KILLED YOURSELF! YOU JUST KILLED YOURSELF!
I HAVE ALL OF YOUR POWERS! I HAVE ALL OF YOU NOW.
NOT QUITE ALL.

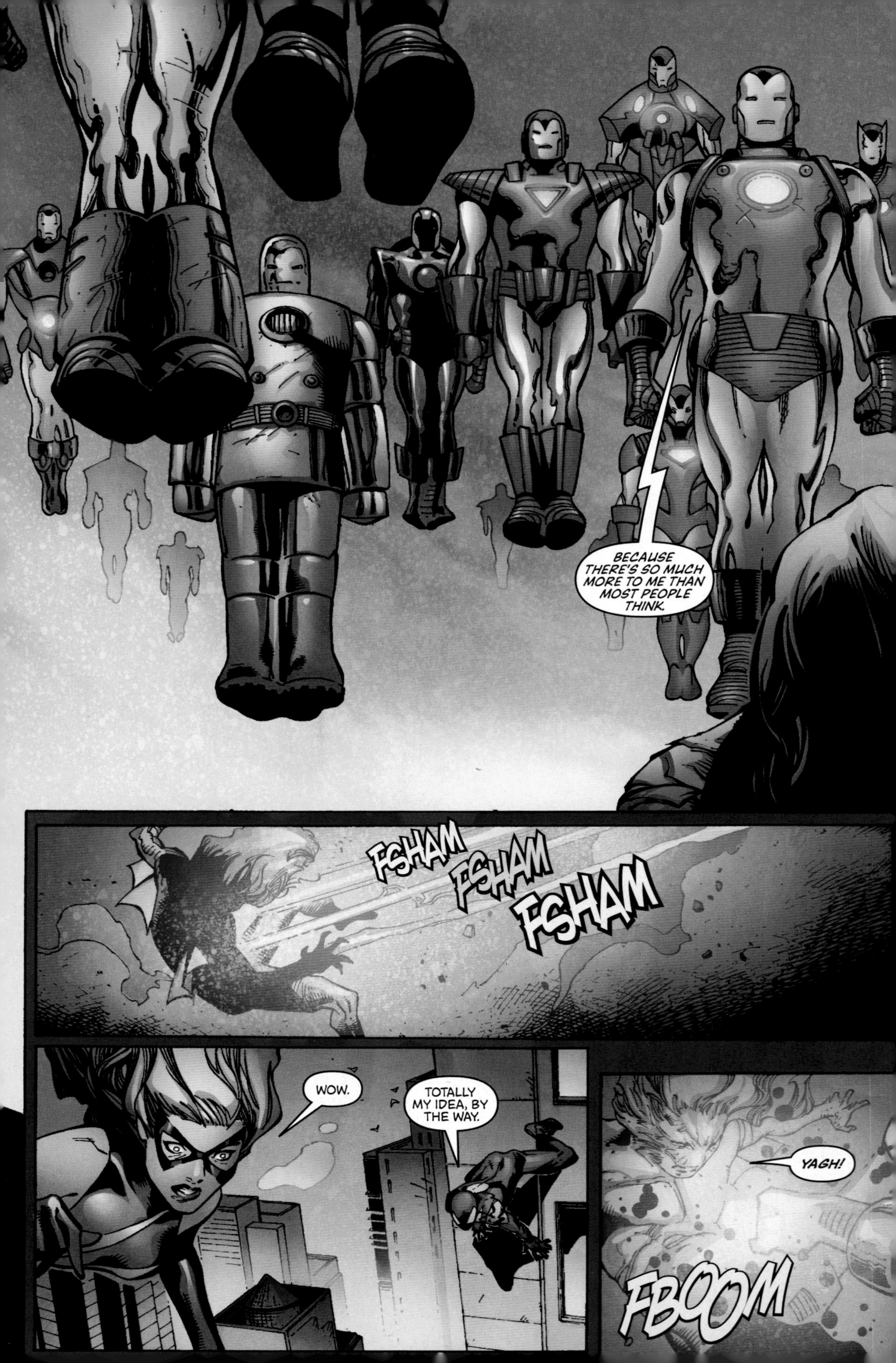
BECAUSE THERE'S SO MUCH MORE TO ME THAN MOST PEOPLE THINK.
FSHAM FSHAM FSHAM
WOW.
TOTALLY MY IDEA, BY THE WAY.
YAGH!
FBOOM

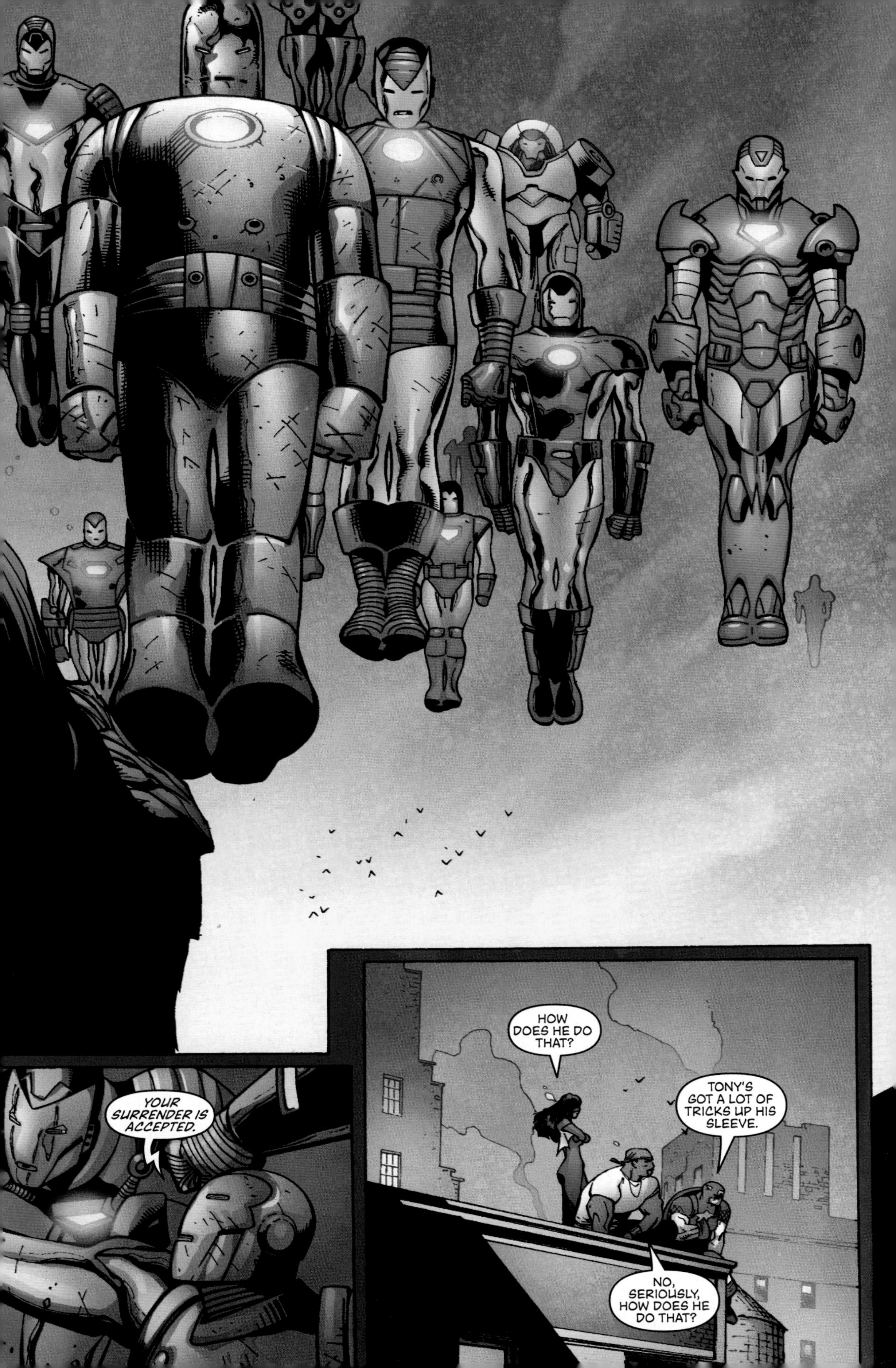
HOW DOES HE DO THAT?
TONY'S GOT A LOT OF TRICKS UP HIS SLEEVE.
NO, SERIOUSLY, HOW DOES HE DO THAT?
YOUR SURRENDER IS ACCEPTED.

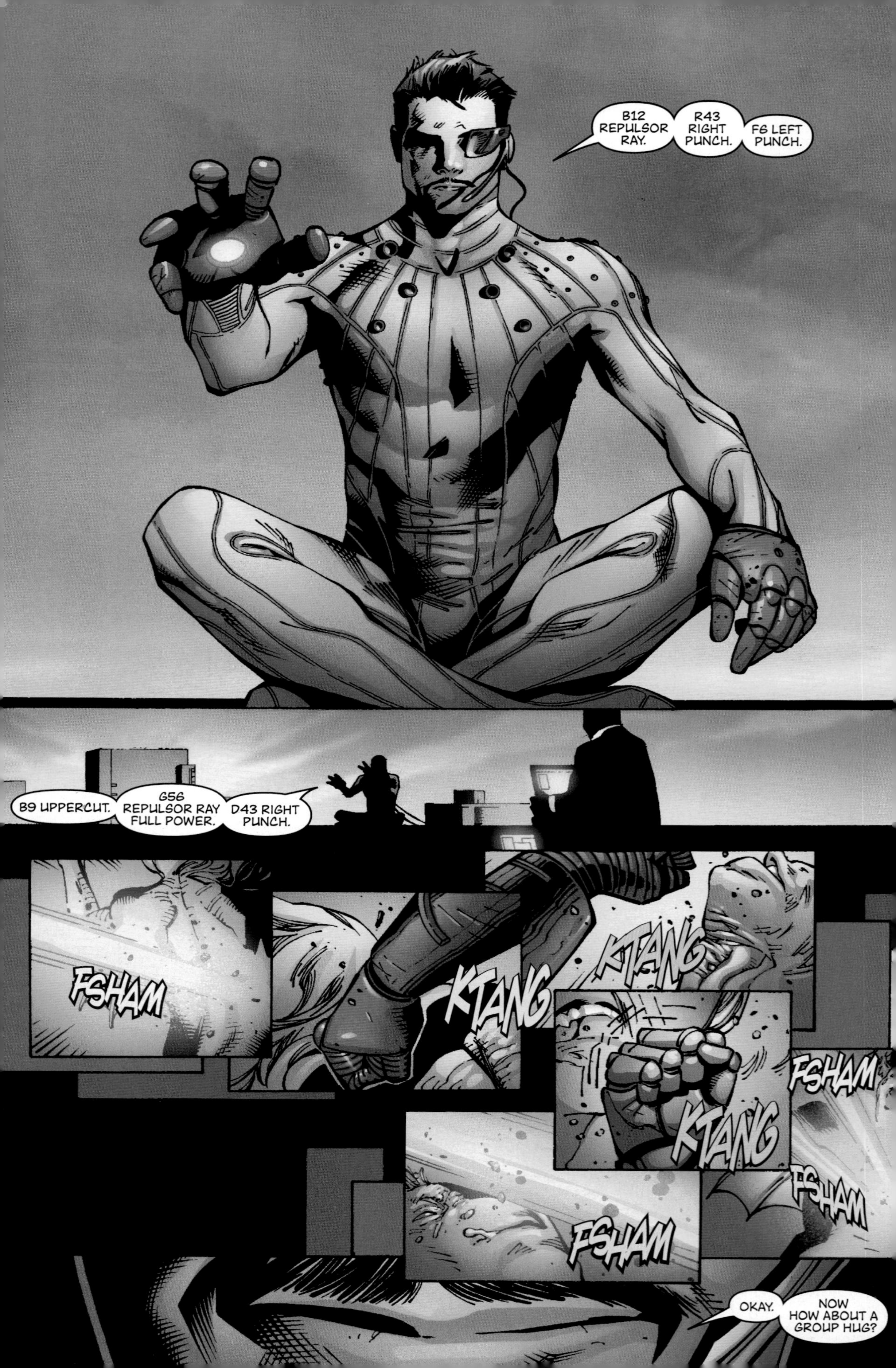
B12 REPULSOR RAY.
R43 RIGHT PUNCH.
F6 LEFT PUNCH.
B9 UPPERCUT.
G56 REPULSOR RAY FULL POWER.
D43 RIGHT PUNCH.
FSHAM
KTANG
KTANG
KTANG
FSHAM
FSHAM
FSHAM
OKAY.
NOW HOW ABOUT A GROUP HUG?

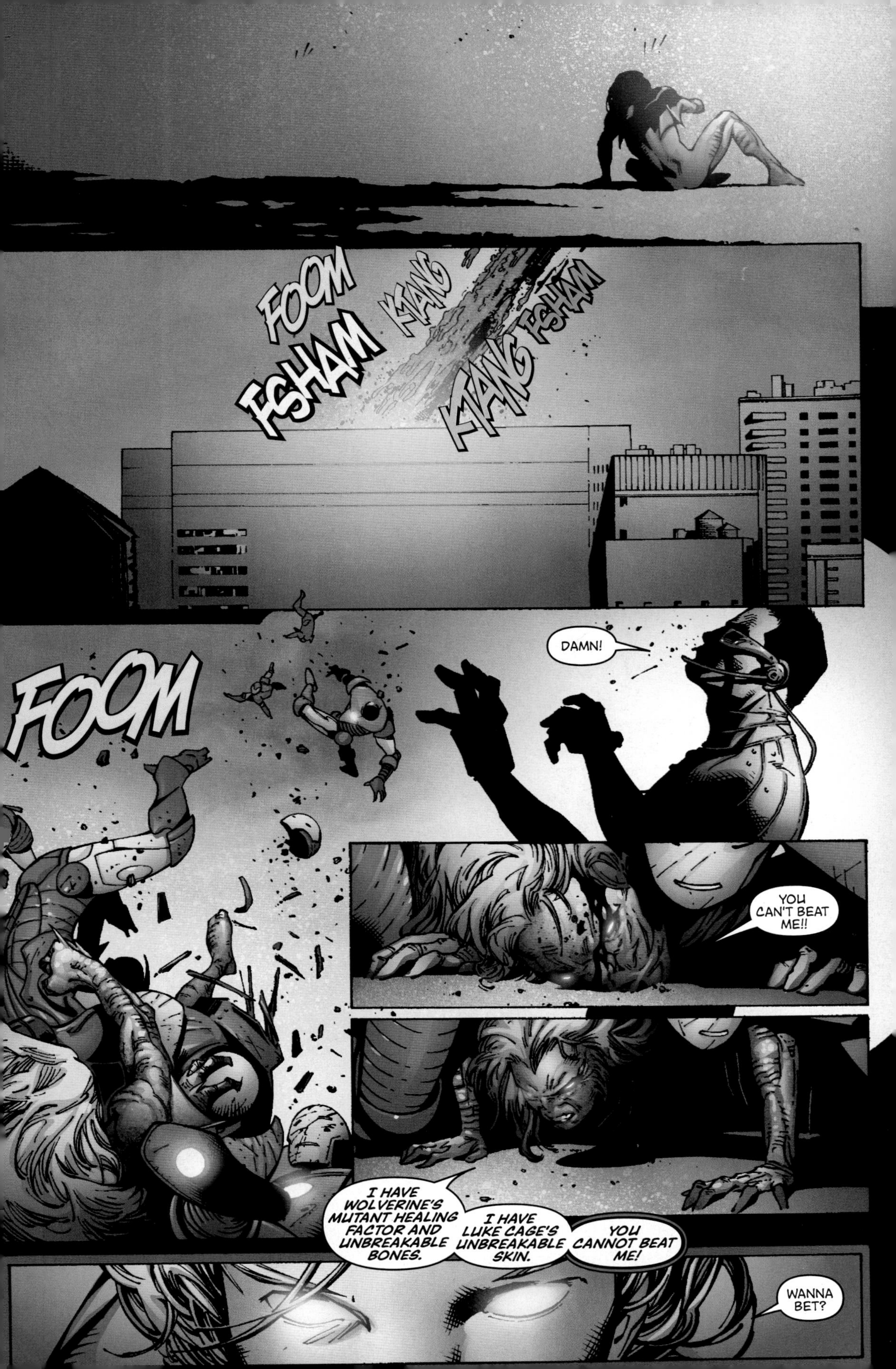
FOOM
FSHAM
KTANG
KTANG
FSHAM
FOOM
DAMN!
YOU CAN'T BEAT ME!!
I HAVE WOLVERINE'S MUTANT HEALING FACTOR AND UNBREAKABLE BONES.
I HAVE LUKE CAGE'S UNBREAKABLE SKIN.
YOU CANNOT BEAT ME!
WANNA BET?

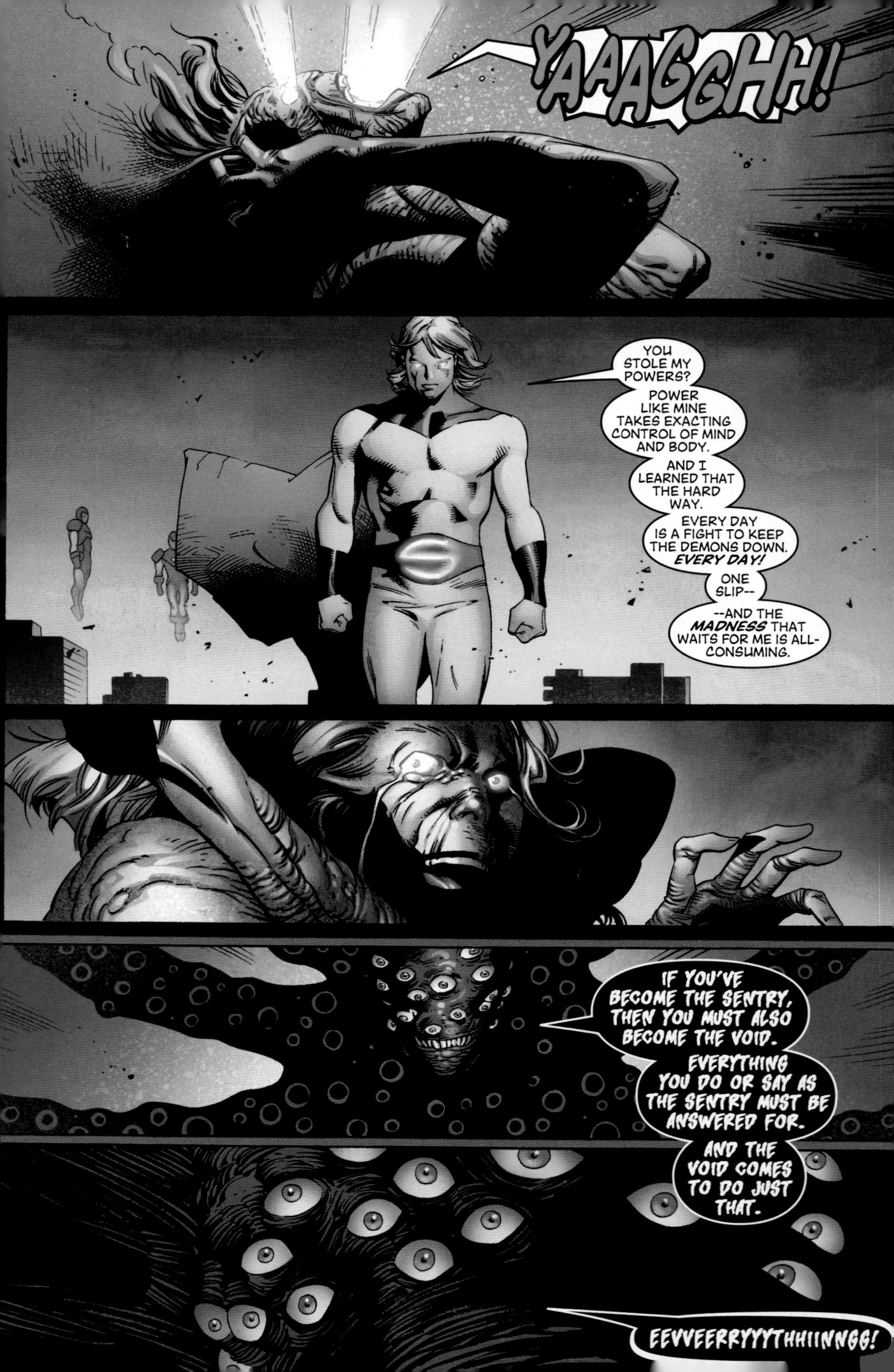
YAAAGGHH!
YOU STOLE MY POWERS?
POWER LIKE MINE TAKES EXACTING CONTROL OF MIND AND BODY.
AND I LEARNED THAT THE HARD WAY.
EVERY DAY IS A FIGHT TO KEEP THE DEMONS DOWN. EVERY DAY!
ONE SLIP--
--AND THE MADNESS THAT WAITS FOR ME IS ALL-CONSUMING.
IF YOU'VE BECOME THE SENTRY, THEN YOU MUST ALSO BECOME THE VOID.
EVERYTHING YOU DO OR SAY AS THE SENTRY MUST BE ANSWERED FOR.
AND THE VOID COMES TO DO JUST THAT.
EEVVEERRYYYTHHIINNGG!

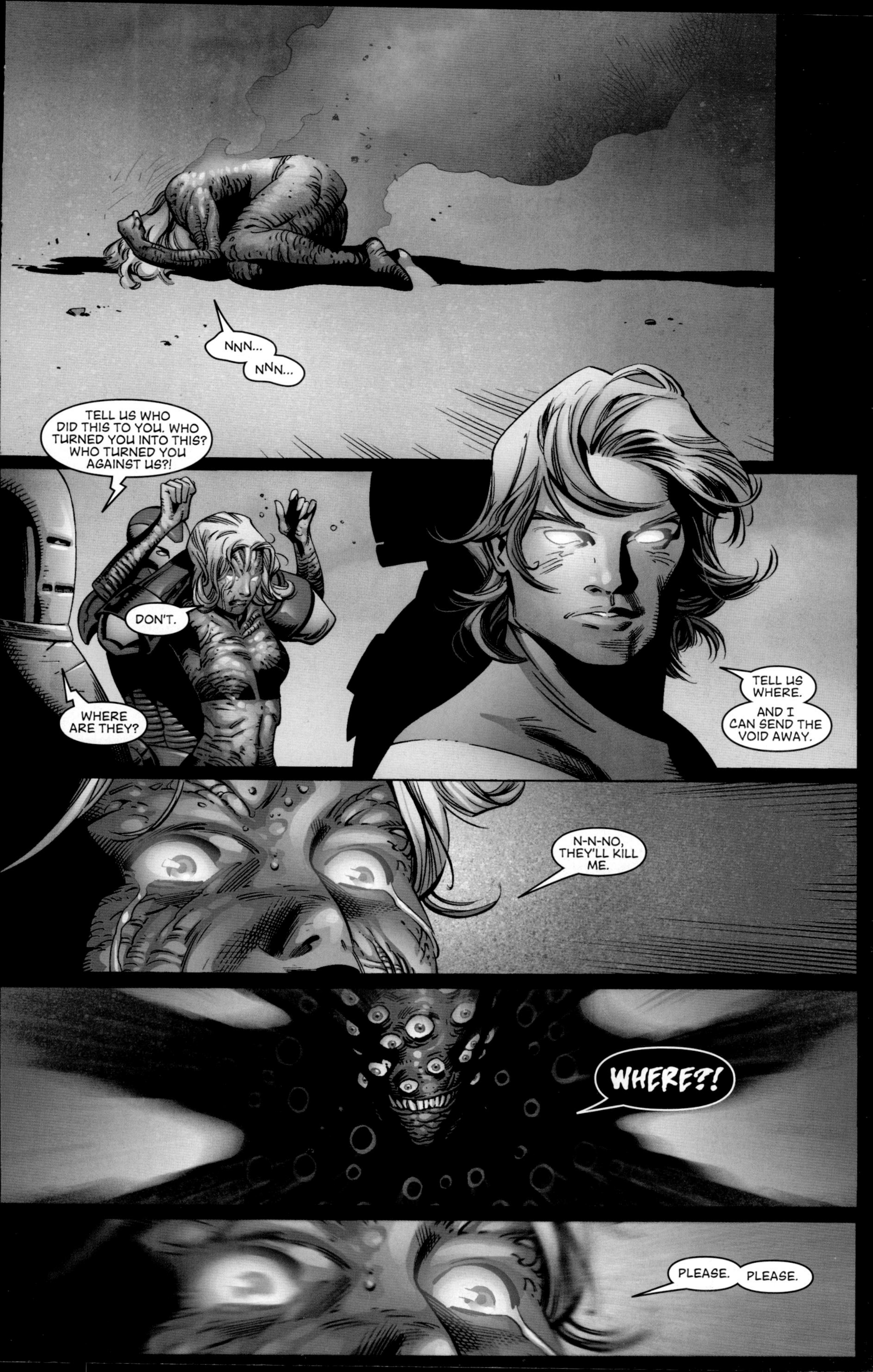
NNN...
NNN...
TELL US WHO DID THIS TO YOU. WHO TURNED YOU INTO THIS? WHO TURNED YOU AGAINST US?!
DON'T.
WHERE ARE THEY?
TELL US WHERE.
AND I CAN SEND THE VOID AWAY.
N-N-NO, THEY'LL KILL ME.
WHERE?!
PLEASE.
PLEASE.

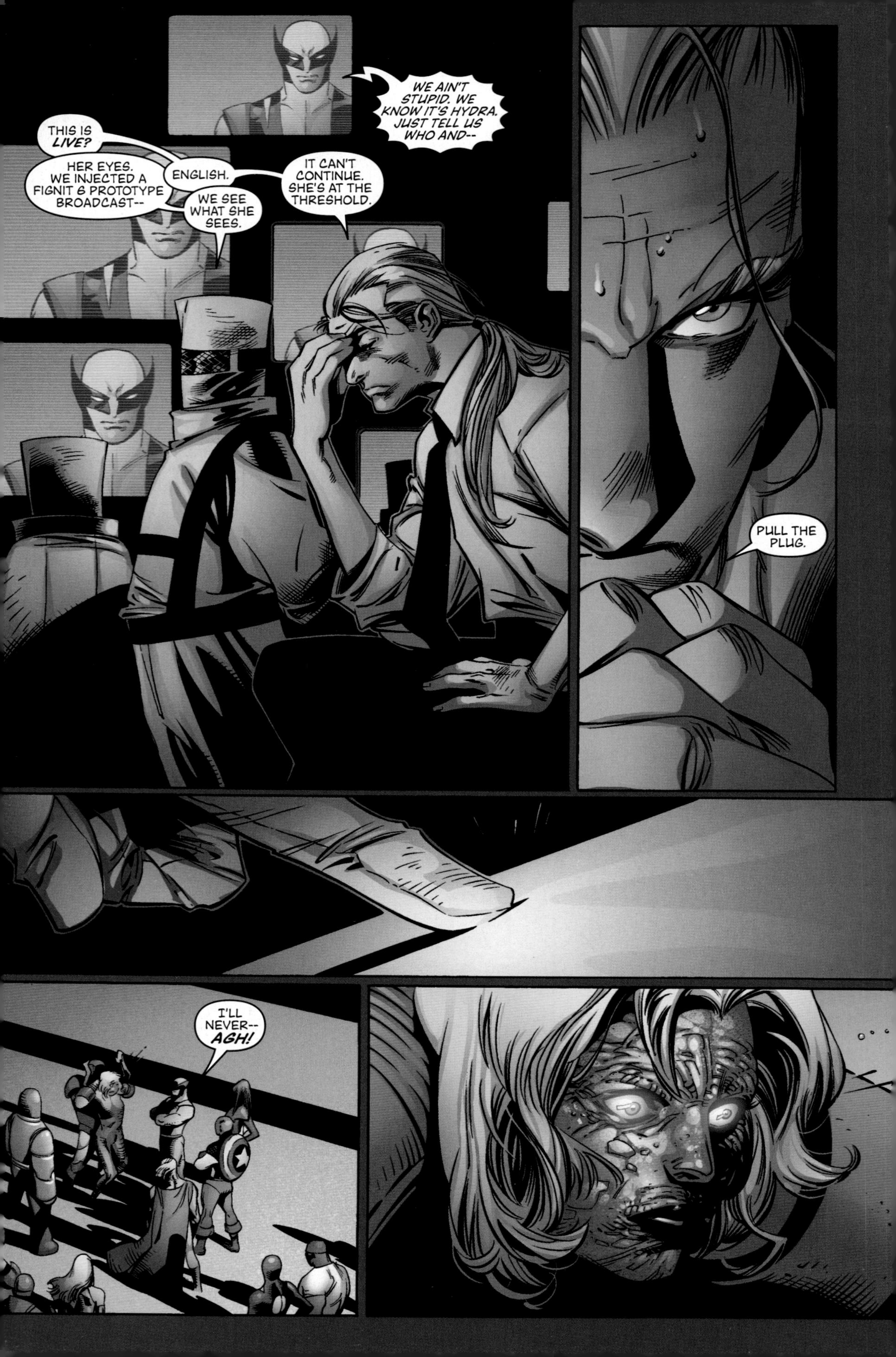
WE AIN'T STUPID. WE KNOW IT'S HYDRA. JUST TELL US WHO AND--
THIS IS LIVE?
HER EYES. WE INJECTED A FIGNIT 6 PROTOTYPE BROADCAST--
ENGLISH.
WE SEE WHAT SHE SEES.
IT CAN'T CONTINUE. SHE'S AT THE THRESHOLD.
PULL THE PLUG.
I'LL NEVER-- AGH!

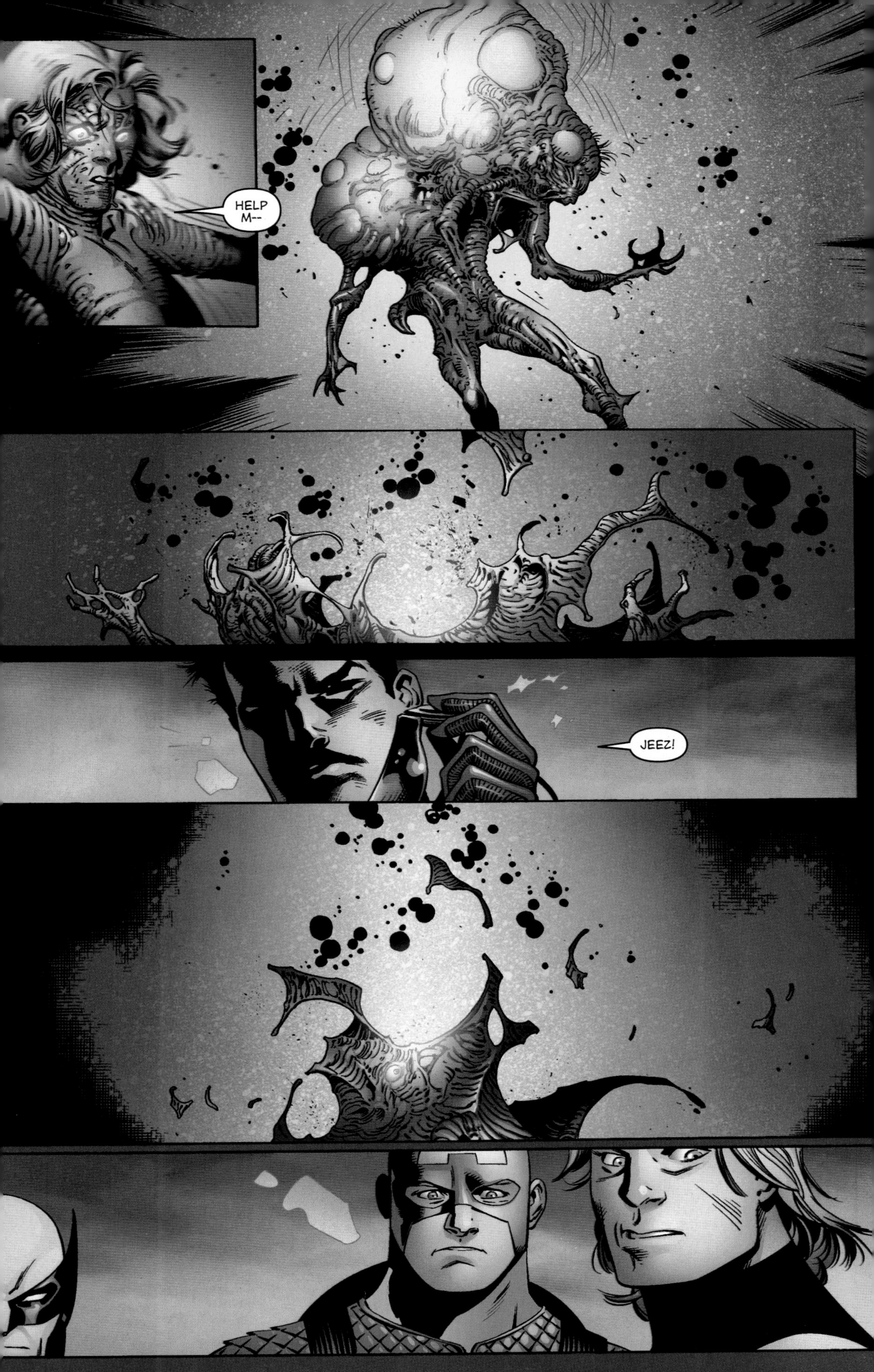
HELP M--
JEEZ!

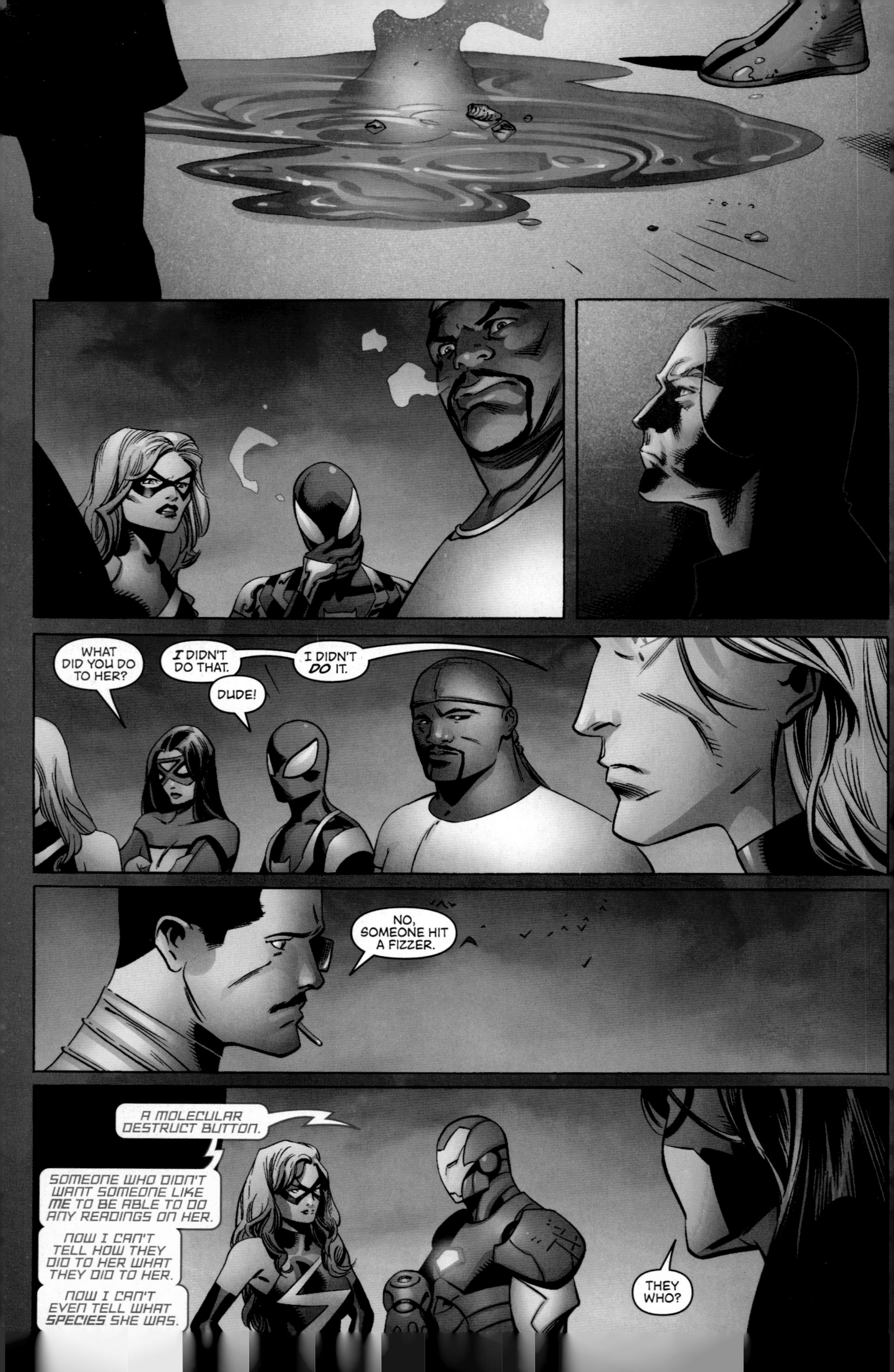
WHAT DID YOU DO TO HER?
I DIDN'T DO THAT.
DUDE!
I DIDN'T DO IT.
NO, SOMEONE HIT A FIZZER.
A MOLECULAR DESTRUCT BUTTON.
SOMEONE WHO DIDN'T WANT SOMEONE LIKE ME TO BE ABLE TO DO ANY READINGS ON HER.
NOW I CAN'T TELL HOW THEY DID TO HER WHAT THEY DID TO HER.
NOW I CAN'T EVEN TELL WHAT SPECIES SHE WAS.
THEY WHO?

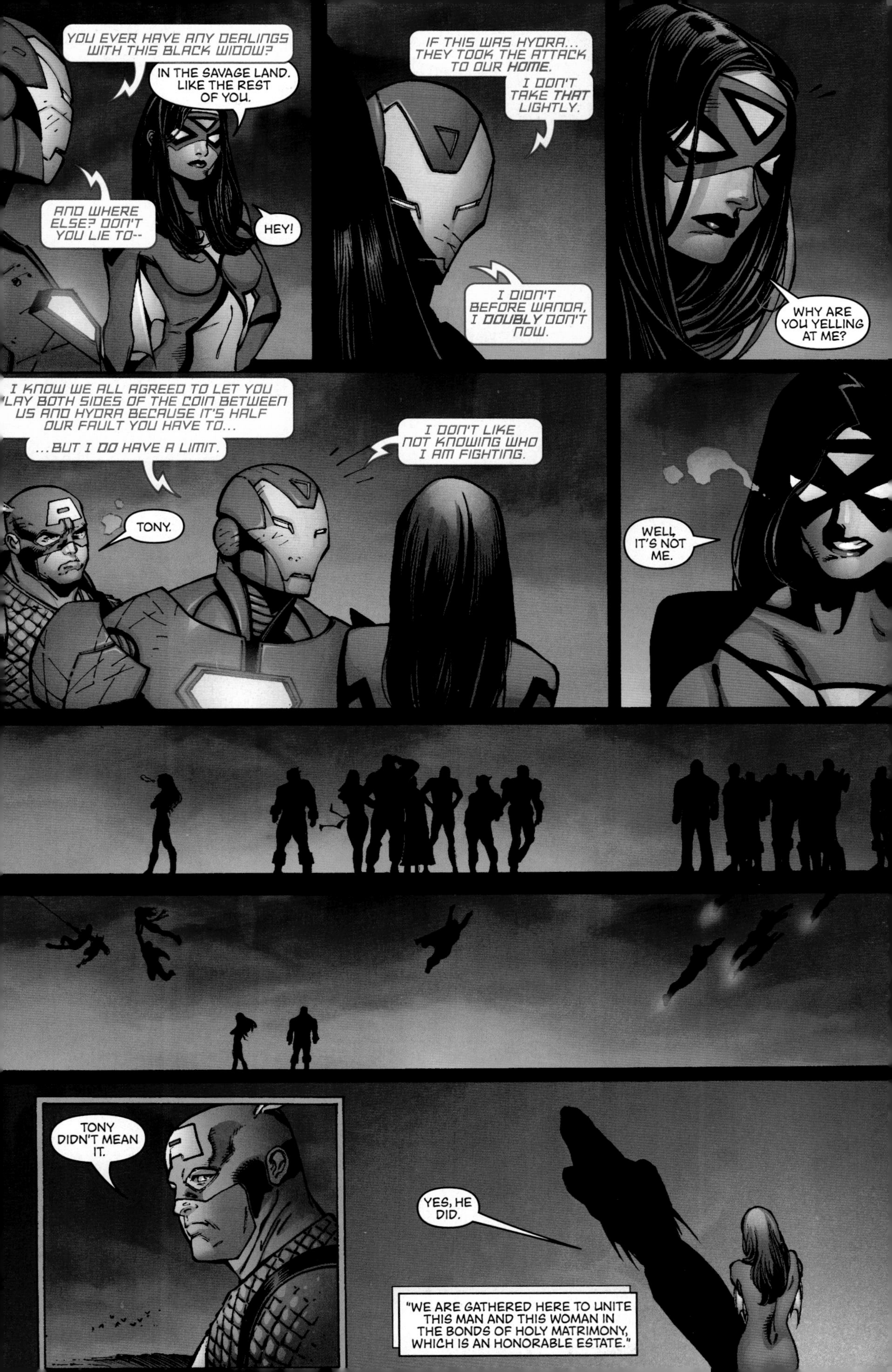
YOU EVER HAVE ANY DEALINGS WITH THIS BLACK WIDOW?
IN THE SAVAGE LAND. LIKE THE REST OF YOU.
AND WHERE ELSE? DON'T YOU LIE TO--
HEY!
IF THIS WAS HYDRA... THEY TOOK THE ATTACK TO OUR HOME.
I DON'T TAKE THAT LIGHTLY.
I DIDN'T BEFORE WANDA, I DOUBLY DON'T NOW.
WHY ARE YOU YELLING AT ME?
I KNOW WE ALL AGREED TO LET YOU PLAY BOTH SIDES OF THE COIN BETWEEN US AND HYDRA BECAUSE IT'S HALF OUR FAULT YOU HAVE TO...
...BUT I DO HAVE A LIMIT.
I DON'T LIKE NOT KNOWING WHO I AM FIGHTING.
TONY.
WELL, IT'S NOT ME.
TONY DIDN'T MEAN IT.
YES, HE DID.
"WE ARE GATHERED HERE TO UNITE THIS MAN AND THIS WOMAN IN THE BONDS OF HOLY MATRIMONY, WHICH IS AN HONORABLE ESTATE."

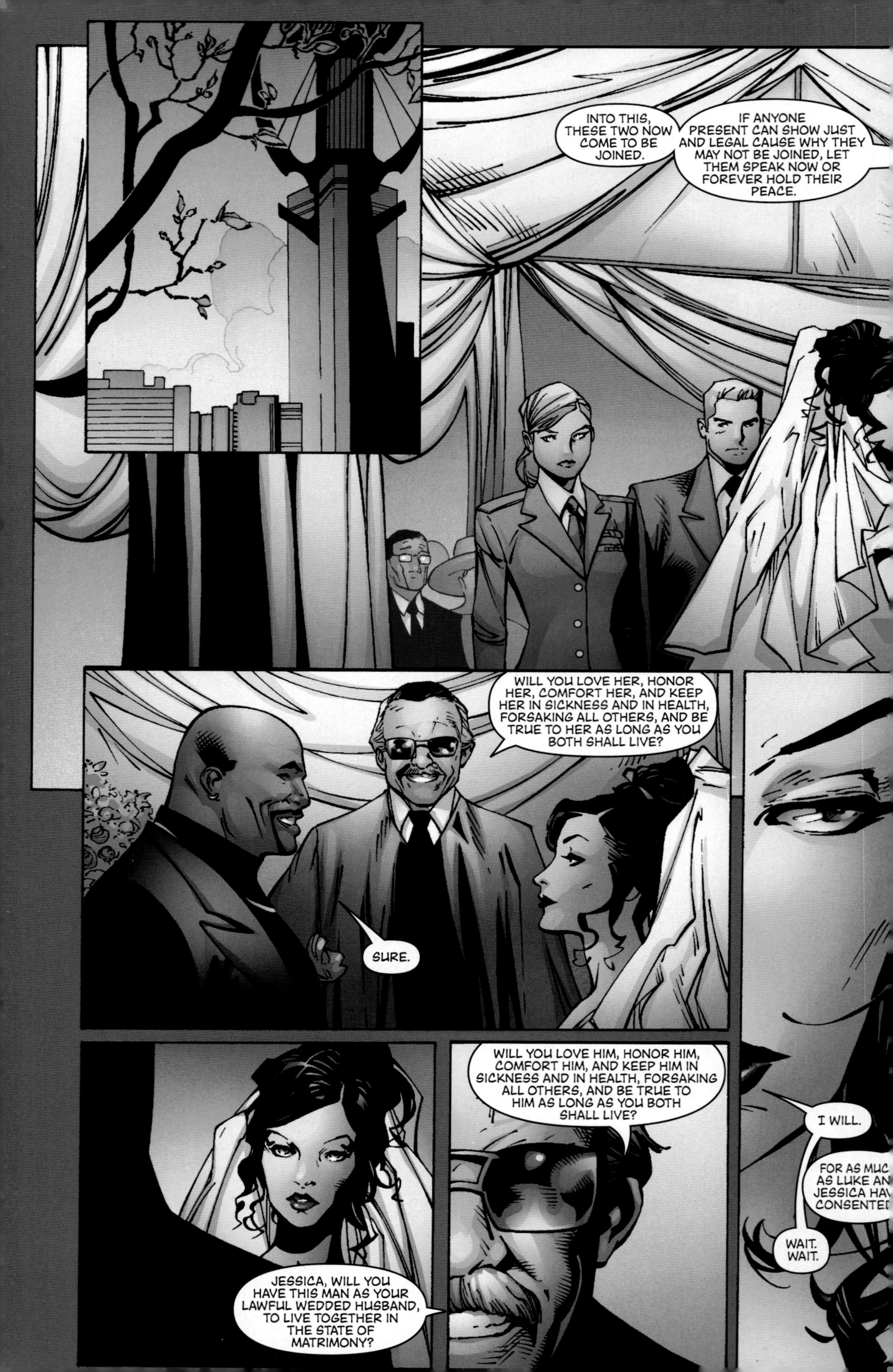
INTO THIS, THESE TWO NOW COME TO BE JOINED.
IF ANYONE PRESENT CAN SHOW JUST AND LEGAL CAUSE WHY THEY MAY NOT BE JOINED, LET THEM SPEAK NOW OR FOREVER HOLD THEIR PEACE.
WILL YOU LOVE HER, HONOR HER, COMFORT HER, AND KEEP HER IN SICKNESS AND IN HEALTH, FORSAKING ALL OTHERS, AND BE TRUE TO HER AS LONG AS YOU BOTH SHALL LIVE?
SURE.
JESSICA, WILL YOU HAVE THIS MAN AS YOUR LAWFUL WEDDED HUSBAND, TO LIVE TOGETHER IN THE STATE OF MATRIMONY?
WILL YOU LOVE HIM, HONOR HIM, COMFORT HIM, AND KEEP HIM IN SICKNESS AND IN HEALTH, FORSAKING ALL OTHERS, AND BE TRUE TO HIM AS LONG AS YOU BOTH SHALL LIVE?
I WILL.
WAIT. WAIT.

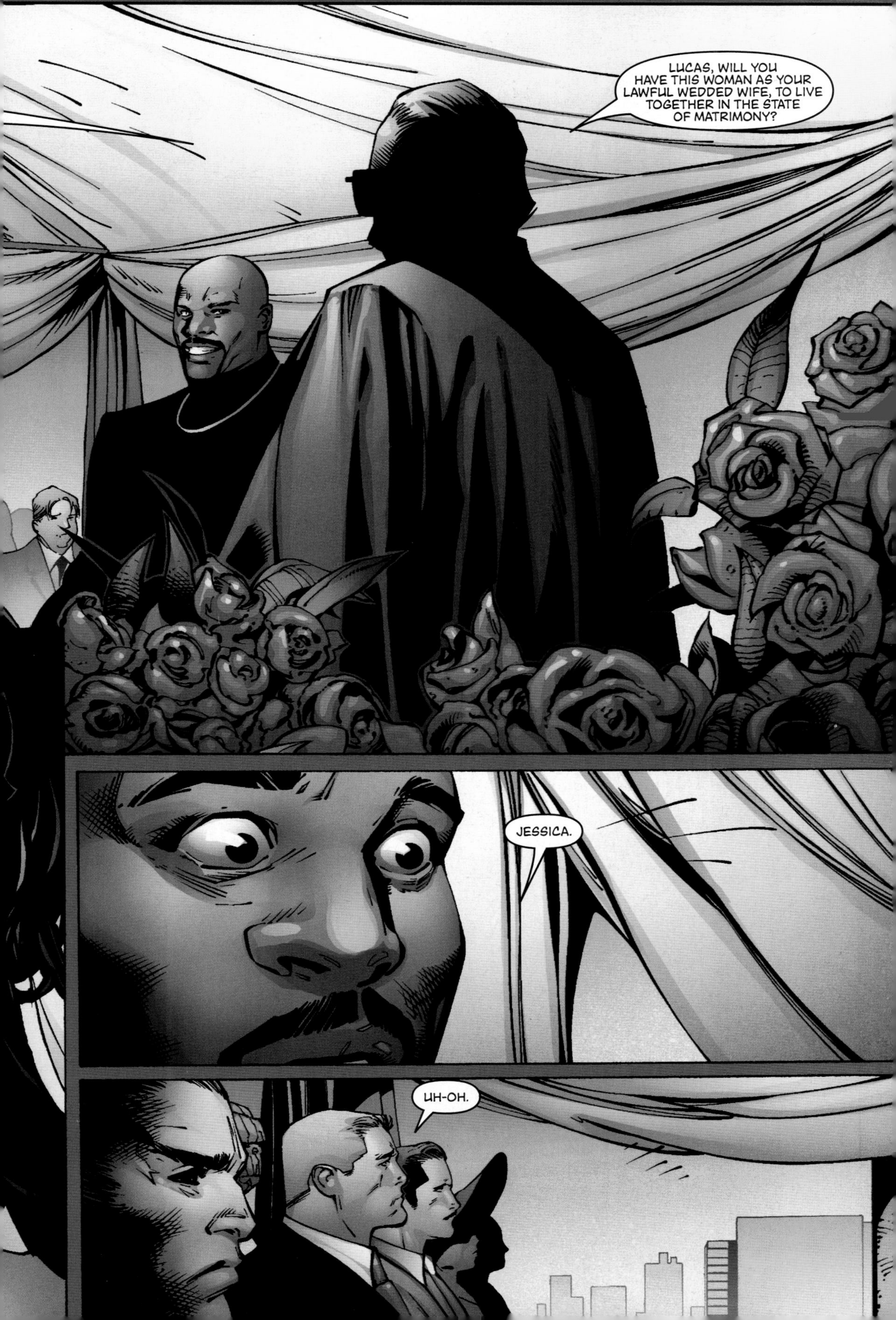
LUCAS, WILL YOU HAVE THIS WOMAN AS YOUR LAWFUL WEDDED WIFE, TO LIVE TOGETHER IN THE STATE OF MATRIMONY?
JESSICA.
UH-OH.

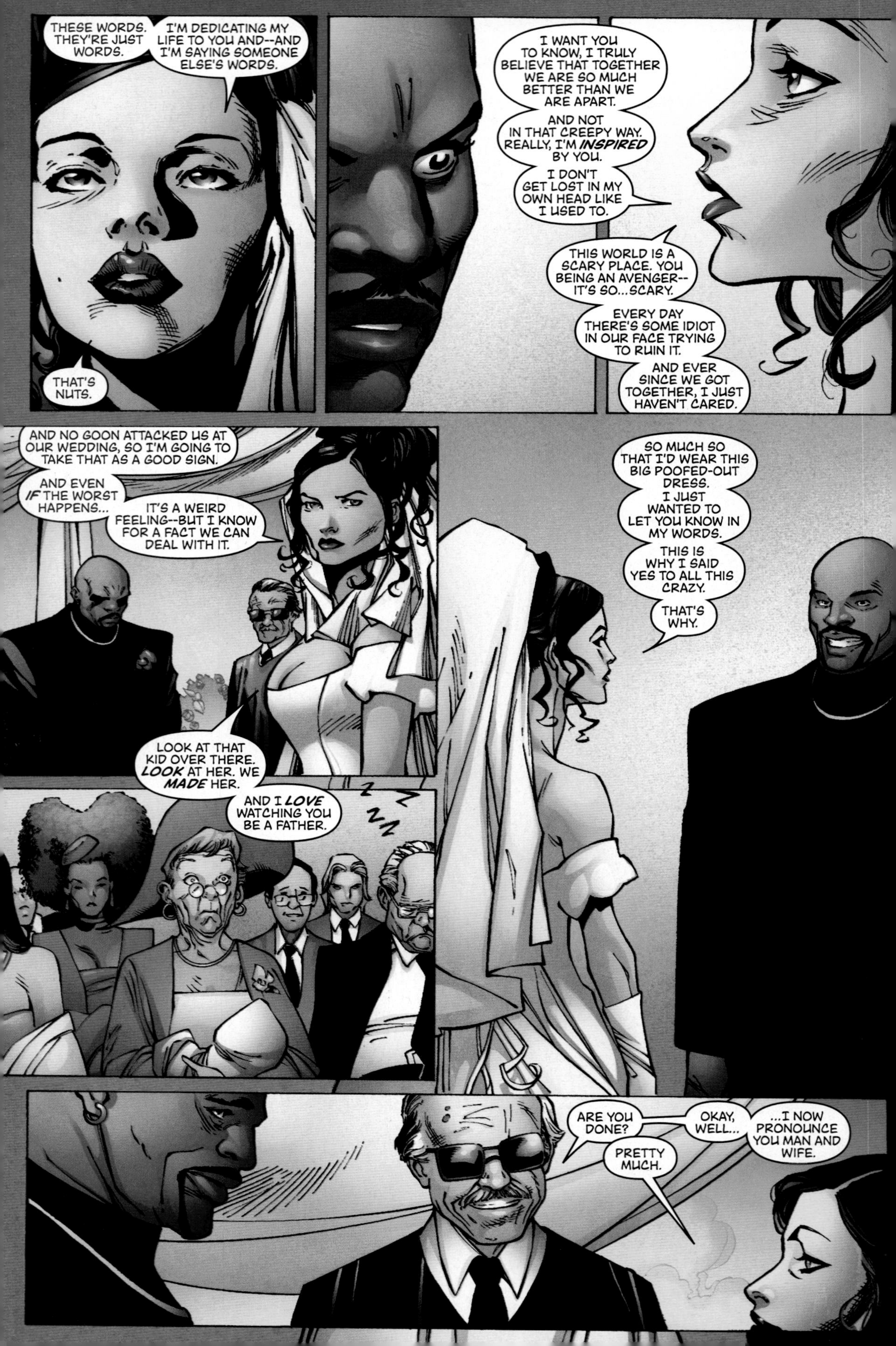
THESE WORDS. THEY'RE JUST WORDS.
I'M DEDICATING MY LIFE TO YOU AND--AND I'M SAYING SOMEONE ELSE'S WORDS.
THAT'S NUTS.
I WANT YOU TO KNOW, I TRULY BELIEVE THAT TOGETHER WE ARE SO MUCH BETTER THAN WE ARE APART.
AND NOT IN THAT CREEPY WAY. REALLY, I'M INSPIRED BY YOU.
I DON'T GET LOST IN MY OWN HEAD LIKE I USED TO.
THIS WORLD IS A SCARY PLACE. YOU BEING AN AVENGER-- IT'S SO...SCARY.
EVERY DAY THERE'S SOME IDIOT IN OUR FACE TRYING TO RUIN IT.
AND EVER SINCE WE GOT TOGETHER, I JUST HAVEN'T CARED.
AND NO GOON ATTACKED US AT OUR WEDDING, SO I'M GOING TO TAKE THAT AS A GOOD SIGN.
AND EVEN IF THE WORST HAPPENS...
IT'S A WEIRD FEELING--BUT I KNOW FOR A FACT WE CAN DEAL WITH IT.
LOOK AT THAT KID OVER THERE. LOOK AT HER. WE MADE HER.
AND I LOVE WATCHING YOU BE A FATHER.
SO MUCH SO THAT I'D WEAR THIS BIG POOFED-OUT DRESS.
I JUST WANTED TO LET YOU KNOW IN MY WORDS.
THIS IS WHY I SAID YES TO ALL THIS CRAZY.
THAT'S WHY.
ZZZ
ARE YOU DONE?
PRETTY MUCH.
OKAY, WELL...
...I NOW PRONOUNCE YOU MAN AND WIFE.

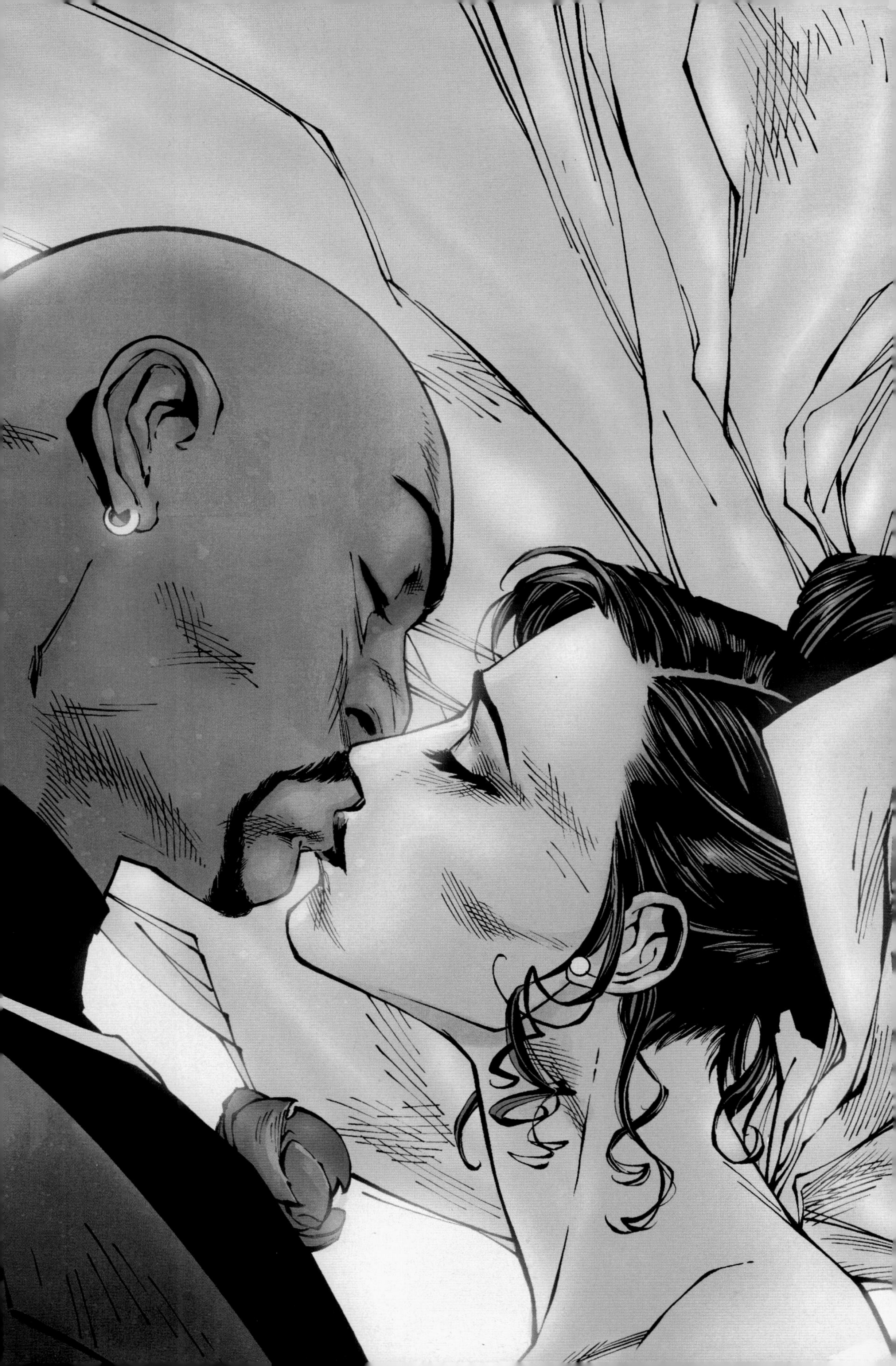

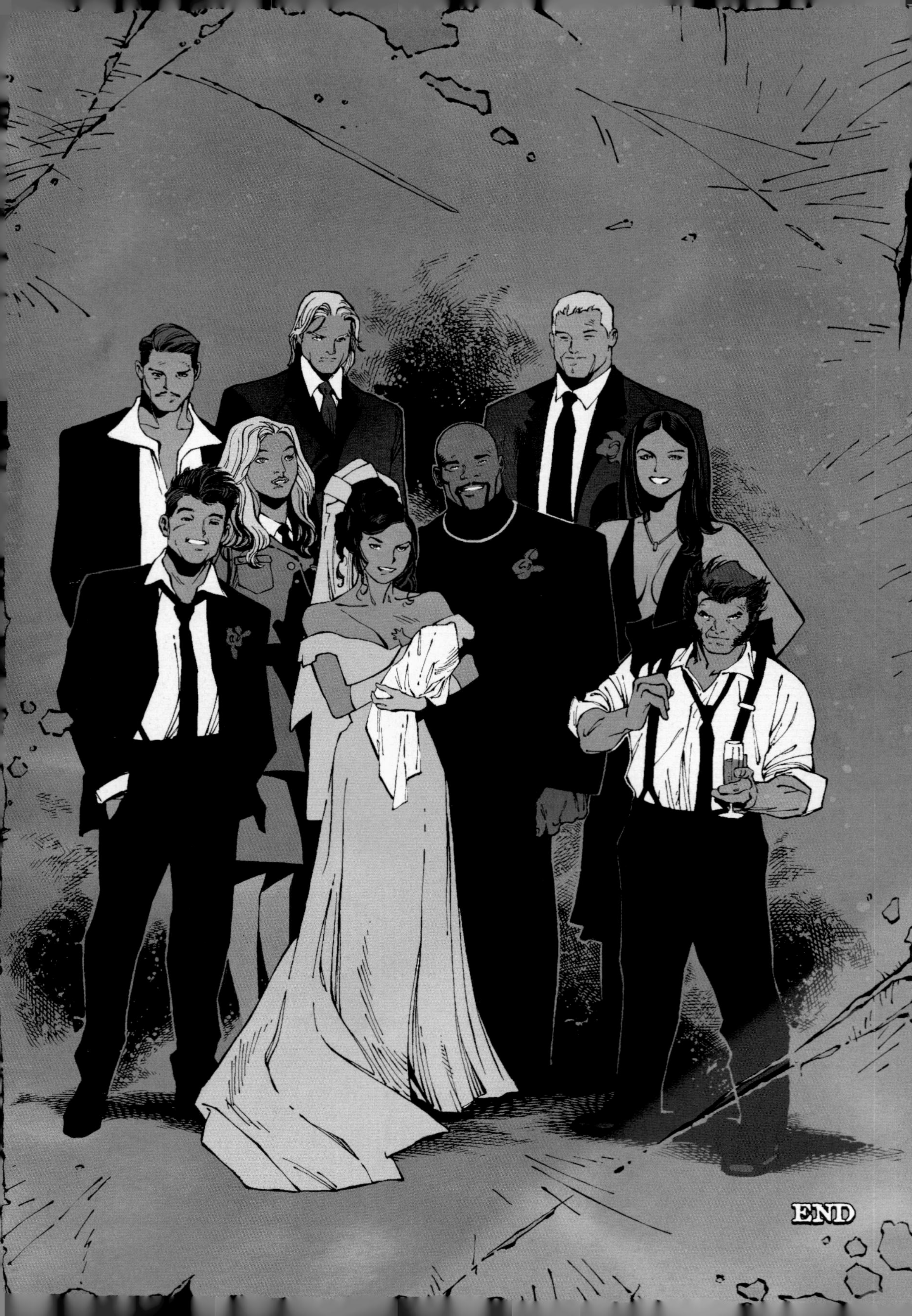
END

THE PULSE

GOODBYE, PULSE!!

Sniff!

I just wrote one of these for DAREDEVIL. I hate writing these. I'm saying goodbye to writing a comic series I completely love writing. Characters I love more than some actual people I know. But, sadly, this is the end of THE PULSE.

WHY??? WHY DO I KEEP DOING THIS TO JESSICA JONES??!!

It's over, is why.

I said what I had to say and we're leaving on a high note, I think. Sadly, the timing of this sucked. We finally got the band back together. Finally we got the entire ALIAS art team back together. Finally Gaydos' schedule and this book's schedule aligned; finally Matt Hollingsworth came back to comics just to paint this book. And now the story is over. The book is done.

Truth is I thought the book would continue after we had left and originally, you might have heard, it was going to, but this is the last issue. Paul Jenkins was supposed to take over this book, but instead will be producing a comic called CIVIL WAR: FRONT LINE that will launch out of the staggering CIVIL WAR event that is coming your way in May. It's the right move for Marvel but sadly, it puts this book on indefinite hiatus. Other books on indefinite hiatus: ROM, SPACEKNIGHTS, US1, and SECRET DEFENDERS. So don't hold your breath :).

But thankfully, we do not leave you empty-handed. You want more Jessica and Luke, look no further than the pages of the NEW AVENGERS ANNUAL that is being drawn even as we speak by my HOUSE OF M pal Olivier Coipel. Will they get married? Will any super-villains crash the wedding? Will we show the honeymoon?

Also, Marvel is in the final stages of production on THE ALIAS OMNIBUS -- every single issue of Jessica Jones' life before THE PULSE in one gorgeous hardcover. It's something I am insanely proud of, and I hope you check it out. Fair warning—it's a Max book and a little raunchy. But if you liked this issue you'll love the Omnibus!

There are so many people to thank. First off, cover artist Mike Mayhew who really delivered some gorgeous, unique, exciting cover work. Three of these covers are my all-time favorite covers I've ever had on any of my comics.

Matt Hollingsworth came back to comics to color this last story and I am eternally grateful.

Michael Gaydos has been with Jessica since day one and this book was not the same without him. Mike is an amazing collaborator and I am just blessed to know him. Mike and I are not done together. Stay tuned.

A very special thank you to Mark Bagley, Brent Anderson and Michael Lark, who really made this unique book a special place for Marvel fans. Andy Schmidt loves this book more than even me and you can tell from his work on it. Thank you, Andy, for all your hard work. Editorial doesn't get the credit it deserves on so many levels. I want you people of the Earth to know, it is not easy to be an editor, it takes a special kind of person.

And of course, you my friends, thank you for making this book successful. Thank you for all your letters and emails about Jessica. Your support for Jessica was seen by Hollywood. In fact, we were this close to getting a Jessica Jones show on TV, maybe one day we still will. That was a crazy experience I'll share with you at a con if you see me.

Though I am leaving this book and it's leaving the shelves, I am not abandoning Jessica, Luke, or the little Cage baby. Promise.

Meanwhile, stop by my Web site Jinxworld.com. The message board is crackling and we'd love to hear from you--unless you're a disgruntled D-Man fan. Then we really don't want to hear from you at all.

See you over at Avengers Tower.

BENDIS!

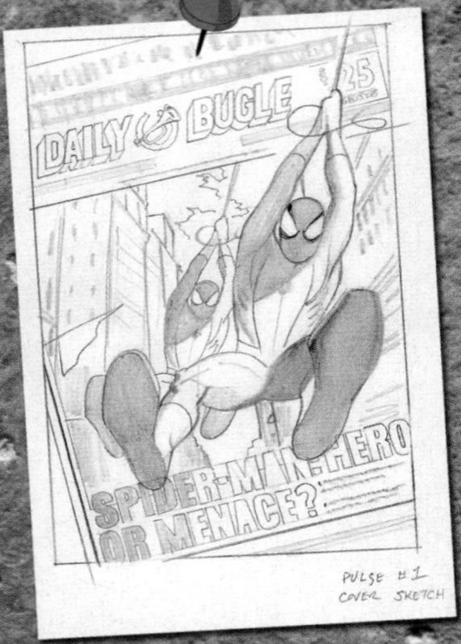
DAILY BUGLE
25
OR MENACE?
PULSE #1
COVER SKETCH

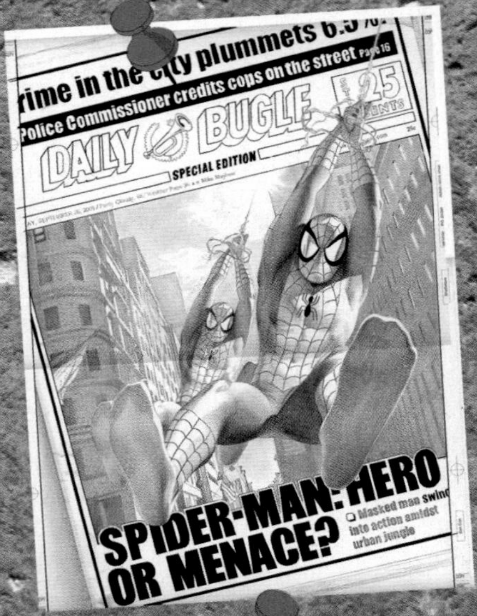
rime in the city plummets 6.5%
Police Commissioner credits cops on the street Page 16
25 CENTS
DAILY BUGLE
SPECIAL EDITION
SPIDER-MAN: HERO
OR MENACE?
Masked man swing
into action amidst
urban jungle

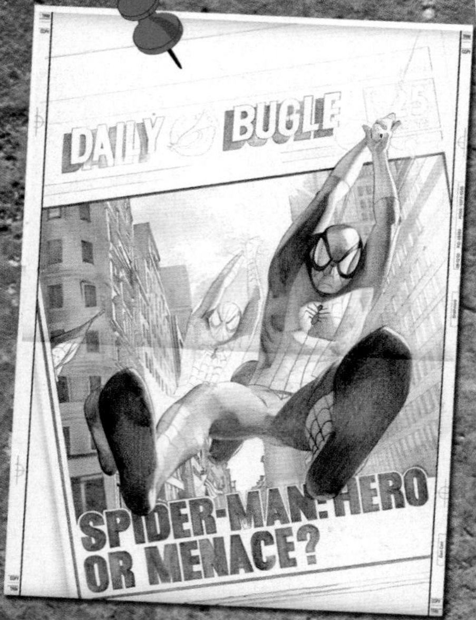
DAILY BUGLE
SPIDER-MAN: HERO
OR MENACE?

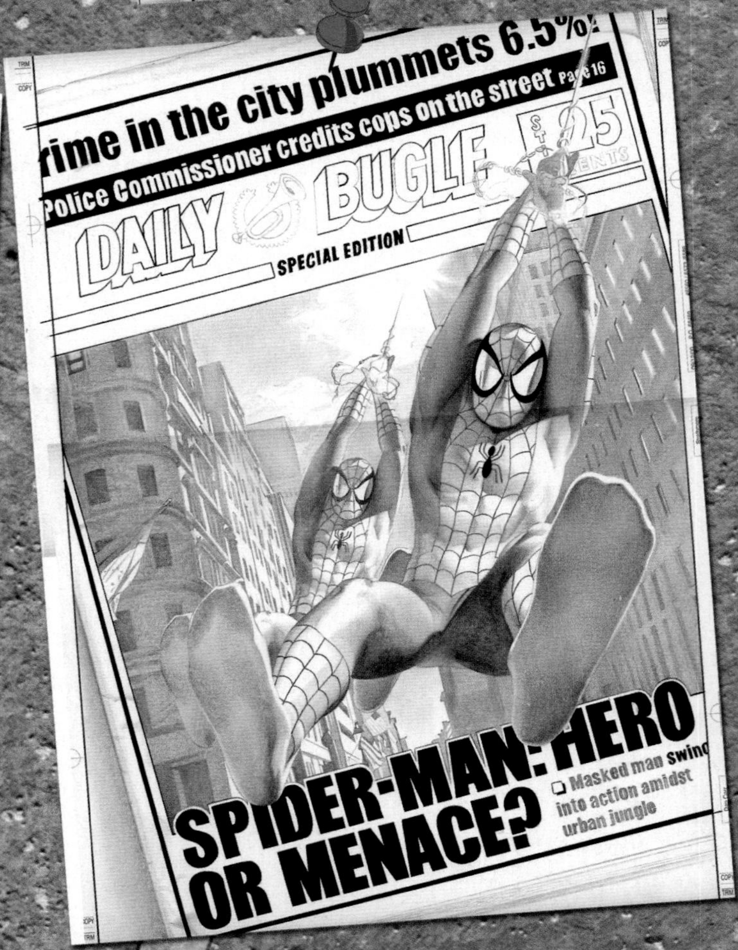
rime in the city plummets 6.5%
Police Commissioner credits cops on the street Page 16
25
DAILY BUGLE
SPECIAL EDITION
SPIDER-MAN: HERO
OR MENACE?
Masked man swing
into action amidst
urban jungle

ISSUE #1 COVER Layouts & Pencils

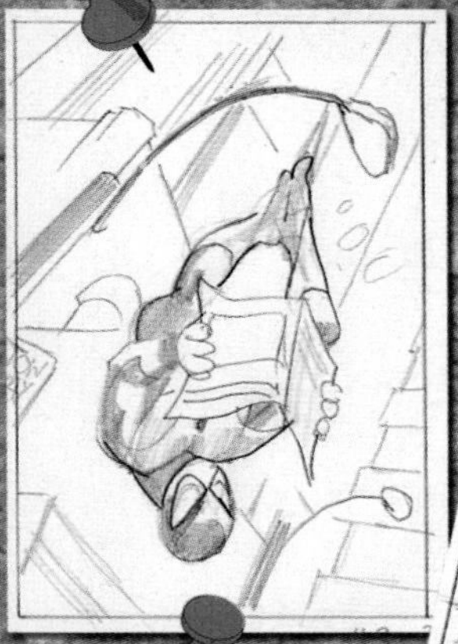

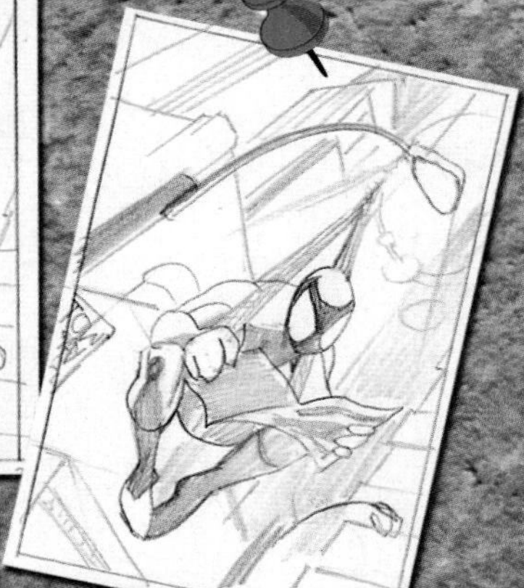

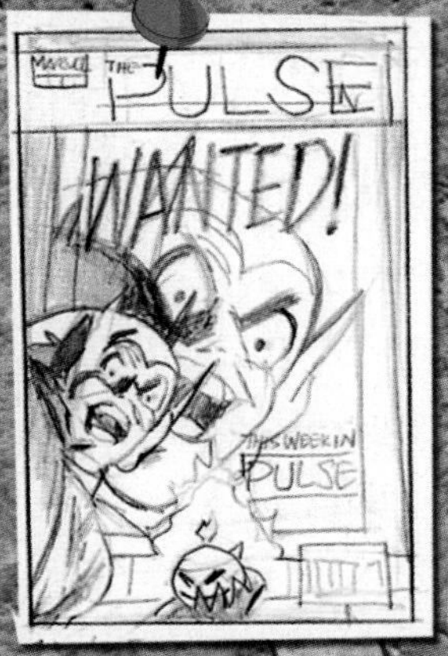
MARVEL THE PULSE
WANTED!
THIS WEEK IN PULSE

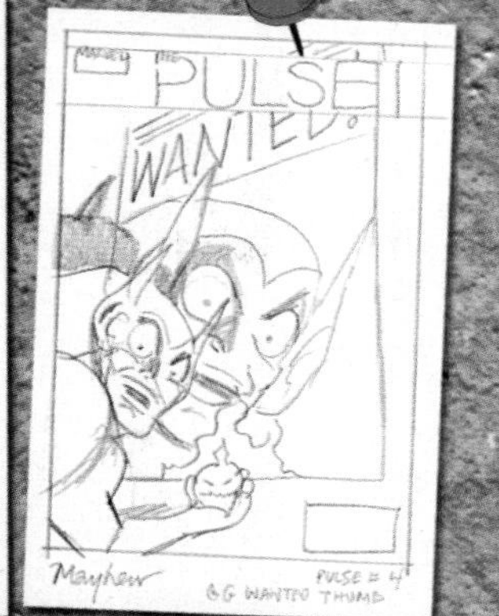
MARVEL THE PULSE
WANTED!
Mayhew
PULSE # 4
GG WANTED THUMB

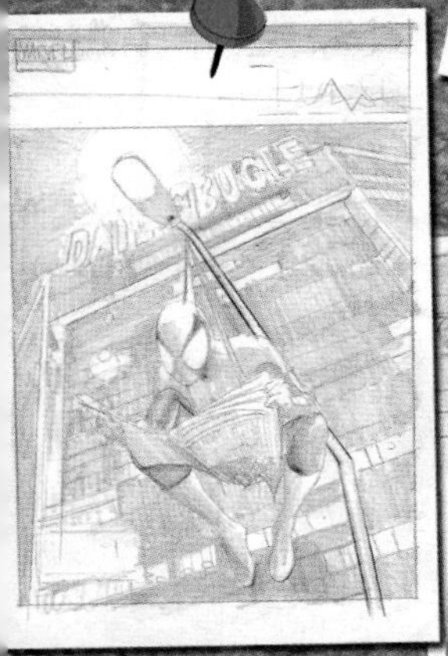
DAILY BUGLE

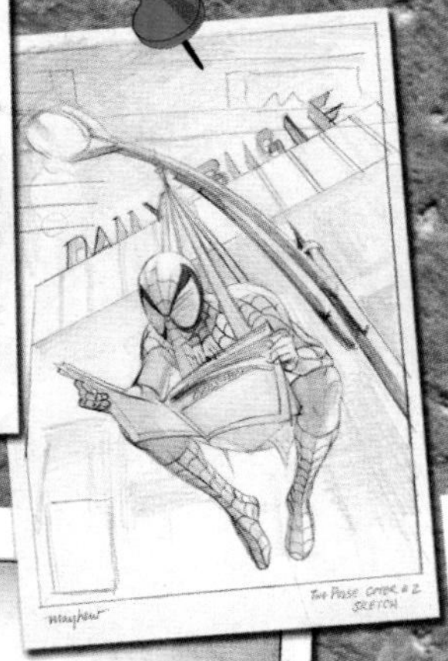
DAILY BUGLE
Mayhew
THE PULSE COVER #2 SKETCH

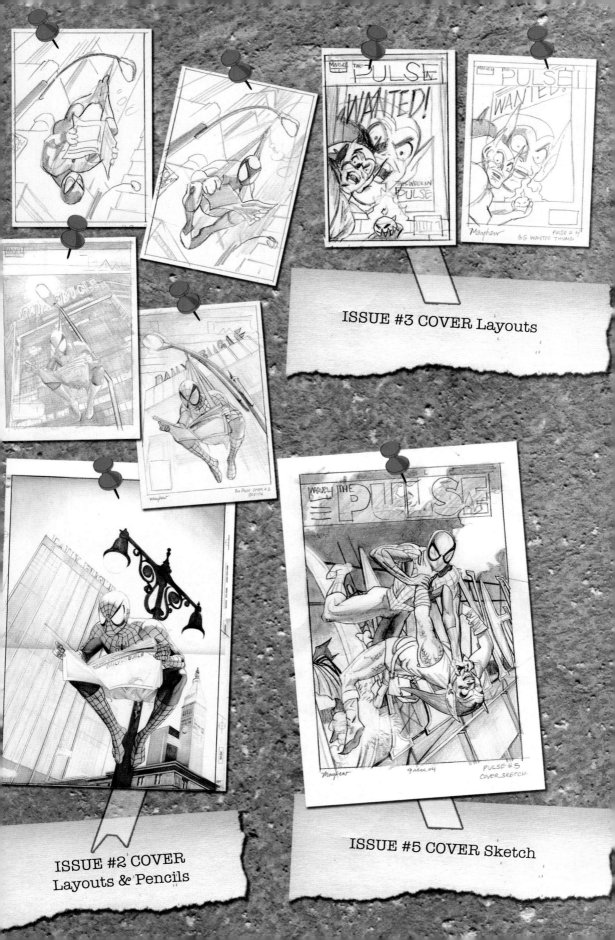

ISSUE #3 COVER Layouts

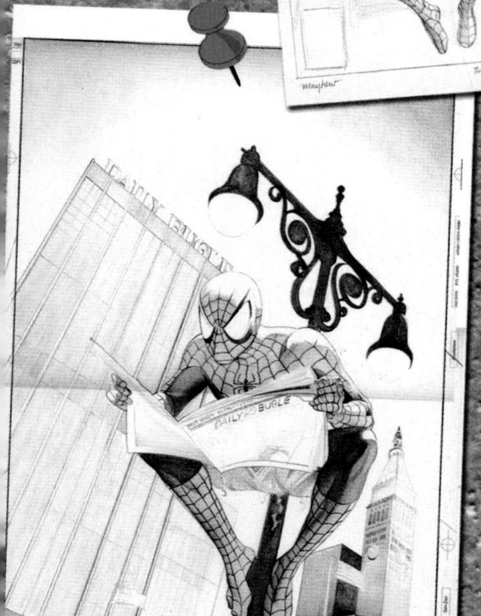
DAILY BUGLE

ISSUE #2 COVER
Layouts & Pencils

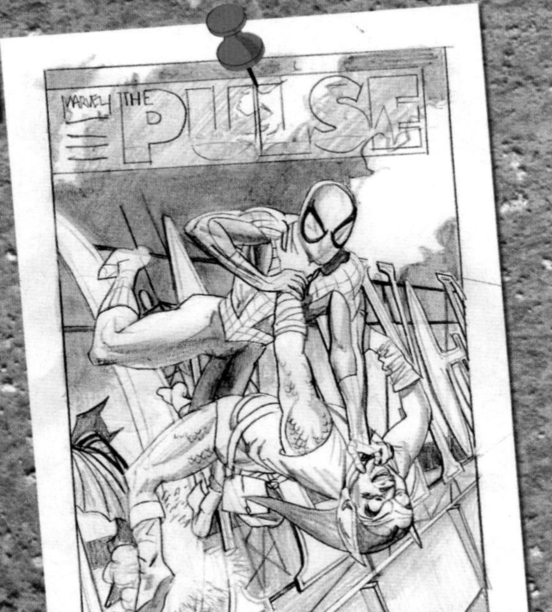
MARVEL THE PULSE
Mayhew
9 MAR 04
PULSE #5
COVER SKETCH

ISSUE #5 COVER Sketch

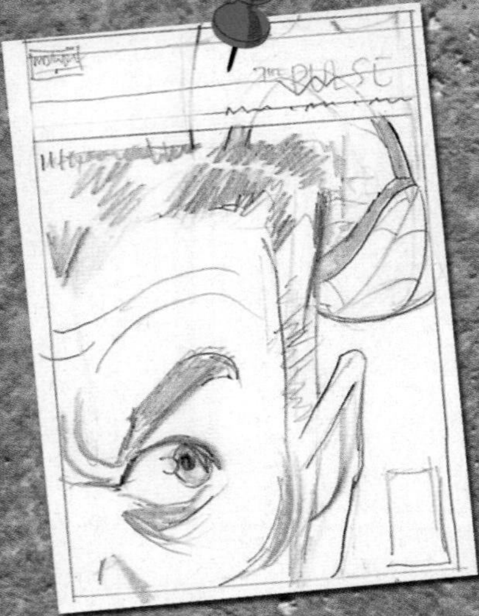
PULSE

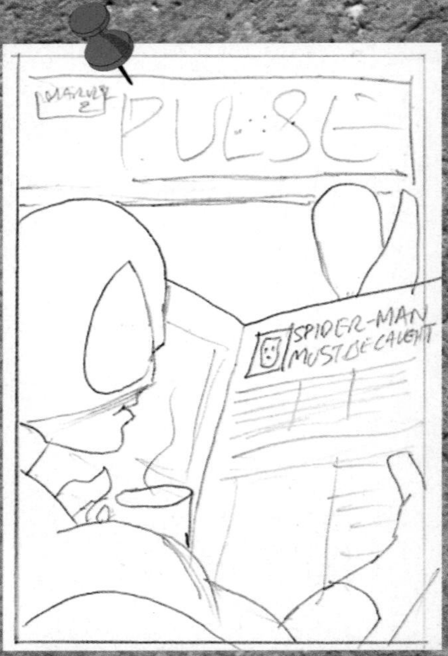
MARVEL
2
PULSE
SPIDER-MAN
MUST BE CAUGHT

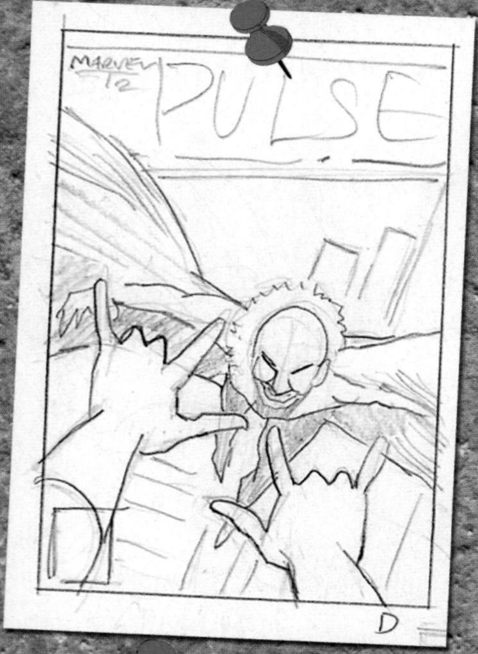
MARVEL
12
PULSE
D

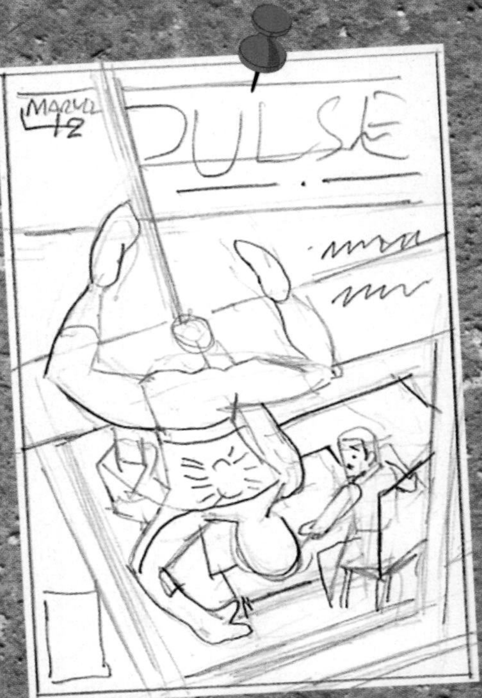
MARVEL
12
PULSE

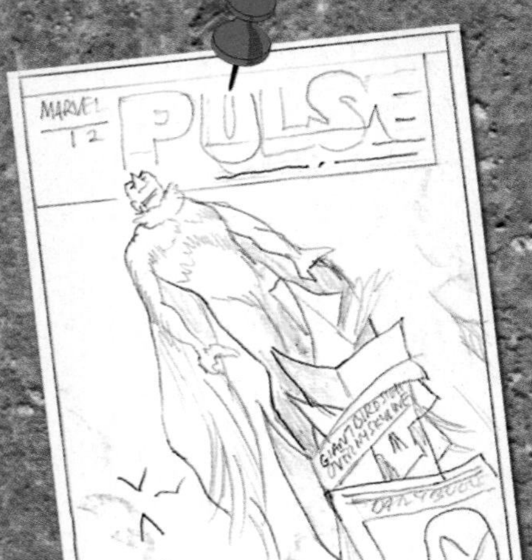
MARVEL
12
PULSE

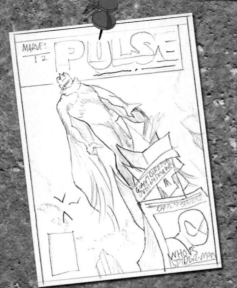

Unused Cover Layouts

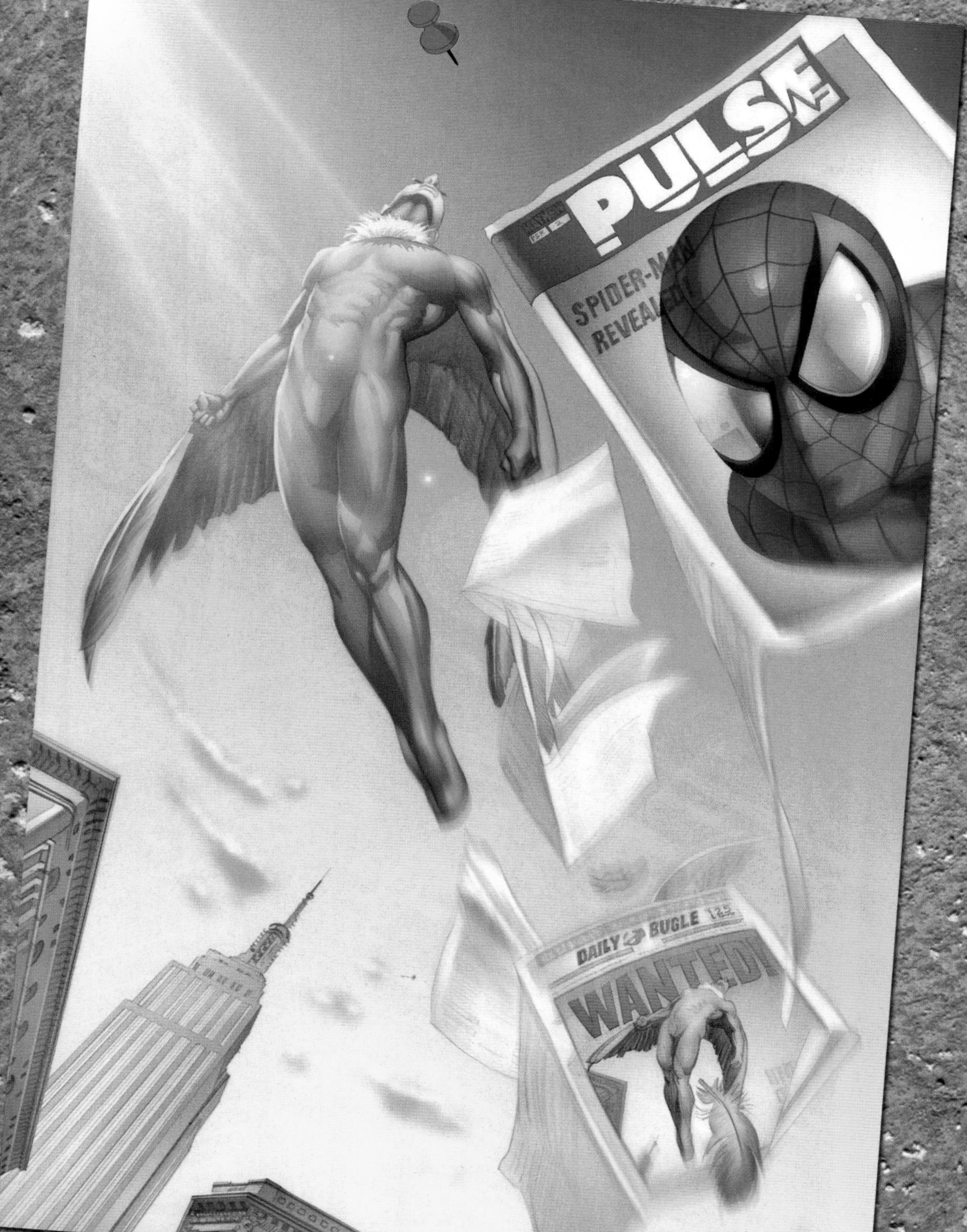

PULSE
SPIDER-MAN REVEALED!
DAILY BUGLE
WANTED!

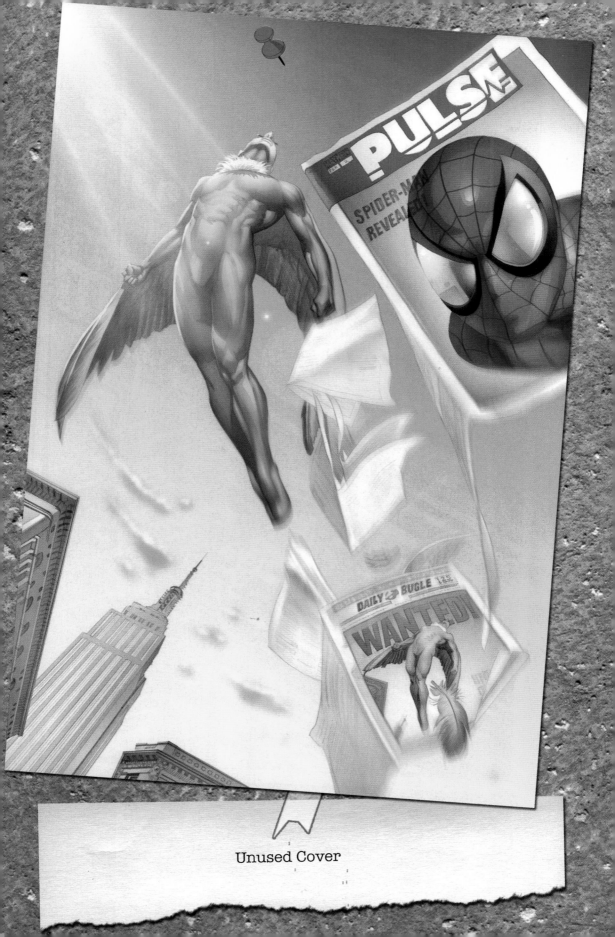

Unused Cover

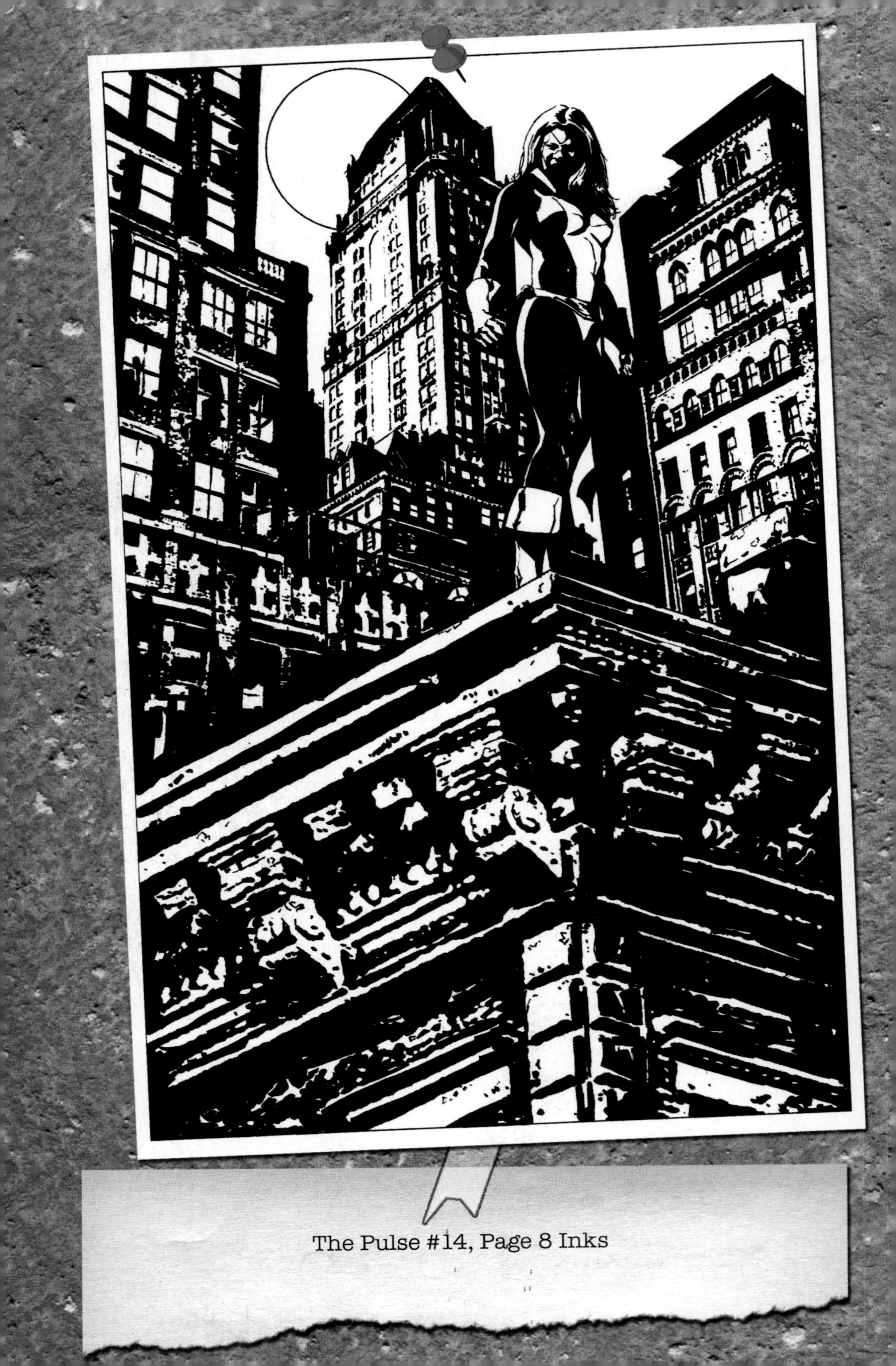

The Pulse #14, Page 8 Inks

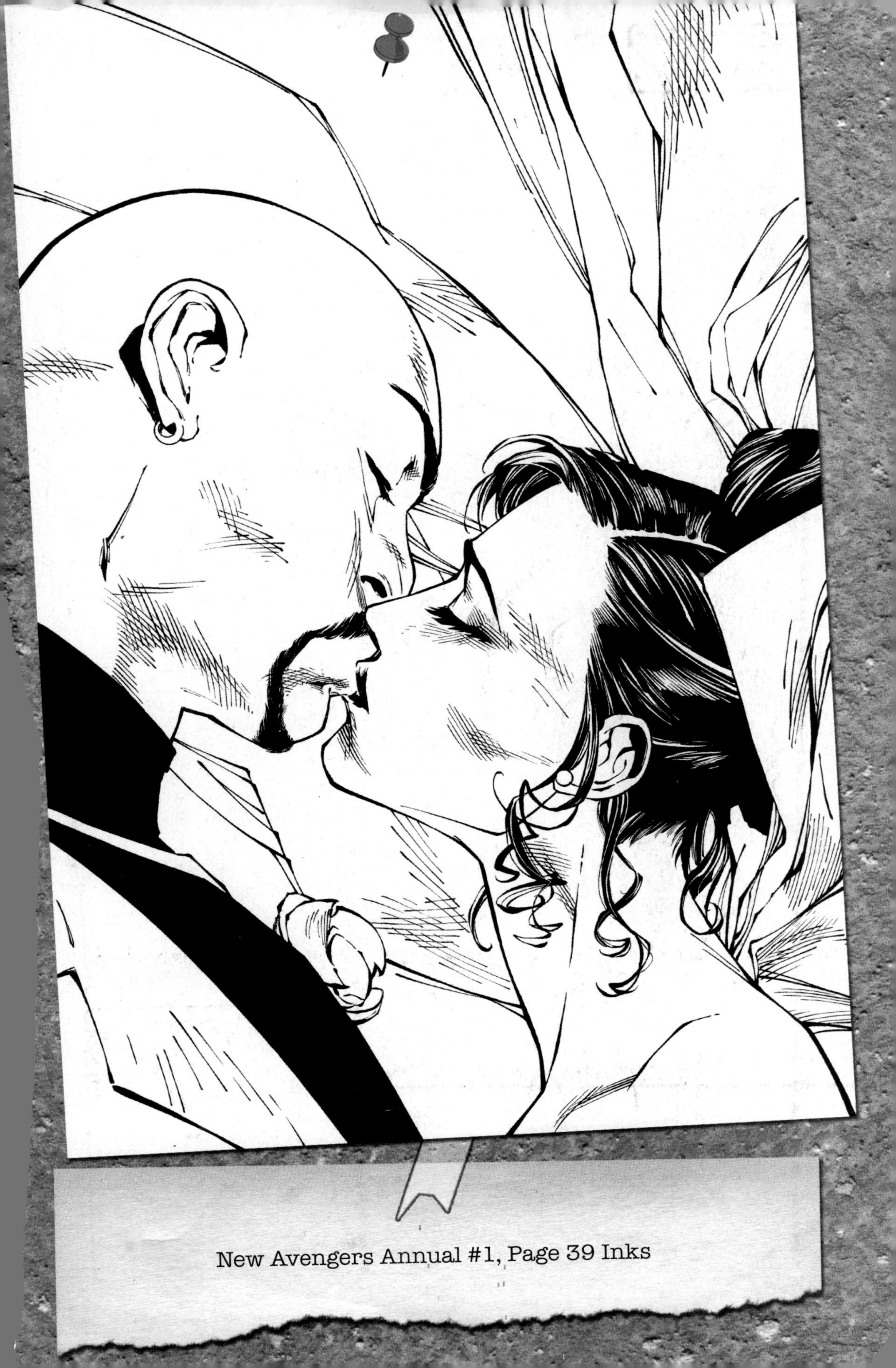

New Avengers Annual #1, Page 39 Inks

AUG 2 7 2016

New Avengers Annual #1, Page 40 Inks